The Unicorn Project

Titles by Gene Kim

Fiction

The Phoenix Project: A Novel About IT, DevOps, and Helping Your Business Win (2013), co-authored with Kevin Behr and George Spafford

The Unicorn Project: A Novel about Developers, Digital Disruption, and Thriving in the Age of Data

Non-Fiction

Accelerate: The Science of Lean Software and DevOps: Building and Scaling High Performing Technology Organizations (2018), co-authored with Nicole Forsgren, PhD, and Jez Humble

Beyond The Phoenix Project: The Origin and Evolution of DevOps (Audio) (2018), co-authored with John Willis

The DevOps Handbook: How to Create World-Class Agility, Reliability, & Security in Technology Organizations (2016), co-authored with Jez Humble, Patrick Debois, and John Willis

Visible Ops Security: Achieving Common Security and IT Operations Objectives in 4 Practical Steps (2008), co-authored with Paul Love and George Spafford

The Visible Ops Handbook: Implementing ITIL in 4 Practical and Auditable Steps (2005), co-authored with Kevin Behr and George Spafford

The Unicorn Project

A Novel about Developers,
Digital Disruption, and
Thriving in the Age of Data

Gene Kim

IT Revolution

Portland, OR

25 NW 23rd Pl, Suite 6314
Portland, OR 97210

First Edition
Printed in the United States of America
24 23 22 21 20 19   2 3 4 5 6 7 8 9 10

Book design by Devon Smith Creative
Cover image by eBoy
Cover design by Joy Stauber, Stauber Brand Studio
Author Photograph by Anna Mayer Photography

Library of Congress Catalog-in-Publication Data

Names: Kim, Gene, author.
Title: The unicorn project : a novel about digital disruption, developers,
and overthrowing the ancient powerful order / by Gene Kim.
Description: First Edition. | Portland, OR : IT Revolution, 2019.
Identifiers: LCCN 2019022761 (print) | LCCN 2019022762 (ebook) |
ISBN 9781942788768 (hardcover) | ISBN 9781942788775 (epub) |
ISBN 9781942788782 (kindle edition) | ISBN 9781942788799 (pdf)
Subjects: LCSH: Computer software--Development--Fiction. |
Knowledge management--Fiction.
Classification: LCC PS3611.I4538 U55 2019 (print) | LCC PS3611.I4538
(ebook) | DDC 813/.6--dc23
LC record available at https://lccn.loc.gov/2019022761
LC ebook record available at https://lccn.loc.gov/2019022762

ISBN: 978-1942788768
eBook ISBN: 978-1942788775
Kindle ISBN: 978-1942788782
Web PDF ISBN: 978-1942788799

For information about special discounts for bulk purchases or for information on booking authors
for an event, please visit our website at www.ITRevolution.com.

THE UNICORN PROJECT

Dedication

To my dad, Byung Kim (1937–2019), who really, really wanted me to get this book done.

To the loves of my life: my wife, Margueritte, and our three sons, Reid, Parker, and Grant, who also really, really wanted me to get this book done.

To the achievements of the DevOps Enterprise scenius, which this book is inspired by and celebrates.

Note to the Reader

The Unicorn Project takes place "in the present day," and is a companion novel to *The Phoenix Project* (which also takes place "in the present day"). The events from both novels take place concurrently, although certain situational elements of *The Unicorn Project* have been altered to account for changes in our industry.

While both books are about Parts Unlimited, *The Unicorn Project* was written to be a standalone book—there is absolutely no need to read or re-read *The Phoenix Project* first! (You may recognize some characters from *The Phoenix Project*—but then again, don't worry if you don't!)

Because the two books were written six years apart, there may be some suspension of disbelief required—for example, everyone's awareness of the Retail Apocalypse and the use of ride-sharing (Uber, Lyft) is much higher now than it was when *The Phoenix Project* was written.

For those who need some concrete waypoints, the characters who appeared in *The Phoenix Project* are indicated as such in the cast of characters, and there is a rough timeline of the two books provided as an endnote (beware, there may be spoilers!).

Parts Unlimited Employee Directory

REDSHIRTS
Maxine Chambers, Developer Lead, Architect
Kurt Reznick, QA Manager
"Cranky Dave" Brinkley, Developer Lead
Shannon Corman, Security Engineer
Adam Flynn, QA Engineer
Dwayne Cox, Lead Infrastructure Engineer
➤Brent Geller, Ops Lead

JUNIOR OFFICERS
Randy Keyes, Dev Manager
Purna Sathyaraj, QA and Release Manager
Rick Willis, QA Manager
➤William Mason, Director of QA
➤Wes Davis, Director of Distributed Technology Operations
➤Patty McKee, Director of IT Service Support

BRIDGE CREW
➤Steve Masters, CEO, Acting CIO
➤Dick Landry, CFO
➤Sarah Moulton, SVP of Retail Operations
➤Chris Allers, VP of Application Development
➤Kirsten Fingle, Director of Project Management
➤Maggie Lee, Senior Director of Retail Program Management
➤Bill Palmer, VP of IT Operations
➤John Pesche, Chief Information Security Officer (CISO)

STARFLEET COMMAND
Alan Perez, New Board Director, Operating Partner, Wayne-Yokohama
    Equity Partners
➤Bob Strauss, Lead Director, Former Chairman, Former CEO
➤Erik Reid, Prospective Board Director

➤Indicates characters who appear in *The Phoenix Project*.

PROLOGUE

From: Steve Masters (CEO, Parts Unlimited)
To: All Parts Unlimited Employees
Cc: Dick Landry (CFO, Parts Unlimited),
Laura Beck (VP Human Resources)
Date: 11:50 p.m., September 2
Subject: Payroll Failure

To fellow employees of Parts Unlimited,

Early this morning, several thousand timecards were corrupted due to a technical failure, mostly affecting employees and contractors in our manufacturing facilities and retail stores.

My goal is to ensure that everyone gets paid as soon as possible. Anyone who was underpaid should get a check in the next twenty-four hours.

As CEO, my job is to ensure that we fulfill our obligations to our employees, who make the daily work of this organization possible. Without you, we would not be able to serve our customers, who depend on us to keep their cars running to conduct their daily lives.

I apologize to you and everyone who depends on you for the problems and inconveniences this payroll issue causes. I commit to you that we will provide all necessary help, including communicating with any bill collectors, banks, etc.

At the bottom of this email you will find a list of Frequently Asked Questions from HR and Business Operations. If you are not getting help quickly enough, please email me or call me on my office phone anytime.

In the meantime, our top priority is to understand what factors led to this failure, and we will do whatever it takes to make sure that it doesn't happen again.

Steve Masters,
CEO, Parts Unlimited

From:	Chris Allers (VP Dev, Parts Unlimited)
To:	All IT Employees
Cc:	Bill Palmer (VP IT Ops), Steve Masters (CEO), Dick Landry (CFO, Parts Unlimited)
Date:	12:30 a.m., September 3
Subject:	Corrective actions for the payroll failure

All—

Because of the high-profile nature of the payroll outage, we have conducted a thorough root-cause analysis. We have concluded that it was due to both human error and a technology failure. We have taken decisive actions to ensure that it will not happen again. The person responsible has been reassigned to a role where they can no longer affect production outcomes.

If you have any questions, please email me.

—Chris

Elkhart Grove Herald Times

Parts Unlimited Flubs Paychecks, Local Union Leader Calls Failure 'Unconscionable'

Automotive parts supplier Parts Unlimited has failed to issue correct paychecks to some of its hourly factory workers, and others haven't received any compensation for their work, according to a Parts Unlimited internal memo. The company denies that the issue is connected to cash flow problems and instead attributes the error to a payroll system failure.

The once high-flying $4 billion company has been plagued by flagging revenue and growing losses in recent quarters. These financial woes, which some blame on a failure of upper management, have led to rampant job insecurity among local workers struggling to support their families.

According to the memo, whatever the cause of the pay roll failure, employees might have to wait days or weeks to be compensated.

"This is just the latest in a long string of management execution missteps by the company in recent years," according to Nestor Meyers Chief Industry Analyst Kelly Lawrence.

Parts Unlimited CFO Dick Landry did not return phone calls from the Herald Times requesting comment on the payroll issue, accounting errors and questions of managerial competency.

In a statement issued on behalf of Parts Unlimited, Landry expressed regret at the "glitch," and vowed that the mistake would not be repeated. The Herald Times will continue to post updates as the story progresses.

PART ONE

September 3–September 18

CHAPTER 1

"You're doing what?" Maxine blurts out, staring in disbelief at Chris, VP of R&D at Parts Unlimited.

Chris smiles weakly from behind his desk. *Even he realizes how absurd he sounds*, Maxine thinks.

"Maxine, I'm really sorry about this. I know it's a terrible way to come back from vacation, but this payroll outage created an incredible crap storm. The CEO and CFO wanted heads to roll. We agonized about this for days, but I think we came up with a pretty good solution...after all, no one is getting fired."

Maxine slaps the printed copy of his email onto his desk. "You say right here that it was caused by 'human error and a technology failure.' And now you say that I'm the 'human error'? After all that time we spent together deciding how to resolve that compliance finding, you're placing all the blame on me? What sort of bullshit is this?" She glares at him furiously.

"I know, I know...It's not right," Chris says, squirming under Maxine's intense gaze. "Everyone here values your incredible skills and talents and your fantastic contributions to the company over the last eight years—no one actually believes it was your fault. But the payroll issue was front-page news! Dick had to give a quote to keep the unions from filing a grievance! Given all that, I felt like we came up with the best solution in a pretty awful situation."

"So you blame the person who was on vacation because that person couldn't defend herself?" Maxine says in disgust. "That's really admirable, Chris. Which leadership book did you get that from?"

"Come on, Max, you know I'm your biggest fan and biggest defender. In fact, take this as a huge compliment—you have one of the most stellar reputations of anyone in IT," Chris says.

Blaming someone for a payroll outage is a strange way of appreciating someone, she thinks.

He continues, "*Everyone* knows that this isn't actually your fault. Just think of this as a vacation—you can work on anything you want, and you won't have any real responsibilities if you don't want."

Maxine is about to respond when she thinks about what she just heard. "Wait, treat exactly *what* like a vacation, Chris?"

"Uh…" Chris stammers, buckling under her stare. Maxine let's him squirm. As a woman in what remains a largely male dominated profession, she knows her directness might be contributing to Chris' discomfort, but she will always stand up for herself.

"…I promised Steve and Dick that I'd put you in a role where you couldn't make any production changes anymore," Chris says, squirming. "So, uh, effective immediately, you're moving from the manufacturing plant ERP systems to help with documentation for the Phoenix Project…"

"You're sending me to…" Maxine can't breathe. She can't believe what she's hearing.

"Look, Max, all you have to do is lie low for four months. Then you can come back and have your choice of any project you want to work on, okay?" Chris says. Smiling weakly, he adds, "See, like a vacation, right?"

"Oh, my God…" she says, finding her voice again. "You're sending me to the Phoenix Project?!" she nearly yells. Maxine immediately kicks herself for this brief moment of weakness. She takes a deep breath, adjusts her blazer, and pulls herself together.

"This is bullshit, Chris, and you know it!" she says right into his face, pointing her finger at him.

Maxine's mind races, thinking about what she knows about the Phoenix Project. None of it is good. For years, it's been the company death-march project, having ensnared hundreds of developers, achieving unprecedented levels of notoriety. Maxine is pretty sure that the reason nothing is going right is simply because they're not doing anything right.

Despite the Phoenix Project's obvious failures, it keeps going. With the rise of e-commerce and the decline of physical stores, everyone knows something has to be done to ensure that Parts Unlimited stays relevant in the increasingly digital age.

Parts Unlimited is still one of the largest players in the industry, with nearly a thousand stores across the nation. But there are times when Maxine wonders how the company will fare beyond its hundredth anniversary, which wasn't that long ago.

The Phoenix Project is supposed to be the solution, the shining hope that will lead the company into the future. It's now three years late (and counting) and $20 million has disappeared, with nothing to show for it except developer suffering. It stinks of impending failure, which will have grave implications for the company.

"You're going to take one of your best people and exile her to the Phoenix Project because you need a fall guy for the payroll outage?" Maxine says, her frustration boiling over. "This is not a compliment—this is the best way that you can say, 'Screw you, Maxine!' Hell, there's probably nothing in Phoenix that is even worth documenting! Unless it's to document incompetence? This is like labeling all the deck chairs on the *Titanic*. Have I said that this is bullshit already, Chris?"

"I'm sorry, Maxine," Chris says, throwing up his hands. "It's the best I could do for you. Like I said, no one is actually blaming you. Just do your time and it'll all go back to normal soon enough."

Maxine sits, closes her eyes, takes a deep breath, and steeples her hands in front of her, trying to think.

"Okay, okay…" she says. "You need a fall guy. I get it. I can take the blame for this whole fiasco. That's cool, that's cool…that's how business is done at times, right? No hard feelings. Just…put me to work in the cafeteria or in vendor management. I don't care. *Anywhere* but the Phoenix Project."

Listening to herself, Maxine's aware that in less than two minutes she's moved from denial to anger and is now in full-blown bargaining mode. She's pretty sure she's missed a step in the Kübler-Ross grief cycle, but at the moment she can't think of which one.

"Chris," she continues. "I have nothing against documentation. Everyone deserves good documentation. But there are tons of places that need documentation *way* more than Phoenix does. Let me go make a bigger impact somewhere else. Just give me an hour or two to come up with some ideas."

"Look, Maxine. I hired you eight years ago because of your amazing skills and experience. Everyone knows you enable teams to do the impossible with software," Chris says. "That's why I fought for you, and why you've led the software teams that are responsible for all our supply chains and internal manufacturing processes for all twenty-three manufacturing plants. I know how good you are…But, Maxine, I've done everything I can. Unfortunately, the decision has already been made. Just do your time, don't rock the boat, and come back when everything blows over," he says, looking so remorseful that Maxine actually believes him.

"There are executives being shot left and right, and not just over this fiasco," Chris continues. "The board of directors just stripped Steve Masters of the chairmanship, so now he's just CEO. And both the CIO *and* VP of IT Operations were fired yesterday, no explanations given, so Steve is now acting CIO too. Absolutely *everyone* is worried that there is going to be even more blood in the streets…"

Chris looks to make sure the door is closed and, in a lower voice, says, "And there are rumors of potentially *even bigger and more sweeping changes coming…*"

Chris pauses, as if he might have said too much. He continues, "Look, whenever you're ready, go get yourself set up with Randy, the Phoenix development manager—he's a good guy. Like I said, think of this as a four-month vacation. Seriously, do whatever you think will be helpful. Heck, you don't need to do anything at all. Just keep your head down. Don't rock the boat. And whatever you do, just stay off Steve and Dick's radar. Sound good?"

Maxine squints at Chris as he name-drops Steve Masters and Dick Landry, the CEO and CFO of Parts Unlimited. She sees them every other month during the company Town Halls. How did she go from a two-week vacation seeing the wondrous sights of Kuala Lumpur to having Chris dump all this crap on her?

"Maxine, I'm serious. Just lie low, don't rock the boat, stay clear of outages, and everything will be fine, okay? Just thank your lucky stars you weren't fired for the payroll issue like the two other people were last year," Chris implores.

"Yeah, yeah. Don't rock the boat," she says, standing up. "See you in four months. And *you're welcome* for helping you keep your job. Super classy, Chris."

Chris is actually getting more spineless each year, she thinks, storming out of the room. She considers slamming the door, but instead closes it…decisively. She hears him say, "Please don't rock the boat, Maxine!"

When she's out of sight, she leans against the wall. Tears well up. Suddenly she remembers the missing step in the Kübler-Ross cycle after bargaining: depression.

Maxine slowly makes her way back to her desk. *Her old desk. Where she used to work.*

Maxine can't believe this is happening to her. Trying to counter all the negative self-talk flying through her head, she reminds herself of her qualifications. She knows that for the past twenty-five years, her job has been to bend technology to do her bidding—efficiently, effectively, precisely, with creativity and flair, and most importantly, competence.

She knows she has unmatched real-world experience building systems that run under adverse and even hostile environments. She possesses a fantastic intuition about which technologies are best suited to achieve the mission at hand. She is responsible, meticulous, and careful about her work, and she insists on the same level of excellence and diligence from everyone around her. *After all, dammit, I was one of the most sought after consultants at the top* Fortune *50 companies*, Maxine reminds herself.

Maxine stops mid-stride. Even though she is a stickler for details and doing things right, she has learned that mistakes and entropy are a fact of life. She's seen the corrosive effects that a culture of fear creates, where mistakes are routinely punished and scapegoats fired. Punishing failure and "shooting the messenger" only cause people to hide their mistakes, and eventually, all desire to innovate is completely extinguished.

During her consulting days, she could always tell, usually within hours, whether people were afraid to say what they really thought. It drove her crazy when people were careful about how they phrased things, speaking obliquely and going to extreme lengths to avoid using certain *forbidden* words. She hated those engagements and would do everything she could to convince the client to end the project, saving them time, money, and suffering.

She can't believe she's starting to see these red flags at Parts Unlimited.

Maxine thinks, *I expect leaders to buffer their people from all the political and bureaucratic insanity, not throw them into it.*

Only yesterday, she and her family were getting off of a nearly twenty-hour flight back from Kuala Lumpur. When she turned her phone on, it nearly melted from all the incoming messages. While Jake and her two kids went to find food in the airport, she finally got ahold of Chris.

He told her about the payroll failure and filled her in on the mayhem. She listened carefully, but her heart stopped when she heard Chris say "…and we discovered that all the Social Security numbers in the payroll database were corrupted."

She broke out in a cold sweat, her hands tingled, and there was ice in her blood. For what felt like a lifetime, she couldn't breathe. She knew. "It was the tokenization security application, right?"

She cursed loudly. Parents all around herded their young kids away from her on the airport concourse. She heard Chris say, "Yep. And there's going to be hell to pay. Get into the office as soon as you can."

Even now, she's still in awe of the scale of the carnage. Like all engineers, she secretly loves hearing disaster stories…as long as she doesn't have the starring role. "Stupid Chris," she mutters as she thinks about dusting off her résumé, untouched for eight years, and putting out feelers for any job openings.

By the time Maxine reaches her work area, whatever equanimity she had managed to muster is gone. She stops before she walks in. Her armpits are sweaty. She smells them to make sure she doesn't stink of the humiliation she feels. She knows she's being paranoid—she put on so much deodorant this morning her armpits were chalky-white. She was glad she did.

She walks into the work area. Everyone knows she is being reassigned but are trying not to let on. Glenn, who has been her manager for three years, comes up and squeezes her shoulder, a pained expression on his face. He says, "Don't worry, Maxine. You'll be back here before you know it. None of us are happy with the way things went down. A bunch of people wanted to throw you a big party, but I was pretty sure that you wouldn't have wanted to make a big scene," he says.

Maxine says, "Damned right. Thanks, Glenn."

"No problem," he says with a wry smile. "Let me know how I can help, okay?"

With a forced smile, she says, "Come on, it's not like I'm dying or being sent into outer space! I'll be closer to headquarters, which is where all the action is. I'll send updates to all you ignorant villagers who aren't good enough to be in the thick of things!"

"That's the spirit. We'll see you back here in four months if all goes well!" he says, giving her a playful jab. Maxine's brow furrows slightly at the "if all goes well" bit. That was news to her.

As Glenn heads to a meeting, Maxine goes to her desk to start packing up. She picks the most critical things she'll need during her exile: her carefully configured laptop (she is very picky about keyboards and amount of RAM), pictures of her family, her tablet, and the USB and laptop chargers carefully selected and accumulated over the years, along with the big sign that hangs over them: "DO NOT TOUCH, under penalty of death!"

"Hi, Maxine! Why are you packing up?" she hears someone ask. Looking up, she sees Evelyn, their promising young computer science intern. Maxine recruited her. All summer long, Evelyn has dazzled everyone with how quickly she picks things up. *She'll have her pick of jobs when she graduates*, Maxine thinks. Which is why all summer long Maxine has been relentlessly selling Parts Unlimited as a great place to work and learn. Which she herself believed, until this morning. *Maybe this isn't such a great place to work after all.*

"I've been temporarily re-assigned to the Phoenix Project," Maxine says.

"Oh, wow," Evelyn says. "That's awful... I'm so sorry!"

You know you're in real trouble when even the intern feels sorry for you, Maxine thinks.

She leaves the building, carrying her plain cardboard box, alone. She feels like she's reporting to prison. *Which is basically what the Phoenix Project is*, she tells herself.

It's a four-mile drive to the corporate headquarter campus. While she drives, she thinks about the pros and cons of staying at the company. Pros: Her husband is a tenured professor, which is why they moved to Elkhart Grove in the first place. Her kids love their schools, friends, and activities.

She loves her work and all the challenges; she loves interacting with the countless and complex business processes that span the entire company— it requires an understanding of the business, incredible problem-solving skills, patience, and the political sophistication to work with sometimes Byzantine and occasionally incomprehensible processes that every large organization seems to have. And the pay and benefits are great.

Cons: The Phoenix Project. Working for Chris. And the feeling that the corporate culture is changing for the worse. *Like how I just got scapegoated for the payroll outage*, she thinks.

Looking around, she sees buildings designed to exude status and success. Parts Unlimited earned that level of prestige by being one of the largest employers in the state, with seven thousand employees. They have stores in almost every state and millions of loyal customers, although every metric shows those numbers declining.

In the age of Uber and Lyft, the younger generation is more often choosing not to own cars at all, and if they do, they sure don't fix their cars themselves. It doesn't take a strategic genius to realize that the long-term prosperity of the organization requires something new and different.

As she drives deeper into the corporate campus, she can't find Building 5. When she circles around for a third time, she finally sees the sign to the parking lot. Her heart sinks. The building's a dump compared to the others. *It even looks like a prison*, she thinks.

Building 5 used to be a manufacturing plant, just like MRP-8, her "old" building. But where MRP-8 is obviously still the pride of the company, Building 5 is where they dump misbehaving IT people like her and throw away the key.

If the Phoenix Project is the most important and strategic project for the company, don't the teams who work on it deserve a better building? Maxine wonders. But then again, Maxine knows that in most organizations, corporate IT is rarely loved and is often parked in the least attractive properties.

Which is odd. At MRP-8, the ERP technology teams work side-by-side with the plant operations people. They're viewed as partners. They work together, eat together, complain together, and drink together.

On the other hand, corporate IT is usually viewed as ranks of nameless faces whom you call when there's something wrong with your laptop or when you can't print something.

Staring at Building 5, Maxine realizes that as bad as the reputation of the Phoenix Project is, the reality is probably much, much worse.

Everyone tells Maxine that one of her most endearing qualities is her relentless and never-ending optimism. She keeps telling herself that as she walks toward Building 5, carrying the cardboard box full of her belongings.

A bored security guard inspects her badge and recommends she take the elevator, but Maxine chooses to go up the stairs instead. She wishes she had a more cheerful bag to carry all her things in instead of lugging this dumb box around.

As she opens the door, her heart sinks. It's a vast cubicle farm with drab gray partitions separating each work area. The maze of cubicles reminds her of the old computer text game *Zork*—she's already lost in a series of twisty passages, all alike.

It's like all the color has been drained from the building, she thinks. Maxine is reminded of her parents' old color TV set when her brother had fiddled with the brightness, contrast, and color dials to make everything look a sickly gray and green.

On the other hand, Maxine is delighted to see that each desk has two massive LCD screens. She's in the right place—these are developers. The new monitors, open code editors, and the high percentage of people wearing headphones are dead giveaways.

The room is so quiet you could hear a pin drop. It's like a university library. *Or a tomb*, she thinks. It doesn't look like a vibrant space where people work together to solve problems. Creating software should be a collaborative and conversational endeavor—individuals need to interact with each other to create new knowledge and value for the customer.

In the silence, she looks around, feeling even worse about her fate.

"Do you know where I can find Randy?" she asks the person nearest her. He points to the opposite corner of the room without even taking off his headphones.

Walking through the hive of silent cubicles, Maxine sees whiteboards and people huddled in groups, speaking in hushed tones. Along one long wall are enormous Gantt charts easily four feet high and thirty feet across, assembled from what looks like more than forty sheets of paper taped together.

Alongside the Gantt charts are printouts of status reports featuring lots of green, yellow, and red boxes. Standing in front of the charts are people dressed in slacks and collared shirts. Their arms are crossed and they look concerned.

Maxine can almost feel the people mentally trying to compress the bars closer together so that they can hit all those promised dates. *Good luck*, she thinks.

As she walks to the opposite corner where she was told to find Randy, Maxine suddenly smells it: the unmistakable smell of people who have slept in the office. She knows this smell. It's the smell of long hours, inadequate ventilation, and desperation.

In technology, it's almost a cliché. When there's a need to deliver capabilities to the market quickly, to seize a market opportunity, or to catch up with the competition, long hours become endless hours, where it's easier to sleep under your desk than to go home only to come right back. Although long hours are sometimes glorified in popular culture, Maxine views them as a symptom of something going very wrong.

She wonders what is happening: Too many promises to the market? Bad engineering leadership? Bad product leadership? Too much technical debt? Not enough focus on architectures and platforms that enable developers to be productive?

Maxine notices that she is wildly overdressed. She looks down at the suit that she's worn to work for years, realizing that she sticks out like a sore thumb. In this building, T-shirts and shorts far outnumber the collared shirt crowd. And *no one* is wearing a jacket.

Tomorrow, I'm going to leave the jacket at home, she thinks.

She finds Randy in a corner cubicle, typing away and surrounded by huge stacks of paper. Randy is a redhead, wearing the management khaki-land uniform—a collared, striped white shirt and khaki pants. Maxine guesses he's in his late thirties, probably ten years younger than her. Judging from his low body fat, he probably runs every day. But he looks stressed in a way that no amount of running can take away.

He gives her a big smile, standing up to shake her hand. She puts her big cardboard box down and realizes how tired her arms are. As she shakes his hand, he says, "Chris told me about how you ended up here. I'm sorry to hear about all that. But trust me, your reputation precedes you, and we're so excited to have someone of your experience on this team. I know it's not the best use of your skills, but I'll take any help we can get. I think you can make a real difference here."

Maxine forces herself to smile because Randy seems nice enough, even earnest. "Happy to help, Randy. What do you need to get done?" she asks, trying to be equally earnest. She does want to be useful.

"I'm in charge of documentation and builds. In all honesty, things are a mess. We don't have a standard Dev environment that developers can use. It takes months for new developers to do builds on their laptops and be fully productive. Even our build server is woefully under-documented," Randy says. "In fact, we've had some new contractors on site for weeks, and they can't even check in code yet. God knows what they've actually been doing. We're still paying them. To do nothing, basically."

Maxine grimaces. She hates the idea of paying expensive people to just sit around. And these are developers—it deeply offends her sensibilities when willing developers are prevented from contributing.

"Well, I'm happy to help out wherever I can," she says, surprised at how much she means it. After all, making developers more productive is always super important, even those working on the Phoenix Project in its fiery, meteoric descent.

"Here, I'll show you where we've got you set up," Randy says.

He leads her past more rows of cubicles, showing her an empty desk, a filing cabinet, and two large monitors connected to a laptop. It's plainer and smaller than she'd like, she thinks, but it's fine. Especially since she'll only be here for a few months. *One way or another, I'll be out of here soon,* Maxine thinks. *Either my prison term will end or I'll get another job somewhere else.*

"We got you a standard developer setup, just like any developer who starts at Parts Unlimited," he says, gesturing at the laptop. "You've got your email, network shares, and printers set up with your existing credentials. I'll send out an introduction email this afternoon. And I've assigned Josh to help you get everything set up."

"That's great," Maxine says, smiling. "I'll take a look at what you have in terms of Dev onboarding and maybe come up with some recommendations. I'd love to get a Phoenix build going on my laptop too."

"That would be great! Wow, I'm so excited, Maxine," Randy says. "I never get senior engineers to work on these problems. Any engineers I have that are any good are always poached away by other teams. They're lured away by feature work that customers see instead of working on boring infrastructure... Now, where is Josh?" he mutters, looking around. "There are so many contractors and consultants running around here that sometimes it's hard to find the actual employees."

Just then, a young kid carrying a laptop walks by and sits down at the desk next to them. "Sorry I'm late, Randy. I went to go check on last night's build failure. Some developer broke the build when they merged their changes in. I'm still looking into it."

"I'll help you in a second, Josh. In the meantime, meet Maxine Chambers," Randy gestures at Maxine.

Maxine does a double-take. He looks barely older than her daughter. In fact, they could be classmates at the same high school. Randy wasn't kidding when he said he had junior people on his team.

"Maxine is a senior engineer in the company, and she's been assigned to us for a couple of months. She's the lead architect for the MRP system. Can you show her what she needs to know to get productive around here?"

"Uh, hi, Ms. Chambers. Nice to meet you," he says, holding out his hand and looking puzzled. *He's probably wondering how he ended up being responsible for someone who could be his mom*, she thinks.

"Nice meeting you," she says, smiling. "Please, just call me Maxine," she adds, even though it usually irks her when her daughters' friends call her by her first name. But Josh is a work colleague, and she's glad to have a native guide who can show her around. *Even if he's not old enough to drive*, she jokes to herself.

"Okay, let me know if there's anything you need," Randy says. "Maxine, I'm looking forward to introducing you to the rest of the team. Our first staff meeting is next week."

Randy turns to Josh. "Tell me more about the build failures."

Maxine listens. All those stories about caveman technical practices in the Phoenix Project are actually true. She's learned over her entire career that when people can't get their builds going consistently, disaster is usually right around the corner.

She looks around at the entire floor. Over a hundred developers are typing away, working on their little piece of the system on their laptops. Without constant feedback from a centralized build, integration, and test system, they really have no idea what will happen when all their work is merged with everyone else's.

Josh spins his chair around to Maxine. "Ms. Chambers, I've got to go show Randy something, but I just emailed you what we've got in terms of documentation for new developers—there are wiki pages where I've assembled all of the release notes we've written and the documentation from the development teams. There's also links to the stuff we know we need to write. Hopefully that will get you started?"

Maxine gives him a thumbs up. As they leave, she logs in with her new laptop and is able to get in and open her email, miraculously working the first time. But before looking at what Josh sent, she pokes around to see what else is on her new laptop.

Immediately, she is mystified. She finds links to HR systems, network shares to company resources, links to the expense reporting system, payroll, timecard systems…She finds Microsoft Word and Excel and the rest of the Office suite.

She frowns. *This is fine for someone in finance*, she thinks, *but not a developer*. There are no developer tools or code editors or source control managers installed. Opening up a terminal window she confirms that there aren't any compilers, Docker, Git…nothing. Not even Visio or OmniGraffle!

Holy cow! What do they actually expect new developers to do? Read emails and write memos?

When you hire a plumber or a carpenter, you expect them to bring their own tools. But in a software organization with more than one developer, the entire team uses common tools to be productive. Apparently here on the Phoenix Project, the toolbox is empty.

She opens her email to see what Josh sent. It takes her to an internal wiki page, a tool many engineers use to collaborate on documentation. She tries to scroll up and down the wiki page, but the document is so short there isn't even a scroll bar.

She stares at the nearly empty screen for several long moments. *Screw you, Chris,* she thinks.

Driven by morbid curiosity, Maxine spends the next half hour digging. She clicks around and finds only a handful of documents. She reads PowerPoint slides with architecture diagrams, lots of meeting notes and Agile sprint retrospectives, and a three-year-old product management requirements document. She is excited when she finds tantalizing references to some test plans, but when she clicks on the links, she is prompted by an authentication screen asking for her login and password.

Apparently she needs access to the QA servers.

She opens a new note file on her laptop and types a note to herself to find someone who can give her access.

Giving up on documentation for the moment, she decides to find the source code repositories. *Developers write code, and code goes into source control repositories. There are developers working on Phoenix, ergo, there must be a Phoenix source code repo around here somewhere*, she thinks.

To her surprise, despite almost ten minutes of searching, she can't find it. She adds to her notes:

> Find Phoenix source code repo.

She finds links to internal SharePoint documentation servers, which may have more clues, but she doesn't have accounts on those servers either. She types another note:

> Get access to DEVP-101 SharePoint server.

For the next hour, so it goes—Search. Nothing. Search. Nothing. Search. Click. Authentication screen. Click. Authentication screen. Each time, she adds more notes to her growing list:

> Get access to QA-103 SharePoint Server.

> Get access to PUL-QA-PHOENIX network share.

> Get access to PUL-DEV-PHOENIX network share.

She adds more notes and to-dos, accumulating a list of more user accounts that she needs, adding the QA wiki server, the performance engineering wiki server, the mobile app team wiki, and a bunch of other groups with acronyms she doesn't recognize.

She needs network credentials. She needs installers for all the tools that are mentioned. She needs license keys.

Maxine looks at her watch and is surprised to see that it's nearly one o'clock. She's achieved nothing in two hours except document thirty-two things she *needs*. And she still doesn't know where the development tools or the source code repositories are.

If the Phoenix development setup were a product, it would be the worst product ever.

And now she needs food. She looks around, and seeing the nearly empty floor, realizes that she missed the lunch rush.

It would have been nice if she had followed them, but she had been too engrossed in digging through the labyrinth of Phoenix docs. Now she doesn't know where people find food. She wonders if she should add that to her list too.

Right after "update and send out my résumé."

From: Alan Perez (Operating Partner, Wayne-Yokohama Equity Partners)
To: Steve Masters (CEO, Parts Unlimited)
Cc: Dick Landry (CFO, Parts Unlimited),
Sarah Moulton (SVP of Retail Operations),
Bob Strauss (Board Chair, Parts Unlimited)
Date: 6:07 a.m., September 4
Subject: Go Forward Options, January Board Session
CONFIDENTIAL

Steve,

Good seeing you two days ago in Elkhart Grove. As a newly elected board director, I've been learning a lot and appreciate the time being invested by the management team to get me up to speed. I've been especially impressed with Dick and Sarah (CFO and SVP Marketing, respectively).

Although I'm new, it's clear that Parts Unlimited's failed efforts to increase shareholder value have raised questions of confidence and created need for action. We must work together to break the string of broken promises repeated quarter after quarter.

Given how essential software is to your plans, your decision to replace your CIO and VP of IT Operations seems proper—hopefully this will restore accountability and increase urgency in execution.

To reiterate my motivation for reviewing strategic options at the board level: revenue growth isn't the only way to reward shareholders—we've put so much focus into forcing Parts Unlimited to become a "digital company" that I believe we've lost sight of low risk ways to unlock value, such as restructuring the company and divesting non-core, poor-performing assets. These are just two obvious ways to increase profitability, which increases shareholder value and provides working capital for transformation.

We need to quickly assemble options for the board to review and consider. Given how much time management is spending on the current strategy, the board chair asked me to work with a few key members of the executive team to generate options for the board to discuss. I will work with Dick and Sarah, given their tenure and breadth of experience at the company. We'll have bi-weekly calls to discuss and assess ideas, and we'll be ready to present strategic options to the entire board in January.

Our firm bought a significant interest in Parts Unlimited because we believe there's considerable shareholder value that can be unlocked here. I look forward to a productive working relationship and improved outcomes for Parts Unlimited that we can all be proud of.

Sincerely, Alan

CHAPTER 2

• *Friday, September 5th*

Maxine scans her to-do list, slowly shaking her head in frustration. It's been two days and she is determined to perform a Phoenix build on her laptop, like any new developer should be able to do. This has become her mission. But according to her list, there are over a hundred items that she's missing, and no one seems to know where to find them.

She has done nothing on her list. Except for updating and sending out her résumé. Many friends replied to her right away, promising to look for positions she might be interested in.

Maxine asked her guide, Josh, about all those missing build items, but he didn't know anything about them. The build team used to know these things, but the details are either out-of-date or missing entirely, the knowledge scattered across the entire organization.

She is frustrated, every turn she takes leads to a dead end. There is nothing fun about this challenge. What she is doing, she's pretty sure, is the exact opposite of fun.

She's an engineer at heart, and she loves challenges and solving problems. She's been exiled smack in the middle of probably the most important project in the entire company's history. And somewhere, there's code—almost certainly millions of lines of code written by hundreds of developers over nearly three years. But she can't find any of it.

Maxine loves coding and she's awesome at it. But she knows that there's something even more important than code: the systems that enable developers to be productive, so that they can write high-quality code quickly and safely, freeing themselves from all the things that prevent them from solving important business problems.

Which seems to be completely missing here. Maxine is one of the best in the game, but after four days she still has almost nothing to show for it. Just endless clicking around, reading documents, opening tickets, scheduling meetings with people to get things she needs, trapped in the worst scavenger hunt ever.

For a moment, Maxine wonders if she's the only person having this problem. But she sees developers all around her struggling, so she quickly pushes away any feelings of self-doubt.

Maxine *knows* her kung fu is amazing. Many times in her career she's had to solve problems that seemed hopeless and impossible. Often in the middle of the night. Sometimes without any documentation or source code. One of her most famous escapades is still known as the "Maxine Post-Holiday Save," where all the in-store systems that handled refunds crashed spectacularly on the Friday after Christmas. It's one of the busiest shopping days of the year as people come in to return gifts from loved ones so they can buy something they actually want.

With her team, Maxine worked into the wee hours of Saturday morning to fix a multi-threading deadlock in a database vendor's ODBC driver. She had to manually disassemble the vendor library and then generate a binary patch. By hand.

Everyone said it couldn't be done. But she pulled it off, to the amazement of the scores of people who had worked that outage for over seven hours. The database vendor professional services team was in awe and immediately offered her a job, which she politely declined.

The legends about her kept growing after that. She's classically trained as a developer, and in her career, she's written software to stitch together panoramic graphic images and chip layout algorithms for CAD/CAM applications, back-end servers for massive multi-user games, and, most recently, the ordering, replenishment, and scheduling processes that orchestrate thousands of suppliers into a plant production schedule for their MRP systems.

She routinely lives in the world of NP-complete problems that are so difficult to solve they can take more than polynomial time to complete. She loves the *Papers We Love* series, revisiting her favorite academic papers from mathematics and computer science.

But she has never seen her job as just writing application code, working only pre-deployment. In production, when theory meets reality, she's fixed wildly misbehaving middleware servers, overloaded message buses, intermittent failures in RAID disk arrays, and core switches that somehow kept flipping into half-duplex mode.

She's fixed technology components that were spilling out their guts in the middle of the night, having filled up every disk and log server, making it impossible for teams to understand what was actually happening. She led the effort to systematically isolate, diagnose, and restore those services based on decades of intuition and countless production battles.

She's deciphered stack traces on application servers that were literally on fire, racing to get them safely backed up before the flooding water, halon extinguishers, and emergency power shutdowns destroyed everything.

But deep down, she's a developer. She's a developer who loves functional programming because she knows that pure functions and composability are better tools to think with. She eschews imperative programming in favor of declarative modes of thinking. She despises and has a healthy fear of state mutation and non-referential transparency. She favors the lambda calculus over Turing machines because of their mathematical purity. She loves LISPs because she loves her code as data and vice versa.

But hers is not merely a theoretical vocation—she loves nothing more than getting her hands dirty, creating business value where none thought it could be extracted, applying the strangler pattern to dismantle decades-old code monoliths and replacing them safely, confidently, and brilliantly.

She is still the only person who knows every keyboard shortcut from *vi* to the latest, greatest editors. But she is never ashamed to tell anyone that she still needs to look up nearly every command line option for Git—because Git can be scary and hard! What other tool uses SHA-1 hashes as part of its UI?

And yet, as awesome as she is, at the height of her soaring powers and skills honed over decades, here she sits in the middle of the Phoenix Project unable do a Phoenix build, even after two days. She found where two of the four source code repositories are, and she's found the three installers for some of the proprietary source code management (SCM) tools and compilers.

However, she is still waiting for license keys for the SCM, and she doesn't know who to ask to get license keys for the two other build tools. She needs credentials for three network shares and five SharePoints, and no one knows where to get the ten mysterious configuration files mentioned in the documentation. When she emailed the person who wrote the docs, it bounced. They had long left the organization.

She is stuck. No one responds quickly to her emails, her tickets, or her voicemails. She's asked Randy to help, to escalate her requests, but everyone says it will take a couple of days because they're so busy.

Of course, Maxine never just takes "no" for an answer. She has made it her mission to do whatever it takes to get a build running. She's hunted down almost all of the people who have promised her something. She's found out where they sit and has pestered them, even camping out at their desks, willing to stay there until they get her what she needs.

Sometimes she got what she needed: a URL, a SharePoint document, a license key, a configuration file. But more often than not, the person she hunted down didn't have what she needed—they would have to ask somebody else, so they would open up a ticket on Maxine's behalf. And now they were both waiting.

Sometimes, they had a promising lead or clue on who or where Maxine needed to go to next. Most times, though, it was just a dead end, and she was right back where she started.

Trying to get a Phoenix build going is like playing *Legend of Zelda*, if it were written by a sadist, forcing her to adventure far and wide to find hidden keys scattered across the kingdom and given only measly clues from uncaring NPCs. But when you finally finish the level, you can't actually play the next level—you have to mail paper coupons to the manufacturer and wait weeks to get the activation codes.

If this really were a video game, Maxine would have already quit, because this game sucks. But Phoenix isn't a game—Phoenix is important, and Maxine never quits or abandons important things.

Maxine sits at her desk looking at the calendar she's printed out and pinned to the wall.

She turns back to her computer and runs her finger down her ever-growing list of to-dos again—each item a dependency she requires to get her build going.

She just added two more SharePoint credentials she needs to get from two different Dev managers who, for some reason, run their own Active Directory domains. They're rumored to contain some critical build documentation with some of the information she seeks.

Randy sent her a ton of Word docs, Visio diagrams, and marketing PowerPoint presentations, which she quickly skims for clues. They may be helpful to marketing people and architects, she supposes, but she's an engineer. She doesn't want to see brochures for the car they've promised to build—she wants to see the engineering plans and the actual parts that they're going to assemble the car from.

These documents might be useful to someone, so she posted them on the wiki. Moments later, someone she doesn't know asks her to take them down because they might contain confidential information.

Looking further down her to-do list, she reads:

Find someone who can give me access to Dev or Test environments.

These were referenced in some of the documentation she read yesterday, but she has no idea who to ask to get access.

She has crossed off one item:

~~Get account for integration test environment.~~

This was less satisfying than she had hoped. She poked around the environment for two hours, trying to gain an understanding of the giant application. But in the end, she found it too bewildering—it was like trying to picture the layout of an enormous building by crawling around air ducts without a map or a flashlight.

She types out a new to-do:

Find someone who's actually doing integration testing so I can shoulder-surf while they work.

Watching someone use the Phoenix applications might help orient her. She's baffled that no one knows of an actual person who uses Phoenix. *Just who are they building all this code for?*

Scanning her to-do list again, she confirms that she in fact has nothing to actually do—she has already pestered everybody today and now she's just waiting for people to (not) get back to her.

It's Friday, 1:32 p.m. Three and a half hours to go until five, when she can finally leave the building. She tries hard not to sigh again.

She looks at her to-do list. She looks at the clock.

She looks at her nails, thinking that she needs a manicure.

She gets up from her desk with her coffee mug and walks to the kitchen, passing by groups of people wearing hoodies, huddled together, talking in hushed urgency. Just to have something to do, she pours herself another cup of coffee. She looks down at her mug and realizes that she's already had five cups today, to satisfy the need to be *doing something*. She pours her coffee down the drain.

Along with her ever expanding to-do list, Maxine has kept a daily work diary on her personal laptop for the last decade. In it, she tracks everything she's worked on, how much time she spent on it, any interesting lessons she learned from it, and a list of things to never do again (most recently, "Don't waste time trying to escape spaces in file names in Makefiles—it's too difficult. Use anything else instead.").

She stares at her huge to-do list and her recent work diary entries in disbelief. She has never met a system she couldn't beat. *Is it possible that the utterly mediocre Phoenix Project, totally incapable of anything, is actually defeating me? Over my dead body,* she vows silently, then turns back to her work diary entries.

WEDNESDAY

4 p.m.: Waited around for Josh this afternoon who was supposed to walk me through his setup so I can replicate it. He's dealing with more nightly build problems.

I have a ticket to get access to build server, but was told by security that I need authorization from my manager. Sent email to Randy.

I'm reading every developer design doc I can find, but they're all starting to look the same to me. I want to see the source code, not read design docs.

4:30 p.m.: In one of the design docs I found the most succinct description of Phoenix: "Project Phoenix will close the gap with the competition, allowing our customers to do the same things online that they can do in our 900 stores. We will finally have a single view of our customers, so in-store employees can see their preferences and order history, and enable more effective cross-channel promotion."

The scope of Phoenix is a little frightening. It needs to talk to hundreds of other applications across the enterprise. What could go wrong?

5 p.m.: Calling it a day. Chris stopped by, reminding me to not rock the boat or call too much attention to myself. And to not deploy anything into production.

Yeah, yeah. Sheesh. I can't even get a build going or log into network shares. How would I be able to push anything into production?

Bored out of my skull. Going home to play with new puppy.

THURSDAY
9:30 a.m.: Yes! They've given me accounts on a couple more wikis. I'm eager to dig in. This is progress, right?

10 a.m.: Seriously? This is it? I found some QA docs, but this can't be all of it, right? Where are all the test plans? Where are the automated test scripts?

12 p.m.: Okay, I met William, the QA director. Seems like a nice guy. We were able to meet just long enough to get me user accounts for their network share. Millions of Word docs filled with manual test plans.

I emailed William asking whether I can meet some of his test team. How do they execute all these tests? Seems like they need a small army. And where do they put the test results? I'm on his calendar. In two weeks. Madness.

3 p.m.: I found out where the big daily project stand-up is held: it's 8 a.m. by the whiteboards. I missed it today, but I won't miss it tomorrow.

5 p.m.: I've gotten so little done in two days. Everything I try to do requires an email, a ticket, or trying to find someone. I'm now resorting to asking them out for coffee. Maybe I'll get more responses.

FRIDAY

10 a.m.: The "15-minute stand-up meeting" went for almost 90 minutes because of all the emergencies. I don't know how I missed this meeting yesterday—seems hard to miss because of all the yelling. Wow.

OMG. Almost no one else can build Phoenix on their laptops, either. They're supposed to deploy this into production in TWO WEEKS! (No one is worried. Crazy. They think it will be delayed again.)

If I were in their shoes, I'd be losing my shit. Oh, well.

2 p.m.: I found a bunch of contractor developers brought in two months ago. They can't do builds, either. Shocking. I took them out to lunch. What a disappointment. They know even less than I do. At least the salad was okay.

I shared everything I know with them, which they were extremely grateful for. Always good to give more than you get—you never know who can help you in the future. Networking matters.

Note to self: I must curb my coffee intake. Must have drunk 7 cups yesterday. This is not good—I think I'm getting heart palpitations.

At 4:45, Maxine packs up her things. There's no chance anyone will get her anything this late on a Friday.

She almost makes it to the staircase when she runs into Randy.

"Hi, Maxine. Bummer we couldn't get further on the Dev environment. I escalated a bunch of issues and will make some phone calls before I leave today."

Maxine shrugs. "Thanks. I hope that lights a fire under some people."

"Whatever it takes, right?" Randy smiles. "Uh, I have one more thing that I need?"

Uh oh, thinks Maxine. But she says, "Sure, what's up?"

"Umm. Everyone on the Phoenix Project is required to submit time-cards," Randy says. "We've got to show utilization levels or the project management people take our people away. I sent you the link to our time-carding system. Could you fill it out before you leave? It should only take a couple of minutes."

He looks both ways before whispering, "I especially need *your* hours because when it comes to budgeting next year, it will help me backfill your position."

"No problem at all, Randy. I'll take care of it right now before I leave," Maxine says agreeably, but she is not happy. She understands the budgeting games that need to be played, but that's not what bothers her. Instead, it's that she already knows exactly what she worked on all week, because she keeps such meticulous notes. Absolutely zero real outcomes accomplished. Zilch. Nothing. Nada.

Back at her desk, she logs into the time-carding system. By her name are hundreds of project codes. They're not the project names. Instead, they're project codes that all look like airline reservation numbers—ten characters long with capital letters.

Looking at Randy's email, she copies the project code he gave her (PPX423-94-10) into the field and then dutifully puts in eight hours into each field from Wednesday to Friday and hits submit. She frowns. It won't let her submit until she describes what she did each day.

Maxine groans. She writes something for each day, basically saying some variant of "Working on Phoenix builds but waiting for entire universe to get me something." She spends five minutes modifying the text so that each entry is sufficiently different from each other.

It felt bad enough to be sitting on her butt getting so little done this week, despite her very best efforts, but it feels far worse to have to lie about it in writing.

Over the weekend, Maxine continually scans her phone for updates on her tickets, but only sees them being transferred from one person to another. When her husband, Jake, asks her why she is brooding, she refuses to admit that it's because of the timecard she filled out—it was like rubbing salt in the wound of non-productiveness. She allows herself to be distracted by their new puppy, Waffles, and thoroughly enjoys seeing her kids play with him.

By Monday morning, Maxine has successfully convinced herself to be cheerful, upbeat, and optimistic as she files into the big auditorium for the Town Hall that the CEO of the company, Steve Masters, hosts every other month. She's enjoyed attending these ever since she joined the company. Her first one made a big impression on her because it was the first time she had seen executives directly address an entire company, taking questions from any of the nearly seven thousand employees.

Steve usually presents with Dick, the CFO. About a year ago, Steve also started co-presenting with Sarah Moulton, the SVP of retail operations. She has profit-and-loss responsibility for retail, the second largest business unit generating over $700 million in revenue per year. While Steve and Dick exude a certain amount of trust and authenticity, Sarah seems less trustable and believable. Last year, she had a different pitch every Town Hall, promising a totally different transformation then what had been presented before, causing lots of confusion, organizational whiplash, and eventually ridicule.

Maxine sees Steve preparing off stage, writing last-minute notes on a folded sheet of paper. Someone hands him a microphone, and he walks onto the stage to polite applause. "Good morning, everyone. Thank you so much for joining us today. This is sixty-sixth Town Hall that I've had the privilege of hosting.

"As you know, for almost a century, our mission has been to help our hard-working customers keep their cars running so that they can conduct their daily lives. For most of our customers, that means driving to work so they can collect a paycheck, take their kids to school, and take care of their loved ones. Parts Unlimited helps our customers in many ways. We are one of the world's most admired manufacturing organizations, making the high-quality and affordable parts that our customers need to keep their cars running. We also have over seven thousand world-class employees directly helping our customers in nearly one thousand stores around this great nation. We are often the only thing that keeps their cars out of expensive service stations."

Maxine has heard this almost fifty times from Steve at these sessions— it's obviously important to him to remind everyone who their customers really are. When things go wrong with Maxine's car, she usually takes it to her car dealership because it's still under warranty. But the vast majority of their customers don't have that luxury. Their cars are older, sometimes older than her kids—in fact, their customers may be driving the same make, model, and year of the car she drove as a teenager. They often have little discretionary income. When something goes wrong with their car, it can wipe out whatever savings they have (if any). And when their car is at a repair shop, they not only deplete their savings but they also can't drive to work. And that means they can't provide for their families.

Maxine appreciates these reminders about their customers—when engineers think of "the customer" in the abstract instead of as a real person, you rarely get the right outcomes.

Steve continues, "For almost a century, that mission has remained unchanged, although the business environment certainly has. On the manufacturing side, we now have fierce overseas competitors that undercut our prices. On the retail side, our competitors have opened up thousands of stores in the very same markets we serve.

"We are also in a time of incredible economic disruption. Amazon and the other e-commerce giants are reshaping our economy. Some of the most famous retailers that many of us grew up with are going out of business, such as Toys"R"Us, Blockbuster, and Borders. Just down the road here from corporate headquarters, many of us drive past that space where the old Blockbuster used to be, and that space has remained vacant for over a decade.

"We are not immune to this. Our same-store sales are continuing to decline. Many of our customers would rather order their windshield wipers from their phone from someone else than go into one of our physical stores and talk to someone.

"But I believe people don't want just automotive parts; they want help from people they trust. And that's why our store associates are so important. That's why we invest so much in training. And the Phoenix Project will allow us to bring that expertise and trust to our customers in the channels they want to use, whether it's our physical stores or online.

"Sarah will talk about the progress of the Phoenix Project later, and how it supports the three metrics I care most about: employee engagement, customer satisfaction, and cash flow. If all our employees are excited to come to work each day, and if we're delighting our customers through constant innovation and great service, cash flow will take care of itself.

"But before we go through our top annual goals, let me first talk about something that is probably on all your minds," Steve pauses for several moments. "Recently, I sent out an email that Bob Strauss is taking over as chairman of Parts Unlimited. As many of you know, I've been here for eleven years, and for the first eight of those, I had the privilege of working for Bob. He was the person who hired me back when I was head of sales at another manufacturer. I'll always be grateful to Bob for giving me a chance to be COO of this company and for mentoring me over the years. When he retired, I took over for him as CEO and chairman.

"Effective last week, the board of directors has re-appointed Bob to be board chairman," Steve says, his voice starting to quaver. Maxine watches with amazement as he wipes a tear from his eye. "Of course, I support this move and I look forward to working with Bob again. I've asked Bob to come out and share some words with us and tell us what it means for the company."

Until this moment, Maxine hadn't realized how much of a setback this was for Steve. She had heard that it was a demotion, but to be honest, she didn't really understand or care much about these types of changes at the executive level. Executives came and went, often without much impact on her and her daily work. But she's riveted by the drama unfolding in front of her.

A slightly stooped older man with white hair and a wry smile walks on stage and stands next to Steve.

"Hi, everyone. It's great to be here in front of you after so many years. I even see some familiar faces, which makes me very happy. For those of you who don't know me, my name is Bob Strauss. I was CEO of this company for fifteen years, back when dinosaurs roamed the earth. And even before that, I was an employee at this great company for nearly thirty years. As Steve mentioned, it was with great hope and pride that I recruited him away from another company many years ago.

"Since retiring, I've continued to serve on the board of directors. The job of the board is very simple: to represent the interests of the company shareholders, which includes almost all of you. We want to ensure that the company's future is secure. If you have a pension or have been part of our employee retirement stock purchase plan, this is probably as important to you as it is to me.

"We do this primarily by keeping company executives accountable, by hiring, and, umm, occasionally firing the CEO," he says plainly. Maxine's breath catches slightly—until that moment, Bob seemed like a friendly grandfather. Apparently, he has a stricter side.

"Just by looking at the stock price, you know that the markets don't think we are performing as well as we should be. When our company's stock price goes down while our competitors' shares are going up, something has to change.

"I like to think that companies have two modes of operations: peacetime and wartime. Peacetime is when things are going well. This is when we are growing as a company and can continue business as usual. During these times, the CEO is often also the board chairman. However, wartime is when the company is in crisis, when it is shrinking or at risk of disappearing entirely, like what's happening to us now.

"During wartime, it's about finding ways to avoid extinction. And during wartime, the board will often split the roles of CEO and chairman." Bob pauses, squinting into the bright lights, looking across the entirely silent audience. "I want everyone to know that I have complete confidence in Steve and his leadership. And if all goes well, we'll figure out how to get him the chairmanship again so I can go back into retirement where I belong." The crowd laughs nervously as Bob waves and makes his exit.

Steve steps up to the front of the stage and says, "Could everyone give a round of applause for Bob Strauss?"

After a muted applause, Steve resumes, "The company goals this year were to stabilize our business. Our manufacturing operation makes up two-thirds of our revenue, which has remained flat but still profitable. This has been the mainstay of our business for almost a century, and we've been able to fend off our very fierce Asian competitors.

"However, our retail operations continue to underperform. Our revenue is nearly five percent lower than last year," he says. "Our biggest quarter is still coming up, so there's hope. But hope alone is not a strategy, and you can see how Wall Street has reacted to our performance so far. However, I remain confident that the Phoenix Project will help us adapt to these new market conditions.

"So, without further ado, I'll turn it over to Sarah Moulton, our SVP of retail operations, to describe why the Phoenix Project is so important to the future of the company."

Sarah walks onto the stage wearing a strikingly beautiful royal blue business suit. Whatever Maxine's opinion of Sarah, she grants that Sarah always looks fabulous. In fact, she would look right at home on the cover of *Fortune*—intelligent, aggressive, and ambitious.

"As Steve and Bob mentioned," Sarah begins, "we are in a time of incredible digital disruption in retail. Even *our* customers order online and through their phones. The goal of the Phoenix Project is to enable our customers to order however they want, whether it be online, in our stores, or even through our channel partners. And wherever they order, they should be able to have their product delivered to their homes or to pick it up in one of stores.

"This is what we've been trying to do for years. Right now, our stores are still in the dark ages. That was Parts Unlimited 1.0. The Phoenix Project will create Parts Unlimited 2.0. There are so many efficiencies we can create to help us compete against the e-commerce giants, but we must innovate and be agile. In order to remain relevant, people need to view us as a market leader creating new business models—what worked for our first century may not work for our second."

As always, there's some validity to what Sarah says, Maxine grudgingly acknowledges, but she can be so condescending.

"The Phoenix Project is the most important initiative for our company, and we're betting our survival on it. We've spent nearly $20 million on this project over three years, and customers still haven't seen any value," she continues. "I've decided that it's time for us to finally get in the game. We will be launching the Phoenix Project later this month. No more delays. No more postponements."

Maxine hears an audible gasp from the whole audience and a loud buzz of urgent murmuring. Sarah continues, "This will finally give us parity with the competition, and we will be poised to regain market share."

Maxine sighs in frustration. She understands Sarah's urgency, but it doesn't change the fact that there are over a hundred developers who are nowhere near as productive as they should be, struggling to perform routine builds, spending too much time in meetings, or waiting for things they need. Sarah's speech sounds like listening to a general tell you how important winning the war is and then finding out that all the soldiers have been stuck in port for three years.

On the other hand, at least Sarah hasn't pitched something completely new today.

Steve thanks Sarah and then quickly reviews the company financials, and an injury that happened in one of the manufacturing plants last month. He talks about Hannah, who had her finger crushed by a stamping machine, and how they've replaced that machine with one that has a sensor preventing the plates from closing when anyone is the danger area. He applauds the team for not waiting for budget to act on this, "Remember, safety is a precondition of work."

Maxine loves these report-outs and has always been impressed and emotionally moved by how much Steve cares about employee safety.

He says, "That almost concludes our report-out. We have about fifteen minutes for questions and answers."

Maxine's attention wanders as people ask Steve questions about the revenue forecast, the performance of the physical stores, the recent issues in manufacturing…But when someone asks about the payroll outage, she's jolted alert before shrinking back into her seat while straining to hear every word.

"I apologize to everyone who was affected by this," Steve replies. "I understand how disruptive this was to everyone, and rest assured that we've taken very specific actions to make sure that it never happens again. It was a combination of technical problems and human error, and we think we've remedied both of them."

Maxine closes her eyes, feeling her cheeks turn bright red, hoping no one is looking at her. She can't see how her exile to the Phoenix Project could possibly be considered a remedy.

CHAPTER 3

• *Monday, September 8*

After the Town Hall, Maxine returns to her desk. She looks at her calendar. It's day four of her imprisonment and her quest to perform a Phoenix build, but it feels like it's been nearly a year, the hours passing like molasses.

She gets a notification on her phone, startling her back to reality:

Phoenix Project: stakeholder status update (starting in 15 minutes).

This is a new meeting for her. To further her quest, she has asked everyone to feel free to invite her to any meetings. It beats sitting at her desk, and she's still trying to get the lay of the land. She's hoping to find someone who can get her some of the things she needs. She's been careful to avoid getting assigned any action items or to volunteer to work on fun-sounding features—she cannot be distracted from the Phoenix build.

Everyone around here thinks features are important, because they can see them in their app, on the web page, or in the API. But no one seems to realize how important the build process is. Developers cannot be productive without a great build, integration, and test process.

She arrives early and is surprised that there's no room except in the back. She stands against the wall with five other people. Looking around, her eyes widen—all the movers and shakers in the company are here. Maxine smiles when she sees that Kirsten Fingle is leading the meeting. She heads up the Project Management Office. Maxine loved working with her when she was supporting a major program that had several of Kirsten's project manager ninjas assigned to it—they were typically reserved for the most important projects that required lots of coordination across many groups within the company. They're aces at making things happen. They can escalate and resolve issues quickly, often with a single text message.

At the front of the room is Chris, who gives her a terse nod—he oversees the efforts of over two hundred developers and QA people, dominated by the Phoenix Project. Chris is glaring at someone across the table from him who looks like Ed Harris from *Apollo 13*. When she quietly asks the person next to her who he is, he responds, "Bill Palmer, the new VP of IT Operations. Promoted last week after the big executive purge."

Great, Maxine thinks. But she enjoys seeing the seniority of the people in the room. It's like being up on the bridge of the starship *Enterprise* and watching the officers interact with each other.

She enjoys the first fifteen minutes of the meeting. It's chaos. Everyone is trying to decipher what exactly Sarah meant at the Town Hall when she said that the launch was "later this month." Kirsten says emphatically, "The date is still being negotiated and nothing specific has been communicated to me yet." *Could it really be another false alarm?* Maxine thinks, incredulous.

Maxine guesses that there is extra urgency as they review the business priorities, the top issues needing escalation and attention, and the priorities that need deconflicting. She doesn't know what all the acronyms mean, but she adds the ones that she thinks are actually important to her list and leaves out the insipid corporate argle-bargle.

As the meeting drones on and against all her expectations, she grows bored as the focus turns toward meaningless minutia, passionately pushed by... she honestly has no idea. *Does OEP stand for "Order Entry Protocol" or "Order Entry Program"? Or were they talking about the OPA again? Or maybe they were the same thing? Do I really care?*

Forty minutes later, her eyes are glazed over—it's the "task status" phase of the meeting, and Maxine has lost all interest. If she had anything else to work on, she would have left by now.

Her feet hurt from standing so long, and she is reconsidering her decision to stay in the meeting when she hears someone complaining about how long they've been waiting for something they need. She smirks as she thinks, *Join the club. That's what I do all day long.*

One of the Dev managers responds from the "junior people" side of the table. "Yes, we're definitely behind, but we have a couple of new developers starting this week to help, and they should be up to speed and productive in a week or two."

Ha. I'm really good at this stuff and I've made almost no progress, she thinks, looking at the floor. She smirks to herself. *Good luck, chumps.*

There is a long, awkward silence in the room. Maxine looks up. To her horror, everyone is looking at her—she realizes that she must have said something aloud.

She looks at Chris, who has a stunned expression on his face and is wildly gesturing with his hands at her in a "no, no, no" kind of way.

From the front of the room, Kirsten quickly says, "Great to see you, Maxine! I had no idea you were on Phoenix. We're glad to have someone of your experience helping this effort—you couldn't have shown up at a better time!"

Chris buries his face in his hands. If Maxine hadn't already been standing against the wall, she would have been backpedaling. Mimicking Chris, she waves her hands in front of her. "No, no, no...Sorry, I've only been here a few days. You're all doing an amazing job. Please carry on—I'm just here to help with documentation and builds."

Kirsten, with the earnestness that makes her so effective, doesn't let it go. She leans forward. "No, really. I think you said, 'Good luck, chumps.' I'm always interested in your perspective, given your extensive success in plant operations. I'd love to better understand what made you laugh."

"I'm sorry I laughed," she starts. "It's just that I've done nothing except try to get Phoenix builds going on my laptop since last Wednesday, and I'm basically nowhere. I'm waiting for credentials, license keys, environments, configuration files, documentation, you name it—I know everyone has a lot on their plate and I know that Phoenix is such a large application that getting all the pieces together to do a build must be a pretty immense undertaking, but if we all want our developers to be productive, they need to be able to perform builds on Day One. Ideally, they should be writing code in a production-like environment so they can get fast feedback on whether the code they write works with the system as a whole. After days of trying, I still don't have anything resembling the whole system—I have a box of subassemblies, with a whole bunch of missing parts. And I'm really, really good at this stuff."

She looks around the room and gives a half-hearted shrug to Chris. She really needed to get that off her chest. Chris looks aghast.

"I'm just hoping these new engineers that you've been hiring have better luck than me, that's all," she concludes quickly.

There's a long awkward silence. Randy nods emphatically and crosses his arms, looking smug. Someone from across the table laughs loudly. "She is so right! They'll need a lot more than luck! Getting a Dev environment around here is like going to the local DMV to renew your driver's license—take a number, fill out a bunch of forms, and wait. Hell, I can get a driver's license in a day...it's more like trying to get a permit to start a new construction project—no one knows how long it'll take."

Half the people in the room laugh unkindly, while the other half of the room is clearly offended.

Maxine looks at the wise-cracking person who spoke—he's about forty-five, slightly overweight in an "ex-athlete" sort of way. He's square-jawed, oddly clean-shaven, with big, square glasses. He's wearing a skateboarding T-shirt, and his face has a permanent scowl.

Based on his crankiness, Maxine bets that he's a senior developer—being stuck in an environment like Phoenix for a long period of time must take a toll on people.

Someone from the front of the room starts responding—she recognizes William, the *super nice* Director of QA, who has gone *out of his way* to help her. "Look," he says, "our teams are getting further behind on testing, so we all agreed that in order to hit our dates we would deprioritize environment work—shipping fully tested features would take priority. We all knew that this would increase the lead times for getting environments to our teams. Trust me, my teams are being hit just as hard as yours—QA needs environments to test in too."

The cranky developer immediately responds, "William, you got suckered. That was a terrible decision. This is a disaster. Maxine is right—developers need environments to be productive. You should have an entire *team* of people assigned to fix the environment creation process. I'm on three projects that need staging environments, all of which have been waiting months. In fact, this is so important, I'd like to volunteer to help," he says.

"Denied," says Chris wearily from the front of the room. "Stay in your lane, Dave. We need you focused on features."

William says, "Wait, wait...I'll have you know that we're not actually the bottleneck for environments—we have several environments that are ready to go, but we still need login accounts from Security and storage and mount points from Ops. I've escalated it but haven't heard anything yet."

Chris points a finger accusingly at Bill and turns to Kirsten, "I need help on escalating our needs to Operations."

Bill quickly responds. "If we're the bottleneck, I need to know. Let's figure out how to get William what he needs."

Kirsten nods, appearing slightly exasperated. Maxine assumes it's because more and more dependencies are surfacing. "Yes, good idea, Bill. Alright, let's move to the next milestone on the list."

As Kirsten talks, Chris turns to look at Maxine, his expression screaming, *Which part of "lie low" did you not understand, Maxine?* Maxine mouths the word sorry.

Out of the corner of her eye, she sees a younger man kneel by Kirsten, whispering in her ear while gesturing at Maxine. Instead of wearing khaki pants, he's wearing jeans and is holding a black Moleskine notebook.

Kirsten nods and smiles at him, points at Maxine, and whispers a couple of sentences in return. The young man nods, furiously taking notes.

Maxine decides to make a beeline for the door, leaving as quickly as possible before she does something else stupid.

She makes it into the cool hallway, relieved to be out of that hot, stuffy room. She heads to the kitchen, where it is even cooler. She's thinking about getting a mug of coffee, maybe her fifth today, when she hears someone say behind her, "Hello, you must be Maxine!"

She turns around. It's the young man from the meeting who was talking to Kirsten. He smiles broadly and extends his hand, saying, "Hi, I'm Kurt. I'm one of the QA managers who works for William. I heard in the meeting that you need license keys and environments and a bunch of other things to get a build running? I think I can help."

For a moment, Maxine just stares back at him, not sure if she heard him correctly. For days, her life has been to search every nook and cranny for the components needed to build Phoenix. For days, she's been submitting ticket after ticket into an uncaring and faceless bureaucracy. She's stunned that someone actually seems to want to help her.

Maxine catches herself staring at Kurt's outstretched hand, snaps back to reality, and shakes it. "Nice meeting you. I'm Maxine, and, yes, I'll take any help I can get to get a Phoenix build going!"

She adds, "I hope that I didn't step on anyone's toes back there. I'm sure everyone is doing their best, you know, given everything that is going on…"

He smiles even more broadly, pointing his thumb back toward the conference room that they were in. "Those folks? Don't worry about it. They're in such deep trouble that they're all covering their asses and throwing each other under the bus. I doubt they'll even remember what you said by the end of the day."

Maxine laughs, but Kurt is all business. "So, you need to get Phoenix builds going. How far have you gotten and what do you still need?"

Maxine slumps. "Not nearly as far as I want, and it's not for a lack of trying." She describes in considerable detail what she's done so far and all the steps that still remain. She opens her checklist on her tablet, showing him all the open to-dos, pointing out everything she's waiting for.

"Wow, most people give up long before getting as far as you have," Kurt says. "May I see that?" he adds, gesturing to her tablet.

"Sure thing," she says, handing it to him. Kurt runs his finger down the list, nodding and appearing to compare it with another list in his head.

"No problem, I think I can get you almost all of these things," he says. And with a smile, he adds, "I'll throw in a couple other things that I'm guessing you'll need later. Don't worry, you couldn't have known. We had to learn the hard way too. No one around here documents the build environment very well."

Kurt takes a picture of her list with his phone and gives it back to her. "You'll hear from me in a day or two," he says. "The Phoenix Project is in the Stone Age. We've got hundreds of developers and QA people working on this project, and most can only build their portion of the code base. They're not building the whole system, let alone testing it on any regular basis. I keep pointing this out to the powers that be, but they tell me they have everything under control."

He looks pointedly at her. "You wouldn't put up with that back in your old MRP group supporting the manufacturing plant, right?" he asks.

"No way," she responds quickly. "It's like that guy said in the meeting—developers need a system where they can get fast and continual feedback on the quality of their work. If you don't find problems quickly, you end up finding them months later. By then, the problem is lost in all the other changes that every other developer made, so the link between cause and effect disappears without a trace. That's no way to run any project."

Kurt nods. "And yet, here we are, running the Phoenix Project, the most important project in the company, like we would have run a program in the 1970s. Developers coding all day and only integrating their changes and testing at the end of the project. What could go wrong?" he adds with smirk. "They keep telling me these decisions are above my pay grade."

They both laugh.

Kurt doesn't seem bitter or cynical. He radiates a good-natured vibe with an easy acceptance of the way the world works. He continues, "I envy how much your manufacturing team got done and how many platforms you supported. We've got ten times as many people on Phoenix, but I suspect your old team gets a lot more done than we do."

Maxine nods. She definitely misses her old team.

"Oh, and by the way, there's a rumor that might interest you," Kurt says, looking around as if afraid of being overheard. "Word is that Sarah pushed for Phoenix to launch this week, and that Steve just approved it. All hell is about to break loose. Let me know if you want to tag along as they assemble the release team. That'll be super fun to watch."

After that strange interaction, Maxine sits back at her desk and realizes that she is waiting again. Absentmindedly, she looks at a quote she always has taped to her desk from one of her favorite Dr. Seuss books, *Oh, the Places You'll Go.*

The book describes the dreaded Waiting Place, where people wait for the fish to bite, wind to fly a kite, for Uncle Jake, for pots to boil, or a better break... Everyone is just waiting.

> NO!
> That's not for you!
> Somehow you'll escape
> all that waiting and staying.
> You'll find the bright places
> where Boom Bands are playing.

Everyone on the Phoenix Project is stuck in the Waiting Place, and she is determined to rescue everyone from it.

It's 11:45 a.m. Maxine looks at her calendar. It's only day four of her forced exile. While she hadn't hear back from Kurt, she did manage to get access to the third of four source code repositories. Today, she decides that she cannot wait for other people any longer.

She is going to build something.

Over the next four hours, she tries running every Makefile, maven POM, bundler, pip, ant, build.sh, build.psh, and anything resembling a build script she can find. Most fail immediately when she runs them. Some barf out alarmingly long error messages.

She pores through all the error logs, scanning for any clues on how to get something to actually run, sifting through all the poo for anything resembling a peanut—laborious and unpleasant work. She identifies at least twenty missing dependencies or executables that she needs. Several times she asks around to see if anyone knows where to get these things, opening tickets and sending out emails, but no one knows. She spends three hours searching around the internet for clues, pouring through Google and Stack Overflow.

In a moment of very poor judgment, she decides to try building some of the missing components from scratch, from similar sounding components that she finds on GitHub. Five hours later she's in a terrible mood—exhausted, frustrated, irritated, and absolutely positive that she has just wasted an entire day going down rabbit holes she never should have gone down.

Basically, she tried to forge missing engine parts by melting down aluminum cans. *That was really dumb, Maxine*, she thinks.

That night when she gets home, she realizes that she has brought all the frustration from work with her. She warns her husband and kids that she is currently incapable of conversation and finds two mini-bottles of Veuve Cliquot rosé in the fridge. When her teenage kids see her, they know immediately to avoid her. She is wearing her "Mom is in a super bad mood" face.

While they prepare dinner, she crawls into bed and watches movies.

What an utter waste of a day, she fumes.

She reflects upon the difference between a great day and a bad day. A great day is when she's solving an important business problem. Time flies by because she's so focused and loving the work. She's in a state of flow, to the point where it doesn't feel like work at all.

A bad day is spent banging her head against a monitor, scouring the internet for things she doesn't even want to learn but needs to in order to solve the problem at hand. As she falls asleep, she tries not to think about how much of her life is spent searching the internet for how to make error messages go away.

It's a new day. Fresh from a good night's sleep, she sits at her desk, intent on *not* repeating yesterday's mistake. Just because she felt busy doesn't mean that she actually did anything meaningful. In a terminal window, she pulls up her work from yesterday and, without looking at it, deletes it all.

Then she pulls up all of her open tickets in the ticketing system. She refuses to feel powerless, at the mercy of distant powers, trapped inside a cold bureaucracy actively impeding her goals, aspirations, desires, and needs.

Maxine has a long and complicated history with ticketing systems, both good and bad.

Last year, she funded a Kickstarter project for a mug that promised to keep her coffee or tea at whatever temperature she wanted for hours. It even had a Bluetooth connection so that she could see and set the temperature of her drink from her phone. She loved the idea of it and quickly paid five hundred dollars to help the inventor.

She was thrilled every time she got a notification: when the inventor reached her funding goals, when a manufacturer was selected, when the first production run started, and, most importantly, when her mug had been shipped. It was so satisfying to be a part of the collective journey and to eventually hold one of the first five hundred mugs made.

The Dev ticketing system felt totally different. It was the opposite of the joy and anticipation she had felt with her magic mug. Instead, it reminded her of the horrific experience of getting her first high-speed DSL broadband package working back in the 1990s. Although she received the DSL modem right away, she then had to deal with the internet service reseller (who sold her the DSL service) and the phone company (who owned the copper wires to her house).

Whoever did the installation at her house must have screwed up because nothing worked—and when she called either organization, they told her that it was the other's responsibility to fix it. Sometimes they could find a ticket related to her previous conversations, sometimes not. She was trapped in a cruel, uncaring, Kafka-esque bureaucracy. For four weeks, her awesome DSL modem did nothing except flash a red blinking light. It was as useless as a brick, and she had countless open tickets with both organizations.

One day, Maxine decided to take an entire day off of work just to tackle activating her DSL line. After three hours, she finally managed to talk her way up the chain to a Level 3 escalation support person who had access to both ticketing systems. He was amazing and obviously incredibly savvy, able to thread Maxine's request to the right department, using the right keywords to get the two supervisors from both companies on the phone to line up all the necessary work. An hour later, she finally had her 64 Kbps broadband connection working.

Even decades later, she remembers how grateful she was to that support person. She had told him, "I'd love to talk to someone that matters about what an amazing job you did and how grateful I am for your help." She happily stayed on hold for ten more minutes to talk to a supervisor and then spent ten minutes gushing in great detail about all the help that she had received.

It was so important to Maxine to describe how extraordinary and even heroic everything that Level 3 support rep did and how much she valued his help. Maxine was gratified to hear that he was being considered for a promotion and that her phone call likely sealed the deal.

Afterward, Maxine spent an hour watching the blinking green light and savoring the blazingly fast download speeds.

Remembering that savvy support rep, Maxine reminds herself that she loves solving problems, that she loves challenges, and how important her work is. It will help every developer become more productive.

Taking a deep breath, she summons the relentless optimism she's been accused of having, and carefully scans her email for any new ticket status changes. She ignores all the team status updates, except for the ones where people are yelling at each other in ALL CAPS. She wants to know who the hotheads are so she can avoid them.

Continuing to scroll, Maxine's heart leaps when she sees the subject line:

Notification: change to ticket #46132: Phoenix Dev environment.

Is her Dev environment finally ready?

She tries not to get excited, because she's been fooled before. Twice yesterday she got a notification, but it was only for the most minor status changes on her ticket. The first was when someone finally looked at the ticket; the second was when it was reassigned to someone else.

Maxine clicks on the link in the email, which pulls up the entire history of the ticket on her browser. She squints and leans closer to her screen. She opened the ticket six days ago (if she counts the weekend), and there have been seven status changes as different people worked on her environment request. As of 8:07 this morning, the ticket is marked closed.

She hoots loudly. At long last, the Ops people are done! She is in the build business!

But she's confused. Where's her environment? How does she log in? What's the IP address? Where are the login credentials?

She scrolls to the very bottom to the notes and comments, reading what each person typed in as they were worked on her ticket. It got bounced from Bob, to Sarah, to Terry, back to Sarah, then finally to Derek. At the very bottom of the notes, Derek wrote:

> To get a Dev environment we need approval from your manager. The correct process is documented below. Closing ticket.

Maxine's face turns hot and bright red.

Derek closed my ticket?! After all that waiting, he just closed my ticket because I didn't have an approval from a manager?

Who the hell is Derek?! Maxine yells to herself.

She moves her cursor around the ticketing screen, trying to find anything to click on. But the only clickable link is the policy document that Derek provided. She can't find any way to find out who Derek is or how to contact him. She finds a button to reopen the ticket, but it's grayed out.

Thanks a lot, Derek, you shithead, thinks Maxine angrily.

Fuming, she realizes she needs a break. She stomps out of the building and sits on a bench in front of the office, she takes a deep breath, closes her eyes, and counts to fifty. Then she walks back into the office and sits down at her desk.

She clicks the button to open a new ticket. When the blank ticket appears, with the countless fields that need to be filled in, she almost gives up and goes home. Almost. Instead, she forces herself to smile and summons up her friendliest self:

> Hi, Derek. Thank you so much for working on my environment, which we badly need for the Phoenix Project—please see Ticket #46132 (link below). I'm assuming I can paste my manager's approval (Randy Keyes) in this ticket? I'll get an email from Randy with his approval for you in the next 30 minutes. Can I call you to make sure this gets processed today?

She clicks the Submit button, writes a short email to Randy asking him to okay the creation of a Dev environment, and runs to his desk. She's relieved to see that he's there and not in a meeting. She tells him what she needs and then stands over him as he sends a reply that merely says "Approved."

By the time she gets back to her desk, she feels a sense of grim determination and relentless focus. She will do whatever it takes to get her Dev environment. She sits down, copies and pastes Randy's approval from her email into the service desk ticket, and adds the note:

> Derek, thanks so much. Here's my manager's approval. Can I still get this environment today?

She hits submit.

She pulls up the corporate phone directory and scans for all the Dereks in the IT organization. There's three. The one in the helpdesk department is the most promising.

She emails him a nice, friendly note, CCing Randy, to thank him in advance for all his help and to let him know how grateful she'll be to get builds going for Phoenix, practically begging him not to put her ticket at the bottom of the queue where it will take another week to process.

She hits send. Five seconds later:

> This is an automated response—please put all service desk related tasks into the service desk. I will do my best to read all my emails and respond in 72 hours. If this is an emergency, please call this number...

She curses. She imagines Derek sitting with his feet up on his desk, guffawing at her misery. She prints out everything related to Ticket #46132, her emails, and the names of the three Dereks, looking up where each one of them sits. Helpdesk Derek is two buildings over, lower level.

She steps out of the elevator on Derek's floor and sees rows of small cubicles with people wearing headsets in front of computers. There are no windows. The ceilings are surprisingly low. She can hear the electrical buzz of florescent lights. It's oddly quiet. *There should be more fans running to make the air less stale*, she thinks. She hears people typing and a few people talking politely to people on the phone.

Seeing all this, she feels suddenly very, very guilty about her previous anger toward Derek. She asks someone where he sits. After walking through the maze of cubicles, she finally sees Derek's nameplate, printed by an ink-jet printer without enough ink. Then she sees Derek.

He's not a hardened bureaucrat at all. Instead, he's in his early twenties. He's Asian, with a remarkably earnest expression as he scans something on a small LCD screen. Maxine has had laptops with bigger screens than this budget PC setup. She feels even worse about all the bad things she's thought about him.

There are no extra chairs, so Maxine kneels down beside him. "Hi, Derek," she says in her most friendly voice. "I'm Maxine, the person who submitted the ticket about the Dev environment last week. You closed it this morning because I didn't have a manager's approval. I just got it. And because you closed the ticket, I had to open a new one. I'm wondering if you can help me get this through the system."

"Oh, golly, sorry about closing the ticket. I'm new to all of this!" Derek replies earnestly, obviously distraught that he might have screwed up. "All I know is that I'm supposed to make sure that certain requests that need approvals have them. I can't reopen tickets. Only supervisors can do that. And all new tickets go into the queue where they get assigned to the next open person. Maybe my supervisor can help?"

Maxine slumps, dreading what might be ahead. But looking around at the sea of people, she realizes that if she doesn't get this straightened out now, she will never get her Dev environment.

"Absolutely. That would be great, Derek." He smiles and they walk toward one of the outer offices.

Over the next fifteen minutes, Maxine watches Derek's supervisor expertly navigate through the extensive ticket trail, examining its history. In the time since Maxine left her desk, someone named Samantha has already closed her new ticket, pointing out that approvals cannot be submitted in the "Notes" field.

Maxine refuses to lose her cool. These people are trying to help her. The supervisor apologizes about how inconvenient this is. She merges Maxine's two tickets together, puts Randy's name in the approver field, and resubmits the ticket. "Now Randy just needs to hit one button in the tool and you're good to go! Sorry we can't actually authorize requests— only designated managers can."

"Can he approve it from his phone right now?" she asks, with forced cheer. Apparently not—the helpdesk tool was written before smartphones existed and mobile phones were probably still the size of suitcases capable of showing only seven LED digits.

Maxine sighs, but she thanks them effusively because she is certain she is finally close to achieving her goal. As she turns to leave, Derek asks tentatively, "Do you mind if I ask a stupid question?"

"Of course. There are no stupid questions. Fire away," she smiles, trying not to look manic.

"What's a Dev environment? I've dealt with laptop issues, password resets, and things like that. But I've never heard of an 'environment' before."

And there it is, Maxine thinks, thoroughly humbled. *This week's lesson on patience, kindness, and empathy, brought to you by Derek and the help-desk department.*

Maxine is proud that she has earned a reputation for being level-headed, compassionate, and having empathy for others. But right now, she feels like she demonstrated none of those things. Is being assigned to the Phoenix Project making her a bad person?

She realizes how misdirected her anger at Derek was. This poor guy didn't hold anything against her because she was a developer. He didn't even know what she was asking for, let alone understand how important it was. In his inexperience, he had merely closed her ticket by following the rules set for him. He was only trying to do his job the best he'd been shown how.

Maxine returns to her desk two hours later. She had taken Derek and his supervisor to lunch—out of appreciation for their help and to atone for thinking the worst of Derek. She got the chance to explain the world of development to him, and his earnest curiosity was infectious. She described all the exciting career tracks available for technical people outside of the helpdesk, hoping it might encourage him to explore some of the options available to him.

She goes to find Randy to make sure he approves her request. He's not at his desk. She calls him on her cell phone right away.

"I can't approve it until I'm back at my desk," Randy tells her. "I absolutely promise that I'll approve it when I'm out of meetings. It'll be done before five o'clock."

Maxine goes back to her desk, feeling conflicted. She understands the need for automated workflows. On the manufacturing plant floor, the MRP systems she wrote control everything that thousands of people do virtually every minute of the day. You can't manufacture products in large volumes, costing thousands of dollars, without a rigorous process.

Even the helpdesk process, whether here or at the organization she had to deal with to get her DSL model installed decades ago, is a pretty good way to provide consistent customer service most of the time, even when it's delivered through thousands of call center staff.

So why does the ticketing system here feel so awful? We're all part of Parts Unlimited, so why does everything feel like I'm dealing with a government bureaucracy or an uncaring vendor? Maxine ponders. *Maybe it's because when friends do favors for friends, we don't require them to open a ticket first.*

The next day, Maxine sees that Randy delivered as promised—he approved the Dev environment ticket, but it was too late for anyone to start work on it.

Despite this breakthrough, Maxine is still waiting for a Dev environment. Disappointed, she wanders aimlessly from meeting to meeting, not wanting to be idle at her desk.

Killing time in the kitchen waiting for another pot of coffee to brew, her phone buzzes. Screenful after screenful of email notifications about changes to Ticket #46132 appear. A request to get a virtual machine assigned to the distributed systems group, a request for storage from another group, an IP address from yet another group, a network mount point from another group, application installs from three more groups…

Maxine whoops in delight—progress, at last! Santa just mobilized his magical elf army to start building the Dev environment that she so desperately needs. The cavalry is finally coming!

Exhilarated, she reads through all the tickets. So much work is being dispatched to what appears to be the entire Ops organization. Maxine suddenly becomes alarmed at just *how many people* are required to create one environment.

She works at her desk, planning out what she'll do first with her Dev environment, when her phone starts buzzing incessantly. Opening her emails, her jaw drops at the forty notifications in her inbox. At the top of her screen are a flood of new notifications marking all her tickets as closed.

"No, no, no," she moans, starting to trace through the ticket history from the beginning. She sees that the user accounts were created, the mount points configured, but then she sees a note from one of the storage administrators:

> I'm sorry to have to close your ticket. Believe it or not, we've been out of storage space for the last three months. We have a big order for more storage that we can't expedite until January, and worse, all the controllers are already at capacity. Purchasing says we can only order twice per year to get the best quantity discounts with our vendors. You are near the top of the list, so we'll get this scheduled for February.

Maxine blinks.

It's September.

Phoenix is the most important project in the company. They've spent $20 million over three years. And yet, here she is, trying to help, and they won't spend $5,000 on more disk space. And now she won't get a Dev environment for five months! She buries her head in her hands and silently screams down at her keyboard.

Completely defeated, she takes another walk, to nowhere in particular. It's two thirty p.m. None of the meetings on her calendar seem interesting anymore. It's just people complaining about waiting. Waiting for something. Waiting for someone. Everyone is just waiting. And she wants no part of it right now.

She returns to her desk, picks up her jacket and laptop bag, and decides to leave. She doesn't know where she'll go, but she just can't stay here today.

It isn't until she's behind the steering wheel that she decides to drop by her kids' old school. Not to see her kids—they're at that age where they don't want to be seen with their parents anymore. No, she's going to the lower school where the fifth- and sixth-graders meet for after-school activities. She is proud of having helped the teachers create a coding club three years ago, which has become wildly popular. And she is delighted they've found so many students who are having fun with science, technology, engineering, and math before they go into high school.

Maxine believes learning these skills is incredibly important, because coding is a proficiency that every profession is likely to need in the next decade. It won't be just for developers anymore.

She walks into the classroom and immediately sees Maia and Paige, two of her favorite kids to work with. They're best friends but also fierce competitors, sometimes even archrivals. They're both smart, ambitious, and have a gift for problem-solving.

This is the first time this school year that Maxine has visited. She's surprised at how much older everyone looks and how much their coding skills have progressed. Some are writing what look like games in JavaScript, some are working on web servers, and two students look like they're writing mobile phone apps.

She spends the next hour learning what each group is working on, laughing in delight as they show off what they've created, and loving it when they ask her questions. When Maia and Paige ask her to help solve a problem, she quickly pulls up a chair.

They're trying to complete a classroom exercise to compute the mean, mode, and interquartile ranges of an array of numbers in Python. She immediately sees they've made the same indentation mistake over and over again.

Of course, when they try to run their program, the Python parser vomits at all the indentation errors. They've clearly been struggling to figure out what exactly they did wrong, trying everything they can to make the errors go away.

"May I make a suggestion?" Maxine asks, taking a more active role.

"Of course, Mrs. Chambers," Maia says. Maxine sighs, still not sure how she wants to be addressed by teenagers.

Maxine explains to them how Python indentation works and how it differs from most other programming languages. "But whatever language you're using, the most important thing is to run your program all the time," she says. "When I'm doing something for the first time, I run my program every time I change *anything*, just to make sure it still compiles and runs. That way, I don't make the same mistake for hours without knowing. Better to catch the mistake the first time you make it, right?"

She directs them on how to correctly line up some of the indentation. "Let's see if that fixes the first error..."

She scans the buttons on their editor. "It looks like you can run your program just by hitting Control-Enter. Ah, looks like there's one more little change needed. Yep, you've now fixed that first error. Now fix up the next error until you're back into a working state. If you keep checking after each small change, you'll never have something big you need to fix..."

Reflecting on what she said, she adds, "One of the really nice things about running your program frequently is that you get to see it running, which is fun, and that's what programming is all about."

The girls smile in understanding and stomp out the rest of their errors in quick succession. Maxine grins seeing them use the keyboard accelerator she showed them.

The girls are smiling because their program is actually running now. Looking at the output, Maia notices that something seems wrong. Their computed average is way off.

"Hmm...I think this is an 'off by one' error," Maxine says. "This is one of the most common errors that developers make. It often happens when we are looping through every element in an array, and we miscompute which one is the last element. And that's what's happening here—we missed the last element...and believe it or not, when you accidentally process one element too many, that can cause the program to crash or even be exploited by a hacker."

Maxine can't stop smiling. She's so excited to share this lesson, because over the decades, she's learned that state mutation and looping is so very, very dangerous and difficult to get right. That crashing ODBC database driver she fixed in the middle of the night a decade ago, which made her so notorious, was caused by this type of problem.

This is why Maxine is so dedicated to applying functional programming principles everywhere. Learning Clojure, her favorite programming language, was the most difficult thing she had ever done, because it entirely removes the ability to change (or mutate) variables. Without doubt, it's been the one of her most rewarding learnings, because she's found that about ninety-five percent of the errors she used to make (like the ones the girls just made) have disappeared entirely.

Functional programming is truly a better tool to think with.

"You want to see something cool?" Maxine asks the girls. When they nod, she says, "Here's what I would do. It looks a little strange, but you can get rid of loops entirely by using iterators—it's an easier, and much safer, way to write a loop."

She scans the Python documentation she finds on the internet, and types one line of code in their editor, hitting Control-Enter a couple of times and converging on the right answer.

"Voila! Look at this. It does the same thing as what you wrote, but with no loops or conditional logic, such as checking for the end of the array. In fact, it's only one line of code, with no risk of an 'off-by-one' mistake!" she says, actually feeling proud of what she just wrote.

Maxine is rewarded by "oohs" and "ahs" as the girls' eyes widen at what Maxine shows them. Maxine is pleased, because even this small exercise has banished some unnecessary complexity from the world. It might save the girls from decades of frustration and make the world a safer place.

She spends the next hour floating between the teams, having fun watching kids solve problems and teaching them little tricks here and there to make them more productive and joyful. When the kids adjourn, packing up their huge, heavy backpacks, Maxine realizes that she's in a very good mood.

The joy of teaching people something that they want to learn is awesome. Plus, these are really great kids. She thinks about how easy everything is here. You hit Control-Enter and the program builds and runs. If there is an error, you fix it, hit a key, and try again.

In her current work hellhole, it's the opposite. She still can't build any part of the Phoenix system. Somehow builds have ceased being a part of everyone's daily work.

Maia and Paige made the same indentation mistake for a half hour. At Parts Unlimited, there are a hundred developers probably making bigger mistakes, and it'll be months before they realize they've done something wrong.

Everyone waves goodbye to Maxine, thanking her for all her help. She climbs into her car and slumps in her seat. To her surprise, she feels sad and dispirited—at work, there is none of the joy and learning that she just experienced here. She wonders if this is how everyone on the Phoenix Project feels all the time.

Maxine is about to start her car when her phone vibrates. It's a text message from one of her collaborators on an open-source project she wrote to help her with personal task management. She started this project over five years ago to help her keep awesome work diaries. She's always been a manic record-keeper of how she spends her time.

Initially, it was just to help her be more productive, to triage her incoming tasks from email, Trello, Slack, Twitter, reading lists, and what seemed like a gazillion other places where work is generated. Her app let's her easily push work into GitHub, JIRA, Trello, and the many other tools where she interacts with other people and teams.

Over the years, she's used this program every day to help her run most of her professional and personal life. It's where she sends all her tasks. It's her master inbox, where she can see all her work and move work between all the systems that she works with.

Many other people use her application too, and some have written adapters to other tools they need to connect to. She's constantly amazed that thousands of people around the world use it every day, with over twenty active contributors writing code for it.

She looks at the new pull request from the text message—someone has created a new adapter to the task manager. The proposed change looks fantastic. She's wanted to do it for years. Their change is quite clever, and she approves of the way the automated tests were written to show that his change works without breaking anything else. He also documented his work, writing several paragraphs on what he did and why. She approves of the way he's turned it into a tutorial, so others can do something similar.

She loves seeing other people's ingenuity and their willingness to make the app better. As the project owner, she sees it as her primary responsibility to ensure that any contributor can be productive.

A couple years ago, there were over twenty active pull requests, but for a variety of reasons, she couldn't merge them in—sometimes the changes were conflicting, sometimes her API couldn't quite accommodate what they needed. She knows it's dispiriting when you submit a change to someone's project, but no one ever looks at it or they tell you that it can't be integrated. If that happens enough, people eventually give up or fork your project and splinter the community.

So, when this started happening to her project, she spent every evening for weeks rearchitecting her system so that people could quickly, easily, and safely make the changes they wanted. It took a lot of effort, and she personally rewrote every pull request so that the contributors didn't have to redo their work. But everyone was delighted and grateful when their changes made it in—but not as delighted as Maxine.

Maxine knows that agility is never free. Over time, without this type of investment, software often becomes more and more difficult to change. There are exceptions, like floating-point math libraries that haven't changed in forty years—they don't need to change, because math doesn't change.

But in almost every other domain, especially when you have customers, change is a fact of life. A healthy software system is one that you can change at the speed you need, where people can contribute easily, without jumping through hoops. This is how you make a project that's fun and worthwhile contributing to, and where you often find the most vibrant communities.

She drives home and is delighted that her husband has already taken care of dinner. She regales her kids about her last-minute decision to visit their old middle school and the exciting new generation of geeks.

When they disappear to do their homework, she grabs her laptop and brings up the exciting new pull request. She pulls the code in and spins up the new version on her laptop. She logs in and clicks around, testing some of the corner-cases to make sure he got the details right.

Smiling, she brings up the pull request in her browser and clicks a button, which merges it into the code base. She writes a thank you note to the submitter, complimenting him on his cleverness and initiative.

Before hitting send, she notices something he wrote: "Maxine, I'd throw you a huge party if you could display a desktop notification whenever someone modifies this property…"

Good idea, she thinks. She pulls up her code editor, and in the next fifteen minutes takes a stab at implementing this idea. When it works the first time, she grins and laughs out loud, clapping her hands in gleeful selfcongratulation. She's in a great mood. You can do so much with so little effort because of all these miracles of technology.

She resumes her note to the submitter:

> Again, really nice work. I'm sure everyone is going to love it as much as I do. Thank you! (And I just added your notification feature. Your offer for throwing me a party is accepted.)

Hitting send, she wonders if the universe is sending her a message. Her afternoon with the middle schoolers and the ease with which she added functionality to her application (which is years older than the Phoenix Project) shows her what coding *should* feel like.

She is able to build things with focus, flow, and joy. She had fast feedback in her work. People were able to do what they wanted without being dependent on scores of other people. This is what great architecture enables.

She has been exiled to the most strategic initiative of the company, on which the survival of the entire company hinges. And yet, hundreds of engineers are paralyzed, unable to do what needs to be done.

In that moment, Maxine decides she must bring this level of productivity that she's helped create for middle-schoolers and her open-source project to the Phoenix Project, even if it means personal suffering in the short term.

CHAPTER 4

Thursday, September 11

The next morning, Maxine still feels triumphant from yesterday's numerous victories. But as Kurt predicted, everyone is freaking out. To everyone's shock and disbelief, the launch was not going to be called off or delayed. Instead, the Phoenix Project is going to be launched tomorrow at five.

Captain Kirk apparently hit the warp speed button, despite Engineer Scotty telling him the dilithium crystals were about to blow. So, no boring status meetings today. Instead, every meeting is in a genuine shitstorm, with people on the verge of panic. One meeting quickly devolved into bedlam and pandemonium, full of questions, objections, and shocked disbelief. People were furiously typing away on their phones and laptops, and a third of people in the room were making phone calls. It was like watching an old movie from the '40s, with reporters racing out of the courtroom to the payphones or back to their offices, frantic to break the news first.

Maxine turns to the person next to her, loudly yelling, "Has Phoenix ever been deployed into production before?!"

"Nope," he yells back.

"Is there a release team yet?" Maxine asks.

"Nope. Chris, Kirsten, and Bill are mustering up a formal release team today, but I have no idea who's going to be in charge," he responds and mimics biting his fingernails in nervousness and fear.

Maxine looks back at him, speechless.

Maxine does not delight in the suffering of others, but watching the fireworks surrounding Phoenix is much more exciting than waiting for people to work on her tickets. She groans, realizing that given this crisis no one will be able to work on her tickets now.

Later that morning, Chris announces that William, the QA director, is in charge of the release team. His goal: get everything into a releasable state and to coordinate with Ops, who were blindsided too.

Poor bastard. She knows that they are in big trouble. The Phoenix developers can't even merge their own code together without accidentally leaving parts of it behind or blowing up the build. Pulling off a successful production deployment seems wildly optimistic. *Or plain bat-shit crazy,* she thinks.

"William, when is your release team meeting?" Maxine asks him as he jogs by. She runs to keep up. "Can I help?"

"First meeting is in one hour. We need all the help we can get," he says, not even breaking stride. Maxine is delighted. Finally, a chance to actually use her skills and experience.

This will be an interesting meeting, she thinks. Maxine has seen how Dev and Ops interact around Phoenix. Instead of acting like an actual team, they act more like sovereign states on the brink of war, with diplomats trying to patch together an uneasy peace, complete with embassies, protocols, and official formalities. Even scheduling a meeting between these two groups requires a summit and lawyers present.

Regardless, she's excited to be in the game. In a perverse way, this is the most fun she's had on the Phoenix Project so far. She realizes she's grinning from ear to ear. *Does this make me a bad person?* she wonders. She grins again, not caring.

Despite trying to arrive early, Maxine is late to the war room. They had to move the meeting twice because the crowd kept outgrowing the space.

It's fifteen degrees hotter in the room than in the hallway, and the air is stale. Nearly fifty people are crammed into a space designed for half that number. She sees Chris, Kirsten, William, and a bunch of the lead developers and managers. Kurt, sitting next to William, waves to her.

On the other side of the table is Bill Palmer, surrounded by a phalanx of faces she doesn't recognize. She notices that there's something...different about them.

The largest one of them to the left of Bill has his arms crossed and a huge, unhappy scowl on his face. He shakes his head in disbelief. "What is wrong with you people? You're telling me you don't know how many Windows servers you need, on top of the handful of Linux servers...Tell me again, how many exactly is a 'handful of servers?' Is that in metric or imperial handfuls? While we're at it, you have any Kumquat boxes you need, or perhaps a Tandem?"

Flanking him are a woman and a younger man. The way they snicker makes Maxine immediately think of Crabbe and Goyle, the two mean-spirited goons who were best friends with Malfoy, Harry Potter's rival from Slytherin house.

"Uhh…" says one of the Dev managers. "Actually, there is *one* component that can only run on Kumquat servers. It's an extension we had to build off of the existing message bus. But it's only a small modification. It shouldn't cause any problems, and it should add negligible load…"

Maxine hears groans from around the room, and not just from the Slytherins on the opposing side of the table. The younger man sitting next to the large man, whom Maxine is already thinking of as Big Malfoy, sighs. "Technically, there's nothing wrong with Kumquats—we have over a decade of experience running production workloads on them, and we understand their characteristics pretty well. The problem is that the reboot time for that cluster is almost eight hours. We just need to be careful about anything that could involve restarts, like security patching. I'm concerned that certain changes will require multiple reboots, which could mean a day of downtime… or that they'll never come back at all…"

These are all the Ops people, Maxine realizes. No wonder she hasn't seen them around.

"Wes, trust me, we are as afraid of that scenario as you are," the Dev manager replies from across the table. "We've been trying for three years to get this application re-platformed, but it always takes a backseat to something more important."

"Yeah, you developers always make sure features take priority, and you never clean up all the technical debt you create… typical crap," Big Malfoy says, gesturing angrily.

Bill says to Big Malfoy, without even turning his head, "Stow it, Wes. Work the problem. Stay focused."

"Yeah, yeah. Got it, boss," Wes (Big Malfoy) says. "Handful of Linux servers, handful of Windows servers, and one Kumquat server. Got it. Now who can define a 'handful?'"

Maxine watches all the Dev managers put their heads together, tabulating the compute needs for each of their components. It's clear they're just going on gut, not any sort of thoughtful capacity-planning exercise.

Maxine realizes that this release is in even more trouble than she thought. The developers still haven't merged all their code together. And they haven't defined the production environment that the application needs to run in—describing your environment in "handfuls" definitely does not cut it.

Raising her voice, she asks, "How many transactions per second are we expecting for product displays and orders? And how many transactions per second are the current builds capable of handling right now? That will tell us how many servers we need for the horizontally scalable portions, as well as how far we're off for the vertically scaled components, like the database."

The room falls silent. Everyone turns toward Maxine. They seem startled by her common sense question. The woman sitting to the left of Wes says, "Thank you! That is precisely what we need to know!"

Maxine gives a small nod and winks.

Chris stands up. "This is the highest publicity release in the entire company's history. Marketing has pulled out all the stops. They're going to spend almost a million dollars getting the word out about the Phoenix launch. All the store managers have been given instructions to tell every customer to download the app and hit the website Saturday—they're even having contests to see which stores register the most new mobile customers. They're hitting all the industry and business press. They're trying to get either Sarah or Steve on all the news shows—even *Good Morning America.*

"Here are the best calculations that I've been able to get from Marketing," Chris continues, flipping through his notebook. "Expect one million people to come banging on the Parts Unlimited website and mobile apps. If all goes well, we should be prepared to sustain at least two hundred orders per second."

Maxine hears mutters and curses from all around the room.

Wes scans the room and finally turns to Chris, all sense of jocularity gone. "Okay, that's good to know." He gestures at Maxine, "Our smart architect just asked how many transactions Phoenix can handle right now. Well?"

Chris looks to William, who pulls out a printout. "Hot off the press from this morning. In our tests, Phoenix currently handles about five transactions per second. Anything over that causes the database clients to start crashing due to timeouts, including the mobile apps... I think we're missing a bunch of database indexes, but we haven't figured out which ones yet..."

William looks up. "It's very, very not good, Chris."

Wes sits in stunned silence for a moment. And then in a blunt, world-weary voice, he says to Chris, "We're not going to make it, are we?"

No one says anything. Eventually, Bill asks, "Wes, what help do you need?"

"...I don't even know," he replies. "Maybe just give the teams some air cover so they can stay focused."

At that moment, Maxine hears a loud voice from the doorway. "For the survival of Parts Unlimited, we have to make this work, so of course we're going to make it."

Oh no, Maxine thinks. It's Sarah Moulton.

She's dressed in a bright, expensive looking yellow suit, and her face is so radiant that Maxine wonders how it's even possible. The fluorescent lights in the office usually make people look ghoulish and devoid of color. Maxine wonders if maybe she adds radium to her makeup to make herself glow like a 1950s bedside clock. Sarah has a certain dangerous glamour about her, and everyone in the room seems similarly rapt.

"We are in a market that is shrinking, with fierce competitors taking market share away from us," Sarah says. "Not to mention tech giants like Amazon and twenty new startups that are coming in to disrupt this entire category. As Steve said at the Town Hall, we've had three years to prepare for this. Now it's time for us to go to war and defend what is rightfully ours."

She looks around the room, scanning for signs of resistance or rebellion. "This is the strategy the executives of this company have decided on. Anyone have a problem with that?" she challenges.

Incredibly, Maxine hears herself laughing. Horrified, she covers her mouth. *Keep it together, Maxine!* Quickly, she wipes all expression from her face, like a student caught doing something bad in high school. *Since when have you ever cared what people in authority think about you?* she wonders.

Ever since Chris warned me to keep my head down, she realizes. Maxine forces herself to look calmly at Sarah with her best Lieutenant Saavik expression, radiating only cool, dispassionate logic.

"Something seem particularly funny to you... umm, sorry, what is your name?" Sarah asks, looking at Maxine coolly.

"Maxine," she replies, calmly. "I was laughing because you were talking about *why* you think Phoenix is important. But in this room, we're just trying to figure out *how* to get Phoenix deployed."

"Which is not going terribly well, either," Wes mutters loudly to some nervous laughter.

"I can see that some of you have not bought into our mission," Sarah says, appraising everyone in the room. "Well, as I mentioned in the Town Hall, the skills that got us here are not necessarily the same skills that will take us to where we need to go. As leaders, we need to figure out if we have the right people on the bus. I'll be sure to keep Steve apprised. I know this release is personally very important to him."

Upon hearing Steve's name, Chris looks at Maxine with disbelief and then covers his face with both hands. *Nice job keeping a low profile,* Maxine tells herself.

"Okay, Sarah, that's enough," Bill says, standing up. "Let's go apprise Steve about some of these problems and let the team figure out how to execute the release. We're only getting in the way here."

"Yes, Steve needs to hear about this," she says. Sarah turns to leave, but then looks back at Maxine. "I like that you say what you think. If you're available sometime this week, let's get lunch. I'd like to get to know you better."

What the... Maxine freezes like a deer in headlights.

"As women, we really need to stick together, don't we?" Sarah says with a wink.

With a frozen smile, Maxine says, "Uhh... thank you—I... I'd love to." Immediately, she hates herself, embarrassed that so many people just witnessed her lying so baldly.

"Let's make it so," Sarah replies with a warm smile. "And if you need someone to mentor you, I'd be happy to." She looks at her phone and says, "That's Steve. He needs something from me. I'll leave you to it. Remember, we all need optimism."

When Sarah is gone, Maxine lets out a long breath, not quite believing what happened. She knows how important it is to have a great network, able to find people who can help get important things done. But she's not terribly excited to be associated with Sarah, no matter how influential she is. Maxine is very picky about who she associates with.

For the next hour, Maxine drifts between the various groups as the huge release team tries to fully understand what is required to support the Phoenix launch. There are at least twelve different technology stacks that need to be deployed, more than Maxine had estimated during her build archaeology.

She knew of the various application servers on Windows and Linux, and the front-end applications that run on the web, but she totally forgot about the two mobile applications (one for the iPhone and one for Android), and those all collectively hit at least ten different back-end systems from across the business, all of which required changes in order to accommodate Phoenix.

She had also forgotten that when you throw the Operations teams into the mix, the number of teams involved more than doubles, because getting all those applications running in production requires the server administration teams, virtualization teams, cloud teams, storage teams, networking teams...

All this reminds Maxine of why production deployments are some of the most complex activities of any technology organization, because they require so much coordination between so many different parts of the organization. And Phoenix wasn't just any deployment—it was designed to change how almost every part of the organization interacts with the customer.

The more Maxine hears, the worse she feels. It seems impossible that they can get everything right the first time with this many moving parts. Getting an environment required Maxine to open up scores of tickets, and she still wasn't successful. She's guessing that deploying Phoenix will require hundreds, or maybe even thousands, of tickets.

The project manager in the group she's sitting with says, "Won't we need a bunch of firewall changes too? Not just to external traffic. I don't think some of these systems have ever talked to each other..."

Maxine raises an eyebrow. She hears more groans around the group. "Oh, great. The firewall teams usually need at least four weeks to get change requests through," says the woman who Maxine learns is Patty. "You think our change management process can be slow? We're speed demons compared to Information Security."

Suddenly, Maxine hears a door slam open behind her, and Patty looks up. "Well, speak of the devil. Here's John, our chief information security officer. This should be fun..." she says.

John is in his late thirties. He's about twenty pounds overweight, but his clothes are still baggy on him. Like in an old Western, John is flanked by two people—one male and one female engineer, who looks vaguely familiar. "At last, I've found you all," John sneers, looking around as if he were a sheriff who had hunted down a group of outlaws. "I'm here about this mad plan to deploy the Phoenix application. This deployment will only happen over my dead body."

The woman behind John suddenly looks embarrassed, as if she's seen John say this before. John continues, "The Phoenix Project has millions of lines of new code, and we cannot responsibly deploy it without my team testing it for vulnerabilities. We just came out of a very, very interesting meeting with the auditors, and trust me, they aren't going to take it very kindly if we put something into production that jeopardizes our compliance posture.

"I have it on *pretty* good authority that the CIO and VP of IT Operations were just fired over some compliance audit findings that were no longer tolerable," John continues. "Let that be a warning to you that compliance is not just a moral obligation or a set of contractual obligations...it's also the law."

Maxine wonders how many times John's rehearsed that line. *It's a pretty good line*, she acknowledges.

Kirsten says from the front of the room, "As you know, the decision to ship Phoenix came straight from the top—Steve Masters, the CEO, and Sarah Moulton, the SVP of retail operations. In fact, Sarah was just here, reminding us of that. The release is scheduled to start at five tomorrow so that everything is live when stores open on Saturday morning."

"That's what you think, Kirsten," John says. "I'm going to go speak with Steve right now. Rest assured that I *will* stop this madness."

He turns to Wes. "You were there at the meeting with the auditors—tell them how serious this is and why there is no way the production release can happen tomorrow!"

Wes quickly replies, "No—leave me out of this, John. That train has left the station, and you can't put the toothpaste back in the tube. The only thing we can do is figure out how to keep this rocket from blowing up on the launch pad and killing us all. Pardon the mixed metaphor," he says with a loud laugh, looking around the room to see who's with him.

"Or was that a simile?" Wes asks suddenly, with a puzzled look on his face.

The woman behind John says in a deadpan voice. "It's a metaphor, Wes. When you say something 'is a pile of crap,' that's a metaphor. When you say that something 'is like a pile of crap,' that is a simile."

"Thanks, Shannon," he says with a big smile. "I've always gotten those confused."

John glares at Shannon, and then says angrily to Wes, "I will *not* leave you out of this, Wes. It is your moral responsibility to stop this release!" He turns to the whole room. "It is all of your moral responsibility to stop this release! You all know where I stand—as I said, this release will be deployed over my dead body."

Wes mumbles, "We can always hope."

Maxine hears some nervous giggles as John and his posse leave. Kirsten stands up, looking a bit uncomfortable. "Well, I should take a moment to say that we made a commitment to deploy Phoenix on Friday. But if any of you feel you have a, umm, moral obligation to not participate in this release, please let me know."

Wes chortles. "Kirsten, going down this path is almost certainly the stupidest thing I've seen in my entire career...but to support the team, I promise we'll all do what we can." With an air of weary exhaustion and resignation, he continues, "Let's just get it over with."

Maxine looks around, thinking about the sudden, surreal appearance of Sarah and then John. She's reminded of *Redshirts* by John Scalzi and Wil Wheaton, a funny book loosely based on a *Star Trek*-like universe. It's written from the perspective of one of the redshirts, the nameless low-ranking characters wandering in the background of the show, who learns that interacting with any of the bridge officers is bad news. Whoever is chosen to beam down to the planet with the officers is doomed to die in bizarre ways: an Alteran blood worm, mind virus, carnivorous plants, an errant Klingon disruptor blast. In the book, the redshirts plant sensors everywhere to detect when the equivalents of Captain Kirk or Commander Spock come below deck so that they can hide.

She is disheartened by how Parts Unlimited executives, the bridge officers, are so disconnected from the daily work of the "redshirts" in the technology organization. It was not helpful for Sarah to remind everyone of how "saving the universe" depends on Phoenix. And it was not helpful for John to appeal to their "moral sense of correctness."

We all know the threat the company faces is real, she thinks. The job of the bridge crew is to ensure the company strategy is viable, not to remind them of the strategy or to micromanage everyone to death. Their job should be to ensure everyone can get their work done.

How did this all come to be?

Maxine drags herself back to her desk with a sandwich, exhausted from the endless Phoenix release meetings, surrounded by everyone who has similarly been sucked into the launch vortex. Oddly, she also sees some people happily working at their desks, as if it were just a regular day.

Curious, she asks one of the them why he doesn't seem very worried. He replies with a puzzled look, "I'm a developer—I work on features. I give them to QA and Ops to test and deploy. Then I work on the features for the next release. That keeps me plenty busy."

Maxine leaves, boggling at what he said. She has never in her career abdicated all testing and deployment to someone else. *How can you create anything of value if you don't have feedback on how it's used?* she thinks.

When she gets to her desk, Kurt is there with a black three-ring binder. Seeing her, he flashes a big smile. "I have a present for you!"

It's an eighty-page document full of tabs. Just scanning the section headings makes her heart leap—they're the painstakingly assembled Phoenix build instructions, complete with links to documents, license keys, step-by-step tutorials, and even links to a bunch of videos. One is titled "Getting your uberjar to run in our (very) crazy, screwed up production web cluster (8 min)," and another is "How to monitor your apps despite our Ops groups (12 min)."

She sees twenty-character hexadecimal strings of activation codes and license keys. She sees user names and temporary passwords for network shares. Best of all, there's a link to a four-node virtual machine cluster *with* administrative access! That means Maxine will be able to do whatever she wants without having to fill out another service desk ticket!

She's speechless. She feels her eyes tearing up. *Over license keys?*

She wonders for a moment whether she has lost all sense of perspective. But after being stuck inside the Phoenix Project, having someone actually care about what she needs is...so unexpected and so utterly appreciated.

Maxine is reminded of when she and her family volunteered for a day to help new refugee families. She remembers how her then ten- and eight-year-old kids reacted when families cried when they were given food, soap, and laundry detergent.

There is nothing so rewarding as providing something to someone who really needs your help. She needed help and she received it.

Elated, Maxine flips through the document. She sees a long list of Windows registry keys that need to be set. "Don't worry, Maxine," Kurt says, politely ignoring her emotional reaction. "You have the electronic version of this in your inbox, so you can copy and paste everything."

With a twinkle in his eye, he adds, "And there's a link to a wiki page where you can incorporate any notes if we missed something. There's a bunch of people who really appreciate your work. We've been trying to crack the Phoenix build puzzle for months! But we've never been able to work on this full-time. Your notes helped us put all the pieces together. This saved us months of work!"

Maxine's brow furrows. She has no idea what Kurt is talking about, but she doesn't even care. "Thank you so much! I can't tell you how much this means to me. How can I ever repay you for this?"

"Anything to help another hard-working engineer trying to help other engineers be productive," Kurt says, laughing. But with a serious look on his face, he adds, "If you want to meet the people who made all this happen, despite considerable adversity and huge obstacles that typically prevent feats of greatness like this, come to the Dockside Bar tonight at five. We meet there on Thursdays."

"Wait, hang on a second," Maxine says, suddenly suspicious. "If this all works, how come everyone isn't using it?"

"That is a great question, with some very surprising answers," Kurt says. "The short version is the 'official build team' hasn't exactly authorized these. They seem to view our efforts as a nuisance, or worse, as competition. Which, on the eve of the biggest and potentially most risky application launch in the history of the company, sure does seem odd, doesn't it?

"But by all means, if you like what we've done, feel free to share it with anyone who needs it. I can explain more tonight. Please, try to join us at five—there's a bunch of people who are dying to meet you!" he says. "And good luck with the build!"

Maxine opens up a terminal window on her laptop and starts following the instructions Kurt gave her. Her excitement grows when she realizes that this might be an actual, working Dev environment.

She's exuberant when she's able to log in and type "make" on a command line, which starts streaming screenfuls of happy output onto her screen.

She's delighted as she sees files getting compiled, binaries getting linked, programs being copied, build tools being installed and run...the output keeps going, and going, and going...

Amazingly, things are still building for ten more minutes...fifteen minutes...thirty minutes...she's relieved as it keeps going without an error, but starts to become alarmed at the size of the Phoenix build. It's *huge.*

Forty-five minutes later, she can't hold off going to the bathroom any longer; she was too afraid she was going to miss something if she stepped away. She hurries there and back and is relieved to see that the build hasn't failed, still generating endless output in her terminal window.

She scrolls through the history to see if she missed anything interesting. She decides to skip the next release team meeting just so she can watch the continuing build, which seems a bit irresponsible, but she knows that having a great build process is key to having a good code deployment and release process. And maybe with the help of these mysterious benefactors, she's on the verge of finally conquering the Phoenix build.

The build output is hypnotic and educational, because she's seeing some components of Phoenix for the first time. There's Java JAR files, .NET binaries, Python and Ruby scripts, and lots and lots of bash scripts.

Wait, is that a remote shell and installer that popped up? Before she can figure out what it is, the window is gone. Maxine's awe and concern at the size and variety of Phoenix continues to grow.

She's about to scroll back further when she sees Eclipse being downloaded from somewhere. *What in the world?* she thinks. Twenty minutes later, she could have sworn that she saw an InstallShield installer, but she knows she's getting tired and might be imagining things.

Honestly, after another hour of watching build output, she's having trouble staying focused on the screen. But she can definitely see the different personalities and tech stacks of the different teams working on Phoenix. She had no idea there were so many.

This is crazy, she thinks. *There can't be this many teams working on Phoenix, right?* And she wonders how any one person could possibly understand the system as a whole, especially when it's built from so many different technology stacks.

Maxine isn't usually a fan of rigid standardization, but she's not a fan of everyone getting to choose whatever they fancy in the moment. Each decision is a commitment to support it for years or even decades—these are decisions that go far beyond just one team.

Like most developers, she's very superstitious that if she stops watching the build, it will fail. Finally, nearly three hours after she started the build, she sees the scrolling output from her build window stop. Her heart falls when she reads:

```
builder: ERROR: missing file: credentials.yaml
```

Damn! She's guessing that she needs a login credential that she doesn't have.

She texts Kurt and he quickly replies:

Ah, yes. For that you need to open a ticket to get your login tied to your ActiveDirectory account. Only Susan can issue those. Contact info coming.

Instead of emailing Susan, Maxine goes to Susan's desk and learns that this missing file contains a cryptographic certificate that comes from some distant security group. Susan searches through years of emails to find how to get a new one. When she finds it, Maxine takes a picture of the email address with her phone.

She is so close to getting a Phoenix build going!

CHAPTER 5

Still on a high after getting so far on the Phoenix build, Maxine hops in her car to make the five-minute drive to the Dockside parking lot, right on time for Kurt's mysterious meeting.

She suspects that the shiny new Lexus IS300 in the parking lot is Kurt's. She doubts it's the Datsun 300 she parked next to. It's surprising that the meeting is at Dockside. It's not one of the usual hangouts for technology people, but she knows it's a longtime favorite for many of the factory workers.

Maxine asked some people about Kurt that afternoon. Three people gave her enthusiastic endorsements, describing how competent and helpful he was. One development manager in her old group called him one of the smartest people in the entire technology organization. Curiously, one of her colleagues texted her:

> Kurt? He's not the sharpest knife in the drawer, which is why he's stuck in QA. He's also really nosy. Why do you ask?

This made Maxine even more curious. *What exactly is Kurt up to?* His gift of the binder probably saved her months of waiting. But what is his motivation? He clearly has an inside track on getting things people need. She's pretty sure he isn't pilfering corporate resources—and even if he was, why would he give them to her?

As she walks in the door, she's immediately hit by the smell of hops. She hasn't been here in years. She's relieved to see that it's much cleaner and brighter than she remembers. There's no longer sawdust on the floor, and it's more spacious than it seems from the outside.

The bar is half-full, but it's loud—maybe because of the cleanly swept cement floor.

Seeing her, Kurt smiles and waves her over to a group of tables on the far side of the room by some booths. "Hey, everyone, meet Maxine, the newest member of the Rebellion if I can help it. She's the person that I've been telling you all about."

She immediately recognizes the cranky developer who backed her up in the Phoenix status meeting about environments and is startled to see the petite woman named Shannon who was with John earlier today. There's another man in his late thirties sitting next to someone who looks out of place—he's in his fifties and wearing a bowling shirt. Next to him is Brent, who she also saw in the Phoenix release meeting. He and Shannon are the youngest people at the table.

Everyone has an open laptop in front of them. Suddenly, she wishes she had hers with her—she'd gotten out of the habit of carrying it around lately because she's had so little to work on.

"You remember Dave?" says Kurt, gesturing at the cranky developer. "He's one of the Dev team leads. He complains a lot, but he's probably banging the drum loudest on the need to pay down technical debt and modernize our architecture, platforms, and practices."

Kurt laughs. "The reason Dave is so good is that he never asks for permission!"

Cranky Dave raises his glass at Maxine with the smallest of smiles, as if smiling causes him physical pain, then takes a sip of his beer. Up close, he looks older than her. "Breaking the rules is the only way anyone can get anything done around here," he grumbles. "Can't do anything without twenty meetings." Cranky Dave pauses. "You know, that's the best compliment Kurt has ever given me. You've probably noticed that he's running his own black market inside the company, right?"

Kurt laughs, clearly not bothered by the characterization. "I'm just trying to solve people's problems. If I'm guilty of anything, it's that I care too much about the success of Phoenix, and even the whole company, to allow bureaucracy to kill it! And if that's a crime, I plead guilty! It's a pity no one will ever give us a medal for the great work we do. The satisfaction of helping people must be reward enough, right?"

Everyone groans, and someone from across the table hollers out, "Good one, Kurt."

Ignoring the banter, Kurt points to the man in his late thirties who is wearing a funny vendor T-shirt. "This is Adam, one of my test engineers. But don't let his title fool you—he's a developer at heart, and he's also one of the best infrastructure people I've ever met.

"You can thank him for the all those virtual machines and pre-built containers you got—he built them all. And that's only a fraction of what Adam does. His day job is helping automate a big chunk of the legacy test suite that we inherited from an outsourcer."

Adam smiles sheepishly. "Actually, Brent over there did most of the work," he says. "He's an ace at infrastructure. We've been working together to try to automate environment creation for over a year. It's been a tough road, working evenings and weekends, because it's not officially sanctioned. Despite all the dead ends and cul-de-sacs, we're proud of what we've been able to achieve.

"Your build notes were awesome, Maxine. Brent here almost fell over and died when he was reading through them. He'd been trying to piece that together for months," Adam says.

Brent smiles at Maxine. "That was amazing detective work, Maxine. Documenting all those environment variables was so helpful!"

"Let us know how the environment works for you," Adam continues. "It's such a pain to get things from Operations through normal channels, so we scraped together enough hardware to build a cluster big enough to support a couple of teams. Now you can get an environment on demand, without needing to open up a ticket."

Maxine blurts out, "Wow, thank you so much. The environment worked! I got three hours into the Phoenix build with it until it failed because of a missing certificate."

"Wow! That's amazing," Brent says.

"So where did all that hardware come from if not from Operations?" Maxine asks.

Adam smirks. "Kurt has his ways—a little from here, a little from there, you know? Kurt keeps saying that it's best not to ask where it comes from... I've always suspected there are a bunch of people missing entire server clusters if they'd bother to check."

Kurt feigns a hurt expression. "Server-hoarding is a huge problem," he says. "Because it takes so long for Ops to get anything to us, people always ask for way more than they need. And that makes Ops' job harder and lengthens the lead times for everyone else, making the shortages even worse! It's like being in the old Soviet Union, where you have to wait in line for everything. You could say we're creating a secondary market to ensure that some of those unused environments go where they're needed most.

You know, to ameliorate the mismatch between supply and demand," he says.

Cranky Dave mutters, "Don't get him started," rolling his eyes as Kurt lectures like a professor.

Adam adds, "But Dave is right—Kurt *is* running a black market."

"Pay no attention to them, Maxine," Kurt continues. "Next down the table, we have Shannon, a security engineer who works on building automated security tools. She spent nearly five years in the data warehouse team before that. She's currently working with Brent, experimenting with some machine-learning and data visualization toolkits and standing up some big data infrastructure, trying to get ahead of some of the marketing initiatives that we know are coming. You probably remember her from the full-scale red-team exercises that she ran last year."

Maxine smiles. That's why she looked so familiar. She definitely remembers—it was the first time she had been the target of a no-holds-barred penetration test. They had tried to plant malware by getting physical access to the manufacturing facilities, sending emails with malicious links, pretending to be company executives, and, in one case, one of their most critical vendors.

She had been very impressed. *It takes a lot of balls to run those types of exercises*, she thinks. Maxine remembers one person being fired for trying to do one because he made a bunch of people look bad.

Shannon looks up from her laptop and says, "Nice meeting you, Maxine. I remember your group. You were one of the best-prepared in the whole company. I was very impressed that everyone in your division knew not to click on links in emails, no matter how official they looked. Someone did a great job training everyone."

Maxine nods with respect, saying, "Nice meeting you, Shannon. We spent weeks fixing the problems you all found. Nice work."

Shannon looks back down at her laptop and types something. Suddenly, she looks up at everyone and says, "Oh, by the way, sorry about that episode with John. He's such a tool. But he's my boss."

Everyone laughs, and several people imitate Shannon's expression from earlier today.

"Up next is the aforementioned Brent, who has his hands in everything infrastructure related," Kurt continues. "If it connects to AC power, Brent has probably mastered it. Networks, storage, compute, databases.

But he's not just good with a screwdriver, he's always on the frontier of automation. Unfortunately, he's so good at what he does, everyone seems to have him on speed-dial. And he's on pager duty way too often, which we're trying to fix."

Brent merely shrugs his shoulders. Suddenly, the camera flash on his phone flickers and notifications flood his screen. He picks up his phone and mutters, "Dammit, another outage call. I probably need to jump on this." He drains the rest of his beer and starts dialing his phone.

"Yeah, that's a real problem," says Kurt, watching Brent walk away. "We've got to bring some sanity to his work life. He's brilliant, but because of the way people dump things on him, he hasn't been able to go on vacation without a pager for years…"

He pauses. "In the meantime, last but not least is Dwayne," says Kurt, gesturing to the oldest person at the table. He's not only dressed differently than everyone, his laptop is different too—it's a beast with a massive screen. "He's a senior database and storage engineer from Ops and was the person who brought Brent into this group. They conspire all the time to find better ways to manage infrastructure."

Maxine smiles. To most people on the Phoenix Project, centralized Ops are merely the people on the other side of a ticket. They're the people everyone is always complaining about. But clearly Kurt and this motley crew have a different way of working, bypassing the normal organizational lines of communication, however informal.

Dwayne reaches across the table, extending his hand. "Great to meet you, Maxine."

Maxine realizes that Dwayne is wearing an actual bowling shirt, complete with his initials sewn on it, "DM," and a faded mustard stain right next to them.

"Dwayne has been trying to get automation initiatives going for years, but he and Brent always get shot down," Kurt continues. "So, they've been helping Adam build up our own infrastructure instead. He knows almost everyone in Operations, and he can usually get them to do anything. Like earlier this week when we needed a firewall port opened between two internal networks. Dwayne made that happen."

"All in a day's work," Dwayne says with a friendly smile. "But to be fair, Kurt is really the master of getting the impossible done…I'm just learning from him!"

Maxine is certain Dwayne is exaggerating. Dwayne looks like he's in his mid-fifties. Just how much could he learn from a young guy like Kurt?

Kurt leans back in his chair, arms spread out. "Maxine, your work cracking the code of the Phoenix builds has impressed us all. We are in awe of the technical and social skills you displayed to successfully hunt down almost all the pieces of the environment, which required incredible perseverance, focus, and never taking 'no' for an answer!"

Confused, Maxine looks around, but she sees everyone nodding at her, genuinely impressed at her work. Kurt continues, "We invite you to be a part of the inner-circle of the 'Rebellion.' We're recruiting the best and brightest engineers in the organization, training and preparing in secret for the right time to overthrow the Empire, the ancient, powerful, and unjust order that definitely needs to be toppled."

Everyone chuckles, and Cranky Dave raises his glass, shouting with a laugh, "To the overthrow of the Empire!"

Confused, Maxine looks around the table. These are people from Dev, QA, Security, and Ops—a very unlikely group of people to be socializing, let alone working together. And she notices that everyone has a small sticker of the Rebel Alliance from Star Wars on their laptop, just like the X-Wing pilots wore on their helmets. She grins at their subtle but subversive badges of solidarity.

Seeing Maxine toast with an empty hand, Kurt jumps up. "What do you want to drink?"

"A pinot noir, please."

Kurt nods and heads toward the bar, but before he can take three steps, a tall and somewhat overweight man with graying hair walks up to him and gives him a big hug. In a loud and boisterous voice, he says, "Kurt! Good seeing you again, my young friend. What do you need?"

Noting the attention that Kurt's group gets from the bar staff, Maxine guesses they must come here often. She smiles. For the first time since her move to the Phoenix Project, she feels like she's in the company of kindred spirits.

"Who are you people? Why are you all are here? What are you possibly trying to achieve?" she asks quickly, while Kurt is at the bar.

Everyone laughs. Dwayne says, "As you know, we're a huge Kumquat database shop, which is what I cut my teeth on. I want to migrate us to MySQL and open-source databases wherever we can, because I'm tired of sending millions of dollars each year to an abusive vendor. We're figuring out how to engineer our way there."

Looking around, he says to everyone, "Other companies have done this already. I think that anyone who is still paying Kumquat database maintenance fees is simply too dumb to migrate off it."

Maxine nods in approval. "Smart thinking! We've saved millions of dollars in my old group doing this, which we can now spend on innovation and other things the business needs. And it's been fun. But why this crusade for open-source software?"

"I'll tell you why," Adam says. "For almost five years, back when I was in Operations, I had a team that kept getting pager alerts at two in the morning for some middleware we used. In almost every case, it was because of their database driver. I was the guy who had to generate a binary driver patch! After all that work, the problems started happening again six months later, because when the vendor released their patches, they didn't integrate my fixes into their code. Next thing you know, we're all up at two a.m. doing the same thing over again."

Maxine is impressed. *Adam has great kung fu too. And so does everyone else here.*

Cranky Dave frowns. "I've been at Parts Unlimited for almost five years, and I can't believe how the bureaucracy and silos have taken over. You can't do anything without first convincing a bunch of steering committees and architects or having to fill out a bunch of forms or work with three or four different teams who each have their own priorities. Everything is by committee. No one can make decisions, and implementing even the smallest thing seems to require consensus from everyone. Almost everything I need to do, I have to go up two levels, over two levels, and down two levels just to talk with a fellow engineer!"

"The Square!" cries out Adam, and everyone laughs.

Dwayne chimes in. "In Ops, we often have to do the return path—up, over, down, and then back up, over, and down before two engineers can finally work together to get something done."

"I want to bring back the days when a developer could actually create value for someone who cares, easily and quickly," Cranky Dave says. "I want to build and maintain something for the long haul, instead of shipping the 'feature of the day' and dragging all this technical debt around."

Cranky Dave is on a roll. "This company is run by a bunch of executives with no clue about technology, and project managers who want us to follow a bunch of arcane processes. I'll scream at the next one who wants me to write a Product Requirements Document."

"The PRD!" everyone shouts, laughing. Maxine raises her eyebrows. Those made sense decades ago, when you wanted written justification before you wasted a bunch of developers' time. But now you can prototype most features in the time it takes to even write one page of a PRD. One team can now build things that used to require hundreds of people.

Kurt sits next to Maxine, putting a glass of red wine in front of her. "We're like the redshirts in *Star Trek* who actually get the real work done."

"I was literally thinking that earlier," Maxine says, smiling.

"Right? You've seen firsthand the reality bubble the bridge crew is in," Kurt says. "They know the Phoenix Project is important, and yet they couldn't have come up with a worse way to organize everyone to achieve it. They outsourced IT, brought it back in, outsourced one piece, maybe two pieces, shuffled them around...In many areas, we're organized as if we're still outsourced, and nothing can get done without permission from three or four levels of management."

"Kurt's right," says Cranky Dave. "We're just another cost center, little cogs in a big machine that can be easily outsourced to some random corner of the globe. We're viewed as replaceable and fungible."

"That's why I'm here, Maxine," Shannon says. "We could build a world-class technology organization and create an engineering culture. That's how we survive and innovate for our customers. And my dream is that *everyone* is the custodian of company data. It's not just the job of one department.

"In Steve's Town Hall, he talked about how we're being disrupted and how we need to compete with the e-commerce giants," she says. "Well, we can only win by innovating and understanding our customers, which we can only do by mastering data. I think the capabilities we're building are the future of the company."

Everyone cheers and hoists their glasses.

After everyone is done toasting each other, Dwayne turns to Kurt and asks, "So, how did the meeting go with your boss? You said you pitched William on funding an automated testing pilot."

Everyone leans in.

"You know, I really thought he was going to go for it. I had testimonials from two of the Dev managers and a product owner about how great it would be. One of them had this great line: 'Without automated testing, the more code we write, the more money it takes for us to test.' Ha! I really thought that would scare the pants off of William!" Maxine can feel the mood deflate around the table.

"Don't keep us in suspense, Kurt. What did he say?" prompts Dwayne.

"'Son, let me explain something to you,'" Kurt says, in a shockingly good impersonation of William. "'You're young. You clearly don't understand how this game works. We're QA. We protect the organization from developers. It sounds to me like you've been hanging around too many of them. Do not trust them. Do not get chummy with them. You give developers an inch, and they'll take a mile.'"

Maxine laughs at Kurt's uncanny impression.

"'Son, you're a pretty good QA manager with a half-million-dollar budget.'" Kurt's on a roll. "'If you do your job well, you can be like me with a three-million-dollar budget. And if I do my job well, then I'll get promoted and have a $20 million budget. You go around automating your QA, your budget shrinks instead of grows. I'm not saying you're stupid, son, but you sure don't seem to understand how this game works.'"

Maxine laughs with everyone else. She is sure Kurt is exaggerating.

"William is like a union leader, not a business leader," Shannon says. "He only cares about growing his union membership dues, not about what's right for the business. You see the same thing inside Ops and even Infosec."

A frown crosses Dwayne's genial face. "Trust me, it's way, way worse in Ops. At least Development is seen as a profit center. In Ops, we're a cost center. The only way to fund infrastructure is through new projects. If you don't find new funding sources, you're screwed. And if you don't spend your whole budget, they'll take the money away from you next year."

"Ah, the project funding model... Another big problem here at Parts Unlimited..." Kurt says, as everyone groans in agreement.

"So, what's your plan now, Kurt?" Dwayne asks.

"Don't worry, Dwayne. I've got another plan," Kurt says, confidently. "We're going to lie low and keep doing what we're doing, looking for new potential customers and recruits. We keep our eyes and ears open for opportunities to get in the game."

"Oh, that's a great plan, Kurt," Dwayne says, rolling his eyes. "We hang out at a bar, complain, and drink beer. Brilliant."

Dwayne leans over to Maxine, explaining, "It's actually not that crazy. It's like in that movie *Brazil*, where the number-one fugitive is the rogue air conditioner repairman who fixes people's air conditioners because Central Services never gets around to it. That's us. We're always on the lookout for places we can help. It's a great way to make friends and find potential new recruits for the Rebellion."

"What?" she says in disbelief. "That can't work, can it?"

"Well, it's how we got you here, isn't it?" Dwayne says with a big smile.

"I'm working all the angles," Kurt continues. "I'm even thinking about asking William if I can have a meeting with him and his boss, Chris. I'd tell William that it's really important to me that Chris hears my proposal and that I want him there."

Wow, Maxine thinks. *That's pretty gutsy, maybe savvy, and probably fatal.*

"I'll keep you posted," Kurt says. "Okay, who has new information or intelligence to share?"

Shannon updates everyone on a nascent data analytics group in Marketing she's been working with and how she's setting up a meeting between them and Kurt. "They're working on a bunch of projects to increase customer promotion conversion rates, and boy, they really need help. They're not even using version control! They're struggling with basic data engineering problems, and they're still trying to get what they need from the data warehouse people," she says, visibly bothered by their suffering. Kurt quickly pulls out an org chart on his laptop.

He asks her, "Another data analytics project? Who's funding it? How much budget do they have? Who's leading it?" As she talks, he takes notes.

When it's his turn, Dwayne says, "I've got bad news. The Phoenix release caught everyone in Ops flatfooted—no one had it on their radar until last week. No budget was assigned to support it. Everyone's scrambling to find enough compute and storage infrastructure. This is the biggest launch we've done in almost twenty years, and everything we need, we don't have enough of. It's bad."

"Holy shit," says Adam.

"Yep," Dwayne says. "I've been trying to tell everyone for months, but no one cared. Well, now they do, and everyone's dropping everything to support the Phoenix launch. Today, I heard someone trying to work with procurement so they can break the rules and order outside of the annual ordering process."

Despite the crisis, bean counters are still bean counters, Maxine thinks.

"Everyone is still scrambling to get environments ready for the release tomorrow," Dwayne says. "No one has any build specifications that Dev and Ops both agree on. I gave them the ones we wrote, and they pounced on them and started using them right away. But still, this release is going to go real bad, real fast."

"I think you're right," Maxine says. "I'm really, really good at this stuff, and I spent nearly a week trying to get a Phoenix build going. If it weren't for the environment that Kurt gave me, I'd still be at square one. With the release team only starting today and the launch tomorrow, they are in big trouble."

Kurt leans forward, a serious look on his face. "Tell me more."

Suddenly, Maxine realizes why she was invited and that Kurt is no dummy after all.

Over the next twenty minutes, Maxine describes her experiences, reading from her work diary, which she can access from her phone. She mentally kicks herself again for not bringing her laptop. Everyone takes notes, especially Brent when he returns. He and Adam pepper her with questions as if she were a captured secret agent being debriefed by the CIA. Everyone's interested in how she was able to piece together the Phoenix build puzzle faster than anyone else had done. They ask lots of questions about who she talked to, what teams they were on, where she got stuck, and so forth.

"That's really impressive, Maxine," says Cranky Dave. "Years ago I put together a build server that my team could use on a daily basis. But that was when Phoenix only had two teams; now we have over twenty. The build team is completely out of their league, with people who, I'm sorry to say, are the people who didn't have enough experience to be application developers."

Adam says, "We're really close now. I think we're down to just one missing signed certificate for the payment processing service."

"He's right," Brent says. "Maxine, can you show me the build logs? I bet we can create that certificates ourselves—it wouldn't actually be valid, but it would be good enough for a Dev or Test environment."

Maxine curses, mentally picturing her laptop still on her desk. "I can show you first thing tomorrow," she sighs.

"This is great, people. Here's what we still need: we need an automated way to create environments and perform code builds," Kurt says, counting off on his fingers. "We need some way to automate those tests and some automated way to get those builds deployed into production. We need builds so that developers can actually do their work."

"So, who's willing to volunteer some of their time to help Maxine get those Phoenix builds going?" Kurt asks. To Maxine's surprise, all hands shoot up.

"Maxine, would you be able to lead this effort, with the help of any or all of these willing and talented volunteers?" Kurt asks.

Maxine is overwhelmed by the sudden support of all these people. Last week, she was unable to get help from anyone and was thinking about interviewing at other places. Suddenly, she's not so sure.

She takes a moment to collect herself and says, "Yes, I'd love to. Thank you, everyone. I look forward to working with you all."

Maxine is excited. She's genuinely amazed at what this group has been doing and that she's been chosen to help. *I've finally found my tribe,* she thinks. *And this is what an effective network is all about—when you can assemble a group of motivated people to solve a big problem, even though the team looks nothing like the official org chart.*

I'm pretty sure I'll learn and achieve more with this group then I would by having lunch with Sarah, she thinks. She wonders if she's being small-minded and petty. She still wonders if she should take the meeting or just wait for Sarah to forget about her.

"Excellent! Let me know if you need anything from me," Kurt says to the table. To Maxine, he says, "We try to meet every week. We typically have only two agenda items. First, we share intelligence on who needs help and other people to potentially recruit. After that, we usually share about something we've learned lately or new technologies that we think could change the game here at Parts Unlimited. I propose we add a third agenda item, which is discussing the progress of Phoenix builds, yes?"

Everyone nods.

Kurt looks at his watch. "Folks, one more thing before we adjourn. I'm starting a betting pool on when the release team will have the Phoenix application successfully running in production."

The most optimistic bet comes from Cranky Dave, who guesses Saturday at two a.m., fully eight hours after the deployment starts. Most bets are scattered between three and nine a.m., with Maxine betting six a.m.

"After all," she says, "the in-store point of sales systems need to be up by eight on Saturday morning."

To everyone's surprise, Dwayne bets Sunday evening, "You people have no idea how unprepared we really are for this release—this one will go down in the record books."

From: Alan Perez (Operating Partner, Wayne-Yokohama Equity Partners)

To: Dick Landry (CFO, Parts Unlimited), Sarah Moulton (SVP of Retail Operations)

Cc: Steve Masters (CEO, Parts Unlimited), Bob Strauss (Board Chair, Parts Unlimited)

Date: 3:15 p.m., September 11

Subject: Maximizing Shareholder Value **CONFIDENTIAL**

Sarah and Dick,

Thanks for the call today, and for walking me through the strategy and the Phoenix Project. I agree that an omni-channel strategy is required for any retailer to survive these days, especially given the e-commerce threat. And selling products manufactured in-house with low cost of sales is intriguing.

However, I'm concerned at how much cash you've diverted from Manufacturing ($20MM) to invest in Retail over the last three years, with no obvious return. The question becomes what return you could have gotten if this were invested elsewhere in the business or just returned to shareholders. As of right now, investing in lottery tickets would have made more economic sense.

Stories about innovation and omni-channel are nice, but the board needs more than stories and PowerPoint slides.

Good luck with the Phoenix release tomorrow. I know a lot rides on it.

—Alan

CHAPTER 6

• *Friday, September 12*

Friday goes by in a blur for Maxine as the emergency release preparations continue. She sees endless mayhem as Dev, QA, and Ops try to line up hundreds of moving pieces for the deployment. *Dwayne was right*, she thinks. And it's too late to change her bet to Sunday in the betting pool.

At five p.m. the release starts on schedule. There are rumors of last-ditch attempts to call it off, because William, Chris, and Bill are nowhere to be seen. These hopes are crushed when an email comes out from Sarah and Steve, making it very clear that the release is to proceed as scheduled.

Maxine is still at the office at ten that evening. By now, there's a sense of genuine panic that things are going very, very wrong. So spectacularly wrong that even Dwayne, who was the most pessimistic in the Phoenix release betting pool, mutters to Maxine, "This is going worse than I thought it would."

That's when Maxine becomes genuinely frightened.

By midnight, it's clear that a database migration is going to take five hours to complete instead of five minutes, with no way to stop it or restart it. Maxine tries to be helpful, but she isn't familiar enough with the Phoenix systems to know where she would be the most useful.

In contrast, Brent is being pulled every which way, needed for just about every problem, from the huge database meltdown in progress to helping people fix their configuration files. Seeing this, Maxine organizes a team to play goalie, protecting Brent from interruptions and fielding problems that don't require him.

Maxine notices something else. There must be two hundred people responsible for some portion of the release, but for most of them, it's only about five minutes of work. So, they have to wait around for hours to perform their little part in this excruciatingly long, complex, and dangerous operation. The rest of their time is spent watching and…waiting.

Even in the middle of this crisis, people are just sitting around, waiting.

By two a.m. everyone realizes there is a very real risk that they are going to break every point-of-sale register in every one of the nearly thousand stores, knocking Parts Unlimited back into the Stone Age. And with all the promotion that Marketing has been doing, the stores will be filled with angry customers unable to buy what they were promised.

Brent asks her to join a SWAT team to figure out how to speed up the database queries, still nearly a thousand times slower than they need to be in order to handle the expected load when stores open up later that morning.

For hours, she works with a bunch of Phoenix developers and Ops DBAs with her IDE and browser open. They are stunned when they discover that clicking the product category drop-down box floods the database with 8,000 SQL queries.

They are still working on fixing this when Wes pokes his head in the room, "Brent, we've got a problem."

"I'm busy, Wes," Brent replies, not even looking up from his laptop. "No, this is serious," Wes says. "The prices have disappeared from at least half of our products on the e-commerce site and mobile apps. Where the price should be displayed, either nothing shows up or it says 'null.' Screenshots are in the #launch channel."

Maxine blanches, pulling up the screenshot. *This is much more serious than slow database queries*, she thinks.

"Dammit, I bet it's another bad upload from the pricing team," Brent says after staring at his screen for several moments. Maxine leans over as Brent pulls up various administrative screens and product tables—some are inside of Phoenix and others on systems she doesn't recognize.

Maxine takes notes as Brent pulls up log files, runs SQL queries against a production database, pulls up more tables in various applications... Only when he opens up a terminal window and logs into a server does Maxine ask, "What are you doing now?"

"I need to inspect the CSV file that they uploaded into the app," he says. "I think I can find one in the temporary directory on one of the application servers." Maxine nods.

When Brent squints at his screen, Maxine does as well. It's a comma-separated text file with column names in the first row—product SKU, wholesale price, list price, sale promotion price, promotion start date... "It looks fine," Brent mutters.

Maxine agrees. She says, "Can you copy that file into the chat room? I'd like to take a look at it."

"Good idea," he says. She imports it into Excel and several other of her favorite tools. It looks fine.

While Wes tries to get one of the development managers on the phone, Brent tries to figure out what is going wrong. It's almost thirty minutes later when he curses. "I can't believe it. It's a BOM!"

Seeing Maxine's confused expression, he says, "A byte-order mark!"

"No way," mutters Maxine, pulling up the file again, this time in a binary file editor. She stares at her screen, stunned that she missed it. A BOM is an invisible first character that some programs put in a CSV file to indicate whether it's big-endian or little-endian. She's been bitten by this before.

Years ago, a colleague gave her a file exported from the SPSS statistical analysis application, and she spent half a day trying to figure out why her application couldn't load it as expected. She finally discovered that the file had a BOM, which got interpreted as part of the first column name, which caused all her programs to fail. *Which is almost certainly what is happening here*, she thinks.

Any intellectual satisfaction she feels at understanding this particular puzzle quickly disappears. She asks Brent, "This has happened before?"

"You have no idea," Brent says, rolling his eyes. "Different problem every time, depending on who generated the file. The most common problems lately are zero-length files, or files with no rows in them. And it's not just the pricing team—we have data problems like this all over the place."

Maxine is appalled. The first thing she would have done right away is write some automated tests to ensure that all input files are correctly formed before they allow them to corrupt their production database, and that the correct number of rows are actually in the file.

"Let me guess. You're the only one who knows how to correct these bad uploads?" Maxine asks.

"Yep," she hears Wes say from behind her. "All roads lead to Brent." Maxine jots down more notes, determined to investigate this and do something about it later.

It's almost two hours later before the pricing tables are corrected. Because of what Brent said, Maxine double-checks the file and is certain that it's missing a significant number of product entries. And because the pricing team wasn't part of the release, no one knows how to get a hold of them in the middle of the night (or early morning as is seems to be). Maxine adds some more things to her list of things that she'll insist on building so that this won't happen again.

At seven a.m., Maxine rejoins the database team. They're still working on speeding up queries—but it's too late. An announcement is made that stores are beginning to open on the East Coast.

The Phoenix release is still nowhere near complete. "We're fourteen hours into the launch, and the missile is still stuck in the tube," Dwayne says glumly.

Maxine doesn't know whether to laugh, smirk, or throw up—when missiles are stuck in the launch tube, it's a very dangerous scenario, because at that point the missile is already armed and too dangerous to approach.

At eight a.m., they are still hours away from having a working point-of-sale system. Sarah and her team are forced to train every store manager on how to use carbon paper imprints, and some stores are forced to only accept cash or personal checks.

For Maxine, the rest of Saturday goes by in a blur. She's unable to go home. The Phoenix rollout was more than just a spectacular outage…it was the most amazing example of production data loss Maxine has ever seen.

Somehow, they managed to corrupt incoming customer orders. Tens of thousands of customer orders were lost, and an equal number of customer orders were somehow duplicated—sometimes three or four times. Hundreds of order administrators and accountants were mobilized, reconciling database entries against paper order slips being emailed or faxed from stores.

Shannon texts everyone in the Rebellion, horrified that boxes of customer credit card numbers are being transmitted in the clear—but in the grand scheme of things, it's just another blip in the Phoenix disaster.

At three p.m., Kurt texts everyone:

> Not to put light on this big pile of suck, but Dwayne wins the betting pool. Congratulations, Dwayne.

Dwayne replies:

Not worth it! FUUUUUUUUUUUU . . .

He posts an image of a burning tire fire.

By Saturday night, Maxine finally manages to go home and sleep for six hours before coming back to the office. *Dwayne was right, this will go down in the record books*, she thinks glumly.

On Monday morning, Maxine is shocked to see her reflection in a mirror. She looks like crap, just like everyone around her—bags under her eyes, hair stringy. Long gone are her carefully pressed blazers. Now it's jeans and a wrinkled jacket to cover up a stain on her equally wrinkled blouse. Today she doesn't look classy. Like everyone else, she looks like she's recovering from a hangover, having slept in her outfit from the night before.

Since Saturday morning, their e-commerce site has been continually crashing under the unprecedented levels of customer traffic. In a status update meeting, Sarah crowed about what a great job Marketing did promoting Phoenix, then demanded that IT pull their weight.

"She's unbelievable," Shannon mutters. "She created this whole disaster! Is anyone ever going to call her on this?" Maxine just shrugs.

The carnage is unbelievable. Most of the in-store systems are still down—not just the point-of-sale registers, but nearly all of the back-office applications that support the in-store staff.

For reasons that continue to mystify everyone, even the corporate website and email servers are having problems, further hampering their ability to get critical information to people who need it—not everyone has access to the developer chat rooms.

In situations like this, technology failures cascade through the organization, like water flooding through a sinking submarine.

Trying to stay alert, Maxine goes to get more coffee from the kitchen. Dwayne's there doing the same thing. They nod at each other, and he says, "Did you hear we have hundreds of people who can't even get into their buildings because their keycards won't work?"

"What?!" Maxine exclaims, exhausted but laughing. She says, "I was just talking to someone who's trying to figure out why a bunch of batch jobs aren't running. He's even saying payroll might be delayed again—umm, I'll leave that to other people to fix," she concludes with a small laugh.

"Huh," he muses. "I wonder if we managed to knock out an interface to an HR application. That might explain these strange errors. We managed to screw up everything else."

All day during the recovery efforts, she hears questions like: Why are all those transactions failing? Where are they failing? How did it get into that state? Of the three ideas that might fix the problem, which one should we try? Will it make it worse? We think we fixed it, but is it really fixed?

Once again, Maxine's sensibilities are offended by how entangled all these systems are with each other. It's so difficult to understand any part of the system in isolation.

At times, it was difficult not to feel panicked. Earlier in the day, it looked like the Parts Unlimited e-commerce site was being attacked by an external party actively stealing credit card numbers. It took over an hour for Shannon and the security team to send out an email concluding that it was an application error—if someone refreshed the shopping cart at the wrong time, the full credit card number and three-digit CVV code of a random customer was displayed.

The good news was that it wasn't an external hack. The bad news was that it was a genuine cardholder data exposure event and likely another reason to be front-page news. All the attention and ridicule exploding on social media only added to everyone's stress.

Taking a break, Maxine walks back to her desk. She sees the developer who was so unconcerned with the release last week. He's wearing fresh clothes and appears to be well-rested.

"Rough weekend, I'm guessing?" he says to Maxine.

Maxine stares at him, speechless. He's still working on features for the next release. The only big change for him is that all his meetings have been canceled because most people have been sucked into the Phoenix crisis.

He turns back to his screen to work on his piece of the puzzle, not caring that none of the pieces actually fit together. Or that the entire puzzle has caught on fire over the weekend, along with the house and the entire neighborhood.

From: Alan Perez (Operating Partner, Wayne-Yokohama Equity Partners)
To: Dick Landry (CFO), Sarah Moulton (SVP of Retail Operations)
Cc: Steve Masters (CEO), Bob Strauss (Board Chair)
Date: 8:15 a.m., September 15
Subject: Phoenix Release **CONFIDENTIAL**

Sarah and Dick,

I've been reading the news headlines about the Phoenix release. Not a great start. Again, I question whether software is a competency Parts Unlimited can create. Maybe we explore outsourcing IT?

Sarah, you mentioned the large number of developers you've contracted to help. How long until they are fully contributing? When you grow a sales team, it takes time for new salespeople to carry full quota capacity. Can new developers really be onboarded fast enough to make a difference? Or are we just throwing good money after bad?

Sincerely, Alan

From: Sarah Moulton (SVP, Retail Operations)
To: All IT Employees
Cc: All Company Executives
Date: 10:15 a.m., September 15
Subject: New production change policy

Thank you for all your hard work helping deliver Phoenix to our customers. This is a badly needed step for us to regain parity in the marketplace.

However, due to the harm that we did to our customers because of unanticipated problems caused by poor judgment exercised by certain members of the IT organization, all production changes must be approved by me, as well as Chris Allers and Bill Palmer.

Changes made without approval will result in disciplinary action.

Thank you, Sarah Moulton

Maxine reads the email from Sarah. There's a new, maybe even sinister, dynamic creeping into the Phoenix Project. In each of the outage calls and crisis management meetings, senior leaders seem to be going out of their way to posture about how they did their job but other people didn't do *their* jobs, sometimes subtly, sometimes very blatantly.

While the redshirts battle to contain the raging engine fire that is threatening the entire ship, the bridge officers continue to cover their asses, Maxine observes. Some are even using the disaster to their political advantage, often to punish individual engineers or entire departments for supposed dereliction of duty.

Apparently, no one in IT leadership is safe—Maxine hears whispers that both Chris and Bill, as the heads of Dev and Ops, are in jeopardy of being fired, and there are rumors of all of IT being outsourced again. However, most believe William, as head of QA, is most likely to be axed.

Which is bullshit, thinks Maxine. *William was assigned to head up the release team less than twenty-four hours before the release! No one can get fired for trying to avert a disaster, right?*

"It's like the TV show *Survivor*," says Shannon. "All the technology executives are just trying to last one more episode. Everyone is freaking out. Steve has been demoted, and Sarah is trying to convince everyone that she can save the company."

Later that afternoon, Brent invites Maxine to join a meeting. "We've got nearly sixty thousand erroneous and/or duplicate orders in the database, and we've got to fix them so that the finance people can get accurate revenue reports."

Maxine helps the group wrangle the problem for an hour. At the end, once they find a solution, one of the Marketing managers says, "This is above my paygrade. Sarah is super-sensitive about changes right now. I've got to get her approval."

Ah, the Square in action, just like Cranky Dave described. But now, decisions that might have needed only to go "up and over one" now have to go "up and over two." Now, all product managers need to run everything by Sarah. Someone mutters, "Don't hold your breath—she never responds right away."

Great, Maxine thinks. *Sarah has effectively paralyzed everyone in this room even further.*

Throughout the day, all decisions and escalations quickly grind to a standstill, even for emergencies, which Maxine didn't expect. She discovers why: every manager insists on being a part of the communication plan. Why? They want to hear any bad news first, so they don't appear out of touch and can massage any messages up the chain.

Maxine is sharing this observation with Kurt when his phone buzzes. Seeing his sour expression, she asks, "What's up?"

"It's Sarah," he says. "She says she's getting conflicting information from Wes and me about the corrupted order data. I need to spend thirty minutes explaining it to her when I've got two actual emergencies going on."

Kurt storms off before she can even wish him good luck. Maxine shakes her head. The lack of trust and too much information flowing around is causing things to go slower and slower.

On Tuesday, Maxine joins a meeting led by Wes about more mysterious, intermittent outages for both the e-commerce site and the point-of-sale systems.

Sarah has been sending out emails, sometimes in all caps, reminding people how important this is. But everyone already knows how important this is—processing orders is one of the most important functions for any retailer.

The room is almost empty, even though this is a Sev 1 outage.

Apparently, everyone has had to go home sick. The Phoenix release forced people to work long hours together in close proximity all day and night, and with little sleep. Now everyone is dropping like flies. Of the people needed on this call, no one is healthy enough to be in the office. In fact, only two people are healthy enough to even be on the conference line.

Maxine looks up when she hears Sarah shouting, "What can you do about this? Who can fix this? Our store managers need our help! Don't people realize how important this is?"

Maxine stares at Sarah in disbelief, noting that she looks tired, not her usual immaculate self. Even Sarah isn't escaping the Phoenix carnage completely unscathed, despite her Teflon-like ability to avoid getting blamed for nearly anything in her three-year tenure at Parts Unlimited.

Wes throws up his hands. "What can we do about it? Nothing. The entire application support team is out sick. Brent just went home sick. The DBAs are out sick. Even though we've got the supremely competent Maxine here, she's like me—we don't know enough about the service to do anything except reboot the systems, which is what the support teams are already doing."

Maxine sees that Wes is sick too—he's congested and looks terrible. Bags underneath his red eyes, hoarse voice...she suddenly wonders if she looks as bad as he does.

"This is not acceptable, Wes," says Sarah. "The business depends on us. The store managers depend on us. We need to do something!"

"Well, these were the risks we warned you about when you proposed proceeding with the Phoenix launch—but you emailed saying that we 'need to break some eggs to make omelets,' right? We're doing everything we can, but unless you want to help reboot some servers, I'm telling you there's nothing we can do."

Wes continues, "But here's something that we should talk about: How do we keep our people healthy enough so they can actually do their jobs? And how do we keep them happy enough so they don't quit? Chris says two of his key engineers quit in the last week. I've lost two people on the Ops side too, and there's a good chance I may lose three more. Who knows how many more are actively looking?

"And when that happens, we will truly be up shit creek, because then we'll have empty meetings like this all the time," Wes says with a half-hearted laugh that turns into coughs.

He grabs his laptop and starts walking out the door. Before he leaves, he says, "Sarah, I know you think it's strange that we have no one left on the bench to solve this important problem, but that's the way it is. If you want to help, learn to be a doctor or learn some middleware. In the meantime, just stay out the way because we're doing our best."

Maxine likes the way Wes rolls—he's fearless and he always says what he thinks.

She makes a mental note to ask the Rebellion about recruiting Wes.

Thinking about the Rebellion, she realizes how important that group is. To her, it's a beacon of hope. Maxine knows she may be manic and loopy from lack of sleep, but the Rebellion has assembled some of the best engineers in the company. And they could liberate everybody from…from…all of this.

We need to keep the Rebellion together and keep this important work going, she thinks.

She texts Kurt right away:

> No matter what, we cannot cancel our Dockside meeting on Thursday.

His reply shows up right away.

> Great minds think alike. In fact, I have a surprise for everyone. See you in two days!

By Thursday, things have stabilized substantially. The most glaring defects and performance problems in Phoenix have been fixed. And it helps that customer traffic is way, way down. Who wants to go to a store or website that can't take orders? The result is that it's no longer necessary for everyone to work all night. Maxine slept in until ten this morning. As she was driving into work, she realized how much she was looking forward to the Dockside meeting that evening.

As promised, Kurt texted everyone in the Rebellion:

> I'll be a little late. Dwayne and Maxine, please run the standard agenda, including the Phoenix environment build. I will be bringing a very special guest.

Maxine is pretty sure everyone will be there tonight.

But despite getting some sleep, she doesn't feel well. She desperately hopes she is not getting whatever illness decimated her fellow co-workers. Despite that, she is very glad to be working on the Phoenix builds again.

That evening, when she arrives at the Dockside, Maxine's excited to see everyone. She wants to find out how to get a Rebellion sticker for her laptop and to trade war stories. She's surprised to see that everyone looks angry and dejected.

Throwing her jacket over the back of a chair, she says cheerily, "Hi, everyone! What's got everyone so grouchy?"

Dwayne looks at her. "Read the email that was just sent out. They fired William."

From: Chris Allers (VP Development)
To: All IT Employees
Date: 4:58 p.m., September 18
Subject: Personnel changes

Effective immediately, Peter Kilpatrick (Front-End Dev Manager) will be leaving the company, and William Mason (QA Director) will be on a leave of absence. We especially appreciate all their contributions.

Please direct all front-end Dev emails to Randy and all QA-related emails to me.

Thank you, Chris

Maxine slumps as she reads the message. The witch hunt has begun. Adam shakes his head angrily. "I wasn't a huge fan of William," he says, "but to blame him for everything is wrong."

In Chris' email there's no mention about his own culpability in the Phoenix disaster. And even though Maxine doesn't believe in punishment or scapegoating, it's doubly unfair that all the blame is being put on the technology organization, and no one from the business or product side is being held accountable.

Cranky Dave looks up from his phone, disgusted. "Ditto for Peter—he was just doing what the business managers demanded. What a complete shit show."

"This is so wrong," Shannon mutters. "I don't suppose it would help to write a petition or anything, right? You know, lodge our protest about their firing?"

Adam says, "No one who matters is being held responsible! We should…"

He suddenly stops talking, staring slack-jawed at something behind Maxine. "Holy shit…" he finally says. Everyone next to Adam is also looking shocked at whatever is behind her.

Maxine turns around and sees Kurt walking through the entrance.

Next to him is Kirsten, the director of project management.

"My God," Maxine hears Adam say. He looks frightened, closing his laptop and standing up, as if he's going to flee the scene.

"Oh, for Chrissakes, sit back down, Adam," says Maxine. "This isn't like the secret police showing up. Not one of us has done anything wrong—have some dignity."

Cranky Dave laughs nervously, but like everyone else, he's already closed his laptop, as if he has something to hide.

Kirsten is wearing a fancy blazer, two steps up from Maxine's usual casual business garb and a full four steps up from the hoodies, T-shirts, and bowling shirts worn by the other engineers around the table. People in the bar are staring, clearly wondering who invited the management suit here.

Maxine knows that she looks slightly out of place at the Dockside, but wow, Kirsten looks *way* out of place, like she was on the way to an event for senior law partners but had a flat tire while driving by with a dead cell phone and had to come in to find help.

Looking around, Kurt smiles and says, "For those of you who don't know Kirsten, she leads Project Management, which is undoubtedly the most trusted organization at Parts Unlimited, despite their association with us technology people." Kurt laughs. "All of the most important company initiatives go through Kirsten and her project management clerics, and she routinely briefs Dick Landry, our CFO, on how they're going."

This is true, Maxine thinks. Kirsten is truly the high priestess of order and discipline. She assigns the score of red, yellow, or green to each major initiative of the organization, which can have career-catapulting or career-ending consequences for the people involved. Besides Sarah and the VP of sales, Kirsten is the person most mentioned by the CFO in his Town Halls.

Sitting, Kirsten pours herself a beer from the pitcher on the table and then pours a glass for Kurt. Kurt introduces everyone to Kirsten and then gestures at Maxine, "Maxine is the latest addition to our elite group of rebels. She was exiled to the Phoenix Project as punishment for the payroll outage, and of course, her vast talents have been completely wasted ever since. That is, until we recruited her to help overthrow the uncaring, ancient, powerful existing order...oh, um..." Kurt suddenly looks embarrassed, realizing Kirsten is part of that order. "Present company excepted, of course," he finishes.

Kirsten merely raises her glass in response.

Kurt continues, "It turns out that Maxine, in her boredom and search for meaning, began working on creating repeatable Phoenix builds, something that has eluded the Phoenix teams for well over a year. We believe in many great and virtuous things, but one thing we all agree on is that getting builds going again is one of the most urgent and important engineering practices we need right now. Once we get continuous builds going, we enable automated testing. We get automated testing, we can make changes quicker, with more confidence, and without having to depend on hundreds of hours of manual testing. And that, I believe, is the critical first step for how we can deliver better value, safer, faster, and happier.

"Without continuous builds, we are like a car manufacturer without an assembly line, where anyone can do whatever they want, independent of the plant goals," he continues. "We need to discover problems only when we are in the build or testing process, not during deployment or production.

"I've wanted to own this for a year, but my boss, uh, rather, my recently departed ex-boss, didn't think it mattered. So, I've been taking people off my team to work on it in secret and seeking out the best engineers in the company who are willing and able to help. And Maxine has been a tremendous help in an amazingly short amount of time," he adds.

Kurt pauses. "Uh, let's all raise a glass to William—he and I had our differences, but he certainly didn't deserve to take the blame for the entire Phoenix fiasco."

Maxine raises her glass, as everyone else does the same. She takes the time to clink glasses with everyone around the table.

Looking at Kirsten, she says, "It sounds crazy, Kirsten, but I really think this group can make a big difference. I've seen developers wait for months to get a Dev environment. The lack of environments and centralized builds slow us down in countless ways. In fact, most Dev teams eventually stop waiting for environments or builds and just write code in isolation, without caring whether it actually works with the system as a whole."

Maxine continues, "Look at what happened last week with the Phoenix release. Better engineering practices would have prevented so much of that. What a waste..."

"We all agree with Maxine," Cranky Dave says. "But, Kirsten, uh, what in the world are you doing here?"

Kirsten laughs. "I've long harbored a suspicion that how we manage technology at this company is not working. And it's not just the Phoenix release catastrophe. Look at all the things we need from Phoenix that are still years away on the project plan.

"Kurt has been telling me for months about the work the Rebellion is doing. But my aha moment was when Kurt pointed out that we've somehow created a system where hundreds of engineers are unable to get simple things done without an incredible amount of communication and coordination," she explains. "Sure, it's our job to safeguard the most important projects in the company. But ideally, everyone should be able to get what they need done without any help from us. Somehow, I think Project Management has turned into an army of paper pushers, being dragged into every single task because of all the dependencies.

"We track the work of nearly three hundred people working on the various parts of Phoenix. But, the real effort is even larger," she continues. "You'd think we have thirty teams of ten people, with each team able to get things done independently. But at times, it's like we have only one team of three hundred people...Or maybe three hundred teams of one. In either case, something is very wrong..."

She turns to Kurt. "What was that term you used? Watermelon projects? Green on the outside, but red on the inside? That's what every one of our IT projects is these days," Kirsten observes wryly.

She continues, "I've been here for fifteen years, and we've been playing this game of outsourcing and insourcing IT the whole time. The last time around, the CIO proclaimed that Parts Unlimited was 'no longer in the people business,' if you can believe that, and outsourced everything.

We eventually brought most of it back in-house, but everything we got back was in worse shape than ever. And we've lost the capability to do some of even the most basic things ourselves. Last year, we had to make a simple schema change for our data warehouse. We put out the request to our normal list of outsourcing partners. It took them about three weeks to get an estimate back to us. They said the work would take about ten thousand hours to complete," she says. "Before we outsourced IT, this was something we could have done in a couple of hours."

Maxine does the math in her head. From her consulting days, she knows one fully loaded engineer works about two thousand hours per year—that's forty hours per week, fifty-two weeks per year, if they don't take any vacation. She bursts out laughing. "That's five engineers working full-time for a year, just to make a database column change?! That's something I could do in fifteen minutes!"

"Yep," Kurt says, with a sad smile. "The data warehouse change requires work from two or three different outsourcers. You'd need to pull together meetings from the account managers from each of those teams. Each account manager would require a change fee and a feasibility study. It takes weeks to get all the technical people to agree upon a change plan, and even then, the tickets bounce back and forth for weeks. It takes a super-heroic effort to actually get the change made."

Dwayne laughs loudly. "You think that's bad? That's nothing! We used to have three networking switches in all of our manufacturing plants. One for internal plant operations, one for employees and guest WiFi, and one for all our equipment vendors that need to phone home to their mothership.

"A couple of years ago, probably during budgeting season, some bean counter looked at those three networking vendors and decided to consolidate them down to one switch. Sort of makes sense, right?" he continues.

"So without asking anyone, they went ahead and did it. And not just in one plant, but in a bunch of the plants. They replaced the three switches with one bigger, beefier switch, and then moved all plant traffic onto it," Dwayne says. "But what they didn't know was that they had three separate outsourcers managing the three different networks. So now all three outsourcers who used to work on their own separate switches had to work on one switch and were suddenly stepping on each other's toes all the time.

"Within a week, one of the manufacturing plants had their entire network knocked offline—absolutely nothing from inside the plant could talk with the outside world. No one could get plant scheduling information, no one could send out replenishment orders, equipment couldn't get maintenance updates...All interfaces were dead!" Dwayne continues, still clearly in awe of the scale of the outage.

"The only thing that worked was the fax machine. Everyone from every department had to wait in line to send out things like weekly production reports to management, orders for raw materials..." Dwayne says.

Maxine bursts out laughing. "I remember that—it was incredible. We had to buy some USB printers from the local office supply store for a couple of systems that couldn't connect to the network printers. It was like going back to the 1970s for almost a week."

Adam mutters from across the table, "Yeah, just like we did to the in-store systems this weekend."

Dwayne takes another drink of beer and leans back, enjoying having everyone's attention. "You're probably wondering why it took a week to restore service. Well, that entire time, no one took responsibility for what happened. All three outsourcers denied that it was them, even when we presented them the log files that clearly showed that one of the them had disabled everyone else's accounts. Apparently someone got tired of having their changes trampled on by the other two, so they just locked them out."

Everyone roars in laughter, but Maxine's jaw drops.

Dwayne continues, "That entire week all three outsourcers kept blaming each other, and the network stayed down for days. It escalated all the way to Steve. Yep. The CEO. Even after he got all the CEOs of all three outsourcers on the phone together, it still took almost twenty-four hours for the network to be restored."

As everyone jeers, Maxine says slowly, "That's so interesting. Consolidating network switches isn't inherently a bad idea. Before, three teams were able to work independently on their own networks. And when they were all put on one network switch, suddenly they were coupled together, unable to work independently, having to communicate and coordinate in order to not interfere with each other, right?"

With awe in her voice, she continues, "You know, after they got put onto one switch, I bet those teams needed to create a master schedule with all of their work on it. And I'm even betting that they needed to bring in project managers where they probably didn't need them before.

"Holy cow," Maxine continues, on a roll. "They did it to reduce costs, but surely, in the end, it was more expensive for everyone all around. And I bet it took everyone longer to do their work, with everyone having to communicate, coordinate, get approvals, with project managers shuffling and deconflicting all the work.

"Oh, my God. It's just like the Phoenix Project!" she exclaims.

Silence falls upon the table as everyone stares at Maxine in a mix of horror and dawning realization.

"You mean everything that's wrong with the Phoenix Project we did to ourselves?" Shannon asks.

Kirsten looks rattled, brow furrowed, but says nothing. "Yes," says Maxine. "I think we did it to ourselves."

"You are correct, Maxine. You are truly on the cusp of understanding the magnitude and scale of the challenges that await you," a voice says from behind Maxine.

CHAPTER 7

The owner of the familiar voice is, to Maxine's surprise, the bartender the last time she was at the Dockside.

He sets a tray of drinks down next to Maxine and gives Kurt a friendly pat on the back. Then he turns to Kirsten, saying, "Oh, ho—if it isn't Ms. Fingle! Long time no see! Welcome to the Dockside, headquarters of the budding Rebellion."

"Holy cow," Kirsten says, staring.

"Uh, you know each other?" Kurt asks, his usual confident tone missing.

Kirsten laughs. "This is Dr. Erik Reid. You may not know this, but Steve and Dick have been trying to recruit him to serve on the board of Parts Unlimited for months. He's worked with the company for decades. In fact, Erik was part of the initial MRP rollout in the '80s, and then he helped the manufacturing plants adopt Lean principles and practices. We were one of the first companies to have an automated MRP system, and he's a genuine hero among the manufacturing ranks."

"Him?" Kurt says in disbelief, pointing his thumb toward the bartender.

Maxine is surprised too. After all, she took over continuing development and operations of the amazing homegrown MRP system years ago. She's always been impressed at how it codified not only a wonderful way of working that led to fantastic flow but also enabled continual learning, for both line workers and plant managers.

"Don't believe everything you hear," Erik says, snorting.

Maxine quickly sizes him up. He appears to be in his mid- to late-fifties, about the right age to be the progenitor of the MRP system. He has the build of someone large who used to be in great shape. He has shoulder-length, graying hair, reminding her of The Dude from *The Big Lebowski*. But instead of being mellow and cool, Erik is clearly sharp and attentive.

He turns to Maxine with a sly smile. "On behalf of everyone in manufacturing operations, thanks for taking such good care of the MRP system. You've helped create and sustain software that is a masterpiece of simplicity and locality. You're not only magnificently meeting the business objectives, you've also created a system where small teams of engineers are able to work productively and independently of each other, with components painstakingly and splendidly isolated from each other, instead of being complected into a giant, ugly, knotty mess.

"A truly magnificent feat of engineering and architecture!" he says, beaming. "The developer productivity you've enabled is a beautiful testament to elegant simplicity. And even more impressive is your ruthless eradication of technical debt as a part of your daily work. I'm pleased to finally meet you!"

Maxine stares at Erik. *It's not every day that a bartender compliments you on the code you've painstakingly written and shepherded for years,* she thinks.

"Thank you—I'll make sure to pass that on to the team," she says, perplexed, but unable to hide her pride.

"Uh, what does 'complected' mean?" Kurt asks.

Erik answers, "It's an archaic word, resurrected by Sensei Rich Hickey. 'Complect' means to turn something simple into something complex.

"In tightly coupled and complected systems, it's nearly impossible to change anything, because you can't just change one area of the code, you must change one hundred, or even a thousand, areas of the code. And even the smallest changes can cause wildly unpredictable effects in distant parts of the system, maybe in something you've never even heard of.

"Sensei Hickey would say, 'Think of four strands of yarn that hang independently—that's a simple system. Now take those same four strands of yarn and braid them together. Now you've complected them.' Both configurations of yarn could fulfill the same engineering goal, but one is dramatically easier to change than the other. In the simple system, you can change one string independently without having to touch the others. Which is very good."

Erik laughs, "However, in the complected system, when you want to make a change to one strand of yarn, you are forced to change the other three strands too. In fact, for many things you may want to do, you simply cannot, because everything is so knotted together.

"And when that happens," he continues, "you've trapped yourself in a system of work where you can no longer solve real business problems easily anymore—instead, you're forced to merely solve puzzles all day, trying to figure out how to make your small change, obstructed by your complected system every step of the way. You must schedule meetings with other teams, try to convince them to change something for you, escalate it to their managers, maybe all the way up the chain.

"Everything you do becomes increasingly distant from the real business problem you're trying to solve," he says. "And that, Dwayne, is what everyone discovered when they switched out the routers in those manufacturing plants. Before, you had three independent strands, with teams able to work independently but at the cost of having to maintain three networking switches.

"When you put them all on one switch, you complected their value streams, all now having dependencies on each other that didn't exist before. They must constantly communicate, coordinate, schedule, marshal, sequence, and deconflict their work. They now have an extremely high cost of coordination, which has lengthened lead times, decreased quality, and, in your story, led to a week-long catastrophe that significantly impaired the business, going all the way up to Steve," Erik says with glee.

"The importance of lead times in software delivery is tantamount, as Senseis Dr. Nicole Forsgren and Jez Humble have discovered in their research," Erik says. "Code deployment lead time, code deployment frequency, and time to resolve problems are predictive of software delivery, operational performance, and organizational performance, and they correlate with burnout, employee engagement, and so much more.

"Simplicity is important because it enables locality. Locality in our code is what keeps systems loosely coupled, enabling us to deliver features faster. Teams can quickly and independently develop, test, and deploy value to customers. Locality in our organizations allows teams to make decisions without having to communicate and coordinate with people outside the team, potentially having to get approvals from distant authorities or committees so far removed from the work that they have no relevant basis to make good decisions," he says, clearly disgusted.

"You should be able to create value by changing one file, one module, one service, one component, one API call, one container, one app, or whatever! Which is why putting cross-cutting concerns in one place is so great, like logging, security, or retry policies. You change it there, and you've changed it everywhere," he says. "Isn't it absurd that when you build a feature, changes sometimes have to be made by the UI team, the front-end team, the back-end team, and the database team?"

"Interesting," Maxine says. "Locality in our code and organization is so desirable, as opposed to what we have now, which is code scattered everywhere!"

"Yes, exactly. Scattered!" Erik says. "And achieving this greatness is never free. It requires focus and elevation of *improvement* of daily work, even over daily work itself. Without this ruthless focus, every simple system degrades over time, increasingly buried under a tundra of technical debt. Just look at the disaster that is the Phoenix build system."

Maxine furrows her brow. "You're saying that Phoenix used to be simple, but now it has become complected beyond recognition. That Phoenix used to have a great build process, but over the years it has become neglected, taking a backseat to features, and eventually bumped out of the car entirely."

"Precisely," says Erik. "Build responsibility moved from Dev to QA to interns. Tech giants like Facebook, Amazon, Netflix, Google, and Microsoft give Dev productivity responsibilities to only the most senior and experienced engineers. But here at Parts Unlimited, it's the exact opposite."

Dwayne laughs, "At least our builds aren't outsourced anymore. Not too long ago, it cost $85 each time a build was performed." Everyone, including Maxine, guffaws in disbelief.

Kirsten says, "I hear engineers complain all the time about technical debt? But what exactly is it, besides being something bad?"

Erik laughs. "There are many definitions, but my favorite is how it was originally defined by Ward Cunningham in 2003. He said, 'technical debt is what you feel the next time you want to make a change.' There are many things that people call technical debt, but it usually refers to things we need to clean up, or where we need to create or restore simplicity, so that that we can quickly, confidently, and safely make changes to the system.

"Sometimes it's a build and test system that doesn't give fast feedback to developers, or when it stops working entirely," he continues. "Sometimes it's when simple components become complected, and you can no longer reason about it or change it without immense effort or risk of catastrophe. Sometimes it's when decision-making processes or the organizational structure loses locality, forcing even small decisions to be escalated—your infamous 'Square.'

"I've started calling all of these things 'complexity debt,' because they're not just technical issues—they're business issues. And it's always a choice," he says. "You can choose to build new features or you can choose to pay down complexity debt. When a fool spends all their time on features, the inevitable outcome is that even easy tasks become difficult and take longer to execute. And no matter how hard you try or how many people you have, it eventually collapses under its own weight , forcing you to start over from scratch."

He looks at Maxine and says, "Which is why what you've done with the MRP system is so remarkable. Your teams are able to add features at a rate that the entire Phoenix team should envy. And that is only possible because you pay down technical debt as a part of daily work. It's a magnificent example of the First Ideal of Locality and Simplicity in our code and organizations. Well done, Maxine."

Erik stands up. "I'm a little short-staffed tonight. I'll catch you later, and great to see you, Kirsten!"

"Oh, one more thing," he says, turning around. "Think about the engagement scores of the technology employees versus the rest of the business and ponder the differences, especially on the Phoenix Project."

As Maxine watches Erik head back to the bar, she hears everyone burst into conversation.

Maxine says, "I have no idea what just happened." Looking at both Kirsten and Kurt, she asks, "What was that all about? And what did he mean by the First Ideal?"

"I have no idea," Kurt says, shaking his head. "I've known Erik for over a year. I had absolutely no idea he had some connection to the company…"

Dwayne says to Kurt, "I never bothered to tell you because, you know, it didn't seem that important. But one evening he asked me whether I knew anything about configuring Kubernetes clusters. That was pretty strange."

"That's odd," Shannon says. "Now that I think about it, I once had a debate with him about how completely you should or shouldn't isolate the cardholder data environment in order to comply with the PCI Data

Security Standard. He even sent me links to the specific subsections in the standard. He seemed very knowledgeable. An expert, even. I thought it was just because this bar took credit card payments..."

"I've heard he's been having many conversations with Bill Palmer, the new VP of IT Operations," Kirsten adds. "Bill told me about how Erik is teaching him something called the Three Ways and the Four Types of Work."

"I've never heard of those," Maxine says. "He only mentioned the First Ideal...I wonder how many other Ideals there are?"

"And what did he mean by engagement scores?" asks Kurt.

"I don't know," Kirsten says. "But I do know that we have some of the highest employee satisfaction scores in our industry...except for the IT department...which I think is negative twenty-seven."

"Is that bad?" Dwayne asks.

Kirsten looks embarrassed. "Very bad."

Maxine is not surprised. And yet, something bothers her. In the Town Hall, Steve talked about how much he cares about employee engagement. What does he think when he sees that the department responsible for the most strategic program in the company is miserable? Shouldn't that worry him?

When Erik walks by with a full beer glass, Maxine gets up and rushes to catch up with him. "Thanks again for the kind words, Erik. You mentioned the First Ideal—How many of them are there and what are they?"

"Ha! That's not the way it works," Erik says, laughing. "In fact, I've got Bill Palmer running hither and yon, trying to find all the Four Types of Work, watch. But...perhaps I can give you all a head start."

Erik and Maxine walk back to the table. "There are Five Ideals," Erik begins. The whole table turns their attention to him. "I've already told you about the First Ideal of Locality and Simplicity. We need to design things so that we have locality in our systems and the organizations that build them. And we need simplicity in everything we do. The last place we want complexity is internally, whether it's in our code, in our organization, or in our processes. The external world is complex enough, so it would be intolerable if we allow it in things we can actually control! We must make it easy to do our work."

Maxine sits back down, opens her laptop (pleased she remembered it this time), and starts taking notes.

"The Second Ideal is Focus, Flow, and Joy. It's all about how our daily work feels. Is our work marked by boredom and waiting for other people to get things done on our behalf? Do we blindly work on small pieces of the whole, only seeing the outcomes of our work during a deployment when everything blows up, leading to firefighting, punishment, and burn-out? Or do we work in small batches, ideally single-piece flow, getting fast and continual feedback on our work? These are the conditions that allow for focus and flow, challenge, learning, discovery, mastering our domain, and even joy."

He looks around the table with a smug expression on his face. "And that's all you get for now. I'll share with you the other three Ideals when you're ready."

"You're kidding me," Maxine says. "You're pulling some sort of Yoda or Mr. Miyagi routine on us? Come on, at least tell us the *names* of the other Ideals!"

"Lucky for you, Young Grasshopper, I don't have time to argue, as there's a line at the bar I need to take care of," he says. "In its briefest form: The Third Ideal is Improvement of Daily Work. Reflect upon what the Toyota Andon cord teaches us about how we must elevate improvement of daily work over daily work itself. The Fourth Ideal is Psychological Safety, where we make it safe to talk about problems, because solving problems requires prevention, which requires honesty, and honesty requires the absence of fear. In manufacturing, psychological safety is just as important as physical safety. And finally, the Fifth Ideal is Customer Focus, where we ruthlessly question whether something actually matters to our customers, as in, are they willing to pay us for it or is it only of value to our functional silo?"

Erik finishes his beer and says with a smile, "Good luck to you all. See you next week."

"Wait, wait, that's it?" Maxine says, but Erik is already gone. Maxine looks down at her quickly typed notes:

The First Ideal—Locality and Simplicity
The Second Ideal—Focus, Flow, and Joy
The Third Ideal—Improvement of Daily Work

Maxine stares at the list—all of the Ideals sound nice, but how in the world are they supposed to use them to change the trajectory of the Phoenix Project?

"That was so strange," Kurt says, saying what everyone is thinking.

Cranky Dave adds, "That bit about the Fourth Ideal hit home. A culture of fear where everyone is afraid to share bad news? That's us."

"Erik is right," Adam says. "No one talks about the real problem. Most people aren't brave enough to say what they think or to do the right thing. They just say 'yes,' whether they agree or not. But maybe this creates an opportunity. There are some big, gaping holes in the org chart now," he says to Kurt. "You should throw your name into the hat for one of them. Maybe even for William's position?"

Silence descends upon the table as everyone turns to look at Adam and Kurt.

"That's a pretty good idea, Kurt. You could make a huge difference in the QA organization. You know all of us would be pretty happy about that," says Shannon, with everyone around the table murmuring assent.

"Maybe," says Kurt, nodding slowly. "But you know, if we really want to make a difference, there's another move. I'm thinking about telling Chris that I want Peter's position."

Maxine hears some gasps around the table, followed by Cranky Dave's loud laugh. "You're right, Kurt. You would definitely make a much bigger difference by taking over a Dev team. We all know we need to change how QA does testing, but the best place to start is by changing how *Dev* does testing. And that requires being a Dev manager...but that brings up a teeny, tiny, little problem...they'll never give you that position, Kurt," he says. "You know, because you're 'just a QA manager.'"

Maxine winces. Cranky Dave is voicing an all-too-popular prejudice that developers have about QA people, which embarrasses her. QA is often viewed as an underclass, but at least they're above Ops. *All of which is crap*, Maxine thinks. After all, she started her Ops career in high school, rotating backup tapes, and later, before graduate school, QA—if it weren't for that background, she wouldn't have become the person she is today. Technology is still too often a caste system.

Adam says to Kurt, "You know I'm a big fan and I love working with you—you're a fantastic leader—but I agree with Dave. There's no way that a bunch of Dev managers are going to let a QA manager take that spot. Maybe you should just settle for William's old role. After all, someone has to lead QA out of the Stone Age and bring automated testing to the rest of the Phoenix Project."

"I have to agree with your friends, Kurt," Kirsten says. "You and I both know that William was never a big fan of yours. He never spoke very highly of you in meetings. They're probably going to bring in someone from the outside."

Kurt grins, seemingly not bothered by Kirsten's observation. In his great William impersonation, Kurt says, "'Yes, Kirsten, you are right. Although Kurt shows some potential, it's clear to me that he doesn't understand the testing game. Maybe in a couple of years he'll have the maturity to run the QA organization.'"

Everyone laughs. Kurt continues in his normal voice, "Folks, here's an opportunity for us to make a difference. But I don't think we can do it from anywhere in the QA organization—QA as we know it is changing. We can't keep being the people who test after the fact. We need to get into the game, and that means finagling our way into the development teams that are actually responsible for shipping features and the quality of their outcomes. Anything else is a waste of our time."

He continues, "In fact, if we can take over Peter's team, my goal will be to show that we can out-perform every other Dev team in the Phoenix Project. Gathered around this table is some of the best technical talent in the company, and we've already created the infrastructure that can bring some great technical practices to the game."

Kurt leans forward. "If I can get Chris to give me that chance, would you all be willing to join the team and show that we can change the trajectory of the Phoenix Project?"

"Hell yes, Kurt. Count me in!" says Cranky Dave. Maxine is surprised that he's the first to volunteer.

Maxine follows. "And me. This is what I want to work on. And I know we can run circles around all the other teams. I've seen the competition up close," she says with a smile.

Everyone around the table chimes in, excited at the potential opportunity. Cranky Dave says, "Okay, we're all in, Kurt. But frankly, I'm not holding my breath. Adam is right—you getting a Dev team is a long shot."

Kirsten says, "Kurt, I agree with your instincts. If you want, I'll write a letter of recommendation to Chris."

"That would be fantastic, Kirsten," says Kurt, beaming and obviously genuinely surprised and grateful for Kirsten's offer. At that moment, Maxine realizes that Kurt has been operating this entire time without any real leadership air cover. *He could get fired for going rogue*, she realizes.

"Happy to help," says Kirsten. "But let me be clear. I'm willing to write a letter to support Kurt's ideas, but I really can't be seen publicly with you all. At least, not yet. People need to see me as impartial."

"Oh, you're willing to give us a chance to take a risk and get fired, but you want to stay safely on the sidelines?" says Cranky Dave, halfway joking. Kirsten merely raises her glass to Dave.

PART TWO

September 23–November 9

CHAPTER 8

On Tuesday of the following week, Maxine arrives at work to see Kurt beaming. "I got the job," he says exuberantly.

"Really? The Dev job?" Maxine asks.

"Yes, the Dev job!" he says, as if he can't quite believe it himself. "It couldn't have happened without Kirsten's support. I'm joining the Data Hub team, and you're coming with me."

"That's awesome!" Maxine says, jubilant. "How'd you get Randy to approve my reassignment?"

"Well, he wasn't happy about losing you. He kept going on about how you're the best thing to happen to this place since sliced bread, but...well, I have my ways," Kurt says with a sly smile.

Maxine gives him a high five.

He looks around and whispers, "All the managers are talking about something very strange happening. Apparently, the technology executives had an off-site with Steve earlier this week, and one of the things they agreed upon was a one-month feature freeze. Apparently, they're actually hitting the brakes on feature delivery to pay down all the technical debt we've built up over the years!"

"Really?!" Maxine is shocked.

"They realize they need to fix all the crap that's been built," he says. "Ops is halting all work not related to the Phoenix Project so they can pay down technical debt and automate things. And Dev and QA will halt all feature work to pay down their technical debt too.

"This is our moment to shine. Here's our chance to show people what engineering greatness looks like," Kurt exclaims.

Later that day, an email goes out announcing Kurt's new role. Maxine doesn't want to hurt Kurt's feelings, but she's pretty sure that the real reason he got the job was that absolutely nobody else in Development wanted it. Data Hub is being widely touted as the "root cause" of the catastrophic crashes during and after the Phoenix release. Chris even called them out by name during one of the meetings Maxine was in, which she thought was quite unfair.

Blaming the Data Hub team for the smoking crater in the ground that was the Phoenix deployment was like blaming an airline crash on the passenger in the back of the plane who didn't fasten his seatbelt tight enough.

She knows why blaming Data Hub is so easy. It's one of the least glamorous technology areas in the company. Data Hub is part of a big, boring message bus system, which Maxine already loves because it's how most of the major applications and systems of record talk to each other: the product database, pricing database, inventory management systems, order fulfillment systems, sales commissioning systems, company financials, and almost a hundred other major systems, many of them decades old.

Maxine has never liked that there are actually three inventory management systems—two for the physical stores (one was inherited by an acquisition and never retired) and another for the e-commerce channel. And there's at least six order entry systems—three supporting the physical stores, one for e-commerce, another for OEM customers, and another for service station channel sales.

Maxine loves byzantine processes like pediatricians love sick children, but even Maxine is taken aback by just how many systems Data Hub has to talk to.

The more Maxine studies up on what Data Hub does, the more perplexed she becomes. Data Hub just didn't seem like it should be part of Phoenix at all. After all, the majority of Data Hub was written over twenty years ago, which was long before Phoenix was even a concept.

Apparently, Data Hub used to be a collection of smaller applications that were scattered across the company. Some resided in finance with the ERP systems, some inside the manufacturing business units, and others within the Development group under Chris.

As the Phoenix juggernaut started rolling, an incredible number of new demands were put on those teams, and those teams just weren't staffed to deal with it. Tons of new Phoenix functionality was blocked because of competing business priorities in Data Hub, and soon Phoenix features were being delayed, month after month.

Finally, as part of a re-org, all those components were rolled up into a new group called Data Hub and put under the Phoenix Project, making sure Phoenix priorities always came first. And now, everyone is blaming Data Hub for what went wrong.

On Wednesday morning, Maxine and Cranky Dave join Kurt for the first meeting with the Data Hub engineers. Maxine's surprised to see that Cranky Dave was able to join Data Hub so quickly too. She asked him how he managed to swing that.

Cranky Dave merely smiled, saying, "One of the many benefits of my winning personality—no manager passes on the opportunity to give me to a different team. It allows me to go wherever I want."

She stands next to Cranky Dave as the other five Data Hub engineers assemble in the central meeting area.

They're all either her age or fresh out of college, no one in between. She suspects the senior developers have been on the team since the beginning, and the younger engineers will quickly leave for more interesting work and be replaced with other new college grads.

Chris clears his throat and addresses the room. "Good morning, everyone. Please welcome Kurt Reznick, who will be taking over for Peter."

Kurt seems surprised by the short introduction but says cheerily, "Hello, everyone. As you may know, this is the first Dev team I've managed. I believe my job my job is very simple: listen, do whatever you need me to do to help make you successful, and remove any obstacles in your way." It's clear from everyone's unimpressed looks that they're well aware of Kurt's lack of experience.

Kurt continues, "I've talked with our numerous internal customers, and they told me how important Data Hub is. But they also told me about how we're often the bottleneck for changes needed across the enterprise, as well as for the Phoenix Project. And as we all know, when our service goes down, so does Phoenix. I've scheduled a session later this week for us to brainstorm how we can make our service more reliable and resilient."

"Blaming Data Hub and Peter for Phoenix going down is bullshit," says one of the senior developers.

"I totally agree with you, Tom," says Kurt. "And rest assured that I'll be working to correct that perception."

Kurt continues, "I really appreciate that Peter was willing to meet with me before I started. He told me that he's been asking for additional head-count for senior developers for years because the business needs have kept growing, especially around the Phoenix integration. He recommended that I keep trying."

Kurt gestures at Chris. "And I promise you that I'll keep lobbying Chris for more headcount."

"And I'll keep lobbying Steve," Chris replies with a tight-lipped smile. Kurt laughs. "So, in the meantime, I've brought with me two senior developers who have volunteered to join the team. Maxine is the most senior developer from the MRP team, and Dave is a senior developer from the Phoenix back-end server team. They're two of the developers I trust the most."

The Data Hub developers look at them, surprised but genuinely happy that she and Cranky Dave are here.

"There will be a directive coming out soon from Chris about a feature freeze, so we can work on fixing defects that impact our customers and fix problematic areas of our code," Kurt says. "But don't wait for the announcement. The top priority is to fix things you think should be fixed and, for that matter, anything that you think will help you be more productive or make Data Hub more stable. I'll handle any complaints that come our way."

Maxine smiles at the expressions of grudging approval from the Data Hub engineers.

As the new engineers, Cranky Dave and Maxine integrate themselves into the daily rituals of the Data Hub team. They attend the stand-ups and are quick to volunteer to help with things.

Maxine pairs up with Tom, the older developer who had commented on the unfairness of being scapegoated for the Phoenix failure. Tom is in his late forties and wears glasses, jeans, and a T-shirt. She sits at his desk with her laptop open as he explains what he's currently working on.

As he talks, Maxine sees that Data Hub is a mishmash of technologies built up over the decades, including a big chunk that runs on Java servlets, some Python scripts, and something that she thinks is Delphi. There's even a PHP web server.

She doesn't judge or dismiss any of the technology stacks—after all, it's been successfully serving the enterprise for decades. It may not be the most elegant piece of software she's seen, but things that have been in production for twenty years rarely are. Software is like a city, constantly undergoing change, needing renovations and repair. She will, however, acknowledge that Data Hub is not the hippest neighborhood. It's undoubtedly difficult to recruit new college grads who want to learn and use the hottest, most in-demand languages and frameworks.

But at least Data Hub is in much better shape than the Phoenix build systems, which were like uninhabitable, radioactive Superfund sites, or the shelled-out remains of a war zone.

Maxine is sitting at Tom's desk as he explains what he's working on, "I'm working on an urgent defect. Data Hub is occasionally generating incorrect message transactions and is crashing under high loads. It sometimes happens when in-store employees mark customer repair work as complete in the service station application," he says. Looking embarrassed, he continues, "I've spent days working on this. I've finally created a semi-reproducible test case—it happens about one out of ten times. I'm pretty sure it's because of a race condition."

Talk about being thrown in the deep end, Maxine thinks. But she relishes the challenge and is sure that when they solve the problem, it will make a very positive impression on the entire team. After all, race conditions are one of the toughest categories of problems in all of distributed systems and software engineering. If working with the middle-school girls was a yellow belt challenge in karate, what Tom is describing can drive even the most experienced tenth-level black belts to despair and madness.

Maxine is impressed that Tom can even reproduce the problem at all. Someone once called these problems "heisenbugs," referring to the quantum physics phenomena where the act of observation changes the nature of reality itself.

This type of work is very different than how coding is portrayed in the movies: a young, male programmer is typing away furiously, wearing a hoodie, of course, but curiously, also wearing sunglasses (which she has never actually seen a developer do in real life). He has many different windows open, text quickly scrolling by in all of them. Behind him, a crowd of people is watching over his shoulder, waiting anxiously. After a couple of seconds, the coder cries out, "I got it!" and everyone cheers. The solution is created, the feature is delivered, or the world is saved. And the scene ends.

But in reality, when developers work, they're usually staring at the screen, deep in concentration, trying to understand what the code does so they can safely and surgically change it without breaking something else as an unintended side-effect, especially if they're working on something mission-critical.

Tom walks her through the problem. "When there are multiple repair transactions being processed concurrently, sometimes one of the transactions gets the wrong customer ID, and sometimes Data Hub completely crashes," he says. "I've tried putting a lock around the customer object, but it slowed down the entire application so much, it's just not an option. We have enough performance problems as it is."

Maxine nods, because Tom is confirming her long-held belief that multi-threading errors are at the very limits of what humans can reason about, especially since most mainstream programming languages like Java, C#, and JavaScript encourage mutation of shared state.

It is almost impossible to predict how a program will behave if any other part of the program can change data that you're depending on at any time, Maxine thinks. But she's pretty sure she knows how to fix this problem.

"Can we walk through the code path again?" Maxine asks. As they do, Maxine goes through a mental checklist to confirm her hypothesis. There's a thread pool that handles incoming messages. Check. Service records can be handled by multiple concurrent threads. Check. The threads pass around objects, which are being mutated when its methods are called. Check.

Hypothesis confirmed. The problem is almost definitely state mutation going wrong, she thinks. *Just like at the middle school.*

"You're right, it's definitely a race condition," Maxine says. "And I'm pretty sure we can solve this problem without putting a lock around the entire customer object. Can I show you what I'm thinking?"

When he nods, just as Maxine did with the middle-school girls, she proposes rewriting the code path using functional programming principles. Tom's test case has a lot of mocks and stubs to simulate the production environment: a configuration server, a database, a message bus, a customer object factory....

She jettisons all of them, because those are not areas of the system she wants to test. Instead, she pushes all that input/output and side-effects to the edges and creates unit tests around how an incoming repair order message is processed, how customer data is transformed, and what outgoing messages are sent.

She has each thread make its own copy of the customer object. They rewrite each object method into a series of pure functions—a function whose output is completely dependent upon its inputs, with no side-effects, mutations, or accesses to global state.

When Maxine shows Tom a unit test that reproduces the problem 100% of the time, as well as the completely thread-safe fix that now works 100% of the time, Tom stares at her, eyes wide with wonder. "That's...that's...incredible."

She knows why he's impressed. Her code is so simple that it's easy to understand and test for correctness. Eventually, marveling at the screen, he says, "I just can't believe how much you simplified it. How can that achieve the same thing as the complex mess that we had before?" For the rest of the afternoon, he asks questions, obviously trying to prove to himself that Maxine's test case captured the problem and that the rewrite is correct. At last he says, "I can't believe it, but I think you're right. This will definitely work!"

Maxine grins at Tom's reaction. Another testament that functional programming principles are better tools to think with. And they've already made the code way better than when they found it—it's definitely safer, easier to test, and way easier to understand. *This is so much fun,* she thinks. *And a great example of the First Ideal of Locality and Simplicity.*

"Okay, let's get this fix merged in!" he says, opening up a terminal window, typing in some commands. He turns to Maxine. "Congratulations! You just fixed your first defect and checked in your first change!"

Maxine gives him a huge high-five, a big grin on her face. Vanquishing a race condition error on her first day is freaking awesome. "That's great! So, let's get this thing tested and pushed into production." Maxine is excited at the thought of a grateful store manager thanking them.

"Errrr...Uhhhh..." Tom says, pausing. "Testing doesn't start until Monday."

Maxine feels her heart drop. "We can't test it ourselves?"

"We used to be able to, before we got re-orged into Phoenix," he says, wistfully. "The QA group took over the testing. And when they had some problems with different teams using the test environment at the same time, they took everyone's access away. Now they're the only ones who can log in, let alone run the tests."

"Wait," she says. "We write the tests but can't run them?"

He laughs. "No, no. They write the tests. They don't even let us see the test plans anymore."

Maxine deflates even more, knowing where this is going. "And we can't push it into production?"

Tom laughs again. "Nope, not any more. We used to be able to do that too. But now someone else deploys it for us. 'Stay in your lane,' they told us." He shrugs his shoulders. Maxine is pretty sure she knows who said, "Stay in your lane." That'd be Chris.

The joy that Maxine felt all day while working on the problem disappears. After all, fixing the code especially for features is just a fraction of the entire job. It's not done until that customer can use what they've written. And even then, it's probably still a work in progress, because we can always learn more about how to help that customer best achieve their goals.

"Crap," she mutters. *I'm back in the same place I was before, a long way away from the First Ideal. I still can't actually do anything myself,* Maxine thinks. Once again, she is dependent on others to create customer value.

Oblivious, Tom laughs and opens up a new window. "It's not so bad. We just need to go into the ticketing system and mark this issue as 'done.' That lets the QA team know to test it, so it can be promoted into production."

Tom looks at his watch and turns back to her, "That was great. We got a lot done today. Want to pick another defect to work on?" Maxine forces a smile and nods. *This sucks,* Maxine thinks. She likes finishing things, not just starting things.

Maxine continues to work with Tom all day, picking the next most urgent defect to be fixed. Tom once again compliments Maxine on how she thinks about problems. He's impressed at how she writes unit tests that can be run without the need for a complex, integration test environment.

But there are limits—Data Hub's job is to connect systems with each other. There's only so much you can simulate on a single laptop. *It would be nice to rearchitect Data Hub so you could,* Maxine thinks wistfully.

Although she enjoys learning about Data Hub and the parts of the business it connects, there's something about all this work that is deeply unsatisfying to her.

She thinks of Erik's Second Ideal of Focus, Flow, and Joy. All the joy she felt vaporized when Tom told her that they had completed only a small portion of the work needed to create value. That's just not good enough for her. In her MRP team, any developer could test their own code and even push code into production themselves. They didn't have to wait weeks for other people to do that work for them. Being able to test and push code to production is more productive, makes for happier customers, creates accountability of code quality to the people who write it, and also makes the work more joyful and rewarding.

Maxine starts thinking about how to introduce some of the tools being built by the Rebellion. *At the very minimum, we need to make standardized Dev environments available, so I can do builds on my laptop,* she thinks. More things to talk about at the next Dockside meeting.

She continues to grind away, helping Tom with the work that he's been assigned. Together they fix two defects and then tackle a crash-priority feature, this time to create some business rules around extended warranty plans, critical enough to be exempted from the feature freeze.

"Why is this so high priority?" Maxine asks Tom as she reads the ticket.

"This is hugely revenue-generating," Tom explains. "One of the highest margin products are these new extended-warrantee plans. Customers loved the pilot warrantee program, especially for things like tires. Now in-store staff need a way to pull up this information, so they can do the repair work and file the claim with the third-party insurer."

Tom continues, "Great for the customer, great for us, and a third-party insurer is taking all the financial risk."

"Cool," Maxine says, perking up. It's features like this that support everything that Steve said in the Town Hall. It's been a long time since Maxine's done work on the revenue-generating side of the business.

Recommitting herself to feel relentlessly optimistic, Maxine and Tom start studying the feature, trying to figure out what is required to enable this important business capability. She tries not to think about how, even if they get it done today, it'll just sit, waiting for the QA team to test it.

The next morning, Tom and Maxine are at a whiteboard, inventorying all the systems that they'll need to change in order to enable extended warrantees. Two more engineers have joined them as the scope keeps increasing. And then they realize that they'll need to talk with engineers from two other teams, as well. Maxine guesses that they'll have to bring in six other teams because of how many business systems this affects.

Maxine is dismayed as the number of teams that need to be involved keeps growing. This is again the opposite of the First Ideal of Locality and Simplicity. Here, the changes that need to be made are not localized. Instead, their scattered across many, many different teams. This is not the famous Amazon ideal of the "two-pizza team," where features can be created by individual teams that can be fed with two pizzas.

We'll need a whole truckload of pizzas to ship this feature, Maxine thinks, watching as Tom draws another set of boxes on the whiteboard.

Kurt pokes his head into the conference room. "Hey, sorry for the interruption. Someone from Ops and the manager of the channel training management application are on a conference bridge. All their customer logins are failing. They say the connector has stopped working?"

"Not again," says Tom. "Authentication has been flaky ever since the Phoenix deployment. We're on it..."

"Roger that," Kurt says, tapping something on his phone. "I just created a chat channel for all of us, okay?"

Maxine follows Tom back to his desk. As Tom opens up another browser window and types something, a login error appears on his screen.

"Okay, something's definitely not working right. Let's see if we can isolate why..." Tom mutters. "I doubt it's actually a Data Hub connector. More likely it's the enterprise customer authentication service or a problem in the network."

Maxine nods, taking notes as more of the Data Hub universe comes into view. Skeptical, she offers, "Can't we rule out network and authentication right away? If either of those were down, we wouldn't even be able to get to the website, and authentication being down would take out every service..."

"Good point…" Tom says. "Could definitely still be networking, though… we've had a bunch of issues lately. Last week, the networking people accidentally blocked some internal IP addresses that caused us problems."

"Networking. It's always the networking people, right?" she says, smiling. "But if it's always the networking people, why are they calling us?" Maxine asks.

"Yeah, well, all the users know is that they can't connect to Data Hub," he says. "We always explain that it's not us; it's something we need to connect to. But they don't care."

When Maxine sees Tom pull up the Ops ticketing system and create a new ticket, she asks, "What's this for?"

"We need the production logs for Data Hub and its connectors to see if they're handling traffic or if they've crashed," he responds, filling out the numerous fields.

"We can't directly access production logs?" Maxine asks, afraid of the answer.

"Nope. Ops people won't let us," he says, typing into the form.

"So, someone has to respond to the ticket and copy the logs off the server for us?" she asks in disbelief.

"Yes," he says, continuing to type, obviously very practiced at filling it out. He tabs between fields, types, mouses over to hit the drop-down box, hits the submit button, only to find that there's still another required field that needs to be filled in.

Maxine groans. The Data Hub application that they're working on might as well be running in outer space or at the bottom of a deep well. They can't directly access it, they can't see what it's doing, and the only way they can understand what's actually happening is to talk to someone in Operations through the ticketing system.

She wonders whether the ticket will get routed to her friend Derek at the helpdesk.

Tom finally succeeds in submitting the ticket. Satisfied, he says, "Now we wait."

"How long does it usually take?" Maxine asks.

"For a Sev 2 incident? Not too bad—we'll probably get it within a half hour. If it's not related to an outage, it could take days," Tom says. He looks at the clock. "What should we do while we wait?"

Even in the Data Hub team, she can't escape the Waiting Place.

Four hours later, after reviewing the production logs, they confirm that the problem isn't Data Hub. Two hours after that, everyone finally agrees. As Tom had suspected, it was an internal networking change that caused the problem.

Another round of intense finger-pointing ensues between Business Operations, Marketing, and within the technology organization. Eventually, Sarah gets involved and demands that there be severe consequences.

"Uh, oh," says Tom, watching with Maxine from the far end of the table. "This can't be good."

From: Wes Davis (Director, Distributed Operations)
To: All IT Employees
Date: 7:50 p.m., September 25
Subject: Personnel changes

Effective immediately, Chad Stone in network engineering is no longer with the company. Please direct all emails to his manager, Irene Cooper, or me.

For the love of all that is holy, please stop making mistakes so that I don't have to write these stupid emails. (And if they fire me, direct your emails to Bill Palmer, VP, IT Operations.)

Thank you,
Wes

Finally, the day is over, which means another meeting at the Dockside Bar. They've invited the entire Data Hub team to join them. Maxine approves of being over-inclusive rather than accidentally leaving some worthy people out. Tom and three other engineers show up. Maxine is glad they're here. After the last couple days, she's eager to brainstorm ways to dramatically improve developer productivity on the Data Hub team.

Seeing everyone having fun, Maxine observes that this is a group of people who love hanging out with each other. Kurt stands up and addresses the group.

"Hello, new Rebellion teammates! Let me introduce everyone," Kurt says. He introduces all the Rebellion members, as he did for Maxine and Kirsten. "And if you don't mind, now that you've heard about some of the subversive things we're working on to bring joy back to Parts Unlimited engineers, how about you tell us something that could make your lives a little easier?"

Tom's two colleagues go first, introducing themselves and sharing their backgrounds. One has been on the Data Hub team, like Tom, for nearly a decade, but he doesn't come up with anything to complain about, saying, "Life is okay, and I appreciate the invitation for drinks."

When he clearly doesn't have anything more to say, Tom starts. "Like my colleague, I've been on the Data Hub team for a long time. Back when it used to be called Octopus. We called it that because of how it connected to eight applications. Now it connects to over a hundred.

"I've been having a blast pair-programming with Maxine, and I still can't believe we fixed a race condition bug! I'm delighted at her idea to get Data Hub Dev environments that we can all use," he continues. "I'm not proud of this, but there have been times when we've hired new developers and six months later, they still can't do a full build on their machines," he says, shaking his head. "It wasn't always like this. When I started, it was simpler. But over the years, we've hard-coded some things that we shouldn't have, updated some things here, updated other things there, never quite documenting all of it... and now? It's a mess."

Looking up, he smirks at his teammates around the table, saying, "You know the developer joke of 'it worked on my laptop'? Well, in Data Hub, we can't even get it running on most people's laptops."

Everyone laughs. At one point or another, every developer on the planet has had this problem. It usually happens at the worst possible time, like when something crashes in production but mysteriously works perfectly on the developer's laptop. Maxine remembers countless times when she's had to painstakingly figure out what exactly was different between the developer's laptop and the production environment.

"My pain points?" Tom muses. "It's our environments. We used to have a good handle on this, but then we got moved into the Phoenix

Project and they made us use environments from their centralized environments team.

"It's crazy. We're puny compared to the rest of Phoenix. To run Data Hub now, we have to install gigabytes of completely irrelevant dependencies," he continues. "It takes forever to figure out how to get everything to run, and it's so easy to break something by accident. No joke: I back up my work laptop every day because I'm so afraid that my builds will stop working and I'll have to spend weeks figuring out how to fix them."

Tom laughs, "Ten years ago, I lost my *emacs* configuration file and couldn't find a recent backup. I just didn't have it in me to recreate it. I finally gave up and switched editors."

Everyone laughs, adding their own stories of loss, anguish, and grief of having to give up their most treasured tools.

Tom turns to Maxine. "I'd love to spend a couple of days exploring how we can make a Dev environment that all of us could use in our daily work. If we had a virtual machine image or a Docker image, any new team member could do a build on any machine, any time. That would be incredible."

"You and I are definitely going to get along," Maxine says, smiling. "We need developers to be able to focus their best energies on building features, not trying to get builds to work. I have a ton of passion for this too and would love your help."

"That's terrific," Kurt says. "We all know how important environments are. For now, feel free to spend half your time on this—I'll hide it in the timecarding system."

Later in the evening, Kirsten shows up and pours herself a glass of beer from the pitcher on the table. Smiling, she says, "What did I miss?"

"Just plotting the inevitable toppling of the existing order, of course," Kurt says. The new Data Hub team members openly stare at Kirsten as she takes a seat.

Kurt asks, "Kirsten, how's Project Inversion going? The feature freeze? I heard that Bill Palmer convinced Steve to put all feature work on hold so everyone can pay down technical debt."

"Confirmed," she says. "Sarah Moulton is going ballistic, complaining how 'all the idle developers' are jeopardizing the promises the company has already made to customers and Wall Street. I still can't believe she doesn't get how this helps her. But Project Inversion is definitely happening: for thirty days, Ops is not doing anything except things to support Phoenix."

"They're not kidding around," Brent says. "Bill has been awesome. He's told me in no uncertain terms that I'm to work only on Phoenix-related things. He's taken me off of pager rotation for basically everything. He's even taken me off of every mailing list, had me turn off notifications from every chat room, and told me not to answer the phone for anyone. And best of all, he said to absolutely not show up for any outage calls. If I do, he'll fire me."

Hearing this, Maxine is shocked. Bill would fire Brent? Thinking of all the people who've been fired lately, Maxine can't figure out why Brent is smiling.

"It's so fantastic," Brent says, even appearing to be... tearing up? "Bill told me that he can't fire the business unit executives or tell them what to do. He said that the only thing he *can* do is ensure that I'm not wasting time on those things. He said to tell anyone trying to reach me that I'll be fired if I call them back."

Brent laughs, obviously elated, finishing his beer and pouring himself another. "He's assigned Wes to screen all my emails and phone calls and to yell at anyone trying to get ahold of me. Life is fantastic! Seriously, never better."

Maxine smiles. She has seen how engineers can become the constraint many times in her career. It can be fun to be at the center of everything, but it's certainly not sustainable. Down that road, only chronic wakeup calls, exhaustion, cynicism, and burnout await.

Kirsten smiles. "It's working. Brent's name shows up on more critical action items than anyone, and Bill has told everyone that their goal must be to protect his time.

"On the Development side, Chris promises that for thirty days, for all teams working on anything related to Project Phoenix, no new features," Kirsten says, reading from her phone. "'All teams need to be fixing high-priority defects, stabilizing the codebase, and doing whatever rearchitecting is needed to prevent another release disaster.'"

Maxine hears lots of excited murmurs from around the table. Maxine knows something like this is needed—and that this could be a fantastic opportunity for the Rebellion.

"There's still a lot of disagreement among Chris's direct reports on how to roll this out," Kirsten continues. "They've spent so much time legislating what should and shouldn't be worked on that we've already lost a week—lots of teams are still working on their features, business as usual. We're going to need a lot more clarity from leadership on this—at this rate, the entire month will be gone, and we'll have the same amount of technical debt as before, if not more."

"I'm surprised no one is talking about all the problems they're having with environments or automated testing or the lack of production telemetry," Kurt says. "We've built some amazing capabilities that other people can use too. But we can't be the people with a solution, peddling them to people who don't know they have a problem."

Kurt looks stumped. And frustrated.

"I totally want to help with this," Shannon says, raising her hand. "I've worked with a bunch of the Phoenix teams. I could swing by each one tomorrow to start asking them what their constraints are and any ideas they have on how to fix them."

"Good, good," Kurt says, writing down some notes in his notebook.

"I'd love to help too, Shannon," Maxine says. "But Tom and I will be a little tied up on Monday, because Monday is Testing Day. I'm going to finally get my changes tested with the QA folks. Outside of that, I'm yours!" A full tray of beer pitchers and two more glasses of wine appear.

They are soon in deep conversation about technical debt and ideas on how to take advantage of Project Inversion. Maxine turns to see Erik grabbing the seat next to her.

He joins the conversation as if he's been there all along. "With Project Inversion, you are all on the beginning of a great journey. Every tech giant has nearly been killed by technical debt. You name it: Facebook, Amazon, Netflix, Google, Microsoft, eBay, LinkedIn, Twitter, and so many more. Like the Phoenix Project, they became so encumbered by technical debt they could no longer deliver what their customers demanded," Erik says. "The consequences would have been fatal—and for every survivor, there are companies like Nokia who fell from the loftiest heights, killed by technical debt.

"Technical debt is a fact of life, like deadlines. Business people understand deadlines, but often are completely oblivious that technical debt even exists. Technical debt is inherently neither good nor bad—it happens because in our daily work, we are always making trade-off decisions," he says. "To make the date, sometimes we take shortcuts, or skip writing our automated tests, or hard-code something for a very specific case, knowing that it won't work in the long-term. Sometimes we tolerate daily work-arounds, like manually creating an environment or manually performing a deployment. We make a grave mistake when we don't realize how much this impacts our future productivity."

Erik looks around the table, pleased that everyone is listening intently to his every word.

"All the tech giants, at some point in their history, have used the feature freeze to massively rearchitect their systems. Consider Microsoft in the early 2000s—that was when computer worms were routinely taking down the internet, most famously *CodeRed, Nimda*, and of course *SQL Slammer*, which infected and crashed nearly 100,000 servers around the world in less than ten minutes. CEO Bill Gates was so concerned that he wrote a famous internal memo to every employee, stating that if a developer has to choose between implementing a feature or improving security, they must choose security, because nothing less than the survival of the company was at stake. And thus began the famous security stand-down that affected every product at Microsoft. Interestingly, Satya Nadella, CEO of Microsoft, still has a culture that if a developer ever has a choice between working on a feature or developer productivity, they should always choose developer productivity.

"Back to 2002—that same year, Amazon CEO Jeff Bezos wrote his famous memo to all technologists, stating that they must rearchitect their systems so that all data and functionality are provided through services. Their initial focus was their OBIDOS system, originally written in 1996, which held almost all the business logic, display logic, and functionality that made Amazon.com so famous.

"But over time, it became too complected for teams to be able to work independently. Amazon likely spent over $1 billion over six years rearchitecting all their internal services to be decoupled from each other. The result was astonishing. By 2013 they were performing nearly 136,000 deployments per day. Interesting that these CEOs I mention all have a software background, isn't it?

"Contrast that with the tragic story of Nokia. When their market was disrupted by Apple and Android, they spent hundreds of millions of dollars hiring developers and investing in rolling out Agile. But they did so without realizing their real problem: technical debt in the form of an architecture where developers could not be productive. They lacked the conviction to rebuild the foundations of their software systems. Just like at Amazon in 2002, every software team at Nokia was unable to build what they needed to because they were hamstrung by the Symbian platform.

"In 2010, Risto Siilasmaa was a board director at Nokia. When he learned that generating a Symbian build took *a whole forty-eight hours*, he said that it felt like someone hit him in the head with a sledgehammer," Erik says. "He knew that if it took two days for anyone to determine whether a change worked or would have to be redone, there was a fundamental and fatal flaw in their architecture that doomed their near-term profitability and long-term viability. They could have had twenty times more developers, and it wouldn't have made them go any faster.

Erik pauses. "It's incredible. Sensei Siilasmaa knew that all the hopes and promises made by the engineering organization was a mirage. Even though there were numerous internal efforts to migrate off of Symbian, it was always shot down by the top executives until it was too late.

"Business people can see features or apps, so getting funding for those is easy," he continues. "But they don't see the vast architectures underneath that support them, connecting systems, teams, and data to each other. And underneath that is something extraordinarily important: the systems that developers use in their daily work to be productive.

"It's funny: the tech giants assign their very best engineers to that bottom layer, so that every developer can benefit. But at Parts Unlimited, the very best engineers work on features at that top layer, with no one besides interns on the bottom working on Dev productivity.

Erik continues, "So your mission is clear. Everyone has been told to pay down technical debt, which will help you realize the First Ideal of Locality and Simplicity and the Second Ideal of Focus, Flow, and Joy. But almost certainly, you will have to master the Third Ideal of Improvement of Daily Work." Then he gets up and leaves as quickly as he joined them.

Everyone watches him leave. Then Kirsten says, "Is he coming back?"

Cranky Dave throws his hands in the air. "What happened at Nokia is happening here. Two years ago, we could implement a significant feature in two to four weeks. And we delivered a ton of great stuff. I remember those days! If you had a great idea, we could get it done.

"But now? That same class of feature takes twenty to forty weeks. Ten times longer! No wonder everyone's so pissed off at us," Cranky Dave yells. "We've hired more engineers, but it feels like we're getting less and less done. And not only are we slower, those changes are incredibly dangerous to make."

"This makes sense," Kirsten says. "By almost any measure, productivity is flat or down. Feature due date performance is way down. I did some research since our last meeting—I asked my project managers to sample a couple of features and find out how many teams were required to implement them. The average number of teams required was 4.2, which is shocking. Then they told me that many had to interact with *over eight teams*," she says. "We've never formally tracked this, but most of my people say that these numbers are definitely higher than they were two years ago."

Maxine's jaw drops. *Absolutely no one can get anything done if they have to work with eight other teams all the time*, she realizes. Just like the extended warrantee feature she started working on with Tom.

"Well, Project Inversion is our shot to fix some of these things and to engineer our way out of this," Kurt says. "Shannon will find out what the Phoenix teams need help on. How about us? If someone gave us the authority, and we were given infinite resources for one month, what would we do?"

Maxine smiles as she hears the suggestions fly fast and furious. They start making a list: Every developer uses a common build environment. Every developer is supported by a continuous build and integration system. Everyone can run their code in production-like environments. Automated test suites are built to replace manual testing, liberating QA people to do higher value work. Architecture is decoupled to liberate feature teams, so developers can deliver value independently. All the data that teams need is put in easily consumed APIs...

Shannon looks over the list they've generated, smiling. "I'll post the updated list when I'm done interviewing the teams tomorrow. This is exciting," she says. "This is what the developers want, even if they can't articulate it. And that's something I can help them with!"

It's a great list, Maxine thinks. Everyone's enthusiasm is evident.

"That is indeed a great list, Shannon, which could dramatically change the dynamics of how engineers work," Erik says, sitting down next to Kirsten once again. Maxine looks around, wondering where he came from.

Gesturing at Kirsten, he continues, "But consider the forces arrayed against you. The entire Project Management Office aims to keep projects on-time and on-budget, following the rules and enforcing the promises written long ago. Look at how Chris' direct reports act—despite Project Inversion, they keep working on the features because they're afraid of slipping their dates.

"Why? A century ago, when mass production revolutionized industry, the role of the leader was to design and decompose the work and to verify that it was performed correctly by armies of interchangeable workers, who were paid to use their hands, not their heads. Work was atomized, standardized, and optimized. And workers had little ability to improve the system they worked within.

"Which is strange, isn't it?" Erik muses. "Innovation and learning occur at the edges, not the core. Problems must be solved on the frontlines, where daily work is performed by the world's foremost experts who confront those problems most often.

"And that's why the Third Ideal is Improvement of Daily Work. It is the dynamic that allows us to change and improve how we work, informed by learning. As Sensei Dr. Steven Spear said, 'It is ignorance that is the mother of all problems, and the only thing that can overcome it is learning.'

"The most studied example of a learning organization is Toyota," he continues. "The famous Andon cord is just one of their many tools that enable learning. When anyone encounters a problem, everyone is expected to ask for help at any time, even if it means stopping the entire assembly line. And they are thanked for doing so, because it is an opportunity to improve daily work.

"And thus problems are quickly seen, swarmed, and solved, and then those learnings are spread far and wide, so all may benefit," he says. "This is what enables innovation, excellence, and outlearning the competition.

"The opposite of the Third Ideal is someone who values process compliance and TWWADI," he says with a big smile. "You know, 'The Way We've Always Done It.' It's the huge library of rules and regulations, processes and procedures, approvals and stage gates, with new rules being added all the time to prevent the latest disaster from happening again.

"You may recognize them as rigid project plans, inflexible procurement processes, powerful architecture review boards, infrequent release schedules, lengthy approval processes, strict separation of duties...

"Each adds to the coordination cost for everything we do, and drives up our cost of delay. And because the distance from where decisions are made and where work is performed keeps growing, the quality of our outcomes diminish. As Sensei W. Edwards Deming once observed, 'a bad system will beat a good person every time.'

"You may have to change old rules that no longer apply, change how you organize your people and architect your systems," he continues. "For the leader, it no longer means directing and controlling, but guiding, enabling, and removing obstacles. General Stanley McChrystal massively decentralized decision-making authority in the Joint Special Operations Task Force to finally defeat Al Qaeda in Iraq, their much smaller but nimbler adversary. There the cost of delay was not measured in money, but in human lives and the safety of the citizens they were tasked to protect.

"That's not servant leadership, it's *transformational* leadership," Erik says. "It requires understanding the vision of the organization, the intellectual stimulation to question the basic assumptions of how work is performed, inspirational communication, personal recognition, and supportive leadership.

"Some think it's about leaders being nice," Erik guffaws. "Nonsense. It's about excellence, the ruthless pursuit of perfection, the urgency to achieve the mission, a constant dissatisfaction with the status quo, and a zeal for helping those the organization serves.

"Which brings us to the Fourth Ideal of Psychological Safety. No one will take risks, experiment, or innovate in a culture of fear, where people are afraid to tell the boss bad news," Erik says, laughing. "In those organizations, novelty is discouraged, and when problems occur, they ask 'Who caused the problem?' They name, blame, and shame that person. They create new rules, more approvals, more training, and, if necessary, rid themselves of the 'bad apple,' fooling themselves that they've solved the problem," he says.

"The Fourth Ideal asserts that we need psychological safety, where it is safe for anyone to talk about problems. Researchers at Google spent years on Project Oxygen and found that psychological safety was one of the most important factors of great teams: where there was confidence that the team would not embarrass, reject, or punish someone for speaking up.

"When something goes wrong, we ask 'what caused the problem,' not 'who.' We commit to doing what it takes to make tomorrow better than today. As Sensei John Allspaw says, every incident is a learning opportunity, an unplanned investment that was made without our consent.

"Picture this scenario: You are in an organization where everyone is making decisions, solving important problems every day, and teaching others what they've learned," Erik says. "Your adversary is an organization where only the top leaders make decisions. Who will win? Your victory is inevitable.

"It's so easy for leaders to talk about the platitudes of creating psychological safety, empowering and giving a voice to the front-line worker," he says. "But repeating platitudes isn't enough. The leader must constantly model and coach and positively reinforce these desired behaviors every day. Psychological safety slips away so easily, like when the leader micromanages, can't say 'I don't know,' or acts like a know-it-all, pompous jackass. And it's not just leaders, it's also how one's peers behave."

A bartender walks up to Erik and whispers something in his ear. Erik mutters, "Again?" He looks up and says, "I'll be right back. Something requires my attention," and walks away with the bartender.

They stare at Erik walking away. Dwayne eventually says, "He's so right about the Third and Fourth Ideal. What can we do about the culture of fear that's all around us? Look at what happened to Chad. He tried to do the right thing and got fired. I probably have more reasons to dislike Chad than any of you—those rolling network outages during the day drove me crazy. But firing Chad doesn't do a damned thing to make those outages less likely in the future.

"I did some asking around to find out what actually happened," Dwayne continues. "Apparently, Chad had worked four nights in a row, in addition to working his normal daytime hours, to support the store modernization initiative. When I asked why, he told me he didn't want the store teams to get dinged on their status reports because of him."

Kirsten raises an eyebrow. Dwayne continues, "His manager kept badgering him to go home, he finally went home on time on Wednesday. But he was back online at midnight because he didn't want to let the store launch team down. He was so worried about all the work piling up, in tickets and in the chat rooms, he wasn't sleeping through the night anymore.

"So he comes into work early on Thursday morning, still tired from all those late nights, and he takes on an urgent internal networking change that needed to be made," he says. "He opens his laptop, and there's like thirty terminal windows open from all the things he's working on. He types a command into the terminal window and hits enter. And it turns out, he typed it into the wrong window.

"Blam! Most of the Tier 2 business systems become inaccessible, including Data Hub," he says. "The next day, he's fired. Does that seem right to you? Does that seem fair and just?"

"Oh, my God," Maxine blurts out, horrified. She knows exactly how this feel. She's done it several times in her career. You type something, hit enter, and immediately realize you've made a huge mistake, but it's too late. She's accidentally deleted a customer database table thinking it was the test database. She's accidentally rebooted the wrong production server, taking down an order entry system for an afternoon. She's deleted wrong directories, shut down wrong server clusters, and disabled the wrong login credentials.

Each time, it felt like her blood turned to ice, followed by panic. Once, earlier in her career, when she accidentally deleted the production source control repository, she literally wanted to crawl under her desk. Because of the OS it ran on, she *knew* no one would ever know it was her. But despite being afraid to tell anyone about it, she told her manager. It was one of the scariest things she had done as a young engineer.

"That really, really sucks, Dwayne," says Brent. "That could have been me... Seriously, every week I'm in situations where I could have made that same mistake."

She says, "It could have been any of us. Our systems are so tightly coupled around here, even small changes can have a catastrophic impact. And worse, Chad couldn't ask for help when he obviously needed it. No one can sustain those insanely long working hours. Who wouldn't start making mistakes if you can't even sleep anymore?"

"Yes!" Dwayne exclaims. "How did we get into this position where someone is so overworked that they're working four nights in a row? What sort of expectations are being set when someone can't take a day off when they need to? And what sort of message are we sending when the reward for caring so much is that we fire you?"

"An excellent point, Dwayne," Maxine hears Erik say, once again rejoining them at the table. "You'd be surprised how deeply this sense of injustice would resonate with Steve. You'd know that if you've spent any time on the manufacturing floor."

"How so?" Maxine asks. She's spent plenty of time working with the plant floor personnel.

"Did you know that when Steve signed on as the COO and VP of manufacturing, he made it contingent upon the company publicly targeting zero on-the-job workplace injuries? He was almost laughed out of the room, not just by the board of directors but also by the plant personnel and even the union leadership," Erik said, smiling. "People thought he was naive, and maybe even a bit addled in the head. Probably because a 'real business leader' would want to be measured on profitability or due-date performance. Or perhaps quality. But safety?

"Rumor was that Steve told Bob Strauss, who was CEO at the time, 'If you can't depend on the manufacturing workforce to not get hurt on the job, why should you believe anything we say about our quality goals? Or our ability to make you money? Safety is a precondition of work.'"

Erik pauses. "Even these supposedly enlightened days, leaders rarely talk like that. Steve had closely studied the work of Sensei Paul O'Neill, the legendary CEO of Alcoa in the 1980s and 1990s, who prioritized workplace safety above all else. His board of directors initially thought he was crazy, but in the fifteen years of his tenure as CEO, net income increased from $200 million to $1.5 billion, and Alcoa's market cap went from $3 billion to $27 billion.

"Despite that impressive economic performance," Erik continues, "what Sensei O'Neill talks about most is his legacy of safety. For decades, Alcoa has remained the undisputed leader of workplace safety. When he joined, Alcoa was rightly proud of having an above-average safety record. But with two percent of their workforce of 90,000 employees being injured every year, if you worked your entire career at Alcoa, you had a forty percent chance of being hurt on the job.

"Alcoa has far more hazardous working conditions than in your manufacturing plants," he says. "In the aluminum business, you have to deal with high heat, high pressure, corrosive chemicals, end-products weighing tons that need to be safely transported...

"Sensei O'Neill famously said, 'Everyone must be responsible for their own safety and the safety of their teammates. If you see something that could hurt someone, you must fix it as quickly as possible.' He told everyone that fixing safety issues should never be budgeted—just fix it, and they'd figure out how to pay for it later," Erik continues. "He gave out his home phone number to all plant workers, telling them to call him if they ever saw plant managers not acting quickly enough or not taking safety seriously.

"Sensei O'Neill tells a story about his first workplace fatality," Erik continues. "In Arizona, an eighteen-year-old boy died. He jumped into an extrusion machine trying to clear a piece of scrap material. But when he did, a boom released, swinging around and killing him instantly.

"This boy had a wife who was six months pregnant," Erik says. "There were two supervisors there. Sensei O'Neill said, they watched him do it, and probably trained the boy to do exactly what he did.

"In the end, Sensei O'Neill stood up in front of the entire plant and told everyone, 'We killed him. We all killed him. I killed him. Because I clearly didn't do a good enough job communicating how people must not get hurt on the job. Somehow it was possible that people thought it was okay for people to get hurt. We must all be accountable for keeping ourselves and everyone safe.'

"As he later said, 'Alcoans were extremely caring people. Every time people were injured, they mourned and there was always lots of regret—but they didn't understand that they were responsible. It had become a learned condition to tolerate injuries.'"

Erik pauses to wipe a tear from his eye. "One of Steve's first actions was to incorporate Sensei O'Neill's True North of *zero workplace injuries* into every aspect of manufacturing plant operations here at Parts Unlimited. One of his first acts on the job was to institute a policy that every workplace injury must be reported to him directly within twenty-four hours, along with remediation plans. What a magnificent example of the Third Ideal of Improvement of Daily Work and the Fourth Ideal of Psychological Safety."

As Erik stares at the wall for several moments, Maxine suddenly realizes why Steve talks about workplace injuries at every Town Hall. He knows he can't directly influence everyone's daily work. However, Steve can reinforce and model his desired values and norms, which he does so effectively, Maxine realizes.

Maxine stares back at Erik. She's never even talked to Steve. How could she possibly do what Erik suggests?

From: Chris Allers (VP, R&D)
To: All Dev; Bill Palmer (VP, IT Operations)
Date: 11:10 p.m., September 25
Subject: Project Inversion: feature freeze

Effective immediately, as part of Project Inversion, there will be a feature freeze for the Phoenix Project. We will make a maximum effort for thirty days to increase the stability and reliability of Phoenix, as well as all supporting systems.

We will suspend all feature work so that we can fix defects and problematic areas of code and pay down technical debt. By doing this, we will enable higher development productivity and faster feature throughput.

During this period, we will also suspend all Phoenix deployments, except for emergency changes, and our Ops teammates will be working on making deployments faster and safer and increasing the resilience of our production services.

We are confident that doing this will help the company achieve its most important strategic goals. If you have any questions or concerns, please email me.

Thank you,
Chris

From: Alan Perez (Operating Partner, Wayne-Yokohama Equity Partners)
To: Sarah Moulton (SVP of Retail Operations)
Date: 3:15 p.m., September 27
Subject: Strategic Options **CONFIDENTIAL**

Sarah—in confidence…

Good meeting yesterday. I'm glad that I had the opportunity to share with you my philosophy of creating shareholder value—in general, we favor "value" and operational discipline over "growth." Our firm has created outsized returns by investing in companies like Parts Unlimited. My plan would create fantastic and consistent cash flow, at a rate higher than most people even think possible. At other companies, we've created considerable wealth for investors (and company executives).

As promised, I'm introducing you to several CEOs in our portfolio of companies whom you may be interested in talking to. Please ask them about how we helped increase shareholder value.

Sincerely, Alan

PS: Did I understand correctly that there's now a "feature freeze" for Phoenix? Doesn't that put you even further behind? And now what do you do with all those new developers you talked about last time? And what will they work on?

CHAPTER 9

• *Monday, September 29*

On Monday, there's a spring in Maxine's step as she walks into the building. And it's not because of the Dockside meeting. It's because it's Testing Day! Her code will finally be tested and put into production.

She carries five boxes of Vandal Doughnuts she bought on her way in. She even got some of their special "cronuts," a crazy hybrid of a croissant and donut, her favorite.

She's feeling so good that she wonders whether the aroma of sixty freshly made donuts might be elevating her blood sugar levels. *What a great way to break the ice with the people who will be testing her code,* she thinks. It's always easier to make new friends when you bring tasty treats.

Everywhere she walks, people ask her, "Are they for me?"

She happily yells back, "Nope, it's for Testing Day!"

Putting down all the donuts on a table near her desk, she slings her bag by her chair. Tom is already there, editor open, typing away.

"Hurray, it's Testing Day!" Maxine announces happily. "At long last."

"You are very strange," Tom says, not even looking up from his monitor. He sniffs the air. "Wow, are those Vandal Doughnuts?"

"Yes, to celebrate Testing Day!" she responds with a big smile. "I think it's super exciting to finally see whether all our changes actually work or not," Maxine says. "So, when do they start? Can we go watch?"

Tom turns to face her, looking at his watch. "I suppose they probably start today. But it's not just our changes. They're testing changes to all the other big chunks of Phoenix—ours are just a fraction of what they need to do. They might not even get to ours today."

"What!?" Maxine interrupts, shocked. She had been waiting all weekend for this! "Can we see where we are in line? Can we help? In fact, where do the QA people sit? I bought all these donuts for them!"

Tom looks surprised. "Well, I've met a bunch of them—some of them are offshore, some are on-site, but I haven't talked with them directly in a long time. We usually meet the QA manager at the end of next week, when they present the testing results."

"Next week? Next week?!" Maxine's jaw drops. "What are we supposed to do in the meantime? Hey, can we follow along as they work? We'll get notifications on our feature tickets, right?"

"Uh, not exactly," Tom says, frowning. "The QA team uses a different ticketing system. It does their scheduling and reporting and manages all their test cases. We don't have access to it—at least, non-mangers like us don't. After two weeks, they'll send us a spreadsheet with a list of all the defects they've found, labeled with our feature ticket numbers. We'll look through them, copy that information into our ticketing system, and then we'll fix anything that needs fixing."

"... and then?" Maxine asks, fearing the worst.

"QA rolls up everyone's fixes and tests again," replies Tom.

"So, let's suppose that all our changes work perfectly—when would be the soonest that our customers actually get to use what we wrote?" she asks.

Tom starts counting on his fingers. "Two weeks for another testing cycle. Then they open up a ticket with Operations, requesting that they deploy the changes into production. Sometimes it takes a bit of time for them to work it into their schedule ... that could take another three weeks." He looks at his fingers. "So that'd be seven weeks from now."

Maxine crumples forward, groaning as she buries her head in her hands, her forehead on the table.

I am so naive, she thinks. Head still on the table, she asks, "And during that whole time, we're just supposed to work on more defects?"

"Yep," she hears Tom say. "You okay, Maxine?"

"Yeah, I'm fine," she says, trying to not feel depressed. *This is the opposite of the Second Ideal*, she thinks. *We're just a stupid feature factory, pushing out widgets that customers may or may not care about. Work is not fun and full of joy, like I know it should be. There is no flow of features, there is no feedback, and there certainly isn't any learning*, she thinks.

She hears Tom ask, "Umm, can I have one of those donuts?"

"No," Maxine responds. Then she has an idea. She lifts her head and looks up at Tom, smiling. "But you can help me deliver them to the QA people."

Finding the QA people was much more difficult than she thought it would be. Tom hadn't been in the same room with one in over a year. His main interactions with them were through formal rituals—he turned over the code and waited for the list of fixes in a spreadsheet, rinse and repeat until the team got the formal acceptance letter that the release was ready for production.

Of course, it was never that easy. There would be all sorts of escalations up the Dev and QA management chains because of disagreements and problems. Is this defect Priority 1 or Priority 2? When developers couldn't reproduce the problem, they'd close the defect, only for it to be reopened by QA later. Or if QA couldn't reproduce the fix, it would bounce back to Dev.

Maxine and Tom stop at Kurt's desk to tell him about their quest. "Those are a lot of donuts. What a great way to make friends," Kurt says. "You tagging along too?" he asks Tom.

"Absolutely," he responds. "I've always wondered where our work goes after we're done with it. It's always felt like flushing the toilet—you put your code in the toilet bowl, press the lever, and it disappears from sight…"

Kurt snorts. "Given the quality of the code we've seen in Phoenix, your metaphor seems pretty appropriate. Roy is the QA Manager assigned to Data Hub. And he'll be tied up for at least ninety minutes," he says, picking up his phone, tapping out a message to someone. "Go over to Building 7 to deliver those donuts while he's preoccupied. I'll connect you with Charlotte, who is, or was, William's assistant. She's like the mother hen for all the QA people."

Kurt finishes typing. "She's expecting you. I think three boxes will be enough for the Data Hub team. Ask Charlotte how to most strategically deploy the remaining two boxes," he adds with a smile.

"She'll get a conference room for you and bring the Data Hub QA team by," Kurt says. "You'll get a chance to meet all of them. And maybe you'll find some people who are looking for help."

Maxine smiles. This is exactly the support she was looking for. "Thanks, Kurt. We'll go make friends. In fact, how about we get pizza delivered for lunch to give us an excuse to hang out even longer?"

"Perfect," Kurt says. "Tell Charlotte to charge it to my old QA department code. With William gone, I'm sure it'll take them a while to shut that down. Let's take advantage of it," he adds with a grin. "But before you go...can I have a donut?" he asks.

"No. Sorry, they're for our new QA friends," Maxine says.

Maxine and Tom walk across the courtyard to Building 7 with the boxes of donuts. They greet the security guard. When Maxine puts her badge on the electronic card reader on the side of the closed door, the light stays red.

Maxine swipes her card again, but again, red light. Maxine sighs. She hadn't expected to not be able to get into the building.

"Interesting that developers can't get into the QA building," Tom says. "Does that mean QA people aren't allowed into the Dev building?"

Maxine is about to call Kurt when she hears the door open. A cheerful, elfin woman bustling with energy greets them. Right away, Maxine finds her irresistibly likeable.

"You must be Maxine? And Tom? Kurt's told me so much about you both! Come on in...I was pretty sure that your badge wouldn't work in this building. It's only a matter of time before Kurt's stops working too. We're all so happy for him—well, most of us are, that is. Many of us always knew that he was destined for bigger and better things than managing a QA team."

Charlotte's comment about "destined for bigger and better things" makes QA sound like an underclass. *Like Kurt had escaped some sort of ghetto*, Maxine thinks.

"What a wonderful idea to throw a party for QA! I'm not sure anyone's ever done that before. Everyone will love it. I reserved the biggest conference room for the whole day—people will swing by whenever they're not in meetings and such. And I also ordered pizza for everyone in the lunchroom." Maxine is impressed that Charlotte has taken care of every detail so quickly. In the conference room, Maxine sees that Charlotte has already written on the whiteboard, "We Appreciate QA!!!" with hearts on either side of the large lettering.

After looking for a moment, Maxine asks if she can make some changes.

"Sure thing," Charlotte is enthusiastic.

Maxine makes her change: "We Appreciate Our QA Team Members!!!"

She then adds the names of Tom, herself, Kurt, and the other five members of the Data Hub development team at the bottom.

"Good idea," Maxine hears Tom say behind her. "I suppose we should invite all of the Data Hub developers to lunch too? Want me to send an email to them?"

Maxine quickly agrees, adding, "We're going to need more pizza..."

"No problem, I'll take care of it," says Charlotte with a big smile.

Over the next couple of minutes, members of the QA team start trickling into the conference room. Maxine introduces herself to each one. She notices that the QA people are demographically a little different than the developers. No one is in their twenties. Maxine wonders if that's because college grads are applying for developer roles instead?

"So, what is this celebration about?" a woman with an Indian accent asks.

"It's Testing Day!" Maxine smiles, delighted to be asked. "I'm so excited that the features we've been working on for weeks are going to be tested. I thought it would be fun to throw a party, so we could meet the people who are doing this important work and to let you know that we'd love to help in any way."

"Gosh, that's really nice," the woman says, returning Maxine's smile. "I'm not sure if that's ever happened before."

Charlotte hollers from the other side of the room, "I've been here for seven years, and I've never seen it happen. This is such a nice idea, Maxine. Let me introduce you to everyone. Purna is one of the QA leads, and these are her team members..."

And then there's silence. Maxine wonders if everyone expects her to give a speech. As the host of the party, maybe she should.

"So, uh, again, thank you so much. We're having pizza delivered for lunch, and the Data Hub developers will be joining us then," Maxine says. "What are you all working on these days?" That's always a good ice breaker.

They tell her about the projects they're working on, which provides a shared context. Then she asks what they find most frustrating about the testing process.

The flood gates open. Their pain points and stories sound all too familiar to her: waiting for environments, environments not completely cleaned up, the problems that cascade when something goes wrong, the inability to determine whether problems were caused by errors in the code or something wrong with the environment.

Suddenly, she and Tom have lots of common ground and things to talk to them about. After all, everyone loves complaining about work. Maxine starts taking notes. And thus, the party gets fully underway.

After ninety minutes, it's clear to Maxine that it isn't really about Dev versus QA—instead, it's about how Phoenix business requirements change so often, which almost always requires urgent code changes. This reduces the time available for testing, resulting in poorer quality, as evidenced by the latest Phoenix disaster.

Everyone understands that change is a part of life, but the Phoenix Project seems ill-suited to this rapid pace of change. And everyone, absolutely everyone, expresses real concerns about the decreasing quality of the Phoenix Project and the potential consequences to Parts Unlimited. Someone says, "In his Town Halls, Steve talks about what's needed from us. We're just not delivering what's needed—and when we find something wrong, there's not enough time to fix it."

There's lots of enthusiasm about the feature freeze, despite the ambiguity of what exactly will be frozen. People are excited that this indicates a real change of values from the top, and it's definitely for the better. However, many managers are convinced they're somehow exempt from the freeze.

Eventually, the party moves to the lunchroom and fifteen large pizzas of every imaginable variety are on the tables. The smell makes Maxine hungry—she's feeling a bit jittery from eating all those donuts; her heart is racing, and she's even sweating a bit. As a borderline hypoglycemic, she needs to eat some protein soon or she'll have a headache and a serious blood sugar crash.

By now, scores of QA people have arrived. Maxine doesn't really know who is supporting Data Hub and who isn't, but she doesn't care. The goal is to make friends today. A bouncer at the door would have squashed that.

Maxine finishes her second slice of pepperoni pizza and throws away the paper plate in the compost bin. After carefully washing her hands, she follows Purna to her desk. Purna has happily agreed to show Maxine how she performs her daily work. Maxine sees rows of desks packed more closely together than in the developer area, but not as dense as the help-desk area where she met Derek.

On Purna's desk are two large monitors, pictures of her with her kids, and a bottle of eight-year-old single malt scotch. Maxine gestures at it, "Your favorite?"

Purna laughs, saying, "Not even close, but good enough for celebrations here. You need it working on the Phoenix Project." She moves windows around her screen and shows Maxine the release project that she has created in the QA ticketing tool.

At last, Maxine thinks. She's been dying to see the QA team workflow. When Maxine sees the tool, she is momentarily taken aback.

"Is that IE6?" Maxine asks, hesitantly. The last time she saw that version of Internet Explorer was in Windows XP.

Purna smiles, as if she's used to having to explain this to people. "Yes. We've been using this tool for over a decade, and now we have to run the client inside of an old Windows VM. It contains all our test projects and runs some of our automated functional tests. There's thousands of test plans that we've built over ten years in here."

"But IE6?" Maxine asks.

"The vendor has an upgrade that supports a modern browser, but it requires upgrading the server it runs on," Purna says. "We finally got budget for it, but we're still waiting for Operations to provision it."

This isn't the first time Maxine has seen people having to use old versions of Internet Explorer. They had some plant support systems back at her old position where the vendor went out of business long ago. They've managed to migrate off of those systems, with one exception. They had to create a completely air-gapped network called "6.6.6.6" for a mission-critical server. It was running on a known vulnerable version of SunOS, which was completely unpatchable.

Good times, she thinks.

As Purna gives her a tour, Maxine sees that despite its age, the QA workflow application is very well-organized and functional.

Purna pulls up a network share with over two hundred Word documents containing test plans. When Maxine asks, she opens up a couple at random. Some describe the test procedure to test a given user scenario: go to this URL, fill out this form with these values, click this button, verify correct values at this other URL…

Other documents describe the test plan for input validation, to ensure that every field in each form rejects any non-conforming input.

Reading these brings back memories from decades ago for Maxine. After all, her first job was doing software QA. Great QA requires a perverse and sometimes sadistic intuition for what will cause software to blow up, crash, or endlessly hang.

Maxine once heard a joke: "A QA engineer walks into a bar. Orders a beer. Orders zero beers. Orders 999,999,999 beers. Orders a lizard. Orders negative one beer. Orders a 'sfdeljknesv.'"

Great QA people are notoriously good at breaking other people's code. They'll fill in forms with thousands of characters, unprintable Unicode characters and emojis, put negative numbers into date fields, and other wildly unexpected things. As a result, programs crash or wildly malfunction, usually causing developers to slap their foreheads, marveling at the diabolical test case.

Some of these injection errors can be used by hackers to gain complete access and potentially grab all the data from the entire system. This is what led to some of the worst personally identifiably information (or PII) thefts in history.

Finding these errors and vulnerabilities is very important work. Maxine feels awful that Purna and her team must manually perform them. During the next two weeks, how many times will they clean up from the previous test, bring up a fresh Phoenix application state, go to the right URL, type the same information into the fields...?

Purna shows other tests to check whether the feature actually worked as designed. Often, this means connecting it with other business systems in an integrated test environment carefully engineered to resemble what is currently running in production.

Maxine keeps thinking about how many of these great tests could be automated. It would liberate the QA teams from work that is tedious, time-consuming, and error-prone, and free up their genius to find more ways to break the code.

Moreover, these automated tests would be run every time a developer checks in code, giving fast and immediate feedback that Maxine and other developers love. They could find mistakes right away and not make the same mistake day after day, week after week.

Maxine doesn't say any of this aloud. The last thing a QA person wants to hear from a developer they just met is their ideas on how to automate their job away.

Nearly an hour later, Maxine is still eagerly taking notes. Purna is being so nice, but Maxine feels impatient. She's here to see her code run and help the QA team make sure it's correct.

Purna turns to her and says, "Well, that's about all we can do. The QA1 environment still hasn't been reset. We're waiting on a customer test data set from the Data Warehouse team, and the Phoenix Dev teams still haven't started their merge…until we get those, there's really nothing we can do."

"The developers haven't started merging?" Maxine says, her heart sinking. "How long does that take?"

"We usually get something within two or three days…I know they're always trying their best…" says Purna.

Maxine groans. In her short tour of duty with the Phoenix Project, she's experienced almost every side of a ticket transaction. To get a Phoenix build going, she opened up tickets to what felt like half of the QA and Operations organization and waited helplessly while they worked to get the things she needed.

She enjoyed working on some Data Hub development tickets, because they represented things that their customers needed. They marked them for QA as "ready to test," and now that she's hanging out in QA, she discovers that QA is waiting on work still being done back in Dev.

And they're also waiting for other people to vacate the test environments they need to use. They're waiting for Ops to provision a server so they can upgrade their test management system. And they're waiting for refreshed test data from the Data Warehouse team. Where does all this madness end?!

"What exactly do you need from the Data Warehouse team?" she asks, reminded of Brent's data problems during the Phoenix release and Shannon describing her five frustrating years on that team.

"Oh, everyone waits for them," she says. "They're responsible for getting data from almost everywhere in the company, and cleaning and transforming it so that it can be used by other parts of the business. We've been waiting almost a year for anonymized customer data, and we still don't have test data that includes recent products, prices, and active promotions. We always get pushed down the priority list, so our test data is years old."

Interesting, Maxine thinks. Data Hub is actually how the Data Warehouse team receives most of its data.

More and more dependencies, as far as the eye can see, she thinks. *There is no place in this whole screwed-up system where you can get anything done.* It doesn't matter whether you're creating the ticket, processing the ticket, waiting on the ticket, or working the ticket. It doesn't matter. You're trapped in a web of dependencies, completely unable to get anything done, no matter where you are.

"This sucks," Maxine says finally, sighing loudly. "I just hate all this waiting…"

"Actually, it's much better than it used to be," Purna says. This makes Maxine feel even worse.

Purna stares at Maxine. Maxine feels like she needs to explain why she's upset: "I'm pissed off that Dev doesn't have their crap together. We've got to do better than this," Maxine finally blurts out.

"I know we sometimes contribute to the problem too," Purna says.

Oh, great, Maxine thinks. *On top of everything else, we're also suffering from Stockholm syndrome.*

Just then, she hears a loud commotion in the lunchroom behind her. A tall man in his early fifties is angrily yelling at Charlotte and pointing at the pizzas and then at Tom and the other Data Hub developers.

Uh oh. That must be Roy, she thinks. She quickly texts a note to Kurt:

Roy is here. You'd better come!

"Excuse me," she says to Purna, walking quickly to the kitchen.

"…we can't have people here disrupting and interfering with our work. Of course, I certainly appreciate the gesture, but this should have gone through me. Next time, get my approval first, Charlotte!"

"Oh, but it just seemed like such a nice gesture," Charlotte responds. "I mean, donuts and pizza! No one has ever done that for QA before. What a very nice thing for Kurt to do."

"Kurt! Kurt's always up to something. This is just part of some scheme he's hatching," Roy fumes, waving his clipboard at everyone. Watching the scene are about fifteen people standing motionless, eyes wide. Some look frightened; some look amused.

"He's probably put all this food on my department code!" Roy says, turning back to Charlotte. "If so, there's going to be hell to pay."

Maxine strides confidently into the lunchroom, extending her hand. "Hi, Roy. I'm Maxine, one of the developers on the Data Hub team. I'm sorry. This is all my fault. It was my idea to bring in donuts this morning. I just wanted to celebrate Testing Day with you and offer our help."

Roy shakes Maxine's extended hand but looks blankly at her. He finally asks, "To celebrate what?"

"Testing Day," Maxine says simply, unable to stop smiling. Roy's expression is nearly identical to Tom's when she brought up Testing Day to him earlier that morning. "I've had so much fun working on the features for Data Hub that I thought it would be just as fun to offer our help to test the code too."

Maxine points behind her to the conference room whiteboard, which everyone can see from the lunchroom, especially the big, pink hearts that Charlotte drew.

Roy looks at her, speechless. Finally, he releases her hand and says loudly, "Oh, no you don't. I don't know what you all are up to," pointing at Maxine and Tom and five other Data Hub developers who stand out in their T-shirts and hoodies. "I'm pretty sure Kurt is up to no good, as usual. This is probably some empire-building scheme he's running, now that he's trumped up a position for himself in Development. I'll get to the bottom of this, you can count on that."

As Roy turns to go, Maxine wonders how she can reiterate her message of "we come in peace."

As she tries to decide what to do, she sees Kurt stride into the room. "Oh, hello, Roy! I'm so glad you're still here. Sorry for not coordinating with you. We just thought it would be fun to throw a surprise party. QA is the next critical part of the chain, and we want to do whatever we can to help."

At the sound of Kurt's voice, Roy turns around, his face red. "Oh, ho, here he is! I'd like to have a word with you. Right now, please."

Kurt is about to respond when Kirsten walks into the room behind him, saying, "Hi, Kurt. Hi, Roy. Mind if I join you all? Oh, I love pizza."

Maxine is surprised to see Kirsten. Other people are wandering into the lunchroom, watching the drama unfold.

"I'm so glad you could make it, Kirsten." Kurt turns to everyone, "As we were walking here, we were talking about how important the QA effort is and that QA's concerns deserve a bigger voice. Kirsten, would you mind sharing what you told me? I think everyone here would love to hear it."

"Of course, Kurt," Kirsten says, holding a paper plate with a slice of sausage and pineapple pizza. "As everyone knows, the Phoenix Project is the most important initiative in the history of the company. The disaster two weeks ago was a big eye-opener for everyone, especially at the most senior levels of this company. We have a lot riding on the next release. We have three years of promises that we've made to the marketplace that we're finally starting to fulfill.

"We just announced Project Inversion, the first time we've had a feature freeze to shore up quality," she continues. "This is a demonstration of the commitment, at the highest levels of the company, not just to do the right things, but to do the right things *right*. And getting you a code release on time is part of that. I know Development is often late merging their changes.

"In our meeting with all the Dev and QA leadership, they gave their commitment to deliver you something to test by five today," she says. "We know how important it is that you have something stable to test, and that needs great development processes. Improving those processes will be a part of Project Inversion, as well."

People cheer, the QA staff clapping especially loudly.

"We're in a relay race, and we need to get the baton handed to you," she continues, gesturing expansively with her free hand. "Your work is important, and my job is to help you get whatever you need to succeed. Thank you in advance for all your hard work, and please let me know how I can help." The room erupts in applause again, and Maxine joins in. She's reminded of a fancy party she was at in Chicago, where she saw the mayor of the city address the room. She was amazed at how gifted of a communicator he was, making everyone not only feel comfortable, but appreciated and part of something special.

Kirsten has that gift too, Maxine thinks. She's never seen this side of Kirsten before and is impressed.

The crowd starts to dissipate, and several people make their way to Kirsten. Others approach Kurt, shaking his hand, congratulating him on his new role.

Roy is at the back of the lunchroom, glaring at Kirsten and Kurt.

At that moment, Charlotte appears beside her. "Life is always interesting around Kurt, isn't it? I'm going to introduce myself to Kirsten. I've always wanted to meet her. She's so cool. We've had so many interesting people visit us here in QA today!"

Maxine sees Roy approach Kurt. She inches over so she's just close enough to hear him say, "...This isn't over. You somehow managed to find a patron, but she won't be able to protect you forever. You think you're better than us? You think you can come in here, put on airs, and automate everyone's job away? Not on my watch. I'll make sure we bring you down."

Roy strides out of the room. Maxine looks at Kurt, who has an unconcerned smile on his face. He says to Maxine and Tom, who just joined her, "Well, that was fun. Don't worry about a thing. I saw that coming a mile away."

"Worried?" Tom responds, laughing. "*I'm* not worried about anything. This is more exciting than your average day coding. What's going to happen next?"

"Apparently, developers merging their code in a hurry to make a five o'clock deadline," Maxine says, deadpan.

Tom's smile quickly disappears. "Let's go watch." Kurt smiles.

CHAPTER 10

• *Monday, September 29*

Over the decades, Maxine has tried to explain to non-technical people how frightening code merges are. Her best description is having fifty screenwriters simultaneously working on a Hollywood script when they haven't decided who the main characters are, or what the ending will be, or whether it's a gritty, detective story or a bumbling sleuth with a sidekick.

They break up the writing responsibilities between all the writers, and each writer works on their part of the script in isolation, typing away in Word for weeks at a time. Then, right before the script needs to be finalized, all fifty writers get together in a room to merge all their work back together into a single story.

Of course, any attempt to merge their scripts together is a disaster. There's still no agreement on who the main characters are, there's hundreds of extraneous characters, completely disconnected scenes, and gaping holes in the plot...just to name a few of the problems..

And most of the writers didn't read the memo from the executive producers that stated they were making the story a horror movie with giant undersea monsters due to changing market tastes.

Merging code is equally difficult. Editing code isn't like editing in Google Docs, where all the developers can see each other's changes. Instead, like the scriptwriters, they create private working branches of the source code, their own private copy. Like those scriptwriters, developers may work in isolation for weeks, sometimes even months.

All modern source control systems have tools to automate the merge process, but when there are many changes, their limitations become all too evident. Someone may discover that someone else has overwritten their changes, or that they changed or deleted something that everyone else depended upon, or that multiple people made conflicting changes to the same parts of the code...just to name a few things that could go wrong.

Maxine loves it when everyone merges their changes frequently to the 'master branch,' such as once per day. That way, the size of the changes being merged are never allowed to get too large. Small batch sizes, like in manufacturing, create a smooth flow of work, with no jarring disruptions or catastrophes.

On the other hand, you have what Phoenix developers do—a hundred developers work for weeks at a time without merging, and from what Purna says, it usually takes at least three days to merge. Maxine thinks, *Who would ever want to work that way?*

Maxine walks with Kurt and Purna back to Building 5 to the "merging war room," which she thinks is a very appropriate name. The moment she walks into the room, she's hit with a wall of humid air caused by too many people being packed into a hot, crowded room. Looking around, she says to Kurt with certainty, "I don't care what Kirsten says. There is no way we're going to get a release branch today."

Purna walks to the front of the room and takes out her laptop. On the walk over, Maxine learned that Purna is the integration manager responsible for making sure that all the promised features and defect fixes make it into the QA release branch. Everyone affectionately calls her the "merge boss."

Maxine looks at the printed spreadsheet that Purna gave her. There are 392 Dev tickets to be merged. Each row has a ticket number from the Dev ticketing tool, a description of the issue, a checkbox showing whether it's been merged, a link to the QA test plan, the QA ticket number, and on and on…

Purna is responsible for getting all these changes merged so QA can finally test them as a whole, find and report any problems, and make sure that any reported defects are fixed. It's a big and often thankless job.

Maxine grabs a seat at the back of the room with Kurt. Gathered around the table are about twenty-five developers and managers representing each team with changes to merge. They're bunched up in groups of two or three, with at least one laptop in front of them. Typically, one person is typing at their laptop, with the others looking over their shoulder.

There is a low buzz of frustrated conversation. "Sounds like developers merging," Tom says, grabbing the seat next to her.

"You know the joke—what's the plural of 'developer'?" says Maxine. "A 'merge conflict.'"

Tom laughs, opening his laptop. "I might as well merge all of our changes into the release branch now. I usually don't do it right away, because what's the rush? I mean, look around...It usually takes days for everyone to get their changes in."

He opens up the source code management application, drags and drops a couple of things, clicks here and there, and types something. He says, "Done!" and closes his laptop.

"I usually don't stick around," he says. "We barely have any shared code with the rest of the Phoenix teams. I can't remember ever having a merge issue..."

Maxine nods, thinking again about how strange it is that Data Hub is part of Phoenix.

"Do *you* think these people will be done merging today?" Maxine asks.

Tom laughs, pointing at the large TV in front of the room connected to Purna's laptop. "Four changes have been merged. Five, when you include the one that we just did. That's 387 more to go. At this rate, I think it'd be a miracle if they're done tomorrow. Three days, I'm guessing. At least."

Over the next hour, as people have problems with their merges, more developers enter the room to help. When people no longer have room to stand, they create a second war room across the hallway. One of the managers gripes, "I don't know why we don't just pre-reserve two or three conference rooms. This happens every time."

Maxine sees a Dev lead type into a terminal window on his laptop "git pull." He immediately gets a long error message showing forty-three merge conflicts. Maxine actually recoils from his screen in shock. She wonders how long it will take them to untangle that mess.

Later, when she hears another team talk about bringing printouts of the source code for everyone so they can manually reconcile each change, she almost spits out her coffee.

There's a group of ten people crowded around the TV at the front of the room, studying a code diff from four different sets of changes to the same part of a file.

Seeing the expression on her face, Kurt asks, "What's wrong?"

Speechless, she gestures at all the chaos and disruption around her. "Developers should be solving business problems…Not…this…This is madness."

Kurt just laughs. "For sure. All the Dev managers are complaining about how much of a hassle this is. Some are lobbying to do these merges less frequently—instead of once per month, maybe once per quarter."

Maxine blanches. "You're kidding, right?"

"Nope," Kurt says, genuinely amused by Maxine's reaction. "If it hurts, do it less often. That's their reasoning."

"No, no, no," Maxine says, dismayed. "They've got it all wrong. It hurts because the merge sizes are so large. To make it hurt less, they need to do it more frequently, so that the merges are small and create fewer conflicts."

Kurt laughs again. "Yeah, well," he says, shrugging his shoulders, gesturing around the room.

Maxine doesn't laugh, because she doesn't see anything funny. She looks at her watch. It's nearly four thirty. She looks at Purna's laptop screen. Only thirty-five changes are merged, with 359 more to go. They were only ten percent complete.

At this rate, Maxine thinks, *it'll take them another forty hours of work—a full week away.*

The next day, Maxine is slumped in a chair in the lunchroom, surrounded by pizza. It's almost the end of the second day of the code merge. She stares at the big posted signs everywhere, admonishing, "For Merge Teams ONLY."

Maxine doesn't know why they bother. Over the past day and a half, she's guessing that every developer has been in one of the merging war rooms.

"Maxine, there you are," Kurt says, interrupting her reverie. "Holy cow. Uhh, you look like hell, if you don't mind me saying."

Maxine just gives Kurt a tight-lipped smile. She just doesn't have it in her to explain what she's seen and how much it bothers her.

Maxine knows that code merges are never anyone's idea of a fun time, but she wasn't prepared for what she saw over the last two days.

She's seen managers copy source files from computer to computer on USB drives because their teams didn't want to use the same version control system as everyone else.

She's seen people trying to resolve merge conflicts that were over one thousand lines long, splattered across scores of files.

She's seen people forget to merge in their changes, caught only when Purna reconciled her spreadsheet.

She even saw two teams grapple with a genuine semantic merge conflict—a rare occurrence, usually only found in stories that developers tell to scare each other. It's the result of an automated merge that compiles correctly but wildly changes how the program functions. The worst part was that it was a near-miss. They discovered it almost by accident. Frankly, she's amazed that they caught it when someone said, "That doesn't look quite right." Otherwise it would have escaped into production, where it undoubtedly would have wreaked havoc.

She keeps wondering how many similar errors weren't caught that are now in production, sitting there like ticking bombs ready to explode when that code path is finally executed.

Looking back at Kurt, she says, "I've seen things. Unspeakable things, Kurt. Such waste and needless suffering…No developer should have to go through…this…this…madness!" Again, she's at a loss for words.

"Ah," Kurt says, suddenly looking concerned. "Throw that pizza away and come join the rest of the Rebellion. Shannon just reported out the results of her interactions with the Phoenix Dev teams, and she has a great idea."

Maxine looks down at her hands and sees that she's holding a cold, half-eaten slice of pizza, the cheese completely hardened into a white, greasy slab. She didn't remember eating it.

She throws it away and follows Kurt without saying a word.

Kurt brings Maxine to another conference room, far away from the ongoing merge madness. She sees Tom, Brent, Shannon, and Dwayne gathered around the table. They all smile and wave at her. Shannon stares at her for a moment, but unlike Kurt, politely says nothing about her haggard appearance.

"Maxine, I think you're going to love this," Shannon says. "We've all been thinking about how all the Data Hub changes have been merged.

But in order for them to be tested, we have to wait for everyone else to be done merging too.

"We're thinking about what it would it take to get Data Hub decoupled from Phoenix, so that we can test independently," Shannon continues. "If we can, we have QA people ready to work on our changes right now."

It takes several moments for Maxine to understand what Shannon suggested, her mind still shell-shocked and ravaged from the merge. Then it hits her.

"Yes!" Maxine exclaims. "Yes, that's a great idea. We can't do much for the rest of the Phoenix teams right now, but that doesn't mean that we have to suffer along with them."

Kurt says, "I've been talking with Purna and Kirsten. They've assigned two people to help us get Data Hub tested and certified. As long as the Phoenix merge is still going on, they're ours. In fact, I bet we could get *all our changes tested* before then."

Frowning, Maxine says, "But we still need a test environment to run Data Hub in." She thinks for a moment. "I wonder if we could create a Data Hub test environment to run in our cluster. It would be so much smaller and simpler than the Phoenix environments. That way, the QA group could use them anytime instead of the scarce environments everyone is always fighting for."

"The environments team won't be happy about that," Kurt says, with a smile. "What do you need?"

She looks around. "If I had Brent and Adam's help for two or three days, I think we could get at least a simplified environment running by Monday. I know Brent is on a Phoenix lockdown, but, hey, technically Data Hub is still part of Phoenix, right?"

Suddenly, Maxine is excited again. The idea of liberating Data Hub from the Phoenix Project morass is thrilling.

"The First Ideal," says Brent with a smile.

The next day, Maxine, Brent, and Adam are furiously working around the clock to create a slimmed down environment that they can use to run and test Data Hub. It's a race against the Phoenix merge.

Purna gave a thumbs-up on the plan. Kirsten did as well, saying, "We created all these rules, so we can break them too. Especially if this permanently eliminates these damned dependencies. Any project manager would jump for joy." That was good enough for Kurt, telling them to go for it, without bothering to get any approvals from further up the chain.

"I'll ask for forgiveness later if we need to," Kurt had said with a smile.

At the moment, Brent is trying to reproduce the environment build that currently only works on Tom's laptop. Meanwhile, Maxine is working with Adam, trying to get the last Data Hub release to work in their trimmed-down Phoenix environment.

She's delighted that they're cracking yet another piece of the build puzzle that has vexed her ever since she was exiled. They're both watching a scrolling terminal window as Data Hub boots, hoping they resolved the last error. They're still watching the log messages scroll by when she hears commotion from the merging war room.

One of the Dev managers yells out, "I need everyone's attention! We've been having intermittent production issues for the last two hours on the e-commerce site. Something in Phoenix is causing incorrect or incomplete promotion pricing to be displayed when users are in the shopping cart. Does anyone know what could be going wrong?"

Good timing for an outage, Maxine thinks as she walks back to the war room. Virtually all the Dev managers are already in there, so it should be pretty easy to figure out which part of the code is causing the problem. It's like having a heart attack at a cardiologist convention—lots of qualified doctors are around.

As she watches, Maxine approves of their disciplined problem-solving. They are efficient, logical, and there's no hint of any blame as they try to replicate the problem on their laptops and systematically think through what could be going wrong.

Ten minutes later, the middleware Dev manager takes the lead. She makes a convincing case that the problem has to be in her area of the code. In takes only another fifteen minutes for her team to generate a fix. "It's a one-line change. We can just push the change to the current release branch," she announces. "Oh, dammit, no we can't...Only the SCM manager can push to this old release branch. We need Jared. Anyone know where he is?"

"I'll go find him," yells someone, who runs out of the room.

"Who's Jared?" Maxine asks Kurt. Kurt rubs his eyes, trying not to laugh.

The middleware Dev manager next to them says in a tired voice, "Jared is the source code manager. Developers aren't allowed access to production. The only time developers can push changes to the release branch is for P1 issues. This is only a P3 issue," she explains. "So, either we need to ask Ops to change it to a P1 issue, which is never going to happen, or Jared needs to grant me temporary access so I can check in our fix."

"And if Jared were here, what would he do?" Maxine asks, knowing what's coming.

The middleware manager says, "He'd take the commit ID of our fix, manually copy it into the release branch, and promote it into production."

"That's it?" Maxine asks.

"Yep," she replies.

Maxine curses under her breath. To her surprise, she's actually angry. Like, actually mad.

A couple of minutes ago, she thought the timing of the outage was fortunate. *That lucky patient*, she had thought. All the best experts in heart trauma who could correctly diagnose the problem and administer emergency treatment just happened to be in the room.

But here at Parts Unlimited, doctors aren't allowed to touch the patient. Well, except if there's a P1 ticket open. But if the patient *isn't* on the verge of death, like right now, apparently only *Jared* can touch the patient. And then Jared just does whatever the doctors tell him to, because, you know, doctors can't touch the patient. Jared isn't a doctor. He's probably just an administrator, just adding and removing users and making sure things are backed up.

"No one can find Jared. I think he might still be at lunch," says the guy who searched for him.

"Oh, for Chrissakes," Maxine mutters under her breath. *It's happening again*, she thinks, remembering how wrecked she felt in the lunchroom yesterday.

Everyone tries to come up with a backup plan because no one can find Jared. Twenty minutes later, Randy shows up declaring nothing can be done, but he's still working on finding Jared.

Everyone nods, going back to merging their changes.

"How is this okay?!" Maxine says loudly, addressing the entire room, no longer able to just watch. "Why aren't developers able to push their own changes into production? Why do we need *Jared* to push the changes? I mean, I'm sure he's really good at what he does, but why can't we just do it ourselves?"

The entire room falls silent. Everyone stares at her, looking shocked. Like she had just belched loudly at a wedding or a funeral. Finally, someone says, "Compliance." And another person chimes in, "And Information Security."

Around the room, she hears people utter other reasons.

"ITIL."

"Change management."

"SOX."

"PCI."

"Regulators."

She looks around. All of these people are capable and responsible. And yet…"Come on, everybody. Those reasons don't make sense at all. I think I know the real reason we aren't allowed to push our changes…they don't trust us. Doesn't that *bother* you?! How can Jared know more about making changes than the developers who wrote them?"

Scanning the room, Maxine sees that only about ten people are remotely troubled by her epiphany.

"Do they think we'll deliberately sabotage the changes? That someone copying and pasting our changes can do a better job than we can?" Maxine knows she's pretty far out on a limb here, but she can't stop herself. "We're almost all developers in this room. Doesn't it bother anyone that we're not trusted enough to push our own changes into production?"

A couple of people just shrug their shoulders. Several others stare back at her as if she's crazy or hopelessly naive.

Maxine knows she hasn't delivered a stirring *Henry V* Saint Crispin Day rallying speech, but she's dumbfounded that people aren't more bothered by this situation. She was hoping someone would yell out, "Hell yes, that bothers me, and we're not going to take it anymore!"

But instead, there's just silence.

We don't even need guards anymore. We love being prisoners so much, we just think the bars are there to keep us safe.

She is about ready to leave when a young man with a ponytail and a laptop underneath his arm enters the conference room followed by two people.

"Oh, no," Maxine accidentally says aloud. *This is Jared?*

He's even younger than the intern who helped her on her first day here. She has nothing against young engineers. On the contrary, her fondest hopes and aspirations lay in the hands of the next generation, and she does everything she can to help them achieve their goals. But it's so difficult for Maxine to think that Jared is more qualified to resolve this outage than everyone else in the room. *If Jared can deploy changes, we should be able to too,* she thinks.

Maxine watches as he sets up his laptop to perform the code push. It takes him ten minutes to get successfully logged in, get the link to the code that needs to be pushed, confirm with everyone that it's actually the right code... Just like in all the movie scenes about coding that Maxine poo-pooed, a crowd gathers behind Jared, waiting in breathless anticipation as he performs his work. When he finally says, "It's in," people clap him on the back.

Maxine rolls her eyes in frustration. She's glad Jared performed the work, but come on, all he did was a bunch of copying and pasting and clicking a button.

When Maxine asks the middleware manager if the problem has been resolved, the manager replies, "Not yet. Now that Jared put it into the last release branch, he needs to work with the Ops people to get it deployed into production."

The patient still hasn't been saved. He needs to be transported to the next department for that. She decides to follow Jared, more out of a sense of morbid curiosity then any sense of adventure.

Four hours after following Jared out of the room, Maxine is dazed and disoriented. Any sense of well-being and excitement that Maxine had working on the Data Hub environments has vanished. And Maxine is missing something else—she is no longer certain about what is good, what is bad, and the processes that govern her world.

She also feels distinctly unwell. *Am I running a fever?*

It all started when she followed Jared two floors down to the ground floor, where Operations resides. In an Ops conference room, she recognized Wes and Patty, but almost no one else, although they all looked uncannily similar to each other.

The room looked almost the same as the merging war room upstairs. Same furniture, same speaker phone on the table, same projector on the ceiling. But sitting around the table are a completely different group of people discussing the exact same topic as upstairs: how to get this urgent change deployed. Only they're discussing slightly different obstacles: No changes outside of the maintenance windows. ITIL. Security. Change Management. Compliance. Different ticketing system. Same number of fields that need to be filled in, and the same errors when you miss a field. Same escalation processes but different people.

They've pushed an emergency change request to Bill Palmer, the VP of Operations, and Maggie Lee, the senior director of product marketing. And just like upstairs, everyone is standing around waiting for approval.

At five o'clock, someone orders pizza. Maxine follows everyone to the lunchroom, identical to the one upstairs. When she sees the pizza, she almost trips and falls—it's from the same place as the pizza brought in for the merging lunch yesterday.

The same pizza, being eaten by different people, complaining about the same problems. It is then that Maxine starts to really feel sick, the room spinning slightly. *Maybe I'm just hungry?* But the look of the pizza instantly turns her stomach.

Maxine feels like she's replaying the same scene of a movie that she just lived through six hours earlier. *Like some horrible version of* Groundhog Day, she thinks. Like Bill Murray's character, she is doomed to replay the same day over and over. But for Maxine, they keep changing all the actors. First, they're Dev, then they're QA, and they're Ops. But it's all the same.

Up until now, deep down Maxine suspected developers were being imprisoned by a heartless, evil, uncaring bureaucracy. Maybe it was run by Operations or a secret ITIL change management cabal. But after following Jared into the heart of Operations, she sees that Ops is imprisoned by the same wardens as the developers upstairs.

Who profits from all of this? Who benefits by oppressing everyone in the technology organization? Maxine doubts that Chris or Bill are the wardens of this endless sea of prisons. If anything, they're prisoners too.

Maxine throws away her slice of pizza before even taking a bite. Back in the conference room, Wes announces the urgent change was just approved. Maggie (the person who needed to approve the change) had missed their first calls because she was at her own birthday party, but she's stepped out now to join the conference call.

It takes forty minutes to push out the change. Maxine watches as the teams rummage in network shares, wiki pages, source code repositories ... Patty then confirms that the problem has been resolved.

Wes thanks everyone for staying so late, and people start to disperse. Soon, Maxine is alone in the conference room. The lights start to turn off as motion sensors no longer detect movement. In the dark, Maxine wonders how the oppressive bureaucracy gained so much control.

It's just like Erik said. This is the opposite of the Third Ideal, where instead of improving the processes we work within, we blindly follow them, she thinks. *And now the process has fully imprisoned us, sucking out all the joy from our daily work, pushing us ever further away from the Second Ideal.*

In the darkness, Maxine picks up her phone and texts Kurt and the rest of the Rebellion:

> Anyone else still here? I really need some help. And a drink. Can anyone meet me at the Dockside?

CHAPTER 11

• *Wednesday, October 1*

Kurt is already at the brightly lit Dockside, a couple pitchers and a bottle of wine on the table, when Maxine shows up. She's glad to see him, and those pitchers, because it means other Rebellion members are coming. She's grateful for their company.

Maxine rarely drinks to self-medicate, but as soon as she sits down, she does exactly that. She works through two pinot noirs in short order, despite the fact that she knows she'll suffer tomorrow morning.

But tonight it doesn't matter, because the wine is definitely making her feel better. The combination of sugar and alcohol is helping her combat the jarring and jangling emotions she's been reeling from ever since she followed Jared to the Ops Bizarro World.

As people arrive and sit down, the mood around the table is upbeat. Tom and Brent are working at the table with their laptops open, having made terrific progress on getting Data Hub running in a slimmed-down environment. They can't stay long. They're meeting with the QA team tomorrow morning to get them up and running, with the hopes that they can start their testing soon. Apparently, Purna and her team might swing by later.

Shannon has written up her notes from interviewing the Phoenix teams, identifying nearly ten developers who want to use what the Rebellion has created to address problems they face on a daily basis. And with Project Inversion fully underway, they have the time to do it.

Maxine smiles blearily as she listens to everyone sharing stories. Eventually, Kurt pours another round for everyone and turns to Maxine. "So, what's up, Maxine?"

"Kurt, we are so screwed up." She runs her hands through her hair in frustration.

Maxine tries to explain. She's usually extremely articulate and precise, but as she listens to herself talk, she is acutely aware that she sounds raving mad.

Starting over, she tries hard to convey how much this afternoon disturbed her. "Ever since I was exiled to the Phoenix Project, I've opened up hundreds of tickets, trying to get things done. I've followed those tickets around, seeing where they went. Many of them went to Ops, some went to QA. Then, when I joined the Data Hub team, I opened more tickets. But more importantly, I got to work the other side of those tickets, doing work that people needed. But to get that work done, I had to open more tickets. It's just a giant circle of tickets, Kurt, being created and passed around, over and over again, without end.

"Who did this to us?" she finally asks.

Adam smiles sadly. "We did it to ourselves. Long ago, QA used to be a part of Dev, but when I joined, QA had been made independent. We made a bunch of rules about how we needed to be separate from Dev concerns, you know, to protect the business from all those crazy, reckless developers. Each year, we used anything that went wrong as an excuse to create more and more rules to 'make developers more accountable,' which just slowed us down even more. What makes me so excited about the Rebellion is that we're trying to undo all of that."

Dwayne nods. "Adam's right. In Operations, we did it to ourselves too. It started for all the right reasons—we brought in ITIL processes that created some sense of order, which was infinitely better than the chaos we had before. In Ops, it's worse, because we have so many areas of specialization. Complex work like deployments hit every one of those areas. We have servers, databases, networks, firewalls . . . heck, in the last decade, we've created even more silos, like storage, VLANs, automation teams, virtualization, hyperconverged infrastructure, and who knows how many more.

"And with the modern technology stacks, we need people with deep expertise in containers, logging, secrets management, data pipelines, NoSQL databases. No one can be an expert in all of those!" Dwayne says. "So we need a ticketing system to manage those complex flows of work. But it's so easy for people to lose sight of what the purpose of all this work is. It's why the Rebellion is so important. Look how many people are working late to help with the Data Hub effort."

Everyone around Maxine raises their glasses, yelling out, "Hear, hear! To overthrowing the ancient, powerful order!" Maxine raises her glass as well, but says nothing.

She's often heard that IT is the nerve center of the entire organization, because over the last thirty years almost every business process has been automated through IT systems. But for whatever reason, businesses have allowed their nervous system to become degraded, like multiple sclerosis disrupting the flow of information within the brain and between the brain and the body.

Maxine pours one more drink, but she only takes a sip. Suddenly, she doesn't feel well. It has nothing to do with what she drank. She is definitely coming down with something. She quickly bids farewell to everyone, thanking them for joining her tonight.

When she gets home, she hugs her husband, says goodnight to her kids, and is relieved when she crawls into bed after taking a shower.

Later that night, Maxine starts to sweat uncontrollably, then is overcome by chills and chattering teeth, then back to a fever. She has succumbed to the illness that decimated the ranks of her teammates after the Phoenix release.

That night, she has unending dreams about being trapped in a bureaucracy, handed off from one desk to another, put on hold, asked to fill out more forms, shuffled from one department to another, and put back into another line with more forms to fill. The forms go into vast data warehouses where they are pulverized, turned into a steaming, greasy miasma of comma-separated text files, spiked with random byte-order marks.

She sees the heartless machinery of bureaucracy turning, with helpless people trapped inside the countless gears. She hears their helpless screams, until they fall silent, all energy sucked out of them only to be periodically revived to fill out their timecards.

She pushes mountains of paper tickets up a set of stairs, across a section of cubicles, and down more stairs, doomed to traverse this Square of Sisyphus forever as punishment for the payroll outage.

When she wakes up, the sun is rising. Her pillow is drenched with sweat. Her sinuses and lungs are congested. Her chest hurts from coughing so hard. She can barely move.

She forces herself to get out of bed and shower. The hot steam feels good, but when she gets out, another cycle of uncontrollable sweating and chills begins. She shambles downstairs to eat a piece of toast and drink some water only to realize how much her throat hurts.

Her husband tells her to stay in bed, that he'll make sure the kids get off to school on schedule. Grateful, she mumbles thanks. She makes it halfway up the stairs before having to take a break, eventually crawling back into bed.

Barely able to read the phone screen, she texts everyone to let them know she's unable to come into work. She falls asleep and bolts awake, realizing that she left the office without filling out her timecard. But she's too weak to do anything about it. She finally falls back to sleep, groaning from the aches everywhere.

The next day Maxine can barely get out of bed. She has become one of the walking wounded, joining the ranks of the people unable to do their jobs, whether due to illness, bureaucracy, or being stuck in the Waiting Place.

Desperate for more cold medication, she ventures out and walks around the store's aisles huddled in five layers of clothing, looking for relief. To keep her family from getting sick, she buys a surgical mask as if she were a Japanese office worker on a subway. When her husband sees her wearing it, he just laughs.

By midday Friday Maxine starts to feel mildly better, finally able to stay awake for more than an hour during the day. She hasn't touched her phone in nearly two days and, in fact, has hardly spoken at all, except to her husband in forced monosyllables. Tired of reading novels in bed, she heads downstairs and texts Kurt and Purna:

> Are the developers done merging yet?

Within seconds, Maxine receives a reply from Kurt:

> Hahahahaha! Sorry, no. Maybe Monday. But Data Hub and its environment are almost ready to be tested. QA likely starting this evening! If you want to hear more, call me! Hope you're feeling better.

Maxine dials his number. He doesn't even say hi. "Brent and Tom have been working non-stop. They're close to getting Data Hub running in the new, smaller environment. All the Data Hub developers are working with the QA team to write automated tests together. Adam and a bunch of developers are leading coding classes, and some of the QA folks are writing tests without any help. You might have seen those tests being checked into the source code repo."

"And Shannon is paving the road for Security," Kurt says. "Environment images will be automatically patched daily, and maybe soon, application dependencies too!"

Maxine tries to smile. She's impressed by how much they've achieved while she was sick. She looks in the chat channel and sees exciting messages about the progress they're making. She loves seeing all the code commits from both the Dev and QA teams.

Without doubt, Maxine knows that the developers will eventually be responsible for testing their own code, with QA taking a more strategic role, coaching and consulting. It means all the automated tests they're writing will soon run with every check-in once they get their centralized build and continuous integration (CI) server going. They're so close!

"This is great," she croaks, which makes her teeth hurt so much that she tells Kurt that she'll see him next week and hangs up.

Maxine crawls back into bed and closes her eyes, thinking about what's next. If they could get Ops to agree, they might even be able to automate deployments to the production Data Hub service. And, although this seems like a long shot, maybe they could even run the production Data Hub services from their cluster.

It would make things so much easier for everyone, even Operations. For starters, they'd be able to test and deploy their changes immediately after working on them, instead of waiting two weeks for the next test cycle.

The real question, Maxine realizes, is which features they should be working on. She wonders what features in Data Hub would be most important for the business. And which business unit they should focus on. Data Hub is unique in that it touches so many areas of Parts Unlimited, each with their parochial needs and priorities.

She tries to go back to sleep, but she keeps thinking about what the highest business value activity is for Data Hub. Curious, she sits up and opens her laptop, bringing up the ticketing system. But instead of opening a new ticket or working on a ticket from someone else, she just looks around. It's the first time she's done that since her exile.

With a couple of clicks, she figures out how to view all the open Data Hub tickets. There are hundreds of them, nicely color-coded based on what business systems they touch. She winces when she sees how many of these tickets are over a year old. No wonder everyone seems so frustrated.

She wonders which features in this backlog are most important for the company. That last part is easy. Steve tells everyone what the company's top priorities are in the Town Halls. Steve and Sarah consistently talk about the importance of helping customers keep their cars running and providing a way for customers to easily buy what they need. Doing this well should increase revenue per customer, average customer order size, and overall revenue and profitability.

With this in mind, she scrolls through pages and pages of features. It's difficult to know what the features really are from the ticket name or reading their contents. They're long on what and how, but not on why.

Maxine eventually notices a term that comes up over and over: "Item Promotion."

She sees a bunch of tickets related to a summer promotion, offering discounted product bundles of battery replacements, air conditioning, and cooling system maintenance items. They were never started. Maxine sighs. Given that it's already fall, the opportunities associated with that campaign have come and gone.

She wonders what the process is for deleting features that are no longer relevant. There's a very real cognitive and spiritual burden of having to carry so many unfulfilled promises forever into the future, where anyone can ask at any time "Where is my feature?"

Curious, she searches for "Winter Promotion" and sees a string of tickets. She starts clicking into them. One ticket marked as complete was to create a SKU for a bundle of wiper blades and ice scrapers. A ticket still in work is to create a discounted price for the bundle.

She sees another pattern just like this, but for winter tires and chains, chains and windshield de-icing fluid, and many more. There's another string of tickets for "Thanksgiving Promotion." Each of these campaigns requires two Data Hub deployments—one to create the new product in the products database, and another to create special promotional pricing in the pricing database.

That means each discounted bundle always takes two months to create. Feeling like she's onto something, she scans the other requested features in the promotions category. One immediately catches her attention. The ticket was created seven months ago, and the title reads, "Create in one step: new product bundle SKU with associated discount."

Opening the ticket, Maxine reads about how Marketing wants the ability to create and price new SKUs entirely self-service, without having to go through the Data Hub team.

Yes! Exactly as I had thought. The feature description points out that the current process requires almost ninety days for a newly created discount to be available to customers.

The author of the ticket is Maggie Lee, the senior director of products. Suddenly Maxine suspects that Data Hub is sitting on an organizational constraint! She emails Kurt and Maggie. In about five minutes she gets a call from Kurt.

She croaks, "You saw my email?"

"Yep," Kurt says. "I checked out the links you sent me. That's definitely interesting. While you've been gone, I've been trying to figure out who our most important customers are. And I'm also on the lookout for who the heavy hitters are who can give us some air cover as we move Data Hub out of Phoenix. Maggie's name has come up over and over again.

"She works for Sarah, and all the product owners for in-store and e-commerce report to her," Kurt continues. "I'll send you the org chart I dug up. I've already met her admin, and we have a meeting scheduled with her soon."

"Fantastic, Kurt!" Maxine says, but when she smiles, she groans in pain. She's excited to get back to work...when she's healthy again.

Groaning, she hangs up, crawls back into bed, and goes to sleep.

On Monday, Maxine is back at work, discussing Data Hub with Dwayne, Tom, and Kurt in a conference room. Tom is displaying his laptop on the screen in the front of the room. "We worked on this all weekend, making sure it's stable enough to show. Holy cow, I'm excited. We now have the Data Hub environment running entirely in a Docker image, so absolutely anyone can use it. Brent and I based it all off the work Maxine did before she was out sick. Thank you, Maxine!

"Now, instead of waiting weeks to get access to one of the scarce QA environments, you can just run this Docker image on your laptop. It takes a couple minutes to download, but only a couple of seconds to start up. It's incredible..." Tom says, typing into a terminal window. "With Brent's help, I got these environments wired into our CI server so it can run Data Hub tests. We are finally in the build and test business! We're using it with QA to test the four features we got completed since the last release."

Looking at Maxine, he says, "We have enough capacity on our CI server for anyone who wants to use it. We couldn't have done it without your great work, Maxine."

Tom smiles, shaking his head. "We've been wanting to do something like this for years, but we never had the time. I'm so excited because it will completely change how Data Hub developers spend their time. Everyone can be more productive—they'll be able to develop and test so much faster. And maybe, if a miracle occurs, we can even get these features into production faster too."

Kurt cheers, raising his fists in the air. "Now *this* is an amazing success story! We can finally start showing people the value we can deliver."

Maxine is impressed. This is an awesome accomplishment, and she's proud that Brent and Tom, who she met only weeks ago, were able to get so much done without her.

Kurt frowns. "Actually, I take what I said back. This is a Dev and QA success story. We still have angry business stakeholders who don't have their features. How do you get these features into production?"

"Now that is a totally different enchilada," Dwayne says, shaking his head and drumming his fingers on the table. "Maxine is right. There's a long history of not letting developers push things directly into production. There's entire institutions whose only purpose is to prevent that from happening."

"Who's the most powerful opposition?" Kurt asks.

"Security, most definitely," Dwayne says. "They're going to want to do a security review of the code before it goes into production—that's enterprise policy. And Operations won't be so keen on this, either. And for that matter, there are so many people in the business that have been screwed over by bad changes that most of *them* won't be jumping for joy when you propose this...So, yeah, basically what I'm saying is that everyone is against developers deploying directly into production," he says with a humorless smile.

Maxine nods. "Security is already very familiar with Data Hub. It's not like we're popping an entirely new application on them. We just need them to schedule their review of Data Hub separately from Phoenix."

"Let's meet with them. The worst they can say is no, and it's not like we haven't heard that before, right?" Kurt says. "So besides Security, what is the official process to get approval with Operations?"

Dwayne sighs, not responding for several moments. Finally, he says, "We probably need to go through TEP-LARB."

"Oh," Maxine says. Kurt flinches as if something just stung him. Tom looks around the table, confused. "Is that bad?"

"Well, there are certainly easier things to get through than the TEP-LARB..." Kurt says, staring at an empty spot on the table in front of him.

Dwayne says, "Actually, that's a bit disingenuous, Kurt. The truth is there is *nothing* more difficult than getting through TEP-LARB. *Nothing* gets through TEP and LARB. And I should know, I'm *on* the LARB."

"He's right, Kurt," Maxine says. "In all my years here, I've never been able to get anything through. It's a ton of work to even fill out their forms, and I've never seen them actually approve anything. They're the Grand Pointless Council of No."

She looks at Dwayne and says, "No offense."

He quickly replies with a smile, "None taken."

"What is TEP-LARB? And why do they always say no?" Tom asks.

"'LARB' stands for Lead Architecture Review Board," Dwayne explains. "It was a committee created decades ago after a whole bunch of bad things happened in technology, long before I joined the company. Someone decided to create a bunch of rules to make sure anything new was 'properly reviewed,'" Dwayne says, air quoting with his hands.

"It's a committee of committees. There are seven Ops architects, seven Dev architects, two Security architects, and two Enterprise architects. It's like they're frozen in time, still acting like it's the 1990s," he says. "Any major technology initiative needs their sign-off.

"And to pitch anything to them, you first have to fill out the Technology Evaluation Process form, or the TEP," he explains. "Maxine is right. It's a lot of effort. It's about fifty pages these days."

Maxine's eyes widen. Assembling all the information to fill out the TEP was an incredible ordeal the last time she attempted it. And it was only about half that size then. She asks, "If you're on the LARB, why haven't you made the process easier?"

Dwayne says, "It's a committee. They all think their job is to say no. I'm the lone radical voice in the whole group, and without more kindred spirits, it's impossible for me to drive a yes vote or bring in younger committee members. Trust me, I've been trying."

Kurt drums his fingers for a moment. "Dwayne is right. Any major technology initiative needs to go through TEP-LARB. If we don't, they'll kill our effort before we even get started."

He takes a deep breath. "It pains me to say this, but I think we need to prepare a TEP and pitch the LARB. Just like we're going to have to ask Security, even though we already know they're going to say no too."

Maxine replies, "You know, we could just run Data Hub ourselves. Like, run it completely without any help from Operations, similar to how we ran our own MRP system in my old group. Besides, whenever something goes wrong with Data Hub, it's not like we're not being escalated to eventually."

Everyone looks at Maxine, shocked. In particular, Dwayne and Shannon look scandalized, as if Maxine has just proposed doing something illegal or maybe even immoral. Brent says, "But how? What about Information Security? And compliance? And the TEP-LARB?"

Maxine snorts, recalling that these were exactly the same reasons she heard for why only Jared could deploy code.

She watches Dwayne switch between nodding and shaking his head, as if two wildly opposing views were violently battling inside of his head. "Oh, wow, that would be great. But they'd *never* let us run this type of enterprise-class service ourselves. It's not like we don't have the skills on the team…we'd just have to be responsible for all the data, make sure it's backed up and all. It would be amazing, because we could run it the way we want…"

His voice trails off. Maxine acknowledges his concerns, "That's right. We run our own MRP system, which all our manufacturing plants rely on. That's about as mission-critical as you can get. We do all the backups, preventive maintenance, patching…It's not easy or simple, but it's not exactly rocket science, either. But we've got some of the best Ops people in the company in this room. We can do it."

Brent says, "Hell, yes. I fear nothing in production."

Dwayne slowly nods. "Okay, I'm in. We need this badly, and of course, I *know* we can run everything ourselves just fine."

Kurt smiles wide. "Okay, we have a Plan B. If all else fails, we operate Data Hub ourselves. This will require getting Chris on board, of course."

Maxine chokes on her coffee, but nods with everyone in agreement.

Tom is clearly excited at the idea that everything that he's helped build could soon be running in production. Suddenly, he frowns. "Wait, wait, wait. Does that mean we're all going to have to wear a pager?"

"Yes," says Brent, adamantly. "You build it, you run it."

Tom's excitement visibly fades.

Maxine laughs.

Even Maxine is stunned by how quickly the entire Data Hub Dev team starts using the new environments. Everyone is using one in some fashion or another. They've spread like wildfire. Some are just using the Docker images on their laptops, some are using environments in *vagrant, Git,* or *terraform* configurations, simulating both Dev and test environments.

More importantly, Purna and the QA teams are using the Data Hub environments as well; once features are flagged as "Ready to Test," they're tested within hours. And because tests are being checked in with the code themselves, it's easy for the developer to quickly reproduce and fix the problem.

This new way of working means that many defects and even a couple of features are completely implemented and tested in one day. Because of some reporting requirements that Maxine doesn't quite understand yet, they're still having to use two separate ticketing tools. But the Dev and QA teams are coordinating more closely than ever. In fact, many of the QA teams are sitting side by side with developers each day. Some in Building 5 and some in Building 7.

Watching how the teams work reminds Maxine of her startup days, where everyone was working together toward a common goal. She's amazed at how quickly attitudes changed in Data Hub.

Over the next three days, they close out more fixes as "shippable" than they used to in most months, and everyone's energy is high and enthusiastic. More importantly, Maxine knows that everyone is having fun.

Maxine and Tom finish another issue, marking it as done in the ticketing system. Within a minute, two engineers in the chat room say that they'll review and test it within the hour.

Maxine stands up. "Unless you need me, I'm heading over to visit Cranky Dave and Purna to see how they're doing."

"Hey, I'm coming with you," says Tom, grabbing his laptop. "I'm going to help them test our fixes."

They find Purna with Cranky Dave and another Data Hub developer, all looking closely at something on her monitor. "Whatcha doing?" Maxine asks.

"We're finally testing the surplus inventory functionality," Purna says.

Cranky Dave adds, "It's to support one of the biggest Phoenix initiatives. It's the critical glue that enables Promotions to scan the in-store inventory systems for products that have been sitting on the shelves gathering dust and ship them to one of the regional warehouses, making them eligible to be promoted on the e-commerce site."

"This is the first time we've been able to get it running," Purna says. "This feature was completed over six months ago, but in the last two releases, we couldn't get it to work. The first time it wouldn't connect with the inventory and customer profile systems. The next time, it couldn't connect with the purchasing history systems. Both times there was some environment or configuration problem, but there just wasn't time to figure it out."

"We had to yank this feature out of the release, otherwise it would have made all the other features late too," Purna says.

This is one of the great things about using Docker containers, Maxine thinks. Containers are immutable, unable to be changed after they're created, so if it works in Dev, it will almost certainly work in Test.

Immutability is another concept from functional programming that is making the world a more predictable and safer place, Maxine thinks, smiling.

"We're on step twenty of the eighty-step test," Cranky Dave says, with no trace of crankiness at all, Maxine observes. "I have a good feeling about this. We found one problem earlier today, but I fixed it in less than five minutes, and we kept marching down the list. This is great!"

Even Cranky Dave can't be that cranky when his features are working, Maxine thinks.

He continues, "Every developer knows that in the next interval, they need to write automated tests as they write the feature, not afterward. Which reminds me, we should really have some of the QA team permanently co-located with us. It seems so silly that we have to walk to a different building to pair on small problems."

"Great idea," Maxine says. "Let's give that one to Kurt—dealing with all the politics of office space and facilities is definitely in his bailiwick. But I think it would be terrific."

"By the way, you should check out what Adam and Shannon are doing over in the conference room. I think it'll make you smile," Cranky Dave says, obviously trying very hard not to spill the beans.

Maxine sees Adam and Shannon at a large table with six other Dev and QA engineers around them, laptops open. Adam is projecting his laptop screen on the TV.

"Holy cow, is that what I think it is?" Maxine asks, stopping midstride and staring at the screen.

"If you mean, does this look like a continuous integration server that is doing code builds and automated tests on Data Hub for every check-in, running in the environments that you helped build? If so, then you would be absolutely right," says Adam, a huge smile on his face.

Maxine recognizes the CI tool immediately. Everyone thinks that Data Hub is so archaic and backward, and yet it's now running under continuous integration. They now have better technical practices than most of Phoenix.

"This is incredibly beautiful," Maxine says, feeling misty-eyed. "Everyone from Data Hub has access? When will other teams be able to use this?"

Shannon looks up from her laptop and says, "Everyone from Data Hub is in. And as you know, getting their code into CI was one of the top requests from the Phoenix teams. Adam and I are onboarding the first teams and getting them trained. We're going to do whatever it takes to make sure they're successful. When they're up and running, we've got a line a mile long to be the next onboard," she says.

Maxine savors the moment. This is what she had been hoping since her first day on the Phoenix Project. Every developer deserves to have this infrastructure to make them productive and a team of experts to help them get up and running.

She looks at the screen and sees that in the last four hours, five Data Hub developers have checked in code changes, and in two cases, the tests failed but were corrected within ten minutes.

Erik would be proud, she thinks. This fast and frequent feedback is such a big part of achieving the Second Ideal of Focus, Flow, and Joy. And all of this was enabled by properly elevating the improvement of daily work over daily work itself, as dictated by the Third Ideal.

"I *love* the idea of co-locating QA and Dev," Kurt says, addressing everyone assembled at Dockside. "Although when I brought this up with some of the other Dev managers, they found the idea quite scandalous," he adds with a smile.

"Right before I came over, I showed some proposed floor plans to the director of Facilities," he continues. "When he saw them, he almost hit the ceiling. I actually think he wanted to confiscate them." Kurt laughs. "He started telling me about all the rules they have about conforming to the space guidelines that HR came up with. Apparently, there are rules about how large the spaces can be based on job titles..."

"Sounds like the USDA rules about the sizes of cow pens," says Cranky Dave. Everyone looks at him. "What? I came from a family of farmers. I had to deal with the occasional USDA audit."

"Great," Shannon says. "He's calling engineers livestock now."

"What's the timeline, Kurt?" asks Adam.

"Nine months," Kurt says.

Maxine hears several people repeat back, "Nine months?!" Some just guffaw.

"Yeah, well..." Kurt says, looking at his notes. "Anything that Facilities does will take forever. We'd have to order the officially supported chairs and desks through Purchasing and schedule the furniture installation with the Facilities staff..."

"Can we just do it ourselves over the weekend?" Dwayne says. "It wouldn't affect anyone outside the team. We could just go to an office supply store or furniture store, buy the bare minimum, and move it into the building. We can use my truck."

"But what happens when Facilities shows up with their badges and says that we don't have the right permits or that we're out of code?" Cranky Dave asks.

Kurt bursts out laughing, "Facilities isn't going to haul it away themselves because no one will give them the budget." He thinks for a moment. "Let's do it. But let's make sure to bring in some furniture that can't be carried away easily...like a couple of bookshelves, and we'll fill them up with books. Maybe a goldfish tank. What do you think?"

Cranky Dave and Shannon laugh. Adam nods thoughtfully, "Possession is nine-tenths of the law. But shouldn't you get Chris's go-ahead first?"

Kurt snorts. "No way. He'd never go for it. Let's just do it."

"Since we have limited space, how about we move some of the QA people to the Dev area, and move some of the developers to the QA area?" Shannon suggests.

"Great idea, Shannon," Maxine says. She's delighted that the team is organizing itself, just as Erik predicted.

CHAPTER 12

• *Monday, October 13*

Over the past week, it's clear to Maxine that Data Hub has figured out how to deliver better value, sooner, safer, and even happier. But it's also clear that a new constraint has emerged. The constraint used to be getting environments—no one could ever get one, and when they did, it was never quite right. Then the constraint became testing, which started only when Development was finished with all their features; finding and fixing defects would take weeks instead of the hours or days it takes now.

Now it is obvious that the constraint is deployment—they are now able to quickly get features production-ready, but they still have to wait weeks for Ops to deploy their code into production.

Figuring out how to get Data Hub into production more quickly is no longer an academic concern. Tom is standing in the front of the conference room with the rest of the Data Hub team. He says, "Maxine, the suspicions that you had while you were out sick were right on target. According to Maggie and all her product owners, creating effective promotional bundles is one of the most critical and urgent Phoenix priorities.

"Kurt, the meeting we have with Maggie is scheduled for tomorrow, and you asked me to study up on this beforehand," Tom continues. "Here's what I've learned: Marketing is constantly experimenting with promotion campaigns to accelerate sales, and this is incredibly important as we approach the holidays, our peak sales season. For example, now that it is snowing in many areas, they want to create a winter promotion bundle: tire chains, ice-melting salts, and window scrapers. They also need to create a discounted price for that bundle, say twenty percent off. They also do promotions to customer segments—if you buy lots of windshield wipers, you may get offered a bundle of wiper fluid and glass defoggers, knowing that you may only need the smallest nudge to buy.

"Conceptually, it sounds easy. But here's all the insane steps they need to go through to get this done: First, every new product bundle needs a new SKU, just like every other item we sell. These SKUs are used by almost every application in the business: inventory tracking, in our supply chain, our in-store registers, our e-commerce sites, even the mobile apps...

"We only create new SKUs in large batches every six weeks. After the SKUs are created, we also need to push all the application and business logic changes for these new SKUs. These are pushed to every application that needs to know about them. That's often scores of back-end and front-end applications across the enterprise. You might have seen these go out at eight on Friday nights. And when that's done, sometimes we even need to manually refresh certain production databases.

"Here's problem number one: we only create new SKUs every six weeks, which is way too slow. Thanksgiving is a month away, and we're already in danger of not getting those product bundle SKUs created in time.

"And the real truth is that it often takes us much longer than six weeks. We need to change so many applications during those pushes that if anything goes wrong during testing, the entire release is canceled... You can't have new SKUs out there when some of the applications don't know how to deal with them. There's just not enough time to fix these things during the test period, so it's all-or-nothing.

"And on top of that, Promotions also needs to rapidly experiment and iterate to discover which bundles customers are actually interested in and what specific factors lead to an actual purchase. Right now, iterating only once every six weeks is not fast enough to learn and adapt—our e-commerce competitors are doing multiple experiments per day," Tom concludes.

"Wow, that's really incredible," Maxine says, looking at all the boxes he's drawn on the whiteboard. "This is so much like the Phoenix architecture, which makes it so difficult for any team to independently develop, test, and deploy value to our customers. The architecture that supports the Promotions value stream that you've just drawn on the whiteboard shows how it's almost impossible to move any work quickly to where it needs to go."

She gestures at his diagram. "At every step, it's entangled with so many other value streams. We have to synchronize with everyone else's release schedules. If any of *them* can't be released, then we can't be released... It's just crazy."

"It really is. It's frustrating that Data Hub is so tightly coupled to Phoenix and the BWOS," Tom says.

"What's a BWOS?" Maxine asks.

"Oh, that's what we call the…you know, the big wad of…umm, crap. You know, the hundred-plus applications we connect to," Tom says.

Maxine laughs. "I really think if we could deploy Data Hub changes into production on demand and fully decouple them from the Phoenix release schedule, we'd be so much better off…That way, if we have to cancel a release, we could at least try again the next day. With some practice, I bet we could get SKU creation down to one or two days."

"I definitely agree," Tom says. Maxine smiles, satisfied that they're on the right track. *And the value of doing this will be huge*, she thinks.

"This may not be related, but I think it's worth mentioning," Tom says. "We have other huge problems being connected so closely to Phoenix. It sometimes sends us tons of messages that hammer the back-end systems that we connect to. We routinely see massive waves of transactions that cause huge reliability and throughput problems, and sometimes even data integrity problems. Sometimes it's Data Hub crashing, but most of the time, it's the systems that we're calling that are the ones crashing."

Cranky Dave piles on. "Dealing with those systems of record are a huge a pain in the ass. We don't have any real API strategy around here. No one knows what APIs are available, and even if you do, no one knows how you get access to them or deal with their crazy authentication or pagination schemes. Everyone's documentation is crap, and some of these teams don't even care if their APIs don't work as advertised.

"And once you *do* get someone's API working, they'll break it however and whenever they want, especially since they probably don't version their APIs. So transactions start failing for our customers, and they blame *us*," he continues. "They never give you all the data you need, so when you actually have an API change you want, you have to go through all these committees to get them approved!"

"It's enough to drive anyone crazy," Cranky Dave says, exhausted.

"We can definitely stop this madness," Maxine says with certainty.

As promised, the next day, Kurt, Maxine, and the Data Hub team meet with Maggie. As usual, Kurt introduces all the Data Hub team members to Maggie and then asks Maggie to introduce herself.

"Many of you already know me," she says with a smile. "My name is Maggie Lee. I'm senior director of retail program management. What that really means is that I have the P&L responsibilities of all the products and programs behind our stores, which includes physical stores, e-commerce, and mobile. My group of product managers own strategy, understanding the customer and market, customer segmentation, identifying which customer problems we want to solve, pricing and packaging, and managing the profitability of everything in our portfolio."

She continues, "We bridge the business goals and everything that's required to actually achieve them. That includes business operations, business analysts, and product managers, who work with Chris' technical teams. I also have all the operational pieces required to deal with Sales, Finance, and Operations on my team.

"When Kurt said that you had some ideas on speeding up how we create promotion product bundles, you certainly got my attention," she says. "Sorry I couldn't meet even earlier, but as you can imagine, we're all buried with a million things right now. It's definitely a make-or-break quarter for us. For *all* of us."

Maxine is already impressed. Maggie is in her mid-forties and has an unmistakable intensity about her. She is the same height as Maxine and obviously competent. She's a no-nonsense type and always has a serious expression on her face. Maxine suspects that she's Sarah's forebrain, handling the million things required to keep a billion-dollar retail operation going.

Kurt explains what they've been working on.

Maggie looks at Kurt. "So you're telling me that you could enable Marketing to create promotions entirely self-service, like our e-commerce competitors can? And that other changes could potentially be pushed into production on the same day?" Maggie says. "Holy shit, folks. If you can actually do what you say, this might be the miracle we've been hoping for. I'm not prone to overstatements, but I'm not kidding when I say that this could potentially save the quarter. And maybe even the company."

Maxine smiles. "From everything we've studied, it's clear that it's way too difficult and takes too long to get those promotional bundles created. We'd love to fully empower your teams to do what it takes to create new promotions anytime you want and have them pushed out to all your sales channels within hours. There's a lot we don't understand, but conceptually, we should be able to do it. We just wanted to explore whether this would be valuable to you."

Maggie nods. "Hugely valuable. Look, Steve has promised all the analysts that this holiday season we're finally going to see an uptick in revenue. This is after years of over-promising and under-delivering. Everything hinges on Promotions being able to move the needle on sales. If you really think you can make this happen, we'll do whatever it takes. What exactly is in the way?" she asks.

"Who isn't in the way?" Kurt laughs. "We're meeting with Information Security tomorrow, who could kill this effort on a whim. But the real threat is the TEP-LARB. We've put together a team to create our proposal, but people usually wait six to nine months to get in front of them," Kurt says. "Unless, of course, there's an urgent business need with a powerful sponsor."

Maggie finally smiles, in not an entirely kind way. "For this, I think we need to bring in the big guns."

"Who's that?" asks Maxine, curious who could possibly be a more powerful sponsor than Maggie.

Maggie grins. "Sarah. Take it from me, there is *no one* more effective at busting down inconvenient barriers than she is. She's like a chainsaw, great at cutting down trees."

"...and sawing off hands," Kurt mutters under his breath.

The next day, Kurt and Maxine meet with Ron, the security manager that Shannon introduced them to. They walk into the conference room and see that Shannon has arrived early.

"There's no way I'd miss this," she says, smiling. "I should have brought popcorn."

Ron, who is in his mid-thirties, comes in and sits down. After introductions, Kurt walks him through their idea to decouple Data Hub from the rest of Phoenix.

Ron says, "Interesting idea. I remember when Data Hub was still called Octopus. Why the need for such a big change? It seems to be working well enough now."

Kurt walks through all the reasons, and to Maxine's surprise, Ron nods agreeably. *This is going better than I thought it would,* Maxine thinks.

"That's exciting," he says, agreeably. But then he takes off his glasses and puts them on the table. "Look, I really want to help, but I can't. I'm responsible for making sure applications in my portfolio meet all applicable laws and regulations and that all those applications are secure. Given how radical of a change you're making, I'm afraid we need to perform a complete due-diligence effort. And you simply can't jump the entire queue. You have twenty people ahead of you who would scream bloody murder," he says.

"But the Promotions capability is one of the most important features inside Phoenix, which is the most important initiative for the company," responds Shannon. "Surely you see that ours should have higher priority, right?"

"Yes, but…" Ron says, shaking his head. "I don't set the priority or order of the applications. That comes from the business. You know, our customer."

"But we are 'the business!' And those 'customers' you're talking about aren't our customers—they're our colleagues! Our customers are the ones who actually pay us money!" Shannon says, bright red with exasperation. "Everyone knows what the top goals are. The top priorities are what Steve always talks about in all the Town Halls. What else is more important than getting Data Hub successfully decoupled from Phoenix, so that the Promotions team can meet the holiday sales goals?"

Ron shrugs his shoulders. "If you want to change the order, you'll have to talk to our boss, John."

Kurt closes his laptop, clearly concluding that there's nothing to be gained in this meeting.

"Fine, fine, fine," Shannon says, resigned as well. Then she turns up the charm, saying, "Hey, could you at least give us all of the testing procedures that you'll use to certify Data Hub, along with a list of tools you use to scan it? We'll do our best to replicate it in our automated test suite. Maybe we can generate security audit reports for you on-demand."

"That's a great idea, Shannon," he responds. "Come to my desk and I'll show where all the documentation for the previous audits are."

Maxine loves how Shannon takes every opportunity to get people on their side.

Watching them leave, Kurt looks at Maxine, shrugging his shoulders. "Could have gone worse, I suppose. Maybe we'll fare better with the LARB."

Maxine sighs. She wonders what is required to generate a true sense of urgency. When her dad had a stroke two years ago, she had remarked on all the bewildering processes in the hospital to one of her doctor friends. Her friend responded, "You were lucky. The processes in a stroke ward tend to be superb, because everyone knows that every minute counts and waiting could be the difference between life and death.

"The worst systems tend to be in mental health and elderly care, where there is less urgency and often no patient advocate," she had said. "You can get lost in the system for years. Sometimes even decades."

Maxine remembers what it felt like to be the patient advocate for her dad, doing whatever it took to get him through the healthcare system. Now, she recommits herself to doing whatever it takes to get her teams through the company bureaucracies—the Data Hub team's sense of mission and urgency deserve no less.

Relentless optimism, she reminds herself.

As Maggie promised, they are on the LARB agenda on Thursday. Maxine is amazed and wonders what strings Sarah must have pulled to get them in so quickly. Then she wonders what Maggie had to do to convince Sarah.

Although Maxine recognizes the political necessity of pitching the LARB, she still resents all the time the team spent filling out the TEP—engineers should be writing code, not filling out forms.

It had many valid questions about architecture and security, but some questions seemed dated, reminding her of TOGAF architecture diagrams from decades past, clearly written for a different era: software development and testing phase gates, datacenter specifications, HVAC specifications, Check Point firewall rules (if applicable, of course)...

The Data Hub gang responsible for putting the proposal together is all here, sitting in the back of the room: Tom, Brent, Shannon, Dwayne, Adam, Purna, and Maxine. At one table sit all the senior Dev and Enterprise architects, and at the other table sit all the Ops and Security architects. They are all close to Maxine's age, but mostly white males with a couple of Indian and Asian males in the mix. Maxine notices there's not a single woman at either table.

Data Hub is second on the agenda. First up is a group pitching to re-platform all of their applications from a commercial product onto

Apache Tomcat, a battle-tested and fully open-source Java application server. A younger woman confidently presents their case, which she delivers in a very thoughtful and competent manner. But when Maxine hears that all they're looking for is permission to *use* Tomcat, she's aghast.

Having to ask permission to use Tomcat in production is like asking permission to use electricity—maybe it was once considered dangerous, but now it's commonplace. Worse, it's apparently their second time pitching the LARB. Maxine's heart sinks. If Tomcat is considered risky and controversial, their Data Hub proposal is going to get laughed out of the room.

After twenty minutes of skeptical questions from the LARB, the young engineer throws up her hands in exasperation. "Why are we so frightened of running software we wrote? We're a manufacturing company. We wrote our own MRP and we run it *ourselves*. And for Tomcat, we don't need to rely on a commercial vendor anymore. Some of the largest companies in the world use it. We'd not only save the company hundreds of thousands of dollars a year, we could finally do things that our current vendor won't allow us to do. There's so many capabilities we need to better serve our customers."

Maxine gets goosebumps—not because the presenter mentioned her old MRP system, but because the presenter is clearly a brilliant engineer, fearlessly doing what she thinks needs to be done and not afraid to run things in production.

While the young engineer fields more questions from the LARB, Maxine texts the Rebellion in the chat channel:

> Who is this engineer presenting? She's awesome! She's obviously Rebellion material. We should recruit her.

Adam texts back:

> That's Ellen. She's one of the best Ops people around

Everyone nods at Maxine, agreeing with Adam's assessment. Brent adds in the chat channel:

> Agreed. I had no idea she was working on this. This is great!

Maxine looks up when she hears Dwayne talking. "You have got to be kidding me. We created TEP-LARB to help evaluate new technologies. Apache Tomcat was created decades ago, and it's either the second or third most widely used application server out there. If we aren't brave enough to run Tomcat, we should get out of the technology game once and for all. I vote yes. And if you don't, I think we all need to hear why."

Someone from the Ops delegation says, "I don't have anything against Tomcat. I'm just not comfortable with our ability to support this given our current staffing levels. We're stretched thin as it is, and while I appreciate that this technology isn't bleeding edge, we still need people to operate and maintain it..."

Dwayne interrupts, "But you *just heard* Ellen say that her team is willing to support it!"

Not even acknowledging Dwayne's comment, the Security architect joins in, "And there's the security risks. I'd like to get a historical report of Tomcat vulnerabilities, how quickly patches were made available, and any reported problems in patching. Maybe then we can come to a decision."

Dwayne mutters, "For crying out loud. *Ellen* is the person who would write the security and the patching guidelines."

"Thank you for your proposal. We look forward to this team presenting the requested information at our next meeting," the Ops architect says, not looking up from the note he's writing.

At the front of the room, Maxine sees Ellen and her teammates slump in exasperation. Ellen closes her laptop, nods respectfully to all the assembled architects, and takes a seat at the back of the room.

Maxine gives Ellen and her teammates the most enthusiastic thumbs up she can manage.

"Next up is Maxine and Adam on the proposal to move Data Hub into a new environment, running on containers, with automated code builds, tests, and deployments?" the Ops architect prompts.

Adam stands up, but after seeing the last presenter, Maxine already knows they're sunk. No matter how well prepared they are, they'll never be able to convince the LARB.

"...and to summarize, the urgent needs of the Promotions team requires us to get Data Hub functionality more quickly to our internal customers.

We need a radically different way to store and retrieve data that allows us to be decoupled from the rest of the Phoenix teams," Maxine concludes. "We've found a set of technologies that can help us achieve that, which have been battle-tested and used in production for over a decade at some of the largest internet properties on the planet: Google, Netflix, Spotify, Walmart, Target, Capital One, and many more. Based on our trials over the past several weeks, we are confident in our ability to support it, and we're willing to support it ourselves if necessary."

Brent, who joined them at the front of the room, adds, "The team supporting Data Hub production would be some of the most experienced people we have in Ops. Personally, I can't even describe how excited I am by this effort. I think these technologies have applicability far beyond Data Hub and could really improve things for almost every application we support. We are willing to be available and responsible to resolve anything that goes wrong. Utilizing these techniques will help every Dev and Ops person at Parts Unlimited."

Maxine sees Kurt smile at the team from the back of the room. Maxine is proud of everyone. It was a solid presentation. She sees Ellen grinning wildly, obviously impressed. But Maxine knows that it's all for naught. The LARB was designed to be an organizational immune system to prevent dangerous changes—they are just too powerful and conservative.

Dwayne tries to rally support. "The LARB should foster innovative efforts like this, picking technologies that can help us win in the market-place. We used to set the industry direction, making bold choices that left our competitors in the dust. People laughed when we created our own MRP system, saying we were idiots, but history has shown that that was the right thing to do. We were the first company in our industry to use thin clients in our factories, and because of that and hundreds of brilliant technology decisions, we became one of the most efficient and effective manufacturers in the country."

Maxine looks around the room and sees some stirrings of excitement and renewed curiosity among the Dev architects. However, she sees all the Ops and Security architects shaking their heads. One of them says, "Dwayne, I appreciate what you're saying, but we've never done anything even remotely similar to this. It's embarrassing that we can't even support Tomcat—but that shows you exactly why we can't possibly support this.

Unless there's a group willing to volunteer to support this initiative as a side project, I think we need to table it."

Dwayne speaks up, "Hell yes, I volunteer. And I'll grab some people I know who would love to help the Data Hub team with the support responsibilities."

"I'd love to help," says Ellen from the back of the room. "I've been using Docker and the other tools you've mentioned for years. These are competencies we need at this company."

"You're in," Maxine says to Ellen, smiling.

The Ops Chair looks surprised but says, "I appreciate your enthusiasm, but I'm afraid that we cannot support your initiative at this time. Let's pick this up in six months and see if conditions have changed by then."

Hearing enough, Kurt stands up and addresses the room. "Didn't you hear the business context? Both Maggie Lee and Sarah Moulton have clearly stated that the company's survival depends on this. This is so important that if you can't support it we're going to have to support it ourselves in Development."

"We hear business people say things like that all the time," the Ops Chair says. "We invite you back in six months to discuss it again. And now to other matters..."

Defeated, the team leaves the meeting, reassembling in a nearby conference room that Kurt booked in advance. Maxine invites Ellen and the three other engineers who presented the Tomcat proposal.

"Wow, that was so great. Are you really going to go rogue and run all this yourselves?" Ellen says, smiling ear to ear, not affected by the glum faces all around her. "If so, count me in. I'm Ellen, by the way," she says, extending her hand to Maxine and then introducing her team.

"Good seeing you again, Ellen," Adam says with a big smile. "Welcome to our merry band of rebels. If I'm reading the tea leaves right, I think we're going to need your help soon."

Ellen smiles. "The fact that you have Brent onboard is enough for me. What you presented was amazing. I had no idea anyone was working on these types of things here at Parts Unlimited."

Brent smiles modestly, "But we still got our asses kicked, right?"

Kurt says, "We did indeed. But if all goes according to plan, by the end of the day there will be a memo going out from Chris and Sarah announcing a small re-org that will allow Data Hub to operate outside the conventional Ops and QA processes. That will be the official go-ahead to do whatever we need to do."

Everyone on the Data Hub team cheers, surprised at the good news. Maxine hears Ellen mutter, "Wow. That's some pretty powerful mojo you have on your side."

Brent mutters back, "You have no idea. I'll tell you later." Adam laughs in agreement.

While almost everyone is celebrating, Dwayne is glum. When Maxine asks why, Dwayne says, "I just can't believe the LARB didn't support these efforts. We let you all down. What was *supposed* to happen was that they would see the grave danger on the horizon. They were *supposed* to support our cause. They were *supposed* to help...Like Gandalf getting the support of the White Council in *Lord of the Rings*..."

Maxine is surprised when Dwayne puts both of his hands on his temples, groaning. After a minute, he finally says, "But it didn't work out that way at all."

Brent laughs. "You've got it wrong, Dwayne. The Fellowship of the Ring wasn't ever officially sanctioned by the White Council. Gandalf warned everyone that the One Ring was at large, but Saruman refused to help because he was already working for the evil Sauron. So, Gandalf went rogue. He went it alone. Just like we're going to do."

"Damn right," says Kurt. Turning to Ellen and her team, he says, "You all doing anything after work? There's a bar that we go to..."

"What the hell have you gotten me into?!" Chris says, fuming at Kurt. "Maggie and Sarah tell me that you've proposed to create your own Ops organization inside of Dev?! And that you've gotten some sort of exception waiver to start running some new Tier 2 services in the cloud?! I don't suppose you ever thought to ask me first?"

Maxine is in Chris' office with Kurt, Dwayne, and Maggie. Chris is clearly not happy, but Maggie goes to extraordinary lengths to describe the business outcomes that need to be achieved and the grave consequences of not doing so.

Chris stares out his window for several moments and then turns to Maxine. "Do you think we really have the chops to keep all this from blowing up in our faces?"

"Absolutely, with the help of Dwayne and Brent from Ops," she says with certainty. "I'll do everything in my power to make sure things go smoothly. I really think we've got this, Chris. And I promise to take the blame for anything that happens."

At the mention of Dwayne and Brent, a pained expression appears on Chris' face. He looks at her, obviously thinking, *What about 'don't rock the boat' and 'stay in your lane' do you not understand?*

Maxine shrugs. She knows that Chris supported mission-critical services early in his engineering career, over twenty years ago. But ever since then, he's only been responsible for the code, no longer running the actual services that it enables. Maxine could almost see him tabulating all the inconveniences this could create, all the things that could go wrong, balancing it against what could happen if he refuses.

"Fine, fine, fine. I'll do it," he says reluctantly. "You people are going to give me a heart attack," and then shoos them out of his office.

As promised, Chris sends out a memo to everyone announcing a re-org—the Data Hub team is now reporting directly to him, and as an experiment, they'll be exempt from the normal rules and regulations around changes, able to test their own code, deploy it, and operate it in production themselves.

"The email just went out," Kurt says, grinning wildly. "We're in the deployment and operations business!"

"Wow, that's incredible," Maxine says, still staring at the email on her phone. "You know, despite everything we did, I was pretty sure it wasn't really going to happen."

Kurt laughs. "I don't think Chris had that much choice in the matter. Both Maggie and Sarah took this all the way up to Steve."

With the Data Hub re-org, the team is now committed. They are working furiously to automate the production deployments and to figure out how to do production operations without centralized Ops. To what extent they needed to really divorce themselves from Ops for things like backup was still unclear and being negotiated.

The enormity of the challenge is exhilarating. The goal is clear: enable fast and safe deployments into production, and for the first time in years, do it using the same environments across Dev, Test, and Production. And everyone wants to prove that they can get everything up and running before the rest of the Phoenix Project even finishes their testing cycle.

Once again, they are in an imaginary race against the lumbering Phoenix Project.

Maxine is working with Dwayne, Adam, Shannon, and Brent, making slow but sure progress on getting the Data Hub production services to run on something besides the fastest bare-metal servers that money can buy…a decade ago. Many things in Data Hub blew up when installed on a current OS version…from *this* decade. They found several binary executables that no one could find the source code for. Data Hub had become this fragile and irreproducible artifact. *That's great if you're an art collector*, Maxine thinks, *but utterly unacceptable when you're running a mission-critical service.*

They work methodically to create a Test and Production service that behaves like the old one, but can be spun up instantly in a container. For days, she's mired again in the messy world of infrastructure, dealing with Makefiles, YAML, and XML configuration files; Dockerfiles; purging secrets from their source code repositories; and using all her experience to speed up build and test times. This, unfortunately, required lots of Bash scripts.

Maxine remembers a quote from Jeffrey Snover, the inventor of PowerShell. He once said, "Bash is the disease you die with, but don't die of." Maxine shares this sentiment. Infrastructure is messy work, almost the opposite of the pure functional programming she loves—in infrastructure, almost everything you do has a side-effect that mutates the state of *something* in the environment, making it difficult to isolate and test changes, as well as diagnose problems when things go wrong.

But she knows how important this work is, and every bit of knowledge and expertise that she can put into these environments and CI/CD platforms will elevate the productivity of every engineer at Parts Unlimited.

Looking around, she realizes that now some of the best engineers in the company are working on making everyone else more productive. *That's the way it should be*, she thinks.

By the next Thursday, Maxine is thrilled at how much they've been able to accomplish with all the restrictions lifted. But something strikes

Maxine as odd. She notices that all the Data Hub engineers are pitching in. She certainly appreciates their help and she knows that Project Inversion was supposed to disallow feature work, but still, there's almost always some urgent feature that needs working on.

Suspicious, she asks Tom what's going on. He says, "This sounds strange, but technically there isn't any feature work even ready. Believe it or not, every feature is waiting on something from Product Management," he says. "It's everything from a customer requirement that needs clarification, a question about a wireframe, a choice that needs to be made between different options or priorities...Sometimes it's something small, like where a button should go. And sometimes it's something big, like them not showing up to the demo to validate what we've built." Tom laughs. "They think we're the bottleneck, but we're always waiting for them."

"Can you show me?" says Maxine. None of the things Tom described sounded good, but the part about the product manager not showing up for the demo pisses her off. What a disrespectful thing to do to engineers who built what you asked them to.

She watches as Tom pulls up a tool she hasn't worked with before, this one used by the product managers to capture ideas from customers: the ideal customer journey, value hypotheses, manage experiments, and so forth.

"What are all those blue cards?" she asks.

"Good eye. That's exactly the problem," he says. "Those are all the features that we're working on, but we're blocked because of something we need from Product Management. Like all those reasons I mentioned before. Oh, and here's some yellow cards which are the features we've completed but that haven't been accepted by the business stakeholders yet. This one has been waiting for forty days."

Maxine feels her face turn red, indignant that as much as Product Management complains about the need to get features to market quickly, all these blue and yellow cards represent where *they* are in the way, not Development. *How can we keep Product Management accountable?* Maxine thinks. *Time to bring in Kurt.*

Ten minutes later, Kurt is with them, staring at the sea of blue cards. "I get it. This is not good, but I have an idea," he says. "By the way, did you know that Sarah put a huge design agency on retainer, and now they're flooding some of the other teams with wireframe diagrams that will probably never get worked on? And no matter how much the Dev managers ask them to stop sending wireframes, they still keep coming."

"Why?" Maxine asks.

"I think it's because Sarah needs to show off the apps she wants to build," he says. "But what's funny is that when the designers came here, the last thing they wanted to do was wireframes. They wanted to learn about our customers, and they did a bunch of exercises to better clarify goals around the personas we used. There was even one session where *we* all drew wireframes," Kurt says, laughing.

Working with designers fascinates Maxine. Early in her career, the ratio of UX and designers to developers was 1:70. These days, great teams doing consumer-oriented products have ratios of 1:6 because it's that important to create products that people love. Every consumer these days knows what a professional app feels like. Apps that don't have great designers are often ridiculed as "enterprisey."

She's seen teams still waiting to be assigned designers, eventually making their own wireframes, HTML and CSS styling, and icons just to keep feature flow moving. *These are the projects that teams are actually embarrassed to show other people*, she thinks.

The good news is that Sarah got a bunch of great designers. The bad news is that she put them all where they weren't needed and were actually slowing important development work down by flooding their backlogs with things that didn't matter.

That evening after dinner, while her family played with Waffles, she opened up her laptop. Something about the sea of blue cards that Tom showed her earlier had been bothering her, and she's determined to get to the bottom of it.

That sea of blue cards is a part of the tool that the product managers use to manage the funnel of ideas to achieve business outcomes. This is a process that starts long before a feature is created in the Dev ticketing system. She logs into that tool using the credentials that Tom gave her. Browsing around, she can see when ideas were first conceived and brainstormed and all the various phases until it becomes an approved feature.

She searches for the first feature that she worked on with Tom about extended warrantee programs. When she finds it her jaw drops. That feature was first discussed almost two years ago. It started off as a small feature but was rolled up into a larger warrantee initiative, which then had to be pitched to a steering committee. When it was approved, they wrote up detailed specifications, which were pitched six months later. Only then were they approved (a second time) and finally funded.

This idea bounced around in the marketing and project management organization for almost two years, and then turned into a super-crash priority feature that had to ship by the end of the year.

For something this important, we wasted almost two years, she thinks. In the ideal, they should have just assigned a team that included developers to explore the idea and build a solution together. *Instead of one product manager working on this the entire time, we could have had five people working on it. And we could have been learning the whole time*, Maxine thinks.

She wonders how much of this specification document that was written two years ago is now out of date.

She pulls up the Dev and QA ticketing system and copies some dates into the spreadsheet. She spends nearly ten minutes Googling around, trying to remember how to do date conversions and date arithmetic correctly.

She stares at the screen, shocked. She does the formula a couple different ways, but she still gets the same number.

She texts Kurt:

We've got to meet tomorrow. I have something to show you.

Maxine is with Kurt, Tom, and Kirsten in a conference room projecting her laptop on the screen. Everyone is staring at it in disbelief, which she totally understands. She's been thinking about this number all night. "Can that actually be right?" Kurt finally asks.

"I'm afraid so," says Maxine. Kurt looks over at Kirsten, who is still staring at the numbers.

"Only 2.5 percent of the time required to go from *concept* to *customers actually using the feature* is spent in Development?" she finally asks, the disbelief evident in her voice. She stands up and walks to the large TV screen to look more closely at the spreadsheet. "Where is all the time going?"

Maxine says, "Long before the feature ever gets to Development, it goes through the funding approval process, which often takes over a year.

And then once the feature is created, most of the time isn't spent in-work, it's waiting for a product manager to respond to a question. It's the Square again. Teams are spending too much time waiting for product managers to get them what they need...

"And then once they're done with the feature, they're waiting for QA and deployment," Maxine says. "This is terrible. We've spent all this time hiring more developers, but they often don't have things ready to be worked on. And when they do finish a feature, it takes forever to actually get things into production so that our customers can use it. And often the only feedback we get are the annual focus groups.

"We don't have a fast value stream," Maxine says. "What we've got is more like a stagnant value pond, full of scum, breeding malaria."

"Time to call Maggie," Kurt says.

That afternoon, Maggie comes up with an elegant solution. She decides to move the Data Hub product manager from the Marketing building to a desk right by Maxine starting Monday.

In the conference room, Maggie tells him, "You're the bottleneck. Your top priority now is to make sure any questions that the technology teams have are quickly answered. Nothing else takes priority over that."

He balks and then proceeds to describe all the other demands on his time. Talking with customers, helping sales with negotiations and trying to break them of bad habits, briefing internal executives, working with business operations, arguing with business stakeholders to agree on a product roadmap, escalating things up the chain to get approvals for urgent issues... And way down the list was answering questions from developers.

Maxine listens with interest, realizing that no one can get anything done when you're pulled in that many directions. Maggie also listens patiently, nodding and occasionally asking questions.

When he's done, she says, "If you're too busy to work with the technology teams, I'll move you into a pure product marketing role, and you don't have to move your desk. Right now, I need product managers who are working side by side with the teams who are building what will achieve our most important business objectives. If you still want to be a product manager, I'll figure out how to clear your plate and get those other responsibilities assigned to someone else.

"Don't give me an answer right now," Maggie says. "Think about it and let me know first thing Monday morning."

Maxine is impressed. *Maggie does not mess around*, she thinks.

By mid-day Monday, that product owner moved his desk right next to Maxine. The dynamic immediately shifts. To get answers, things no longer wait on tickets. Engineers are able to just swivel their chairs around and ask him. Things that normally took days are being resolved in minutes. And better yet, engineers start gaining a much better understanding of the business domain.

Maxine smiles. The team of teams keeps growing, and it feels good.

From:	Alan Perez (Operating Partner, Wayne-Yokohama Equity Partners)
To:	Dick Landry (CFO), Sarah Moulton (SVP of Retail Operations),
Cc:	Steve Masters (CEO), Bob Strauss (Board Chair)
Date:	7:45 p.m., November 5
Subject:	Strategic Options **CONFIDENTIAL**

Dick and Sarah,

For our next meeting, I've asked an investment banker we've used in the past to brief us on the market outlook for the retail and manufacturing sides of the Parts Unlimited business. Could you present a high-level briefing on the Phoenix initiative so we can get their thoughts?

Given the criticality of the upcoming holiday sales performance, I thought it might be useful to introduce ourselves to them sooner rather than later. Hopefully any valuation estimates will be anchored before any disasters. (You never want to talk to bankers when you really need them. They can always smell fear.)

Sincerely, Alan

CHAPTER 13

It's six thirty on Thursday evening, and Maxine is again in a conference room, along with the entire extended Data Hub team. Everyone is tense and on edge, looking at a large screen that has all the production telemetry and dashboards showing the health of the test and production Data Hub services. Maxine is pretty sure that everyone is holding their breath, just like she is.

The team had been deploying into a Test environment for weeks before having the confidence to start deploying into Production, which required days of negotiations with seemingly every area of the business. An agreement was reached that production pushes would occur after business hours, after internal business users had gone home but before thousands of internal batch jobs run at midnight.

For the past two days, at the same time each day, as a test, they've been pushing "whitespace changes" into production—adding a couple of blank lines to the end of HTML or configuration files, which in theory should not change functionality in any way.

Of course, reality is much, much messier. It was the "world as imagined" colliding violently with the "world as it actually is." They discovered that they accidentally forgot some critical files in their container images, which knocked Data Hub offline for nearly a half hour. Three hours later, after a painstaking investigation, they were able to execute the whitespace deployment without crashing anything.

The next day, they performed a second whitespace deployment, but absolutely nothing happened. It took them another hour to discover a configuration error they had made earlier in the day had broke all their pipelines. It was messy and imperfect, but the fact that they were quickly solving these problems gave Maxine confidence that they were on the right track.

Today, Tom and Brent are about to start the first push of Data Hub application code into production.

"Okay, here we go," says Tom. "Starting code deployment." He clicks a button and some new boxes appear on the CI/ CD pipeline page, showing that a new deployment has been initiated. They all watch with bated breath as the log files start scrolling by.

Over the next ten minutes, Maxine sees notifications of the tests being run, the tests passing, files being copied onto the production system, Data Hub being restarted, more log messages as it starts up, and then the log messages stop.

On the screen in front, the big circle representing the health of Data Hub goes from green to red, and stays red.

"Uh oh," Tom says. "Data Hub just crashed on startup..." He types quickly into a terminal window.

Maxine hears people swearing all around her, and Maxine joins Tom at his laptop as he tries to figure out what went wrong. She sees him scrolling through seemingly endless Java stack traces, looking for any clue on why Data Hub crashed. He yells out, "It's some type of uncaught exception, but I can't find a useful error message..."

Shannon calls out from the other side of the table, "Folks, I'm not seeing any active connections to the database."

Brent looks up with an expression of horror on his face. "Shit, did I forget to change the database connection string?"

When he just stares off into space, Maxine gently asks, "Good hypothesis, Brent. What are you thinking? How can we test your idea?"

As if jolted out of a trance, Brent looks back at Maxine. "I can't remember where the database connection string is stored! Is it an environment variable? Or is it in a configuration file? Does anyone know?"

"It's an environment variable. I'm pasting where it's set in the chat room," Purna says. Maxine watches as the team jumps into action.

Twenty long minutes later, the necessary fixes are made, and Data Hub is back up and running. Everyone breathes a sigh of relief. The transactions that had been blocked have all been processed and everything is green again. "Okay, we found two other places where we missed some configuration settings in environment variables. Those are now all in version control. It should work this time. Is everyone ready to try again?" Tom asks, and everyone gives a thumbs up, if not as confident as earlier.

Again, they watch as the Data Hub deployment starts...tests are run in the test environment, files are pushed into the production server, Data

Hub is stopped, the new files copied onto the server, Data Hub is restarted, and the startup messages start to scroll by.

This time, there is only a half-second pause where they got stuck before, and then screenfuls of logging messages scroll by faster than anyone can read. Tom whoops in delight, but he still watches his laptop, knowing that lots of things still need to go right before Data Hub is properly handling requests again.

Moments later, the red indicator next to the Data Hub health turns green. Some people clap, but most people realize that any celebration is premature as eyes quickly turn toward the production telemetry. Maxine sees the logging messages come to a crawl and then stop, and the production graphs start climbing again.

The entire room erupts in cheers. Almost the entire room. Maxine notices that Brent looks upset, as if he's angry at himself for the first database connection error.

Tom confirms, "Data Hub is processing transactions again. We're in the deployment business!" He looks around with a big smile. "Who wants to go to the Dockside to celebrate?"

"Now that everyone is here, I can properly hoist a glass to all of you for your amazing work!" says Kurt with a big smile. "Rest assured that you've earned the attention of some *very important people* who have decided to join us today!"

Kirsten raises her glass. "My congratulations to you, everyone. And you did it all without even one project manager from my team, which makes it even better!"

Everyone laughs and applauds. Even Brent is smiling now.

"Ah, what great timing," Kurt continues, raising his glass to someone walking toward them

Maxine turns around to look. *Holy cow*, she thinks.

It's Maggie Lee. The crowd at the Dockside keeps getting classier and classier. Kurt smiles and says, "Meet our newest visiting VIP."

"Hello, everyone," Maggie says, sitting next to Maxine. "I'm delighted to be here to celebrate the successful Data Hub code push."

Kurt introduces all the Data Hub team members to her, and Maggie stands up and introduces herself to everyone. "What you're doing with

Data Hub is amazing, and trust me, all my product managers are incredibly excited about how what you're doing could help us quickly create new product bundles," Maggie says. "We know so much about our customers, and we want to use that information to help them solve their problems. If we do this right, this will naturally lead to achieving our revenue goals. That's the bet we're making. I don't need to tell you all how important the upcoming Thanksgiving and Christmas season is.

"I just want to thank you for being willing to help us, and I'm really looking forward to working with you all," Maggie says. "The work you're doing is important, and I think it's critical to the success of the company."

She raises her glass to everyone's loud applause.

Over pitchers of beer and glasses of wine, Maggie tells the group more about their struggles, some of which surprises and worries Maxine. They have only completed integrations with two systems of record. They are still waiting for nearly twenty API integrations, including product, pricing, promotions, purchases...

They've hired a bunch of data scientists to help create more effective offers, but they're still waiting on the Data Warehouse team: purchasing history from all of the disparate systems, car service histories, their customer loyalty programs, and their branded credit cards. When it's not an executive asking for data for a board presentation, even the simplest data requests take six months, as their requests lumber through the Data Warehouse Dev and QA processes. And like Brent found, the data they get is often malformed, unreadable, incomplete, or, worse, inaccurate.

When Maggie and team complain, the Data Warehouse manager emails everyone a graph showing that they're keeping up with incoming data requests, but that's only because people have given up and stopped asking them for anything.

After the challenges in front of them become clear, Kurt turns to Maxine. "Maggie already has a bunch of development teams assigned to support the Promotions effort, but they clearly need some help. Based on what you've heard, who would you want to take with you to make the biggest difference?" He gestures at everyone around the table. "You have the pick of the entire litter. You can have anyone from the Data Hub Dev and QA teams. Heck, anyone from the Rebellion."

"Pick of the litter. Nice, Kurt," Maxine snorts, trying not to picture their best engineers as if they were a basket of puppies at the Humane Society.

She ticks through the mental list she's been accumulating. "We'll need someone with experience with architecture and decoupling components that are deeply entangled with each other. We'll need someone really good at databases, because we'll probably need to reduce our reliance on the big, centralized Phoenix databases and all those systems of record. We'll need some serious infrastructure skills to support a new deployment and operations model. And because we'll likely be running things in production ourselves again, we'll need people with superb skills in Security and Ops."

She thinks for a minute. "I'd take Cranky Dave, Adam, and Purna on Dev and architecture. Dwayne and Brent on databases, infrastructure, and Ops. Shannon on security and data."

As she calls off people's names, they smile, sitting up straighter. She points at Dwayne and Brent. "I think we'll probably need two or three more people on infrastructure and databases, since we'll probably be spinning up a bunch of new things, probably in the cloud. Can you think of anyone you'd want on the team?"

Dwayne and Brent look at each other. Dwayne says, smiling, "I think we can come up with a short list of awesome engineers."

To Kurt, she says, "I haven't met any of the Promotion developers, so I don't know their skill levels. Ultimately, if we need to make a difference in time for Thanksgiving, we need to get heads-down in the code soon and ensure that all those Promotions teams are productive—either we onboard them onto the platforms we've already built or we build or buy what they need."

She points at Tom. "I'd want to take three or four developers to go native in the Promotions teams. Tom, do you know who you'd pick?"

When he nods, she says to Kurt, "That's twelve people. I have no idea how you're going to convince everyone to let us strip the benches. None of those managers will want to lose their best people."

Kurt looks at Maggie. "We'll have to convince the higher-ups to make a massive investment in speed to achieve your goals. Do you think you can swing that?"

"Hang on a second. You'd all do that for me?" Maggie said, suddenly looking a little suspicious. "What's in it for you?"

Kurt smiles. "Ma'am, you're looking at a renegade group of engineers who want to solve big problems that actually matter to the business. Our attempts to go through the normal channels haven't worked, so here's our chance to work directly with the business instead of through technology middle managers. If we succeed, we get credibility. We'd love your endorsement supporting these new ways of working."

Kurt shrugs, continuing, "If it doesn't work, we all pretend like it never happened and promise not to bug you again."

"You've got a deal," Maggie says after thinking a moment. "And here's the good news. I don't need approval from anyone—it's my call. Sarah is already onboard. It's my belief that the survival of the company depends on this."

Almost on cue, Maggie looks down at her phone, saying, "Hang on a second, it's Sarah," as she taps out a reply. "Uh, she's getting heat from some people because Data Hub was down earlier today, and she wants to know what's going on, who caused the problem, and if we need to make an example of them."

Oh great, Maxine thinks. By working with Maggie, they're falling even deeper into Sarah's orbit.

The next morning, Kurt, Maxine, Kirsten, and Maggie are once again in front of Chris. When Kurt proposes temporarily swarming the Promotions efforts, not surprisingly Chris seems exasperated.

"You want my job, Kurt? Cause you're sure acting like it," he grumbles. But Maggie implores him on the importance of the need for accelerating the work to support the Black Friday holiday promotions and how it could generate very visible and quick wins, and Kirsten reassures him that the other efforts can absorb the temporary reassignments.

Chris furrows his brow. Just like last time, he turns to Maxine. "What do you think, Maxine? Do we really need to do this?"

Maxine studies him, realizing how uncomfortable he is with the constantly changing plans, very different from the static plans that characterized the Phoenix Project.

"Without a doubt, Chris. This is clearly where the company needs developers most. We can't be hamstrung by our org chart or, for that matter, the annual plan we made last year," Maxine says, reassuringly.

He looks at her for another moment, grunts his approval, and again briskly shoos them out of his office.

Maxine and Kurt give each other discrete thumbs-up as they walk out.

Despite Sarah's loud demands to find someone to blame on the temporary Data Hub outage yesterday, Kurt refuses to do anything along those lines. Instead, he gathers everyone in a conference room.

Kurt starts the meeting, saying, "Every time we have an outage, we'll be conducting a blameless post-mortem like this one. The spirit and intent of these sessions are to learn from them, chronicling what happened before memories fade. Prevention requires honesty, and honesty requires the absence of fear. Just like Norm Kerth says in the Agile Prime Directive, 'Regardless of what we discover, we understand and truly believe that everyone did the best job they could, given what they knew at the time, their skills and abilities, the resources available, and the situation at hand.'

"Let's first start by assembling a timeline and gathering details on what happened. To help with the process, Maxine pulled together our production telemetry and logs, as well as our chat rooms, just to provide a framework for discussion. The goal is to enable the people closest to the problem to share what they saw, so we can make our systems safer. The only rule is that you can't say 'I should have done X' or 'If I had known about that, I would have done Y.' Hindsight is always perfect. In crises, we never actually know what's reallyl going on, and we need to prepare for a future where we have an equally imperfect understanding of the world."

He looks over at Maxine, indicating for her to proceed. Maxine is impressed and wonders briefly if Kurt has been coached by Erik before this meeting. If so, she's glad. But despite Kurt's strenuous declaration that people shouldn't be afraid to talk, everyone seems reticent to react... even the members of the Rebellion. Given the ever-growing culture of fear and blame, Maxine has been prepared to model the behaviors you'd see where there's real psychological safety—Erik's Fourth Ideal.

But before Maxine can start, Brent blurts out, "I'm so sorry, everyone. It was all my fault. I can't believe I missed the database connection string. I never make that type of mistake, but I was in such a hurry..."

Brent looks so distraught, as if he'd been wanting to make this confession for days. Kurt puts his hand on Brent's shoulder and says, "Brent, let's go back to the Agile Prime Directive. No one is at fault. Everyone did the best they could, given what they knew. Let's just stick with assembling the timeline. Maxine, please lead the way."

"My pleasure," Maxine says, winking at Brent, projecting her laptop on the TV. "I'm choosing to start our timeline at 6:37 p.m., which is after Tom initiated the deployment, after all the tests passed but the app failed to start. The health indicators went red, and Tom was the first to notice. Tom, what exactly did you see?"

"I was watching the logs scroll by in the deployment tool, and I saw the startup messages, as you'd expect, and then I saw a bunch of error messages and a stack trace," he says, his face darkening, reliving the crisis.

"Got it," she says, adding to her notes that everyone can see on the TV in the front of the room. "What happened next? I remember feeling almost borderline panic, because despite all our preparation, we were clearly in uncharted waters." With a wry smile, she adds, "Umm, that's code for 'I was so scared I was crapping in my pants.'"

People around the table laugh, and Tom says, "Yeah, me too. I've spent decades looking at stack traces, but I've never seen them in our deployment tool. I couldn't stop the window from scrolling on me, and I couldn't see anything long enough to read it."

Maxine had no idea, because Tom had seemed so calm and was so effective at making sense of the logs. She is typing when Tom says, "You know, I should have rehearsed looking at logs in this new tool."

"I totally get that, and I've been there…and it totally sucks to feel that way," Kurt responds. "But remember, we're doing this so that we can be better prepared for the next crisis, when we will be equally ignorant of entirely new things that are just as important and will be just as obvious in hindsight…This is great stuff, Tom. Keep going. What happened next?"

Over the next hour, Maxine and the group assemble an amazingly detailed and vivid timeline of what actually happened. Once again, she marvels that anything can run in production at all given all the imperfections and sharp edges present in their daily work. Log files scrolling by too fast to read, configuration settings scattered across scores of locations, potential failure points hiding in almost every nook and cranny, surprises lurking around every corner...*Given all this, it's amazing that Data Hub has worked mostly without incident for over a decade*, she thinks.

Maxine is certain that everyone has learned something about how Data Hub actually works, in stark contrast with their mental models of how they *thought* it works. She records a list of five things people will change right away that will likely prevent future outages and will certainly make fixing certain problems faster in the future.

As they adjourn, Maxine smiles and says to Kurt, "Nice job running the meeting." She means it. It was a pitch-perfect example of improving daily work and fostering a culture of psychological safety, as Erik described in the Third and Fourth Ideals.

Reflecting on the meeting, Maxine now appreciates how tenuous and fleeting the conditions that enable psychological safety can be. It depends on the behavior of leaders, one's peers, their moods, their sense of self-worth, wounds from their pasts...*Given all this, it's amazing that psychological safety can be created at all*, she thinks.

Later that day, Kurt, Maxine, and the rest of the newly selected team are gathered in a conference room to meet with Maggie and the rest of the Promotions team leads.

During introductions, Maxine notes that most of the twenty people in the existing Promotions team are front-end developers—they own the mobile application, the product landing pages for the e-commerce site, in-store applications, and all the applications that Marketing staff use to manage the product promotions lifecycle.

Maggie is presenting. "Thank you to Kurt, Maxine, and the rest of the engineers from the Data Hub team who have volunteered to help us achieve some badly needed near-term wins. I put together some slides to frame some of the higher-level business outcomes that this team was created to make happen.

"Our market share is declining, primarily because we have little presence in the e-commerce market, the fastest growing part of the broader market," she says. "This is where our competitors and the e-commerce giants are taking share from us. The good news is that we have fiercely loyal customers…the bad news is that the average age of our customer base continues to increase. Our competitors are clearly winning younger customers, a real market segment, despite declining car ownership because of the rise of ride-sharing, such as Uber and Lyft. But the number of car-miles driven per year keep growing, although who's doing the driving is definitely changing. But without doubt, demand for car maintenance should grow, not shrink."

Maggie continues, "For our loyal customers, we know what they buy and how frequently they buy it. We're focused on enabling personalization and knowledge of current inventory to drive promotion. Until recently, we've never been able to use this information to create compelling offers for them.

"We know from our customer research that our core market uses mobile phone apps extensively—in fact," she points to the projected slide, "here is a picture of Tomas, a customer we interviewed during our market research. He's a fifty-two-year-old public school teacher. For decades, he's done all his own car maintenance. It's something he did with his dad and now it's something he does with his two teenage daughters and son. He wants his kids to focus on STEM, but he insists that they understand mechanical basics and learn self-reliance.

"He also maintains his wife's car, and when he has time, his parents' cars too," Maggie says. "Tomas doesn't consider himself to be very technical, but he has six computers at home that he supports for his entire family.

"Right now, he uses a spiral notebook and these file folders to keep records for each car he maintains. He uses his mobile phone all the time, primarily for messaging but also Amazon. He would love to have more of the maintenance routine codified. He loves using Parts Unlimited, but he says he would far rather look in the app for parts rather than having to call the store. He says he likes the in-store employees and knows many of them by name, but complains about our terrible automated phone system and hates having to listen for which button to push to get to a real person."

Maxine laughs. No one likes those things.

"For the Thanksgiving and Christmas season, we want to find inventory that we have too much of, combine it with our personalization data, create compelling promotions, and deliver them through our e-commerce site, email, and our mobile apps. We want to drive real revenue through these promotions and increase the average monthly usage of the app to prove that we're actually building something that they value.

"The Phoenix teams have already identified all the needed interfaces to all the various systems where this data is stored: the customer and orders database, the POS transactions, fulfillment systems, the e-commerce website, and the ad campaign data from the Marketing team.

"One of the most critical sources of data is the in-store inventory systems. We want to promote overstocked items, but we've got to be very careful that we don't promote items that we don't have on hand in that region.

"We finally rolled out a customer relationship management or CRM system a couple of years ago. But as I described last night, connecting data about the customers, such as which automobiles they own and some demographic information, with the vast wealth of other data we have is a real struggle.

"You can see what we're trying to achieve, right? If only we had a single view of the customer: top of funnel, bottom of funnel, as well as their complete history with the company. Not only what they purchased, but also what they did on our site, what they browsed, searched for, their credit card transactions, repair history... There's so much potential!

"If we could combine all this information, we would know so much about what they need, and we'd be so much better able to help them," she says, almost wistfully.

Maxine nods, impressed. She says, "After analyzing even the small amount of data that we've been able to combine, we've built some customer profiles based on their behavior. The archetypes we've created so far are: Racing Enthusiast, Frugal Maintainer, Meticulous Maintainer, Catastrophic Late Maintainer, and Happy Hobbyist."

"For now, we are focusing on the Meticulous Maintainers and the Catastrophic Late Maintainers, because we think these groups have the highest probability of buying for the types of campaigns we're thinking of," Maggie says. "We know the Meticulous Maintainers purchase things like oil change products every month without fail. On the other hand, the purchase history of Catastrophic Late Maintainers suggests that they are constantly accumulating more expensive tools and engine parts, just needing a nudge to complete their work.

"On the screen, you can see a bunch of hypotheses we have. These are offers we think will be a big hit with these customer segments. And this report shows the attributes of customers that we're at risk of losing entirely," Maggie says. "The problem is that executing on any of these ideas requires months. Anytime we want to do something, we've got to make a million changes across all of Phoenix. Phoenix has been rolling for three years, and we haven't made one targeted promotion yet. And if we can't experiment, we can't learn!"

"You haven't been able to execute even one of these promotion ideas?" Maxine asks, surprised. "How is that possible?!"

Maxine hears grumbles from around the room from the Promotions team. They start describing why.

"We're still waiting for access to all those back-end systems. The only one we have access to is the inventory management system," someone complains. "We already have all the data from the TOFU—top of the funnel. We need information about the customer lifetime value from BOFU—bottom of the funnel."

"The integration teams take six to nine months to create any new integration for us," says someone else.

"When we do query the inventory management systems, they often shut us down because of the CPU load we generate or the amount of data we copy," says a third person.

"The APIs from many of the back-end systems don't deliver the data we need. We've been waiting for months for those teams to implement the necessary API changes."

"We're still waiting for correct data from the Data Warehouse team, because their reports are always wrong. Last time we found people's last names in the zip code field."

"We're still waiting on getting new database instances created for us." And on and on.

There were twenty developers on the Promotions team, with a ton of good ideas that could deliver on so many of the Phoenix promises, but they were all bottlenecked on the back-end systems.

Suddenly, Maxine is very sure that they can help. But another part of her is aghast at how helpless these developers have been, unable to complete their work.

Maxine and the rest of the engineers from the Data Hub team smile at each other. Seeing this, Kurt folds his hands in front of himself, smiling. "I think we can help."

After nearly ninety minutes of excited discussion and brainstorming, everyone adjourns. Maggie takes Kurt and Maxine aside. "That was amazing. We've been crying out for help for so long, but this was the first time that we've been able to engage like this with anyone."

"Well, we haven't done anything yet," Kurt says. "But hopefully by the end of next week, we'll have something that we can point to as progress."

Maxine nods emphatically. She looks at Maggie for several moments and then asks the question she's been wanting to ask since last night. "Just what does it take to build great products? And how can we as developers help?"

"Where do I start?" Maggie says. "It usually begins with understanding who our customers are, both current and desired. Then we typically segment the customer base, so we know what set of problems each faces. Once we know that, we can understand which of those problems we want to solve, based on market size, ease of reaching them, and so forth. Once we know that, we think about pricing and packaging, offer development, and more strategic issues, such as the overall profitability of the product portfolio and how it affects the achievement of strategic goals.

"I need each of my product managers to be able to live in this domain," Maggie continues. "Almost all great product organizations create customer personas so that everyone can better understand and relate to the people who you're building products for. That's the reason behind so much of the UX and ethnographic research we do. For these personas, we articulate their goals and aspirations, figure out what causes problems for them during a typical day, and describe how they do their daily work. If we do things well, we end up building a set of user stories, framed inside of the business outcomes we want. We should be testing and validating all these assumptions in the marketplace and learning all the time."

Maxine says, "I love this relentless focus on understanding the customer—it reminds me of the Fifth Ideal."

Maggie looks at her quizzically.

"I'll explain later," Maxine says.

"You know, if you're that interested in the customer, you could do the same in-store training that all employees and managers do. Two weeks ago, all the new sales managers flew here to headquarters to spend a week with our local store. You missed that, but if you want, there's a new employee training happening on Saturday. Want to join them?" Maggie asks.

Maxine's jaw drops. She's always been envious of people who have been able to do this program, and Maggie just offered her the chance to take part in it. "Holy cow, I'd love to. Frankly, I'm a little bummed that I've been here for almost seven years and have never been offered this."

"I require all my product owners and everyone at the manager level and above to go through it," Maggie says. "I'd be happy to get it arranged."

"Sign me up!"

It's Saturday morning. Maxine is in front of the bathroom mirror making sure her "Hello, My Name Is Maxine: How Can I Help?" name tag is straight.

She's very excited to finally take part in this program. Famously at Parts Unlimited, every leader at the director-level or higher must work in the stores as a front-line employee twice a year. Not as a high-falutin' store manager, but as a regular employee behind the register or out on the floor. This is something that Parts Unlimited has been doing since they opened in 1914.

Maxine quickly says goodbye to her family, who are lounging in the living room on various forms of technology, and dashes to her car. She doesn't want to be late for her first day of in-store training. Maxine is a stickler for punctuality and expects that the store manager she'll be reporting to is likely the same way.

The previous evening, she spent three hours watching YouTube videos on home car maintenance with her kids. She's relieved that changing the oil on a 1984 Toyota Tercel is exactly the same as it was twenty years ago. An oil change is an oil change since the invention of the internal combustion engine. Even now, Maxine still refills the windshield wiper fluid in her family's cars, refusing to pay someone to do it for her. However, it's been decades since she's changed her own oil or transmission fluid.

When Maxine walks into the store, she immediately feels out of place. She sees four young men and one woman, all in their twenties, and an older man in his forties.

Mildly irritated that she's not the first person here, she joins the semi-circle facing the store manager, Matt. Maxine recognizes him from having been in the store before. He's in his early thirties and looks almost like a drill sergeant. He glances at his watch and gives Maxine a small nod and smile of recognition.

"Good morning. I'm Matt, the store manager. I'm here to help orient all of you, our new employees, who will be working at either this store or one of the four stores within a sixty-mile radius. You're all lucky; since Elk Grove is where our corporate headquarters is, there are some store amenities here that none of the other nearly one thousand stores have.

"Parts Unlimited was started in 1914, and we still pride ourselves on being the very best at catering to the needs of the home mechanic. We don't sell luxury items to the rich and famous. We serve the needs of people like us, who depend on our cars to get to work every day, to drive our kids to school, who need reliable transportation to go about our daily lives.

"At our stores, we aim to provide our customers the parts they need to keep their car running. Often, we are all that exists between a working car and a very expensive trip to the garage or service station that ties up their car for days. Our job is to help them avoid that fate."

Maxine has goosebumps. She is struck by how consistently Matt communicates the company vision. It could be Steve delivering these lines from the Town Hall. It's so great to hear this from the store managers. It's very different from hearing executives or plant managers say it, because it's here on the front lines where it matters most.

"Over the next two days, I'll be showing you the duties of working at a Parts Unlimited store and all the tools you need to become experts at helping our customers," Matt says. "And there is a test at the end, so pay attention—nearly one-quarter of the people who go through this training do not pass their first time. So to help you keep notes and prepare for the exam, here's a set of Parts Unlimited manuals and notebooks and pens so you can take notes. There is a prize for the highest score."

She looks around at her fellow students, resisting the urge to view them as the competition. *They're just kids,* she thinks.

Matt begins a tour of the store floor, describing the broad categories of items and why they stock them. He points to a rack of large, thick books. "These are the books that you'll use to help your customers." They look like the huge phone books Maxine grew up with, four inches thick with razor thin newsprint paper.

"Your customers will often come in looking for a replacement part or with a problem that you need to diagnose," Matt explains. "Your job is to help them find what they need. If we have it in stock, you will sell it to them. If we don't have it in stock, you will do what it takes to find one of our stores that does stock it. We have a website that anyone can use, but it's very difficult to actually source the parts you need. The best way to find the answers are in these books."

Maxine looks dubiously at the row of books. She hates the idea of technology being beaten by a pile of books and makes a note to find out what makes the current application so cumbersome to use.

"It is very important that you get this part right," he says. "If you sell someone the wrong brake pads, they may find out only after they've jacked up their car, taken all the wheels off, and struggled to figure out why the parts won't fit. Or worse, they find out when they are trying to slow down on a highway or after they've crashed into a tree.

"We think of ourselves like doctors," Matt continues. "We do not want to hurt our customers. And the best way to avoid doing that is by making sure we get them the right parts the first time. We do that through these books."

Matt picks one up and asks everyone to do the same. "You have a customer that has a 2010 Toyota Tacoma, and he needs floor mats for the back seat. What part number should we sell them?"

Maxine reluctantly picks up one of the books. *In this century*, she thinks, *in a modern commercial enterprise, we still rely on looking up things in a paper book? This is like using a card catalog at the library.* Which, she remembers, her kids have never heard of.

She flips through the book. It's organized alphabetically by make, then model, and then by year. She flips three-quarters through, jumping to the Toyotas, the Tacomas, and then 2010.

She groans at what she sees. Even for the 2010 model year, there's table after table of all different configurations. Number of engine cylinders, size of engine, standard cab, extended cab, short wheelbase, long wheelbase...and for variation, there are a bunch of parts.

One of the younger men says, "Depends on what configuration the truck is. What kind of cab is it?"

"Exactly," Matt says, smiling. "Finding the right part is based on a number of factors. And often, the customer won't know. When that happens, you walk out to their car with them and help them find the information. The fastest way is to record all the information on this little sheet." He holds up a piece of paper. "This helps ensure you only have to go out to their car once."

"Yes, Maxine?" Matt says when Maxine raises her hand.

"Isn't there a way to use the computer to find out this information?" she asks, not wanting to give away that she already works for Parts Unlimited.

Matt chortles. "Trust me, this is so much easier. After I show you how to do this on paper, we'll use the computer systems and you'll see why we recommend everyone just do it by hand."

This is embarrassing, she thinks. *We go through all the trouble of building these systems to serve our employees, but what we generate for them is so inadequate that they still use antiquated paper systems.*

By the end of the day, Maxine is exhausted. She's learned far more about car maintenance and diagnosis than she expected. She had no idea how much time the in-store employees spend helping customers figure out why cars won't start or what the strange noises coming from their engines mean.

Accurately diagnosing the problem is important, because they can help the customer avoid going to a service station. There are many examples of service stations taking advantage of their customers, charging for work they don't need.

Helping their customers fix problems themselves often saves them thousands of dollars. On the other hand, employees also need to know which problems are way beyond the scope of do-it-yourselfers, such as when there is actual damage to an engine or when the problem involves the electronic engine management systems.

But Maxine is also exhausted from seeing the constant inadequacies of the computer systems supporting in-store employees. Matt was right— using the system was a nightmare. Once you knew the VIN and the part you needed, looking up certain out-of-stock parts required using a 3270 terminal session and keying in commands. This is the famous "green screen" mainframe interface, which most people have seen but few have used.

Maxine is always in awe when she sees the best airline gate agents use systems like this for making complex flight changes at the airport. Someone needs to book a flight to Boston, because their flight was canceled, but needs contiguous seats for their family, but doesn't want to incur a change fee. An experienced agent will rapidly type out all the keystrokes required to find what options are available, running circles around another agent using the "modern graphical user interface."

There's no question that with practice some of these in-store applications are extremely efficient. After all, Maxine loves the SPSS statistics package that was born during the mainframe era, battle-tested for decades, so she can run circles around people using the more modern tools, such as Jupyter notebooks, Python, R, and Tableau. But despite her evangelizing and objective evidence of superiority, people find SPSS alien and strange.

That's why Maxine knows that some of these in-store systems prolong the period required for employees and managers to learn how to effectively manage a Parts Unlimited store. And she knows people on many mainframe teams want to improve their UX but have been denied budget for years.

The process of ordering out-of-stock parts is even worse. You pull up inventory reports from other stores, which are months old. Then you need to pick up the phone and call each store to verify that they have a certain part, reciting eleven-digit product codes.

If the part is in stock, the person on the other end of the phone keys in a parts transfer order into the system. The easiest part in the entire process is carrying the part to the loading dock, where it will be picked up by a delivery truck and delivered in the next day or two.

When she couldn't take it anymore, she asks Matt, "If you could have a system that, you know, looked like Amazon to do parts lookups and execute transfer orders, would that be useful to you?"

Matt immediately answered, "Oh, my gosh, yes. I don't *actually* want my employees spending twenty minutes looking things up in books or talking to other store employees by phone. I want them in front of our customers. In our regional operations meetings, we've complained endlessly about it for years, but corporate keeps saying they're working on it. It would be a gamechanger for us. We'd have faster service, happier customers, and the right parts in-stock more often."

He points at the counter behind the register. "Inside those cabinets are racks of tablets that corporate deployed to the stores. Trouble is, all the apps make you fill out so many fields that they're even harder to use than the computers. At least the computers have real keyboards. No one has used a tablet in months."

In her head, Maxine does a silent face-palm. Clearly, not enough technologists are spending time in the stores observing the outcomes of the products they create.

After she gets home, she plays with their *second* new puppy, Marshmallow, a dog disguised as a big, cute, white ball of fluff. Incredibly, it was Jake's idea, and Maxine couldn't believe that they drove two hours yesterday to pick him up with their kids.

After the kids disappear into their rooms and her husband insists on taking the two dogs for a walk, Maxine takes out her laptop and spends an hour typing up a trip report. She lists all her observations divided by area of the store employee's daily work and applications they have to interact with. It's nearly twelve pages by the time she's done.

She's always been a prolific notetaker. She remembers reading somewhere, "In order to speak clearly, you need to be able to think clearly. And to think clearly, you usually need to be able to write it clearly." Which is why she takes the time to write out the document, so that people can understand what she observed. She objectively describes what she observed, often attaching pictures she took with her phone, and in other places she makes recommendations.

Before Parts Unlimited, Maxine worked for a CEO who actually wrote white papers himself, which were widely read among their customers and employees. She once asked why he bothered to spend time writing when he had Marketing staff to do things like that.

He said he thought it was important to think through problems clearly, and for him, writing things down enforced a logical rigor that he thought was very important for leaders to have. "How can you send a company down a strategic path when you haven't thought through what all the implications are?"

That left a lasting impression on Maxine. Ever since then, especially as she has become more senior, she makes sure that she takes the time to write things out, which also enables her to more broadly influence things.

She knows some things that she observed yesterday don't belong in her head. They need to be in front of the people whose daily work it is to write and maintain the applications that the in-store employees rely on.

When she finishes her draft an hour later, she closes her laptop. She knows everyone won't read her document, which means she'll have to give a presentation on it. Luckily, she took lots of pictures today, but far fewer than she normally would have—none of the other trainees were taking any and she didn't want to stand out.

She quickly sends a note to Kurt and Maggie in a chat room:

> Here's my Day 1 trip report. I'm seeing tons of things I can't unsee. Lots of easy things we can address that will help advance Promotions' goals.
>
> I'm attaching my unedited report. Kurt, can you join me in training tomorrow? There's a bunch of things that we could help with, even if it's not right away.

The next morning, Maxine takes the shirt she was wearing yesterday out of the dryer, cursing when she realizes she's going to need to iron it. *There's no way I'm showing up in a wrinkled shirt*, she thinks.

She shows up at the store fifteen minutes early, just as she likes it. To her delight, Kurt says he'll be able to make it later in the morning.

When the other trainees arrive, they all follow Matt to the service garage. There has been a multi-year pilot to outfit some of their larger stores with these garages. They've been an incredible hit with customers.

This morning's training was diagnosing car batteries. One of the top reasons customers come to the stores is because their cars won't start.

"This is just an introduction to the basics. You won't be able to do this solo until you work with someone who's already been trained and certified." They stand next to a fifteen-year-old Honda Accord with a technician wearing a Parts Unlimited coverall uniform working on attaching cables to the battery and connected to a stack of instruments.

Matt explains the steps as the technician works. "And now she enters the data into the computer, which we use to generate a diagnostic report for the customer." Maxine watches with interest as Matt continues his explanation, occasionally asking the technician questions about the work she is doing.

Kurt walks into the service bay while they're watching the technician work. He's wearing a Parts Unlimited uniform just like her, complete with a "Hi, My Name Is Kurt" name tag. His shirt is slightly wrinkled. He must have been in a hurry this morning because he's typically pretty fastidious.

Kurt stands next to Maxine, and Matt nods at him and smiles.

Maxine watches the technician work. After a minute, she can't help asking, "Why do we have to enter so much data? If this person is a repeat customer, do we still have to type all of this in?" Maxine tries to sound as much like her peers as possible. This is their onboarding experience that she is intruding upon, and she doesn't want to do anything that will detract from it.

Matt laughs, turning to the technician, "How much rekeying of information do you have to do for each diagnostic?"

The technician, wearing a "Hi, My Name Is Emily" name tag, shakes her head. "It feels like a lot. Typing the customer address takes time, but the Vehicle ID Numbers are the worst. They're seventeen characters and very easy to mistype. And I still have to put in the make, model, and year. In most of our other systems, all that is filled in for us from the VIN. Some people around here just put garbage into the VIN fields, but that doesn't seem right to me."

"I still don't get it. Why do we have to type in so much information?" the youngest trainee asks.

"Corporate wants us to," Matt says, eliciting laughs from the trainees. Even the twenty-somethings seem world-weary, as if they've already dealt with back-office bureaucrats.

They have no idea what being trapped in a real corporate bureaucracy is like, Maxine thinks, recalling her ordeal in the Phoenix prison.

"Seriously, though," Matt continues, "we want this information because the company is working on customer profiles. Someday, when a customer walks into a store, we'll know who they are, what cars they own, what the makes and models are…so that eventually we won't have to rekey that information. I know there's an initiative, years in the making, to get portable scanners in here so that we can just scan the VINs."

Maxine sees Kurt purse his lips in frustration, even though he's been here less than five minutes. *Good,* Maxine thinks. *Now I'm not the only one who is frustrated.* She has confidence Kurt will translate that frustration into action, somewhere, somehow.

Maxine peers at the computer in the diagnostic rack. It's some sort of desktop PC attached to an LCD screen, as well as some sort of peripheral bay that has USB and serial ports and some other attachment that she doesn't recognize.

She hears Matt say, "When you've got customers coming in repeatedly for battery problems, it's probably because they're not driving the car frequently, letting the battery charge drop below the levels needed to start it." He continues, "When you see this, recommend getting a car battery charger that can keep those batteries topped off. I love mine, and since I've had it, I've never had to jump-start any of my cars. We have a bunch of different types, from twenty-five to a hundred dollars. I bought this forty-nine dollar model."

Maxine notes how Matt has repeatedly linked the customer symptoms with car parts that they likely need. She sees why certain store managers outperform others, not just in customer satisfaction, employee productivity, and retention, but also with the best sales per square foot. Matt is teaching all these desired behaviors to the new employees.

"It would be great if the computer systems could tell us who's purchased multiple batteries so that we could proactively make that recommendation," Kurt adds.

"That would be terrific," Matt says. Turning to include the trainees in the discussion, he continues, "As you know, we don't pay sales commissions, because we've found that this sometimes leads people to do things that aren't in the best interest of our customers. But everyone gets a handsome bonus if we exceed our sales targets, and that will naturally happen if we all do what's right for them.

"So now you know something about battery inspection, which results in this report that you'll give the customer," Matt says, showing a seven-page report.

As her second training day winds down, Maxine thinks about the hardships the in-store employees face when using the systems they've built. Instead of feeling discouraged, Maxine is inspired. Fixing these problems will make the jobs of in-store employees easier, who will then be able to better keep their customers' cars running.

Throughout the weekend, Maxine had also been getting a steady stream of updates from the rest of the Rebellion. They've been working furiously to help the Promotions teams get the data they need for the big, upcoming Black Friday holiday campaign. But they're starting to encounter challenges, including conflicting definitions of data across all the enterprise silos, tough choices about what database technologies would best support the Promotions effort, and lots of unanticipated problems now that they're working directly with the data scientists and analysts.

Maxine is looking forward to seeing everyone tomorrow and seeing everything up close and personal. There are so many exciting things to do!

PART THREE

November 10–Present

CHAPTER 14

On Monday morning, Maxine is startled. The team has exceeded her expectations once again. They are all gathered in a conference room to quickly review status and talk about areas where they need help.

"Before we start, there's something I think we need to do," Maggie says. "We really need a code name for this effort. If we're working toward something big, we need to have a name. The more we accomplish, the more we're going to have to talk about what we're doing, and we can't keep referring to ourselves as the Rebellion."

"What's wrong with Promotions?" someone asks.

"Well, that's the name of the team," she responds. "But the team has changed so much since our friends from Data Hub have joined, and there are so many new initiatives we've started. I think we need a new name because the way we're working is so different than before."

The ideas start flying fast and furious. Serious names are proposed: Ulysses, Phaethon, Iliad...and names from the US space program: Mercury, Apollo, Gemini...

"They're so serious, and they sound too much like Phoenix," Shannon says. "I wouldn't want anyone to think there's any similarity between what we're doing and the way the Phoenix Project turned out."

"Totally," Brent says. "It wouldn't bother me at all if we salted the ground to make sure no program is ever named 'Phoenix' again."

"How about from movies? Like *Kill Bill*, *Blade Runner*, *Star Wars?*" suggests Shannon. Others propose names of music bands, Pokémons, board games, weapons from Dungeons and Dragons...

"How about the Unicorn Project?" suggests Dwayne, obviously half-joking. "That's pretty distinctive."

Maxine laughs out loud. She loves it. The term "unicorn" is often used to reference high-flying tech startups and the FAANGs that Erik talked about—the Facebooks, Amazons, Apples, Netflixes, and Googles of the world. Parts Unlimited is a century-old horse, but they are out to prove that they can do everything the unicorns can, with the right culture, technical practices, and architectures to support them. In fact, what is a unicorn besides a horse with a horn and painted up with some fancy rainbow colors?

And in our case, Maxine thinks, *our competition is not the FAANGs— it's the other horses in our industry and tiny little software startups that are encroaching on our market.* Startups have lots of ability to do things, she knows from personal experience, but they're always lacking the resources to do them.

This is not a story about small beating large; it's fast beats slow. What the past couple of months have decisively proven to her is that greatness can be stifled, but it can also be restored.

"I love it," Maxine says. "Can you imagine Steve saying 'unicorn' during every Town Hall? Let's do it."

Everyone laughs. Dwayne says, "Umm, are you sure this will fly? Do we need to get approval for this?"

Maxine laughs out loud. "Approval? Since when do you feel like you need approvals from anyone? No, this is up to us. Yeah, the Unicorn Project," Maxine tries it on for size. "Let's do it."

They decide that the Unicorn Project is the new name for the customized recommendation and promotion capabilities that, among many other things, will power the Black Friday and holiday promotion campaigns, and hopefully many more in the future. Orca is the name for the analytics and data science teams who will be working alongside and supporting the Unicorn promotion efforts. And Narwhal is the new database and API gateway platform that is being created that Unicorn will use. Unikitty is the name of the continuous integration and deployment platform being used by the Data Hub team, and some other carefully chosen teams in Phoenix.

Maxine is pleased. In hindsight, giving the team a unique name is probably long overdue. She's always loved the Tuckman phases of teams, going through form, storm, norm, and perform. She's ready to start norming and performing!

And team names help create an identity for the entire group, not just for individuals, and they reinforce the notion that team goals are more important than individual goals.

"You know, I'm also going to have say 'unicorn' in front of everybody," grouses Maggie. But Maxine suspects that Maggie is secretly pleased.

Later that morning, Maxine is back in the auditorium for the bi-monthly Town Hall, her second since her exile, and the first since the disastrous release a month ago. She is especially interested to see how Steve will address that topic. Maggie told the team that she'll be presenting one slide to the entire company about their hopes and aspirations for the Black Friday campaign.

Just like the last time, Maxine grabs a seat as close to the stage as possible. But this time, she's surrounded by her teammates. Kurt is sitting in the row behind her, and she is excited to see Maggie backstage being wired up with a microphone.

At exactly nine, Steve comes on stage and welcomes everyone to his sixty-seventh Town Hall. He promises to talk about vision and mission, as well as annual goals. He says, "I also want to take some time to address all the problems associated with the Phoenix rollout and our hopes for the upcoming Black Friday campaigns."

As he has in every previous Town Hall, he talks passionately about the Parts Unlimited mission to help hard-working customers keep their cars running so they can conduct their daily lives. After spending an entire weekend working with the in-store manager and new frontline staff, Maxine has gained a tremendous appreciation for how Steve's relentless repetition of these organizational goals are reflected in the daily work of so many people at the company.

"Our business is one that depends on operational excellence and superb service. We make a simple promise to customers: that we will provide parts and services that help keep their cars running. When we released Phoenix into production, we let everyone down. We let our customers down, we let our employees down, and we let our investors down.

"We made promises to customers that we couldn't keep. Merchandise we offered them wasn't in stock or couldn't be purchased, and we even accidentally disclosed hundreds of credit card numbers. We've given away millions of dollars in vouchers to customers we let down, but we can't buy back the trust we lost.

"And it's not just our customers. Many of our critical internal systems were down, preventing thousands of employees from doing their daily work. As CEO of the company, I take responsibility for this.

"I want to recognize everyone in this room who did absolutely everything they could to help fulfill our obligations to our customers. Many of you know that for the last two months, I've also been acting as the head of technology," he says. "Don't laugh, because as you know, I need a lot of help with anything technology-related. And I want to acknowledge all the amazing things that the technology teams did.

"Since then, I've been working with Chris Allers, VP of R&D, and Bill Palmer, VP of IT Operations, to do some radically different things. Among them was the thirty-day feature freeze. Everyone in technology worked on fixing problems and paying down technical debt.

"For those of you not in technology, 'technical debt' is what creates hardship, toil, and reduces the agility of our software engineers," he continues. "It's like a spreadsheet that's grown over years to the point that you can't change it anymore without breaking formulas or introducing errors. But technical debt affects us at a much vaster scale, involving systems that run the most complex processes in the company.

"I've been hearing from people across the organization that this was badly needed," he says. "Just like in manufacturing, where I come from, it's important to have a sustainable work pace and to limit our work in process to make sure that work keeps moving through the plant. And that's what we're doing here.

"This quarter is make or break. We promised the world that we'd get Phoenix out in September, but because of all the features we delayed, we're not getting the sales benefits that we hoped for. Now we're well into the quarter, with the holiday buying season right ahead of us. We are out of time.

"Here to talk about what we've learned is Maggie Lee, our senior director of retail product marketing," he says. "Come on out, Maggie."

Maggie looks as nervous as Maxine has ever seen her, but most people would never notice. Maggie says, "As you know, Phoenix has always been about helping customers buy high-quality parts they need from us faster, easier, and cheaper. Over the years, we've built the groundwork to make that happen, but we haven't been able to activate those capabilities...yet.

"Thanks to Steve, Chris, and Bill, I've had the privilege of working with a team made up of a cross-section of the entire company, including Finance and Accounting, Marketing, Promotions, Retail Operations, and of course, an incredible technology group to figure out how we can deliver a small but extremely important set of Phoenix goals. We want to generate great customer recommendations and enable the Promotions team to sell profitable products that we have in inventory," she says. "We have years of customer purchasing data, and because of our branded credit cards, we know our customer demographics and preferences. If we can get those promotions to the customer, we think we can make a real difference to the company and create incredible value for our customers.

"And that's why I'm excited to introduce the Unicorn Project," she says, smiling as everyone in the audience laughs at the whimsical name. "I'd like to recognize Kurt Reznick and Maxine Chambers who approached me a short time ago with a radical idea to make this happen, along with a group of engineers who wanted to help. We have all been working with the support of the entire Phoenix Project, toward the goal of having incredibly effective campaigns in support of Black Friday, one of the highest selling seasons of the year. Our goal is to break all the records and make it the top selling day in company history."

Maggie continues, "We will be conducting a series of tests over the next two weeks to ensure that things go right when we launch the campaign to millions of customers on Black Friday," she says. "Thank you and wish us luck," Maggie smiles, waving to everyone and shaking Steve's hand before exiting the stage.

"Thank you, Maggie," he says. "There are some who say this won't work, including some people who championed the Phoenix Project for many years. But Maggie and her team have made me a believer. In my career, I've found that whenever you have a team of people who are passionately committed to achieving a mission and who have the right skills and abilities, it's dangerous to bet against them, because they'll move heaven and earth to make it happen. So...good luck to the Unicorn Project!"

Maxine cheers and whistles loudly. She also notes Steve's oblique reference to Sarah and her absence today. She looks around and confirms that she is nowhere to be seen, wondering whether that's good news or bad news.

For the next couple days, the team is entirely focused on the work required to generate winning promotions by Black Friday. Everyone is buried with urgent work. Maxine again brings up with Kurt the need for more experienced people to help.

"I'm way ahead of you," he says. "I got Chris to bring in William from his leave of absence and I'm bringing him over to help the Unikitty team."

"No way," Maxine says, incredulous. She laughs, thinking about how Chris probably reacted. "How'd you manage to get him back from his indefinite leave of absence?"

Kurt laughs. "Let's just say I called in every favor built up over years of doing good. I had them all lobby Chris to bring back William. There's no better person to help us get these environments working. It also feels great that he's back from his unjust exile."

Maxine heartily agrees and is again impressed with Kurt's ability to deliver the things that the teams need, able to navigate the organization in a way very different than the official org chart would suggest.

Meanwhile, the Narwhal team is trying to figure out a workable API gateway and database solution given all the things the various teams need. The stakes are very high. The amount of data they'll be dealing with is huge, and the consequences of it not working would be disastrous.

This is an ambitious undertaking, but one that dazzles Maxine. Narwhal will shield everyone from almost all the API problems that Cranky Dave had complained so much about, often without any need to change the back-end systems. It will serve as a central place where developers can easily access the data they need and easily find other company data that might be able to help solve their business problems, often from distant silos. And Shannon has been helping ensure that Narwhal will keep all this data secure, enforcing policies around authentication and PII anonymization.

A major part of Narwhal is that it will often store copies of the major company systems of record—anytime that the back-end systems are too slow, too difficult to change, or too expensive to actually conduct all the transactions they need.

"We've got to make a decision," Dwayne says in a big meeting that he pulls together late Wednesday afternoon. To Maxine he says, "Believe it or not, all of us are strongly in favor of a pure NoSQL solution. We think it's the fastest way to get all the data we need into a place that we control and satisfy the performance needs of the Unicorn team.

"Brent and the team have two NoSQL clusters running, one for Test and one that we could use for Production," Dwayne says. "And data ETL process...uhh extract, transform, and load...is going better than we thought. We have an extended team cobbling together a bunch of technologies to copy data from nearly twenty different systems of record into our database, using a combination of commercial and homegrown tools. The good news is that it's going faster and more quickly than we thought…

"But here's our conundrum," he says. "We were planning to keep all the data in both NoSQL and MySQL databases, just in case the NoSQL option blows up. But after the ETL experiences and some large-scale tests, we think we should 'burn the ships' and go pure NoSQL. Supporting two back-end databases is going to slow us down, and we won't get any of the productivity advantages we were aiming for."

"Whoa," she says, surprised. This was a much more daring approach than Maxine expected. In fact, it was probably decisions like this that caused people to create the TEP-LARB.

No one in the company had used NoSQL in production in a significant way, let alone for something so large and mission-critical. Usually Maxine thinks prudence and practicality would disqualify such a risky approach for such a high-stakes project, especially when there's so little time to research and gain real-world production experience. She says as much to the team.

"Normally I'd agree, Maxine. You'd think the biggest risk would be operational," Brent says, seeing her concerned expression. "But I think the far bigger risk is losing relational integrity between all these tables that we're copying from everywhere in the enterprise. As you know, a NoSQL database won't enforce relational integrity like most databases we're used to. But I'm comfortable that we can enforce it at the API level."

Although nerve-wracking, Maxine admits that it is exciting to see technologists at the top of their game working to solve an urgent business problem. Maxine asks a bunch of questions, sometimes repeatedly, and scrutinizes their thinking. But by the end, they've all convinced each other to go all-in on NoSQL.

"Okay, let's burn the ships," Maxine finally says. There's just no time for any other option. She does not like this level of uncertainty, but she trusts the team.

The developer agility this will enable is undeniable, but more than ever, Maxine realizes how engineering constrained they were. To work with more systems, they really needed a bigger team. She reminds herself that this again will be the first topic to discuss in her next meeting with Kurt.

Over the next two days, the teams work on their portions of the Unicorn Project. Maxine spends most of her time on what she views as the riskiest part of the whole operation, which is getting all the data into the Narwhal NoSQL databases and enabling all the teams to be able to access what they need. She knows that they are now well past the point of no return, having torched the ships they knew how to sail.

The most difficult part was not the mechanics of importing the data from twenty different business systems. Instead, it was trying to create a unified vocabulary and taxonomy that they could use, because almost every business system had different names for similar things.

Physical stores have five different definitions of in-store sales, including from a company acquired decades ago. There are six different ways that products are catalogued. Product categories and prices don't line up. The business rules around pricing and promotion are exercises in forensic archaeology. They pulled in business analysts from across the company to help make sense of it and make decisions about how they should be represented.

Maxine found herself constantly switching between insisting on clarity and consistency to ensure accuracy to saying "good enough for now" and deferring decisions that would require days of consensus-building because they would impact Parts Unlimited for decades to come. Without her extensive experience working with enterprise systems, she's sure she wouldn't have had the judgement necessary to make these types of calls, especially given the deadlines involved.

Everyone is focused on the big, upcoming Demo Day, where each team will show their portions of the system on the final days before Black Friday. Maggie will be leading it, and almost all the stakeholders will be there, as well as all the technology executives, ending with a final "go/no go" launch decision.

Because of the high stakes involved, Maxine makes sure that she attends all of the daily engineering team standups, where team members quickly share progress and, more importantly, what help they need. She approves of how quickly and efficiently these meetings are run, with blockers being urgently handled by the team leads.

On this tight timeline, every day counts. Thanksgiving is just over a week away. She listens intently as she sits in the Unicorn standup. One of the two most senior data scientists from the Promotions team is visibly flustered. "We still don't have the fields we need in the one percent subset of the customer list from the Data Warehouse team, and we still can't match up nearly half of the physical store order data.

"And for our data analysis, the Narwhal database is incredibly fast, compared to what we're used to. But because of all the joins we need to do, the query times are still orders of magnitude too slow," he continues. "Given the deadlines, we only have one or two shots at this, and if the results are like the ones we're getting right now, we will not be ready for the Black Friday launch. And if we use the data we have right now, the promotions are guaranteed to be a real dud. Just this morning I found a case where we would have sent offers for snow tires to people in Texas."

Oh, shit, thinks Maxine. This is what you get for waiting too long to invite the data scientists to the engineering meetings. She says out loud, "Okay, I'll pull together an emergency single-topic meeting later this morning. I'll make sure Kurt and Maggie are there, as well as the Narwhal team. Could you prepare a ten-minute briefing about these problems and some ideas on how to solve them?"

When he nods, Maxine takes out her phone and calls Kurt.

Two hours later, everyone is gathered in a conference room listening to the problems that the Analytics and Promotions teams are having. After fifteen minutes, Maxine is feeling genuinely daunted at the sheer scale of the problem.

It's no wonder the Analytics team has made so little progress—what they want to do is simply impossible with the infrastructure they've built. The data sets are orders of magnitude larger than what they can handle. Maxine immediately sees that the queries the data scientists are building are a complete mismatch to what they've built Narwhal for. Narwhal is stellar at handling API requests from all the various teams across the company, but now they're learning that it's spectacularly not great for what the Analytics teams need to do.

Worse, the Unicorn teams still can't get the data they need. It takes the Data Warehouse team four months to get twenty lines of SQL from Dev to QA to Production. And every time they do, reports break or show incorrect data. Apparently last month, a schema change somewhere broke almost every report in the company. To Maxine, it's the same problems they had with the Phoenix Project, but instead of code, it's for the data that the Unicorn teams need.

Moreover, the Data Warehouse teams still haven't reconciled the different definitions of product, inventory, and customer from the physical stores and e-commerce stores. The newly created Narwhal teams were already way ahead of them.

Maxine drums her fingers. She cannot believe that they've run smack into another Phoenix-scale bureaucratic quagmire—the Data Warehouse is sitting on so many things they need.

As people continue talking, Maxine stares at the numbers on the whiteboard. *This is not going to work*, she thinks. She decides that she needs to discretely signal Kurt to step out into the hallway so she can tell him that there's just no way that the Promotions plan can realistically work as currently envisioned. They'll need to convince the Unicorn team to drastically scale down their plans. Or maybe the Rebellion should abandon them and find another program to work with to generate a business win.

In order for the Unicorn team to succeed, they somehow need to be decoupled and liberated from the giant data warehouse, and maybe even Narwhal, to support the massive calculations and queries they need to do.

"I know what you're thinking," Shannon says, just as Maxine is about to get Kurt's attention. "This looks impossible, right? But I spent nearly five years on the Data Warehouse team thinking about this. Let me show you something I've wanted to do for years."

Over the course of the next thirty minutes, Shannon presents a breathtaking plan that she's obviously been thinking about and studying deeply. She is proposing to build a Spark-like big data and compute platform, fed by an entirely new event-streaming bus, modeled closely to what the tech giants all have built to solve their data problems at scale. It would allow hundreds, even thousands, of CPU cores to be thrown at the computations, allowing analyses that currently take days or weeks to be done in minutes or hours.

Maxine is familiar with these techniques. Their use exploded after the famous 2004 Google Map/Reduce research paper was published, which described the techniques Google used to massively parallelize the indexing of the entire internet on commodity hardware, using techniques at the core of functional programming. This led to the invention of Hadoop, Spark, Beam, and so many other exciting technologies that transformed this space, just like NoSQL revolutionized the database landscape.

Shannon describes how this new data platform would be fed by a new event streaming technology. "Unlike Data Hub, where almost every business rule change also requires a change from the Data Hub team, this new scheme would allow a massive decoupling of services and data. It would enable developers to change things independently, without needing a centralized team to write intermediary code. And unlike the centralized Data Warehouse, the responsibility for cleaning, ingesting, analyzing, and publishing accurate data to the rest of the organization would be pushed into each business and application team, where they have the most knowledge of what the data actually means."

She continues, "The importance and urgency of keeping this data secure, making sure that we don't store PII that we shouldn't, the need to encrypt it at rest, and the risks of what could happen to Parts Unlimited if this data were stolen are tantamount." It's obvious that Shannon is passionate about how this platform must ensure the security of all this data, not leaving it to each individual team.

And most appealing to Maxine, it could also support an immutable event sourcing data model, which would be a massive simplification compared to the current morass of complexity built up over decades.

It was also fast. It would have to be, because Data Hub and potentially every application in the enterprise would eventually be throwing everything into this new message bus: all customer orders, all customer activity from their CRM, everything from their e-commerce site and marketing campaign management systems, all customer activity from their in-store and garages...all of it.

When Shannon is done presenting and has answered questions from the team, Kurt looks pale. "You're kidding me. We don't even have approval to get Narwhal off the ground yet. And adding all of...this...would quadruple our compute and storage footprint...and potentially put even more sensitive data out in the cloud," he says, gesturing at the whiteboard. "Oh, man, Chris is going to lose his shit. There is no way he'll go for this."

Even Brent looks slightly ill. "I've always wanted to run something like this, but...it's just so much new infrastructure to build at once. This seems a bit reckless, even to me."

Maxine studies Kurt's expression, and then Shannon and her drawings that cover two full whiteboards. Then she laughs, momentarily enjoying Kurt and Brent's discomfort. But she knows how they feel. Gamblers who lost everything at the casino probably had moments of reflection and prudence like this before they went all-in.

She says, "Are we playing to win and to establish the technical supremacy we need to keep up with what the business needs, or do we just keep limping along, shackled to things built decades ago, and tell our business leadership to throw in the towel and stop having good ideas?"

Maxine thinks Shannon's idea is a good one, even though it seems suicidal. Maxine says, "All my intuition and experience says that our data architecture has created another bottleneck that affects every area of the company. This is a problem that's far bigger than just developers. Anyone who needs data as part of their daily work isn't getting what they need."

"Yes," Maggie says, looking like she's been hit by a bat. "That's absolutely right! I've got twenty-five data scientists and analysts across five teams who never have the data they need. But it's not just them—almost everyone in Marketing accesses or manipulates data. Operations is mostly about data. Sales operations and management is all about data. In fact, I'd bet half of all Parts Unlimited employees access or manipulate data every day. And for years, we've been handcuffed by the way everything has to go through the Data Warehouse team.

"And frankly, we need pros like you to help," she says, embarrassed. "We have a few data visualization platforms that we manage internally, but we're not software people. In fact, earlier this year we managed to corrupt all our order data when the vendor told us to change the server time zone."

Brent groans, and Maxine is relieved that he manages to refrain from saying anything demeaning about the vendor or Maggie's server administrators.

Seeing Kurt's sudden expression of rapt interest and calculation, Maxine smiles. She knows that hearing this sort of distress and suffering is exactly what motivates him into action. She says, "Let's start small, with the most critical capabilities to enable the Unicorn team. We leverage all the ETL work we're already doing with Narwhal, and we use fully managed and battle-tested data platform services in the cloud that could reduce a lot of the operational risk. Here's what I'm thinking…"

Maxine congratulates herself that over the next four hours, no one leaves the room. Or quits. Instead, they wrangle over the whiteboard and come up with an outline of a plan that everyone tentatively agrees to explore. They defer the event streaming platform, but Maxine and Shannon will lead the creation of something that can provide more bulletproof data transformations, get things under version control, build automated testing to confirm the correct shape and size of data before it's ingested, and so many other things to prevent all these data accidents she's seen and heard about.

Kurt and Maggie promise to start the delicate discussion with Chris and Bill to head off a political battle with the Data Warehouse team, who might feel threatened. *Which is not unreasonable*, thinks Maxine. The Data Warehouse team has been the custodian of this data for decades, and now we'd be liberating it, making it available to anyone who wants it, on demand, without opening a ticket.

Despite all these plans, everyone knows that there is a real chance of total failure. She hears Brent mutter from the whiteboard, "I love it, but there's just no way we can get all of this done by Thanksgiving…"

As Maxine's teenagers would say, Brent is not wrong. But clearly, the way they're doing data now is not working, and here's an opportunity to show that there's a better way. *If there's any time that deserves courage and relentless optimism, it's now*, she thinks.

When Brent finally says, "Let's call this Project Panther," Maxine knows that there's a shot of making this all work.

On the night before Demo Day, many teams work late into the evening. The next morning, everyone is there as the Black Friday Promotion demos begin in the lunchroom. Kurt asks Maggie to kick off the session to help frame the "why" behind all of their efforts, but everyone knows that Black Friday is just days away. Everyone working on the Unicorn Project knows that it's not an exaggeration that the survival of the company depends on their efforts.

The Unicorn Project is now high-profile. And Maxine knows that if things don't go well today, it will not be good for the company, and it will be very not good for Maggie, Kurt, and herself.

Maggie begins, "As everyone knows, Black Friday is right around the corner. Our goal is for the Unicorn Project to drive real revenue, made possible by the Orca, Narwhal, Panther, and mobile app teams. Our focus is on using inventory information and personalization data to drive promotion and to get useful information into our apps, such as inventory availability. Specific outcomes we want to affect are revenue, repeat engagement in our mobile apps and e-commerce site, and campaigns that generate a positive response."

Maggie pauses. "And we have a special guest in the room, Bill Palmer, our VP of IT Operations, who helped create Project Inversion, which allowed us to focus so much energy on the Promotions effort. We also have a big contingent from Ops here who are helping fast-track all these initiatives. First up is Justine to present for the Orca team."

"I'm Justine, and I'm on the team responsible for generating the data used to create the promotions. As Maggie mentioned, our goal is to give Marketing the ability to create the best promotions based on everything we know about our customers.

"Data is the lifeblood of the company," she continues. "In Marketing, almost all of us access or manipulate data to guide the efforts of the company. For the first time, thanks to the Panther platform that Shannon and team created, we can finally get the data we need, trust that it's correct, and use all sorts of statistical techniques and even things like machine learning to predict what our customers might need. This is what we use to craft offers and promotions. I have no doubt that the future of the organization will be built upon understanding our customers and providing them what they need…and we are best able to do that by understanding this data."

Shannon smiles as Justine goes on to outline Orca's successes. "Over the last two weeks, our goal was to get all the queries needed to support the top priority use cases: we need to find out what the top-selling items are, which customer segments have purchased them, and vice versa. For each customer segment, we need to determine the products they buy most frequently.

"A great promotion is one where we can sell inventory we already have, but also at the optimum price. We don't want to unknowingly sell products lower than what customers are willing to pay. And we can only learn what that price is through experimentation," she says.

"We built a simple web application where everyone can generate and run these queries, build candidate promotions, and share them with each other," she continues. "On the screen, you'll see all the top-selling items along with their photos. This is pretty great but also boring, and it's very difficult to quickly understand what all these SKUs actually are. We realized that the e-commerce site has images for all these products. So we asked Maxine and the Narwhal team if they could give us those links too, which they did within hours and without needing to open a ticket! By the end of day, with only ten lines of code, we were showing these images in our app, which helped everyone on the team generate more compelling offers more quickly and effectively. That's been a crowd pleaser," she says with a smile.

Maxine sees Tom, her former Data Hub coding partner, join Justine at the front of the room. He says, "Once we understood what the Promotions team was trying to do, generating this app was easy. The Narwhal people gave us the API, and we just used one of the modern web frameworks to display it. Justine is absolutely right about how awesome the Narwhal database API is. And it's blazingly fast. I'm used to queries that take minutes or hours to run on big servers. So, hats off to the Narwhal team—I'm blown away. We couldn't have done it without them."

Maxine grins and sees that Brent and Dwayne also have huge smiles on their faces.

Justine shows her last slide. "We're working with the Marketing teams to finalize the promotion campaigns for the two highest-priority customer personas: the Meticulous Maintainers and the Catastrophic Late Maintainers. For each of those, using the Panther data and compute clusters, we've generated candidate-recommended products and recommended bundles, which they're still reviewing and tweaking. Once they're done, we'll help get those loaded into the product and pricing databases so we can execute the campaign."

Unprompted, one of the senior Marketing people walks to the front of the room and says, "I want to acknowledge and thank everyone's hard work. This is incredibly exciting and impressive. I've been amazed at how much this team has done in a couple of weeks. We've been at this for almost two years, but I've never been as excited as now. We're taking all the data from the Orca team and fine-tuning the offers that we'll be presenting throughout the Thanksgiving weekend. I think there's millions of dollars of revenue that we can unlock!"

Maggie thanks him and Justine, applauding with the crowd. She then calls up Mark, the lead developer for the Parts Unlimited mobile app. He's a tall man in his mid-thirties. His laptop is so covered in stickers of technologies and vendors that you can't even tell what kind of laptop it is. "Good morning, and I'd like to just answer the question that you're probably thinking. The answer is, yes, we're the team that built the current mobile apps—both of them. We're not proud, and we're just glad users can't rate an app with zero stars."

People laugh. The Parts Unlimited app has been an embarrassment for years. "There's so much we wanted to fix, but we were all put on other projects, so until recently, there's been no full-time developers on the mobile apps. But as Maggie said, that has changed. Mobile is how our customers want to interact with us, so we've reconstituted the team, with a persona-driven approach that focuses on what our customers want," he continues. "We've been working closely with the product owners to generate some quick wins and taking full advantage of what the Narwhal team has done.

"We've never had access to a store's inventory levels before. We loved the idea of showing which stores nearest to the customer have a particular part in stock. We can use the geolocation data from the customer's device, or they can have them put in a US zip code. Here's what the page looks like now…"

He brings up an iPhone simulator and the Parts Unlimited app on the screen. "Getting inventory information from Narwhal was incredibly easy. So, when we click into the product page, you can see the item availability for all the stores around them. They can now reserve the item, so it'll be guaranteed to be there for them to pick up, which again was made entirely possible by Narwhal. And now, we're collecting information on how parts availability affects purchasing so we can compute how much of an effect this has."

Wow. Maxine is impressed. She hasn't seen any of this work before, and she loves what they've created.

And even though Mark had apologized about the app, Maxine thinks it looks really good. She's always amazed by how great most mobile applications can look, presenting an incredibly rich amount of information—even the Parts Unlimited app. She's used to engineering prototypes that she and other developers build, which look more like 1990s-era websites. It's clear that the mobile app team had professional designers working on it. This polish is something that consumers now demand. If an app looks shabby, they'll likely won't use it, let alone open it a second time.

"All these changes have already been pushed out to the app stores. All we need to do to enable it for customers is flip a switch," he says. "We're also logging a ton more data back to Narwhal to help the Marketing teams perform experiments. We're especially interested in what exactly should and shouldn't be presented to the user in the search results and on the product pages to increase conversion rates. Narwhal performance is awesome—none of it slows down the user experience."

He continues, "We've done hundreds of iterations internally, and we're ready to use all the user telemetry to perform experiments with real customers. We've never been able to do anything like this before. This has been a fantastic experience for me and my team. Keep up the great work!"

Maggie thanks Mark and everyone claps in appreciation, then she turns to address the room again. "You've just seen demos of the progress we're making. All these give us confidence that we'll be able to execute some very exciting Thanksgiving promotions.

"We spent the month trying to come up with the best promotions, slicing and dicing the data in many different ways," she continues. "We were able to spin up a bunch of compute resources in the cloud to do the necessary computations. We start the recommendations reporting run every evening and spin up hundreds of compute instances until we're done, and then we turn them off. We've been doing this for the past four days, and it's working well—really well. Right, Brent? Right, Shannon?"

Brent and Shannon are sitting at the front of the room, and they are beaming. Maxine is delighted that Brent, in particular, is so invested in the outcome. She's never seen him so happy and having so much fun, which makes her thinks of the Second Ideal. And Shannon is rightly proud of getting Panther off the ground. There is absolutely no way that the teams could have generated these promotions without this new platform.

Panther was already making a huge difference in how teams worked with data. Errors in data uploads were being caught right away through automated tests. The teams could easily access any data from across the organization, and easily add new data, contributing to the entire collective knowledge that could be tapped to experiment and try out new ideas. It's enabled scores of new reports and analyses to be conducted, leveraging an incredible variety of tools, many that Maxine has never heard of.

And to Maxine's amazement, even the output of these discoveries and experiments are making it back into the Panther data platform, further enriching the data already there. Seeing and spreading learnings, as per Erik's Third Ideal, Improvement of Daily Work.

Maggie shows a slide with a bunch of products on it. "These are the Unicorn promotions generated for my customer account. As you can see, it's looked at my buying history and is letting me know that snow tires and batteries are fifteen percent off. I actually went to our website and purchased both because I need them. The company just made money because those are all items that we have excess inventory of and that have high profit margins.

"And here are the Unicorn promotions for Wes," she continues, going to the next slide with a smile. "Looks like you got a discount on racing brake pads and fuel additives. That of any interest to you?"

"Not bad," hollers out Wes.

"Given the incredible success of these initial experiments, here's my proposal," Maggie says. "As planned, I'd like to do an email campaign to one percent of our customers to see what happens. If everything goes well, we'll go full blast on Black Friday."

Maggie looks at the Ops leadership. "Sounds like a great plan," Bill says. "Wes, is there any reason why we shouldn't do this?"

From the front of the room, Wes says, "From an Ops perspective, I can't think of any. All the hard work has already been done. If Chris, William, and Marketing have confidence that the code is working, I say go for it."

Maggie cheers and says, "Everyone, we have a plan. Let's make it happen!"

Maxine is cheering, along with everyone else. Suddenly curious, she looks around—again, Sarah is nowhere to be seen. You'd think she'd want to be here at a time like this, if anything to take all the credit. Her absence is conspicuous. And it makes Maxine nervous.

CHAPTER 15

Despite the jubilant mood, everyone knows they're a long way from being fully prepared for the Black Friday promotions. As Maggie said, the plan is to do a trial run against a small subset of customers to test their readiness for the full-scale campaign on Friday—so at eleven a.m. they will conduct a campaign to just one percent of their customers. They're doing this in the middle of the day, when everyone will already be in the office and able to quickly respond to emergencies. This will help them find vulnerabilities and weaknesses in the process so they can fix them before Friday.

To Maxine, this decision alone shows how much has changed in the organization. A couple of months ago, they would not have conducted any trials. And they would surely have scheduled the campaign to start at midnight, requiring the teams to be in the office throughout the entire night.

At nine a.m. everyone is in the war room furiously dealing with last-minute details in preparation for the one percent mini-launch. The Orca team is still fine-tuning the customer offers. Maxine is a little alarmed to learn that they're still deciding which one percent of the customer base they're targeting—but if they aren't panicking, she won't panic either. They've earned that level of trust over the last several weeks.

Even though they're sending an email to only one percent of their customer mailing list, the stakes are still huge. They'll be sending nearly one hundred thousand emails to all the persona profiles, not just the Meticulous Maintainers and the Catastrophic Late Maintainers, to learn how each segment responds.

Countless things could still go wrong. If the response rate isn't in the same ballpark as in their early experiments, all the hopes and dreams riding on the Unicorn Project will be dashed. If they promote the wrong items, or if those items are not in stock, or if they screw up the fulfillment, they will anger their customers.

This campaign represents many firsts for Parts Unlimited. It is the first time that emails will open up the mobile app if they are being read on a mobile phone. It's the first time they're presenting promotions through the app—people with the app installed will get a notification about this limited-time offer, which the Promotions team believes will have higher response rates than even their carefully designed emails.

Over the last week, they've been continuously performing experiments in their mobile app, zeroing in on what maximizes conversion rates, such as presenting promoted items differently, using different pictures, picture sizes, typography, and copywriting. Those lessons and learnings were then considered for the email campaigns too.

The results of all these experiments were being poured back into Panther to guide the next round of experiments and trials, along with all customer activity within the app. It was a lot of data, but it had the Analytics team salivating for more. People's appreciation for the Panther data platform kept growing.

The mobile app team has also been working around the clock to make sure that things display properly and that the buttons actually do what they are supposed to, but they are also trying to streamline the purchasing process as much as possible. Noticing that many customers dropped off when prompted for a credit card, they licensed some technology to input this information by using their phone camera and offering different payment options like PayPal and Apple Pay in the hopes that one of these might reduce order abandonment rates.

The big gamble is that all this investment in their mobile app will result in significantly higher sales than just using the mobile phone browser. It's a gamble, but a well-informed gamble, made by an organization that is obviously and constantly learning.

But preparation and practice time is over; now it's game time, Maxine thinks. She sees many of the technology teams starting to assemble, but the Narwhal data team is already huddled around their screens, going through checklists and whispering back and forth, making sure that everything can handle the traffic they're expecting. Over the last week, Brent and his team have been stress-testing the entire system, routinely causing parts of the technology landscape to blow up. And then in a blameless post-mortem, they'd all work together to figure out how to fix things so that they'll survive the actual launch.

The results of these "Chaos Engineering" exercises resulted in some surprising things breaking. But everyone has been working diligently, trying to ensure that they are as prepared as they can be for the big launch event. A few days ago, a small test run of the offer generation process kept crashing because they didn't increase the limits for an external service they used. They had gotten in the habit of scaling everything down to save on costs, and someone had forgotten to scale it up before the test.

We still have so much to learn before we're experts at this, Maxine thinks.

At times, it's difficult to know who works on which team, because people are moving so fluidly between them. When everyone knows what the goals are, as Erik predicted, teams will self-organize to best achieve those goals. To Maxine, it's been amazing to see how people are acting and reacting to each other, especially when compared to the big Phoenix launch two months ago. People across different disciplines—Dev, QA, Ops, Security, and now even Data and Analytics—are working together daily as fellow teammates instead of adversaries. They are working toward a common goal. They realize that they are on a journey of learning and exploration, and that making mistakes is inevitable. Creating ever-safer systems and continual improvement is now viewed as part of daily work.

This is worthy of the Third Ideal of Improvement of Daily Work that Erik painted many weeks ago, Maxine thinks.

Thanks to the pioneering work by Data Hub, code is now being promoted into production multiple times per day, smoothly, quickly, and mostly without incident, with any issues being resolved quickly and without blame or undue crisis. Even now, Maxine sees that there are production deployments happening, as teams are pushing out last-minute changes to ensure the success of the mini-launch.

Twenty minutes ago, someone noticed that one API was returning a bunch of "500" HTTP errors. Apparently, yesterday, someone had committed a code change that accidentally misclassified "400" user-caused errors as "500" server-caused errors. Wes pulled together a huddle, and Maxine was astonished when Wes recommended pushing out a fix, even though it was less than an hour before the mini-launch.

"If we don't fix it, these errors could potentially hide important signals if we have a real outage," he said. "We've proven repeatedly that we can push out these one-line changes safely."

The best part was it was a developer who detected the error and who pushed out the fix. *We finally trust developers*, she thinks. If someone had told her a month ago that Wes would support something like this, she would have never believed it.

And best of all, Maxine's worst fears about developers going amok and ruining the integrity of the data in the Narwhal platform never materialized. Left to their own devices, development teams will often optimize everything around themselves. This is just the parochial and selfish nature of individual teams. *And that's why you need architects,* thinks Maxine.

Because they provided access to the data through versioned APIs, things remained very controlled and teams were able to keep working independently. Maxine is not just relieved—she's elated. They designed these platforms to optimize for the system as a whole and ensure the safety and security of the entire organization.

"Sending emails and notifications to the mobile apps in 3, 2, 1…now. Here we go, everyone," says the marketing launch coordinator in a calm voice. Maxine looks at her watch. It's 11:12 a.m. Emails and mobile app notifications are now going out to a hundred thousand customers.

The launch is starting twelve minutes late because of a couple unforeseen issues—a configuration problem was found in the Narwhal systems and someone noticed that there were too many email addresses in the campaign, requiring a recalculation and regeneration of the email list in Panther. Maxine gave a thumbs-up to Shannon when the Unicorn teams quickly generated and uploaded the new data in record time.

On the one hand, Maxine is mildly irritated that these details were caught so late in the launch process. But on the other hand, that's what rehearsals are for and why everyone is assembled in the war room. Everyone needed to make these types of last-minute calls are in the room and everyone agreed that it made sense. Maggie, Kurt, the team leads, and many others are assembled here, as well as Wes and key Ops people.

Maxine looks around. Again, Sarah is nowhere to be seen. Maxine wonders if she's the only one who is suspicious that Sarah might up to no good.

She turns her attention to what everyone else in the room is watching— the large monitor hanging on the wall. Everyone is holding their breath.

On the screen are a bunch of graphs, dominated by the number of emails sent and the order funnel: this shows how many people viewed a product page, added a product to the shopping cart, hit the checkout button, had their order processed, and had their order fulfilled. The bottom shows where the most drop-offs are occurring, as well as the number of orders and revenue booked.

Underneath those graphs are the technical performance metrics: CPU loads for all the various compute clusters, number of transactions being processed by the services and databases, network traffic, and much, much more.

She could see several spikes associated with the massive calculations enabled by Panther. But now, most of the graphs are at zero. Several of the CPU graphs are at twenty percent. Those are the services that need to stay warm to make sure they don't go to sleep. In one of their launch rehearsals, they were horrified when this happened to a key system, requiring six minutes for the system to wake up and scale out.

Nothing happens. One minute goes by. Another minute goes by. Maxine is starting to get worried that the launch was a complete dud. Maybe something terrible has happened in their infrastructure. Or maybe something terrible has happened that prevented the emails from being received. Or maybe their worst fears about terrible recommendations had come true, and they had accidentally sent offers of snow tires to people who don't live near snow.

Maxine audibly sighs in relief when the graph for product page views suddenly jumps to ten, twenty, fifty... and keeps going up.

Everyone cheers, including Maxine. She is staring at the technical metrics, praying that the infrastructure doesn't fall over like during the Phoenix release. She's relieved when the CPU loads are starting to climb across the board, showing that things are actually being processed.

Minutes later, almost five thousand people are in various stages of the order funnel. *So far, so good*, Maxine thinks, watching the numbers continue to creep up. Again, people cheer as the number of processed orders continues to climb... Ten orders completed, then twenty, and it still continues to climb. To her excitement, the revenue generated from this campaign surges past $1,000.

Everything is working as designed. She smiles as she hears a smattering of applause throughout the room but continues to stare at the graph.

She frowns. The number of completed orders graph has flatlined, stuck at 250. She looks at the other graphs to see if they're stuck too, but they're still climbing. Maxine sees a bunch of people crowded around the TV, pointing at the stuck graph.

Something is definitely going wrong.

"Let's have some quiet here!" Wes hollers out. He remains silent for a couple of moments before he turns around and finally says, "I need people to try ordering products on the web and on mobile and tell me what is actually happening! Something is preventing orders from going through!" Maxine already has the app open on her phone. She hits the Add to Shopping Cart button and blinks in surprise. She calls out, "Mobile app crashes when you add an item to the cart on an iPhone...app crashes and disappears."

"Dammit," she hears someone say from the other side of the room. Someone else calls out, "Getting error message on Android. I see a dialog box that says 'An error has occurred.'"

Right next to her, Shannon hollers out, "Web shopping cart is generating an error—web page renders after you hit submit, but I'm getting a blank webpage! I think something on the back end is erroring out when we query whether items are available to ship."

Wes says from the front of the room, "Thank you, Shannon. Get all these screenshots into the #launch channel. Okay, everyone, listen up! We're getting errors on all client platforms—Shannon thinks it's one of the back-end calls we make: maybe the 'available to promise' API call or 'available to ship.' Anyone have any ideas?"

Maxine jumps into action, appreciating how great it is that Wes is running the war room. *Yeah, he's cantankerous,* she thinks, *but he's handled more outages than everyone else in the room combined.* Having that type of experience during this high-stakes launch is a very good thing. *We developers are great at what we do, but these types of crises are a part of everyday life for Ops.*

It doesn't take long to confirm that Shannon's hypothesis is correct—it was a problem in the order entry back-end systems. All the systems in that particular cluster are pegged at one hundred percent CPU usage; unfortunately, the system being hit is part of the main ERP, which handles almost all the core financials of the company. It's been running for over thirty years, but it's stuck on a version that is almost fifteen years old. It's been so customized that it's been impossible to upgrade. At least it's put on newer hardware every five years. But there's no easy way to throw more CPU cores at it to speed it up.

Apparently, even the small one percent promotion is causing it to get backed up. Maxine sees that queries are taking longer and longer to return, and client requests start timing out. All those clients start resending the queries, causing even more requests to overload the back-end database.

"Thundering herd problem," Wes mutters, referring to when simultaneous client retries end up killing a server. "We can't do anything on the back end. How do we get all the clients to back off on the retries?"

"We can't change the mobile apps, but we can get the e-commerce servers to wait longer before they retry," Brent says. Wes points at Brent and Maxine and says, "Do it."

Maxine and Brent work with the e-commerce teams to push out new configuration files to every web server. They are able to push out all these changes into production in less than ten minutes.

Luckily, this is enough to stave off disaster. Maxine watches in relief as the database error rates start decreasing and the number of completed orders starts creeping up again. Several other things go wrong over the next two hours, but none of them are as heart-stopping as the 'available to promise' server issue that she and Brent had to deal with.

Another forty-five minutes later, they cross over their goal of three thousand completed orders, grossing a quarter million dollars in revenue, and the orders are still coming in strong. Maggie must have snuck out, because two hours later Maxine sees her come back into the room with a bunch of people carrying champagne bottles. Maggie opens one up and starts pouring glasses, handing the first to Maxine.

After everyone has a glass in hand, Maggie raises hers with a big smile. "Holy cow, everyone. What a day! And what an amazing team effort! I want to share with you some of the early results, and, wow, they are great…people are continuing to respond to the promotions, but at this point, almost a third of the people responded to our campaign. This is, without a doubt, the highest conversion rate we've ever achieved by at least a factor of five!"

She pulls out her phone and peers at the screen. "Here are some early calculations from the team. Over twenty percent of people who received our offer went to view the products we recommended, and over six percent purchased. We've never seen any numbers like this! So thank you to everyone here who helped make this happen.

"And remember, almost all the items we promoted are high-margin items or were sitting on shelves gathering dust. So each sale we made today will have an unusually large effect on profits!" Maggie cheers and drains her glass. Everyone laughs and follows suit.

She says, "Based on these results, the Unicorn promotion campaign to our entire customer base on Black Friday is a GO! If the results are anywhere near what we saw in this test campaign, we are going to have a blowout holiday season…

"Uh, just a reminder, this is insider information. If you use this information to trade Parts Unlimited stock, you can go to prison. Dick Landry, our CFO, told me to tell you that he will assist in your prosecution as per your employment contract," she says, and then smiles. "But having said that, there's no doubt we're going to *crush it* on Black Friday!"

Everyone cheers loudly again, including Maxine. Maggie motions for everyone to quiet down and asks Kurt and Maxine to speak. Maxine laughs, motioning Kurt to go. He says, "What an amazing effort, everyone! I'm so proud. Maxine?"

Maxine hadn't wanted to say anything, but being cornered like this, she stands up and raises her glass. "Here's to the Rebellion showing the ancient, powerful order how kickass engineering work is done!"

Again, everyone cheers and laughs. When that all dies down, Maxine says, "Okay, enough of that. On Black Friday we can safely expect one hundred times the load as today. We'll surely run into tons of problems we've never encountered before, so we've got our work cut out for us between now and then. Let's figure out how to best prepare for it."

Kurt adds, "I'd like to send as many people home on time tomorrow as possible, given that it's Thanksgiving on Thursday. So let's get to work! And we'll need people in the office early on Friday to support the launch."

They agree to stagger the emails and mobile app notifications to prevent the systems from being slammed all at once and to better protect those unexpectedly delicate back-end servers. Brent comes up with an idea to reconfigure the load balancers to rate-limit the transactions. This will cause customer errors on the mobile app and e-commerce servers, but everyone agrees this is far better than those back-end systems crashing again.

"We'll get on it. I think we'll be in good shape and get everyone out of here in time for Thanksgiving!" Brent says with a big smile. "Happy Thanksgiving, everyone!"

As Brent predicted, all the work is done before five the next day. With just a couple of exceptions, people start heading out. Maxine is making the rounds, trying to shoo the stragglers home. It's the day before Thanksgiving, and Maxine wants to get out of here by five thirty. She's proud that she even got Brent to leave.

One team that couldn't leave were the data analysts. Now that the one percent test proved to be a smashing success, they had to finish generating all their recommendations for millions of customers by Friday. The resulting compute loads on Panther keep growing, and they keep updating the promotions data in the Narwhal data platform. Maxine thinks with a grin, *We're racking up a heck of a bill with the cloud computing providers, but absolutely no one in Marketing is complaining because the business benefits are so spectacular.*

She swings in to say goodbye to Kurt but freezes mid-stride when she sees Sarah having a heated discussion with him.

"...and I walk around this building after five and there's barely anyone here. Kurt, I don't know if you realize this, but the company is on the verge of extinction. We need everyone pulling their weight," Sarah says, fuming in righteous indignation. "I think we need some mandatory overtime. Buy them more pizza and they'll be happy to stay and do the work.

"And if that weren't bad enough," she continues, "I just saw a bunch of people sitting around reading books! We don't pay people to read books; we pay them to do work. That should be pretty clear, right, Kurt?" Kurt's expression remains deadpan.

"You'll have to bring that up with Chris. Banning books from the workplace is above my paygrade." She gives him a dirty look and storms out.

Kurt makes a motion to Maxine, indicating that he wants to hang himself. "It's so strange," he says. "She thinks we pay developers just to type, instead of paying them to think and achieve business outcomes. And that means we pay them to learn, because that's how we win. Can you imagine banning books from the workplace?" he says, laughing and shaking his head.

Maxine just stares at Kurt. Sarah's beliefs are like the antithesis of the Third Ideal of Improvement of Daily Work and the Fourth Ideal of Psychological Safety. Maxine knows that the only way they could have achieved what they had was by creating a culture where people felt safe to experiment, to learn and make mistakes, and where people make time for discovery, innovation, and learning.

"No argument from me, Kurt. Let me know if you convince her," Maxine says smiling, waving goodbye. "Happy Thanksgiving."

Maxine has a fantastic Thanksgiving. It's the first since her father died, and she enjoys having everyone over, even if she is surreptitiously looking at her phone all the time to see how the Black Friday preparations are going.

The highlight of Thanksgiving is when Waffles, now not so little, tipping the scale at forty pounds, grabs a big piece of turkey off the table in front of everyone, to Maxine's horror. It was the first time he had ever done that, Jake promises everyone.

Everyone pitches in to clean up after, and Maxine goes to bed early.

She needs to be in the office early the next morning.

At three thirty a.m. she's in the office with the rest of the team. The technical teams had been going through their launch checklist, getting ready for the surge in demand that would start in a couple of hours. They grab another conference room for the extended teams who can't fit in the first. It's a larger affair than the one percent test they ran on Tuesday. Each conference room has a similar configuration of big, U-shaped tables with about thirty people seated. She starts her day in the room where the technical teams are assembled.

In the extended war room are the Narwhal and Orca teams, next to the monitoring team, the web front-end teams, the mobile teams, and the numerous back-end service teams responsible for products, pricing, ordering, and fulfillment. There are many more technical teams on standby in the chatroom.

All of these services have to run seamlessly for products to be presented to a customer and for orders to be placed. On the huge TV monitor on the wall are more technical graphs showing the number of visits to the website, stats on the top product pages, as well as health checks and most recent errors from all the services represented in the room.

In the primary war room, they've set up a second TV where some of these technical metrics are displayed. And today, they have more representatives from business and technology leadership, the entire Unicorn and Promotions team, and even people from Finance and Accounting. Everyone who matters is here to see how the campaign goes.

At four thirty a.m. Maxine is hanging out with Kurt and Maggie in the primary war room. She is looking for something to help with, but everyone seems to know what they're doing. At this point, all she can do is get in the way. They are thirty minutes away from the beginning of the campaign launch.

Sarah is here too. As far as Maxine can tell, she appears to be haranguing someone about the pricing and promotional copy for one of the offers.

Maggie is also in the huddle, not looking happy, saying, "Look, I know we want the offers to be perfect, but the time to make changes was yesterday. The risk of making changes in the copy is just too high for something going out to so many people. It might delay the launch by another hour."

"This may be good enough for you, but it's certainly not good enough for me. Get this fixed. Now," Sarah says, eliminating any further discussion.

Maggie sighs and walks away, rejoining Kurt and Maxine. "We're going to have to make some changes," she says, rolling her eyes. "Undoubtedly, this is going to push back the launch by at least an hour."

"I'll go tell the technical teams next door," Kurt says, grimacing as he leaves the room.

An hour later, things are again finally ready to go. Maggie asks from the front of the room, "If there are no objections, let's launch at six a.m. That's fifteen minutes from now."

When the launch begins, Maxine is in the business war room watching the large TV monitor like everyone else. Within two minutes, over ten thousand people have hit the website and are going through the order funnel, and the rates of arrivals keep climbing. And again, all the CPU loads start climbing, much higher than in the test launch.

People clap as the number of completed orders passes five hundred. Maxine is amazed at the scale of customers who are being mobilized by this launch.

She holds her breath, hoping that all their hard work hardening their systems will make this launch boring. She watches as the number of orders continues to climb...until they flatline, just like on Tuesday.

"Dammit, dammit," Maxine mutters. Something is definitely going wrong again. And in the same portion of the order funnel. Something is preventing people from the shopping cart checkout.

Wes hollers out, "Someone tell me what's going wrong with the shopping cart! Who has any relevant data or error messages?"

Shannon is the first to speak up again. Maxine marvels at Shannon's uncanny ability to be first on scene. "Web shopping cart is generating an error. Fulfillment options aren't being shown! I'm guessing some fulfillment service is failing. Posting screenshot in the chatroom."

Someone from the other side of the room hollers out, "iOS mobile app crashing again." Wes swears. The mobile app Dev manager swears.

Suddenly, Maxine tunes everything out, because in that moment, she's suddenly afraid that maybe Data Hub is causing the problem. She's still trying to think this through when she hears someone from the mobile team holler out: "Wes! The app just crashed after I hit the checkout button, right when it should have presented all the transaction details. I think a call to a back-end service is timing out. I thought we fixed all the places where that can happen, but we obviously missed one. We're trying to figure out which service call is causing the problem."

"Could that be a call to Data Hub?" Maxine whispers to Tom.

"Not sure," Tom says, thinking. "I don't think there's any direct calls from the mobile app to us..."

On her laptop, Maxine pulls up the logs from the production Data Hub service, looking for anything unusual, grateful that she can do this herself now. She sees a couple of incoming order events, which generate four outgoing calls to other business systems. They all appear to be succeeding.

Seeing nothing, she turns her attention back to the front of the noisy room where Wes, Kurt, and Chris are convening. Seeing that they're actively in discussion, Maxine joins them. She hears Wes ask, "...so what service *is* failing?"

Chris and Kurt pow-wow for a bit, and Wes apparently loses patience. He turns to the entire room and hollers over all commotion, "Listen up, everyone! Something in the transaction path between bringing up the shopping cart and completing an order is failing. Maxine, what are the names of each of these transactions and service calls?"

Although she is surprised at being prompted, she quickly rattles off eleven API calls and services off the top of her head. Brent calls out three more. "Thank you, Maxine and Brent," Wes says.

Turning to the room, he hollers, "Okay, everyone, prove to me that each one of those services are working!"

Minutes later, they discover the problem. When a customer views the shopping cart, they are presented with the order details, payment options, and shipping options. When all that is correct, the customer hits the place order button.

Apparently, when displaying this page in the mobile app and on the web, a call is made to a back-end service to determine which shipping options are available based on their location, such as next-day air and ground shipment, as well as providers such as UPS and FedEx.

This service calls out to a bunch of external APIs from the shipping providers, and some of those are failing. Brent suspects that they are being rate-limited by one of them, because they'd never had Parts Unlimited servers send so many queries like this before.

Maxine can't believe that a service that seems so trivial is jeopardizing the entire launch. She smiles and makes a note of this, because she knows that this will likely be the new normal. *But for something this mission-critical, there's no way we should depend on external services,* she thinks. *We need to gracefully handle the case when they're down or when they cut us off.*

Maxine joins the technology team leaders huddling in the front of the room. She suggests, "When we get shipping API failures, maybe we present just the ground shipment option. We know that this type of shipping is always available...Thoughts?"

The fulfillment service team lead nods, and they quickly work through the details with Wes and Maggie. They decide that, effective immediately, if they can't get information from all shippers, they'll just present ground shipment as the only option.

After all, it's better to take their order and ship it slowly as opposed to giving them an error page.

The team lead says, "Give us ten or fifteen minutes to push the code change out. I'll keep you posted," and runs from the room.

Ten minutes later, Maxine is pacing, waiting for the fulfillment team to announce that they're pushing their fix into production. When that happens, everyone will high-five each other and celebrate. She's still waiting when someone yells out, "Wes! Web server page requests are timing out and front-end servers are crashing! These aren't '404' errors. Two servers are actually rebooting and clients are starting to get 'unable to connect' errors!"

Maxine looks at the dashboards and is shocked at what she sees. The entire web server farm is pegged at a hundred percent CPU utilization, with some of them X'ed out because they have hard-crashed. Page load times have gone from 700 milliseconds to over twenty seconds, which is basically forever, and still climbing.

This means some people going to their webpage won't see anything at all because the requests for the page are not being fulfilled.

Wes is staring at the graphs too, and then attempts to load the webpage on his phone. "Confirmed. Nothing is loading in my mobile browser. Web server team, what's going on?" he hollers out.

"They're in the next room," Kurt says. "I'll go find out." Maxine follows.

In the next ten minutes, they learn just how bad the problem is. A record number of people are hitting the e-commerce site. They had anticipated this, which is why Brent had blasted their site with a homemade bot army, making sure they could actually handle such a heavy load.

But apparently, they missed something important. They hadn't tested for real customers coming to their site, who were presented product recommendations based on their customer profile. This was a new component they had created in the last week. The component wouldn't render for bots, only for actual customers who were logged in."

As real customers hit their sites, this component made a bunch of database lookups from the front-end servers, which were never tested at this scale. Now those front-end servers are crashing under the load like a house of cards.

"I need ideas on how to keep those front-end servers alive, I don't care how crazy!" Wes says from the front of the room. The enormity of the problem is clear to everyone. Seventy percent of all incoming traffic is through the web. The largest portion of their order funnel is still the web, and if that stays down, all Black Friday goals will go down with it.

"Get more servers into rotation?" someone says. Wes responds immediately, "Do it! No, Brent, not you, you stay here. Get someone assigned to it... Other ideas, people?"

More ideas come out, and almost all of them are shot down. Brent says, "The recommendation component is what's causing the unusual server load. Can we disable it until traffic dies down?"

Maxine groans inwardly. They had worked so hard to get it working, and now they might have to tear it out to keep the site running.

"Interesting. Well, can we or can't we?" Wes says, asking the room.

A group of managers and technical leads huddle with Maxine and Brent, and they quickly brainstorm ideas. They finally decide to just change the HTML page, commenting out the recommendations component. A brute force approach that Maxine appreciates, because no code changes are needed. The front-end team lead says, "We can change the HTML page and push it out to all the servers within ten minutes."

"Go!" Wes says.

Maxine watches over the shoulders of two engineers as they carefully modify the HTML file. They're careful because a mistake in the HTML can break the website as thoroughly as any code change. When he's done, they review it together, commit the change into version control, and initiate the push into production.

They're surprised when there is no impact to the front-end performance, even after three minutes. They keep waiting to see a change, but servers keep dying. "What's going on? What did we miss?" the engineer says, obviously trying to stay calm, confirming over and over that his modified HTML file is being loaded in the browser.

"I can see your changes in the HTML served by the site," Maxine announces loudly. "There must be another path that displays the recommendations component?"

Wes is watching from behind them. "Everyone, the new HTML file has been pushed into production, but we're still getting excessive CPU load. I need confirmation that recommendation component is still getting rendered somewhere. Give me hypotheses and ideas!"

It takes four more minutes for them to discover that there is one more place where the component can be rendered. Maxine watches as they push another HTML file and is relieved to see that sixty seconds later the CPU load drops by thirty percent.

"Congratulations, team," Wes says, pausing to smile. He continues, "But that's not enough to keep our servers up. What else can we do to reduce the load, people?"

More ideas are proposed, more ideas are shot down, but some are jumped on immediately. The server load finally dips another fifty percent when the most common graphic images are offloaded from their local web servers and moved to a Content Distribution Network (CDN). This takes almost an hour to fully execute, but it's enough to prevent the site from going down entirely.

And so it goes for the rest of the day—hundreds of things going wrong, some big, some small, and never just one problem at a time. Like in their post mortems, they learn how imperfectly they understand this incredibly vast and complex system they've created and now must keep operating under extreme conditions.

Hours fly by. There are moments of tired smiles and high fives as heroic acts keep everything running. The number of completed orders continues to climb, and Maxine is relieved that incoming order rates peak around three p.m., giving people a reason to hope that the worst might be behind them.

Strangely, Maxine has a brief glimpse of Sarah looking sour on the sidelines—but even this doesn't bother her. Maxine's so proud of how well her teams did, handling every crisis that was thrown their way, quickly adapting and learning. And absolutely everyone knows that all this adversity is a great thing, because it is a consequence of the outrageous success of the Black Friday promotion made possible by the Unicorn Project.

By four, it's clear that the worst is behind them. Order traffic is still incredibly high, but off fifty percent from their peak earlier in the day. The number of failures and near-misses are down to a less bewildering rate, and people are actually starting to relax. As evidence of this, Wes is now wearing a Parts Unlimited baseball hat with a unicorn and large flames emblazoned on the side. He is laughing and joking with the people around him, handing out hats to everybody who walks by.

Shortly before five, Maggie goes to the front of the room, and the champagne bottles and plastic cups are carried in by her staff. When everyone has a cup, she says, "What a day, everyone! We made it!"

Everyone cheers, and Maxine drains her glass. She's exhausted, but she can't wait to hear the business results from everything they've done today.

"This is the largest digital campaign that this company has ever done," Maggie says. "We sent more emails today than ever. We pushed out more mobile app notifications than ever. We had the highest response rates. The highest conversion rates. We had higher e-commerce sales today than any other day in the company's history. We will likely have the highest margin on sales today than any single other day. How's that for the Unicorn Project pulling through?"

Maxine laughs uproariously and cheers loudly, along with everyone around her.

Maggie continues, "It's going to take days to get final numbers, but you can see on the screen behind me that we've booked over $29 million in revenue today alone. We blew away last year's sales record by a mile!"

Maggie looks around the room for a moment, cheers again, and then says slowly, "This is a watershed moment for Parts Unlimited. This is what we've been reaching for, for years. This shows that even horses can do unicorn-like things. Trust me, this will turn a lot of heads, and our job now is to start dreaming bigger. We've shown what an incredible business and technology team working together can do, and we've got to elevate the dreams, goals, and aspirations of our business leadership.

"Bigger and better things are yet to come, everyone," she says. "But in the meantime, we've all earned the right to celebrate. Uh, that is, when Wes says it's safe for us to celebrate. Kurt and Maxine, get on up here and say a couple of words."

Kurt joins Maggie, laughing as he beckons to Maxine to join him at the front of the room. "Here's to a kick-ass technology team that supported the Promotions team! We took a bunch of risks, and we did things that have never been done before in this company. As Maggie just said, we have a chance to make a material difference to the performance of the company."

Kurt turns to Maxine, obviously expecting her to say something. Maxine looks at everyone for a moment. "I'm so proud to be a part of this effort. Kurt is right in that we all took a bunch of risks to get here, and I think we've all learned so much in this journey. I can't believe how much we've gotten done since I was first exiled to the Phoenix Project only a couple of months ago. Working on the Unicorn Project has been one of the most rewarding and fun things I've ever done, and I've never been as proud as I am today.

"And I can't wait to celebrate with all of you tonight, because I heard that Kurt is buying drinks at the Dockside. But there is one thing I need to say," she says, waiting for people's cheering to quiet down. "As awesome and amazing as what we pulled off today was, we're a long way from being done. We're basically Blockbuster, who just figured out how to do paper coupon promotions. If you think that's enough to save Parts Unlimited, you must be smoking something.

"Maggie's right. We're just at the beginning of our real fight. We haven't blown up the Death Star yet. Not by a long shot. It's still out there. What we did today was we finally figured out how to fly our X-wings. Our world is still in grave danger," she continues. "But we finally have the tools, the culture, the technical excellence, and the leadership to win the fight. I can't wait for the next chapter to prove that we're not a Blockbusters or Borders, Toys"R"Us or Sears. We're in it to win it, not to be another causality of the Retail Apocalypse!"

Having said what she wanted to say, Maxine looks up and sees the shocked looks on everyone's faces. *Oops*, Maxine thinks, realizing that she maybe should have saved that speech for a private conversation at the Dockside. Then she hears Maggie say, "Holy cow, Maxine is so right! I'm totally going to use that line with Steve and Sarah. I can't wait for Round 2!"

Everyone laughs and then people start applauding and cheering, Maggie loudest of them all. Although at the mention of Sarah, Maxine looks around, puzzled. She's nowhere in sight. *This is a very bad sign*, Maxine thinks. *Usually she'd be here to claim credit. Or pounce on someone if something went badly wrong.* But Maxine is feeling too exhilarated to really care.

Kurt and Maxine are the first ones at the Dockside. They push a bunch of tables together and pre-order a bunch of pitchers of beer for the large group that will be assembling there soon. Kurt looks squarely at Maxine. "By the way, this is a great time for me to tell you how much I appreciate everything you've done. We couldn't have done this without you…the Rebellion changed when you arrived on the scene."

Hearing this, Maxine smiles. "You're welcome, Kurt! We make a great team. And I'm so grateful that you sucked me into all of this."

She sits down as people start to file in and takes a sip of her wine, thoroughly enjoying it. She discovered a couple of weeks ago that Erik had instructed the bartender to always serve her from a special stash of wine from a vineyard owned by a friend of his.

She looked into buying a bunch of bottles but balked when she found out how much it cost. Apparently, Erik drastically subsidizes the cost for her here. She bought one bottle for her and her husband to drink on a special occasion.

As if he knew she was thinking about the wine, Erik arrives, grabbing the seat next to her. "Congratulations to you both—you did terrific today. Now, you need to show Steve and Dick how the future requires creating a dynamic, learning organization where experimentation and learning are a part of everyone's daily work. It's funny, when Steve was VP of manufacturing, he was very proud that hundreds of plant worker suggestions were put into production to improve safety, to reduce toil, to increase quality, and to increase flow. That too is also a form of continual experimentation. You now need it at a much larger level, liberated from the tyranny of project management and functional silos.

"The Fifth Ideal is about a ruthless Customer Focus, where you are truly striving for what is best for them, instead of the more parochial goals that they don't care about, whether it's your internal plans of record or how your functional silos are measured," he says. "Instead we ask whether our daily actions truly improve the lives of our customer, create value for them, and whether they'd pay for it. And if they don't, maybe we shouldn't be doing it at all."

Erik gets up, and one of the bartenders arrives with a newly opened bottle of wine. Erik takes it and places it in front of Maxine with a wink. "Congratulations, Maxine. Catch y'all later tonight!"

He leaves just as six more of their teammates walk through the door. Maggie turns to Maxine and Kurt and asks, "What was that all about?"

"I'm trying to figure that out myself," Maxine says. "But it's nothing that can't wait until next week. Maybe we can find a moment to talk later tonight... But in the meantime, let's celebrate!"

The next morning when Maxine wakes up, her head is pounding. On top of the Dockside celebration, she and her husband had a couple more drinks while watching their favorite TV series late into the night. She didn't actually remember falling asleep, such was her sudden exhaustion.

She wants to go back to sleep on this Saturday morning, but she scans her phone. There is some chatter in the chatrooms about an ongoing issue in the stores. Apparently, store managers are having problems because of overwhelming demand for promoted items. They were completely out of stock, and it was taking them fifteen minutes per customer to create rain check orders, having to key each one into another clunky in-house ordering system.

The in-store app teams were dispatched to the stores to figure out how to speed things up. Someone thinks they could write a simple tablet app to simplify the process. Maxine likes the idea, and she has full confidence that they'll come up with a fix that will delight the in-store managers and staff.

She smiles, satisfied that this problem could be solved without her. Over the past month, she has grown to trust and respect her teammates and appreciate what they're doing.

Maxine grins as she looks at the tickets to Comic-Con that Jake bought yesterday for her and the whole family.

She smells bacon and eggs. *Jake must be making breakfast*, she thinks. Maybe she can go back to sleep after eating. *Life keeps getting better.*

CHAPTER 16

Friday, December 5

One week later, Maxine is sitting in the fanciest conference room she's ever seen. She's in Building 2, where all the top executives have their offices. The building is nearly seventy years old, one of the oldest and tallest on the corporate campus, complete with wood-paneled walls.

For Maxine, it's surreal to look at who's sitting at the table. Never before has she been in a meeting with so many top executives. At the head of the table are Steve, Dick, Sarah, and three other executives she doesn't recognize. This is the first time that she's been in the same room with Steve and Dick, outside of the Town Halls.

Maxine is surprised that Erik is sitting at the table too. Steve and Dick don't give him much notice, as if they're used to having him around.

While Maggie is at the front of the room getting ready to present, Maxine stares around the room representing the opulence of a bygone era. She feels like she needs to tell Kurt not to touch any of the paintings or steal any of the fancy things hanging on the walls.

It's like the bridge crew decided to invite the red shirts from Engineering into the captain's quarters for tea, asking for their advice on how to deploy their starship fleet.

Which is, it occurs to her, what's actually happening. Maggie's briefing the top company executives on the blindingly awesome success of the Unicorn Project, the looming remaining threats that Maxine had warned about, and to present their proposals.

When Steve nods, Maggie begins her presentation, reviewing the amazing Black Friday statistics. Even though Maxine has seen her present before, she's still blown away by Maggie. She's on fire, brilliantly describing what the team did and the amazing business outcomes they generated.

"...All that activity resulted in what you've seen in these official revenue numbers. Because of the Black Friday campaign, we posted nearly $35 million of revenue on top of our run-rate business. Almost

• The Unicorn Project

all of those orders came in through the web or our mobile apps," she says. "For a variety of reasons, we believe this is mostly additive revenue. In other words, revenue that wouldn't have been attained were it not for these campaigns. Which was the result of thousands of experiments, analyzing our customer base in ways we've never been able to before. This was made possible by the five incredible technology platforms we created and using all the data in our systems to make fantastic predictions on which promotions would most effectively drive sales.

"We moved inventory that had been sitting on shelves, often for a year or more, freeing up badly needed working capital," she says. "Looking forward, assuming we can generate some equally exciting promotions over the holidays, I'm thinking we could be looking at $70 million of upside revenue. That's twenty percent above what we've been signaling to analysts and Wall Street."

That generates smiles and a buzz of conversation, especially from Dick. "That would lift our net margins to levels we haven't seen in four years, Steve," he says. "It's been way too long since we've actually surprised analysts, in a good way, that is."

There's laughter around the table, and Steve has a happy but tight-lipped smile on his face. People are in a good mood, Maxine sees. Except Sarah, who is scowling, periodically taking out her phone and tapping furiously to someone.

Maxine stares at Steve and Sarah, mystified at the strange dynamics between them. Maggie continues, "There's more good news. We've put a huge amount of focus on improving the in-store systems to better help store managers incorporate the practices that we know every one of our rock star store managers use. We've put a bunch of new capabilities into the tablets that employees use, making it easy for them to do things like look up the availability of parts and ship them from other stores.

"Maybe more importantly, in every tablet app, we took out any question that slowed down the ability for our in-store employees to help our customers," she says. "We used to ask them for the customer name or phone number first, with no way to skip. No wonder our employees stopped using those tablets!

"In the last sixty days, in-store sales for our pilot stores are up almost seven percent," Maggie explains. "To put this into perspective, the non-pilot stores have had flat or negative same-store sales. This performance is extremely noteworthy and shows that better customer service enables more sales, which has always been a Parts Unlimited core value.

"Like most businesses these days, we use the Net Promoter Score to rate customer satisfaction. We ask our customers, on a scale of 0 to 10, how likely it is that they would recommend our stores to their friends. The 9s and 10s are promoters, the 7s and 8s are neutrals, and the rest are detractors. To compute the score, we subtract the percentage of detractors from the percentage of promoters. An NPS score of thirty is considered good, and above fifty is great.

"For nearly a decade, we've hovered around fifteen, which puts us right in the middle of the pack among our competitors. But that's also what most airlines get, so it's really not something we brag about," she says. "We did a little experiment after the Black Friday promotion. We compared people who bought a promoted item versus the population at large. Customers who bought something during our promotion swung eleven points higher than the rest. And when you look at the pilot stores with ship-to-store and the new in-store apps, they swing almost fifteen points higher.

"I've never seen anything like this in my career," she says. "Those stores are now scoring higher than any of our competition. They're now on par with some fantastic retailers, like Ikea. For a store that sells windshield wiper fluid, I think that's pretty amazing."

She moves on to the next slide: "Our store managers are also reporting improvements in employee engagement and morale. Here's a quote from one store manager that I keep reading over and over again: 'My in-store staff love the new in-store systems. One of my staff actually cried. She said that the old system not only made her feel stupid and helpless but also frustrated, because she couldn't help our customers. Thank you so much to you and your team for making a real difference to my team and our customers!'"

Maxine hears impressed murmurs all around the table. Steve smiles broadly. "It's been true for hundreds of years and probably thousands more: employee engagement and customer satisfaction are the only things that matter. If we do that right, and manage cash effectively, every other financial target will take care of itself."

Maxine can't help herself. She says to Dick, "As a numbers person, do you really believe what Steve said? That's quite a bold claim, isn't it?"

Dick smiles, as if he really appreciates the question. "I do believe it, especially as a numbers guy. Some of the most revered and admired companies all had that in their heyday, like Xerox, P&G, Walmart, Motorola…Now, it's Toyota, Tesla, Apple, Microsoft, Amazon…How you achieve those metrics have changed, but the importance of those metrics are still the same."

"Amen to that, Dick," Erik says. "Well done, Maggie, Kurt, and Maxine."

"It's so exciting to see happen, and I really think we're moving the needle," Maggie says, smiling almost as broadly as Maxine is. "I've saved the best for last. Six months ago, we had one of the worst mobile apps in our industry. I'm guessing that all of you have installed the app but none of you have spent more than a couple of minutes in it."

Maggie smiles, looking around the room at the sheepish grins around the table. She says, "Don't feel too bad, because I hadn't, either. Everyone knew that this was a real problem. If we can't create a compelling reason to use the app, if we don't solve an actual problem that our customers care about, why did we even build it in the first place?

"We've spent a lot of time studying our customers, trying to figure out their wants and needs," she says. "So, we made a couple of bets, looking at what we could build that would keep customers coming back for more. Here's one bet we made."

She advances to the next slide, showing a picture of a VIN sticker that is on every car manufactured since 1954.

"Typing in these VIN numbers is the bane of almost every Parts Unlimited employee," she says, resulting in knowing chuckles from all around the room. "All of you have worked in-store. You know how difficult and error-prone this is. We now enable customers to use their app to create a profile for all of their cars. They just scan the VIN on their car using their phone camera, and we automatically populate the information of their car: make, model, year, and we can even pull in records from Carfax and other services.

"Now they can walk into a store, and our in-store employees can scan a QR code on their phone to pull up their customer's record. Our employees don't need to walk out to the customer's car, sometimes in the rain and snow, to write down that fourteen-digit VIN on a piece of paper.

"One of our store managers said, 'This is a game changer. Besides being great for our customers, it's great for our employees. For the first time, it's like we're doctors who have their patient's charts on hand. We know our customer's history, what's important to them, and we can better help keep their cars on the road. I've been told thank you more times in the last month than I have in most years!'

"This could create some exciting business opportunities: we could potentially create all sorts of maintenance programs for them. We could explore subscription programs, where they automatically receive parts based on their consumption. We could potentially partner with service stations to get any needed work scheduled, or even do it ourselves," she says, advancing to the next slide.

"To me, the success of all of these programs suggest that there are some opportunities that could dramatically reshape the future of Parts Unlimited," she says, looking more serious than she has during the entire briefing.

"After the Black Friday promotion, Maxine said that we were still a long way from winning the war. Just like a better coupon campaign wouldn't have saved Blockbuster, we are still a long way from figuring out how to survive the 'digital disruption' or 'retail apocalypse.' As good as the quarter may turn out, we haven't blown up the Death Star. It's still out there, and we need to figure out how to engage it in battle and win. Otherwise, we risk decline, irrelevance, or, worse, extinction."

Maxine feels herself blushing but keeps her attention on the executives. She knows Maggie is starting her pitch.

"Project Unicorn could just be the beginning of learning how we can dominate the market by understanding our customers better than anyone else does," she says. "After all, we created this market almost a century ago. Our proposal is that we fund more teams to explore the most promising business ideas, to find the next winner like the Unicorn Project.

"What I've learned in Promotions is that it's an extremely experimental process, an exercise of exploration and learning. Not every idea is a winner," she says. "For every winning idea, there are many losing ideas. And some of the winners seemed outright crazy and never would have been approved by the typical middle-manager or committee. The literature suggests that in general, only one out of every three strategic ideas has a positive result, and only a third actually move the needle in a material way.

"And that's for the big, strategic ideas," she says. "For feature promotions, A/B tests, or algorithmic testing, you may be thrilled to even have five percent of tests work.

"We need a group that is dedicated and empowered to explore a broad range of business ideas that take advantage of our unique position in the marketplace, to quickly make bets, and then explore and validate them," she says. "We need to have some way to quickly shut down bets that don't pan out and to double-down on the winners.

"Project Unicorn shows that we have the capability to do this," she says. "But this time around, we need to do it with the sponsorship and support of the highest levels of the organization."

Maxine sees Steve smile, looking not just interested, but delighted. He applauds loudly, but before he can say anything, Erik speaks up.

"Ms. Lee is exactly right, Steve," Erik says, looking up from his notebook, which appears to be full of doodles. "You are in charge of a century-old business that might finally be climbing out of its doldrums, thanks to the heroic work of Maggie, Kurt, and Maxine. Everything around you has been built upon the success of your Horizon 1 or cash-cow business. And as Maggie is alluding, you have nothing in Horizons 2 or 3."

Maxine looks around and confirms that she's not the only person confused by what Erik just said. Steve doesn't appear to be phased by Erik's non sequitur. Instead he asks, "What are Horizons 1, 2, and 3, and why are they important?"

"A great question," Erik says, standing. "The concepts of Horizons 1, 2, and 3 were popularized by Sensei Dr. Geoffrey Moore, who is most famous for his book *Crossing the Chasm*, which introduced the customer adoption curve into modern business planning. He observed that customer adoption is a Gaussian distribution curve, naming them the innovators, early adopters, early majority, late majority, and laggards. And yet, as brilliant as this was, I think he will be best-known for the Four Zones, which help us better organize ourselves to win in all Three Horizons.

"Horizon 1 is your successful, cash-cow businesses, where the customer, business, and operational models are well-known and predictable. For you, that's your manufacturing and retail operations, which make up sixty and forty percent of revenue, respectively. Both of these businesses generate over $1 billion in annual revenue but are under fierce attack by competitors and disruptors," he says.

"Almost all businesses fade over time, because any profitable operation will attract competitors. The economic logic of selling reductions in transactional cost is irresistible and inevitable," he says. "Which is why

Horizon 2 lines of business are so important, because they represent the future of the company. They may introduce the company's capabilities to new customers, adjacent markets, or with different business models. These endeavors may not be profitable, but this is where we find higher-growth areas. It is from here that enterprising leaders create the next generation of Horizon 1 businesses. For you, this transition happens when your Horizon 2 business revenue hits $100 million.

"You may have guessed that Horizon 2 efforts come from Horizon 3, where the focus is on velocity of learning and having a broad pool of ideas to explore," he says. "Here, the name of the game is to prototype ideas and to answer as quickly as possible the three questions of market risk, technical risk, and business model risk: Does the idea solve a real customer need? Is it technically feasible? And is there a financially feasible engine of growth? If the answer is *no* to any of them, it's time to pivot or kill the idea.

"If the answer is *yes*, then the idea is continually developed until it earns the right to graduate to Horizon 2, where the business builders take over," he says, pausing for a moment. "Your obvious problem is that you have virtually no Horizon 2 businesses, and absolutely no Horizon 3.

"Steve, your intuition serves you well. You know you need to explore Horizon 3 opportunities. And you know how different Horizon 1 and 3 are," he says. "Horizon 1 thrives on process and consistency, on rules and compliance, and on bureaucracies, which create extraordinary resilience. These are the mechanisms that allow greatness to be consistently delivered over decades.

"In contrast, in Horizon 3, you must go fast, you must be constantly experimenting, and you must be allowed to break all the rules and processes governing Horizon 1," he continues. "As Maggie says, it's about fast iteration, making lots of bets, and doubling down on the winners until they graduate to become Horizon 2 businesses. This is where the new methods are forged and mastered, which will likely help the organization survive into the next century.

"And in this age, and nowhere more than in Horizon 3, speed matters," he says. "In the pharmaceutical business, the effort required to create a market offering is huge: billions of dollars are spent over a decade to create a new drug. The instant you have an idea, you patent it, which gives you only twenty years of IP protection before generic copies are allowed and your ability to charge a price premium disappears.

"There, Sensei Dr. Steven Spear observed that for each day you can get to market faster, you can often capture upwards of millions of dollars of additional revenue. If you're first to market, you will capture fifty percent of the revenue that the entire product category will ever yield. Second place will capture twenty-five percent, and third place will get fifteen percent. For any later entrants, it will surely have been a complete waste of time and money.

"Speed matters. Or more precisely, lead time from idea to market offering matters," he says. "And regardless of what horizon you're in, this is the Age of Software. Almost all business investment now involves software. And that means we must elevate developer productivity, as Maxine has so splendidly done."

Erik looks at his watch and starts gathering his things. "I will leave you with one last caution. Horizon 1 and Horizon 3 are often in conflict with each other." He gestures at Sarah meaningfully. "Left unchecked, Horizon 1 leaders will consume all the resources of the company. They will note correctly that they are the lifeblood of the company, but that's only true in the short term. There is an instinct to maximize profitability and take cash out of the business instead of reinvesting it. This is the 'manage to value' thesis and is the opposite of 'manage to growth.' If you want growth, Steve, you must protect Horizons 2 and 3, and any learnings generated there must be spread throughout the company."

Erik looks to Maxine. "You saw how all the learnings from Data Hub and the Unicorn Project made it possible to achieve the original goals of the Phoenix Project. There are plenty more learnings to be had. And in fact, I suspect creating a learning organization will become front and center soon."

Erik looks back at Steve. "You created one of the safest and most admired manufacturing organizations in the world by creating a unique learning culture, where physical safety is embraced by everyone in the organization," he says. "What if psychological safety is as much of a precondition to dynamic, learning organizations as physical safety?"

He looks at his watch again. "I've got to run, folks," he says, heading to the door. "I have a lunch date that I can't miss. I wish you the best of luck! The survival of the company surely depends upon it."

Everyone stares as Erik leaves the room, pulling his suitcase behind him. Maxine looks back at Steve, who looks thoughtful. With some awe, she remembers Erik suggesting that she must enlist Steve's help to change the culture of fear of the technology organization. *I can't believe he teed that up for me,* she thinks.

Maxine is trying to think of what she must do when Sarah stands up. She says, "Steve, as much as I appreciate what Maggie and her little team have done, I think this is a losing proposition. Your chairman and boss, Bob Strauss, has grave doubts about the future of the company," Sarah says. "We cannot drive up R&D expenses for any wild-eyed ventures, these so-called 'Horizon 3' activities. We have demonstrated over and over that we simply do not have the DNA to compete against all the startups on the low end, and we cannot continue to fight a two-front battle on the manufacturing and retailing side on the high end at the same time.

"Our two Horizon 1 businesses are struggling. At this point, Bob's idea of splitting up the company and selling off the pieces is our only prayer of salvaging shareholder value. Absolutely no one is interested in buying them together," she says. "During our preparation for the January board meeting, Bob and our new board director, Alan, have convinced me that the growth path is just too risky. In fact, I'm convinced we should do another round of headcount reductions immediately to shore up profits.

"This is the right thing to do for our shareholders, and it will undoubtedly make us more attractive to acquirers when we start the roadshow with the investment bankers," she continues. "This is what I'll be recommending in my meeting with Bob and Alan in our special board subcommittee."

Sarah gathers her things. With an expression that Maxine can only characterize as sinister, she says to Steve, "I notice that you were not invited to that meeting. Too bad. I'll let you know how that meeting goes and what we decide."

Maxine watches with everyone else as she opens the door and exits, wondering why Steve can't just fire Sarah. Why does he put up with her antics? The excitement and pride she was feeling moments ago is gone. Could Sarah really disregard everything that the Unicorn Project had achieved? Was it all for nothing? She thinks back to when everyone was celebrating after the successful Black Friday launch, except Sarah, who had mysteriously disappeared.

Watching the door close, Maxine realizes that her worst fears about Sarah dismissing or undermining their efforts aren't so crazy after all.

Steve stares at the door for several moments before he lets out a long sigh. He turns to the rest of the room. "Unlike Sarah, my bets are on the growth thesis. If we're not growing, we're shrinking, and that's not why I'm here at Parts Unlimited. There's no question that we need to make Horizon 3 bets. Dick and I have already modeled this scenario. I propose carving out $5 million to fund Maggie's innovation efforts," he says.

Maxine's heart leaps, realizing that Maggie's proposal may still have a chance. Then Steve says, "But Sarah might be able to cut us off at the knees if she convinces Bob to cut staff and expenses."

"Maybe Bob and the rest of the board won't be that short-sighted," Dick replies. At Steve's skeptical expression, he says, "Well, if it happens, we'll figure something out. In the meantime, what would we do with that five million? How do we put it to work?"

Over the next three exciting hours, an outline of a plan emerges. Kurt, Maggie, and Maxine will be part of the Innovation team, reporting directly to Bill Palmer. Kurt and Maggie will be "two in a box," occupying the same position in the org chart, sharing responsibility for the business and technical outcomes.

"You will be responsible for nurturing new, promising ideas and exploring market risk, technical risk, and business model risk," Steve continues to summarize. "Each initiative will have clearly defined business outcome measures, such as customer acquisition, repeat customer usage, or customer satisfaction. At the end of each quarter, we'll review progress on each initiative, and we'll make a decision: continue funding the project; kill it, reassigning the team to the next best idea; double-down on the project; or graduate it to Horizon 2. We'll also decide whether the entire program needs to be grown or shrunk.

"Your charter is to find new ways to use technology to better enable supporting the nearly century-old vision: help our customers keep their cars running so they can conduct their daily lives"

Steve turns to Bill and says, "To capture the best ideas, go create an Innovation Council. Find fifty of the most respected people from across the entire organization, including store managers, sales managers, technicians, engineers, and of course, the technology organization."

Bill nods, taking notes on his clipboard. Maxine sees everyone around the table nodding in agreement.

As they adjourn, Steve says to everyone, "I have the utmost confidence in Bill, who will be leading this effort. This is something that we've never done before, so it will be new to almost everyone. So, let us know what we can do to support you and your effort."

"Roger that," Bill says. Gesturing at his clipboard, he says, "I already have a list of things I'd like your help on." As Bill rattles them off, Steve quickly mobilizes resources from across the entire company. Maxine marvels at how efficiently Bill gets what he needs from Steve, and the resources Steve is putting at Bill's disposal.

After the meeting, Bill asks Kurt, Maggie, and Maxine to walk with him back to Building 5. The entire walk back, Maxine hears Kurt and Maggie share how elated they are at how the meeting went. Maxine is excited to be working with Bill, who has always seemed level-headed and a straight-shooter, and he's already demonstrated how effectively he can drive large initiatives.

To Maxine, it seems like Rebellion victory is within sight, with all the sponsorship, funding, support, and energy they need to win.

But there's still the question of Sarah. *If she succeeds in convincing Bob Strauss to break up and sell the company, then the Evil Empire will have won. But not even Sarah can pull that off, right?*

CHAPTER 17

"What do you mean we're losing all our people?" Kurt says, looking shocked.

It's one week after the meeting with Steve and Dick, and Maxine has been pleased with how the agreed upon plan is rapidly progressing. Bill, Maggie, and Kurt are starting to put together the Innovation Council, and work within the Unicorn Project is going faster than ever, preparing for the massive Christmas holiday promotion launch.

The Orca team continues to study the data from the Thanksgiving campaign, and they are certain they'll have an even higher response rate this time around by incorporating what they've learned. All their experiments and results are again being poured back into the Panther data platform. They are also continuing to harden the infrastructure to handle the resulting onslaught.

However, many of the things they took for granted after last Friday's exciting meeting with Steve and Dick no longer seem certain. Which is why Chris summoned Kurt and Maxine to his office.

"They were never 'your people,' Kurt. You were temporarily loaned a bunch of engineers for the Unicorn Project," says Chris. "All those engineers were already assigned to other projects in the new fiscal year, which starts in a few weeks. They're all important business projects with people depending on them being fully staffed. All those business managers are raising hell because we've reassigned those resources, and they've banded together in revolt."

"But why now?" Kurt asks, incredulous. "What got everyone so riled up?"

Chris laughs humorlessly. "Sarah is stirring the pot, egging them all on. Bill is pulling together another meeting with Steve and Dick to figure out how to deal with the shenanigans she's pulling."

"I can't believe Sarah is stirring up a counter-rebellion, to umm, counter our Rebellion," Kurt mutters, sounding offended that Sarah had stolen his playbook.

Later in the day, Bill writes:

> Continue as planned. We'll figure out how to backfill those positions.
> We are stuck in the middle of a huge political battle. Sarah and a board
> faction are on one side, and we're on the other side with Steve and Dick.

Throughout the day, they discover that Sarah is indeed an incredibly effective corporate guerilla fighter, having successfully raised an insurgency army against them over the past week.

Maxine is grudgingly impressed with her resourcefulness, despite driving her batshit crazy. She wants nothing more than for Sarah to just give up and go away.

"In so many ways, Sarah is a remarkable person," she tells her husband at dinner. "In a slightly different universe, Sarah could have been an amazing force for good. If this were a superhero movie, she'd be the gifted person who turns into the villain after some traumatic life event. And now she goes out of her way to crush all sparks of joy she can find."

Monday morning, Kurt and Maggie meet with Bill to stave off Sarah's efforts to undermine them. Maxine stays behind, resuming her work with Cranky Dave on a technical issue jeopardizing both the Unicorn promotions campaign and the core Phoenix application. Over the last month, they had started building tons of automated tests for Phoenix so that they could better and more safely make changes. The effort was incredibly successful. However, with so many tests, running them now takes hours, and developers are starting to avoid checking in their changes, not wanting to wait for the long test times.

Worse, some of the automated tests were failing intermittently. Last week, she cringed watching as a developer, whose tests failed, just ran them again, and they also failed. So, he ran it a third time, as if it were slot machine in a casino. This time it passed. *This is no way to run a development shop*, Maxine thought with embarrassment and distaste.

Recognizing that this will soon become a new bottleneck for developers, she had the teams work on parallelizing the Phoenix tests so they could be run across multiple servers. But they discovered that running parallel tests caused Phoenix to occasionally deadlock or crash entirely—and if it's crashing during testing, it's probably crashing in production too.

"Maxine, we've narrowed it down to an uncaught exception somewhere in the Phoenix order fulfillment module," says Cranky Dave. Maxine is with Cranky Dave and another engineer with laptops open. When she pulls up the code on her laptop, she physically recoils. "Wow," she says, speechless as she scrolls down the file…and scrolls…and scrolls…

"Yeah," says Cranky Dave, laughing. "This is two thousand lines of code to determine whether we can ship to the order location. A bunch of architects made this framework fifteen years ago, predating Phoenix. Even the TEP-LARB came around and realized this was all a terrible mistake, but the people who wrote that framework are long gone."

Maxine keeps scrolling and scrolling, gob smacked that she can't find any business logic, just boilerplate code: loops iterating through orders, order items, line items, just as dangerously as the middle school girls had done so many months ago. There's null checking everywhere, as well as type tests, downcasting, coercing, and all sorts of horrible contortions to get at the desired data, through enumerated types or polymorphic supertypes without concrete subtypes. There's so many object methods that she can't keep them straight in her head: getOrderLines, getItemLines, getShippingLines…

She opens her mouth, but nothing comes out. "This is…incredible," she says at last, with apoplectic horror and disbelief. She closes her eyes, trying to summon some relentless optimism, thinking of the Hoare principle: "There are two ways to write code: write code so simple there are obviously no bugs in it, or write code so complex that there are no obvious bugs in it."

"Gentlemen, we are going to clean up all this crap," Maxine says, with a level of confidence that she realizes may be foolhardy. Even Cranky Dave looks cowed. She exhorts, "This should be simple code. All we need to do is retrieve the locations from the order, right? We can do this!"

They spend two hours writing tests around the code to make sure they really understand how it works, and then they start pulling out common operations, putting them where they belong. Maxine modifies the class hierarchy to their best advantage, but adheres to functional programming principles, using modern types and their idiomatic map, reduce, and filter functions, just like the famous Google Map/Reduce paper that inspired Shannon's Panther project.

By noon, they've reduced the two thousand lines of code to five hundred lines. Cranky Dave grins. "That is amazing, Maxine. This is probably the first time in over five years that anyone was brave enough to touch this code."

"Eight years," says the other developer. "This code is beautiful! And I think I found the problem. Here's some code that isn't wrapped in a try/catch block."

Looking over at his laptop, Maxine immediately knows they've found the issue. "Nice work!" Now that they've drained the swamp of the muck, the problem is obvious.

While they go get lunch, Maxine stays behind, wanting to try an idea out. She opens up a new window on her laptop. She copies the data that the team has been manipulating all morning and starts redoing the code from scratch in Clojure.

Forty-five minutes later, Cranky Dave is back and hands Maxine her sandwich. He asks, "What are you grinning at?"

"Oh, just the results of a little experiment," she says. "I rewrote our code in a functional programming language, using its built-in data types and standard library, to see if I could make it even simpler, smaller, and get rid of the need for exception handling."

"And?" prompts Cranky Dave. She turns her laptop around to show him.

"Holy shit," he says, staring at her screen in disbelief. "Fifty lines of code."

Maxine laughs, knowing that they'll be inspired to try to match or exceed her results. Even for her, this was an incredible display of achieving the First Ideal of Locality and Simplicity.

The work they did this morning will enable parallelized testing and make it blazingly fast, surely creating huge productivity dividends long in the future, allowing developers to keep moving fast, getting even faster feedback on any errors. It's like the opposite of technical debt. It's like when compounded interest works in your favor. If they could make developers a little more productive all the time, it would always pay off in spades.

Maxine smiles as she sees Cranky Dave open his laptop, still giddy with excitement over their successes. He says, "Uh oh."

On his screen is the Unikitty CI status page. Maxine looks to see whether the fix that they checked in before lunch passed the automated tests. But instead of getting all green lights, she sees that the tests aren't running at all. There are over fifty jobs in front of them, all waiting to start.

"This is bad," Cranky Dave says. "The entire Unikitty CI cluster is down. Everyone's builds are stuck."

Annoyed, Maxine looks over at his screen. She curses. This is ruining what is supposed to be their shining moment of triumph and glory.

He says, "The #ci-unikitty channel is going nuts. No one can run their tests."

Whenever Unikitty goes down, they have a bunch of angry customers: their fellow developers. What better proof that Unikitty is an internal platform that they must manage like a product, not just as a project. It's never done, if they want to keep their customers happy.

They look all over for the Unikitty team. They find Dwayne, Kurt, and two other engineers in a conference room, crowded around Brent's laptop.

"Good timing. All the Dev managers are screaming that their teams can't get their work done," Kurt says, looking up from the huddle. Maxine is surprised at how haggard he looks. He has bags underneath his eyes. *Kurt's having a rough couple of weeks*, she thinks. "We can't afford this distraction right now, of all times…"

"This is what we always wanted, right? Customers!" Maxine says with a big smile. "You wanted people to value the infrastructure we're creating? Well, your wish has been granted. After all, if they didn't care, they wouldn't even bother complaining."

The adoption of CI practices has been astounding, with nearly one third of all engineering teams using Unikitty in their daily work. But they're having problems scaling it to keep up with demand.

She looks at her watch. It's almost noon. Every developer tended to check in their code before heading out to lunch, which probably caused something in Unikitty to fall over. *Unikitty is having more than its share of growing pains*, Maxine thinks.

Kurt sighs. "If you look in the chat room, many of the Dev managers are saying that they're tired of our flaky build servers and that they're pulling their teams out of Unikitty. They're going to go back to doing builds the old way."

Maxine's smile freezes on her face. "You're kidding." Going back to the bad old days like her first days on the Phoenix Project would be…intolerable. That wouldn't be a setback—that would be a genuine disaster.

What was happening? It felt like all the progress they had made with the Phoenix developers and with the achievements of the Black Friday launch and the Unicorn Project were slipping away. They were slowly being pulled back into the morass, dragging all the engineers that they had liberated and made productive back in with them.

It's almost four thirty when the Unikitty team finally gets things back up. But there are so many builds and tests backed up, it will be almost midnight before all the jobs finish running.

"I can't believe it was a networking switch failure," Dwayne says.

Maxine shakes her head in disbelief. Another Unikitty hardware failure is embarrassing. From the beginning, it had been cobbled together from whatever equipment Kurt and the team were able to scavenge from almost every corner of the organization.

They've had disk failures, power failures, and now network hardware problems. She hates seeing highly skilled engineers walking around with screwdrivers, opening up server cases, and mucking about with physical infrastructure.

Sure, she has many fond memories of working on hardware, both in her career and with her kids. When she was a young engineer, she had loved opening those huge boxes full of the newest, hottest equipment on the loading dock, and then racking and stacking them. But back then, she also loved rotating the backup tapes.

Now, this type of work seems so low-value, especially when compared to the opportunity cost of the work they *should* be doing, which is figuring out how to blaze the digital future of Parts Unlimited.

Their job was to build code, not muck with the actual hardware that the code runs on.

"I hate to say it, but I think Unikitty is on her last legs," Maxine says to Dwayne. "We can't keep running something this mission-critical with hardware that Brent finds under his desk. And it's not just hardware issues—each build server is still slightly different. Like when my compile job doesn't run on Build Server #3, it takes ten times as long. We're spending too much time keeping it running. We've got to do something about this—soon."

"No argument from me. We're all just so busy right now," Dwayne says, shrugging his shoulders. Maxine can't argue with that.

As was predicted, there is hell to pay. Tuesday morning during Kurt's team meeting, Kurt says, "Chris not only chewed me out in front of everyone at his staff meeting, but he invited Rick too. He presented his plan to create a competitive CI service to compete with Unikitty."

"Rick?!" Dwayne asks, expressing the complete shock and disbelief that Maxine feels. "He wouldn't recognize a CI service if it bit him in the ass!"

Kurt slumps. "Sarah has apparently started shouting from the rooftops that Unikitty is jeopardizing the entire company and that we should be shut down."

Silence falls over the entire table.

"Amazing how people are blaming us for anything bad that happens around here. The toilets broke on the second floor yesterday, and we're being be blamed for that too," says Cranky Dave.

Kurt's phone buzzes. He picks it up and stares at the screen for several moments. He looks at Maxine. "We gotta go. Bill just pulled together a meeting with Maggie. More bad news, I think."

Maggie sees Bill look up when his assistant Ellen lets her, Kurt, and Maggie into his office. "We've got problems," he says, standing up and picking up his clipboard. "We're meeting Steve and Dick in fifteen minutes in Building 2. I'll brief you on our walk over."

As they walk outside, he says, "Sarah convinced Bob and the rest of the board to freeze all expenses, effective immediately. And Steve just found out that they're denying the $5 million he was going to allocate to the innovation efforts."

Bill shakes his head. "That Sarah is something, isn't she?"

"I have learned so much from her. She's an incredible expert in merchandising, but she's never led software projects," Maggie says. "She creates high expectations for everybody, which is great, but she definitely has some blind spots when it comes to managing people and teams ... she's not exactly a nurturing type."

"No, I suppose I don't," Bill says, grimacing. "I have a really bad feeling about this meeting."

When they walk into the grand conference room, Maxine immediately knows something is wrong. Steve and Dick are here, as well as Chris. But surprisingly, so are Kirsten and, very ominously, Laura Beck, the VP of HR.

Having the head of HR in a meeting is never a good thing, Maxine thinks. To her surprise, she spots Erik standing at the back of the room, looking at the historical pictures hanging on the wall. He gives her a quick wave.

At least Sarah is nowhere to be seen, Maxine thinks.

"Grab a seat, everyone," Steve says, looking up from a printed spread-sheet, a grim expression on his face. "You probably heard that Sarah successfully convinced the board that we shouldn't increase our costs until after we release earnings.

"Unfortunately, that's not all the bad news," he says. "Last night, the board instructed me to reduce costs across the entire company by three percent. Sarah and our new board director, Alan, have convinced everyone that the success of the Black Friday promotions have unlocked huge new efficiencies; therefore, we don't need as many people."

Maxine hears gasps from around the room. She feels like she's going to throw up. Or cry. Or both.

I cannot believe this is happening, Maxine thinks. *I feel like I'm partially responsible. After all, I had a lot to do with making the Unicorn Project so successful and planting the seeds of the Innovation effort.*

And somehow, those successful efforts that she is so proud of are now going to cause a bunch of innocent people to lose their jobs. *Dammit, Sarah,* she thinks.

"Sorry, folks. I know this is surprising news, given the increased revenue from Unicorn. I really thought we had more time with the board," Steve says.

"You've probably already done the math," he continues. "To hit this goal, we're going to have to reduce headcount across the company by about 150 employees. And to fund the innovation efforts from internal operations, we're going to have to find an additional $5 million of costs to cut or reduce headcount by another forty people."

Maxine hears more gasps around the table as the casualties keep mounting. She can't breathe, and she feels her eyes tearing up.

She looks at Laura, the VP of HR. *So this is going to be one of those meetings.* Now that the reduction targets have been set, everyone will first defend their turf, trying to maintain their slice of the pie. Once the allocations have been agreed to, everyone will come up with a list of names of people to eliminate. Then they'll have to decide whether Sally is more important than Sam, or vice versa.

Maxine is filled with dread. Looking around the table she says, "These are real people. People with families who depend on them. These are people who will be walked out the door with all of their things. One after another, everyone will watch people leave, dreading that their name will be called next, wondering when the managers will finally be done piling up the bodies. Only then will Steve's scheduled email go out to the entire company, announcing that the purge is over, including saccharine remarks of optimism and, of course, asking everyone to do more with less."

Everyone drops their heads. Suddenly, Maxine doesn't want anything to do with any of this. She wishes things could go back to the way they were. She wishes she had never joined the Rebellion. She only wanted to get the builds going, to help make developers productive. She had never imagined that it would be the Rebellion that would be helping decide who would get to stay and who must leave.

If I had known that joining the Rebellion would lead to all this, she thinks, looking around, *I would have kept my head down, stayed in my lane, not rocked the boat, just like Chris told me to.*

"I really thought they'd give us until at least January," Dick says, shaking his head. "The purpose of this meeting is to prepare a plan to submit to the board that takes down operating expenses by $15 million. And if we want to fund the innovation efforts, we need to take costs down by $20 million.

"Steve and I have already met with the heads of each business, and we've asked them to put together a plan to cut their part of the $20 million target," he says. "Which is why you're all in the room. We need you all to come up with a plan to eliminate $2 million from the IT organization— that's about fifteen people across all of your groups."

Maxine does the math. That's more than four percent of all the technologists in the company. "No! This is horrible. We can't fund the Innovation effort given all this. It's just not worth letting all those people go," Maxine says. She sees everyone turn toward her, some with expressions of hardened weariness and some with sympathy, as if she were a child who just discovered Santa didn't actually exist.

"Maxine, around this table we're all too used to doing layoffs," Bill says. "I'm guessing that all of us believe that our most important work today is finding a way to fund the Innovation effort. Otherwise, everything you've done and achieved will go to waste. We'll just be choosing a slightly slower death. If we don't invest in doing new things, we'll still end up where we started: outgunned and outmaneuvered in the marketplace."

Chris turns to Maxine. "Bill is right. It's the right thing to do."

Maxine just shakes her head, still aghast at the human toll.

Steve looks at Maxine. "Yes, protecting the Innovation effort is our most important task. If I didn't believe this, I would have just threatened to resign. After all, they can cut costs without me. But this work is so important that we must do everything we can to make sure the Innovation group gets its chance."

This all makes Maxine feel even worse.

"But why? Why is this Innovation effort so important to you?" Maxine finally asks Steve.

Steve looks thoughtful for a moment. "What Erik said last week was right. As a company, we must show that we have a viable growth thesis and that we can create value in ways besides just cutting costs. By the book, there's two extremes for how to run companies, which affects how you plan and how the investment community perceives you. On one extreme, you have Alan and Sarah's way of creating value, which is just by cutting costs. You squeeze every bit of margin you can out of the operation. Some companies thrive at this, and some manage to malinger for decades, but most eventually fade and disappear," Steve explains.

"But when you're in this mode, you're often just playing financial engineering games," Steve says, gesturing at Dick. "In order to stem our losses, we've had to do a couple of asset sales to generate cash. But this can be like selling the furniture to pay the mortgage bill. Eventually, you run out of things to sell and you can no longer fund daily operations, which means more layoffs.

"On the other end of the spectrum, you can choose to build the company for growth. Like I said, if you're not growing, you're slowly dying. The Unicorn Project has proven to all of us that we can actually grow: by creating new offerings that customers want, by taking market share away from our competitors, by doing things that great companies do," Steve says with a thin smile. "And when we grow revenue, we eventually grow profits too. And we earn the ability to innovate and place more bets in the marketplace, which accelerates growth and ensures our relevance in the future.

"Investors reward growth," he says. "Already our stock price is up, and we haven't even reported earnings yet. Analysts are starting to raise their price targets. This means Wall Street is rewarding us with higher multiple on revenue. A couple of months ago, we were valued at less than 1.0x trailing revenue, which is almost an insult, because they're *expecting* us to shrink. When we announce the results of this quarter, hopefully they'll start valuing us as they would any healthy retailer. And in time, they may value us much higher, as someone who is defining and leading, and maybe even disrupting our market.

"Bill is absolutely right, Maxine," he says. "The easier thing to do is to just do what the board says. But the right thing to do is ensure that the Innovation program has its shot. It sucks, but as leaders there should be no doubt that cutting deeper is the right thing to do, because it creates a potential path to long-term growth."

Maxine still feels sick as the managers start to negotiate which departments will eliminate eighteen positions. They debate whether they will eliminate a few experienced engineers or, for the same price, a larger number of junior engineers. Axe the managers or individual contributors. Eliminate employees or contractors.

When she can't take it anymore, Maxine excuses herself to take a walk, just to get out of the room.

When she gets back a half-hour later, she sees that Chris has agreed to RIF (reductions in force) two Dev and five QA positions, most likely underperforming engineers and several managers. Bill must RIF seven positions, targeting the helpdesk, server, and network administration positions, as well a manager. Maxine hopes that Derek will survive this, not to mention her old MRP team.

Surprisingly, Kirsten has put on the table seven project managers, noting that the Rebellion has changed the way teams work. "Long term, we don't want to manage our dependencies, we want to eliminate them," she says. "That's the system of work and the company architecture we need to create, which means fewer project managers. Maxine has shown repeatedly how this can be done. And we have so much further to go."

On the one hand, Maxine is impressed by the professionalism being displayed by everyone in the room. But hearing some of the names being proposed for the RIF and being held up as the reason to let go more of Kirsten's team, Maxine feels like she's going to throw up again.

"You'll probably have to cut even deeper than you think," Erik says from across the table, speaking for the first time since the meeting started. Maxine had nearly forgotten he was there.

"Oh, *great*," Bill says.

"Last time we met, I mentioned Sensei Geoffrey Moore's Three Horizons, but I didn't have time to explain his concept of Core versus Context, which are what the Four Zones are about," Erik says. "Sensei Moore observed that many businesses understand the Three Horizons but are still unable to properly invest in the next generation of innovation. In other words, they underinvest in *Core*, because they are being controlled by *Context*.

"Cores are the central competencies of the organization. These are things that customers are willing to pay for and what investors reward," he says. "Context is everything else. It's the cafeterias, shuttles between buildings, and the thousands of things companies must do to operate. They're often mission-critical, such as HR, payroll, and email. But our customers do not pay us for the great payroll services we provide to our employees.

"Not properly managing Context is what Sensei Moore called the *killing ground* of great companies. Companies who become too burdened by Context are unable to properly invest in Core. There is a strategy for transforming a company, but it also takes ruthless focus and tenacity."

Erik looks at Bill and Steve. "You know that technology must become a core competency of this company and, indeed, that the future of Parts Unlimited depends upon it. But how much of the $80 million of your technology spending is Core, actively building competitive advantage, and how much of it is Context, which is important and maybe even mission-critical, but still needs to be standardized, managed down, and maybe even outsourced entirely?"

Bill bristles, turning red. Up until now, he always appeared remarkably stoic and reserved, but apparently Erik had touched a nerve. "You're talking about outsourcing? After all we've been through, Erik, haven't we already agreed that outsourcing IT has caused many of the problems we're currently cleaning up?"

"Hardly!" Erik scoffs. "You've all proven that you can jeopardize the First, Second, and Third Ideals plenty without outsourcing. Instead, think of the Fifth Ideal, of being truly customer-centric instead of being silo-centric. As Sensei Moore asks, of the applications and services that you manage, which of them are customers willing to pay you for? Which ones truly enhance competitive advantage? And which can you rely on vendors for?

"A hundred years ago, most large factories had a CPO—a chief power officer—who ran the electricity generation processes. It was one of the most important roles in manufacturing, because no electricity, no production. It was a Core process," he says. "But that role has disappeared entirely. Electricity has become infrastructure that you buy from a utility company. It is interchangeable, and you choose suppliers primarily on price. There is rarely a competitive advantage to generating your own power. It is now merely Context, no longer Core. You don't want to be the organization that has a large staff providing internal power generation.

"As Sensei Clay Christiansen once stated, one keeps what is 'not good enough' and outsources what is 'more than good enough,'" he says. "Why did you choose to outsource your cafeteria point-of-sale system?"

Bill looks thoughtful, scratching his chin. "I had my team work with John, the CISO, to figure out which applications stored PII or credit card data. That's like toxic waste. We shouldn't waste time or energy protecting it; we get rid of it. We looked for those applications, and where we could, we retired them. And if we couldn't, we looked for an external vendor who could run it for us as a service."

"Precisely," Erik says, standing up. "I challenge you and the technology team to think deeply about the Fifth Ideal and identify areas of Context that you can unload, freeing yourself from decades of technical debt, things that have been shackling you for years or maybe even decades. Imagine what you can get done without all those things dragging you down. Even though it may be more painful in the short term, you will find some unexpected and critical dividends long term.

"Steve, lucky for you, according to Sensei Moore, the person best suited to manage Context is someone just like Bill and Maxine," Erik says. "This is never easy. You need someone who truly understands the business, someone hard-nosed who can drive standardization across the company, who truly has the best interests of the entire organization at heart, and who knows what technology can and can't do.

"Imagine a world where you can make decades of technical debt disappear..." he says. "Where you rid yourself of bad automation built on top of bad business processes. Imagine what it could feel like to deliberately and carefully choose what to leave behind and where you could spend your time and energy instead. Dick knows that simplicity enables effectiveness, and that complexity conspires against it. How much of getting business done here is impeded by your internal systems and processes?"

This makes Maxine pause. The notion of simplifying the business and technical landscape of the company is breathtaking. She loves working on complex business problems, but it would be so much better and easier if they weren't obstructed by the decades of senseless complexity and accumulated neglect.

"Lastly, to everyone else, especially Steve," he continues, "think carefully about how each and every position you eliminate might disrupt flow, especially when you don't have locality in decision-making, as embodied by the First Ideal. For instance, what happens when you get rid of managers when you already have situations like the Square happening all the time?

"Those middle managers are your interface between strategy and execution," he says. "They are your prioritizers and your traffic cops. We all have this ideal of small teams working independently, but who manages the teams of teams? It's your middle managers. Some call them derisively the 'frozen middle,' but you'll find that properly developing this layer of people is critical to execute strategy.

"I wish you the best of luck," Erik says, turning to leave. "And hang in there, Maxine. If you choose wisely, better days are most assuredly ahead of you, however dismal it may appear now."

Everyone remains silent on the walk back to Building 5. Finally, Maxine says to Bill, "You don't talk much, do you?"

"Sometimes," he says with a tight-lipped smile.

"Uh, what do you think of that last meeting?" she asks, the question that's likely on everyone's mind.

Bill stops to look at Maxine for a moment. "It sucked ass. On the one hand, it looks so much like the same drill that everyone in Ops deals with all the time. Do more with less. Outsource this. Outsource that. In the past, this has led to some incredibly unwise decisions, and people like us are left cleaning up the mess afterward for years. And when everyone's realized that we crapped the bed, we often have to bring everything back in-house. There's nothing fun about that.

"But this time it could be different," he says, resuming his fast-paced walk. "Steve and Erik are absolutely right. We must find a way to protect the Innovation efforts. That is the key to our long-term future. For the first time in my career, I think we can change the way we manage technology and do it right, with the support of the highest levels of the company.

"But this is not going to be easy," he says. "I like what Erik said about Context and Core. There are services we should get out of the business of operating. One of the places I'm thinking about is my old mid-range group. We've created the Galapagos Islands of technologies, which served us well for decades, but we've drifted so far from where the entire industry has gone that we haven't been able to benefit from all the things the industry vendors have created. Maybe it's time to build a bridge back to the mainland...or maybe vacate the island completely."

He continues, "I wonder if we can re-skill everyone on my old team and find new roles for them without driving up operating expenses. There's going to be a bunch of new positions in the Innovation effort. I want them to have a shot at it. They have so much domain expertise and institutional knowledge. It'd be a huge loss if we lost them. Same with Kirsten's project managers..."

Bill continues to think in silence as he walks. Which is fine, because Maxine is feeling even more troubled than before. Has her old MRP group become inhabitants of their own Galapagos Islands too?

"I think this *all* sucks," Kurt says, brooding.

For the rest of the day and into the next, Maxine and Kurt tag along as Bill, Chris, Kirsten, and their teams struggle to come up with a plan to deliver the needed headcount reductions. Although Steve told Dick that his job is to help both sides of value and growth, Dick assigns two of his direct reports, the director of business operations and the corporate controller, to help them.

Maxine is very impressed by them. They are two hard-nosed business people who seem to know every nook and cranny of the company.

But it's still very grim work.

Maxine is often tempted to take a walk or skip these meetings entirely, because she sometimes feels overwhelmed at the human toll that all of this has put into motion. But she knows that this is important, even critical, to get right. And she absolutely wants a say in what happens.

At first, each department manager divided their people into three categories: critical, desired, and RIF. Of course, only a few people ended up on the third list. Seeing the three names, it was clear that managers were using this as an opportunity to get rid of people that should have been eased out long ago.

But that wasn't nearly enough. So Chris and Bill started turning the screws on each manager, scrutinizing and comparing people on their managers' "desired" lists. After nearly an hour of this exhausting wrangling, Maxine is reminded of something Erik said.

"Wait. Erik cautioned us on the need to examine things from the perspective of flow," Maxine says. "We can't do this by department or by some popularity contest. If we take random people out of a value stream, we could do as much damage as what the bean-counters did in Dwayne's story of the three manufacturing plant network switches.

"And in our world, where we currently don't have sufficient locality in our decision-making," she says, "it's actually our managers who are figuring out how to expedite the most important work. Erik called them the traffic cops and prioritizers."

Both Bill and Wes stare at her. Bill says, "Good idea. Let's put this aside for a moment and instead focus on trying to distinguish Core versus Context. What are the broad areas of technology that we can eliminate?"

Maxine is acutely aware that the ultimate goal of this exercise is to reduce operational expense. They need to reduce the number of people on payroll.

Obviously, unhappy at being asked to figure out how to dismantle the empire that he's helped build over the last decade, Wes mutters, "This feels so wrong, Not so long ago, these were things we were arguing we needed." But even he acknowledges that there is an urgent and important business imperative to do this. When he sees Bill put up his old mid-range group on the list of candidate technologies to eliminate, he groans.

"Holy crap. I'm sorry, Bill. That's rough," he says, staring at the whiteboard. "Sure, I've made fun of them for being frozen in time like *Encino Man*, but they're good people. And I sure haven't had any reason to complain about their work."

"Thanks, Wes," Bill acknowledges. "But honestly, there are SaaS vendors out there who we can pay to do much of what we've built. And that will give us five people. And we'd eliminate a whole technology stack, along with all the software licenses and maintenance contracts associated with it. That's another $100,000 of annual spend, which is another half of a head right there."

Wes sits in silence. "Well, if you put it that way...I'd pay anyone in duffel bags of unmarked bills to get rid of our helpdesk system. Of course, we'll have to get a replacement service, but I'd rather have a vendor managing it anyway. And our email servers. And Lotus Notes, which we still have pockets of, believe it or not, because a couple managers complained loudly. I think we finally have the clout to override their objections.

"Combined, the workload of managing all those things is easily three people," Wes says. "Of those, two I'd want to keep around. All I'd want is the opportunity to take a sledgehammer to some of those servers before we haul them out."

Maxine stares at Wes and Bill. They're not exactly being magnanimous, but they aren't being cold-hearted bastards, either. In fact, she much prefers this approach to comparing lists of names between departments.

Inspired, Maxine gathers up her courage and says, "Maybe we should take a look at the Manufacturing Resource Planning group too." When Chris looks at her in surprise, she says, "There are certain pieces that are absolutely critical for competitive advantage, such as the scheduling module that we're changing from 'build to forecast' to 'build to order' to support on-demand manufacturing. But the rest of it could be moved onto a commercial package...I'd keep five developers on the team to finish the transition, but that would free up ten developers and QA people, and maybe two other Ops people..."

She feels ill. The people she's reduced to numbers are the wonderful people who wished her well when she was exiled. This was the system she helped build and maintain for nearly six years. Even Erik said it was an architectural marvel.

She quickly adds, "These are some of the best engineers in the company. I personally vouch for each and every one of them. If they could work on projects like Unicorn or in the Innovation areas, their contribution to the company would be much higher than on the MRP system..."

"You're right," Chris says, looking proudly at Maxine. She feels relieved to finally suggest this, which is something she's been dreading all day.

Bill adds Maxine's old MRP group to the whiteboard, joining mid-range financials, cafeteria POS, helpdesk, email, and Lotus Notes on the list. Together, they identify eighteen positions that they can eliminate. The software services to replace them would cost $500K annually.

Bill adds another column. "If the Innovation effort is fully funded at $5 million, that could potentially create thirty-three technology positions in Core. We could potentially hire all these people back, as Maxine pointed out, doing work that is far more valuable.

"So, let's keep pushing. Come on, what else might we want to unshackle ourselves from so that we can reallocate more people to Core? What are things running in our datacenters that customers will never pay us for? We've already outsourced payroll. What other back office functions might we want to consider?"

"We have three ERP systems," Maxine offers. "It's a pain to have to integrate with all of them. In fact, all three of them are owned by one company now. Maybe now's the time to bite the bullet."

Wes nods. "If we switched to one, that would free up another two or three Ops people to do something else."

"I like where this is going," Bill says. "How about our HR systems. And sales commissioning tools and compensation planning...and our timecarding systems in plants..."

At the mention of the timecarding systems, which were at the epicenter of the payroll failure that led to her exile, Maxine mutters, "Good riddance."

"Yeah, and our desktop backup systems," Wes adds. "Maybe even our telephone systems and PBXes. We're a manufacturer and retailer, not a phone company..."

Wes' face lights up. "And there's two datacenters that we should have shut down years ago. Between them and what's in them, they probably cost us a million dollars annually to run. And if we actually got rid of them, that's another four people...Oh, and those damned Kumquat servers...Let's get rid of them once and for all. That's another $100K in maintenance costs."

Looking at the growing list of ignoble Context on the whiteboard, Maxine doesn't feel dread. Instead, she feels inspired thinking about how jettisoning these things will liberate the company from things that slow it down and present the opportunity for engineers to work in areas of far higher value. There is one more thing bothering her, though.

"Our Unkitty CI cluster is on its last legs," Maxine says. "It's important Context, but still Context. We have our best people working on Unikitty. It's made a world of difference elevating developer productivity, but we should find a commercially supported SaaS vendor and get our best people working on things that we can't find commercial vendors for. Come on, Kurt, how much time have Dwayne and Brent spent propping Unikitty up?"

"Damn," Kurt says. But after a moment, says, "But yeah, add it to the list."

Dick's finance team presents their tabulations. Everyone stares. They've identified nearly $4 million of expenses that could be reduced, with twenty-six positions being eliminated.

But if they opened up thirty-three positions in Innovations, they could hire almost all of them back. If they were willing to learn new things.

Maxine smiles.

Maxine is amazed by how quickly Bill is able to get on Steve and Dick's calendar, impressed that he has that type of working relationship with the CEO. They are presenting to both of them by the end of the day. In contrast, there are times when it takes weeks for Maxine to get on Chris' calendar. She briefly wonders if the problem is her or Chris.

When Bill presents their plan, Steve and Dick take notes, ask questions, and eventually nod in approval.

Steve especially liked how the team identified areas to eliminate by value stream while maintaining flow. But when Bill talks about their desire to move talented engineers and retrain them so they could contribute to the Innovation efforts, Steve becomes visibly excited.

"During my manufacturing days in the 1990s, I had to oversee a massive reskilling of the workforce," he says. "We made huge investments to make sure every worker could survive and thrive in a new era where everyone was being paid not to just use their hands but also their heads. It was one of the most fulfilling and rewarding things I've ever done. We must do the same with the technology workforce.

"And I don't mean just putting up posters on the wall," he says. "I mean we *really* invest in our people. Maybe we create a Parts Unlimited University or some other long-term training where we create the next generation of leaders and engineers we need for the long-term survival of the company. We pay them to get the skills they need."

Steve looks excited and alive in a way that Maxine has never seen before. Even Dick looks excited.

"I need your help on this one already, Steve," Bill says. "Take my old mid-range team that I used to manage only four months ago, before you put me in this role. Through no fault of theirs, they're in a business process that is Context, not Core. We need to do right by all our people and help make sure that we prepare those people to have long and productive careers. They have valuable knowledge that we'd be idiots to let walk out the door."

"You bet," Steve says. Maxine breathes a sigh of relief. *Maybe this whole thing can be a force for good after all,* Maxine thinks. *Even though it was Sarah who lit the fuse.*

Dick has been taking notes and occasionally tapping on his calculator. "We need $15 million in cost reductions. With the numbers you provided, we're nearly there," Dick says, looking at his staff, who nod in return. "In manufacturing, we'll be shutting down production of our lowest-margin category of products. This affects fifty workers, of which fifteen will be filling currently open positions.

"The head of supplier management plans on saving another $2 million by reducing our number of suppliers," he says. "We're using this to negotiate higher discounts and reduce logistics overhead, and it shouldn't create much hardship at all.

"On the retailer front, we'll be shutting down ten of the lowest-performing stores, which will save us about $3 million," Dick continues. "And the rest will be gained through early retirement and some elimination of positions."

Dick pauses to look at the spreadsheet. "I think this is a pretty good plan. The biggest risk I see is the operational risk from transitioning to these new systems. They're Context, but they're mission-critical. We've never changed this many business processes, let alone all at the same time. And I'm sure we're going to have a bunch of very unhappy people who will come up with a bunch of reasons why we can't."

"Just so you know, some of those objections are undoubtedly correct. This is just a working list, created by us, a bunch of spreadsheet jockeys," Bill says. "At our level, we don't really know what the implications of shutting these systems down are and what it takes to transition. We need time to work with our teams to figure out what's even possible and come up with a realistic timeline."

"That's a good plan, Bill," Dick nods. "Steve, you need to find a way to buy him some time."

Steve looks at the spreadsheet on the screen. "Maybe we ask the board that instead of the three percent cut they asked for, we deliver a plan to cut two percent in January before the quarterly earnings announcement and get to four percent by the end of the next year. That should satisfy them..."

"Not bad," Dick says with a smile. "That will make Alan and his voting bloc very happy."

"Okay, I'll work on socializing this with the board," Steve says. "Once we get approval, I'd like to announce this to the company and be as open about it as possible, so people can prepare for it."

To Dick, he adds with a small smile, "Sorry, Dick...We may need a couple more quarters of that financial engineering to keep the numbers going in the right way."

Maxine is so relieved that her worst fears about the cost-reduction plan haven't come true. However, she doesn't feel carefree. Instead, her acute fears of the worst happening are replaced with a dull, constant, gnawing sense of unease.

For the rest of the day, she feels utterly spent and exhausted, her left eyelid keeps twitching and her stomach constantly hurts. Sometimes she can't quite look people in the eye. A quick Google search confirms that this is probably all due to prolonged stress. All these types of people management issues are why she always veered clear of management roles.

That night, she forces herself to relax, having a couple of glasses of wine and watching the "Red Wedding" episode of *Game of Thrones* with her husband, eager to be distracted from anything related to work. She's stunned by the ruthless cruelty and senseless violence of the massacre at the end, and she and Jake laugh about how lucky they are that modern work environments don't involve wholesale slaughter—even though Sarah had certainly given it her best shot.

CHAPTER 18

When she wakes up on Thursday morning, she feels well-rested and excited about the day. Part of it is from having gotten a full night of dreamless sleep. But it's also because today is when the finalists for the Innovation ideas will be pitching the entire Innovation Council. As promised, Bill picked fifty of the most respected people from across the company, making them responsible for choosing the first three Innovation ideas to be staffed and explored.

Those three winning submitters would each have a team hand-selected by Maxine, and they'd have ninety days to explore the viability of the idea, investigating market risk, technical risk, and business model risk, and hopefully achieving some fantastic agreed-upon business outcomes. This would be the Horizon 3 work that they were fighting so hard to protect.

Maxine was astonished that back when Steve announced to the entire company that anyone could submit an idea, within a week they had hundreds of submissions. Being on the committee, Maxine read all of them and was inspired by their creativity and thoughtfulness. Almost all of them attempted to address real problems that their customers had, and many of them displayed ingenious ways that Parts Unlimited could help.

She marveled at how strong people's intrinsic motives were to explore these problems. The committee deliberated and picked the top thirty proposals, and today, all of them are pitching the entire Innovation Council in the big auditorium where they normally held the Town Halls.

Each of the pitching teams had been able to rehearse with some of the committee members during the week, getting any desired coaching and guidance. Maxine loved how committee members were so generous with their time, especially right before the holidays. For the people pitching, these interactions would help create useful networks and would likely help advance their careers.

Maxine walks to her desk, eager to get the most urgent work done so she can go the auditorium and help with the Innovation pitch preparations.

As she sits down, she sees a text message from Cranky Dave:

Holy crap. Check your email.

When she pulls up her email and sees the subject line, she breaks out in a cold sweat, whispering, "Oh, no..."

From: Sarah Moulton (SVP, Retail Operations)
To: All IT Employees
Cc: Company Executives
Date: 8:05 a.m., December 18
Subject: Changes to personnel and responsibilities

Effective immediately, Maggie Lee (Sr. Director of Retail Product Marketing) has been reassigned to assist with an urgent inventory audit at our retail stores.

Because of the time-criticality of these issues, she is relieved of all duties, including any Innovation Council work. Please direct all those communications and decisions to me.

Furthermore, Kurt Reznick (QA Manager) is suspended of all responsibilities, for reasons I cannot responsibly disclose. Please direct all Innovation Council related issues to Rick Willis (QA Manager) and all other issues to Chris Allers (VP R&D).

Thank you, Sarah

Shocked, Maxine stares at the email. She cannot quite fully comprehend the enormity of what just happened. Sarah has effectively decapitated the Horizon 3 effort. To defend Horizon 1 and her quest for value, she has ensured that the Innovation Council work dies before it even gets started.

Oddly, Maxine feels neither angry nor sad—she feels numb and suspects it's because all her mental fuses have been blown from Sarah's incredibly bold move. With some disbelief, she realizes that Sarah has engineered her own Red Wedding at Parts Unlimited.

She picks up her phone and frantically tries to call Kurt and Maggie, but neither one of them answer their phones. She texts them, asking them what is going on. She gets no response from either of them.

She stares off into space for a long time, trying to think of what she can do. She looks up and notices that people are gathering around her desk—Cranky Dave, Dwayne, Brent, Shannon, Adam, Purna, Ellen…In a frantic voice, Cranky Dave asks, "What the hell is going on? Does anyone even know?"

No one has any idea. Nobody can reach Kurt or Maggie. Or Kirsten. Or Chris. Or Bill, for that matter.

The junior officers and bridge crew have all disappeared, leaving the redshirts completely on their own.

For the third time, Maxine sends another text message to Kurt:

What's going on? Where are you? Everyone is freaking the hell out!

"Is the Rebellion over?" Brent asks the question that's on everyone's mind. "Are we all going to be shut down?"

"Get a grip," Shannon says, rolling her eyes. But Maxine can tell that she's shaken too, because no one actually knows what's going on. Maxine tries to be the mature adult in the room, calming everyone's fears, but deep down she's rattled to the core.

Maxine looks at Brent. Maybe this grand adventure really is over. Maybe Bill is next on the chopping block. How high up does a corporate coup like this go? Maybe Steve is gone too. Has Sarah just really won the war?

Maxine pictures Sarah sitting in the captain's chair on the bridge of the starship *Enterprise*, grinning triumphantly with an all-new bridge crew, having completed her purge of the old guard. Maybe she'll have all the heads of her vanquished foes mounted on posts to deter the next would-be rebels.

Would she reach all the way down into the engine room and purge all the redshirts who were associated with Kurt and Maggie? Normally she would have dismissed this idea as absurd. Bridge crew don't care about redshirts, right?

But the way Sarah has conspired to undermine all their efforts makes her rethink that idea. It's not difficult to imagine her going through the entire redshirt roster, dividing them into naughty and nice lists, with the naughty people being beamed into exile to the planet Ceti Alpha V, like Kahn and his followers had been fifteen years before he took revenge on Captain Kirk.

Not Sarah... She'd probably arrest them all right now and just beam them into the middle of a star to prevent any possibility of future wrath, Maxine thinks. Say what you want about Sarah, but she can definitely think ahead.

Maxine looks at her watch. There's only forty-five minutes until the pitches are scheduled to start in the auditorium. Maggie is missing in action and won't be able to lead the session as planned, and she's guessing that Steve will be a no-show too.

Who is going to save Horizon 3? She looks around.

In that moment, she realizes that it's all up to her now.

She picks up her desk phone and calls Steve's extension on the landline, getting his assistant, Stacy.

"Hi, I'm Maxine Chambers. I was in the meetings with Steve and Dick regarding the Innovation Council, along with Kurt and Maggie. We're all a little freaked out at the message about Kurt and Maggie being suspended. Steve was scheduled to present at the Innovation pitches at nine o'clock. Will he still be able to make it?"

"Hi, Maxine," she hears from the other end of the line. "Amazing timing. I was just about to call you. Steve has a message for you. He says, 'Take charge of the Innovation Pitch meeting. Good luck!' He will be there if he can, but he'll likely only be able to stay for a couple of minutes."

Steve's assistant asks for her cell phone number so that Steve or Dick can text her later today. After Maxine gives it to her, she says, "Hang in there, Maxine! We're all rooting for you."

Maxine hangs up the phone and stares at her desk for the briefest moment, girding herself for what she must do.

"Come on, everyone," she says. "We need to get to the Innovation Pitch meeting."

"But Maggie and Kurt have been rounded up by Sarah! Who is going to lead it?" Shannon asks.

"We are," Maxine says, gathering up her things.

In the front row of the big auditorium, the focused excitement and nervousness of all the teams getting ready to present is palpable. If anyone dropped out because they saw Sarah's email, Maxine doesn't notice.

Maxine climbs up on the stage, looking for the people who are running the operation. She finds the person who seems to be managing the A/V and asks for a microphone so that she can address the room at nine. That's in three minutes.

Brent hands her the printed schedule of the teams presenting their proposals and then tells the stage manager to start lining people up backstage. Maxine thanks Brent, who grins back. "Good luck, Maxine! Tell us if you need anything!"

Maxine looks into the audience and sees all the committee members chosen to judge the proposals sitting in the front row. They'll be listening to each of the teams give their ten-minute pitch. Behind them are hundreds of people who have come to watch the teams pitch their ideas.

Maggie had taken extraordinary care to mitigate the "HIPPO effect" (or Highest Paid Person's Opinion), referring to people's unhealthy tendency to only care what the highest-level decision-maker thought. To counter this, Maggie instructed the entire Innovation Council to listen to each pitch, ask any questions, but keep their votes and ratings secret.

She looks around for Steve but can't find him. She looks at her watch. It's time. She waves at the stage manager and motions that she's ready to go. The stage manager says something in her headset, and then motions counting down from 3, 2…

"Hi, my name is Maxine Chambers," she says into the microphone, squinting into the bright lights. "Umm, Maggie Lee was supposed to lead this meeting, but as you may have read in the email, she's been put on an urgent mission to do an inventory audit."

She hears laughter in the crowd, which surprises her. She hadn't intended that to be funny.

"And Steve was supposed to say some words about the proud history of the company and how we must help keep our customers' cars running. He was also going to talk about how important he thinks fostering innovation within the company is, but he's unable to join us at the moment. We've assembled an amazing group of some of the most respected people in the company to judge these pitches. We had hundreds of proposals, and I read every one of them.

"They're all amazing, and it was so difficult to choose just thirty of them. But we did, and they will all present to you today," she says, hoping her voice isn't cracking and that her nervousness isn't showing. She wishes she had worn her jacket to hide the sweat pouring from her body. "Each team will get ten minutes, and then we'll have five minutes for Q&A. At the end of the day, the Council will deliberate, and Steve will announce the three winners at the next Town Hall.

"My team and I will have the privilege of working with each of these teams to test the viability of their ideas," she says with a big smile. She thinks about the events of this morning and her eyes start welling up with tears. She says, voice cracking, "We have made a bunch of sacrifices to make this happen, so I'm grateful to all of you for putting so much work into your pitches, and I promise you that we'll do our best to make them a reality."

She smiles and feels teary-eyed as she hears everyone clap and cheer. She looks at the stage manager, who smiles and gives her a big thumbs up. Maxine looks at the sheet of paper in front of her, shaking visibly in her hands, and calls the first team up on the stage.

As she goes backstage, she sees Brent appear next to her, saying, "Holy crap, Maxine. That was awesome. I'm so glad everyone is going to be able to pitch their ideas... Even after all that... You know?"

Maxine smiles back, giving Brent a quick hug, thanking him for his help. She turns her attention to the team pitching. Maxine is delighted by what she hears. One store manager presents her idea of helping rideshare drivers, such as Uber or Lyft drivers, with their unique needs. Another proposes a concierge service for common maintenance tasks.

But the first idea that generates buzz throughout the auditorium is a rating system for garages and service stations, which immediately gets the nickname "Yelp for Garages." The idea is to have Parts Unlimited customers share their experiences about service stations with other customers.

Another proposal that excites Maxine comes after the morning break. A senior sales manager presents an idea to create a four-hour delivery service to their service station customers. This would enable those stations to offer more repair services, knowing that needed parts could be quickly delivered as needed. A competitive startup had recently emerged offering four-hour delivery, and the Parts Unlimited business unit that sold directly to service stations already cut their revenue forecasts for next year by ten percent because of them.

This team is convinced that Parts Unlimited can take on this competitor and win, and that it will improve their relationships with their most important service station customers. When its ringleader says, "Given all our capabilities, I think we can wipe this startup completely off the map," the auditorium erupts in cheers.

Some of the other presentations are also very good, but by mid-afternoon Maxine sees the pitch that she falls in love with, only partly because it is being pitched by Brent, Shannon, Dwayne, and Wes. She can't resist cheering for them as they take the stage. She is so proud of them.

Their idea is to sell an engine sensor and create a huge array of offerings around it. Initially, it will focus on earlier detection of car problems while they are small and before they can snowball into big, expensive problems, like oil changes and engine wear. Stores could provide these repair services for discounted rates to their customers, because the work could be scheduled during slow periods.

Many months ago, Wes saw that one of the items recommended for him on the app (powered by the Unicorn Project) was an engine sensor that they recently started selling in their stores. It had been flying off the shelves. It was a surprisingly neat device. It attached to the Onboard Diagnostic Port 2 (ODB-II) that every car has these days, required by the landmark 1994 California Air Resources Board Act. This standard data connector enables monitoring of engine characteristics, including, most famously, emissions levels.

Maxine is surprised to learn that even new electric cars like the Tesla have ODB-II ports, even though they don't have an internal combustion engine.

The idea is to either OEM or resell one of these sensors, and then build a world-class software ecosystem around it to help with everything from on-site diagnostics, advisory services to customers, and better preventive maintenance. They also describe ideas such as working with insurance companies to help reduce premiums and making apps to help parents track their kids' driving habits.

This was so compelling to Maxine that she immediately bought the sensor during the pitch on her phone. Maxine is always terrified of her kids driving too fast. At the end of the pitch, despite her desire to be impartial, Maxine leaps to her feet and cheers. In her mind, it's ideas like this that can take Parts Unlimited to exciting, new, and vibrant places.

There are other pitches that catch her attention too, but she knows who she is going to vote for. At the end of the day, Maxine takes the stage again and says, "Thank you all so much for presenting all these amazing ideas. We'll be collecting all the ballots at the end of the day, and Steve will be announcing the winner at the January Town Hall. See you then!"

She waves at everyone and hands the stage manager back her microphone. She's exhausted. Her legs are shaking, her back hurts from standing, and she prays that she doesn't stink from all her nervous sweating and standing under the hot lights.

As she rejoins her fellow Rebellion members, she thinks about the day. Maxine feels relieved and energized about the Innovation pitches. As wrenching as the reorganization and workforce changes will be, if they enable exciting things like this to happen, it will be worth it. And better yet, she will always have the satisfaction of having helped make it a reality. But now, they need to figure out what happened to Kurt and Maggie and, for that matter, the rest of the bridge crew who have gone missing.

And whether the Innovation effort will happen at all.

It's after five, so they all decide to meet at the Dockside as usual.

As people arrive at the bar, Maxine keeps asking if anyone has any updates or news. Or even new rumors to share. But no one has heard anything. There has been complete radio silence. Aside from Sarah's email, there have been no further official company communications or announcements.

Maxine says to everyone, "Look, whatever happens, even if Maggie and Kurt have been fired, we still must do everything we can to make those Horizon 3 projects succeed. Even if it means working with those teams over the holidays. We need to help them get a running start and increase the chances of those projects succeeding...I have the names of the three winning teams here. Who's with me?"

"Count us all in, Maxine," says Shannon. "Even if it means helping the competition."

"We're all on the same team, Shannon," Brent says, rolling his eyes. "We're not *actually* competing against each other; we're competing against the market."

"You know what I meant," Shannon says. "Who are the winners?"

Maxine looks around and sees that everyone is nodding, committed to helping the three pilot teams. She says, "It was pretty decisive. It wasn't even close. The judges' top choice is the Engine Sensor project…"

Before she can announce the others, everyone cheers and slaps Shannon, Brent, and Dwayne on the back, congratulating them. "Wes is on his way," says Shannon. "I'm texting him the news now."

"…and the other two winners are the Service Station Ratings team and the Four-Hour Parts Delivery team," Maxine says with a smile. "I'd love to help the Four-Hour Delivery project, because it deals with so many different parts of the organization. I love that stuff."

Cranky Dave raises his hand, saying, "I'll help the Service Station Ratings project." And when they divide themselves into teams, with the exception of the Engine Sensor group, Maxine smiles. "I'll email you introductions to each of the team leads."

Dwayne pours beer for everyone and Maxine sips her favorite "Erik Special" wine. They order food, and she decides to invite the three teams down to join them at the Dockside. If they make it, they could get a head start on planning.

Maxine takes a deep breath. She has now successfully discharged her obligations to get the Horizon 3 efforts rolling. She has done everything she can. The mood is a mix between relief and a somber, anxious, fretting impatient waiting, like people waiting in a hospital for a baby delivery, awaiting word on news of both the mother and the newborn. Wes eventually shows up but has no news on Bill or the others, either.

It's six. *Surely there should be some resolution to whatever is happening up on the bridge by now,* Maxine thinks.

Thirty minutes goes by. An hour. Two hours.

And then she hears Wes holler out, "Holy flaming tamales. Check your email!"

Maxine checks her phone.

From: Steve Masters (CEO, Parts Unlimited)
To: All Parts Unlimited Employees
Date: 7:45 p.m., December 18
Subject: Maggie Lee reinstated

Maggie Lee is resuming her responsibilities for retail operations and the Innovation Council. If you have any questions about roles and responsibilities, please email me.

I look forward to sharing more news about the exciting future of Parts Unlimited soon. See you at the next Town Hall!

Thank you, and happy holidays! Steve

Maxine hears cheering all around the table, but the still-uncertain fate of Kurt, let alone Sarah, dampens the mood. Wes looks at his phone and hollers out with a big smile on his face, "Bill and Maggie and Kurt are on their way."

Someone orders a bunch more pitchers of beer, just in time. Kurt walks through the door, smiling, both arms stretched triumphantly above his head. Behind him are Maggie, Kirsten, and Bill.

A round of cheers erupts from their table, with the rest of the Dockside Bar joining in, as well. Eventually, they sit at the table, downing their drinks, and the tale finally comes out.

"It was just like the movie *Brazil!*" Kurt says proudly, laughing. "I got killed with paperwork. Sarah opened up an investigation with HR about all the rules I broke: Failure to submit timecards. Failure to follow expense report policies. Failure to follow capital spending guidelines. Failure to follow budgeting processes. Inaccurate coding of personnel."

Maxine sees Bill eyeing Kurt. She wonders if he's going to keep closer tabs on him now.

"...and, well, there was another thing," Kurt says. "One alleged inappropriate relationship with another manager. But we never worked for each other, she was actually senior to me, and we told HR about it right away. We've been happily married for five years now, so I'm pretty sure that won't stick."

"Oh, Kurt," Maxine says, relieved that it wasn't something more serious. "Can Sarah really get away with this?"

"For now. I'm suspended with pay for sixty days, pending further investigation," he says. "Steve got Maggie off the hook for now too. Sarah is still at large, though. Apparently, everything is hinging on the success of the Horizon 3 projects. Steve is betting his job on it. If these efforts don't pan out, Sarah will become the new, and likely last, CEO of Parts Unlimited as we know it."

Maxine quickly fills Maggie, Kurt, and Bill in on what happened today and how they'd organized themselves into three teams to support the three Innovation projects.

Maxine sees Maggie burst into a big smile. "That's absolutely amazing, Maxine. Great work. Let's pick this back up tomorrow. But in the meantime, I'd like to buy you all a drink! It's been a helluva day!"

"We're still in business, everyone!" Bill says. Almost as an afterthought, he gestures to Kurt with a smile, "Well, most of us... See you in sixty days, Kurt."

He turns to Maxine and says, "Good job on the Horizon 3 stuff today. The next month is critical, so don't screw it up." With a smile, he adds, "Let me know how I can help. There is literally nothing else more important."

Despite the late night out on Thursday, work begins early on Friday, the last day before most people leave on holiday for two weeks. But everyone knows that the fate of the Innovation pilots is uncertain. No one needs any convincing to get as much done as quickly as they can. The idea of having something, anything, to show at the January Town Hall is an inspiring goal.

But the peak holiday selling season is also upon them, and work continues unrelentingly on the Unicorn Project. On the infrastructure side, people are more confident than ever because of Brent's Chaos Engineering efforts. Over the last several weeks, they've increased production load testing and even injected faults into the production environment to ensure that they've exposed the failure modes that the incredible onslaught of orders coming from the Unicorn campaign could create.

Brent has proven to be incredibly devious in designing these tests, including unplugging a bunch of network cables during the middle of one of the drills. Incredibly, everything kept limping along instead of blowing up spectacularly like during the Phoenix launch over three months ago.

For several days, the Rebellion works furiously to support the holiday promotions launch. To Maxine's relief, the holiday launch goes more smoothly than the Thanksgiving launch, and the early business results look very good.

Maggie was right—creating great promotions is a game of learning, and it's obvious that the entire Unicorn team has learned a lot and that Parts Unlimited is benefiting tremendously from it.

As soon as holiday sales peak, the entire Rebellion shifts their focus to helping the three grateful Innovation teams. But not before having a blameless post-mortem, even though they didn't have an outage.

For that matter, nothing even terribly bad happened. But as Kurt reminded them, the purpose of these meetings is to learn.

It was a fantastic and riveting hour, and Maxine learned about several near misses that could have resulted in something more serious happening. People enthusiastically volunteered for engineering work that could make the system even safer. That's when Maxine realizes how many people from outside the team have come to watch.

People are always invited to join these blameless post-mortems, but she never expected so many engineers to show up. In fact, there wasn't enough room for everyone, so many people joined online. These forums now had a reputation for being the fastest way to learn about the most innovative and exciting things in the company.

"Where is she?" asks Debra, the director of sales, looking at her watch as she paces around the conference room.

"Don't worry, she'll be here," Maxine says.

"Don't worry? Are you kidding? I'm worried about everything!" Debra says. "We're driving up costs everywhere, and if I were a store manager, I'd be freaking out at all these manual processes we're proposing. Bill is even suggesting that we stockpile parts at the service stations to create a safety buffer, without them even paying us for it in advance! And he's pushing us to do our first test market pilot two weeks sooner than planned!"

"It makes sense to me," Maxine says, smiling. "The fastest way to kill the pilot is let these service stations down. If Bill is willing to pay for the added inventory, let him. Usually he's the one pushing for more constraints, not more slack."

Debra stops mid step. "Right. Customer Focus. The Fifth Ideal."

"Exactly," Maxine says. "We'll certainly be testing how much Steve really believes his schtick around how great customer satisfaction and employee engagement will lead to great cash flow."

"You know, it's incredible how enthused and engaged the store managers are," Debra says, smiling for the first time. "We're relying so heavily on them. They're going to be bringing in more in-store staff to handle the load, and in a pinch, they'll be personally delivering these parts if no one is available…

"I think it's because the data is so persuasive," she continues. "Thanks again for your help pulling it all together. If there's anything I've learned managing salespeople, it's that you never want to bring opinions when you're playing a game that needs facts."

Maxine laughs. "I didn't do that much. It was your team that pulled together all the analysis. We just made sure that all the data they needed was in a place where they could access it."

"I wouldn't minimize your contribution," Debra says. "There are so many bets we're making. We needed purchasing histories for each of the pilot service stations, line it up with our parts availability and lead times, their distance from our distribution centers and stores, cross-shipment costs, not to mention all the uncertainties about how to build up a transportation capability…and there's still so much we don't know!"

Maxine nods. Despite (or maybe because of) the high stakes, Maxine is having fun, very much in the spirit of the Second Ideal of Focus, Flow and Joy. Working with the team to generate the analyses, working with the distant silos across the company, studying the transportation challenges…She imagines this is better than any MBA project, because they're doing it for real.

Although Debra frets about all the manual processes, Maxine knows that this is all about creating a Minimum Viable Product to test their offerings and confirm their hypotheses of what capabilities are required to fulfill them. This rapid iteration and learning before they invest heavily in rolling out a big, disruptive process is a great example of the Third Ideal of Improvement of Daily Work.

Similarly, having all the expertise within the team and the data they need at-hand is a great example of the First Ideal of Locality and Simplicity, and the crazy ideas that people are willing to offer up certainly shows the presence of the Fourth Ideal of Psychological Safety.

"Why are you smiling?" Debra asks, staring at her.

Maxine just shakes her head, and instead, greets the Director of Operations as she and her staff file into the conference room.

CHAPTER 19

• Tuesday, January 13

From: Steve Masters (CEO, Parts Unlimited)
To: All Parts Unlimited Employees
Date: 8:45 a.m., January 13
Subject: Sarah Moulton is no longer with the company

Effective immediately, Sarah Moulton is taking a leave of absence to spend more time with her family. Maggie Lee will be taking over all retail-related concerns, and Pamela Sanders will be taking over product marketing, analyst relations, and public relations. For other matters, please refer them to me. We thank her for all her contributions to the company over the last four years.

See you at the next Town Hall! Steve

From: Alan Perez (Operating Partner, Wayne-Yokohama Equity Partners)
To: Steve Masters (CEO)
Date: 3:15 p.m., January 13
Subject: Congratulations on a remarkable quarter

Steve—in confidence…

Congratulations on a remarkable quarter. As they say, two data points don't make a trend, but it is still exciting to see. Your record-breaking Black Friday and Christmas holiday sales performance and contributions to profits are noteworthy and definitely change the financial posture of the company. I can see the glimmer of a growth story taking shape.

I am glad we supported you throughout this turnaround. Good luck closing the books, and I look forward to seeing the final numbers for the quarter.

Cheers, Alan

PS: It's too bad Sarah never fully bought into your vision. She could have been a fantastic asset.

Maxine is sitting in the second row at the January Town Hall. She can't stop smiling from the news of Sarah's departure. And better yet, Chris sent out a memo saying that Kurt had been reinstated and cleared of all wrongdoing. Kurt is sitting next to her, and against all her wildest expectations, they both have a minor role in today's agenda.

At ten a.m. sharp, Steve turns on the microphone and addresses everyone in the audience. "Good morning and Happy New Year to you all. And given the fantastic holiday season and the earnings call that I just got off of, here's to this year being the best year for the company yet!" Everyone in the auditorium applauds and cheers. Maxine had seen the fantastic press about the company's amazing quarter. Steve goes through his usual reiteration of the company mission, and then gives more specifics about the incredible performance of the company during December. To roaring applause, he asks Maggie to take the stage. "Congratulations on a job well done helping with the urgent inventory audit, and your new position as the SVP of retail operations!"

Until this Town Hall, it had always been Sarah talking about the company strategy. Maxine is so delighted and proud that Maggie has taken her place and is being recognized in front of the entire company.

"Thanks, Steve," she says, looking sharp in her designer suit. "I'll make this really short. In December we set records all across the board:

revenue, average order sizes, conversion rates for promoted items, and margins. Even customer satisfaction.

"Because of all the amazing groundwork that Phoenix laid down, the Unicorn teams were able to quickly create promotions capabilities to drive people to our mobile app, e-commerce site, and physical stores. Of course, it wasn't just Marketing. It was an amazing combined effort that included in-store staff and the technology teams," she says. "In particular, I want to call out the amazing work of Kurt Reznick and Maxine Chambers and the entire Unicorn Project team."

Maggie points out Maxine and Kurt from the stage, insisting they stand up and wave to everyone from their seats. Maxine waves at everyone, gritting her teeth.

Maggie walks through a series of graphs. "...In short, due to this incredible performance, Steve and Dick announced our first profitable quarter in almost two and a half years."

Maxine hears people cheer wildly and realizes how significant this is to the future of the company. Maggie says with a big smile, "Rest assured, this is just the beginning. Steve won't let us rest on our laurels. In fact, he's raised our targets, and we're scrambling, trying to figure out how to meet them. Thank you all very much!"

Steve takes the microphone back from Maggie, thanking her again for her great work. "I'd like to officially announce the winners of the Innovation Contest that we held in December. Over thirty teams were selected to pitch their ideas to a group of judges we picked from across the company," he says. "There were a lot of incredible ideas, and I'm so delighted by the committee's decisions."

To Maxine's utter delight, she watches as Brent, Shannon, Dwayne, and Wes go up on stage to be recognized by Steve, as well as the teams who pitched the service station ratings and the four-hour parts delivery.

Pointing at the people on stage, Steve says, "Incredibly, each of these teams have already worked with Maxine and her teams to explore, prototype, and validate these ideas. We will report the results to you quarterly."

Each team gives a five-minute presentation of what they're planning, and each are able to show a demo of what they've already created, what they plan on doing next, their goals for the next three months, and the help they're looking for.

Maxine is very, very impressed with what they've all created.

Steve thanks them, asking each team to share a learning, whether from a mistake or from an experiment. "It's important to share our wins *and* losses," he explains.

"Our future depends on innovation," he says. "That doesn't come from process. It comes from people." He describes the Three Horizons to everyone, as well as the steps he's taking to move people from Context to Core.

"As a company, we don't want to leave anyone behind. We want to invest in you at a level we haven't since the 1920s, when the founder of Parts Unlimited made it his mission to create the most skilled workforce in the nation.

"To that end, I'm increasing the frequency of these Town Halls from bi-monthly to monthly, and I invite everyone to submit questions in the chatroom we've created for this, or you can even just post an emoji," he says, projecting all the questions and emojis behind him.

This is exciting and new, Maxine thinks.

Before he adjourns, Steve says, "Oh, one more piece of news. I'd like to congratulate Bill Palmer, who has been promoted to chief information officer, allowing me to vacate that position. And I'm pleased that I've gotten board approval to make him provisional chief operating officer, provided that he doesn't wash out of a special program we've created for him over the next two years."

Maxine looks over at Bill in surprise. She had absolutely no idea this was coming. No wonder it seemed like Bill had such a great relationship with Steve. She punches him on the shoulder and says, "Congratulations, Bill."

As promised, Steve has another Town Hall in February. From the stage he says, "Every month in between our normal Town Halls, I'll have one like this. It's only an hour, and it will be mostly for small announcements and then open questions and answers." He talks again about the vision of the company and the focus on enabling Core by managing down Context.

He says, "Before Q&A, I have an announcement to make. I said last time that we must become a learning organization or we will lose to another organization that is. To help advance this, thanks to Maxine Chambers, we are creating something called Teaching Thursdays."

Maxine's heart leaps at the mention of this. This was something she had lobbied for, and now she's getting it. Not just for the technology organization, but for everyone in the company.

"Every week we will create time for everyone in the company to learn. For two hours, everyone is expected to teach something or learn something. The topics are whatever you want to learn: cross-train in another silo or business unit, take part in our famous in-store training program, spend time in our stores or manufacturing plants, sit with your customer or our helpdesk, learn about Lean principles or practices, learn a new technology or tool, or even how to better manage your career. The most valuable thing you can do is mentor or learn from your peers. And you can expect to see me there too. Learning is for everyone, and it is from there that we will create competitive advantage."

In that moment, Maxine feels an incredible sense of professional pride, and by announcing his participation, Steve has gone a long way to reduce the embarrassment that often comes with learning something new. Leaders must model the behaviors they want.

"Good job, Maxine," Bill says, who is sitting right next to her. "This is absolutely awesome."

Maxine can't stop smiling. As Steve starts fielding the Q&A, the #ask-steve-town-hall chatroom is projected behind him. As promised, he asks how people feel about the company, asking them to fill out a poll question where the answers are emojis. The majority of people answer with a heart or smiley face. About five percent answer with the poo emoji, which results in Steve encouraging them to email him about their complaints or with any suggestions.

The next Thursday, Maxine is sitting at the front of the lunch room with over forty other people. It's Teaching Thursday, and Shannon and a data scientist are in the front of the room giving a tutorial on creating machine learning models using real company data from the Panther data platform. Everyone, including Maxine, has their laptops open, following along with the lab assignment.

Steve is sitting next to her with his laptop open. When Maxine stares at the machine learning book next to his laptop, he says, "What? I was in logistics for decades. I actually wanted to study math in graduate school but didn't have the money to go. I used to love linear algebra and statistics. I'm still the best at Excel of anyone I know. But I've got a lot to learn too."

Maxine is impressed. Looking around the room, she sees many of her former MRP teammates, as well as some of the project managers and QA and Ops engineers whose positions were going to be eliminated. A few appear to be here only grudgingly, but most have jumped in with gusto, including Derek from the helpdesk. *Good for him*, she thinks.

As painful as the RIF exercise was, to see all these people here eagerly learning some of the hottest and most-desired skills makes Maxine smile. It removes all doubt that it was the right thing to do, not just for the company but for these engineers as well.

Maxine acutely understands the psychological barriers that sometimes come with learning new things. Which is why she is here too, showing that even she needs to be learning new things.

Many years ago, when she took a workshop at MIT, her instructor said that adult learners often hide the fact that they're trying to acquire a new skill, whether it's learning a new language, swimming, or even taking golf lessons. It usually comes from embarrassment or being afraid of being seen doing something that they're not good at.

Indeed, decades ago she wanted to learn to be a better swimmer. She couldn't even swim one lap without stopping in the middle of the pool. She was embarrassed, imagining that the other swimmers, both kids and adults, were laughing at her. She was incredibly self-conscious about the lifeguards sitting in those chairs whose job it was to watch everyone.

She remembered that she even started walking with a fake limp, so that the lifeguard would excuse her for being a bad swimmer. Finally, she started taking lessons at the same time as her kids, and after years of practice, she is proud that she can swim laps for an entire hour.

She never wants any engineer to feel embarrassed, like she did in that pool. Everyone is a learner. And this is why Maxine has such a deep sense of satisfaction about how many people Teaching Thursdays is reaching.

Two weeks later, Maxine finds herself standing around a big pile of Kumquat servers in the parking lot right outside the loading dock of Building 5. There's still snow surrounding the parking lot and the weather is still freezing, but that doesn't stop nearly fifty people from crowding around.

Maxine knows why so many people are here. In addition to working on the four-hour delivery service, Maxine has been working tirelessly to help Brent and Dwayne migrate everything off of the Kumquat servers. And now that their work is complete, all these people want to give these old Kumquat servers the farewell they deserve.

To her astonishment, Steve, Dick, and Bill are here too. Steve says, "My heartiest congratulations to Wes and team for successfully retiring these old, tired servers. Our job is to serve our customers, and quite frankly, they don't care about these things. Through all your hard work, we can harvest all the energy that used to be spent propping these things up and redeploy them in Core, where we can further delight our customers. I'll be having Wes share this story at the next Town Hall so we can all celebrate it together.

"With that, Wes, I turn it over to you," he says, to the applause of everyone gathered round.

Wes steps forward, addressing the crowd. "Thank you all for coming. This is the first of many ceremonies we will hold as we bid adieu to these things that used to inhabit our datacenters, tormenting us on a daily basis. I grew up with Kumquat servers nearly twenty years ago," he says. "I learned almost everything I know on these things. Back then, they were a technological marvel, on the absolute cutting edge of what was possible. But these days, they are the bane of our existence. The middleware it ran made it difficult for anyone to get new work done. They're prone to crashing, and worse, the entire cluster takes almost a half day to reboot because of the filesystem disk checking.

"We've worked hard over the past months to migrate all the applications off of these machines, either onto commodity servers or entirely into the cloud," Wes says. "And now that it's complete, we're able to haul them out of our datacenters and out of our lives."

Wes pulls a giant sledgehammer from behind him. "As the person who has been on more late-night outage calls because of these ancient hulks, I'm giving myself the privilege of taking the first swing at it. And then anyone can give a speech and smack the crap out of them too."

With that, Wes raises the sledgehammer over his head, screams out, "Goodbye, you awful pile of 1990s 8U garbage!!" and slams the sledgehammer into the pile of servers. There is a cacophonous sound of fragile parts breaking, and Maxine cheers. Wes takes a couple more swings at it, whooping with joy. He laughs, yelling out, "Wow! That felt good!"

He hands the sledgehammer to Brent, who picks it up and yells, "This is for waking me up almost every night five years ago!" He then swings the sledgehammer, resulting in more horrible noises. He yells, "And this is for ruining my last vacation while my family and I were at Disneyland!" and swings it again.

As Brent continues to exact his revenge on the now-inert servers, Maxine, along with everyone else, is recording the carnage on her mobile phone, smiling maniacally. Brent finally passes the sledgehammer on to the next person. As Maxine gets in line to bid her own goodbye, Wes smiles at her, "You know, this is really amazing. We've hauled away almost eight thousand pounds of equipment out of the datacenter to be recycled. Only fifteen more tons to go!"

Weeks later, Maxine is hanging out at the Dockside with the Rebellion crew. Everyone is sharing what they're working on, and Maxine is delighted that everyone seems to be having as much fun as she is.

"These engine sensors are such cool devices! They're manufactured in China, but the company that designed them is based not so far from here. I think it's a very small shop," Shannon says. "We've done some experiments modifying the software on the devices. They have ARM processors that run Linux. I've managed to change the configurations and reflash the devices, so now they're sending their sensor data to our back-end servers instead of theirs."

She laughs. "I'm pretty sure what we're doing isn't legal, because it violates their Terms of Service, but it's so fun. We'll be sending a team to talk with them about entering into some sort of joint venture, or maybe we OEM their products outright.

"Their data ingest and webpages are crap. It crashes at least daily," Shannon continues. "We want to build a huge data ingest mechanism in the cloud and then pour it all into the Panther data platform. We'll build something that can easily handle millions of devices," she says, obviously excited. "I want to show the people who make these devices what we're building and show them that the smartest thing they can do is partner with us. Or it'll be the last mistake they ever make."

Seeing Shannon's fierce grin, Maxine is reminded of just how competitive Shannon is, in the best possible way.

"By the way, would you be willing to join our team?" Shannon asks. "We could really use your help on the application and data side. Working on this with Brent and Dwayne is a blast. It's such an incredibly fun project!"

Maxine blinks. She's honored at the request, and she's very tempted. "Who would we backfill onto the four-hour delivery service?"

Shannon looks around, pointing at all the new faces. "I'd bet that any one of these people from the MRP and mid-range teams would jump at the chance," she says with a smile.

Maxine nods, smiling. She's sure they would too.

During the March Town Hall, Steve looks more upbeat than ever. Of course, he starts by talking about the corporate mission, and then he describes how excited he is by all the novel ways the company can help keep their customers' cars on the road.

He brings Maggie onto the stage, who shares the recent updates from the second meeting of the Innovation Council, tasked with reviewing the progress of the three chosen initiatives after ninety days of experimentation and execution.

The garage recommendation service had seemed promising. The in-store managers liked having the data, but the complications created by sales account managers who owned the relationship with those garage owners with lower scores was sufficiently problematic. The business lead needed more time to come up with a better policy of what to do with those organizations. It was decided that further development of this idea would be suspended, and the Innovation Council decided to start the next most highly rated proposal, which was the idea to provide services for rideshare drivers.

"In contrast," Maggie says, "the four-hour delivery team is exceeding our expectations."

Maxine sees Debra join Maggie on stage, describing how their service station salespeople loved the offering. In the pilot markets, they were able to sign up more customers than they could handle, serving them a limited number of important parts where speed of delivery mattered.

Debra says, "We've learned that many service stations have multiple locations, and they often need to have their mechanics drive urgently needed parts from one location to another, which means they're not working on cars. To them, it was a no-brainer to use our service instead.

"We're excited that they're starting to share with us the parts they need to cross-ship most often, and we're figuring out which ones we can deliver, some as soon as thirty minutes," she says.

As Debra leaves the stage to loud applause, Maggie introduces Shannon and Wes, who give an update on the engine sensor project. They show off a prototype of the mobile app and website they're building, and they describe how they're in negotiations with two sensor companies, pitting them against each other to land an exclusive deal with Parts Unlimited.

"A bunch of us are using some prototype sensors in our cars, and all of us can't imagine life without them anymore," Shannon says. "Here's an example of being able to see daily driving patterns, showing it on a map, highlighting where the car exceeded the speed limit. And here are dashboards that show maintenance programs and alerts that could indicate urgent mechanical issues, like oil temperature overheating or when tire pressures are low. Just think about all the amazing features or apps we can make to help our customers!

"We want to have sensors on sale by the May Town Hall," she says. "As soon as we line up a partner and confirm that all the pieces fit together, we'll start taking orders. It'll be a small-batch production run, but we want to see if there's real customer demand. And we need to make sure we get security right. We don't want to collect data that creates liability for the company, and we need to protect our customer's privacy."

Maxine applauds with everyone else, and she's pleased beyond words that she's now a part of the engine sensor team, as are many of her former MRP teammates.

As promised, Steve brings Wes and his team to celebrate the hauling away of all the Kumquat servers, thanking them for enabling the company to focus even more on creating value for Parts Unlimited customers.

Steve is really good at this, Maxine thinks. And she never would have guessed how Wes and his team would be so proud of dismantling an empire they helped create.

During the May Town Hall, Maggie talks about the updates for the engine sensor product, and Shannon shares the good news: "When we showed the engine sensor company executives what we've built and how strong our channel to their target market is, they were excited to partner," she says with a grin. "Or maybe they were frightened at what we'd do if they didn't partner. Either way, they agreed to make modified sensors to our desired specs.

"We are now taking orders for thousands of engine sensors per week, and it's taking everything we've got to keep up with demand," she continues. "And I'm so pleased that our investments into the Narwhal database and Panther data platform are paying off. All our pilot sensors are sending their data to our platform and are being analyzed by our data scientists and product team."

Thanking Shannon, Maggie then says, "Surprisingly, we're bringing an entirely new category of customers into our stores," says Maggie. "We've found that many customers are car fleet managers and solo rideshare drivers, people whose livelihoods depend on keeping their cars running. We know we can help these people in many ways!

"And another surprise is that many customers are installing our sensors in luxury cars, many of them electric. They're very tech-savvy and love the information we provide them. They love the historical data and mapping. This demographic is extremely desirable, which could open up many opportunities for the company, including all sorts of add-on subscriptions," she continues.

"In fact, we're doing an experiment to contact them when we detect that their tire pressures are low," she says. "We found that a large number of Tesla owners are driving around for weeks with low tire pressure. We tested an offering to drive out to their car and refill their tires and their fluids, and we were all stunned at the high conversion rate.

"This is a market that is not very price sensitive," she says with a smile. "We confirmed that we can charge a much higher fee. I suspect there are many other problems we can solve for them, with high margins."

Maggie presents on a new initiative using machine learning to analyze in-store camera footage to examine foot traffic. They've already discovered certain endcap displays that were incredibly effective at capturing attention, resulting in dwell times much higher than normal, which meant they could sell more products, charge a higher price, or even create new related product offerings. They also found stores with unusually high queue abandonment rates, where customers waited so long in lines that they just left. They found that increasing in-store staff in these stores paid off big time.

Similarly, there was an in-store pilot that notified store managers whenever a high-value customer entered the store with their app installed. These managers loved it, able to use their already broad discretion to make sure these customers were always delighted. If the customer wasn't using the app, the store manager was notified when they presented their loyalty card or swiped their credit card. Already, these customers have noticed and expressed their appreciation.

Next up, Debra shares the exciting updates on the four-hour delivery project. As Debra wraps up, she says, "Sorry, I have to tell you one last story. Last time, I asked for help, about how we needed ideas to more quickly find couriers in new markets. Someone noticed that ninety per-cent of our current couriers were engine sensor customers too. So in our latest pilot market, we tried sending an email to engine sensor customers in the area who were known to be professional drivers. The response was amazing. We had ample capacity within a week. This is an incredible competitive advantage, so thank you to Darrin Devaraj who suggested this!"

When Steve thanks her, he adds, "Remember, our business is built on customer trust. We have made a commitment to our customers that we will protect their privacy and data. I want to thank Shannon Corman for creating the Panther platform that is enabling us to turn data into a competitive advantage and also protect it for our customers."

Maxine smiles. She knows that none of this would have been possible without Shannon's initial proposal that led to Panther. They say that 'data is the new oil,' and these are only some of the many ways that they've enabled the entire company to harness value from it.

By democratizing the data, they've made it available to anyone who needs it. They may have decentralized teams, but they can access the vast expertise across the company. This learning and sharing dynamic has obviously and vastly amplified the effectiveness of some of the most strategic efforts in the company. *Erik would be proud*, she thinks.

Taking a break from the endless and exciting whirlwind of the engine sensor project, Maxine goes for a walk. Without a doubt, this project is already a runaway success. Sales have recently hit over ten thousand sensors a week, and rumor has it that their mobile app was just nominated for an interactive design award.

Maxine and her team are having a blast, but they need help. They started lobbying Maggie for another five engineers to accelerate building out all the awesome ideas on the roadmap.

On a whim, Maxine decides to go into the datacenter. She looks around, amazed at how it's changed in the last five months.

Before, it was packed from wall-to-wall, filled with servers from floor to ceiling mounted on nineteen-inch racks. But now, there's an area one hundred feet long and nearly fifty feet wide that is entirely empty, the racks having been hauled away.

On the floor are pieces of masking tape and paper tombstones indicating the business systems that used to reside on those servers.

"Email Server: $163K annual savings."

"Helpdesk: $109K annual savings."

"HR Systems: $188K annual savings."

There are nearly thirty tombstones, and on a nearby wall is a sign that reads, "Rack Funerals: Over ten tons of obsolete equipment removed and recycled…So far…May they rest in peace." The "ten" has been crossed out and replaced with a hand-written "thirteen."

Also posted on the board are pictures of removed equipment. Seeing the picture of the wrecked pile of Kumquat servers still makes Maxine smile.

Maxine knows that later in the year, large portions of her old MRP system will be replatformed to a commercially supported offering so it can be safely retired. She is helping Glenn, her old manager, in that effort. Glenn's newly stated goal is to build the "world's best manufacturing supply chain," As reported by one of the industry trade organizations, he vowed. "I'm so pissed off we fell off the top ten. Give me three years, with your support and Steve's, and we'll be the envy of the industry."

They will finally consolidate from twenty different warehouse management systems down to one. They will finally migrate to a current version of their ERP system. Almost all customizations will be converted to what the vendor provides, unless it creates competitive advantage, such as certain key MRP modules—any customizations would be done outside the ERP in separate applications.

When Glenn declared his incredibly ambitious goal, it became clear that they needed more top-talent engineers, and he has no problems getting budget to do it—everyone knows that this effort will help Parts Unlimited for decades to come.

There were other surprises, as well. They used a technique called Wardley Maps to better localize what parts of various value chains were commodities and should be outsourced, which should be purchased, and which should be kept in-house because they created durable, competitive advantage. They used this exercise to methodically disposition their technology stacks, given the business context.

In doing so, they found another technology gem right next to the MRP group: it was an event bus that ingested all the equipment sensor data from their manufacturing plants, which had been running flawlessly for years.

When Maxine found this tech stack, she couldn't believe it—it was exactly what Shannon had wanted when she had first pitched Panther but had to be taken out of scope. Although Maxine kicked herself for not thinking of it sooner, she knew exactly what to do with it.

It is now at the center of Project Shamu, forming the foundation of a massive architectural change that will eventually touch almost every back-end service and API across the entire company. Maxine knows that this is one of the most important technology initiatives in the company, because it solves something that has been bothering her for over a year. In the first Unicorn mini-launch, the transportation options service took down the entire order funnel. It was just one of twenty-three deeply nested API calls made whenever someone checked for product availability.

Even after a year, this problem remained unfixed. It was simply too expensive to shore up all twenty-three APIs to be a Tier 1 service—an SLA that requires five-nines of uptime, guaranteed response within ten milliseconds, and all sorts of other things that cost tons of money.

What's always bothered her was why twenty-three API calls were needed in the first place, why they had to respond within milliseconds, and why they had to be so expensive to run. After all, it's not like the transportation and shipping options changed every millisecond—they changed monthly. Product categories only changed once per quarter. Product descriptions and pictures only changed every few weeks.

Many thought caching the results solved the problem. But for Maxine, functional programming and immutability showed a much more elegant, even beautiful, solution. If they could represent all these API requests for information as values that were re-computed every time one of their inputs changed, they could reduce the number of API calls from twenty-three... to one.

Maxine never tires of the aha moments that people have when she explains this use of the event sourcing pattern, "Instead of calling twenty-three APIs to tell the customer when they can get their order, she asks them to think of this process instead... "It's like leaves on a tree, all sending data that eventually end up at the trunk. One service knows only about products, another service only knows about zip codes or warehouses. Another service combines these, to describe what products are in-stock in each warehouse. Another service combines this information with shipping options to tell customers how soon they can have that product delivered. And all this information ends up in a specialized delete key/value store.

"It's no longer twenty-three API calls that all must be available and respond quickly. Instead, it's just one API call that takes a product ID and zip code, and returns the shipping options and delivery times without having to compute anything," she would say. "Doing it this way will save millions of dollars per year!"

But that's just the beginning and a fraction of the value it will create, Maxine thinks, smiling. This will be such a massive simplification over the mess they've lived with for decades. They will do this for customer orders, inventory availability, customer loyalty programs, service station jobs... almost everything.

It will decouple all of these services from each other, allowing teams to make changes independently, no longer reliant upon the single Data Hub team to implement their business rule changes. If all goes well, and Maxine will make sure it goes well, Shamu will replace Data Hub and all the point-to-point API calls across the entire company.

It will make the tracking of data and state across the enterprise simpler, safer, more resilient, easier to understand, cheaper to run, faster to deliver... It will lead to better business outcomes, happier stakeholders, and happier engineers.

This is not functional programming principles applied in the small—it will be applied to how the entire enterprise is organized and architected. Their technology landscape will now resemble the tech giants and enable an agility that is difficult to even imagine right now. She can think of no better manifestation of the First Ideal of Locality and Simplicity. She knows with certainty that it will enable competitive advantage, even if she doesn't know exactly how—any company who doesn't do something like this will continue their slow, but inevitable, decline. This will be the biggest triumph and achievement of her entire career.

Thinking about everything she's achieved and all the triumphs that are sure to come, Maxine looks around at the datacenter again, so much emptier than when she was here last.

It is still difficult for her to believe how much has happened to her since she was exiled to the Phoenix Project. Back then, all she wanted to do was get a Phoenix build going on her laptop. Even undertaking that modest task, she faced adversities and obstacles that seemed insurmountable at the time, even with her vast experience and skills.

She had almost given up when Kurt approached her to join the Rebellion, asking for her help to liberate developers so they could get done what needed to get done. They were a seemingly crazy group of misfits who were out to overthrow the ancient, powerful order...and against all odds they did.

They started off as a group of redshirts, trapped in the engine room. They were later joined by brave and like-minded junior officers who pitched in to help. And in the strangest turns of events, they eventually found themselves working side-by-side with the bridge officers, helping turn the tide in their collective fight for survival, and they were even drawn into political battles with Starfleet Command, who wanted to break up their ship and sell it off for parts..

Maxine smiles. She thinks about how much she's learned, how many times she was about to give up, and how the Five Ideals guided her on which battles to fight and why those battles mattered. And how she couldn't have done it without a team of teams around her, supporting her quest for excellence.

She stares at the servers that run the MRP system she shepherded for six years. She thinks about how later this year, she'll be standing in the parking lot celebrating the completion of the MRP migration, telling everyone about how proud she is that the MRP systems served their mission so well, and now they could be retired and hauled away.

Steve will say some words, and then Wes will hand her the sledgehammer.

Thinking about it all, she smiles and makes her way back to her desk.

EPILOGUE

• One Year Later

Maxine walks out of the Town Hall. Steve and Maggie had talked about the incredible achievements of the company. The company is growing and becoming known as one of the most innovative in the industry.

Steve had once again reclaimed the role of board chair, and he thanked Bob Strauss for his service to the company.

The technology group is nearly twice the size of what it was when she was first exiled to the Phoenix Project. And Maxine is so proud that engineers in the company are presenting at nearly every technology conference around, showing off what they've built and, of course, letting everyone know that they're hiring.

Every business unit is desperate for more engineers. Maxine spends nearly a third of her time looking for or interviewing talent. They've already hired every good engineer within driving distance, so they're now hiring remote engineers everywhere and actively recruiting from almost every college campus.

They even found that an unexpected way of attracting great talent was through all the amazing new Parts Unlimited open-source projects that Maxine and the teams have created. Just like the tech giants, they've decided to open source various technologies that don't create competitive advantage, and now many are becoming industry standards. For prospective engineers, the opportunity to work with the luminaries who created them is undeniably compelling.

Thanks to Maxine's endless and relentless lobbying, the TEP and LARB have both been disbanded. Proudly hanging on her desk is a certificate that says, "Lifetime Achievement Award to Maxine Chambers for Abolishing TEP-LARB," which is signed by everyone from the original Rebellion.

The engine sensor project is a monster runaway success, by far the fastest growing part of the company. Nearly two hundred thousand units have now been sold, generating $25 million in revenue.

The engine sensors were the surprise hit of the last holiday shopping season. Despite all their preparation, the company couldn't keep enough in stock. They were not only impossible to keep on store shelves, but they were out of stock on the e-commerce site as well. They were back-ordered for three months, even with the massive production orders they had started earlier in the year trying to get ahead of the holiday season.

But it was their mobile app that made all the difference. People were buying the engine sensors because they loved the app so much. An entirely new demographic was entering the store. Many of the store managers had told her that it was the first time they'd seen so many people in their twenties coming to Parts Unlimited.

Maggie is convinced that a huge market will be car rental fleet managers, as well as agencies that recondition cars for the huge car auction market. They are even exploring connecting their enthusiastic ranks of home mechanic customers to car manufacturers, who desperately need to reduce their backlog of getting safety-critical recall work done—an "Uber for Auto Mechanics."

The wildly popular Parts Unlimited mobile app won a bunch of industry interactive design awards from some of the most prestigious firms in the nation, to the pride of the entire team. And because of savvy deal-making, the profit margin on each unit sold was fantastic. Maxine's part of a secret team that is actively in talks to acquire the sensor manufacturer, which would increase profit margins even more. She's certain that the real money to be made is in selling subscription services to people with these sensors. Everyone agrees that this could be a $100 million business within a couple of years.

Bill has been assigned to lead the acquisition discussions. If the deal goes through, the founders of the sensor company will be independently wealthy, contingent that they stay with Parts Unlimited for another three years.

Maxine would welcome working with them. They, too, would help shape the future of a thriving Parts Unlimited. And they should be extremely happy with the arrangement, because they'd still be working out of their garage if it weren't for the amazing software capabilities that Shannon, Brent, Dwayne, and Maxine had built for them.

One of them told her, "You made all our dreams come true. This is why we created this engine sensor, but we didn't have the software skills to make it this successful." That made her day.

Even though the acquisition will cost Parts Unlimited tens of millions of dollars, Steve is adamant that this money will be extremely well spent because it will further reinforce that Parts Unlimited is setting the direction for the entire industry. Dick reports that even skeptical Wall Street analysts think this will be a great move for the company.

In contrast, Maxine thinks about the four-hour delivery team. As predicted by Debra, Parts Unlimited had a tremendous advantage over its startup competitor, having vastly more resources, knowledge of the market, existing commercial relationships with service stations, and a willingness to put in whatever funding was necessary to win. In comparison, the startup was running out of money.

Debra and her team were able to grow revenue to $10 million, with no signs of slowing down. The entire direct sales force had been assigned quotas to sell this new offering, and it was quickly becoming their favorite thing to sell. Their customers love the service so much that the amount they order from Parts Unlimited is skyrocketing.

Maxine had recommended to Maggie that they graduate them to Horizon 2. She's working with Bill and the executives to figure out which organization should own it, with the Service Station Direct Sales division being the most logical choice. She thinks that's where it belongs, closest to the people who care most about it and are willing to happily fund it. Technology needs to be embedded in the business, not external to it or merely "aligned with it."

A couple of weeks ago, Maxine learned that this defeated startup competitor had approached Steve, exploring whether he might be interested in acquiring them. Steve tasked Bill with conducting the due diligence. After a week, Bill dismissed the idea as a bad one. Quite simply, Parts Unlimited had already replicated or exceeded all their intellectual property, know-how, and software.

"Rumor is they're now being shopped around by some bankers," Bill had told her, laughing. "I'm sure they're going to all our competitors to see if they'll bite, trying to provoke us to reconsider. But given how we've already won in the marketplace, I really doubt that would be a threat to us."

This is precisely what Sarah had wanted to do with Parts Unlimited nearly one and a half years ago. During those dark days, Sarah was trying to sell the company off for parts, while Maxine and team tried to figure out how to find $15 million to fund the Innovation efforts.

Once again, they're at Dockside Bar. They just opened up a new patio area in the back, which the Rebellion has taken over to better enjoy the June summer evening. There's nearly forty people here, including Maggie and Kirsten and leaders from all areas of the business. And she's thrilled that her husband is here too.

Maxine is happy to be here with her fellow Rebellion members. Although, as the months go by, calling this group the Rebellion seems a bit anachronistic. The Rebellion has won.

Earlier today, Bill had taken her aside to let her know that she was being promoted. She was going to be the first distinguished engineer in the company's history, reporting directly to Bill. She loves her proposed job description. Among other things, her charter is to help create a culture of engineering excellence across the entire company. She'll meet regularly with the top company leadership to understand their goals and strategize on how technology can be used to achieve those goals, which of course helps the company win in the marketplace.

Maxine is excited that there is finally a career ladder for individual contributors and brilliant technologists without having to become managers. Her job is not is to come up with the best ideas. It's to ensure that the entire company can ship the best ideas, wherever they come from, quickly, safely, and securely. She made a note to herself to find the best designer in the company. After spending two days at an interactive design conference, she knows that this discipline is critical to the company's success too.

Kurt's now reporting directly to Chris. Rumor has it that he will soon be promoted to engineering director, and that Chris is trying to figure out how to finally retire and open up a bar in Florida. In the meantime, Chris has eliminated QA as a separate department, distributing them into the feature teams. Ops is quickly turning into a platform team and internal consultants, with the goal of providing developers the infrastructure they need, complete with a vast army of experts who are there to help, looking for ways to make developers productive.

Patty now has a fascinating new role. To help accelerate moving more developers from Context to Core, she volunteered to manage over one hundred fifty applications, moving them all into maintenance mode, supported by a small group of talented and motivated engineers, with the goal of managing them at the lowest cost or killing them entirely. She is also helping to build a customer support function within the engine sensor product team, supported by Derek!

And in a suprising turn of events, earlier this week Maxine finally had that lunch meeting with Sarah, who had reached out to her. It was not at all what Maxine expected. Despite her initial wariness, she had fun and even learned some things. Maxine thinks they may even have built a degree of mutual respect. Maybe. They promise to meet again.

When she can't stand the pestering any longer, Maxine stands up and clinks her glass. "Thank you all for being here tonight. We've got a lot to celebrate. As the Rebellion, we set out to overthrow the ancient, powerful, and unjust order! And against amazing odds, I think we've actually done it!" Maxine hollers out.

Everyone hoots and cheers, and several holler out, "Congratulations on your promotion, Maxine!" She raises her arms in the air in victory, then sits back down.

"Indeed, way to go, Maxine," says Erik. "Large, complex organizations like yours are truly like sleeping giants that are awakening. Your engine sensor product shows that you identified a $300 million market you wanted to go after, and within a year, you have captured nearly ten percent of it. That's an amazing feat. What startup could have ten percent of a $300 million market in one year? If a startup had done that, it'd be a miracle. They'd be on the cover of all the magazines and newspapers. A real unicorn.

"And this is surely the nature of this new economy. The power to disrupt the customer experience is no longer just the domain of the FAANGs: the Facebooks, Apples, Amazons, Netflixes, and Googles," Erik continues. "Instead, it is within reach of almost any organization that wants to disrupt the market. And who better to disrupt things for the benefit of customers than the organizations that already have a decades-long relationship with them?

"Companies like Parts Unlimited already have the customer relationships, the supply chains, the understanding of the customer's wants and needs as they progress through their own life journey. Compared to startups, the modern enterprise has more resources and expertise. What's needed is focus and urgency, and the modern methods of managing the value creation process.

"As evidence, look at how Wall Street is valuing this company," Erik says. "It's at an all-time high, over 2.5 times higher than when you joined the Rebellion. Parts Unlimited is now being valued at six times trailing sales, almost four times higher than before. Parts Unlimited now has one of the highest multiples of any physical store retailer, making them the talk of the industry and an emerging success story of surviving and thriving in the era of digital disruption.

"And this is just the beginning. We are undoubtedly in the earliest stages of a new golden age that will lead to decades of economic growth, creating prosperity for all segments of society.

"We are at the dawn of the Age of Software and Data. Steve and Maggie are even thinking about what data is most important to the long-term success of the company, exploring ways of buying data from our customers and even potentially acquiring strategic data sources. And Steve already knows that technologists are some of the most important people in the company. Which is why you're a distinguished engineer," Erik says. "Did you know that Steve keeps a book by his bed of the most important people in the company, so that he'll always recognize them, even in a crowd at Disneyland. And did you know that you're in it, as well as Kurt, Brent, and Shannon? A decade ago, only the top plant managers and store managers were in there. Now, there are engineers in there too.

"Great times are truly ahead, Maxine," he says.

"You're so right, Erik. Small doesn't beat big," Maxine says. "Instead, fast beats slow. And fast and big will win almost every time. The Unicorn Project has shown us that."

From:	Alan Perez (Operating Partner, Wayne-Yokohama Equity Partners)
To:	Steve Masters (CEO)
Cc:	Dick Landry (CFO)
Date:	4:51 p.m., January 11
Subject:	Meet up for drinks?

Steve,

I'll be the first to admit that when I heard you present to the board a little over a year ago, I thought you were crazy. Even if I did believe you about "employee engagement, customer satisfaction, and cash flow" being the only things that matter.

Frankly, I could not see Parts Unlimited being a growth play, let alone doing it through software. But you've vaulted the company into the highest range of growth that we see in our portfolio. And given the significantly higher multiples that the markets put on growth (vs. value and profitability), your company was one of the best performers in our portfolio last year.

Despite my initial skepticism, I'm very happy that you've proven me wrong. Suddenly, I've become a bit of a hero in our firm. We've got many investments, some of which were once the most recognized brands in their respective industries. They could definitely benefit from a similar digital disruption. I now wonder how we can help those companies win in their markets.

I'll be in Elkhart Grove for the next board meeting. Let's meet for drinks the evening before? I'd love to learn more about how you did it and get your thoughts on how it might be applicable to some of our other portfolio companies.

See you soon, Alan
_____

JOB DESCRIPTION: DISTINGUISHED ENGINEER

Sponsor and cultivate a culture of technical excellence through the following activities:

- Grow our next generation of technical leaders through mentoring, sponsorship, and formal training programs.
- Establish and participate in cross-team guilds focused on technology areas like security, performance, site reliability.
- Guide the creation of a governance and architecture review function that can evolve and ensure company obligations are fulfilled for years to come.
  - Review important issues that management is concerned about.
  - This function will include risk and assurance, information and e-records, and architecture.
  - Provide technical assistance to any team seeking feedback on their approach.
  - Develop measures to keep governance capabilities and their staff hands-on and relevant.
- Be the company spokesperson to technical audiences to advance the company brand and facilitate recruiting, competing with the top technology companies for talent.
- Oversee the architecture, design, and implementation of *Shamu*, the enterprise event-sourcing platform to replace Data Hub, and timeline to transition all enterprise services to use it.

THE FIVE IDEALS

The First Ideal: Locality and Simplicity

The Second Ideal: Focus, Flow, and Joy

The Third Ideal: Improvement of Daily Work

The Fourth Ideal: Psychological Safety

The Fifth Ideal: Customer Focus

Timeline

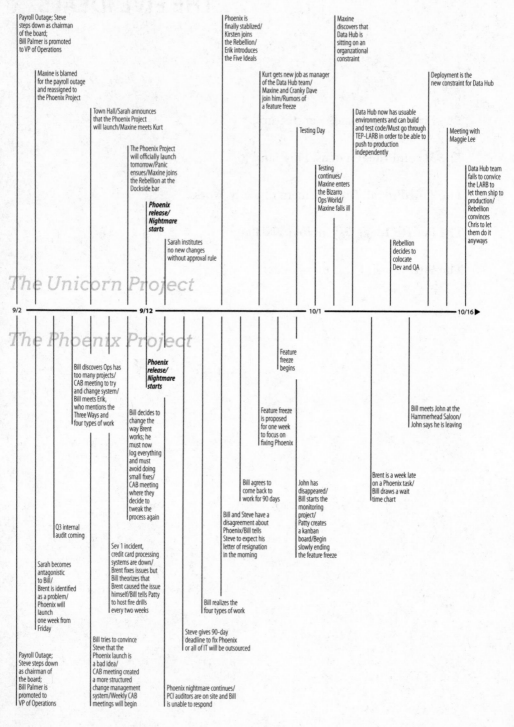

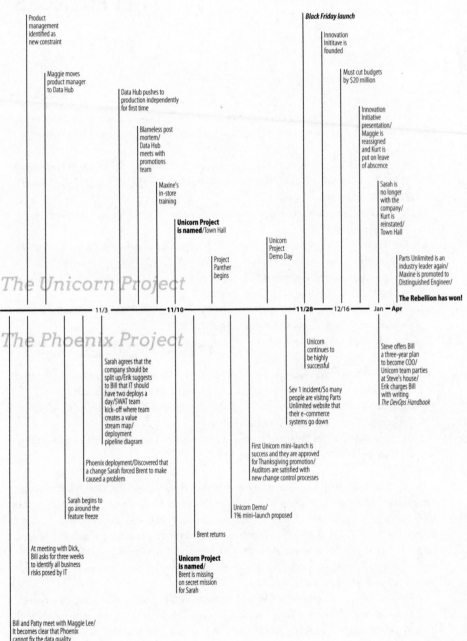

The Unicorn Project

Product
management
identified as
new constraint

Maggie moves
product manager
to Data Hub

Data Hub pushes to
production independently
for first time

Blameless post
mortem/
Data Hub
meets with
promotions
team

Maxine's
in-store
training

**Unicorn Project
is named**/Town Hall

Project
Panther
begins

Unicorn
Project
Demo Day

Black Friday launch

Innovation
Inititave is
founded

Must cut budgets
by $20 million

Innovation
Initiative
presentation/
Maggie is
reassigned
and Kurt is
put on leave
of abscence

Sarah is
no longer
with the
company/
Kurt is
reinstated/
Town Hall

Parts Unlimited is an
industry leader again/
Maxine is promoted to
Distinguished Engineer/

The Rebellion has won!

—— 11/3 ————————— 11/10 ——————————————— 11/28 —— 12/16 —— Jan ➤ Apr

The Phoenix Project

Sarah agrees that the
company should be
split up/Erik suggests
to Bill that IT should
have two deploys a
day/SWAT team
kick-off where team
creates a value
stream map/
deployment
pipeline diagram

Phoenix deployment/Discovered that
a change Sarah forced Brent to make
caused a problem

Sarah begins to
go around the
feature freeze

At meeting with Dick,
Bill asks for three weeks
to identify all business
risks posed by IT

Brent returns

**Unicorn Project
is named**/
Brent is missing
on secret mission
for Sarah

Bill and Patty meet with Maggie Lee/
It becomes clear that Phoenix
cannot fix the data quality
problems it was supposed to

Unicorn Demo/
1% mini-launch proposed

First Unicorn mini-launch is
success and they are approved
for Thanksgiving promotion/
Auditors are satisfied with
new change control processes

Sev 1 incident/So many
people are visitng Parts
Unlimited website that
their e-commerce
systems go down

Unicorn
continues to
be highly
successful

Steve offers Bill
a three-year plan
to become COO/
Unicorn team parties
at Steve's house/
Erik charges Bill
with writing
The DevOps Handbook

REFERENCES

The Unicorn Project was heavily influenced by many books. Listed below are, in my opinion, some of the best in the relevant bodies of knowledge from which we drawn upon most:

Accelerate: The Science of Lean Software and DevOps: Building and Scaling High Performing Technology Organizations by Nicole Forsgren, PhD, Jez Humble, and Gene Kim (IT Revolution, 2018).

The Goal: A Process of Ongoing Improvement by Eliyahu M. Goldratt and Jeff Cox (North River Press, 1984).

The High-Velocity Edge: How Market Leaders Leverage Operational Excellence to Beat the Competition by Steven J. Spear (McGraw Hill, 2010).

The Principles of Product Development Flow: Second Generation Lean Product Development by Donald G. Reinertsen (Celeritas, 2009).

Project to Product: How to Survive and Thrive in the Age of Digital Disruption with the Flow Framework by Mik Kersten (IT Revolution, 2018).

A Seat at The Table: IT Leadership in the Age of Agility by Mark Schwartz (IT Revolution, 2017).

Team of Teams: New Rules of Engagement for a Complex World by Gen. Stanley McChrystal with Tantum Collins, David Silverman, and Chris Fussell (Portfolio, 2015).

Technological Revolutions and Financial Capital: The Dynamics of Bubbles and Golden Ages by Carlota Perez (Edward Elgar Pub, 2003).

Transforming NOKIA: The Power of Paranoid Optimism to Lead Through Colossal Change by Risto Siilasmaa (McGraw-Hill, 2018).

This story was inspired by so amazing and heroic stories from the DevOps Enterprise community. Many infrastructure elements were inspired by Jason Cox (The Walt Disney Company) and Fernando Corango (adidas), architectural and development elements inspired by Scott Prugh (CSG), and event sourcing architecture by Scott Havens (Walmart Labs). The Dockside Bar was modeled after Café Intención, where adidas held regular meetings to plan and eventually pitch their leadership on a digital transformation. This led to the creation of their platform team.

Over the years, I've also been inspired by many lectures, talks, videos, articles, tweets, and personal correspondence with people I admire. I've included many of the ones that directly influenced moments in *The Unicorn Project* below, presented in the order that they appear in the book.

Chapter 2

"Fireside Chat with Compuware CEO Chris O'Malley," YouTube video, posted by IT Revolution, from DevOps Enterprise Summit Las Vegas 2018, https://www.youtube.com/watch?v=r3H1E2lY_ig.

Chapter 3

Zachary Tellman, *Elements of Clojure* (LuLu.com, 2019).

Chapter 6

"The PMO is Dead, Long Live the PMO - Barclays," YouTube video, posted by IT Revolution, from DevOps Enterprise Summit London 2018, https://www.youtube.com/watch?v=R-fol1vkPlM.

"Better Value Sooner Safer Happier - Jon Smart," YouTube video, posted by IT Revolution, from DevOps Enterprise Summit London 2019, https://www.youtube.com/watch?v=ZKrhdyjGoM8.

Chapter 7

Rich Hickey, "Simple Made Easy," *InfoQ*, recorded at QCon London 2012, posted June 20, 2012, https://www.infoq.com/presentations Simple-Made-Easy-QCon-London-2012/.

Nicole Forsgren, PhD, Jez Humble, and Gene Kim, *Accelerate: The Science of Lean Software and DevOps: Building and Scaling High Performing Technology Organizations* by Nicole Forsgren, PhD, Jez Humble, and Gene Kim (IT Revolution, 2018).

Ward Cunningham, "Ward Explains Debt Metaphor," wiki.c2.com, last edited January 22, 2011, http://c2.com/cgi/wiki?WardExplainsDebtMetaphor.

Chapter 8

"What people think programming is vs. how it actually is," YouTube video, posted by Jombo, February 22, 2018, https://www.youtube.com watch?v=HluANRwPyNo&feature=youtu.be.

Ryan Naraine, "10 Years Since the Bill Gates Security Memo: A Personal Journey," ZDNet, January 13, 2012, https://www.zdnet.com article/10-years-since-the-bill-gates-security-memo-a-personal-journey/.

Bill Gates, "Bill Gates: Trustworthy Computing," *Wired*, January 17, 2012, https://www.wired.com/2002/01/bill-gates-trustworthy-computing/.

Risto Siilasmaa, *Transforming NOKIA: The Power of Paranoid Optimism to Lead Through Colossal Change* (McGraw-Hill, 2018) Kindle, 49.

John Cutler (@johncutlefish), "Case in point (from actual org) * In 2015 reference feature took 15-30d. * In 2018 same (class of) feature took 150-300d primarily bc of 1) tech debt, and 2) fast track silver bullets to drive success theater and/or acquisitions (for same effect) Cc: @realgenekim @mik_kersten" Twitter, September 29, 2018.

John Allspaw, "How Your Systems Keep Running Day After Day – John Allspaw," YouTube video, posted by ITRevolution, from the DevOps Enterprise Summit Las Vegas, 2017, https://www.youtube.com/watch?v=xA5U85LSk0M.

Charles Duhigg, "What Google Learned From Its Quest to Build the Perfect Team," *New York Times*, February 25, 2016, https://www.nytimes.com/2016/02/28/magazine/what-google-learned-from-its-quest-to-build-the-perfect-team.html?smid=pl-share.

"Guide: Understand Team Effectiveness," ReWork, accessed August 21, 2019, https://rework.withgoogle.com/print/guides/5721312655835136/.

Team of Teams: New Rules of Engagement for a Complex World by Gen. Stanley McChrystal with Tantum Collins, David Silverman, and Chris Fussell (Portfolio, 2015).

"Quote by W. Edwards Deming," The W. Edwards Deming Institute, February 1993, https://quotes.deming.org/authors/W._Edwards_Deming/quote/10091.

The Principles of Product Development Flow: Second Generation Lean Product Development by Donald G. Reinertsen (Celeritas, 2009).

The High-Velocity Edge: How Market Leaders Leverage Operational Excellence to Beat the Competition by Steven J. Spear (McGraw Hill, 2010).

"Convergence of Safety Culture and Lean: Lessons from the Leaders," YouTube video, posted by IT Revolution, from DevOps Enterprise Summit San Francisco 2017, https://www.youtube.com/watch?v=CFMJ3V4VakA.

Jeffrey Snover (@jsnover), "I literally (and yes I do mean literally) wanted to hide under my desk. I knew that they wouldn't be able to tell who did it (downside of DomainOS) so ... making the phonecall was one of the hardest things I've every done." Twitter, November 17, 2017, https://twitter.com/jsnover/status/931632205020913664.

"Paul O'Neill of Safety Leadership," YouTube video, posted by Steve Japs, February 7, 2014, https://www.youtube.com/watch?v=0gvOrYuPBEA&t=1467s.

"Paul O'Neill The Irreducible Components of Leadership.wmv," YouTube video, posted by ValueCapture, Mar 22, 2012, https://www.youtube.com/watch?v=htLCVqaLBvo.

Chapter 9

Bill Sempf (@sempf), "QA Engineer walks into a bar. Order a beer. Orders 0 beers. Orders 999999999 beers. Orders a lizard. Orders -1 beers. Orders a sfdeljknesv." Twitter, September 23, 2014, https://twitter.com/sempf/status/514473420277694465.

Chapter 12

Mik Kersten, "Project to Product: Thrive in the Age of Digital Disruption with the Flow Framework," YouTube video, posted by IT Revolution, from DevOps Enterprise Summit London 2019, https://www.youtube.com/watch?v=hrjvbTlirnk.

Chapter 13

John Allspaw, "How Your Systems Keep Running Day after Day – John Allspaw," YouTube video, posted by IT Revolution, from DevOps Enterprise Summit San Francisco 2017, https://www.youtube.com/watch?v=xA5U85LSk0M&t=2s.

DD Woods, *STELLA: Report from the SNAFUcatchers Workshop on Coping with Complexity* (Columbus, OH: The Ohio State University, 2017) https://snafucatchers.github.io/.

Gene Kim, Jez Humble, Patrick Debois, and John Willis, *The DevOps Handbook: How to Create World-Class Agility, Reliability, and Security in Technology Organizations* (IT Revolution, 2016).

Gene Kim and John Willis, *Beyond The Phoenix Project: The Origins and Evolution of DevOps* (IT Revolution, 2018).

"DOES15 – Courtney Kissler & Jason Josephy – Mindsets and Metrics and Mainframes… Oh My!" YouTube video, posted by DevOps Enterprise Summit, from DevOps Enterprise Summit 2015, https://www.youtube.com/watch?v=88_y1YFsRig.

Chapter 14

Jeffrey Dean and Sanjar Ghemawat, *MapReduce: Simplified Data Processing on Lage Clusters*, (Google Inc., 2004) https://static.googleusercontent.com/media/research.google.com/en//archive/mapreduce-osdi04.pdf.

Christoper Bergh, Gil Benghiat, and Eran Strod, *The DataOps Cookbook: Methodologies and Tools that Reduce Analytics Cycle Time While Improving Quality* (DataKitchen, 2019).

"From Startups to Big-Business: Using Functional Programming Techniques to Transform Line of," YouTube video, posted by Microsoft Developer, May 8, 2018, https://www.youtube.com/watch?v=dSCzCaiWgLM.

"Forging a Functional Enterprise: How Thinking Functionally Transforms Line-of-Business Applications," YouTube video, posted by IT Revolution, from DevOps Enterprise Summit London 2019, https://www.youtube.com/watch?v=n5S3hScE6dU&amp=&t=5s.

Chapter 16

Stacey Vanek Smith, "Episode 724: Cat Scam," *Planet Money,* NPR, March 13, 2019, https://www.npr.org/sections/money/2019/03/13/703014256/episode-724-cat-scam.

"Digital Transformation: Thriving Through the Transition – Jeffrey Snover, Microsoft," YouTube video, posted by IT Revolution, from DevOps Enterprise Summit London 2018, https://www.youtube.com/watch?v=nKyF8fzed0w&feature=youtu.be.

"Zone to Win – Organizing to Complete in an Age of Disruption, by Geoffrey Moore," YouTube video, posted by TSIA, November 6, 2017, https://www.youtube.com/watch?v=FsV_cqde7w8.

"GOTO 2016 – Zome to Win – Geoffrey Moore," YouTube video, posted by GOTO Conferences, December 7, 2016, https://www.youtube.com/watch?v=fG4Lndk-PTI&t=391s.

"Digital Transformation: Thriving Through the Transition – Jeffrey Snover, Mircosoft," YouTube video, posted by IT Revolution, from DevOps Enterprise Summit Las Vegas 2018, https://www.youtube.com/watch?v=qHxkcndCQoI&t=1s.

"Discovering Your Way to Greatness: How Fining and Fixing Faults is the Path to Perfection," YouTube video, posted by IT Revolution, from DevOps Enterprise Summit London 2019, https://www.youtube.com/watch?v=h4XMoHhireY.

Chapter 17

"DOES14 – Steve Neely – Rally Software," YouTube video, posted by DevOps Enterprise Summit 2014, November 5, 2014, https://www.youtube.com /watch?v=BcvCR5FDvH8.

"Typescript at Google," Neugierig.org, September 1, 2018, http://neugierig.org/software /blog/2018/09/typescript-at-google.html.

Chapter 19

Kim, Humble, Debois, and Willis, *The DevOps Handbook.*

"More Culture, More Engineering, Less Duct-Tape (DOES17 US) – CSG International," YouTube video, posted by IT Revolution, from DevOps Enterprise Summit San Francisco 2017, https://www.youtube.com/watch?v=rCKONS4FTX4&t=247s.

XI IOT - Facefeed Application Deployment Guide," Nutanix Workshops website, accessed August 20, 2019, https://nutanix.handsonworkshops.com/workshops/e1c32f92-1de8 -4642-9d88-31a4159d0431/p/.

Compuware (compuwarecorp), "The racks keep leaving and space keeps opening up in our #datacenter, but our #mainframeswill never leave! #alwaysandforever #ibmz #hybridIT #cloudcomputing #cloud" Instragram, September 7, 2018, https://www .instagram.com/p/Bnb8B4iAQun/?utm_source=ig_embed.

"Keynote: Crossing the River by Feeling the Stones – Simon Wardley, Researcher, Leading Edge Forum," YouTube video, posted by CNCF [Cloud Native Computing Foundation], May 6, 2018, https://www.youtube.com/watch?v=xlNYYy8pzB4.

XI IOT - Facefeed Application Deployment Guide," Nutanix Workshops website, accessed August 20, 2019, https://nutanix.handsonworkshops.com/workshops/e1c32f92-1de8 -4642-9d88-31a4159d0431/p/.

Epilogue

"Open Source is the Best Insurance for the Future: Eddie Satterly Talks About IAG," YouTube video, posted by The New Stack, December 5, 2017, https://www.youtube .com/watch?v=k0rcNAzLzj4&t=2s.

"DevOps at Target: Year 3," YouTube video, posted by IT Revolution, from DevOps Enterprise Summit San Francisco 2016, https://www.youtube.com/watch?v=1FMktLCYukQ.

Technological Revolutions and Financial Capital: The Dynamics of Bubbles and Golden Ages by Carlota Perez (Edward Elgar Pub, 2003).

"Risto Siilasmaa on Machine Learning," YouTube video, posted by Nokia, November 11, 2017, https://www.youtube.com/watch?v=KNMy7NCQDgk&t=3721s.

The Dockside Bar was modeled after Café Intención, where adidas held regular meetings to plan and eventually pitch their leadership on a digital transformation. This led to the creation of their platform team.

ACKNOWLEDGMENTS

I am so grateful to Margueritte Kim, my wife and partner, whose love and support makes all my work and life possible. And to our sons, Reid, Parker, and Grant.

Thank you to Anna Noak, Kate Sage, Leah Brown, Ann Perry and the entire IT Revolution team for helping me throughout all the stages of development of this book—if you only knew how much they had to put up with!

I want to thank the following people for the incredible amount of time they spent sharing their expertise with me—this book would not be possible without them. I learned so much from them about the automotive parts industry, architecture principles, business and technology leadership, functional programming, and so much more!

John Allspaw (Adaptive Capacity Labs), Josh Atwell (Splunk), Chris Bergh (Data Kitchen), Cornelia Davis (Pivotal), Charles Betz (Forrester), Jason Cox (Disney), John Cutler (Amplitude), Stephen Fishman (Salesforce), Dr. Nicole Forsgren (Google), Jeff Gallimore (Excella), Sam Guckenheimer (Microsoft), Scott Havens (Jet.com/Walmart Labs), Dr. Rod Johnson (Atomist), Rob Juncker (Code42), Dr. Mik Kersten (Tasktop), Dr. Tom Longstaff (CMU/SEI), Courtney Kissler (Nike), Chris O'Malley (Compuware), Mike Nygard (Sabre), Joe Payne (Code42), Scott Prugh (CSG), Mark Schwartz (Amazon), Dr. Steven Spear (MIT/The High-Velocity Edge), Jeffrey Snover (Microsoft), and John Willis (Botchagalupe Technologies).

And thank you to the following people who provided such amazing feedback on the manuscript: Paul Auclair, Lee Barnett, Fernando Cornago, Jennifer Davis, Dominica DeGrandis, Chris Eng, Rob England, Alan Fahrner, David Favelle, Stephen Feldman, Bryan Finster, Dana Finster, Ron Forrester, Dawn Foster, Raj Fowler, Gary Gruver, Ryan Gurney, Tim Hunter, Finbarr Joy, Sam Knutson, Adam Leventhal, Paul Love, Dr. Steve Mayner, Erica Morrison, Steven Murawski, Scott Nasello, Shaun Norris, Dr. Tapabrata Pal, Christopher Porter, Corey Quinn, Mark Schwartz,

Samir Shah, Nate Shimek, Randy Shoup, Scott Stockton, Keith Swett, Dr. Branden Williams, and Michael Winslow.

To everyone who helped me over the years, and to anyone who I may forgotten, my deepest thanks. And if you want to learn more about the concepts covered in the book, I've included a list of resources in the reference section.

Practical
Electrocardiography

SEVENTH EDITION

"For he who'd make his fellow-creatures wise
Should always gild the philosophic pill."

W. S. GILBERT

Practical

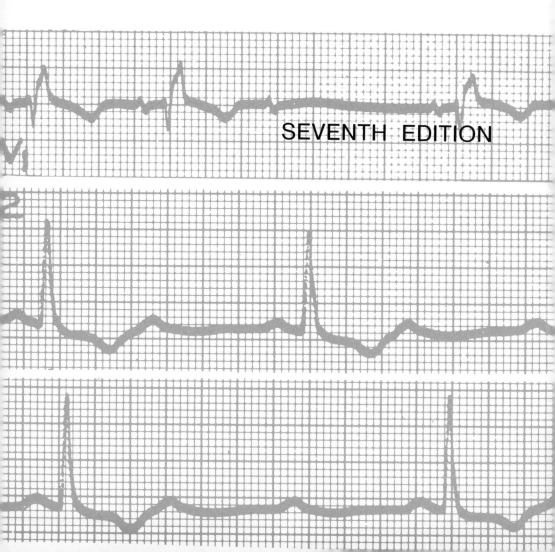

SEVENTH EDITION

Electrocardiography

Henry J. L. Marriott, M.D., F.A.C.P., F.A.C.C.

Director of Clinical Research, Rogers Heart Foundation, St. Petersburg, Florida; Director of Electrocardiograph Department, St. Anthony's Hospital, St. Petersburg, Florida; Clinical Professor of Medicine (Cardiology), Emory University School of Medicine, Atlanta, Georgia; Clinical Professor of Pediatrics (Cardiology), University of Florida, Gainesville, Florida

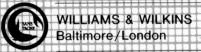
WILLIAMS & WILKINS
Baltimore/London

Made in United States of America

First Edition, 1954
    Reprinted 1954
Second Edition, 1957
    Reprinted 1958, 1961
Third Edition, 1962
    Reprinted 1964, 1965, 1966
Fourth Edition, 1968
    Reprinted 1969, 1970, 1971
Fifth Edition, 1972
    Reprinted 1974
Sixth Edition, 1977
    Reprinted 1978, 1979, 1980, 1981

Library of Congress Cataloging in Publication Data

Marriott, Henry Joseph Llewellyn, 1917–
    Practical electrocardiography.

    Includes index.
    1. Electrocardiography. I. Title. [DNLM: 1. Electrocardiography. WG 140 M359p]

RC683.5.E5M3 1983   616.1′207547   82-11170
ISBN 0-683-05574-7   AACR2

Composed and printed at the
Waverly Press, Inc.
Mt. Royal & Guilford Aves.
Baltimore, Md. 21202

TO

Jonni

Who "sat like patience on a monument
Smiling"—and shaping unsubmissive pages!

Preface to the Seventh Edition

At about the time the first edition of this book appeared, electrocardiography as a subject for profitable progress and investigation was widely regarded as "dead." Developments since then indicate that this prophecy of doom represented a gross misjudgment. Far from suffering a decline, electrocardiography has enjoyed robust health and has increasingly flourished.

The advent of various forms of constant or intermittent monitoring (including coronary care, telemetry, Holter and transtelephonic), the development of His-bundle recordings and the great advances made in electrophysiological investigation, the phenomenal progress in the technology of pacemakers and the refinements and experience in exercise testing, each in their several ways, because of their fundamental dependence on electrocardiography, has made a signal contribution to its growing importance.

This edition has been extensively rewritten and expanded. In place of the 21 chapters in the Sixth Edition, there are now 30. The chapters on the hemiblocks, supraventricular tachycardia, preexcitation, escape and dissociation, A-V block (two chapters) and artificial pacemakers have been entirely rewritten and expanded. Also, in this edition, the following topics which were but sections of chapters in the previous edition have been accorded a chapter to themselves: systematic approach to diagnosis of arrhythmias; extrasystoles; supraventricular tachycardia; atrial flutter; atrial fibrillation; ventricular tachycardia; accelerated idioventricular rhythm and parasystole; fusion beats; junctional rhythms; sinus rhythms and the sick sinus; the growing pains of A-V block; and the effects of digitalis and quinidine on the electrocardiogram.

Major additions and revisions have been made in the chapters on bundle-branch block, aberrant ventricular conduction, coronary insufficiency and related matters—including a greatly expanded section on exercise testing.

Other significant additions include material on XYZ leads, the QT interval, U waves, electrical axis, chamber enlargement, Holter monitoring, transtelephonic monitoring, incidence of arrhythmias and blocks in normal populations, ladder diagrams, sick sinus syndromes, myocardial infarction, coronary mimicry, cor pulmonale, pericardial disease, hypokalemia and hypertrophic cardio-myopathy.

Approximately 500 new references have been included and the illustrations—probably the most important part of any book on electrocardiography—now number almost 500, including more than 150 new ones. As before, review tracings after each of the last 20 chapters serve as a cursory refresher course.

In all of this extensive revision and expansion, I have drawn freely from the text and illustrations of my CME course, *Contemporary Electrocardiography*, published by the Williams & Wilkins Company in 1980.

The index has again received a special measure of tender loving care in this edition. It has been meticulously prepared by Mary Conover (bless her heart!) and all the leading words are NOUNS, since this makes one's search easier, quicker and more logical. For example, you do not have to wonder whether you will find "atrial tachycardia" under "Atrial" or under "Tachycardia" since you know in advance that it will be indexed only under the noun, "Tachycardia."

Aphorisms have always been helpful in teaching and learning because, as Osler picturesquely put it, they are "burrs that stick in the memory." I have therefore again inserted at strategic points in the text several homespun epigrams that have seemed helpful, and these are appropriately tagged with**.

The aims and scope of this book are unchanged and simplicity remains the central theme. The text is designed to be digestible for beginners, yet it contains a wealth of material of potentially great value to the more sophisticated reader. Once again the publishers have graciously given me a free and unconventional hand in arranging the layout of pages so that I have been able to place illustrations and descriptive text in as convenient proximity as possible.

H.J.L.M.

Preface to the First Edition

Books on electrocardiography seem to possess one or more of several disadvantages for the beginner: the introductory chapters on electrophysiology are so intricate and longwinded that the reader's interest is early drowned in a troubled sea of vectors, axes and gradients; or only certain aspects of the subject are dealt with, for example, the arrhythmias may be entirely omitted; or illustrations are deficient and frequently situated uncomfortably far from the descriptive text.

For several years I have been attempting to introduce fourth year students to the comparatively easy technique of interpreting electrocardiograms. During this period I have been unable to recommend any single text that deals with the subject quickly and simply and yet is sufficiently comprehensive. This book is an attempt to supply such a manual. Its aims are: (1) to emphasize the simplicities rather than the complexities of the electrocardiogram; (2) to give the reader only those electrophysiologic concepts that make everyday interpretation more intelligible without burdening him with unnecessary detail; (3) to cover all diagnostically important electrocardiographic patterns; and (4) to provide adequate illustrations and in every instance to have the illustration conveniently situated to the reader as he reads the descriptive text. To achieve this last desideratum, the publishers have generously waived publishing conventions and given me a free hand in the arrangement and spacing of illustrations and text.

This book is designed for those approaching electrocardiography from the point of view of the clinician. It is hoped that it will enable the beginner to acquire a rapid but thorough grasp of a sophisticated yet simple discipline.

H.J.L.M.

Acknowledgments

It is a great pleasure to acknowledge my indebtedness:

To Mary Conover for again volunteering to prepare the index and doing it with cheerful, accurate zeal.

To Marcie Etheridge Perry and Raymond Rochkind for their excellent line drawings; to Dr. William Schuman for coining the mot juste, electrocardiographogenic; to Dr. Carrol Moody for improving my approach to the electrical axis.

To the following colleagues for graciously providing me with illustrative tracings: Dr. L. E. Bilodeau for figure 22.2, Dr. Harold H. Bix for figure 23.17, Dr. Diego Bognolo for figure 25.15, Dr. Joseph Bowen for figure 22.3, Dr. Richard Cuthbert for figure 24,3, Dr. William Everett for figure 18.14, Dr. Morris Fulton for figure 29.5, Dr. Martin Grais for figure 8.4, Dr. Emory Hollar for figure 23.18, Dr. Leonard Leight for figure 25.13, Dr. Alan Lindsay for figure 8.9, Dr. Robert Mahon for figure 27.10, Dr. Nathan Marcus for figure 28.14, Dr. Pierre Nizet for figure 10.14, Dr. Breffni O'Neill for figure 29.3, Dr. Jack Pyhel for figure 18.16, Dr. Thomas Ross for figure 16.4A, Dr. Leo Schamroth for figures 17.19 and 23.15, Dr. Victor Schulze for figure RT-30.1, Dr. Roger Sutton for figure 18.10, and Dr. Edward Swanick for figure 27.9.

To the electrocardiograph departments of the Mercy Hospital in Baltimore, the Tampa General Hospital and St. Anthony's Hospital in St. Petersburgh as the sources of most of the remaining tracings; and especially to technicians—past and present—for their interest and zeal in capturing good records of arrhythmias.

To innumerable students and many colleagues and nurses who have stimulated me with encouragement or criticism.

To the publishers, whose gracious cooperation has now been patient and unfailing through seven gestations.

H.J.L.M.

Contents

Introductory Note

Much of electrocardiography is simple, but it does not always provide a clear-cut answer. Our knowledge of the electrocardiogram has definite limitations which must be appreciated. In the arrhythmias and blocks it often gives a clear and irrefutable answer, but with myocardial disease there is much less specificity. Every interpreter, no matter how experienced, encounters tracings he cannot unravel. Not infrequently a tracing is "borderline" or "abnormal but nonspecific" and must be classified as such—an unsatisfying situation for both the interpreter and the patient's physician, yet one which should be frankly and humbly faced.

Profession and laity alike are inclined to lay too much stress on mechanical devices in diagnosis. The electrocardiograph is no exception. A patient with a normal tracing may unexpectedly drop dead of a coronary attack, while another, with a grossly abnormal tracing, may live on without cardiac symptoms for many years.

The electrocardiogram should always be read in the clearest light of clinical observation. All pertinent data should be in the hands of the interpreter. Ideally the clinician in charge of the patient reads his own tracings; failing this he should see to it that his interpreting colleague is furnished with full details, including his own clinical impression, for only so will he and his patient derive maximal benefit from expert interpretation.

As electrocardiographic interpretation and clinical observation are, or should be, inseparable, a few clinical notes of practical diagnostic value are included in this primarily electrocardiographic text.

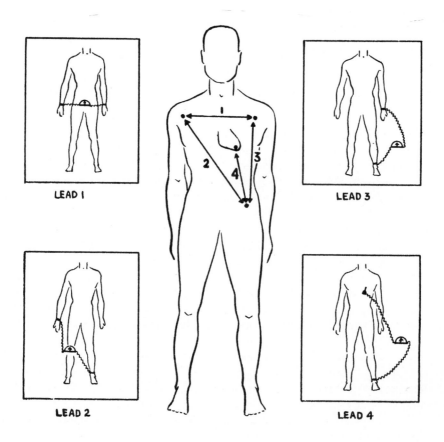

Figure 1.1. The standard limb leads and the original precordial lead. *Caution:* The double-headed arrows in the diagram are not intended to represent Einthoven's triangle.

1

Electrodes and Leads

Contraction of the heart's muscle is the dynamo that powers life; and the spark that initiates that contraction is an infinitesimal electrical current that is generated and discharged by the sinus node. Small as this current is, it can be recorded from the surface of the body as it traverses the cardiac muscle. The machine that records it is the electrocardiograph and the recording is the electrocardiogram (ECG).

To make a recording, it is necessary to complete an electrical circuit between the heart and the electrocardiograph. To this end, electrodes are placed at two (or more) sites on the body and, as the sites vary, so does the "view" of the heart's electrical impulse. Each different "view," derived as it is from the varying placement of the recording electrodes, is known as a "lead."

Standard Limb Leads

These are three in number and have been in use for 80 years. We therefore have had a far longer acquaintance with these than the numerous additional leads more recently introduced. Probably 80 to 90% accuracy in diagnosis can be achieved by inspecting these leads alone. Many arrhythmias and most types of heart block are easily diagnosed from them.

The connections of these leads are illustrated in figure 1.1. Lead 1 connects the two arms; lead 3 connects the left arm with the left leg; and lead 2, the hypotenuse of the triangle, connects the right arm with the left leg. Each lead records the difference in potential between the two connected limbs. Although the electrodes are attached at wrists and ankle, this is purely a matter of convenience—it is easiest to attach bracelets to those parts of the limbs. It is more accurate to think of the potential as derived from the roots of the respective limbs, i.e., from the two shoulders and the left groin. The heart is approximately in the center of the triangle so formed (fig. 1.1).

It is worth noting **Einthoven's law**, which states, in effect, that a complex in lead 2 is equal to the sum of the corresponding complexes in leads 1 and 3 (2 = 1 + 3). This is a helpful rule to remember when the technician has wrongly

1

labelled the leads. For example, if the P wave is seen to be upright in all three leads, you know at a glance that the lead with the tallest P is lead 2.

Precordial Leads

The standard limb leads have two disadvantages: (1) each is derived from *two* points *distant* from the heart and (2) the three electrodes are all in the same plane, i.e., the frontal plane of the body. It is not surprising that we can gain additional information by placing electrodes closer to the heart and moving them round the bend of the thorax to obtain "views" of the heart from different angles. The first precordial or chest lead, introduced in 1932, connected the left leg with the apex beat and was called lead 4 (fig. 1.1). This was a successful innovation and soon a series of precordial points was introduced whose positions are illustrated in figure 1.2. Point 1 is just to the right of the sternum in the fourth interspace; point 2, just to the left of the sternum in the fourth interspace. Point 4 lies in the midclavicular line in the fifth interspace. Point 3 is halfway between 2 and 4. Points 5, 6 and 7 are at the same level as 4 in the anterior, middle and posterior axillary lines, respectively.

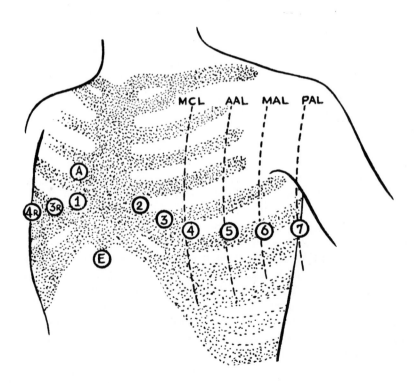

Figure 1.2. Precordial points from which chest leads are derived.

Most cardiologists employ precordial positions from 1 to 6 routinely. Sometimes it is desirable to take additional leads from further points; some of these are also illustrated in figure 1.2. Point E is situated over the ensiform process. The atrial lead point (A) is just to the right of the sternum in the third interspace. The locations of further right precordial points, 3_R, 4_R, etc., correspond with the locations of their opposite numbers on the left side of the chest. Occasionally it is desirable to take leads from the posterior thorax; points 8 and 9 are at the angle of the scapula and over the spine, at the same level as 4, 5, 6 and 7. At times, especially for the purpose of unravelling difficult arrhythmias, it may be useful to obtain a tracing from behind the left atrium by means of an esophageal electrode[2, 5, 8, 9]; or from the cavity of the right atrium by means of a transvenous wire electrode.[11]

In a standard lead the two electrodes are about equally remote from the heart and each is therefore about equally important in its contribution to the tracing. When, however, one electrode is placed in one of the precordial positions while the other electrode is on a limb, it is natural that the closer chest electrode should contribute more to the tracing, and the limb electrode less. The limb attachment of such a lead is therefore called the **indifferent electrode** and the chest electrode is referred to as the **exploring electrode**, since it is moved in an exploratory fashion from point to point across the chest. If the indifferent electrode is attached to the left leg, the connection is designated CF; if to the right arm CR; if to the left arm CL. According to the precordial point employed, a subscribed number is added to the CF, CR, or CL label. Thus, for example, lead CF_5 indicates that the exploring electrode is placed at point 5 in the anterior axillary line while the indifferent electrode is attached to the left ankle. The "MCL" leads, which have become popular for monitoring, are modifications of the CL hookup.

V Leads

Though the exploring electrode exerts a far greater influence on the tracing than the indifferent electrode, the indifferent electrode nevertheless has considerable influence. It was discovered empirically, however, that if all three limb electrodes were connected, through resistances of 5000 ohms each, to form a common **central terminal**, this afforded a more truly indifferent connection—the potential at such a central terminal was practically zero throughout the cardiac cycle. Thus, theoretically at any rate, such a connection leaves the exploring electrode as sole dictator of the pattern. The hookup of the V leads is diagrammatically shown in figure 1.3.

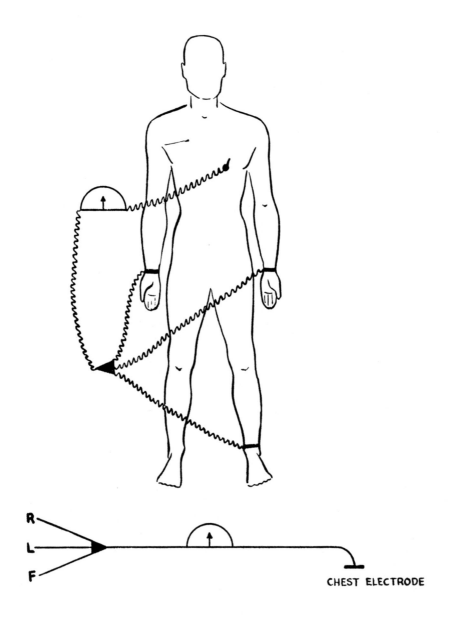

Figure 1.3.   The hookup for V leads.

Although theoretically the V lead connections should given the most reliable precordial pattern, in practice it is not so certain that they always do[4]; and at least one authority[6, 7] insisted that the CR connection was the most satisfactory. At any rate, it is worth appreciating the expected differences between the various precordial connections. These may best be summarized by stating that the CR leads tend to emphasize positive (upright) deflections, while the CF leads lend emphasis to negative (downward). The pattern of V leads usually lies somewhere in between. It may sometimes be useful to take advantage of the "emphasizing" tendencies of the CR and CF connections, rather than to rely slavishly on the V leads because they are theoretically superior. Such employment of the CR or CF leads may be likened to the use of a magnifying glass to detect otherwise invisible or questionable changes. CL connections found little favor or use until a modified CL ("MCL") hookup came into its own for the constant monitoring of patients in coronary care units (see Chapter 9).

aV Leads

The standard limb leads are strictly **bipolar**, representing as they do the difference in potential between two points. CF, CR and CL leads are also clearly bipolar, in that they too record the difference in potential between two points. In the standard leads the two points involved exert approximately equal influences, whereas in the C leads, as stated above, the precordial point is more influential than the more distant limb connection. With the V leads comes the virtual exclusion of this distant influence because the central terminal shows practically zero potential throughout the heart cycle. They are therefore referred to as **unipolar** precordial leads. From this development it is only a short step to the unipolar *limb* leads. By using the central terminal as the indifferent connection and placing the exploring electrode on one limb, the resulting tracing might well be expected to record the potential at the root of the "explored" limb exclusively. Such leads are labeled VR, VL and VF according to the limb with which the exploring electrode is connected. The connections of VF are diagrammatically shown in figure 1.4*A*. The deflections in such a lead are small; but the amplitude of complexes in such leads can be materially increased by disconnecting the central terminal attachment to the explored limb (fig. 1.4*B*). This device increases the size of the deflections (thus making them more readable) without significantly altering their shape. This *augmentation* of potential is designated by a prefixed "a"—aVR, aVL, aVF.

Relation of Bipolar to Unipolar Limb Leads

In a sense, the unipolar limb leads are the algebraic bricks of which the bipolar leads are built. Lead 1 represents the difference between aVR and aVL; lead 2 the difference between aVR and aVF; and lead 3 between aVL and aVF.

Now, quite arbitrarily, as originally ordained by Einthoven, the polarity of the electrodes is arranged as in figure 1.5 (Einthoven's triangle). F is positive in relation to R in lead 2 and relative to L in lead 3; while in lead 1 L is positive in relation to R. In other words, F is always relatively positive and R is always relatively negative, while L is variable as between leads 1 and 3. The relation-

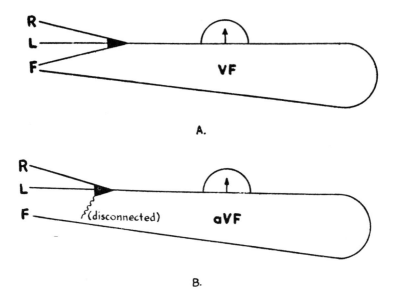

Figure 1.4.   (*A*) The hookup for lead VF. (*B*) The hookup for augmented VF (aVF).

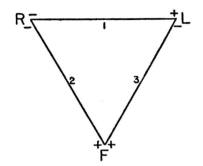

Figure 1.5. Polarity of electrodes in the standard leads.

ships between the bipolar and unipolar limb leads can thus be summarized in the following equations:

$$Lead\ 1 = aVL - aVR$$
$$Lead\ 2 = aVF - aVR$$
$$Lead\ 3 = aVF - aVL$$

The information available from the six limb leads can be deduced from any two of them. In theory, therefore, it is only necessary to take two of the limb leads, but in practice it is valuable to acquire a working knowledge of all six. If only two leads are taken, the most suitable and informative pair are 1 and aVF.[10]

XYZ Leads

With the increased popularity of three-channel ECG machines, leads X, Y and Z are frequently encountered and it is necessary to know their derivation and significance.[1] Lead X has its positive electrode in the left axilla with its negative electrode in the right axilla; it therefore recognizes right-to-left, and left-to-right forces and records them as positive and negative deflections respectively. The scalar mind may think of it as an approximate V_6. Lead Y has its positive electrode on the front of the lower chest and its negative electrode on the neck. It therefore recognizes up-down forces, recording a downward force as a positive and an upward force as a negative deflection; it can be roughly equated to lead aVF. Lead Z uses the anterior chest electrode as its positive with an electrode on the back as the negative pole, and it is therefore the approximate equivalent of an inverted lead V_2.

The XYZ leads are the "orthogonal" (perpendicular to each other) leads from which the vector loop is derived and therefore, theoretically, contain all the information that is contained in the derived loop.

Conclusion

In a routine screening ECG, 12 leads should be employed: the three standard limb leads, the three aV leads and six V leads from 1 to 6 inclusive. For certain purposes, however, this number of leads is inadequate, while for other purposes 12 leads are quite unnecessary. In following the progress of an arrhythmia a single lead, V_1 or 2, is usually ample, whereas in a doubtful case of myocardial infarction it may be expedient to explore additional higher and more lateral areas of the precordium. There should be no rigid routine. While the usual 12 leads are generally adequate and necessary, the number should be freely modified or supplemented by an intelligent understanding of the particular requirements.

REFERENCES

1. Castellanos, A., et al.: XYZ electrocardography. Correlation with conventional 12 lead electrocardiogram. Cardiovasc. Clin. 1977: **8**, 285.
2. Copeland, G. D., et al.: Clinical evaluation of a new esophageal electrode, with particular reference to the bipolar esophageal electrocardiogram. Am. Heart J. 1959: **57**, 862 and 874.
3. Douglas, A. H., and Cohen, N.: The vector and algebraic relationship of the CF and V chest leads. Am. Heart J. 1954: **48**, 340.
4. Editorial: Are the V leads always superior? Ann. Intern. Med. 1952: **36**, 1548.
5. Enselberg, C. D.: The esophageal electrocardiogram in the study of atrial activity and cardiac arrhythmias. Am. Heart J. 1951: **41**, 382.
6. Evans, W.: *Cardiography*, Ed. 2. Butterworth, London, 1954.
7. Evans, W., and Lloyd-Thomas, H. G.: The infrequent normal electrocardiogram in cardiac pain. Am. Heart J. 1961: **62**, 51.
8. Hammill, S. C., and Pritchett, E. L. C.: Simplified esophageal electrocardiography using bipolar recording leads. Ann. Intern. Med. 1981: **95**, 14.
9. Prystowsky, E. N., et al.: Origin of the atrial electrogram recorded from the esophagus. Circulation 1980: **61**, 1017.
10. Schaffer, A. I., et al.: A new look at electrocardiographic leads. Am. Heart J. 1956: **52**, 704.
11. Vogel, J. H. K., et al.: A simple technique for identifying P waves in complex arrhythmias. Am. Heart J. 1964: **67**, 158.

2

Rhythm and Rate

In every electrocardiogram 10 features should be examined systematically:

1. Rhythm
2. Rate
3. P wave
4. P-R interval
5. QRS interval
6. QRS complex
7. ST segment
8. T wave
9. U wave
10. Q-T duration

A suggested form for recording routine interpretations is given on page 13.

Rhythm

A glance is enough to determine whether the rhythm is regular or irregular. If it is regular, the interpreter should state whether it is sinoatrial (S-A)—as it usually is—A-V junctional, or idioventricular. If it is irregular, a preliminary survey should be made to determine whether there is a definite pattern to the irregularity, e.g., beats grouped in pairs, every fourth beat dropped, etc., or whether the irregularity is erratic, as in atrial fibrillation.

Measuring Intervals

The tracing is inscribed against a background of millimeter squares and every fifth line is thicker than the intervening four. The horizontal span between two consecutive thick lines is ⅕ sec (0.2 sec); the time elapsing between two consecutive thin lines is ¹⁄₂₅ sec (0.04 sec). The basic interval for timing electrocardiographic events is thus 0.04 sec. In practice, if an interval is to be measured, one counts the number of small squares horizontally contained within the interval and multiplies this number by 0.04. It is an easy matter to

9

multiply by 4 and adjust the decimal point. In figure 2.1 about two squares are horizontally contained between the beginning and the end of the QRS complex; the QRS interval interval is therefore $2 \times 0.04 = 0.08$ sec. The P-R interval (from beginning of the P to the beginning of the QRS) measures 3½ small squares and is therefore 0.14 sec.

Estimating Rate

Most electrocardiographic paper conveniently provides marginal markers at 3-sec intervals. On such records the simplest and quickest method for estimating rate is to count the number of cardiac cycles in 6 sec and multiply by 10.

When such markers are not available, we use the thick lines as points of reference. As there are 300 fifths of a second in a minute (5×60), it is only necesary to determine the number of fifths of a second between consecutive beats (if the rhythm is regular) and divide this number into 300. For convenience we select a complex which coincides with a thick line and then count the number of fifths elapsing before the same complex recurs. The QRS complex is usually employed, but it is obvious that any wave will serve provided the rhythm is normal and regular. Should there be only ⅕ sec between consecutive beats the rate would be 300; if ⅖, 150; if ⅗, 100; and so on. Table 2.1 gives the

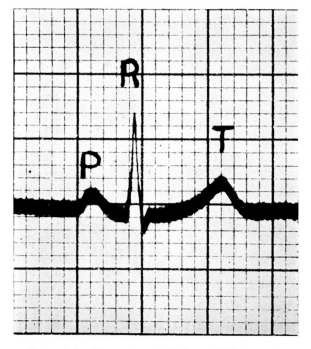

Figure 2.1.   Measurement of P-R and QRS intervals.

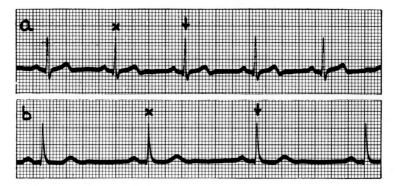

Figure 2.2. Estimation of heart rate (two examples). See text and figure 2.3.

rates prevailing if from 1 to 10 fifths elapse between consecutive beats. For rates between 30 and 100, it is obvious that reasonably accurate approximations can rapidly be made.

In the second example (*b*) in figure 2.2, the QRS marked *x* coincides with a thick line. There are then 6½ fifths of a second (thick lines) before the next QRS is reached. Thus the rate will obviously lie about halfway between 50 and 43 and may be called 46 or 47 with assurance that the approximation is within 1 or 2 beats of the actual rate. This method is obviously quite accurate enough for all practical purposes, and the slower the rate the more accurate the approximation. For even greater accuracy, the intermediate figures provided in

Table 2.1

With This Number of Fifths between Consecutive QRS Complexes	The Rate Is:
1	300
2	150
3	100
4	75
5	60
6	50
7	43
8	37
9	33
10	30

the guide in figure 2.3 may be employed. These figures are obtained by dividing into 1500 (25 × 60) the number of 25ths of a second elapsing between consecutive beats.

When the rate is over 100, the margin of error rapidly increases and, to determine the rate more accurately, it is better to count the number of cardiac cycles occurring in 5, 6 or 10 sec and multiply the number by 12, 10 or 6. This method must also be adopted, regardless of the rate, when the rhythm is irregular. Figure 2.4 illustrates this method for estimating a rapid rate.

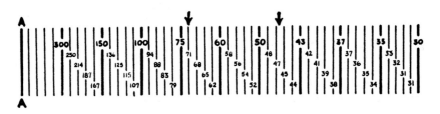

Figure 2.3.   Guide for rapid estimation of heart rate. In any tracing select a QRS complex that coincides with a thick line (e.g., those marked *x* in the two examples in fig. 2.2). This thick line is represented by the first thick line, *AA*, in the guide above. Note with which line the next QRS in the tracing coincides (*arrows* in fig. 2.2) and read off the rate from the corresponding line of the guide: first arrow, rate 71 (tracing *a*); second arrow, rate 46 (tracing *b*). *NOTE:* UNLIKE MANY MANUFAC-TURERS' RULERS, THIS GUIDE IS NOT DRAWN ON THE SAME SCALE AS THE CLINICAL TRACING AND IS OBVIOUSLY NOT INTENDED FOR DIRECT APPLICA-TION TO IT. IT IS A DIAGRAM *REPRESENTING* THE LINES IN THE TRACING AND IS INTENDED AS AN AID TO MEMORIZING KEY FIGURES.

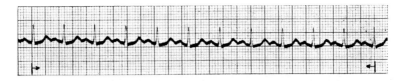

Figure 2.4.   Estimation of rapid rates. In the 5 sec between the two markers, there are 11 cardiac cycles. The rate is therefore 11 × 12 = 132 per minute.

SUGGESTED FORM FOR ROUTINE RECORDS

RHYTHM: RATE:

P-R INTERVAL: QRS INTERVAL: Q-T DURATION:

P WAVE: axis:

QRS COMPLEX:
   axis:
   Q waves:

ST SEGMENT:

T WAVE: axis:

U WAVE:

IMPRESSIONS:
  (1)
  (2)
  (3)
  (4)

COMMENT:

3

Complexes and Intervals

When a complex is partly above the baseline and partly below it, it is **diphasic**. When its excursions above and below the line are approximately equal, it is **isodiphasic** or **equiphasic**.

P Wave

This is the first wave of the electrocardiogram and represents the spread of the electrical impulse through the atria (**activation** or **depolarization** of atria). It is normally upright in leads 1 and 2 but is frequently diphasic or inverted in lead 3. It is normally inverted in aVR and upright in aVF and in left chest leads (V_{4-6}). It is variable in the other leads. Its amplitude should not exceed 2 or 3 mm in any lead, and its normal contour is gently rounded—not pointed or notched.

Abnormalities that should be looked for are, therefore:

1. *Inversion* in leads where the P wave is normally upright, or the presence of an upright P wave in aVR (where it should be inverted); such changes are usually found in conditions where the impulse travels through the atria by an unorthodox path—as in ectopic atrial or A-V junctional rhythms (fig. 3.1 C).
2. *Increased amplitude*: this usually indicates atrial hypertrophy or dilation and is found especially in A-V valve disease, hypertension, cor pulmonale, and congenital heart disease.
3. *Increased width*: this usually indicates left atrial enlargement or diseased atrial muscle. The normal P wave does not exceed 0.11 sec in duration.
4. *Diphasicity*: an important sign of left atrial enlargement when the second half of the P wave is significantly negative in lead 3 or V_1 (see fig. 30.1 B, p. 456).
5. *Notching*: when the left atrium is mainly involved (as in mitral disease) the P wave often becomes wide and notched and is taller in lead 1 than in lead 3—**P-mitrale** (fig. 3.1 A). Notching is considered significant when the distance between peaks exceeds 0.04 sec.

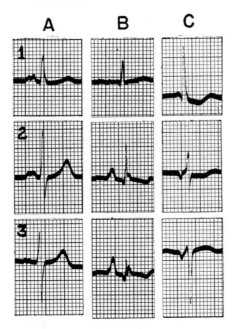

Figure 3.1. Abnormal **P waves**. (*A*) **P-mitrale**; note broad, notched P waves taller in lead 1 than in lead 3. (*B*) **P-pulmonale**; note flat P in lead 1 with tall, pointed P wave in leads 2 and 3. (*C*) **A-V junctional rhythm**; note inverted P in leads 2 and 3 with short P-R interval.

6. *Peaking*: right atrial overload usually produces tall pointed P waves taller in lead 3 than in lead 1—**P-pulmonale** (fig. 3.1*B*).
7. *Absence* of P waves: this occurs in some A-V junctional rhythms and in S-A block.

In summary, P waves are:

> Normally upright in 1, 2, V_{4-6} and aVF
> Normally inverted in aVR
> Variable in 3, aVL and other chest leads.

T_P Wave

This wave, formerly called Ta,[43] represents repolarization of the atria, and is directed opposite to the P wave—if the P wave is upright it is inverted, and vice versa (fig. 3.2C). It is usually invisible because it coincides with the QRS complex. It can best be seen in A-V block, where the P waves are not followed by QRS complexes and there is consequently an opportunity for the T_P wave to show itself (see fig. 23.12, p. 331).

P-R Interval

This is measured from the *beginning* of the P wave to the *beginning* of the QRS complex. It measures the time taken by the impulse to travel all the way from the S-A node to the ventricular muscle fibers, and this is normally from 0.12 to 0.20 sec. It is customary to examine several intervals and record that which appears the longest. The interval varies with heart rate, being shorter at faster rates. Up to a rate of 140 to 150, exercise shortens the P-R interval, mainly through withdrawal of parasympathetic tone.[3] If the conducting system is diseased or affected by digitalis, the P-R may lengthen as the rate increases. Similarly, if the atria are paced artificially the P-R increases as the paced rate quickens.[6] The P-R is proportionately shorter in children, averaging 0.11 sec. at 1 year, 0.13 at 6 and 0.14 at 12 years. An interval prolonged beyond normal limits is regarded as evidence of A-V block (fig. 3.2C).

At relatively slow rates a few apparently normal people, with no evidence of heart disease, have been found to have intervals ranging considerably above 0.20 sec.[45] In a group of over 67,000 apparently healthy airmen, 0.52% were found to have prolonged P-R interals.[5] Most of these prolongations (80%) ranged from 0.21 to 0.24 sec, while in the remaining minority the P-R interval ranged up to 0.39 sec. In another study, 59 of 19,000 healthy aircrew applicants (0.31%) had P-R intervals of 0.24 sec or more.[8] Standing often reduces such prolonged P-R intervals to normal.

P-R prolongation is more likely to be a pointer to otehwise latent rheumatic or coronary disease, but one must not brand an individual as a "cardiac" whose only stigma is an unconventionally long P-R interval. Obviously it is a signal for a thorough search to exclude cardiac abnormality, but if none is found, the heart should be acquitted with reservation.

Biological values do not submit to arithmetical laws, and one must bear in mind all the physiological factors that may influence P-R duration. An elephantine man with a correspondingly large heart will generally have a longer interval than a petite woman less than half his size. She may have true block with an interval of only 0.19, while he may well have a normal duration of 0.21 sec. Biological variations too often are lost sight of in attempting to regiment natural values.

The P-R interval is abnormally short when the impulse originates in the A-V node (fig. 3.1C) instead of the S-A node, and also when the passage of the

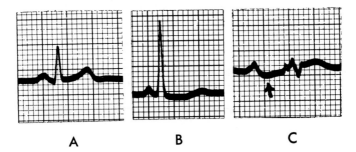

Figure 3.2. P-R intervals. (*A*) Normal interval of 0.14 sec. (*B*) Short P-R interval of 0.10 sec, from hypertensive patient shortly after an episode of atrial flutter. (*C*) Prolonged P-R interval of 0.30 sec; note shallowly inverted T$_P$ wave (*arrow*) immediately following P wave.

impulse to the ventricle is accelerated as in the Wolff-Parkinson-White syndrome. A short P-R interval is also sometimes seen as a normal variation (fig. 3.2*B*); but this combination (normal P, short P-R and normal QRS) is perhaps not so benign as might be thought, because it is found often in association with hypertension[9] and with the tendency to develop paroxysms of tachycardia.[7]

In summary, the P-R interval is

Prolonged	*Shortened*
(a) In A-V block (p. 322) due to coronary disease, rheumatic disease, etc.	(a) In A-V junctional and low atrial rhythms (p. 290)
(b) In some cases of hyperthyroidism	(b) In Wolff-Parkinson-White syndrome (p 257)
(c) As a are normal variation	(c) In Lown-Ganong-Levine syndrome (p. 272)
	(d) In glycogen storage disease
	(e) In some hypertension patients
	(f) As a normal variation

P-R Segment

This is the baseline between the *end* of the P wave and beginning of QRS. Normally isoelectric, it may be displaced in atrial infarction and in acute pericarditis.

QRS Complex

This complex is the most important in the electrocardiogram, as it represents spread of the impulse through the ventricular muscle (**activation** or **depolarization** of ventricles).

Proper labelling of the component waves of this complex should first be mastered (fig. 3.3):

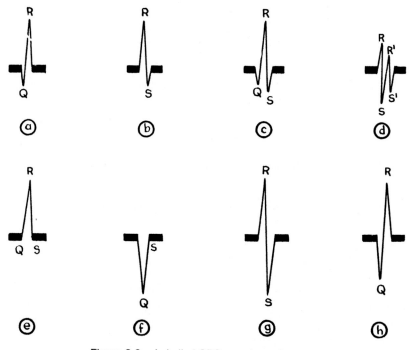

Figure 3.3. Labelled QRS complexes (see text).

1. If the first deflection is downward (negative), it is a **Q wave**.
2. The first upright deflection is an **R wave**, whether or not it is preceded by a Q.
3. A negative deflection following an R wave is an **S wave**.
4. Subsequent excursions above the line are labelled successively R′, r″, etc; similarly later negative excursions are labelled S′, S″, and so on.

If the QRS complex consists exclusively of an R wave, the points at which the complex begins and ends may be labelled Q and S, respectively, though there are no actual Q or S *waves*. When the complex consists exclusively of a Q wave it is described as a QS complex. A word-saving convention is the use of small and large letters to signify the relative sizes of the component waves. Thus, in figure 3.3, (*c*) is conveniently labelled qRs, which is quicker and simpler for the reader's eye than "a small Q, a tall R and a small S wave." In the figure (*a*) would be labelled qR, (*b*) Rs, (*g*) RS, (*h*) QR, and so on. The term "QRS complex" may always be used as a sort of collective noun to describe the ventricular complex no matter what waves actually compose it. Thus all the examples in figure 3.3 may also quite correctly be referred to as QRS complexes.

In interpreting the QRS complexes there are at least seven features that should be routinely inspected:

1. Their *duration* (the QRS interval)
2. Their *amplitude* (or "voltage")
3. The presence of Q *waves* (or equivalents)
4. Their *electrical axis* in the frontal plane (limb leads)
5. The relative prominence of the component waves in the precordial leads, V_1 to V_6, noting the *transitional zone*
6. The timing of the *intrinsicoid deflections* in various unipolar leads
7. The general configuration of the complex, including the presence and location of any slurring or notching.

The *duration* of the normal QRS complex is usually given as 0.05 to 0.10 sec. The QRS interval is measured from the beginning of the QRS to its end, usually in the standard limb leads. The chest leads frequently display a slightly longer QRS spread (0.01 or 0.02 sec longer) than the standard leads; the explanation for this is not clear. A measurement of 0.12 sec or more is indicative of abnormal intraventricular conduction and usually means block of one of the bundle branches or a ventricular arrhythmia.

The *amplitude* of the QRS complexes has wide normal limits. It is generally agreed that, if the total amplitude (above and below the isoelectric line) is 5 mm or less in all three standard leads, it is too low to be healthy; such low voltage is seen in diffuse coronary disease, cardiac failure, pericardial effusion, myxedema, primary amyloidosis and any other conditions producing widespread myocardial damage. It is also found in emphysema, generalized edema and obesity. The minimal normal QRS amplitude in precordial leads waxes and wanes from right to left across the chest, being generally accepted as 5 mm in V_1 and V_6, 7 mm. in V_2 and V_5 and 9 mm in V_3 and V_4. Some define low voltage as an *average* voltage in the limb leads of less than 5 mm with an *average* in the chest leads of less than 10 mm.[12]

It is more difficult to set an arbitrary upper limit to normal voltage. Amplitudes up to 20 or even 30 mm are occasionally seen in lead 2 in normal hearts, while the generally accepted maximum in a precordial lead is 25 to 30 mm.

The amplitude or "voltage" recorded on the tracing is dependent on many factors besides the health of the heart; for example, the distance of the heart from the recording electrode (as determined by size of chest, thickness of chest wall, presence of emphysema, etc.) profoundly affects the size of the recorded deflections. Such factors must receive due consideration before the voltage of any complex is judged too high or too low.

The significance of Q *waves* is one of the most important, and sometimes the most difficult, assessments in the tracing. Size is important, and yet a diminutive Q wave of less than 1 mm. may have real significance, while a QS complex of 10 mm. in certain leads may sometimes be within normal limits. A small narrow Q wave of 1 or 2 mm is a normal finding in leads 1, aVL and aVF, and in chest leads over the left ventricle, e.g., V_5. Indeed, the absence of the expected small Q waves in these leads may be an abnormal sign.[11] On the other hand, deep QS or Qr complexes are a perfectly normal finding in aVR, the Q in aVR being the equivalent of an initial R in other leads—since aVR, for reasons to be explained in Chapter 4, is an "upside down stepchild"; and QS complexes are occasionally found normally in lead 3 and in leads V_1 and V_2. The Q wave should not be more than 0.03 sec in width. To gauge their importance Q waves must be viewed in the light of the overall picture and one must take into account (1) their depth, (2) their width, (3) the leads in which they appear and, most important, (4) the clinical setting.

ST Segment

This segment is that part of the tracing immediately succeeding the QRS complex (fig. 3.4). The point at which it "takes off" from the QRS is called the J (junction) point. Two features of the ST segment should be observed: (1) its *level* relative to the baseline, i.e., whether it is elevated or depressed below the T-P segment, and (2) its *shape*.

Normally it is on the same level as the T-P segment, i.e., it is **isoelectric**, or only slightly above or below it. It is sometimes normally elevated not more than 1 mm in the standard leads, and even 2 mm in some of the chest leads; it is never normally depressed more than half a millimeter or so. An interesting exception is sometimes observed, particularly in healthy young black men[15, 16] where the ST segments may be markedly elevated (sometimes as much as 4 mm) in one or more precordial leads (fig. 3.5), a configuration often described as "early repolarization" (see pp. 414 and 463)."

In shape the ST segment normally curves gently and imperceptibly into the proximal limb of the T wave. It should not form a sharp angle with this limb, nor should it pursue a frankly horizontal course. Horizontality of the ST

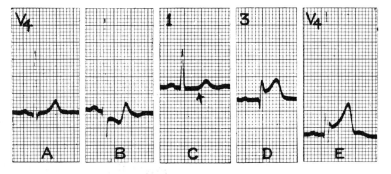

Figure 3.4. ST segments. (*A*) Normal. (*B*) Same lead, same patient as A; 2 min after exercise, showing ST depression. (*C*) ST segment is minimally depressed (certainly less than 0.5 mm) but is horizontal and forms a rather sharp-angled junction with proximal limb of T wave (compare with *A*). (*D*) ST elevation from myocardial injury (acute infarction). (*E*) ST elevation as a normal variant in a healthy black man.

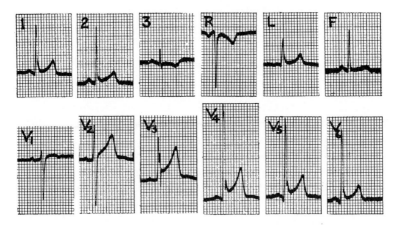

Figure 3.5. From a normal black man of 29 years. Note marked ST elevation in precordial leads,

segment, which is highly suspicious of myocardial ischemia, has also been called "plane depression" (fig. 3.4C).

Frank displacement of the ST segment is, of course, the hallmark of myocardial ischemia or injury and is seen with any of the syndromes of coronary artery disease. ST depression in the precordial leads is said to indicate subendocardial, and ST elevation subepicardial or transmural injury or ischemia. Temporary injury, as with DC cardioversion, may produce transient ST elevation.[14]

T Wave

The T wave represents the recovery period of the ventricles, when they recruit their spent electrical forces (**repolarization**). We particularly notice three of its features: (1) its *direction*, (2) its *shape*, and (3) its *height*.

The T wave is normally upright in leads 1 and 2, and in chest leads over the left ventricle (except in infants and very young childen); it is normally inverted in aVR; in all other leads it is variable. Certain general rules govern this variability: (1) The T wave is normally upright in aVL and in aVF if the QRS is more than 5 mm tall, but may be inverted in the company of smaller R waves. (2) In the precordial leads the tendency to inversion of T waves over the left ventricle (V_5 and V_6) rapidly diminishes with increasing age, and in adult males it is generally considered abnormal if the T waves are inverted as far to the left as V_3; in normal women the T wave in V_3 may be shallowly inverted. The T in V_1 may be inverted normally at any age (indeed it is more often inverted than upright); and in V_2 it is also sometimes normally negative. In normal hearts, when the T wave in V_1 is upright, it is almost never as tall as the T wave in V_6.[32]

We may summarize the direction of the normal adult T wave as follows. It is:

> Normally upright in 1, 2 and V_3 to V_6
> Normally inverted in aVR
> Variable in 3, aVL, aVF, V_1 and V_2.

The *shape* of the T waves is normally slightly rounded and slightly asymmetrical. When T waves are sharply pointed or grossly notched,[17] they should be regarded with suspicion, though either of these characteristics may sometimes occur in precordial leads as a normal variant. Notching of the T waves is particularly common in normal children (fig. 3.6); on the other hand, it is sometimes found in pericarditis. A sharply pointed symmetrical T wave (upright or inverted) is suspicious of myocardial infarction (fig. 3.7).

The *height* of the T waves is also important. They are normally not above 5 mm in any standard lead, and not above 10 mm in any precordial lead. Unusually tall T waves (fig. 3.7 *B* and *D*) suggest myocardial infarction or potassium intoxication. Tall T waves are also seen in myocardial ischemia without infarction (fig. 3.7*B*), in certain forms of ventricular overloading (see p. 58), in psychotics and in patients with cerebrovascular accidents. In obesity, the T waves tend to be flattened, regaining their normal amplitude as the excess weight is lost.[17a]

Q-T Duration

This interval, measured from the beginning of the QRS to the end of the T wave, gives the total duration of ventricular systole. It varies with heart rate, sex and age, and its normal values are most conveniently determined by consulting a prepared table based on the calculations of Ashman (table 3.1). A useful rule of thumb is that the Q-T interval should be less than half the preceding R-R interval. This holds good for normal sinus rates. However, as

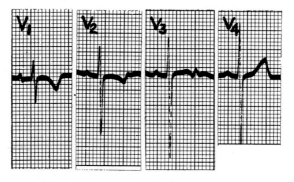

Figure 3.6.   T waves in a normal child. Note marked notching in V_3; this is a common normal transitional form of T wave between the normally inverted T in V_2 and the normally upright T in V_4.

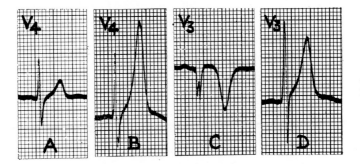

Figure 3.7. T waves. (*A*) Normal T wave. (*B*) Tall T wave of myocardial ischemia in a patient with angina but without infarction. (*C*) Deeply inverted symmetrical T wave of anterior infarction. (*D*) Tall upright symmetrical T wave of inferior infarction.

Table 3.1
Normal Q-T Intervals and the Upper Limits of the Normal [a]

Heart Rate per Minute	Men and Children (sec)	Women (sec)	Upper Limits of the Normal	
			Men and children (sec)	Women (sec)
40.0	0.449	0.461	0.491	0.503
43.0	0.438	0.450	0.479	0.491
46.0	0.426	0.438	0.466	0.478
48.0	0.420	0.432	0.460	0.471
50.0	0.414	0.425	0.453	0.464
52.0	0.407	0.418	0.445	0.456
54.5	0.400	0.411	0.438	0.449
57.0	0.393	0.404	0.430	0.441
60.0	0.386	0.396	0.422	0.432
63.0	0.378	0.388	0.413	0.423
66.5	0.370	0.380	0.404	0.414
70.5	0.361	0.371	0.395	0.405
75.0	0.352	0.362	0.384	0.394
80.0	0.342	0.352	0.374	0.384
86.0	0.332	0.341	0.363	0.372
92.5	0.321	0.330	0.351	0.360
100.0	0.310	0.318	0.338	0.347
109.0	0.297	0.305	0.325	0.333
120.0	0.283	0.291	0.310	0.317
133.0	0.268	0.276	0.294	0.301
150.0	0.252	0.258	0.275	0.282
172.0	0.234	0.240	0.255	0.262

[a] Reproduced with kind permission of the publishers from *Essentials of Electrocardiography* by R. Ashman and E. Hull, The Macmillan Company, New York, 1945.

the rate slows below 65 the maximal normal Q-T duration falls further and further below half the preceding R-R interval; and as the rate increases above 90 the normal Q-T duration gradually exceeds half the preceding R-R. These points will provide a near enough guide for most practical purposes. The diagnostic value of the Q-T duration is seriously limited by the technical difficulties of measuring it exactly.[29]

Q-T prolongation may be idiopathic[33] or acquired. It may accompany congestive heart failure or it may be due to ischemic heart disease,[21] rheumatic fever[19, 20, 28] or other causes of myocarditis[22, 23]; a lengthened Q-T duration may result from cerebrovascular disease,[24] or from electrolyte disturbances.[27, 31] Careful measurement showed that it was not lengthened in hypokalemia unless there was an associated deficit in calcium.[30] Drugs, including quinidine, procaine amide and the phenothiazines may cause Q-T prolongation,[26, 27, 36] as may hypothermia[18] or stringent dieting.[25, 35] A prolonged Q-T means that there is delayed repolarization of the ventricular myocardium, and this is associated with an increased predisposition to reentry (see p. 127), thus favoring the development of serious ventricular tachyarrhythmias, syncope and sudden death.[33, 34] It is often prolonged in patients with mitral valve prolapse.[18a] The Q-T is shortened by digitalis, calcium excess and potassium intoxication.

U Wave

This is usually a small wave of low voltage, sometimes seen following the T wave. Its normal polarity is the same as that of the T wave (i.e., when the T wave is upright, it too is upright, and vice versa), and the normal wave is often best discerned in lead V_3. It is rendered more prominent by potassium deficiency (fig. 3.8), and its polarity is often reversed in myocardial ischemia and left ventricular overload secondary to hypertension, or aortic or mitral regurgitation[37a] (fig. 3.8). Negative U waves in the resting ECG are claimed to be a faithful index of significant stenosis of the left main or left anterior descending coronary artery.[37] These are the conditions in which its alterations are of most value in diagnosis, but it is affected by numerous other factors; digitalis, quinidine, epinephrine, hypercalcemia, thyrotoxicosis and exercise all increase its amplitude.[38, 41]

Its source is uncertain; some have postulated that it represents repolarization of the papillary muscles, and others that it represents repolarization of the Purkinje system.[37a] In the cardiac cycle it coincides with the phase of supernormal excitability during ventricular recovery,[40] and in this connection it is interesting to note that most ventricular extrasystoles occur at about the time of the U wave.

Some common artifacts are illustrated in figures 3.9–3.12.

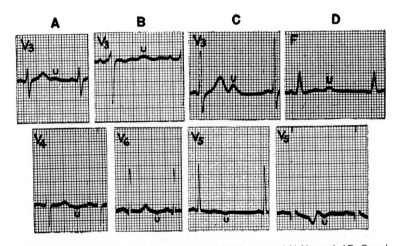

Figure 3.8. U waves. *Upper row*—upright U waves: (*A*) Normal, (*B, C* and *D*) Prominent U waves in hypokalemia. *Lower row*—inverted U waves: (*A*) Tracing from which this was taken showed no abnormalities except for U wave inversion in several leads; this situation is referred to as "isolated U wave inversion." (*B*) From a patient with hypertension whose tracing showed left ventricular strain including inverted U waves. (*C*) From a patient with coronary insufficiency but without hypertension. (*D*) Note marked inversion of T wave as well as U wave; from a hypertensive.

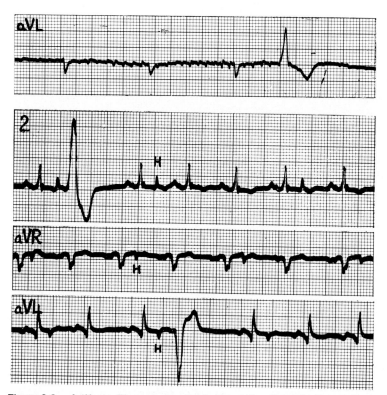

Figure 3.9.   Artifacts. The uppermost strip shows the effect of an involuntary muscular tremor affecting the left arm. The lower three strips are from a patient with hiccups; each lead shows the effect of three or four hiccups, one of which is indicated (*H*) in each lead.

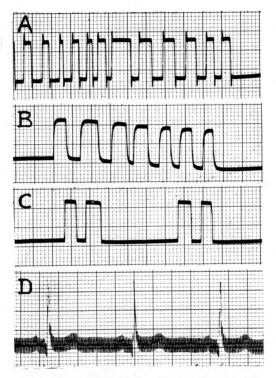

Figure 3.10. Artifacts. *A* and *B* show common errors in adjustment of the stylus—overshoot (*A*) and over-damping (*B*)—which can significantly distort the QRS complexes. Proper standardization is shown in *C. D* illustrates 60-cycle AC interference.

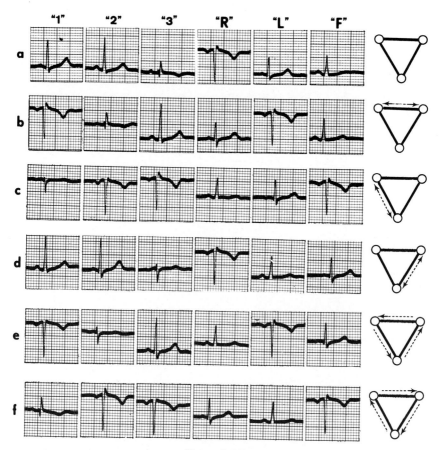

Figure 3.11

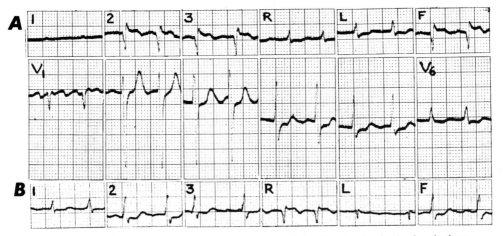

Figure 3.12. (*A*) **Atrial fibrillation** and pseudo-inferior infarction due to **electrode misplacement**. With Q waves and ST elevation in leads 2, 3 and aVF, and with reciprocal depression of the ST segment in aVL and the chest leads, this tracing suggests acute inferior infarction. But lead 1, with virtually no deflections, is the tip-off: the two arm electrodes are on the two legs (and the leg electrodes are on the arms). (*B*) Limb leads with the electrodes attached correctly.

Figure 3.11 (*opposite page*). **Electrodal confusion.**

    a. Electrodes properly placed. Leads are as labelled.

    b. Arm electrodes (lead 1) reversed:
> "1" is mirror image of 1
> "2" is 3, "3" is 2
> "R" is L; "L" is R

    c. Right arm and left leg (lead 2) electrodes reversed:
> "2" is mirror image of 2
> "1" is mirror image of 3
> "3" is mirror image of 1
> "R" is F; "F" is R

    d. Left arm and left leg (lead 3) electrodes reversed:
> "3" is mirror image of 3
> "1" is 2; "2" is 1
> "L" is F: "F" is L

    e. All three electrodes rotated counterclockwise:
> "1" is mirror image of 2
> "2" is mirror image of 3
> "3" is 1
> "R" is F; "L" is R; "F" is L

    f. All three electrodes rotated clockwise:
> "1" is 3
> "2" is mirror image of 1
> "3" is mirror image of 2
> "R" is L; "L" is F; "F" is R

REFERENCES

P Wave

1. Thomas P., and Dejong, D.: The P wave in the electrocardiogram in the diagnosis of heart disease, Br. Heart J. 1954: **16**, 241.

P-R Interval

2. Alimurung, M. M., and Massell, B. F.: The normal P-R interval in infants and children. Circulation 1956: **13**, 257.
3. Atterhog, J.-H., and Loogna, E.: P-R interval in relation to heart rate during exercise and the influence of posture and autonomic tone. J. Electrocardiol. 1977: **10**, 331.
4. Blizzard, J. J., and Rupp, J. J.: Prolongation of the P-R interval as a manifestation of thyrotoxicosis, J.A.M.A. 1960: **173**, 1845.
5. Johnson, R. L., et al.: Electrocardiographic findings in 67,375 asymptomatic individuals, Part VII. A-V block. Am. J. Cardiol. 1960: **6**, 153.
6. Lister, J. W., et al.: Atrioventricular conduction in man: effect of rate, exercise, isoproterenol and atropine on the P-R interval. Am. J. Cardiol. 1965: **16**, 516.
7. Lown, B., Ganong, W. B., and Levine, S. A.: The syndrome of short P-R interval, normal QRS complex and paroxysmal rapid heart action. Circulation 1952: **5**, 693.
8. Manning, G. W., and Sears, G. A.: Postural heart block. Am. J. Cardiol. 1962: **9**, 558.
9. Scherf, D.: Short P-R interval and its occurrence in hypertension. Bull. N.Y. Coll. Med. 1941: **43**, 116.
10. Scherf, D., and Dix, J. H.: The effects of posture on A-V conduction. Am. Heart J. 1952: **43**, 494.

QRS Complex

11. Burch, G. E., and Pasquale, N.: A study at autopsy of the relation of absence of the Q wave in leads I, aVL, V_5 and V_6 to septal fibrosis. Am. Heart J. 1960: **60**, 336.
12. Unverferth, D. V., et al.: Electrocardiographic voltage in pericardial effusion. Chest 1979: **75**, 157.
13. Lepeschkin, E., and Surawicz, B.: The measurement of the duration of the QRS interval. Am. Heart J 1952: **44**, 80.

S-T Segment

14. Chun, P. K. C., et al.: ST-segment elevation with elective direct current cardioversion. Circulation 1981: **63**, 220.
15. Edeiken, J.: Elevation of the RS-T segment, apparent or real, in the right precordial leads as a probable normal variant. Am. Heart J. 1954: **48**, 331.
16. Goldman, M. J.: RS-T segment elevation in mid- and left precordial leads as a normal variant. Am. Heart J. 1953: **46**, 817.

T Waves

17. Dressler, E., Roesler, H., and Lackner, H.: The significance of notched upright T waves. Br. Heart J. 1951: **13**, 496.
17a. Eisenstein, I., et al.: The electrocardiogram in obesity. J. Electrocardiol. 1982: **15**, 115.

Q-T Duration

18. Abildskov, J. A.: The nervous system and cardiac arrhythmias. Circulation 1975: **51** (Supp. III), 111–116.
18a. Bekheit, S. G., et al.: Analysis of QT interval in patients with idiopathic mitral valve prolapse. Chest 1982: **81**, 620.
19. Carmichael, D. B.: The corrected Q-T duration in acute and convalescent rheumatic fever. Am. Heart J. 1955: **50**, 528.
20. Craige, E., et al.: The Q-T interval in rheumatic fever. Circulation 1950: **1**, 1338.
21. Elek, S. R., et al.: The Q-T interval in myocardial infarction and left ventricular hypertrophy. Am. Heart J. 1953: **45**, 80.
22. Fox, T. T., et al.: The Q-T interval in the electrocardiogram of children with tuberculosis. Circulation 1950: **1**, 1184.

23. Gittleman, I. W., Thorner, M. C., and Griffith, G. C.: The Q-T interval of the electrocardiogram in acute myocarditis in adults, with autopsy correlation. Am. Heart J. 1951: 341, 78.
24. Hersch, C.: Electrocardiographic changes in subarachnoid haemorrhage, meningitis and intracranial space-occupying lesions. Br. Heart J. 1964: **26,** 785.
25. Isner, J. M., et al.: Sudden, unexpected death in avid dieters using the liquid-protein-modified-fast diet. Observations in 17 patients and the role of the prolonged Q-T interval. Circulation 1979: **60,** 1401.
26. James, T. N.: QT prolongation and sudden death. Mod. Concepts Cardiovasc. Dis. 1969: **38,** 35.
27. Khan, M. M., et al.: Management of recurrent ventricular tachyarrhythmias associated with Q-T prolongation. Am. J. Cardiol. 1981: **47,** 1301.
28. Kornel, L., and Braun, K.: The Q-T interval in rheumatic heart disease. Br. Heart J. 1956: **18,** 8.
29. Lepeschkin, E., and Surawicz, B.: The measurement of the Q-T duration of the electrocardiogram. Circulation 1952: **6,** 378.
30. Lepeschkin, E., and Surawicz, B.: The duration of the Q-U interval and its components in electrocardiograms of normal persons. Am. Heart J. 1953: **46,** 9.
31. Loeb, H. S., et al.: Paroxysmal ventricular fibrillation in two patients with hypomagnesemia; treatment by transvenous pacing. Circulation 1968: **37,** 210.
32. Meyer, P., and Herr, R.; L'interet du syndrome eléctrocardiographique TV1 > TV6 pour le dépistage précoce de troubles de la repolarisation ventriculaire gauche. Arch. Mal. Coeur 1959: **52,** 753.
33. Moss, A. J., and Schwartz, P. J.: Sudden death and the idiopathic long Q-T syndrome. Am. J. Med. 1979: **66,** 6.
34. Schwartz, . J., et al.: The long Q-T syndrome. Am. Heart J. 1975: **89,** 378.
35. Singh, B. N., et al: Liquid protein diets and torsade de pointes. J.A.M.A. 1978: **240,** 115.
36. Surawicz, B., and Lasseter, K. C.: Effects of drugs on the electrocardiogram. Prog. Cardiovasc. Dis. 1970: **13,** 26.

U Wave

37. Gerson, M. C., and McHenry, P. L.: Resting U wave inversion as a marker of stenosis of the left anterior descending coronary artery. Am. J. Med. 1980: **69,** 545.
37a. Kishida, H., et al.: Negative U wave: A highly specific but poorly understood sign of heart disease. Am. J. Cardiol. 1982: **49,** 2030.
38. Lepeschkin, E.: The U wave of the electrocardiogram. Arch. Intern. Med. 1955: **96,** 600.
39. Lepeschkin, E.: The U wave of the electrocardiogram. Mod. Concepts Cardiovasc. Dis. 1969: **38,** 39.
40. Mack, I., Langendorf, R., and Katz, L. N.: the supernormal phase of recovery of conduction in the human heart. Am. Heart J. 1947: **34,** 374.
41. Palmer, J. H.: Isolated U wave negativity. Circulation 1953: **7,** 205.
42. Symposium: The U wave of the electrocardiogram. Circulation 1957: **15,** 68–110.

General

43. Committee on Electrocardiography, American Heart Association: Recommendations for standardization of electocardiographic and vectorcardiographic leads. Circulation. 1954: **10,** 564.
44. Kossman, C. E.: The normal electrocardiogram. Circulation 1953: **8,** 920.
45. Manning, G. W.: Electrocardiography in the selection of Royal Canadian Air Force aircrew. Circulation 1954: **10,** 401.
46. Packard, J. M., Graettinger, J. S., and Graybiel, A.: Analysis of the electrocardiograms obtained from 100 young healthy aviators. Ten-year follow up. Circulation 1954: **10,** 384.

Electrical Axis

The QRS Axis

The orientation of the heart's electrical activity in the frontal plane may be expressed in terms of "axis" or "heart position." The axis may be "normal" or there may be right or left "axis deviation"; and the electrical positions may be "horizontal," "vertical," etc. (see p. 39). But this approach leaves something to be desired. The description, "left axis deviation, horizontal heart," is, like "an elderly old man," both inexact and redundant. Just as we should be precise and say "a 76-year-old man," so we should specify the axis and say, for example, "minus 40°"; this, in a single and relatively accurate figure, combines both "axis" and "position."

The axis can be determined approximately from any two limb leads, but it is most readily and accurately determined if all six limb leads are available for simultaneous inspection. To calculate the numerical axis, one must know the "hexaxial reference system." By taking the three sides of Einthoven's triangle (fig. 4.1*A*), each of which represents one of the standard limb leads, and rearranging them so that they bisect each other, we obtain a "triaxial reference system" (fig. 4.1*B*). If we add to this system three further lines to represent the unipolar limb leads (fig. 4.1*C*), the final figure consists of six bisecting lines, the hexaxial reference system (fig. 4.1*D*), each line of which represents one of the six limb leads. By convention, the degrees are arranged as shown in fig. 4.1*D*, with 0° at 3 o'clock and successively greater negative degrees progressing counter-clockwise to −180° at 9 o'clock, and with corresponding positive degrees ranging clockwise.

One further principle: the electrical impulse writes the largest deflection on the lead whose line of derivation is parallel to its path, and it writes the smallest deflection on the lead perpendicular to it. For example, an impulse travelling parallel to lead 1 will produce the maximal deflection on this lead and a minimal deflection on the lead at right angles to it, i.e., aVF.

In general, axes between 0° and +90° correspond with "normal axis." Axes between 0° and −90° represent "left axis deviation," and between +90° and +180° "right axis deviation." This leaves the quadrant between −90° and

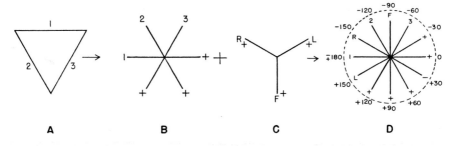

Figure 4.1. Constitution of the hexaxial reference system. (*A*). Einthoven's triangle, the sides of which represent the three standard limb leads. (*B*) The triaxial reference system composed of the three sides of Einthoven's triangle rearranged so that they bisect one another. (*C*) Lines of derivation of the three unipolar (aV) limb leads. (*D*) The hexaxial reference system composed of the lines of derivation of the six limb leads (*B* + *C*) arranged so that they bisect each other.

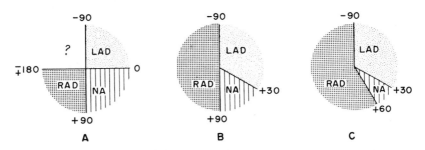

Figure 4.2. Illustrating inconsistencies in the definitions of axis deviations. NA = normal axis. LAD = left axis deviation. RAD = right axis deviation. (*A*) Convenient and realistic boundaries of axis deviation (adopted in this book). (*B*) Boundaries recommended by the Criteria Committee of the New York Heart Association. (*C*) Boundaries described by Sodi-Pallares.

−180° without identity ("no-man's-land"): does it represent extreme right or extreme left axis deviation (fig. 4.2*A*)? This quandary is resolved by using the precise numerical axis.

A further difficulty arises from the fact that authorities define the bounds of "axis deviations" differently; according to Sodi-Pallares[7] "slight" left axis deviation begins at +30° (fig. 4.2*C*), whereas most authorities more conveniently place 0° as the rightmost limit of left axis deviation. Similarly, "slight" right axis deviation begins at +60° for Sodi-Pallares, but for others it begins at +90° (fig. 4.2*B*). The Criteria Committee of the New York Heart Association[4] applies left axis deviation to the segment lying between −90° and +30° and right axis deviation to the area between +90° and −90° (fig. 4.2*B*). As normal axes range between −30° and +120°, the most realistic boundaries would seem to be those diagrammed in figure 4.2*A*; this applies "normal axis" to the range between 0° and +90°. "Slight left axis deviation" then applies to the still normal 0° to −30° segment, and pathological deviations of the axis to the left (−30° to −90°) are referred to as "marked LAD." Similarly, "slight RAD" is applied to axes still within the normal range of +90° to +120°, while axes of +120° to +180° are called "marked RAD."

By using the quadrant system illustrated in figure 4.2*A*, the axis now can be calculated. The two leads that divide the "clockface" into its four quadrants are leads 1 and aVF. In figure 4.3 the positive field of lead 1 is shaded vertically and the positive field of aVF is indicated with horizontal shading; thus, the quadrant assigned to "normal" axis is where the positive fields of both leads overlap. If the QRS is upright in both leads, as shown in figure 4.3*b*, the axis is "normal." On the other hand, if it is positive in 1 but negative in aVF (fig. 4.3*a*), it is in the left-axis quadrant. If it is positive in aVF but negative in 1 (fig. 4.3*c*), it is in the right-axis quadrant; and if it is negative in both leads (fig. 4.3*d*), the axis is in "no man's land." Using only these two leads, it is easy to place the axis in its appropriate quadrant.

But clearly it is not enough to state that the axis is between 0° and −90°; one must know whether it is −30°, or −45°, or −80°, and this finer adjustment is achieved by comparing the size of the complexes in the two leads. For example, as shown in figure 4.3*b*, if the R wave in aVF is about twice the size of the R in 1 (the area enclosed by the complex should be estimated, not just its amplitude), the axis will point twice as close to the positive pole of aVF as it will to the positive pole of 1, i.e., about +60°. On the other hand, if the complex (fig. 4.3*a*) is twice as positive in 1 as it is negative in aVF, the axis will be twice as close to the positive pole of 1 as it is to the negative pole of aVF, that is, about −30°. If it is about equally positive in aVF and negative in 1 (fig. 4.3*c*), the axis will be equidistant from the negative pole of 1 and the positive of aVF, or +135°. Finally, if it is almost equally negative in both leads (fig. 4.3*d*), the axis will be about equidistant from the negative poles of the two leads, or −135°. Using just those two leads one can get to within 5 or 10 degrees of the axis in a few seconds. Since the axis may shift more than that with normal respiration, a fairly close approximation is all one can hope to achieve.

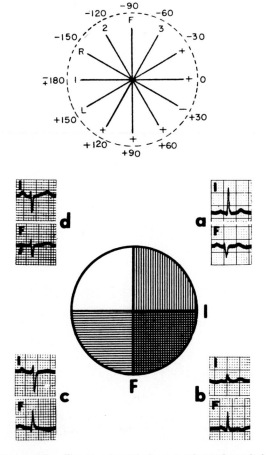

Figure 4.3. The four frontal plane quadrants bounded by leads 1 and aVF. The positive "field" of lead 1 is shaded vertically, the positive "field" of aVF horizontally. Examples of an axis in each quadrant occupy the four corners (leads are from the same tracings as *A, B, D* and *E* in fig. 4.4).

Another approach complements the 1/aVF method: the smallest deflection shown in any of the six limb leads indicates that the axis is roughly at right angles to that lead in the hexaxial clockface. For example, the tracing in figure 4.4C shows that aVR has the smallest QRS complex. At right angles to aVR is −60° or +120°; but from an initial glance at leads 1 and aVF, it can be seen that the axis is in the left axis quadrant, so the answer is −60°, not +120°. But the QRS is a little more positive than negative in aVR; and so, in search of maximal accuracy, swing the axis a shade towards the positive pole of aVR and call it −70° rather than −60°. With a little practice using this combined approach, it soon becomes a simple matter to place any axis accurately within a few seconds.

In short, the determination of an axis is accomplished in two swift stages: (1) look at leads 1 and aVF and place the axis in its appropriate quadrant; then

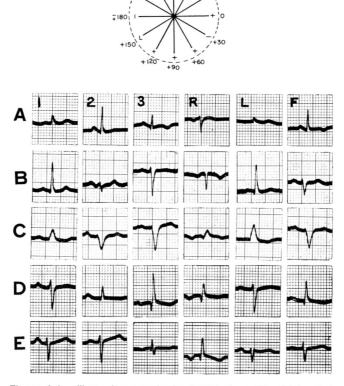

Figure 4.4. Illustrating axes in the frontal plane. The QRS axis in each tracing is as follows: (A) +60°. (B) − 30°. (C) − 70°. (D) +135°. (E) − 135°.

Figure 4.5. A simple triaxial reference figure illustrating the plotting of QRS (minute hand) and T (hour hand) on the clockface of the frontal plane. The axes plotted are those of the tracing in figure 4.4*B*.

(2) look for the lead with the smallest QRS deflection and place the axis at right angles (perpendicular) to it in the quadrant predetermined in stage 1. This is the best and fastest way to get the frontal plane axis—and it is accurate to within a few degrees.

In some circumstances, a single axis is meaningless. For example, when the QRS is virtually equiphasic in all the limb leads, the axis is usually and lazily described as "indeterminate." But of course no axis is actually indeterminate; and if, in such a case, the axis is really required, it is necessary to find two axes, "initial" for the first half of the QRS and "terminal" for the second half. The same applies when one is determining the axis in right bundle-branch block where the initial and terminal forces are usually widely separated. On the other hand, in left bundle-branch block the initial and terminal forces usually point in much the same direction and a single axis suffices.

These same principles and methods can and should be applied to determine the axis of the T waves, and of the P waves. It is well to plot the QRS and T axes routinely and to symbolize them with a long and a short arrow respectively, as in figure 4.5. These can be conveniently graphed on a simplified axial system, from which unnecessary lines and symbols have been omitted, as is illustrated in figure 4.5. Rubber stamps of both the labelled hexaxial system and the simplified triaxial form are useful toys.

The T wave axis normally points in the same general direction as the QRS axis; if they diverge by more than 50°, a myocardial abnormality (not necessarily structural) is almost always responsible.[3]

One of the advantages of applying the hexaxial reference system is that it teaches us to appreciate the interrelationship of the limb leads and to view the frontal plane record as a whole rather than in fragments. When one grasps this interrelationship it becomes absurd to consider the pattern of a single lead out of its hexaxial context. For example, some writers have stressed the importance of a prominent R wave in aVR in the diagnosis of right ventricular hypertrophy. But, from our knowledge of the mutual interdependence of all the limb leads in the hexaxial reference system, we know that for the QRS in aVR to be mainly positive the mean QRS axis must be *either* further to the right than +120° *or* further to the left than −60°. That is, it may mean either marked right or marked left axis deviation. Obviously it only means *right* ventricular hypertrophy when it is part of a significant *right*ward shift in the axis and says no more than that right axis deviation to more than +120° suggests right ventricular hypertrophy.

During the first 6 months of life, the normally vertical axis moves leftward because the left ventricle grows faster than the right. By the age of 6 months, adult proportions have been reached and the axis then remains stable until, with advancing age in later life, a leftward drift sets in again.[1, 5]

The range of the frontal plane axis in normal adults is wide. Although the great majority of supposedly normal subjects have an axis between −30° and +110°, a few supposed normals have axes that lie beyond these limits: in about 10 per thousand the axis is between −30° and −60°, with about 3 per thousand between +110° and +135°.[2, 8]

This discussion has so far represented the axis in one plane only, the plane of the limb leads, the frontal plane. But the cardiac axis obviously has direction in innumerable other planes, being oriented in three-dimensional space. However, the only other plane that our routine leads at all portray is the horizontal plane, the plane in which the chest leads lie. Unlike the limb leads, which symmetrically encircle the clockface of the frontal plane, the chest leads do not encircle the chest but span only a quarter of its circumference. They are sufficient, however, to determine whether the axis is pointing relatively forward or backward.

When the T-wave axis points anteriorly (TV_1 taller than TV_6) it is often a sign of myocardial abnormality.

Causes of Axis Deviation

The electrical QRS axis may be shifted to the right (beyond +90°) or to the left (beyond 0°) in the following circumstances:

Right	*Left*
Normal variation	Normal variation
Mechanical shifts—inspiration, emphysema	Mechanical shifts—expiration, high diaphragm from pregnancy, ascites, abdominal tumors, etc.
Right ventricular hypertrophy	
Right bundle branch block	
Left posterior hemiblock	Left anterior hemiblock
Dextrocardia	Left bundle branch block
Ventricular ectopic rhythms	Endocardial cushion defects, and several other congenital lesions, both acyanotic and cyanotic
Wolff-Parkinson-White syndrome	Wolff-Parkinson-White syndrome
	Emphysema
	Hyperkalemia
	Ventricular ectopic rhythms

In considering mechanical shifts, note that such disturbances as pneumothorax and pleural effusion usually cause a wholesale shift of the mediastinum, heart and all, toward the opposite side, and do not necessarily affect the heart's axis—they push it to one side without necessarily rotating it.

Axis Deviation of P Waves

With axis deviation of the QRS understood, one can see that the pattern of right atrial hypertrophy already referred to (p. 15), with P_1 lower than P_3, is an expression of a tendency toward right axis deviation of the P wave; and similarly the P wave pattern characteristic of mitral stenosis, with P_1 taller than P_3, and P_3 sometimes actually inverted, indicates a shift of the atrial axis toward the left. A P-wave axis to the right of +60° is considered good evidence of chronic lung disease.

Electrical Heart Position

For descriptive purposes, the heart's "electrical position," as determined from leads aVL and aVF, is sometimes referred to. The five generally recognized positions are **horizontal, semi-horizontal, intermediate, semi-vertical** and **vertical**. If the main deflection of the QRS is positive in both leads, the position is called intermediate. If the main deflections are divergent, the heart is horizontal; if convergent, vertical. Semi-horizontal and semi-vertical positions are halfway stations between the intermediate position and the horizontal and vertical extremes.

In other words, horizontal, semi-horizontal, intermediate, semi-vertical and vertical positions respectively represent axes of about −30°, 0°, +30°, +60° and +90°. Although the use of these five terms to describe electrical position has little to recommend it, there are times when it is convenient to refer to a heart with an axis in the neighborhood of 0° to −30° as a horizontal heart, and to one with an axis between +60° and +90° as a vertical heart.

Normal Findings in aV Leads

aVR: All three complexes—P, QRS and T—are inverted. This is to be expected, since the lead is an inverted stepchild in the hexaxial system—its negative pole is flanked by the positive poles of leads 1 and 2 (see fig. 4.1*D*, p. 33). The inverted QRS complex usually presents an rS pattern, but may be QS or Qr in form.

aVL: All the complexes in this lead are variable; P, QRS and T all may be upright or inverted, according to the heart's electrical position. If the QRS is as much as 6 mm tall, the accompanying T wave should not be inverted. Any pattern of the QRS can be normal, even QS when the voltage is low. However, if the R wave is 6 mm or more, the Q wave should be small by comparison—not more than 1 to 2 mm deep and less than 0.03 sec in duration.

aVF: The complexes in this lead are also variable, depending mainly on the heart's position. The P wave is usually upright but may at times be inverted. Again, as in aVL, if the R wave is 6 mm or more the T wave should be upright and the Q wave should be relatively small—not more than half the amplitude of the R and less than 0.03 sec in duration.

REFERENCES

1. Bachman, S., et al.: Effect of aging on the electrocardiogram. Am. J. Cardiol. 1981: **48,** 513.
2. Ewy, G. C., et al.: Electrocardiographic axis deviation in Navajo and Apache Indians. Chest 1979: **75,** 54.
3. Grant, R. P.: *Clinical Electrocardiography. The Spatial Vector Approach.* McGraw-Hill, New York, 1957.
4. *Nomenclature and Criteria for Diagnosis of Diseases of the Heart and Blood Vessels.* New York Heart Association, New York, 1955.
5. Perloff, J. K., et al.: Left axis deviation; a reassessment. Circulation 1979: **60,** 12.
6. Pryor, R., and Blount, S. G.: The clinical significance of true left axis deviation. Am. Heart J. 1966: **72,** 391.
7. Sodi-Pallares, D.: *New Bases of Electrocardiography.* C. V. Mosby, St. Louis, 1956.
8. Soffer, A.: Range of frontal plane QRS axes. Electrocardiograms of subjects in a multiphasic screening program. Chest 1977: **72,** 477.

Practical Points

Enough variables influence the tracing without introducing unnecessary technical ones. Care should therefore be exercised to ensure that technique is uniform from tracing to tracing and day to day, so that allowances do not have to be made for variations in technique. The following points are of importance.

1. Effective *contact* between electrode and skin is essential. Electrode jelly contains electrolytes and an abrasive; the abrasive is intended to break down the waterproof horny layer of the skin so that the electrolytes of jelly and body may form a continuous conductor. The jelly should therefore be rubbed briskly, not delicately smeared, on the skin before the electrode is applied.

   On the other hand, special jelly is seldom necessary, and Lewes obtained equally good records using a variety of contact substances including handcream, mayonnaise, mustard, ketchup, toothpaste, K-Y jelly and even tap water!

2. *Standardization* should be consistent. It should always, if possible, be full and should be adjusted exactly. When 1 mv is thrown into the circuit, the baseline should deflect exactly 10 mm. If standardization varies from tracing to tracing, it may be difficult to evaluate slight changes. Moreover, the interpreter is given considerable and unnecessary extra work if he has to take note of inconsistencies in standardization and make allowances for them.

3. *Placement of the precordial electrode* is often too casual. Kerwin found that placement by the same technician on the same patient in serial tracings varied by 2 to 3 cm in both vertical and horizontal directions. But placement should be as exact and constant as possible. For this reason only bony landmarks should be used in locating the precordial points (p. 2). Especially in leads close to the transitional zone (p. 46 and fig. 5.4), small displacements of the electrode may produce considerable changes in the pattern.

4. *Position of patient* while the tracing is being taken is of importance. He should be lying uniformly flat. If for some reason he has to be in any other position, a note to this effect should be made. Lying on either side, or sitting up, usually alters the heart's electrical axis and transitional zone; thus serial tracings, if taken in a variety of positions, are difficult to compare.

REFERENCES

Bradlow, B. A.: *How To Produce a Readable Electrocardiogram.* Charles C Thomas, Springfield, Ill., 1964.

Kerwin, A. J., et al.: A method for the accurate placement of chest electrodes in the taking of serial electrocardiographic tracings. Can. Med. Assoc. J. 1960: **82**, 258.

Lewes, D.: Electrode jelly in electrocardiography. Br. Heart J. 1965: **27**, 105.

Schnitzer, K.: *Electrocardiographic Techniques,* Ed. 2. Grune & Stratton, New York, 1960.

Genesis of the Precordial Pattern

The Intrinsicoid Deflection

Over the normal heart, the R wave becomes taller and the S wave smaller as the electrode is moved from right to left across the chest. To understand this it is helpful to consider the patterns that result when an electrode is placed at various points along a single strip of stimulated muscle.

In figure 5.1 the muscle strip *ABC* is stimulated at the *arrow* and the wave of activation spreads from left to right to the other end of the strip. If the electrode is placed successively at points 1, 2 and 3 the illustrated patterns are respectively derived: from point 1 an rS complex; from point 2 an RS; and from point 3 an Rs complex. It is easy to deduce from these patterns that as long as the impulse is travelling toward the electrode, a positive deflection (R wave) is produced, while a negative deflection (S wave) is inscribed when the impulse has passed the electrode and is travelling away from it.

A convenient way to rationalize this finding is to think of the impulse as a

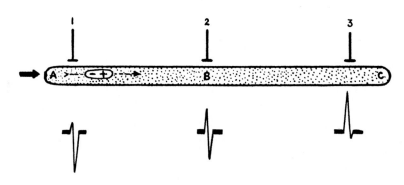

Figure 5.1

moving dipole (or doublet), i.e., a pair of charges, one positive and one negative, travelling together with the positive charge always leading. This is a crude but convenient approximation of what actually occurs when an impulse travels through stimulated tissue. Let us consider in terms of the dipole what happens when the electrode is placed in the middle of the muscle strip (point 2) and the strip is then stimulated. As the dipole travels from left to right, the leading positive charge gets nearer and nearer to the recording electrode; as it approaches it exerts a stronger and stronger influence on the electrode and the tracing becomes more and more positive, until it reaches maximal positivity (peak of R wave) at the moment that the positive charge is immediately under the electrode. A split second later the dipole has moved on and the negative charge is now immediately under the electrode exerting its maximal influence. So the tracing makes a quick swing (the downstroke) from maximal positivity to maximal negativity. Then, as the dipole continues on its journey, its negative tail recedes from the electrode and its influence diminishes. The tracing becomes less and less negative until, when the whole muscle strip has been activated, it regains the isoelectric line.

The downstroke which represents the abrupt swing from maximal positivity to maximal negativity is called the **intrinsic deflection**. It is a deflection of great practical importance, for it tells us the moment that the impulse (dipole) has arrived under the electrode. We know that the start of the upstroke marks the moment that the impulse started from the arrow; we now also know that the start of the downstroke marks the moment that the impulse arrived at *B*. We can thus measure the time it takes for the impulse to travel the distance from the *arrow* to *B*. This, of course, like all timing, is measured horizontally as illustrated in figure 5.2. This simple principle has been used for decades in

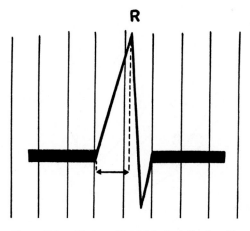

Figure 5.2. Timing of the intrinsic deflection. The time that elapses from the beginning of the QRS complex to the peak of the R wave is measured horizontally.

experimental physiology. Lewis used it to plot the times of impulse arrival at various points in the atria when he was attempting to prove his theory of circus movement; Prinzmetal used it even more extensively in his experiments on the atrial arrhythmias; and modern electrophysiologists today make use of the same principle.

In the light of this let us now examine what happens when electrodes are placed in contact with the myocardium of normally functioning ventricles, either in the experimental animal or in man with the heart surgically exposed. If an electrode is placed in contact with the surface of the right ventricle, a mainly negative (rS) deflection is inscribed; if placed in contact with the left ventricle, a mainly positive (qR) complex is registered. For all practical purposes the patterns are the same as those obtained clinically from precordial points to the right and left, say V_1 and V_5. To appreciate the reason for this one must recall the sequence in which the ventricular muscle is depolarized (fig. 5.3).

The impulse apparently descends the left bundle branch rather more rapidly than the right, with the result that the left septal surface is activated about 0.01 sec before the right septal surface. The net result is that the septum is activated mainly from left to right (*1* in fig. 5.3). Then both ventricular walls are activated simultaneously, but because the right wall is much thinner than the left, the impulse traverses its perpendicular path through the right wall (*2*) and arrives at the epicardium well before impulses on the left have reached the epicardial surface. Then, finally, the left ventricular muscle is "penetrated," first at the apex and then successively toward the base (*3–5*).

Now if an electrode is placed over the thin wall of the right ventricle (*A* in fig. 5.3), the first impulse (dipole) to influence it will be that traversing the septum from left to right (*1*); this is travelling toward the electrode and the deflection produced will therefore be positive. The next impulse (*2*) is also

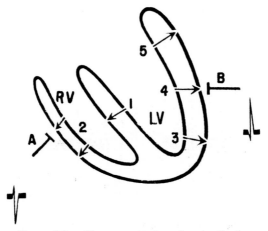

Figure 5.3. The approximate order of activation of the ventricular myocardium, and the form of ventricular complex derived over each ventricle.

travelling toward A and therefore augments the already positive deflection. From this time on, the only dipoles left in the picture are those activating the left ventricle. These are all travelling away from the electrode A and therefore cause a negative deflection. The wall is thick and the impulses have a relatively long journey, so the S wave is relatively deep. The composite picture produced is thus an rS complex.

When an electrode is placed over the left ventricle (B in fig. 5.3), again the first influence felt is (1). This is now travelling away from our electrode and therefore causes a small initial negative deflection (Q wave). From now on the electrode is under the influence of the approaching impulses travelling toward it through the left ventricular wall. Therefore the remainder of the tracing is positive, and the composite picture is a qR complex.

Thus over the right ventricle a deep S wave represents activation of the left ventricle, while over the left ventricle itself its activation is represented by a tall R wave. From both sides of the heart the major deflection represents activation of the major (left) ventricle. As in the single muscle strip, the downstroke from the peak of the R wave is the intrinsic deflection and tells us when the impulse has reached the epicardial surface of the ventricle over which the electrode is placed. As the right ventricle has a much thinner wall, the impulse over this ventricle naturally reaches the surface much earlier than it reaches the surface of the left ventricle; i.e., the peak of the small R wave over the right ventricle is reached earlier than the peak of the tall R wave over the left ventricle.

In clinical practice we obviously cannot take **direct** or **epicardial leads**, and the best we can do is to place the electrode on the chest wall at strategic intervals across the precordium. The resulting series of **semidirect** or **precordial leads** produces patterns very similar to those taken with the electrode in direct epicardial contact. In these clinical leads the downstroke is the analogue of the intrinsic deflection and is therefore called the **intrinsicoid deflection**. This deflection should begin, i.e., the peak of the R wave should be reached, within 0.02 sec in V_1 and within 0.04 sec in V_6. If it takes longer than this for the intrinsicoid deflection to start downward, it means that the impulse is late in reaching the epicardial surface of the ventricle under the electrode, and this indicates either that the wall of the ventricle has become thickened (ventricular hypertrophy) or dilated (so that the conducting paths have been lengthened), or that there is a block in the conducting system to the ventricle concerned (bundle-branch block).

This application of the dipole concept to the complex process of activation of the entire heart is obviously an over-simplification, though a most convenient and practical one. Regardless of what term—impulse, dipole, wavefront, electromotive force or vector—is used in describing the phenomena of myocardial activation, the principles enunciated above are helpful in visualizing the train of electrical events.

"Clockwise" and "Counterclockwise" Rotation

Between the definite "right ventricular" pattern (rS) of V_1 and the definite "left ventricular" pattern (qR) of V_6, there are transitional patterns—the S wave becomes less deep as the electrode is moved toward the left while the R wave becomes progressively taller. The **transitional zone** is the area in which the QRS is equiphasic (an RS complex), and this usually appears in V_3 or V_4 or between them. In figure 5.4 five series of precordial leads from V_1 to V_6 are recorded. The first three show normal transitional zones (T): in *A* lead V_3 shows the equiphasic complex; in *B* lead V_4 shows it; in *C* the actual transitional pattern is not shown, but V_3 presents an rS pattern while V_4 shows an Rs; the transition from one to the other has occurred between the two.

The last two series in the figure show abnormal transitions. In *D* the transition occurs between V_1 and V_2—the Rs pattern is recorded unusually far to the right of the chest. In *E* the transition occurs between V_5 and V_6—an rS pattern is recorded unusually far to the left of the precordium.

In explaining this we picture the heart to have rotated about its longitudinal axis. In describing rotation about this axis we are asked to look *up* at the heart from *under* the diaphragm. Thus if the front of the heart revolves toward the left we have, from our subphrenic viewpoint, **clockwise rotation**. If the front of the heart rotates toward the right we have **counterclockwise rotation**. Clockwise rotation will obviously move the zone between the two ventricles toward the left so that the transitional zone in the precordial tracing shifts to the left (*E* in fig. 5.4), while counterclockwise rotation will shift the transitional zone toward the right (*D* in fig. 5.4). Such rotations are not necessarily abnormal.

Note on Use of Terms "Ventricular Lead" and "Ventricular Pattern"

A precordial record is not derived exclusively from one underlying area of the myocardium. No matter what lead is used, the resulting tracing is always a composite picture, an electrical resultant of all the many simultaneous impulses, or dipoles, that are travelling in various directions through the whole myocardium. It is true that the area of myocardium subjacent to the electrode may make a major contribution to the record—the so-called "local pickup" effect—because an important factor determining recorded voltage is the nearness of the electrode to the electrical force, and therefore a nearby force will exert more influence than a distant one on the pattern produced. As an example, if the electrode is placed at position 6, the impulses travelling through the wall of the left ventricle are appreciably nearer to it than those traversing the right ventricular wall, and the left ventricle therefore exerts a greater influence than the right; but as long as forces continue to be generated in the right ventricular wall, they will be making some contribution to what we have been calling the "left ventricular pattern." The "vector" electrocardiographers (see below) in particular have de-emphasized the "local pickup" effect and rightly point out

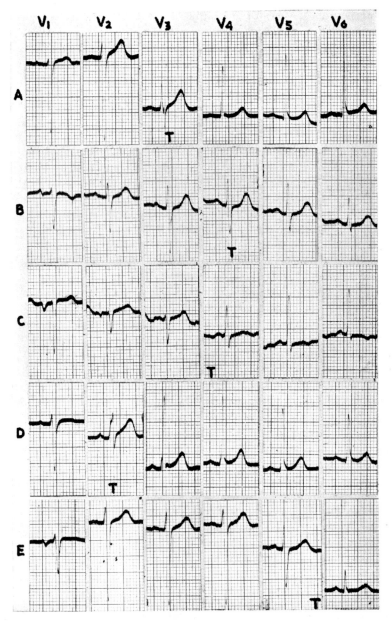

Figure 5.4. Transitional zones (*T*). (*A*, *B* and *C*) Normal transitions. (*D*) Counterclockwise rotation. (*E*) Clockwise rotation.

that, no matter where the electrode is placed, the resulting pattern is a product of the total electrical forces generated in the myocardium and is not derived from the subjacent area of the heart.

In other words, a right or left ventricular pattern means the type of pattern produced *when the electrode is placed over* the right or left ventricle rather than the pattern produced by the subjacent ventricle. Indeed it is obvious that the so-called right ventricular pattern is mainly derived from left ventricular forces (the deep S wave in V_1 represents *left* ventricular depolarization). Provided one appreciates what is meant by right and left ventricular lead and right and left ventricular pattern, these are useful descriptive terms.

A Word about Vectors

The leads so far described are known as "scalar," and the system employing them is scalar electrocardiography. It seems appropriate to give a word of integration with vector electrocardiography (or vectorcardiography). Students of vector methods have introduced ideas that are helpful and illuminating in our everyday reading of scalar tracings, and the beginner should at least be acquainted with vector terminology and should appreciate the close correlation between scalar and vector methods. The two methods are complementary and should not be thought of as rivals.

Vector is a technical term for force and as applied to electrocardiography obviously means electrical force. As all electrocardiography deals exclusively in electrical forces, all electrocardiography is necessarily vectorial. However, by association and implication, the term has become reserved for that form of electrocardiography in which the heart's forces are represented by arrows and loops, rather than by waves and complexes. *Spatial* vectorcardiography indicates that the arrows or loops are disposed in three-dimensional space—not just two-dimensional symbols on paper like the complexes of the scalar tracing.

Like any other force, a vector has size and direction. Both of these attributes can be conveniently embodied in an arrow whose length is proportional to the size of the force. An instantaneous vector represents the resultant of all the heart's electrical forces at a given moment (any of the thin arrows in fig. 5.5 *A* and *B*). The mean vector is the average or resultant of all the instantaneous vectors (thick arrow in fig. 5.5 *B*). The loop (fig. 5.5 *C*) substitutes for a set of innumerable arrows a single continuous line and is obtained by joining up the heads of all the arrows; conversely the instantaneous vector for any given moment can be derived from the loop by drawing an arrow from the "center" of the loop to a point at its periphery.

There are two methods for deriving a vectorcardiogram:

1. The routine 12-lead electrocardiogram can be translated into the necessary vectors from which the loop is artificially constructed. This is the method that Grant[2] popularized and its advantage is that the only equipment it requires is a standard electrocardiograph and a nimble mind. Its disadvantage is that it derives the vectors from only two planes, the frontal (limb leads) and horizontal (precordial leads), and it obviously can provide no additional information that is not contained in the scalar tracing from which it is derived.

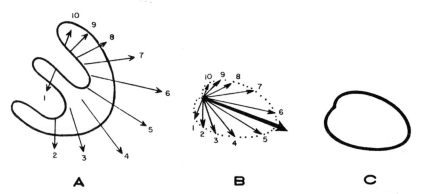

Figure 5.5. The **vector loop**. (*A*) Diagram of successive instantaneous axes (or vectors) as the ventricular muscle mass is depolarized. (*B*) Regrouping of the instantaneous vectors in A as though they all originated from a single "center"; the thick arrow represents the *mean* vector, being the resultant of the 10 instantaneous vectors. If the heads of the vector *arrows* are joined by a continuous line the vector loop is formed (*C*).

2. The loop may be directly written by means of the cathode ray oscillograph. For this purpose electrodes are placed on the torso in such a way that three leads are obtained whose planes are at right angles to each other (orthogonal leads). Thus each of the three planes—frontal, horizontal and sagittal—is equally represented in the resulting vectorcardiogram. As all three planes are represented, this obviously results in additional information in certain cases, and this is the main advantage of the method. Such a vectorcardiogram may be of particular value in distinguishing between right ventricular hypertrophy and right bundle-branch block, and between right ventricular hypertrophy and posterior infarction; and in recognizing atrial abnormalities, lateral ischemia, infarction in the presence of LBBB, and inferior infarction in the presence of left anterior hemiblock.[3] Disadvantages of the method are that the equipment is relatively costly, and that it has little or no place in the diagnosis of arrhythmias.

   Two further points are noteworthy: vectorcardiographers cannot agree on the most suitable placement of electrodes for obtaining the most accurate spatial record though most espouse the Frank system; second, the derived loop cannot contain more information than scalar leads recorded with the same electrode positions; and therefore, if one had adequate experience with such leads, one could obtain all the information that the vectorcardiographer can obtain from the loop. Unfortunately scalar leads of this kind have not received the attention and study they probably deserve.

   In summary, vectorcardiography is an interesting and valuable research tool, necessarily of rather limited clinical value; limited because it affords only modest additional information over conventional scalar leads, because it cannot take the place of conventional tracings in diagnosing arrhythmias, and because of the more expensive equipment it requires. An interesting survey revealed that established experts in vector interpretation achieved greater diagnostic accuracy from scalar tracings than from the corresponding vectorcardiogram.[7]

REFERENCES

1. Grant, R. P.: The relationship between the anatomic position of the heart and the electrocardiogram. A criticism of "unipolar" electrocardiography. Circulation 1953: **7**, 890.
2. Grant, R. P.: *Clinical Electrocardiography. The Spatial Vector Approach.* McGraw-Hill, New York, 1957.
3. Hoffman, I.: Clinical vectorcardiography in adults. Am. Heart J. 1980: **100**, 239 and 373.
4. Johnston, F. D.: The clinical value of vectorcardiography. Circulation 1961: **23**, 297.
5. Milnor, W. R., Talbot, S. A., and Newman, E. V.: A study of the relationship between unipolar leads and spatial vectorcardiograms, using the panoramic vectorcardiograph. Circulation 1953: **7**, 545.
6. Scherlis, L.: Spatial vectorcardiography: 3-dimensional study of electrical forces in heart. Modern Med. 1957: p. 172 (Feb. 1).
7. Simonson, E., et al: Diagnostic accuracy of the vectorcardiogram and electrocardiogram. Am. J. Cardiol. 1966: **17**, 828.

6

Chamber Enlargement

With the genesis of the normal precordial tracing fresh in mind, the natural pattern to turn attention to is that of ventricular hypertrophy. In so doing, one should keep in mind the discouraging fact that the signs of hypertrophy are not sensitive though reasonably specific (see p. 181).

Left Ventricular Hypertrophy

The pattern of left ventricular hypertrophy (LVH) is what one would predict. If the wall of the left ventricle is thicker than normal, the impulse will take longer to traverse it and arrive at the epicardial surface. Therefore the QRS interval will increase toward or to the upper limit of normal, the intrinsicoid deflection may be somewhat delayed over the left ventricle and the voltage of the QRS complexes will increase—producing deeper S waves over the right ventricle and taller R waves over the left (as in the precordial leads in fig. 6.1).

Many criteria have been proposed for the diagnosis of LVH, and they are all unreliable. Though quite specific, they lack sensitivity; according to Devereux,[10, 29] all the usual electrocardiographic and vectorcardiographic criteria attain a limit of about 60% sensitivity when they approach 95% specificity.

The ancient, honorable and much-quoted criterion for LVH proposed by Sokolow and Lyon[37] simply adds the depth of the S wave in lead V_1 to the height of the R wave in either V_5 or V_6 (whichever is the taller), and if the sum amounts to more than 35 mm LVH is present. This criterion correlates well with the thickness of the left ventricular walls and the diameter of the left ventricular cavity as determined by echocardiography.[39]

One of the most popular formulas so far developed is Estes[13] scoring system: (1) *3 points* if the largest R or S wave in the limb leads is 20 mm or more, *or if* the largest S wave in V_1, V_2 or V_3 is 25 mm or more, *or if* the largest R wave in V_4, V_5 or V_6 is 25 mm or more; (2) *3 points* if there is any type of ST shift opposite in direction to the QRS, provided no digitalis is being taken (if digitalis is being taken, the shift must be of classical "strain" type—see below—and only 1 point is scored); (3) *2 points* if there is left axis deviation to −15° or more; (4) *1 point* if the QRS duration is 0.09 sec or more; (5) *1 point* if the

51

intrinsicoid deflection in V_{5-6} begins at 0.04 sec or later; (6) *3 points* if the "P-terminal force" in V_1 is 0.04 or more. With a maximum of 13 points, 5 indicates LVH and 4 probable LVH. For comparison, the criteria proposed by Scott[32-35] are listed in an adjacent "box." For good exercise, apply these three sets of criteria to figures 6.1 to 6.4, assuming that none of these patients was taking digitalis.

Estes' Scoring System for LVH

1. R or S in limb lead: 20 mm or more
   S in V_1, V_2 or V_3 25 mm or more   }   3
   R in V_4, V_5 or V_6 25 mm or more

2. Any ST shift (without digitalis)   3
   Typical "strain" ST-T (with digitalis)   1

3. LAD: $-15°$ or more   2

4. QRS interval: 0.09 sec or more   1

5. I.D. in V_{5-6}: 0.04 sec or more   1

6. P-terminal force in V_1 more than 0.04   3

     Total   13
     (5 = LVH; 4 = probable LVH

Scott's Criteria for LVH[32-35]

Limb leads:

R in 1 + S in 3:	more than 25 mm
R in aVL:	more than 7.5 mm
R in aVF:	more than 20 mm
S in aVR:	more than 14 mm

Chest leads:

S in V_1 or V_2 + R in V_5 or V_6:	more than 35 mm
R in V_5 or V_6:	more than 26 mm
R + S in any V lead:	more than 45 mm

Early in the disease, septal forces (q in leads 1, aVL, V_5 and V_6; r in V_1) tend to increase, but as time goes by and conduction in the left ventricle becomes impaired, they shrink and may disappear (fig. 6.3).[9]

"Strain" is sometimes applied when ST-T-U abnormalities develop. Over the left ventricle (V_5, V_6) the ST segments become depressed with an *upward*

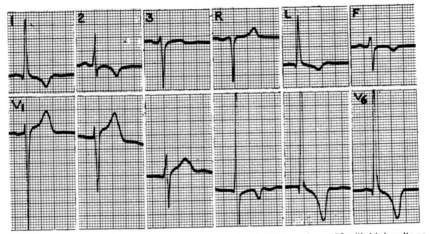

Figure 6.1. Left ventricular hypertrophy and strain. Note: axis −10° with high voltage of QRS complexes in limb and precordial leads; secondary ST-T changes in 1, 2, aVL, aVF and V$_{4-6}$.

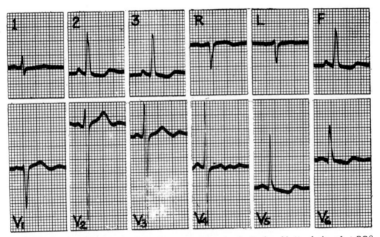

Figure 6.2. Left ventricular hypertrophy and strain. *Note:* Axis of +80° and therefore secondary ST-T changes in 2, 3, aVF and V$_{5-6}$. Notice QRS amplitude of over 40 mm in V$_3$ and V$_4$.

convexity whose final downward curve blends into an inverted T wave (fig. 6.1). The same ST-T changes are usually evident in limb leads having the form (qR) of left ventricular leads. Thus when LVH appears in a heart with left axis deviation, lead 1 and aVL will show ST-T changes (fig. 6.1), whereas in a vertical heart the ST-T changes will appear in lead 3 and aVF (fig. 6.2). If the tracing shows tall R waves in all three standard leads, the ST-T changes may be present in all three. In leads where the QRS is predominantly negative, as in V$_1$, the ST segment is reciprocally elevated with an *upward concavity*. A further example of LVH is seen in figure 6.3 which shows gigantic precordial QRS voltage, loss of q waves in leads 1, aVL, V_5 and V_6 with loss of r in V_1, and characteristic ST-T displacements.

Not uncommonly, the earliest indication of left ventricular strain is inversion of U waves in left ventricular leads (fig. 6.4).

"Strain" is a useful, non-committal term. The exact mechanism that produces its pattern is not completely settled, but there are several factors believed to contribute to it. It is known to develop in those who have shown the pattern of LVH for some time, and the pattern intensifies when dilation and failure set in; its development correlates well with increasing left ventricular mass as determined by echocardiography.[10a] Myocardial ischemia and slowing of intraventricular conduction are important among the factors which probably contribute to the pattern.

Left axis deviation is not an invariable accompaniment of LVH; indeed, significant left axis deviation implies the presence of myocardial disease in the left ventricle apart from pure hypertrophy.[7, 8]

Along with the left ventricle the left atrium also may suffer; in such cases the stigmata of left atrial enlargement (p. 59) may accompany the pattern of ventricular hypertrophy.

Much the commonest cause of LVH is hypertension. Less frequently the pattern is found in aortic stenosis, aortic insufficiency, coarctation of the aorta, hypertrophic cardiomyopathy and occasionally in other conditions.

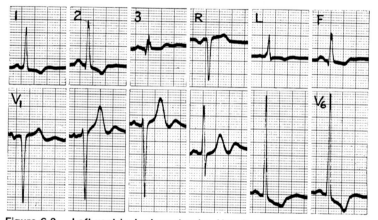

Figure 6.3.   **Left ventricular hypertrophy.** Note huge amplitude of QRS in V_5 and V_6 with high voltage in all chest leads. Axis is $+40°$, and ST-T pattern is typical.

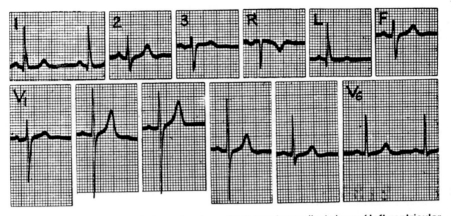

Figure 6.4. From a severely hypertensive patient showing earliest signs of **left ventricular strain**—inverted U waves seen in 1, 2 and V$_{4-6}$, T wave in aVL abnormally low.

Right Ventricular Hypertrophy

When the left ventricle hypertrophies, the normal dominance of the left ventricle becomes exaggerated and we have seen that the associated electrocardiogram reflects this by exaggerating the normal precordial QRS pattern—tall R waves get taller and deep S waves get deeper. On the other hand, when the right ventricle hypertrophies the normal balance of power is upset and finally reversed, and this is reflected in the electrocardiogram by a reversal of the normal precordial pattern—R waves assume prominence in right precordial leads while deepening S waves develop in left precordial leads.

Most of the criteria for recognizing right ventricular hypertrophy (RVH) center around the QRS pattern in the right chest leads. As the right ventricle hypertrophies, there is an increase in the height of right precordial R waves with concomitant decrease in depth of the S wave and consequent increase in the R:S ratio. If this ratio exceeds 1.0, RVH can usually be diagnosed. There is evidence that V$_{4R}$ is a more useful and reliable lead than V$_1$, in that it not infrequently reveals an abnormal ratio of more than 1.0 while that in V$_1$ remains normal.[5] In the fully developed picture of RVH, the precordial pattern is completely reversed so that tall R waves (R, qR or Rs) are written in V_1 with deep S waves (rS) in V_6 (fig. 6.5). An incomplete right bundle-branch block pattern (rSr') in right chest leads may signal RVH; and this pattern seems particularly common in the RVH of mitral stenosis (see fig. 30.1B, p. 456). In the limb leads right axis deviation usually develops and at times prominent Q waves, simulating inferior infarction, appear in leads 2, 3, and aVF (fig. 6.6). In children, the $S_1S_2S_3$ pattern (i.e., S wave deeper than R in all three standard leads) is a reliable index of RVH.[24]

A pattern short of RVH is often seen. This consists in rS complexes all across the precordium (clockwise rotation), with right axis deviation in the limb leads. Such a tracing is seen in many cases of emphysema (fig. 6.7).

Right ventricular "strain" manifests itself in ST-T changes similar to those seen in left ventricular but in different leads, namely in those over the right ventricle (V_1, V_2) and in leads 2, 3 and aVF. The changes of well developed RVH are seen in figures 6.5 and 6.6. In infants, after the first day or two of life, an upright T wave in V_1 is good evidence of RVH.[44]

The fully developed pattern of RVH is much less commonly seen than that of LVH, because the causes of right ventricular overloading are less common and because it requires a greater overload to produce the mature pattern. In LVH the left ventricle is already the "major" ventricle and as it hypertrophies its majority becomes accentuated, so that early hypertrophy is fairly readily seen as an exaggeration of the normal pattern. In RVH, on the other hand, the right ventricle, starting as the minor ventricle, has a good deal of overtaking to do before it becomes the major ventricle and materially alters the tracing.

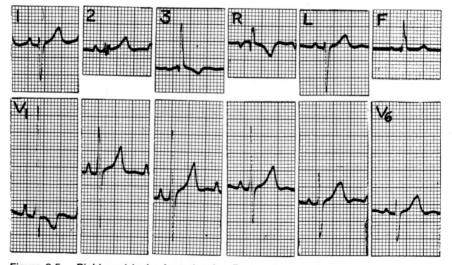

Figure 6.5.   Right ventricular hypertrophy. From a 5-year-old boy with a tetralogy of Fallot. *Note*: Marked right axis deviation (+145°), enormously tall R in V_1 and rS in V_6. The P waves indicate right atrial hypertrophy and are typical for P-congenitale.

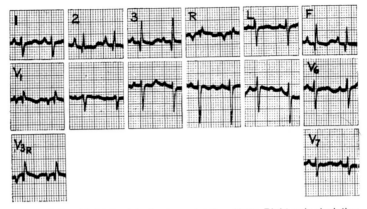

Figure 6.6. Right ventricular hypertrophy. *Note*: Right axis deviation (+130°) with prominent R in V₁; in V₃ᵣ the R:S ratio is definitely greater than 1.0, while rS complexes are seen in the remaining V leads.

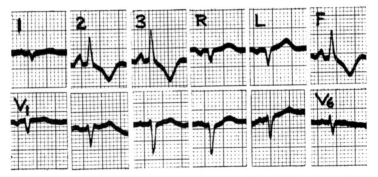

Figure 6.7. From a patient with **emphysema**. *Note*: Right axis deviation (+95°) with rS complexes all across the precordium. The ST-T pattern of right ventricular "strain" is fully developed in leads 2, 3 and aVF. The P-wave pattern suggests P-pulmonale with an axis of +80° and pointed, though not very tall, P waves in 2, 3 and aVF.

In the presence of RVH, the right atrium may also suffer. In such cases the stigmata of right atrial enlargement (p. 58–59) are added to the pattern of ventricular overload. If pure mitral stenosis is the cause of the RVH, the P-mitrale pattern (fig. 30.1*A*, p. 456) may appear.

The main causes of RVH are congenital lesions, such as the tetralogy of Fallot, pulmonic stenosis and transposition of the great vessels; acquired valvular lesions, including mitral stenosis and tricuspid insufficiency; and chronic lung diseases, especially emphysema.

Salient Features of Right Ventricular Hypertrophy
1. Reversal of precordial pattern with tall R over right precordium (V_1, V_2) and deep S over left (V_5, V_6); or rS across precordium
2. QRS interval within normal limits
3. Late intrinsicoid deflection in V_{1-2}
4. Right axis deviation
5. ST segment depression with *upward convexity* and inverted T waves in right precordial leads (V_{1-2}) and in whichever limb leads show tall R waves

Patterns of Systolic and Diastolic Overloading

The patterns of ventricular overload have been subdivided into "systolic overloading" and "diastolic overloading."[3, 4] When the heart has to pump against an obstruction, it is in systole that the strain is felt; when the blood overfills the ventricle, as in aortic regurgitation, the predominant strain is diastolic.

With systolic overloading of the left ventricle, as seen in hypertension and aortic stenosis, the classical pattern of hypertrophy as outlined on pages 51–54 is found, but when the main load is borne in diastole, as in pure aortic regurgitation, mitral regurgitation or in patent ductus, a different pattern appears; this consists of prominent upright T waves as well as tall R waves over the left ventricle (V_{5-6}) as seen in figure 6.8.

With systolic overloading of the right ventricle, as in pulmonic stenosis or pulmonary hypertension, the classical pattern in figure 6.5 is produced; but when the main load is diastolic, as in atrial septal defect, the pattern of complete or incomplete right bundle-branch block (see Chapter 7) results. This pattern apparently does not result from blockade of the right bundle branch but rather results from hypertrophy of the basal portions of the right ventricle.[43]

Combined Ventricular Hypertrophy

Enlargement of both ventricles is suggested if there are voltage criteria for LVH in the chest leads combined with right axis deviation in the limb leads; or if there are criteria for LVH in left chest leads combined with prominent R waves in right chest leads; or if a shallow S wave in V_1 is associated with a strikingly deeper S wave in V_2—the "shallow S-wave syndrome."[35]

Atrial Enlargement

A P-wave axis to the right of $+70°$ ("**P-pulmonale**") suggests right atrial enlargement (RAE) from chronic lung disease; in congenital heart disease with RAE, the axis is usually not so far to the right ("**P-congenitale**"). Both may

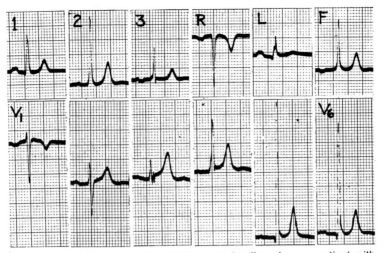

Figure 6.8.   Left ventricular diastolic overloading, from a patient with rheumatic mitral regurgitation. R waves in V_5 and V_6 are unusually tall and are accompanied by tall and pointed T waves. The P waves show P-mitrale pattern, being rather broad and notched with a leftward axis shift to about $-15°$.

show narrow, pointed P waves in limb and right chest leads; but sometimes, when the right auricle enlarges sufficiently to extend toward the left across the front of the heart, the P waves of RAE may be inverted in V_1 and so create the illusion of *left* atrial enlargement (LAE) (see fig. 29.14 on p. 452). In tricuspid disease the P waves may be tall and notched, with first peak taller than second ("**P-tricuspidale**").[14]

Suggestive as these P-wave features are, it is intriguing to realize that QRS criteria are probably better! A qR in V_1 (in the absence of myocardial infarction) correlates best with echocardiographically determined RAE; and the next best criterion is the finding of small QRS voltage in V_1 with abrupt increase (threefold or more) in the QRS voltage in V_2.[28]

In LAE the P wave is often widened to 0.12 sec or more, notched, and its terminal part may be deviated backward and to the left; i.e., it becomes frankly negative in V_1[1] and may become negative in leads 3 and aVF ("**P-mitrale**").[25] The product of width (in seconds) × depth (in millimeters) of the terminal part of PV_1 ("P-terminal force") is used as an index of LAE;[25] if the product is more than 0.04 mm sec, LAE is indicated. The widened P waves are often notched, the interval between peaks being greater than 0.04 sec, in fact fulfilling the criteria for intra-atrial block (see p. 319). Indeed there is good evidence that the pattern of LAE is more often due to a conduction disturbance than to atrial enlargement and it has even been suggested that the term left atrial enlargement be replaced with "intra-atrial conduction defect."[21] In some patients with pure left heart disease, with no reasons for *right* atrial enlargement and every reason for *left*, an unexplained **pseudo-P-pulmonale** pattern may develop.[8]

REFERENCES

1. Arevalo, A. C., et al.: A simple electrocardiographic indication of left atrial enlargement. J.A.M.A. 1963: **185,** 359.
2. Beach, C., et al.: Electrocardiogram of pure left ventricular hypertrophy and its differentiation from lateral ischemia. Br. Heart J. 1981: **46,** 285.
3. Cabrera, E., and Monroy, J. R.: Systolic and diastolic loading of the heart. II. Electrocardiographic data. Am. Heart. J. 1952: **43,** 669.
4. Cabrera, E., and Gaxiola, A.: A critical reevaluation of systolic and diastolic overloading patterns. Prog. Cardiovasc. Dis. 1959: **2,** 219.
5. Camerini, F., et al.: Lead V4R in right ventricular hypertrophy. Br. Heart J. 1956: **18,** 13.
6. Carter, W. A., and Estes, E. H.: Electrocardiographic manifestations of ventricular hypertrophy; a computer study of ECG-anatomic correlations in 319 cases. Am. Heart J. 1964: **68,** 173.
7. Chou, T., et al.: Specificity of the current electrocardiographic criteria in the diagnosis of left ventricular hypertrophy. Am. Heart J. 1960: **60,** 371.
8. Chou, T., and Helm, R. A.: The pseudo P pulmonale. Circulation 1965: **32,** 96.
9. Das, G., et al.: Natural history of electrical interventricular septal force in the course of left ventricular hypertrophy in man. J. Electrocardiol. 1981: **14,** 109.
10. Devereux, R. B., and Reichek, N.: Left ventricular hypertrophy. Cardiovasc. Rev. Rep. 1980: **1,** 55.
10a.Devereux, R. B., and Reichek, N.: Repolarization abnormalities of left ventricular hypertrophy. J. Electrocardiol. 1982: **15,** 47.
11. Davies, H., and Evans, W.: The significance of deep S waves in leads II and III. Br. Heart J. 1960: **22,** 551.
12. Engler, R. L., et al.: The electrocardiogram in asymmetric septal hypertrophy. Chest 1979: **75,** 167.
13. Estes, E. H.: Electrocardiography and vectorcardiography. In *The Heart*, Ch. 21, Ed. 3, edited by J. W. Hurst and R. B. Logue. McGraw-Hill, New York, 1974.
14. Gamboa, R., et al.: The electrocardiogram in tricuspid atresia and pulmonary atresia with intact ventricular septum. Circulation 1966: **34,** 24.
15. Gooch, A. S., et al.: Leftward shift of the terminal P forces in the electrocardiogram associated with left atrial enlargement. Am. Heart J. 1966: **71,** 727.
16. Grant, R. P.: Left axis deviation. Circulation 1956: **14,** 233.
17. Grant, R. P.: Left axis deviation. Mod. Concepts Cardiovasc. Dis. 1958: **27,** 437.
18. Griep, A. H.: Pitfalls in the electrocardiographic diagnosis of left ventricular hypertrophy: a correlative study of 200 autopsied patients. Circulation 1959: **20,** 30.
19. Holt, J. H., et al.: A study of the human heart as a multiple dipole source; IV. Left ventricular hypertrophy in the presence of right bundle branch block. Circulation 1977: **56,** 391.
20. Johnson, J. B., et al.: The relation between electrocardiographic evidence of right ventricular hypertrophy and pulmonary artery pressure in patients with chronic pulmonary disease. Circulation 1950: 31, 536.
21. Josephson, M. E.: Electrocardiographic left atrial enlargement; electrophysiologic, echocardiographic and hemodynamic correlates. Am. J. Cardiol. 1977: **39,** 967.
22. Mazzoleni, A., et al.: Correlation between component cardiac weights and electrocardiographic patterns in 185 cases. Circulation 1964: **30,** 808.
23. McGregor, M.: The genesis of the electrocardiogram of right ventricular hypertrophy. Br. Heart J. 1950: **12,** 351.
24. Moller, J. H., et al.: Significance of the $S_1S_2S_3$ electrocardiographic pattern in children. Am. J. Cardiol. 1965: **16,** 524.
25. Morris, J. J., et al.: P-wave analysis in valvular heart disease. Circulation 1964: **29,** 242.
26. Myers, G. B.: The form of the QRS complex in the normal precordial electrocardiogram and in ventricular hypertrophy. Am. Heart J. 1950: **39,** 637.
27. Parkin, T. W.: Problems in the electrocardiographic diagnosis of ventricular enlargement. Circulation 1962: **26,** 946.
28. Reeves, W. C., et al.: Two-dimensional echocardiographic assessment of electrocardiographic criteria for right atrial enlargement. Circulation 1981: **64,** 387.
29. Reichek, N., and Devereux, R. B.: Left ventricular hypertrophy: relationship of anatomic, echocardiographic and electrocardiographic findings. Circulation 1981: **63,** 1391.
30. Roman, G. T., et al.: Right ventricular hypertrophy. Correlation of electrocardiographic and anatomic findings. Am. J. Cardiol. 1961: **7,** 481.

31. Romhilt, D. W., et al.: A critical appraisal of the electrocardiographic criteria for the diagnosis of left ventricular hypertrophy. Circulation 1969: **40**, 185.
32. Scott, R. C., et al.: Left ventricular hypertrophy. A study of the accuracy of current electrocardiographic criteria when compared with autopsy findings in one hundred cases. Circulation 1955: **11**, 89.
33. Scott, R. C.: The electrocardiographic diagnosis of left ventricular hypertrophy. Am. Heart J. 1960: **59**, 155.
34. Scott, R. C.: The correlation between the electrocardiographic patterns of ventricular hypertrophy and the anatomic findings. Circulation 1960: **21**, 256.
35. Scott, R. C.: Ventricular hypertrophy. Cardiovasc. Clin. 1973: **5(3)**, 220.
36. Scott, R. C.: The electrocardiographic diagnosis of right ventricular hypertrophy; correlation with the anatomic findings. Am. Heart J. 1960, **60**, 659.
37. Sokolow, M., and Lyon, T. P.: The ventricular complex in left ventricular hypertrophy as obtained by unipolar precordial and limb leads. Am. Heart J. 1949: **37**, 161.
38. Soloff, L. A., and Lawrence, J. W.: The electrocardiographic findings in left ventricular hypertrophy and dilatation. Circulation 1962: **26**, 553.
39. Toshima, H., et al.: Correlations between electrocardiographic, vectorcardiographic, and echocardiographic findings in patients with left ventricular overload. Am. Heart J. 1977: **94**, 547.
40. Walker, C. H. M., and Rose, R. L.: Importance of age, sex and body habitus in the diagnosis of left ventricular hypertrophy from the precordial electrocardiogram in childhood and adolescence. Pediatrics 1961: **28**, 705.
41. Walker, I. C., Helm, R. A., and Scott, R. C.: Right ventricular hypertrophy; I. Correlation of isolated right ventricular hypertrophy at autopsy with the electrocardiographic findings. Circulation 1955: **11**, 215.
42. Walker, I. C., Scott, R. C., and Helm, R. A.: Right ventricular hypertrophy; II. Correlation of electrocardiographic right ventricular hypertrophy with the anatomic findings. Circulation 1955: **11**, 223.
43. Walker, W. J., et al.: Electrocardiographic and hemodynamic correlation in atrial septal defect. Am. Heart. J. 1956: **52**, 547.
44. Ziegler, R. F.: The importance of positive T waves in the right precordial electrocardiogram during the first year of life. Am. Heart J. 1956: **52**, 533.

7

Bundle-Branch Block

Of the various forms of intraventricular block, bundle-branch block is most common and best recognized. Other forms result from delayed conduction or block in a subdivision of the left bundle branch (hemiblock—see chapter 8); from diffuse slowing of the impulse throughout the conduction system of one ventricle; or from conduction disturbances in the ventricular wall. In our current state of knowledge, the terms arborization, parietal and periinfarction blocks appear to have outlived their usefulness.[11]

It is appropriate to consider bundle-branch block (BBB) next for two reasons: first, its patterns are in many ways exaggerations of the corresponding ventricular hypertrophy and strain patterns that we have just dealt with; and second, for those whose main interest is the study of arrhythmias and conduction disturbances (for example, coronary care nurses and anesthesiologists), these are the patterns that probably should be mastered first because they provide a morphologic peg on which to hang one's diagnostic hat.

General Principles

If one of the branches of the bundle of His is blocked by disease, the impulse travels down the branch to the other ventricle first. Having activated this ventricle, the impulse spreads through the septum to the ventricle on the side of the block and in turn activates it. In other words, the ventricles will be activated one after the other instead of simultaneously, in series instead of in parallel—as the physicists say.

There are two main situations in which the ventricles are activated successively instead of simultaneously: BBB and ectopic ventricular rhythms. There is, therefore, in these conditions a marked fundamental similarity in the bizarre patterns produced: in each there is prolongation of the QRS interval and the ST segment slopes off in the direction opposite to the main QRS deflection. A premature ventricular beat, a run of ventricular tachycardia and two artificially stimulated ventricular beats are illustrated side by side with bundle-branch block in figure 7.1. The similarity of pattern common to all is evident.

In BBB—since the impulse has to worm its way slowly through the thickness of the septum before the second ventricle can be activated—the QRS interval is prolonged to 0.12 sec or more, and it tends to be more prolonged in left than in right branch block. When the left branch is blocked the impulse reaches the right ventricle punctually but is late in activating the left ventricle. The intrinsicoid deflection over the right ventricle (e.g., in V_1) therefore begins on

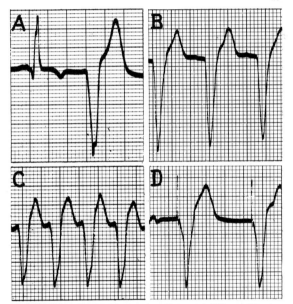

Figure 7.1. Comparison of patterns of (*A*) **ventricular extrasystole,** (*B*) **bundle-branch block,** (*C*) **ventricular tachycardia** and (*D*) ectopic ventricular rhythm driven by **artificial pacemaker.** Note that each pattern has in common (1) prolonged QRS interval and (2) ST segment sloping off to T wave in direction opposite to main QRS deflection.

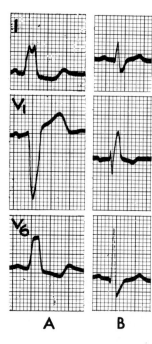

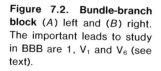

A   B

Figure 7.2. **Bundle-branch block** (*A*) left and (*B*) right. The important leads to study in BBB are 1, V_1 and V_6 (see text).

time, whereas over the left ventricle (e.g., in V_6) this deflection is much delayed (fig. 7.2*A*). On the other hand, when it is the right branch that is blocked, just the reverse occurs—the intrinsicoid deflection is on time in left ventricular leads but is late over the right ventricle (fig. 7.2*B*).

Genesis of the Precordial Pattern in BBB

To understand the genesis of the pattern in the V leads, one must visualize the sliced heart (fig. 7.3) as we did for the normal pattern in Chapter 5. In left bundle-branch block (LBBB), the impulse must enter the right ventricle first and so the septum is activated from right to left. These electrical forces are dominant over the weaker free wall forces of the right ventricle and, since they are travelling away from lead V_1 and toward V_6, they write a negative deflection in V_1 and a positive deflection in V_6. That accounts for approximately the first half of the QRS. Once the septal crossing has been completed, the march continues in the same direction as the impulse activates the left ventricle. Thus it is that in LBBB there is a marked tendency toward monophasic complexes— QS in V_1 and monophasic R in V_6. However, in about 30% of LBBB, a small initial r wave is found in V_1—as in figure 7.2; this is generally explained by assuming that, for some reason, perhaps because septal branches of the RBB are diseased, the free wall of the right ventricle is activated momentarily just before the septum.

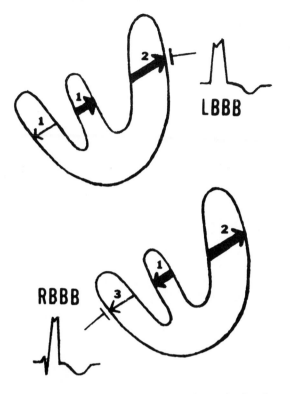

Figure 7.3. Sequence of ventricular activation in BBB. In LBBB (*upper diagram*), the septum is activated (*1*) exclusively from the right side at the same time that the free wall of the right ventricle (*1*) is activated. The meager forces of the free wall are overshadowed by the much stronger septal forces. Once the septum and the right ventricle have been depolarized, the left ventricle alone remains and the direction of its activation (*2*) is similar to that of the septum; hence the complex of LBBB tends to be monophasic and is upright in V_6. In RBBB (*lower diagram*), the septum is first activated, as in the normal heart, from the left side (*1*); a moment later activation begins in the left ventricular free wall (*2*) but, since septal forces are simultaneously spreading in the opposite direction, the free wall deflection (S wave in V_1) is dwarfed. Once the septum and left ventricular free wall have been depolarized, all that is left is the right ventricular free wall. Its feeble forces now have it all their own way and, since they are unopposed, now write the largest deflection of the ventricular complex (R' in V_1).

In right bundle-branch block (RBBB), provided there is no associated delay on the left side, the impulse activates the septum normally on the left and the beginning of the QRS remains normal—r in V_1 and q in V_6. But now, in contrast with the normal state of affairs, there are no opposing forces advancing from the right side to neutralize the left-to-right septal forces and consequently these left-to-right forces are available to oppose those activating the free wall of the left ventricle which normally inscribe a sizeable S wave in V_1. As a result of this opposition, the S wave in V_1 is relatively shrunken and usually measures only 1 to 5 mm in depth (fig. 7.2) as opposed to the usual 7 to 15 mm (fig. 5.4). The height of the R wave in V_6 is not affected to the same extent—probably because of the proximity of the V_6 electrode to the free wall of the left ventricle.

Now comes delayed activation of the right ventricle—the relatively feeble ventricle that normally contributes little to the QRS pattern. But at this point in RBBB, there is nothing left to counteract its feeble forces—the septum and the rest of the left ventricle have already been depolarized—and so it comes into its own with a vengeance and writes the most prominent component of the ventricular complex in V_1: a large, wide R' wave (fig. 7.2). The corresponding S wave in V_6 is much less prominent, probably for two reasons: *distance*—V_6 is comparatively remote from the right ventricle; and *direction*—spread is much more directly toward V_1 than away from V_6.

Classical 12-lead examples of BBB are illustrated in figures 7.4 and 7.5. In the example of LBBB (fig. 7.4), note the *mono*phasic complex (QS in V_1; monophasic R in V_6); in RBBB (fig. 7.5), note the *tri*phasic complexes—rsR' in V_1 and qRs in V_6.

We have seen (p. 44) that the septum is normally activated from the left side first. This fact is responsible for a striking difference between the patterns of left and right BBB: when the right bundle branch is blocked, the impulse still travels normally down the left and as usual activates the left side of the septum first. Because of this, the first part of the QRS in pure RBBB remains normal and unchanged. On the other hand, if the left branch is blocked, the normal initial activation of the septum is disturbed and the first part of the QRS is altered. Normal septal activation writes a Q wave in left chest leads (p. 45) which therefore disappears when LBBB supervenes, and one of the hallmarks of uncomplicated LBBB is this absence of normal Q waves in left precordial leads.

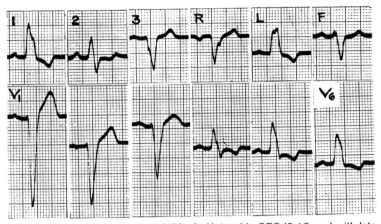

Figure 7.4. Left bundle-branch block. Note wide QRS (0.16 sec) with late intrinsicoid deflection in V_{5-6}. There is left axis deviation with the mean QRS axis $-20°$. Note absence of Q waves in lead 1 and V_{5-6}.

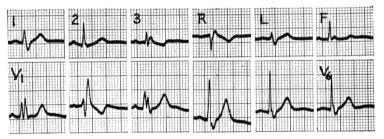

Figure 7.5. Right bundle-branch block. Note wide S_1, M-shaped QRS with late intrinsicoid deflection in V_1 and early downstrokes with wide S waves in V_{5-6}.

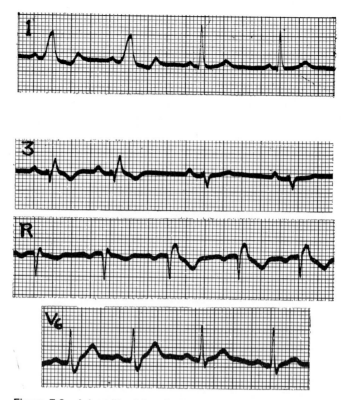

Figure 7.6.   Intermittent bundle-branch block. The first strip is lead 1 from one patient; the remaining three leads are from another patient. In the first strip the first two beats show *left* bundle-branch block; the last two are of normal duration and shape. Note that the initial portion of the blocked QRS complexes differs from the initial part of the normal complexes. In the bottom three strips some complexes show *right* bundle-branch block while others show normal conduction; note that the initial deflection is identical in normal and blocked beats.

    These features are in the tracings in figure 7.6. In the top strip, two complexes showing *left* BBB precede two showing normal intraventricular conduction. Note that the beginning of the blocked QRS is definitely altered compared with the normal QRS. On the other hand, the bottom three strips show intermittent *right* BBB; note in this case that the initial portion of the QRS complex in each lead is identical in both normally conducted and blocked beats.

Limb Leads in BBB

Characteristic, though somewhat less reliable, changes also develop in the limb leads. Leads 1 and aVL usually have the same general features as V_6—not surprising, since these leads have as their positive pole the nearby left shoulder—showing no Q wave and a monophasic R wave in LBBB (figs. 7.2 and 7.4), and a qRs contour in RBBB (fig. 7.2). LBBB is often associated with left axis deviation (LAD) (fig. 7.4), but there is some evidence that this implies additional disease besides the blocked bundle branch. Certainly it is not uncommon to see a normal axis (fig. 7.7), and it is even possible to have frank right axis deviation (RAD) (fig. 7.8). When LBBB is associated with left axis deviation, the prognosis is less favorable than when the axis remains normal.[8, 10]

The *significance* of LAD complicating LBBB is more evident than its *cause*. When LAD is present, the LBBB is associated with a higher incidence of myocardial dysfunction, more advanced disease of the conduction system and an earlier mortality than is LBBB with a normal axis.[8]

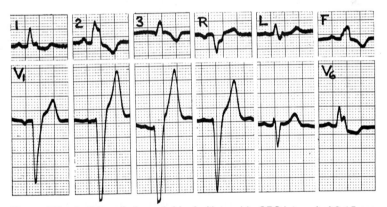

Figure 7.7. Left bundle-branch block. Note wide QRS interval of 0.15 sec with late intrinsicoid deflection in V_6. The mean QRS axis is normal, being about +50°. Note absence of Q waves in leads 1 and V_6.

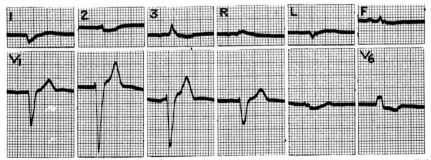

Figure 7.8. Left bundle-branch block. There is *right* axis deviation, but the precordial pattern is typical of *left* bundle-branch block.

Whether LBBB itself produces LAD has been argued for decades. Among 29 men without previous evidence of heart disease, the development of LBBB was associated with a mean leftward shift of the axis of 22 degrees; and the risk of sudden death increased more than 10-fold compared with the control group without LBBB.[31] One explanation for the combination of LBBB with LAD is that the LBBB is incomplete in the presence of anterior hemiblock, though this is probably not the *usual* reason.[39]

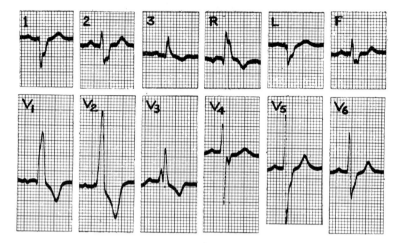

Figure 7.9.   Right bundle-branch block with marked right axis deviation—the "uncommon" type of RBBB.

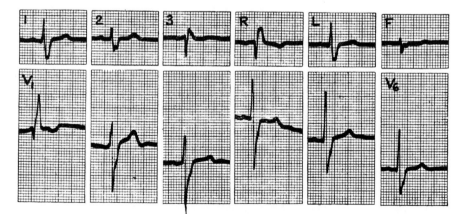

Figure 7.10. The Wilson type of **right bundle-branch block.** Note slender tall R preceding wide S wave in lead 1. Axis of terminal part of QRS is about 180°, while T-wave axis is +15°. QRS-T angle is therefore 165°.

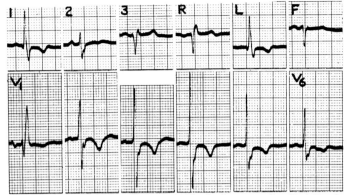

Figure 7.11. Right bundle-branch block. An example with *left* axis deviation. Note the wide S waves in 1 and V_6 and the rsR′ pattern with late intrinsicoid deflection in V_1. Since the T waves in 1, aVL, and V_{2-6} are in the same direction as the terminal QRS forces, these are *primary* T-wave changes (see p. 72).

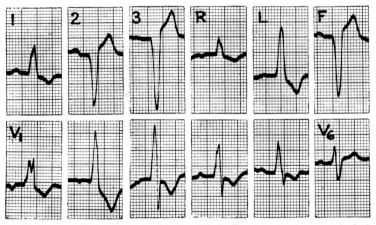

Figure 7.12. Atypical intraventricular block. The limb leads are typical of *left* BBB, while the precordial leads indicate *right* BBB (M-shaped QRS in V_1 with late intrinsicoid deflection; wide S waves in V_6).

RBBB also can be associated with a normal axis or with right or left axis deviation. If the S wave in lead 1 becomes sufficiently deep, and the QRS complex in lead 3 is upright, frank RAD may be produced (fig. 7.9). The common type (sometimes still called Wilson block) presents a tall, slender R wave in lead 1 which exceeds in amplitude the S wave (figs. 7.10 and 7.11). When frank RAD accompanies the RBBB (the "uncommon" type), or when frank left axis appears (figs. 7.11 and 7.12), the cause is usually to be found in an associated block of one of the divisions of the left bundle branch (see Chapter 8).

An interesting hybrid pattern has been described in which the limb leads suggest *left* BBB while the chest leads indicate *right* BBB (fig. 7.12). Such tracings probably represent RBBB with left anterior hemiblock and are associated with extensive disease of the ventricular myocardium.[41]

ST-T Changes

In BBB the T wave is usually directed opposite to the latter portion of the QRS complex; e.g., in figure 7.4 the T wave in lead 1 is inverted while the latter part of the QRS is upright, and in figure 7.10 the T wave in lead 1 is upright while the latter part of the QRS is negative. This opposite polarity is the natural result of the depolarization-repolarization disturbance produced by the block, and the T-wave changes are therefore known as "secondary"—they are part and parcel of the BBB pattern and mean no more than the block itself. If, on the other hand, the direction of the T wave is similar to that of the terminal part of the QRS (fig. 7.13), this is no longer the natural consequence of the conduction disturbance. Such T-wave changes are called "primary" and they imply myocardial disease in addition to the BBB.

One method of gauging the prognostic severity of T-wave changes in BBB is to measure the angle between the axis of the T wave and that of the terminal part of the QRS complex. Obviously, if the two are oppositely directed (as they are with secondary T-wave changes), the angle between them will be wide and may approach 180°. It is proposed[12] that if this angle is less than 110°, serious organic heart disease is indicated. In figure 7.10 the angle is about 165°, whereas in figure 7.13 it is only a few degrees, each axis being close to 180°.

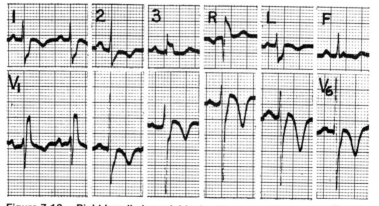

Figure 7.13. **Right bundle-branch block** with primary T-wave changes. The direction of the terminal part of the QRS and that of the T wave are similarly directed in the frontal plane and in V$_{2-6}$.

	Salient features of bundle-branch block:	
Leads	Left Bundle-Branch Block	Right Bundle-Branch Block
V₁	QS or rS	Late intrinsicoid, M-shaped QRS (RSR' variant); sometimes wide R or qR
V₆	Late intrinsicoid, no Q waves, monophasic R	Early intrinsicoid, wide S wave
1	Monophasic R wave, no Q	Wide S wave

Comparison with Ventricular Hypertrophy

The pattern of BBB in many ways is like an exaggeration of the pattern of ventricular hypertrophy. Compare *A*, *B* and *C* in figure 7.14. The differences are that the QRS interval is longer in block, the intrinsicoid deflection over the blocked ventricle is correspondingly later, and the secondary ST-T changes are more pronounced. The QRS deflections in block are often of lower voltage and are more likely to show definite notching than in ventricular hypertrophy and strain. One further important detail should be noted: whereas the normal Q waves over the left ventricle may be present or exaggerated in ventricular hypertrophy, in LBBB these normal Q waves are absent. This is because, as the left branch is blocked, the septum is entirely activated from its right side. Figures 7.14 and 7.15 illustrate how LVH sometimes progresses to LBBB.

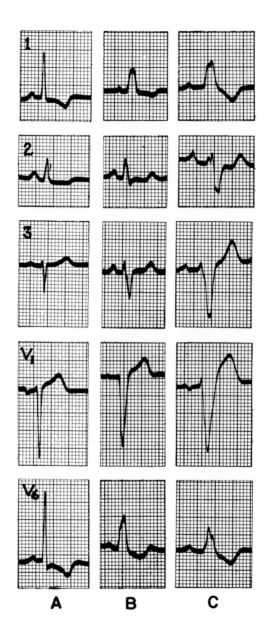

Figure 7.14. Left ventricular hypertrophy and strain (*A*), **incomplete left bundle-branch block** (*B*), and presumably **complete left bundle-branch block** (*C*) compared.

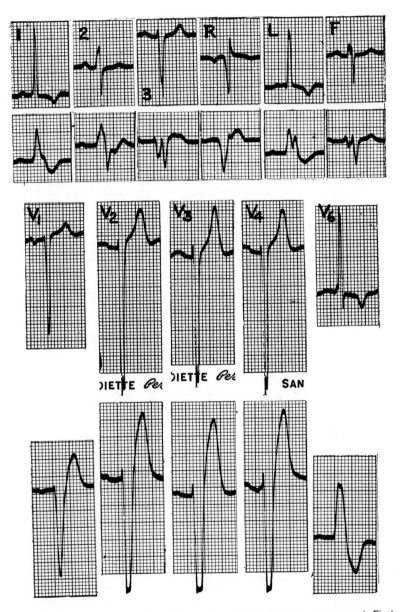

Figure 7.15 Two tracings from the same patient, taken two years apart. First tracing (first and third rows) shows **left ventricular hypertrophy and strain;** because of the initial slurring of R wave and absent Q in leads 1 and V_6 some would call this incomplete LBBB. Second tracing (second and fourth rows) shows fully developed **left bundle-branch block.**

Intermittent and Incomplete BBB

Intermittent bundle-branch block, i.e., prolonged QRS complexes present at times but not at others (fig. 7.6), usually represents a transition stage before permanent block is established.

The designation **incomplete bundle-branch block** has been assigned to those patterns whose QRS intervals place them in the no man's land of 0.10 to 0.11 sec. with a LBBB pattern (fig. 7.14*B*), of 0.09 to 0.10 sec. with RBBB pattern (fig. 7.16).

Sodi-Pallares' criteria[38] for diagnosing incomplete LBBB are initial slurring of the upstroke of the R wave, with or without small preceding Q waves, in left ventricular leads; at a more advanced stage, the Q wave is definitely lost, the slurring is greater and T waves are inverted. All these features are shown in the first tracing in figure 7.15. The incidental finding of the pattern of incomplete RBBB in apparently healthy men carries with it a definite though slight risk that "complete" RBBB will develop.[32]

The problem of secondary R waves (R′) in right precordial leads, in the presence of normal or borderline QRS duration, is sometimes vexing.[24] Are they due to late but physiological activation of the basal region (outflow tract) of the right ventricle, or do they represent abnormal delay in right ventricular activation as a result of incomplete right bundle-branch block or right ventricular hypertrophy? Although there are no foolproof criteria for separating normal from abnormal, the following pointers are helpful[40]:

1. The R′ is probably *normal* if it is present as part of an rSr′ complex in V_1 and/or V_2, but absent in V_{3R} or in a low V_1 taken two interspaces below the conventional V_1 position (fig. 7.17).
2. It is probably *abnormal* if it persists in the lower right precordial leads, or if it is 6 mm. or more tall in V_1 or V_{3R}, or if the R′:S ratio is more than 1.0.

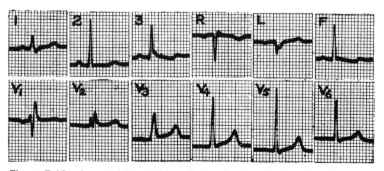

Figure 7.16. Incomplete right bundle-branch block. Note the salient features of the right bundle-branch block pattern—wide S in lead 1 with late intrinsicoid deflection in V_1—but with QRS duration of only 0.10 sec.

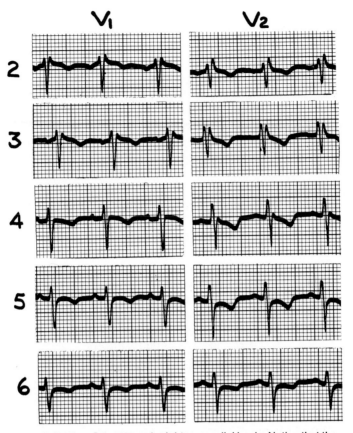

Figure 7.17. rSr′ patterns in right precordial leads. Notice that the r′ wave, present in the higher interspaces, decreases in amplitude and disappears in the lower interspaces. (Figures at the left indicate the interspace in which the electrode was placed.)

Incidence and Etiology

It is generally thought that RBBB is considerably more common than LBBB, and that RBBB is more likely to be found without other evidence of heart disease. But in fact they occur with about the same frequency.[35] In the famous Framingham study, at the initial examination of over 5000 participants, there were 17 with LBBB and 16 with RBBB; and in the subsequent 18 years of follow-up, LBBB developed in 55 while RBBB developed in 70. The majority of both had evidence of cardiovascular disease.[35]

On the other hand, both RBBB and LBBB are occasionally seen in apparently normal hearts.[5, 15, 18, 42] Among 122,000 asymptomatic airmen there were 231 with RBBB and 17 with LBBB; in 44,000 under the age of 25, no instance of LBBB was found.[13]

The common causes of BBB in this country are Lenegre's disease, Lev's disease and ischemic heart disease. In other countries where the condition is indigenous, Chagas' disease is a potent cause of RBBB. Other causes are rheumatic disease, syphilis, trauma, tumors, cardiomyopathy and congenital lesions. As many as 14% of patients with *severe* aortic stenosis may have LBBB.[43] Surgical correction of the tetralogy of Fallot or closure of an uncomplicated ventricular septal defect often produces RBBB.[14]

Transient BBB may occur in acute heart failure, acute myocardial infarction, acute coronary insufficiency and acute infections. Transient RBBB is often produced during right heart catheterization and may complicate monitoring with a Swan-Ganz catheter.[2, 22]

Remember that everything that we call "bundle-branch" block is not necessarily due to a lesion in the branch itself. The fibers destined to form each branch may be involved within the His bundle and so result in the pattern of BBB. This assumption is supported by the facts that *left* fascicular block can be produced, along with RBBB, by a catheter in the *right* ventricle[2]; and that bifascicular (RBBB + left anterior hemiblock) aberration can appear and disappear simultaneously[22]—as though the product of a single central lesion. Further, the fact that pacing the distal His bundle can normalize a RBBB pattern[9] indicates that the lesion causing the BBB is proximal to the pacing site.

Prognostic Considerations

LBBB, statistically at any rate, carries with it a less favorable prognosis than RBBB.[16, 25, 37] It is obvious, however, that the ultimate outlook depends not on the conduction disturbance per se but on the disease that is causing it. Therefore, in any given instance of coronary disease causing BBB, the prognosis should be based, not on which bundle the disease process has happened to affect, but one's estimate of the severity of the underlying coronary disturbance. For example, in acute anteroseptal infarction, the development of RBBB carries with it a mortality of 65%[27, 28]; and the development of block in either bundle branch is a potent predictor of late in-hospital death.[21]

On the other hand, the incidental finding of RBBB in apparently healthy men, even when associated with an axis shift presumably indicating an associated left fascicular block, has no adverse effect on long-term prognosis.[32]

Rate-Dependent BBB

At times intermittent BBB is determined by the heart rate. If the rate accelerates, the R-R interval shortens and the descending impulse may find one of the bundle branches still in its refractory period so that block of that bundle is registered for a few beats (fig. 7.18); if the heart then slows, descending impulses may arrive after the refractory period of the branch is over and normal conduction is resumed. The rate at which conduction changes is known as the "critical rate." Knowledge of this phenomenon is of importance because the

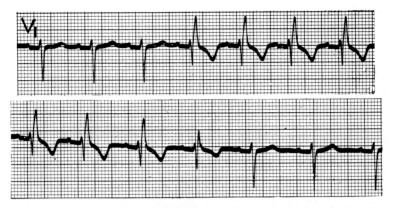

Figure 7.18. Intermittent right BBB—showing "critical rate." As the rate accelerates in the upper strip from 98 to 102, RBBB develops. In the lower strip the RBBB persists as the rate slows to about 90; the first three beats in this strip show presumably complete RBBB, while the fourth shows incomplete RBBB, and then normal conduction resumes. As usual, the critical rate is faster during acceleration than during slowing.

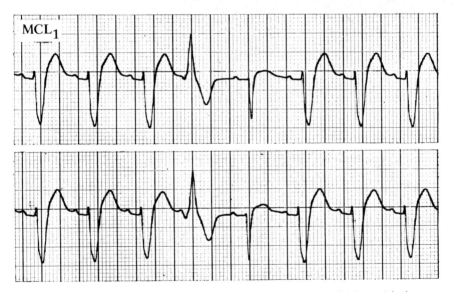

Figure 7.19. Rate-dependent LBBB revealed by the more normal intraventricular conduction at the end of the longer postextrasystolic cycles—the somewhat shorter sinus cycles all end with LBBB.

appearance or disappearance of BBB is often wrongly regarded as evidence of deterioration or improvement when it may be merely the result of a minor rate change. One can also recognize that the BBB is rate-dependent when the longer cycle following an extrasystole permits normal conduction (fig. 7.19).

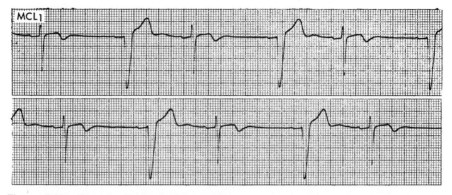

Figure 7.20. Bradycardia-dependent LBBB (paradoxical critical rate). All beats are conducted sinus beats and they are grouped in pairs suggesting 3:2 sinus Wenckebach periods (see p. 325). Those ending the shorter cycles are conducted normally while those ending the *longer* cycles develop LBBB.

Rarely, the intermittent BBB develops only when the cycle lengthens rather than shortens (fig. 7.20); it is then referred to as "paradoxical critical rate" or as "bradycardia-dependent" BBB.[23, 33]

Further discussion of this subject will be found in Chapter 16.

Bilateral Bundle-Branch Block (BBBB)

The patterns of BBBB are varied. If both bundle branches are completely blocked, no impulse can reach the ventricles and the picture is one of complete A-V block. If one branch is completely blocked and the other only partially, the BBB pattern is associated with either a prolonged P-R interval ("first degree A-V block") or dropped beats ("second degree A-V block"). If both bundles are incompletely but equally blocked, only P-R lengthening results with a normal QRS complex. The evidence for BBBB therefore may take five forms:

1. First degree A-V block
2. First degree A-V block + BBB
3. Second degree A-V block + BBB
4. Complete A-V block
5. Sometimes RBBB, sometimes LBBB

Of all of these, only the last is absolute evidence that both bundle branches are involved, since any of the first four manifestations can be produced by blocks other than BBBB.

RSR' Variants and Dominant R Waves in V$_{1-2}$

This is a good place to summarize the causes of RSR' patterns and dominant R waves in right precordial leads[24]:

Causes of RSR' variants in V_{1-2}

1. Occurs in 5 per cent of normal young people[7]
2. Frequently associated with pectus or straight back deformities[6]
3. Incomplete RBBB (fig. 7.16)
4. RV hypertrophy (fig. 30.1*B*)
5. Acute cor pulmonale
6. RV diastolic overloading (fig. 29.7)
7. Wolff-Parkinson-White syndrome
8. Duchenne dystrophy[30]

Causes of dominant R waves in V_{1-2}

1. Occasionally a normal variant
2. RV hypertrophy (fig. 6.5)
3. True posterior (fig. 26.24) or lateral myocardial infarction
4. Wolff-Parkinson-White syndrome (fig. 18.1)
5. Left ventricular diastolic overloading
6. Hypertrophic cardiomyopathy (fig. 29.9)
7. Duchenne dystrophy[30]

REFERENCES

1. Barrett, P. A., et al.: Electrophysiological factors of left bundle-branch block. Br. Med. J. 1981: **45**, 594.
2. Castellanos, A., et al.: Left fascicular blocks during right heart catheterization using the Swan-Ganz catheter. Circulation 1981: **64**, 1271.
3. Chung, K.-Y., et al.: Wolff-Parkinson-White syndrome. Am. Heart J. 1965: **69**, 116.
4. Cokkinos, D. V., et al.: Electrocardiographic criteria of left ventricular hypertrophy in left bundle-branch block. Br. Heart J. 1978: **40**, 320.
5. DeForest, R. E.: Four cases of "benign" left bundle block in the same family. Am. Heart J. 1956: **51**, 398.
6. deLeon, A. C., et al.: The straight back syndrome: clinical cardiovascular manifestations. Circulation 1965: **32**, 193.
7. DePasquale, N. P., and Burch, G. E.: Analysis of the RSR' complex in lead V_1. Circulation 1963: **28**, 362.
8. Dhingra, R. C., et al.: Significance of left axis deviation in patients with chronic left bundle-branch block. Am. J. Cardiol. 1978: **42**, 551.
9. El-Sherif, N., et al.: Normalization of bundle branch block patterns by distal His-bundle pacing. Circulation 1978: **57**, 473.
10. Evans, W., et al.: The significance of deep S waves in leads II and III. Br. Heart J. 1960: **22**, 551.
11. Hecht, H. H.: Atrioventricular and intraventricular conduction: revised nomenclature and concepts. Am. J. Cardiol. 1973: **31**, 232.
12. Henry, E. I., et al.: Significance of the relation of QRS and T waves in bundle branch block: a useful electrocardiographic sign. Am. Heart J. 1957: **54**, 407.
13. Hiss, R. G., and Lamb, L. E.: Electrocardiographic findings in 122,043 individuals. Circulation 1962: **25**, 947.
14. Hobbins, S. M.: Conduction disturbances after surgical correction of ventricular septal defect by the atrial approach. Br. Heart J. 1979: **41**, 289.
15. Johnson, R. L., et al.: Electrocardiographic findings in 67,375 asymptomatic individuals. VI. Right bundle branch block. Am. J. Cardiol. 1960: **6**, 143.

16. Johnson, R. P., et al.: Prognosis in bundle branch block; II. Factors influencing the survival period in left bundle branch block. Am. Heart J. 1951: **41**, 225.
17. Lamb, L. E., et al.: Intermittent right bundle branch block without apparent heart disease. Am. J. Cardiol. 1959: **4**, 302.
18. Lamb, L. E., et al.: Electrocardiographic findings in 67,375 asymptomatic individuals. V. Left bundle branch block. Am. J. Cardiol. 1960: **6**, 130.
19. Lenegre, J.: Etiology and pathology of bilateral bundle branch block in relation to complete heart block. Progr. Cardiovasc. Dis. 1964: **6**, 409.
20. Lepeschkin, E.: The electrocardiographic diagnosis of bilateral bundle branch block in relation to heart block. Progr. Cardiovasc. Dis. 1964: **6**, 445.
21. Lie, K. I., et al.: Early identification of patients developing late in-hospital ventricular fibrillation after discharge from the coronary-care unit; a 5½-year retrospective and prospective study of 1897 patients. Am. J. Cardiol. 1978: **41**, 674.
22. Luck, J. C., and Engel, T. R.: Transient right bundle branch block with Swan-Ganz catheterization. Am. Heart J. 1976: **92**, 263.
23. Massumi, R. A.: Bradycardia-dependent bundle branch block. Circulation 1968: **28**, 1066.
24. Menendez, M. M., and Marriott, H. J. L.: Differential diagnosis of RSR′ and dominant R wave patterns in right chest leads. J.A.M.A. 1966: **198**, 843.
25. Messer, A. L., et al.: Prognosis in bundle branch block. III. A comparison of right and left bundle branch block with a note on the relative incidence of each. Am. Heart J. 1951: **41**, 239.
26. Myers, G. B.: The form of the QRS complex in bundle branch block and in anterolateral infarction. Am. Heart J. 1950: **39**, 817.
27. Norris, R. M., and Mercer, C. J.: Significance of idioventricular rhythm in acute myocardial infarction. Prog. Cardiovasc. Dis. 1974: **16**, 455.
28. Norris, R. M., and Sammel, N. L.: Predictors of late hospital deaths in acute myocardial infarction. Prog. Cardiovasc. Dis. 1980: **23**, 129.
29. Papp. C., and Smith, K. S.: The changing electrocardiogram in Wilson block. Circulation 1955: **11**, 53.
30. Perloff, J. K., et al.: The cardiomyopathy of progressive muscular dystrophy. Circulation 1966: **33**, 625.
31. Rabkin, S. W., et al.: Natural history of left bundle-branch block. Br. Heart J. 1980: **43**, 164.
32. Rabkin, S. W., et al.: The natural history of right bundle branch block and frontal plane QRS axis in apparently healthy men. Chest 1981: **80**, 191.
33. Sarachek, N. S.: Bradycardia-dependent bundle branch block. Am. J. Cardiol. 1970: **25**, 727.
34. Scherf, D.: Intraventricular block. Am. J. Cardiol. 1960: **6**, 853.
35. Schneider, J. F., et al.: Comparative features of newly acquired left or right bundle branch block in the general population: the Framingham study. Am. J. Cardiol. 1981: **47**, 931.
36. Scott, R. C.: Left bundle branch block—a clinical assessment. Am. Heart J. 1965: **70**, 535, 691, and 813.
37. Shreenivas et al.: Prognosis in bundle branch block. I. Factors influencing the survival period in right bundle branch block. Am. Heart J. 1950: **40**, 891.
38. Sodi-Pallares, D.: *New Bases of Electrocardiography*, pp. 289–292. C. V. Mosby, St. Louis, 1956.
39. Swiryn, S., et al.: Electrocardiographic determinants of axis during left bundle branch block: Study in patients with intermittent left bundle branch block. Am. J. Cardiol. 1980: **46**, 53.
40. Tapia, F. A., and Proudfit, W. L.: Secondary R waves in right precordial leads in normal persons and in patients with cardiac disease. Circulation 1960: **21**, 28.
41. Unger, P. N., et al.: The concept of "masquerading" bundle-branch block: an electrocardiographic-pathologic correlation. Circulation 1958: **17**, 397.
42. Vazifdar, J. P., and Levine, S. A.: Benign bundle branch block. Arch. Int. Med. 1952: **89**, 568.
43. Wood, P.: Aortic stenosis. Am. J. Cardiol. 1958: **1**, 553.
44. Wu, D., et al.: Bundle branch block. Demonstration of the incomplete nature of some "complete" bundle branch and fascicular blocks by the extrastimulus technique. Am. J. Cardiol. 1974: **33**, 583.
45. Wyndham, C. R. C., et al.: Epicardial activation in patients with left bundle-branch block. Circulation 1980: **61**, 696.

Sensitivity and Specificity

These are current "buzzwords" in medicine and need to be understood in evaluating the accuracy of a test, e.g., the 12-lead ECG in recognizing ventricular hypertrophy or the treadmill test for identifying the presence of ischemic heart disease.

Sensitivity expresses the ability of a test to recognize a condition: if the test recognizes every single case, it has 100% sensitivity; if it recognizes only half the cases, it has 50% sensitivity. It can be represented by a fraction in which the numerator is the number of cases recognized and the denominator is the actual number of cases in the sample tested (including those that were missed). To express sensitivity as a percentage, you divide the number of cases recognized by the actual number of cases and multiply by 100:

$$\frac{\text{No. cases diagnosed}}{\text{No. cases present}} \times 100 = \% \text{ sensitivity}$$

Specificity expresses the proportion of positive diagnoses that are correct: if the test makes the diagnosis 100 times but in fact only 50 have the diagnosed condition, specificity is only 50%; whereas, if all 100 diagnosed indeed have the condition, then specificity is 100%. Specificity can be represented by a fraction in which the numerator is the number of correctly recognized cases and the denominator is the number that were diagnosed (including the false positives). To express it as a percentage, you divide the number of times the diagnosis was made, correctly and incorrectly, into the number of times it was correct and multiply by 100:

$$\frac{\text{No. correct diagnoses}}{\text{No. diagnoses made}} \times 100 = \% \text{ specificity}$$

Thus, one may say that sensitivity is limited by false negatives and specificity by false positives.

8

The Hemiblocks and Trifascicular Block

The development of the concepts of hemiblock and trifasicular block is described by Uhley[37] as "one of the most interesting events in the modern history of cardiology."

The Hemiblocks

In a fascinating series of publications, beginning with a 730-page treatise in Spanish and culminating in a 260-page condensation and update in English,[23-34] Rosenbaum popularized the concept of "hemiblock"—his name for block of one of the two main divisions of the left bundle branch (LBB).

The term is neat, comes trippingly to the tongue, and is undoubtedly here to stay, but there has been considerable debate concerning its propriety. First of all, on analogy with kindred words like hemisphere meaning half-a-sphere, hemiblock ought to mean half-a-block or about the distance that a man with severe angina can walk before his pain comes on, rather than block of half a bundle-branch system. Then again, since most hearts appear to have three major divisions of the left branch rather than two,[8, 9] the lesion represents block of a third rather than a half. And the anatomical purists, because of the spatial relationship of the divisions and the territories they supply, would prefer "anterosuperior" and "posteroinferior" as more accurate descriptive terms than plain "anterior" and "posterior" (fig. 8.1). Because of these several grounds for criticism, a significant conclave of critics would rather we talked of "anterosuperior fascicular block" (instead of anterior hemiblock) and "posteroinferior fascicular block" (instead of posterior hemiblock). In deference to Rosenbaum's work, the fewer syllables and the much more common usage, I shall retain the anatomically less accurate term, hemiblock. Moreover, since, as yet, there are no "right" hemiblocks, I shall omit prefixing "left" and refer simply to anterior and posterior hemiblock.

84

Genesis of Hemiblock Patterns

Subsequent investigators have made it clear that in many, if not most, hearts there are three significant divisions—anterior, posterior and centriseptal—in the LBB system,[8, 9] as in fact Tawara clearly depicted as early as 1906. But activation of the septum exerts little influence on the frontal plane axis and so, from the point of view of axis shifts, the bifascicular concept remains a useful one electrocardiographically. Others[9] regard the LBB as a fanlike structure in most hearts with no clear-cut subdivisions. Histologically, however, the patterns of hemiblock are associated with diffusely distributed lesions in the LBB system and localization of the pathological lesion cannot in fact be inferred from the ECG.[22, 35]

The anterior (or superior) division of the LBB runs toward the anterior papillary muscle; the posterior (or inferior) division, toward the posterior papillary muscle; and the septal division initiates activation of the midseptum.

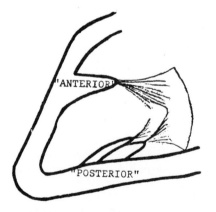

Figure 8.1. The "anterior" papillary muscle of the left ventricle is above, rather than anterior to, the "posterior" papillary muscle.

Figure 8.2 diagrams an approximate frontal view of the left ventricle with the anterior and posterior fascicles of the LBB heading toward their respective papillary muscles. If the anterior division is blocked, as in the left-hand diagram, the initial activation of the myocardium begins at the root of the posterior papillary muscle and travels, from endocardium to epicardium as ventricular activation always proceeds, downward and rightward inscribing, therefore, an r wave in leads whose positive electrode is on the leg (i.e., 2, 3 and aVF) and a q wave in leads whose positive electrode is on the left arm (leads 1 and aVL). Although this q wave is a logical and appropriate element of the anterior hemiblock pattern, it is not absolutely essential to the diagnosis.[12] To activate the rest of the ventricle from this inferior site, the remaining forces must spread upward and to the left; in so doing, they produce a dominant R

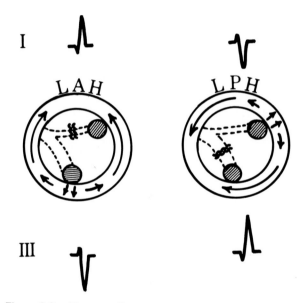

Figure 8.2.   Diagrams illustrating the hemiblock patterns in the limb leads: left anterior hemiblock (LAH) and left posterior hemiblock (LPH). The "anterior" papillary muscle is above and lateral to the "posterior" papillary muscle and the two divisions of the LBB course towards their respective papillary muscles. Thus, if the anterior division is blocked, initial electromotive forces are directed downwards and to the right, inscribing a Q wave in leads 1 and aVL and an R wave in leads 2, 3 and aVF. The subsequent forces are directed mainly upwards and to the left, writing an R wave in 1 and aVL and an S in 2, 3 and aVF, to produce a left axis deviation. In LPH, the initial forces spread upwards and to the left to write an R in 1 and aVL and a Q in 2, 3 and aVF while subsequent forces are directed downwards and to the right to produce right axis deviation.

wave in leads 1 and aVL; a dominant S wave in leads 2, 3 and aVF; and a left axis shift of approximately −60°.

If the posterior fascicle is blocked, the situation is reversed, as depicted in the right-hand diagram. Now initial activation begins at the root of the anterior papillary muscle and first travels upward and to the left, from endocardium to epicardium, inscribing an r wave on leads 1 and aVL and a q wave in leads 2, 3 and aVF. To activate the rest of the left ventricle from this superolateral site, the remaining forces must spread downward and to the right; in so doing, they produce a dominant R wave in leads 2, 3 and aVF; a dominant S wave in leads 1 and aVL; and a right axis shift to about +120°.

In the diagnosis of anterior hemiblock, an additional criterion was added to Rosenbaum's original set by the Mexico school[20]: a delayed intrinsicoid deflection (beyond 0.045 sec) and slurred R wave in aVL. In posterior hemiblock the intrinsicoid deflection is similarly delayed in aVF.

Both hemiblocks, if they are pure, i.e., not complicated by right bundle-branch block (RBBB), will have QRS complexes of normal duration. This is because there is a rich intercommunication between the territories of the fascicles consisting of rapidly conducting Purkinje tissue; and so, although the mean direction of ventricular activation changes dramatically, according to Rosenbaum its duration is little prolonged—at most 0.01 or 0.02 sec, although later work indicates an *average* QRS lengthening of 0.025 sec.[12] From the frontal plane viewpoint, normal ventricular activation spreads simultaneously from two foci (at the roots of the papillary muscles), and many forces are, therefore, travelling in opposite directions and neutralizing each other's influence—the phenomenon of "cancellation." But in the presence of hemiblock, activation of the ventricle proceeds from one site instead of two, and so cancellation is reduced and the amplitude of the ventricular complex increases, sometimes markedly as in Figs. 8.3 and 8.4.

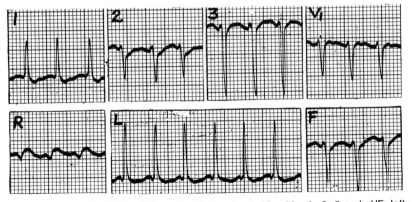

Figure 8.3. Anterior hemiblock: Note q in 1 and aVL with r in 2, 3 and aVF; left axis shift of −60°; normal QRS duration (0.08 sec); large voltage, especially in 3 and aVL, imitating left ventricular enlargement.

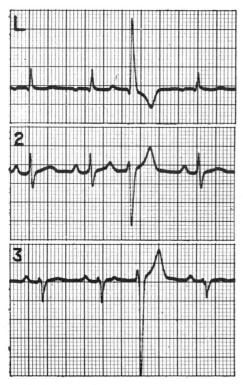

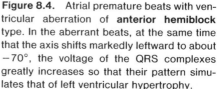

Figure 8.4. Atrial premature beats with ventricular aberration of **anterior hemiblock** type. In the aberrant beats, at the same time that the axis shifts markedly leftward to about −70°, the voltage of the QRS complexes greatly increases so that their pattern simulates that of left ventricular hypertrophy.

Besides being good examples of the increased ventricular voltage occasioned by hemiblock, the tracings in figures 8.3 and 8.4 show typical features of anterior hemiblock. In figure 8.3, note the q waves in leads 1 and aVL; the r waves in leads 2, 3 and aVF; the late intrinsicoid deflection in aVL; and the axis of −60°. In figure 8.4, the first two beats in each lead are sinus beats followed by an atrial premature beat that manifests anterior hemiblock aberration. Apart from the gigantic voltage assumed by the aberrant beat, note the q in aVL and the r in 2 and 3 as well as the superior ("leftward") swing of the aberrant axis.

The cardinal features of pure hemiblock are summarized in the boxes. Note that for left posterior hemiblock (LPH) a special criterion is required: there must be no evidence of or reason for right ventricular hypertrophy. This additional criterion is necessary because right ventricular hypertrophy itself can produce exactly the same pattern in the limb leads as LPH (fig. 29.6, p. 446).

Bifascicular Block

Anterior hemiblock is often and posterior hemiblock is usually accompanied by RBBB, and in either case the resulting duo is a "bifascicular block." In such combinations, of course, the QRS is no longer normally narrow, as it is in the lone hemiblock, but is widened by the associated RBBB. Figures 8.5 and 8.6 present typical examples of RBBB with anterior hemiblock, and figure 8.7

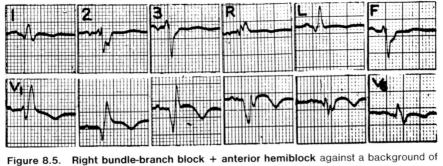

Figure 8.5. **Right bundle-branch block + anterior hemiblock** against a background of extensive anterior infarction.

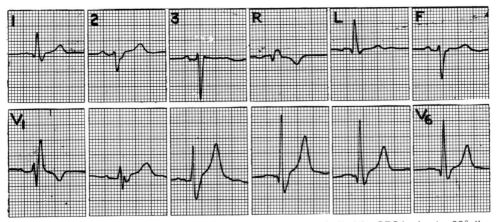

Figure 8.6. **Anterior hemiblock with RBBB.** The axis of the first half of the QRS is about −60°; the QRS interval is widened to 0.15 sec by the RBBB.

Criteria for Left Anterior Hemiblock

1. LEFT axis deviation (usually −60°)
2. Small Q in lead 1 and aVL, small R in 2, 3 and aVF
3. Normal QRS duration
4. Late intrinsicoid deflection aVL (>0.045)
5. Increased QRS voltage in limb leads

Criteria for Left Posterior Hemiblock

1. RIGHT axis deviation (usually +120°)
2. Small R in lead 1 and aVL, small Q in 2, 3 and aVF
3. Normal QRS duration
4. Late intrinsicoid deflection aVF (>0.045)
5. Increased QRS voltage in limb leads
6. No evidence for right ventricular hypertrophy

1/15/67

4/3/68

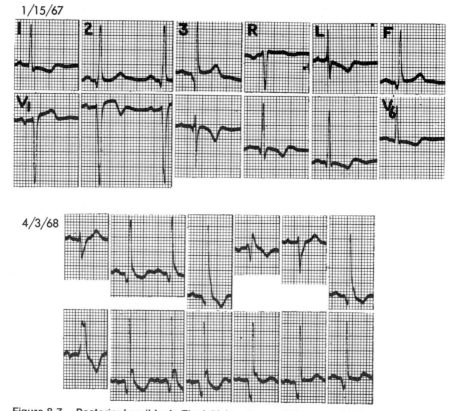

Figure 8.7. Posterior hemiblock. The initial tracing exhibits a normal axis with pathological Q waves in anterior (V_{3-5}) and inferior (2, 3 and aVF) leads. The later tracing illustrates widespread development of wide Q waves in the precordial leads with RBBB and marked right axis deviation, presumably due to left posterior hemiblock.

illustrates the combination of RBBB with posterior hemiblock. In determining the axis in the presence of RBBB, remember to use only the first half of the QRS because a hemiblock involves only left ventricular activation and, in the presence of RBBB, the second half of the QRS is, of course, inscribed by delayed right ventricular activation. Another point worth mentioning is that a hemiblock can upset the "rabbit ears" (see Chapter 11) of RBBB. In figure 8.8, both in V_1 and in the MCL_1 rhythm strip, the left rabbit ear is taller than the right—usually a hallmark of ventricular ectopy. Hemiblock is probably the commonest cause of reversing aberrant rabbit ears and so simulating ectopy.

From time to time, authors have referred to block involving both the right bundle branch and one of the divisions of the left branch as bilateral bundle-branch block (BBBB). But it is better to reserve this term for the situation when the right bundle branch and the main left bundle branch are simultaneously involved; and, when the block on the left side involves only one fascicle of the left branch system, to adhere to the term "bifascicular" block.

Incidence and Prognosis

Anterior hemiblock is much more common than posterior. During the 15 years that Rosenbaum and his colleagues were amassing nearly 900 examples of anterior hemiblock, they encountered only 30 of posterior hemiblock. This degree of preponderance was not found, however, when Kulbertus[14] deliberately induced ventricular aberration: in the course of inducing 116 instances of ventricular aberration by premature atrial stimulation, he produced 38 instances of anterior hemiblock and 22 of posterior hemiblock aberration. Reasons that have been advanced to explain the greater vulnerability of the anterior division include the fact that it is longer and thinner than the posterior fascicle, it is subjected to the stresses and strains of an outflow tract structure, and it has but a single blood supply.

Anterior hemiblock is usually found in people with hearts that are otherwise normal[5] and does not seem to affect longevity. However, there is evidence that men with such axes have a slight but definitely greater risk than average of later developing RBBB.[21] Like BBB, hemiblock may be caused by Lenegre's or

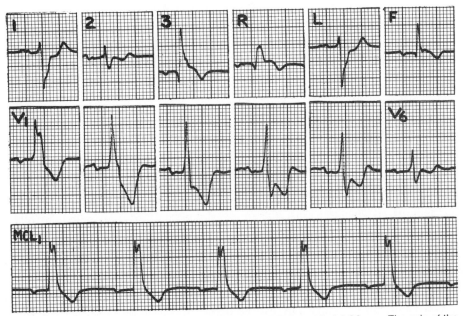

Figure 8.8. Posterior hemiblock with RBBB and a P-R interval of 0.22 sec. The axis of the first half of the QRS is about +120°; the QRS interval is widened to 0.14 sec by the RBBB. Note that the QRS complex peaks early (taller left "rabbit ear") in V₁ and MCL₁ simulating ventricular ectopy.

Lev's disease, aortic valve calcification, cardiomyopathy, or ischemic heart disease. It was found in 17% of 250 consecutive patients with acute myocardial infarction.[18] Temporary hemiblock may result from cardiac catheterization, selective coronary arteriography,[10] or hyperkalemia.[4] Anterior hemiblock may accompany the permanent RBBB that results from surgical correction of the tetralogy of Fallot.[30]

In the past, experts have argued that the development of left bundle branch block (LBBB) does not significantly shift the electrical axis; others have claimed that LBBB can produce significant left axis deviation. Judging by Rosenbaum's study[26] of 98 patients with intermittent LBBB, in which blocked and unblocked complexes could be examined side by side, LBBB often produces a significant left axis shift, sometimes produces even right axis deviation, and leaves the axis unchanged in only a minority.

The combination of LBBB with marked left axis shift is undoubtedly sometimes produced by anterior hemiblock complicating *incomplete* LBBB[26] though, as indicated in the last chapter, this is probably not the usual mechanism.

Miming and Masking

One of the most interesting and important features of the hemiblocks is their ability to both mask and mimic patterns of structural disease. Anterior hemiblock can mask anterior and inferior infarctions,[6, 13] left ventricular hypertrophy, and RBBB[34]; it can imitate anterior[17] and lateral infarctions and left ventricular hypertrophy. Most of these counterfeits are only half-hearted imitations, however, and can often be seen through; but some deceptions may be perfect.

Anterior hemiblock can completely mask inferior infarction by preventing the development of Q waves in leads 2, 3 and aVF. In figure 8.9, the Q waves of inferior infarction are replaced by R waves in the first premature beat in leads 2 and 3 when anterior hemiblock aberration is superimposed on the RBBB. Anterior hemiblock can mask anterior infarction by adding a little r wave to a previous QS complex: If the V_1 or V_2 electrode is placed relatively low, the initial downward forces of anterior hemiblock (fig. 8.2) approach the low-lying electrode and so inscribe an initial positive deflection. The relatively low placement of the chest electrodes in the presence of anterior hemiblock can also mask RBBB[34] which can also be obscured by posterior hemiblock.[16] When RBBB is camouflaged by anterior hemiblock, its presence may be suspected if the QRS interval is wider than expected with hemiblock alone, and confirmed by obtaining high right-sided chest leads which show the typical terminal R'.[34]

Left ventricular hypertrophy can be deprived of one of its salient features when anterior hemiblock lowers the QRS voltage in left chest leads.

Figures 8.3 and 8.4 are excellent examples of the way in which anterior hemiblock can mimic left ventricular hypertrophy in the limb leads. It can imitate anteroseptal infarction by producing a small q wave in front of the

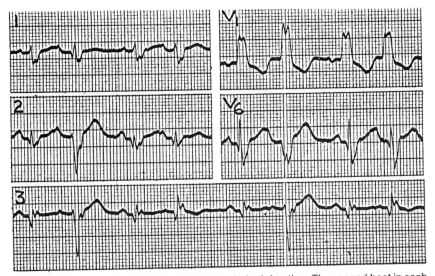

Figure 8.9. Atrial bigeminy with RBBB and inferior infarction. The second beat in each lead, and the sixth beat in lead 3, show **anterior hemiblock** aberration as well. In the limb leads, the development of left anterior hemiblock eliminates the Q waves in leads 2 and 3 and so masks the inferior infarction. (Reproduced from *Hemiblock Lecture Slides*, Tampa Tracings, Oldsmar, Fla., 1971.)

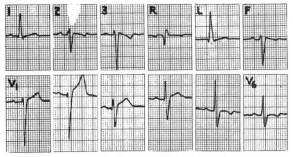

Figure 8.10. **Anterior hemiblock,** axis −60. The q waves in V_{2-3} are probably secondary to the hemiblock rather than anteroseptal infarction.

normal r wave in V_2 and V_3[17] (fig. 8.10): If the electrode is placed relatively high, the initial downward forces of anterior hemiblock (fig. 8.2) move away from the high electrode and so inscribe an initial negative deflection. Anterior hemiblock imitates lateral infarction only to the extent that it causes a Q wave to appear in leads 1 and aVL and shrinks the R wave in V_{5-6}.

	Miming and Masking by Hemiblocks	
	Can Mimic	*Can Mask*
LAH	Anterior infarction	Anterior infarction
	Lateral infarction	Inferior infarction
	Left ventricular	Left ventricular
	hypertrophy	hypertrophy
		RBBB
LPH	Anterior infarction	Anterior infarction

The diagnosis of anterior hemiblock in the presence of inferior infarction presents problems[2, 3, 11]: both produce left axis deviation (LAD), the hemiblock with S waves, the infarction with Q waves in leads 2, 3 and aVF (fig. 8.11). But if the axis is as far leftward as $-60°$, the hemiblock is almost certainly present, with or without the infarction, and it is unlikely to be infarction alone.[11] Also in anterior hemiblock, the QRS in lead 2 ends with a deep S wave and never has a terminal r wave; whereas a terminal r or R in aVR is common. These two features are characteristic of hemiblock, whether or not inferior infarction is also present.

The hemiblocks have written a new and exciting chapter in the annals of intraventricular conduction; but there is still much to learn, and it is only fair to point out that in some patients with hemiblock who have come to autopsy, the location of lesions in the LBB system does not always live up to electrocardiographic expectations.[22, 35]

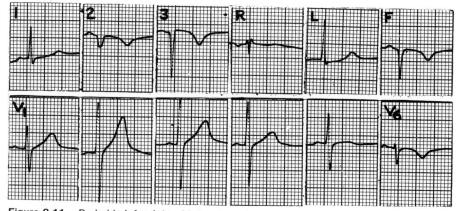

Figure 8.11. Probable **inferolateral infarction** and **anterior hemiblock.** The QS complexes and T-wave inversion in 2, 3 and aVF are diagnostic of inferior infarction, and probable lateral wall involvement is suggested by the shrunken r wave and inverted T wave in V₆. The axis of $-60°$ with terminal r' in aVR and absence of terminal R in 2, 3 and aVF speak for anterior hemiblock.

Trifascicular Block

Semantically, this term can be appropriately applied to simultaneous block, complete or incomplete, in any three of the five ventricular conducting fascicles (His bundle, RBB, LBB, anterior and posterior divisions of the LBB); but it is specifically applied to block simultaneously involving the three peripheral fascicles—the RBB and the two divisions of the LBB. Its manifestations are therefore varied and include all the eight possible combinations of complete and incomplete block in these three fascicles (see table 8.1). If all three fascicles are completely blocked, "complete A-V block" results. If the RBB and the anterior division block completely while the posterior division blocks incompletely, the pattern of RBBB + left anterior hemiblock with "first degree A-V block" appears; and so on.

Table 8.1 lists the eight possible combinations with some of their electrocardiographic expressions. When incomplete block involves two or more fascicles, the number of possible variations is multiplied. For example, combination 8, with incomplete block in all three fascicles, could produce *any* of the expressions of trifascicular block, depending on the *relative* degree of incomplete block in each fascicle.

Notice that this whole concept of trifascicular block ignores the conducting potential of the septal fascicle. The term continues to enjoy common use long since the realization that the ventricular conduction system is usually *quadrifascicular*.

Table 8.1
Manifestations of Trifascicular Block [a]

Combination	RBB	LAD	LPD	ECG Expression
1	C	C	C	complete AVB
2	C	C	I	RBBB + LAH + "AVB"
3	C	I	C	RBBB + LPH + "AVB"
4	I	C	C	LBBB + "AVB"
5	C	I	I	various combinations
6	I	C	I	depending upon relative
7	I	I	C	degrees of incomplete
8	I	I	I	fascicular block

[a] *Key:* C = completely blocked, I = incompletely blocked, and "AVB" = manifestations of first or second degree A-V block.

REFERENCES

1. Anderson, R. H., and Becker, A. E.: Gross morphology and microscopy of the conducting system. In *Cardiac Arrhythmias: Their Mechanisms, Diagnosis and Management*, p. 12, edited by W. J. Mandel. J. B. Lippincott, Philadelphia, 1980.
2. Benchimol, A., et al.: Coexisting left anterior hemiblock and inferior wall myocardial infarction; vectorcardiographic features. Am. J. Cardiol. 1972: **29**, 7.
3. Castellanos, A., et al.: Diagnosis of left anterior hemiblock in the presence of inferior wall myocardial infarction. Chest 1971: **60**, 543.
4. Cohen, H. C., et al.: Disorders of impulse conduction and impulse formation caused by hyperkalemia in man. Am. Heart J. 1975: **89**, 501.

5. Corne, R. A.: Significance of left anterior hemiblock. Br. Heart J. 1978: **40**, 552.
6. Cristal, N., et al.: Left anterior hemiblock masking inferior myocardial infarction. Br. Heart J. 1975: **37**, 543.
7. Das, G.: Left axis deviation; a spectrum of intraventricular conduction block. Circulation 1976: **53**, 917.
8. Demoulin, J. C., and Kulbertus, H. E.: Histopathological examination of concept of left hemiblock. Br. Heart J. 1972: **34**, 807.
9. Durrer D, et al: Total excitation of the human heart. Circulation 1970: **41**, 899.
10. Fernandez, F., et al.: Electrocardiographic study of left intraventricular hemiblock in man during selective coronary arteriography. Am. J. Cardiol. 1970: **26**, 1.
11. Fisher, M. L., et al.: Left anterior fascicular block; electrocardiographic criteria for its recognition in the presence of inferior myocardial infarction. Am. J. Cardiol. 1979: **44**, 645.
12. Jacobson, L. B., et al.: An appraisal of initial QRS forces in left anterior fascicular block. Am. Heart J. 1979: **94**, 407.
13. Kourtesis, P: Incidence and significance of left anterior hemiblock complicating acute inferior wall myocardial infarction. Circulation 1976: **53**, 784.
14. Kulbertus, H. E., et al: Vectorcardiographic study of aberrant conduction. Anterior displacement of QRS: another form of intraventricular block. Br. Heart J. 1976: **38**, 549.
15. Leachman, R. D., et al.: Electrocardiographic signs of infarction masked by coexistent contralateral hemiblock. Chest 1972: **62**, 542.
16. Loperfido, F., et al.: An unusual ECG pattern; left posterior fascicular block obscuring a right ventricular conduction defect. J. Electrocardiol. 1981: **14**, 97.
17. Magram, M., and Lee, Y.-C.: The pseudo-infarction pattern of left anterior hemiblock. Chest 1977: **72**, 771.
18. Marriott, H. J. L., and Hogan, P.: Hemiblock in acute myocardial infarction. Chest 1970: **58**, 342.
19. Massing, G. K., and James, T. N.: Anatomical configuration of the His bundle and bundle branches in the human heart. Circulation 1976: **53**, 609.
20. Medrano, G. A., et al: Clinical electrocardiographic and vectorcardiographic diagnosis of the left anterior subdivision block isolated or associated with right bundle-branch block. Am. Heart J. 1972: **83**, 447.
21. Rabkin, S. W., et al.: Natural history of marked left axis deviation (left anterior hemiblock). Am. J. Cardiol. 1979: **43**, 605.
22. Rizzon P., et al: Left posterior hemiblock in acute myocardial infarction. Br. Heart J. 1975: **37**, 711.
23. Rosenbaum, M. B.: Types of right bundle branch block and their clinical significance. J. Electrocardiol. 1968: **1**, 221.
24. Rosenbaum, M. B.: Types of left bundle branch block and their clinical significance. J. Electrocardiol. 1969: **2**, 197.
25. Rosenbaum, M. B., et al.: Five cases of intermittent left anterior hemiblock. Am. J. Cardiol. 1969: **24**, 1.
26. Rosenbaum, M. B., et al.: The mechanism of bidirectional tachycardia. Am. Heart J. 1969: **78**, 4.
27. Rosenbaum, M. B., et al.: Intraventricular trifascicular blocks. The syndrome of right bundle branch block with intermittent left anterior and posterior hemiblock. Am. Heart J. 1969: **78**, 306.
28. Rosenbaum, M. B., et al.: Intraventricular trifascicular blocks. Review of the literature and classification. Am. Heart J. 1969: **78**, 450.
29. Rosenbaum, M. B.: The hemiblocks: diagnostic criteria and clinical significance. Mod. Concepts Cardiovasc. Dis. 1970: **39**, 141.
30. Rosenbaum, M. B., et al.: Right bundle branch block with left anterior hemiblock surgically induced in tetralogy of Fallot. Am. J. Cardiol. 1970: **26:** 12.
31. Rosenbaum, M. B., et al.: *The Hemiblocks: New Concepts of Intraventricular Conduction Based on Human Anatomical, Physiological, and Clinical Studies.* Tampa Tracings, Oldsmar, Fla., 1970.
32. Rosenbaum, M. B., et al.: Anatomical basis of AV conduction disturbances. Geriatrics 1970: **25**, 132.
33. Rosenbaum, M. B., et al.: Right bundle branch block with left anterior hemiblock surgically

induced in tetralogy of Fallot. Am. J. Cardiol. 1970: **26,** 12.

34. Rosenbaum, M. B., et al.: Left anterior hemiblock obscuring the diagnosis of right bundle branch block. Circulation. 1973: **48,** 298.
35. Rossi, L.: Histopathology of conducting system in left anterior hemiblock. Br. Heart J. 1976: **38,** 1304.
36. Sclarovsky, S., et al.: Left anterior hemiblock obscuring the diagnosis of right bundle branch block in acute myocardial infarction. Circulation 1979: **60,** 26.
37. Uhley, H. N.: The concept of trifascicular intraventricular conduction; historical aspects and influence on contemporary cardiology. Am. J. Cardiol. 1979: **43,** 643.

And Now Arrhythmias*

Detection of Arrhythmias

Since the early 1960s, great strides have been made in the detection and identification of arrhythmias. The introduction of coronary care units (May 1962) was a tremendous stimulus and since that time methods have multiplied and been refined. Until then, the "last word" in diagnosis was the "rhythm strip," and popular leads were 2 and V_1. But with the development of special intensive care areas, continuous monitoring became a necessity (for principles governing such monitoring, see Chapter 10).

Dynamic (Holter) Monitoring

At about the same time, a method to monitor the ambulant patient in his workaday environment evolved. This monitoring mode has proved invaluable and has enjoyed numerous improvements and refinements over the past 20 years. The patient is attached, by means of chest electrodes, to a portable tape recorder which records on one or two leads every heart beat during, usually, 24 hours. The patient keeps a diary of his activities so that any symptoms can be correlated with his then rhythm and any disturbance of rhythm can be correlated with his then activity. Thus he is monitored during real life situations—office encounters and pressures, golf or tennis, domestic squabbles, sexual intercourse, driving in traffic, showering, defecating. Its main use is to detect and identify any arrhythmic cause of symptoms such as palpitations, dizziness, syncope or chest pain; or, alternatively, to rule out arrhythmias as the cause of the symptom.

To give some idea of the likely harvest from Holter monitoring: out of 371 monitored patients, 174 (47%) had their symptoms during the 24-hour period of monitoring. Of these 174, the symptoms coincided with a culpable disturbance of rhythm in only 48 (27%), while the remaining 126 patients (73%) experienced their symptoms while their rhythm was entirely normal. Thus, of the original 371 patients, the Holter gave the answer (symptoms due to

---

* See glossary of terms at the end of this chapter.

arrhythmia or not) in approximately half; but in only about 1 in 8 of the original 371 was arrhythmia the cause of the symptoms.[16]

Holter monitoring is also of value in specific cardiac diseases or situations in which information concerning the heart's rhythm is important for prognosis and management—ischemic heart disease, variant angina, mitral valve prolapse, cardiomyopathy, conduction disturbances, evaluation of pacemaker function, Wolff-Parkinson-White syndrome. It may be helpful in the asymptomatic patient in whom an arrhythmia has been detected on routine examination and about which further information is required. And it may be of value in assessing the therapeutic effect of antiarrhythmic drugs and adjusting dosages; but in this context it is important to realize that there may be spontaneous variation in the frequency of arrhythmia from day to day of up to 90%,[6, 8] and therefore there must be a marked and consistent reduction in its incidence before triumphant conclusions are drawn.

Dynamic monitoring has proved an invaluable diagnostic aid, but the limited span of (usually) 24 hours makes it expensively unsuitable for detecting the *infrequent* rhythm disturbance. It has also been of great value in revealing the unexpected frequency of disorders of rhythm in presumably healthy populations of all ages (see below).

Indications for Dynamic (Holter) Monitoring

1. Symptoms suspected to be of cardiac origin (palpitations, dizziness, syncope, chest pain)
2. Specific cardiac disorders (e.g., ischemic heart disease, variant angina, mitral valve prolapse, cardiomyopathy, conduction disturbances, pacemaker evaluation, WPW syndrome)
3. Asymptomatic patient with known arrhythmia
4. As a guide to therapy of arrhythmia
5. Analyzing frequency of arrhythmias in a given population

Transtelephonic Monitoring (TTM)

The unlikelihood of catching the infrequent arrhythmia by Holter monitoring has been largely overcome by TTM,[5, 7] a method in which the patient carries with him a pocket-sized transmitter and, with a few simple instructions, is able to transmit his rhythm over the telephone when symptoms occur. In this way there can be more efficient and economical coverage for days or, if necessary to catch the fugitive arrhythmia, several weeks.

Valuable as this method has also proved, it still leaves the infrequent, *asymptomatic* arrhythmia uncaught.

Indications for Transtelephonic Monitoring

1. To detect the *infrequent* but symptomatic arrhythmia
2. For continued daily monitoring at home of postmyocardial infarction patient recently discharged
3. As an aid in adjusting dosage of antiarrhythmic therapy

His Bundle Recordings

His bundle electrography in man[3, 4, 14] has been an exciting development for those with a special interest in arrhythmias and conduction disturbances. By proper positioning of a multipolar electrode catheter, it is possible to obtain simultaneous recordings of the electrical activity of the A-V node, the bundle of His and the right bundle branch. Thus for the first time we are able to some extent to dissect and partition the P-R interval into two stages: from atrium to bundle of His (A-H interval); and from bundle of His to ventricles (H-V interval). This has proved instructive in elucidating the mechanisms of A-V block.

The main contribution of the technique to date is in confirming assumptions already ingeniously deduced from clinical tracings—it has converted the game of inference into a science.[9] It has confirmed the fact that concealed retrograde conduction follows ectopic ventricular beats; that concealed A-V junctional extrasystoles exist and can mimic A-V block; and that patterns of concealed conduction into the A-V junction account for the irregular ventricular response to atrial fibrillation.

But in addition to its role in confirmation, it has also provided a fresh approach to arrhythmia research; and, when all else fails, it may be the only means of resolving a difficult arrhythmia. For example, a His bundle recording alone may settle the notoriously difficult differentiation between ventricular aberration and ectopy, since ventricular complexes that result from supraventricular impulses must be preceded by His bundle activation, whereas ectopic ventricular complexes are not. Again, by this technique it has been demonstrated that the site of conduction delay during Wenckebach periodicity is usually in the A-V node itself (prolongation of A-H interval) whereas in type II A-V block, the site of block is always infranodal and usually below the

---

Indications for His-Bundle Recordings[14]

1. Determining the level of A-V block
2. Differentiating ventricular ectopy from aberration
3. Identifying concealed junctional extrasystoles
4. Identifying type of SVT
5. Investigating action of drugs

bundle of His (prolongation of H-V interval). Finally, the technique has yielded precise and useful information concerning the action of antiarrhythmic drugs on A-V conduction.

Incidence of Arrhythmias in Normal Populations

Evaluation of cardiac rate and rhythm must take normal data into consideration; and so, before exploring the incidence and intricacies of arrhythmias in subsequent chapters, it is well to be aware of the frequency with which "abnormal" rhythms are found in normal populations—information which the development of dynamic monitoring has enabled us to obtain.

The extent of normal variation in rate and rhythm in normal children is widely unappreciated. Among 134 normal infants monitored for 24 hours during the first 10 days of life, the maximal 9-beat heart rate reached 220/min, while the minimal rate was 42/min. Atrial premature beats were found in 19 (14%). Sinus pauses occurred in 72% of a subgroup of 71 infants, the longest pause reaching 1.8 sec. Of over 2000 infants screened with a standard ECG and a 10-sec rhythm strip, 0.9% had premature beats, many of them ventricular.[12]

Among 92 healthy children aged 7–11 years[13] the fastest rate attained for 9 consecutive beats was 195/min and the lowest rate was 37/min. Junctional escape as a result of sinus slowing occurred in no less than 45%, in one child lasting for 25 min. First degree A-V block was found in 9 children with P-R interval up to 0.28 sec. Three children had Wenckebach periods, one of whom had 53 episodes. Isolated atrial and ventricular extrasystoles were found in 21% and sinus pauses in two thirds of the children monitored.

Among 131 healthy boys aged 10–13 years,[11] waking maximal heart rates ranged between 100 and 200/min with minimal rates between 45 and 80/min. Maximal sleeping rates were between 60 and 100/min with minimal rates between 30 and 70/min. First degree A-V block was found in 8.4% and type I A-V block in 10.7%. Single atrial and single ventricular extrasystoles were found in 13 and 26%, respectively.

Among 50 young women without heart disease aged 22–28 years,[10] the waking maximal heart rate ranged between 122 and 189/min with minimal rates between 40 and 73. Maximal sleeping rates ranged between 71 and 128/min with minimal rates between 37 and 59/min. Atrial premature beats occurred in 64% and ventricular prematures in 54%. One woman had one 3-beat run of ventricular tachycardia and two (4%) had periods of type I A-V block.

Fifty male medical students without apparent heart disease were similarly monitored.[1] Their waking maximal rates ranged from 107 to 180/min with minimal rates between 37 and 65/min. Maximal sleeping rates were between 70 and 115/min with minimal rates of 33 to 55/min. Half of these young men had sinus arrhythmia sufficient to cause 100% change in consecutive cycles, and 28% had sinus pauses of more than 1.75 sec. Atrial extrasystoles were found in 56% and ventricular in 50%. Three students (6%) had periods of type I A-V block.

It is also not widely known that a significant minority of the supposedly healthy work force has arrhythmias that are generally regarded as of serious prognostic significance including multifocal and R-on-T ventricular extrasystoles, ventricular bigeminy, ventricular tachycardia and second degree A-V block.[2]

Among a healthy elderly population (98 subjects aged 60 to 85 years, all with normal maximal treadmill tests), sinus bradycardia was found in 91%, supraventricular premature beats in 88, supraventricular tachycardia in 13 and atrial flutter in one; ventricular arrhythmias included extrasystoles in 78%—many with pairs or multiform beats—and ventricular tachycardia in four per cent.[3a] Even among young athletes extrasystoles are common: all of 20 male long-distance runners aged 19 to 29 years had atrial and 14 (70%) had ventricular premature beats; and 8 of the 20 had periods of type I A-V block.[13a]

Such have been the largely unexpected revelations of dynamic monitoring.

Ladder Diagrams

Ladder diagrams, or "laddergrams" for short, are indispensable for helping one unravel the difficult arrhythmia, for communicating one's interpretation, and in teaching arrhythmias, both simple and complex. We generally use three tiers (fig. 9.1*A*): atrial (A), junctional (A-V) and ventricular (V). One may need to add a sinus node tier (fig. 9.1*B*) or a tier for an ectopic ventricular focus (fig. 9.1*C*), or divide the A-V junction into 2 or 3 layers; but for most purposes the three tiers suffice.

You place the laddergram immediately under the tracing to be graphed and then there are two steps in using it: (1) first you put in *what you can see*, i.e., you put in appropriate lines or bars to represent the visible P waves and QRS complexes; and (2) then, and only then, you work out the conduction pattern and write it in.

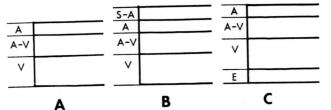

Figure 9.1. The skeletons of laddergrams. For use of each type, see text. (Reproduced with permission from H. J. L. Marriott and R. J. Myerburg: Recognition of arrhythmias and conduction disturbances, in *The Heart*, Ed. 5, pp. 519–556, edited by J. W. Hurst, McGraw-Hill, New York, 1982.)

Various types of beats are represented in figure 9.2. In the *top diagram*, *a* is an ordinary sinus beat; we have a gentle slope indicating the passage of time as the impulse spreads through the atrium; it is slowed in the A-V junction and then it speeds up again in the ventricles. You can put a blob for the point of origin of the impulse, but you do not have to because you can tell which way the impulse is travelling from the slight slope of the line. Then *b* is a sinus beat with first degree block: delay in the A-V junction compared to the normal one. And *c* is an ectopic atrial beat with first degree block and ventricular aberration. This split line is not an accepted symbol but is useful to indicate ventricular aberration.

In the second diagram, *a* represents an A-V junctional beat with activation of the atria before the ventricles; *b* is an A-V junctional beat activating atria after the ventricles; and *c* is an A-V junctional beat with considerable delay back to the atria and normal conduction to the ventricles; the delay back to the atria enables the impulse to spill over into a no-longer-refractory downward tract and we get a reciprocal beat. The *arrowheads*, like the pacemaker blobs, are optional. You do not need them; if you slope the line, it is obvious which way the impulse is going, but the *arrowhead* sometimes helps the eye.

In the third diagram *a* is an ectopic ventricular beat which does not penetrate back into the A-V junction. Then *b* is an ectopic ventricular beat that does penetrate the A-V junction but not to the atria. And *c* is an ectopic ventricular beat with retrograde conduction all the way to the atria.

In the *bottom diagram*, *a* is a dissociated beat—a sinus impulse coming down and meeting an ascending ectopic ventricular impulse in the A-V junction. Then *b* is a ventricular fusion beat—a sinus impulse reaching the ventricles but not occupying the entire ventricular myocardium because an ectopic ventricular impulse has fired and activated part of the ventricles. And *c* is a combination between an ectopic impulse conducted retrogradely to the atria and the sinus impulse; the sinus impulse cannot control the whole of the atria because of the retrograde invasion by the ventricular impulse and now we have an atrial fusion beat.

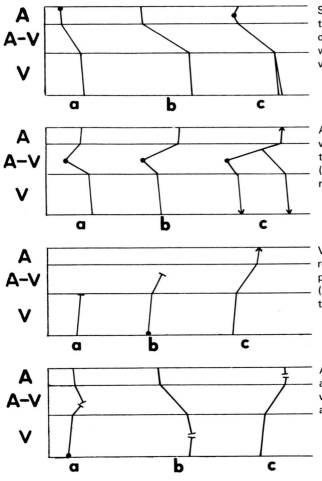

Sinus beats with normal conduction (a) and with prolonged A-V conduction (b); atrial extrasystole with prolonged A-V and aberrant ventricular conduction (c).

A-V beats with atrial-before-ventricular activation (a), ventricular-before-atrial activation (b), and with retrograde delay and reciprocal beating (c).

Ventricular ectopic beats without retrograde conduction (a), with penetration into the A-V junction (b), and with retrograde conduction to the atria (c).

A-V dissociation between sinus and ventricular pacemakers (a); a ventricular fusion beat (b); an atrial fusion beat (c).

Figure 9.2. Laddergrams of various beats.

Now, to get the hang of their use, let us construct a laddergram in the two recommended stages. The tracing in figure 9.3, which is again reproduced in Chapter 11, illustrates a ventricular extrasystole with concealed retrograde conduction prolonging the ensuing P-R interval. The first step is to indicate each of the visible P waves and QRS complexes with an appropriate sloping line. The second step is to indicate conduction of the normally conducted sinus beats by connecting atrial and ventricular lines through the A-V junction. But the sinus beat following the extrasystole is conducted with a prolonged P-R interval, and this requires explanation. Clearly the ventricular extrasystole must have travelled retrogradely into the A-V junction so that the next descending sinus impulse found the junction relatively refractory. We therefore depict the ventricular ectopic impulse travelling backward a certain distance into the A-V junction; and the sinus impulse, conducted normally until it reaches the level to which the ectopic impulse has penetrated, suffering delay below that point.

In subsequent chapters, laddergrams will be freely used as a visual aid to understanding patterns of conduction.

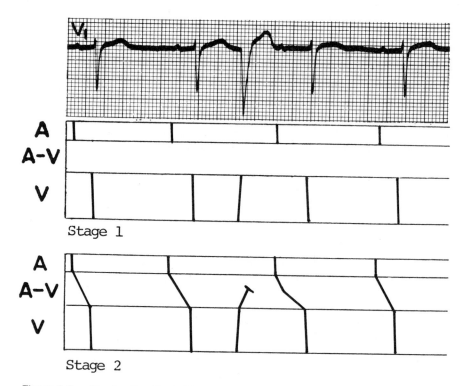

Figure 9.3. Constructing the laddergram of a simple arrhythmia in two stages. For explanation, see text.

Glossary

Aberrant ventricular conduction. The temporarily abnormal intraventricular conduction of a supraventricular impulse, usually associated with a change in cycle length.

Accelerated idionodal rhythm. An automatic A-V rhythm, controlling only the ventricles, at a rate between 60 and 100 beats/min.

Accelerated idioventricular rhythm. An automatic ectopic ventricular rhythm, controlling only the ventricles, at a rate between 50 and 100 beats/min.

Atrial capture. Retrograde conduction to the atria, from A-V junction or ventricles, after a period of A-V dissociation.

Automaticity. The property inherent in all pacemaking cells that enables them to form new impulses spontaneously.

Automatic beat or rhythm. A beat or rhythm arising in a spontaneously beating center, independent of the dominant sinus (or other) rhythm.

A-V dissociation. Independent beating of atria and ventricles.

Block. Pathological delay or interruption of impulse conduction.

Bradycardia. Any heart (or chamber) rhythm having an average rate under 60 beats/min.

Capture(d) beat. A conducted beat following a period of A-V dissociation.

Concealed conduction. Conduction of an impulse within the conduction system, recognizable only by its effect on the subsequent beat or cycle.

Coupling interval. The interval between an extrasystole and the beat preceding it.

Ectopic beat. A beat arising in any focus other than the sinus node.

Ectopy. Ectopic impulse formation.

Escape(d) beat. An automatic beat ending a cycle longer than the dominant cycle and able to appear only because of a slowing or interruption of the dominant rhythm.

Extrasystole. A premature ectopic beat, dependent upon and coupled to the preceding beat.

Fusion beat. A beat resulting from the simultaneous spread of more than one impulse through the same myocardial territory (either ventricles or atria).

Idionodal rhythm. An independent rhythm arising in the A-V junction and controlling only the ventricles.

Idioventricular rhythm. A rhythm arising in and controlling only the ventricles.

Isorhythmic dissociation. A-V dissociation with atria and ventricles beating at the same or almost the same rate.

Parasystole. An automatic ectopic rhythm whose pacemaker is "protected" from discharge by the sinus or other circumnavigating impulses so that it is able to maintain its own uninterrupted rhythm in competition with the dominant rhythm.

Pre-excitation. Activation of a ventricle earlier than its activation would be expected via the normal conducting pathways.

Premature beat. An ectopic beat, dependent upon and coupled to the preceding beat, and occurring before the next expected dominant beat; extrasystole.

Tachyarrhythmia. Any disturbance of rhythm resulting in a heart or chamber rate over 100 beats/min.

Tachycardia. Any heart (or chamber) rhythm having an average rate over 100 beats/min.

Ventricular aberration. Aberrant ventricular conduction.

Ventricular capture. Conduction to the ventricles after a period of A-V dissociation.

Wolff-Parkinson-White   syndrome.   An   electrocardiographic "syndrome" consisting of a short P-R interval (<0.12 sec) with widened QRS complex including a delta wave (slurred initial component).

REFERENCES

1. Brodsky, M., et al.: Arrhythmias documented by 24-hour continuous electrocardiographic monitoring in 50 male medical students without apparent heart disease. Am. J. Cardiol. 1977: **39**, 390.
2. Clarke, J. M., et al.: The rhythm of the normal heart. Lancet 1976: **2**, 508.
3. Damato, A. N., and Lau, S. H.: Clinical value of the electrogram of the conduction system. Prog. Cardiovasc. Dis. 1970: **13**, 119.
3a. Fleg, J. L., and Kennedy, H. L.: Cardiac arrhythmias in a healthy elderly population: Detection by 24-hour ambulatory electrocardiography. Chest 1982: **81**, 302.
4. Goldreyer, B. N.: Intracardiac electrocardiography in the analysis and understanding of cardiac arrhythmias. Ann. Intern. Med. 1972: **77**, 117.
5. Grodman, P. S.: Arrhythmia surveillance by transtelephonic monitoring; comparison with Holter monitoring in symptomatic ambulatory patients. Am. Heart J. 1979: **98**, 459.
6. Harrison, D. C.: Contribution of ambulatory electrocardiographic monitoring to antiarrhythmic management. Am. J. Cardiol. 1978: **41**, 996.
7. Judson, P., et al.: Evaluation of outpatient arrhythmias utilizing transtelephonic monitoring. Am. Heart J. 1979: **97**, 759.
8. Michelson, E. L., and Morganroth, J.: Spontaneous variability of complex ventricular arrhythmias detected by long-term electrocardiographic recording. Circulation 1980: **61**, 690.
9. Pick, A.: Mechanisms of cardiac arrhythmias; from hypothesis to physiologic fact. Am. Heart J. 1973: **86**, 249.
10. Sabotka, P. A., et al.: Arrhythmias documented by 24-hour continuous ambulatory electrocardiographic monitoring in young women without apparent heart disease. Am. Heart J. 1981: **101**, 753.
11. Scott, O., et al.: Results of 24-hour ambulatory monitoring of electrocardiogram in 131 healthy boys aged 10 to 13 years. Br. Heart J. 1980: **44**, 304.
12. Southall, D. P., et al.: Study of cardiac rhythm in healthy newborn infants. Br. Heart J. 1980: **43**, 14.
13. Southall, D. P., et al.: A 24-hour electrocardiographic study of heart rate and rhythm patterns in population of healthy children. Br. Heart J. 1981: **45**, 281.
13a. Talan, D. A., et al.: Twenty-four hour continuous ECG recordings in long-distance runners. Chest 1982: **82**, 19.
14. Vadde, P. S., et al.: Indications of His bundle recordings. Cardiovasc. Clin. 1980: **11**, 1.
15. Winkle, R. A.: Ambulatory electrocardiography and the diagnosis, evaluation, and treatment of chronic ventricular arrhythmias Prog. Cardiovasc. Dis. 1980: **23**, 99.
16. Zeldis, S. M., et al.: Cardiovascular complaints; correlation with cardiac arrhythmias on 24-hour electrocardiographic monitoring. Chest 1980: **78**, 456.

10

Systematic Approach to Diagnosis of Arrhythmias

Disturbances of rhythm are most conveniently divided into (1) supraventricular and (2) ventricular. This corresponds with a simple electrocardiographic difference—arrhythmias originating in the atrium or A-V junction (supraventricular), unless complicated by aberrant ventricular conduction (Chapter 16), are characterized by normal QRS complexes, while ventricular arrhythmias produce bizarre QRST complexes with prolonged QRS interval.

Many disturbances of rhythm and conduction are recognizable at first glance. For example, one can usually spot at once atrial flutter with 4:1 conduction, or atrial fibrillation with rapid ventricular response. But there are a significant number of dysrhythmias that defy immediate recognition, and it is for these that we require a systematic attack. The following approach has evolved after analyzing the reasons for the mistakes I have made and those I have repeatedly watched others make; and the system is therefore designed to avoid the common errors of omission and commission. Undoubtedly, we make most mistakes because of failure to apply reason and logic and not because of ignorance.

Before outlining the systematic five-point approach, it is worth making some observations about the principles of monitoring, since in this day of its widespread use anyone concerned with the interpretation of arrhythmias is likely to be involved in continuous monitoring whether in intensive care, on telemetry, on Holter tapes or during stress testing—and much the same principles apply in each context.

Principles of Monitoring (Table 10.1)

Principle 1. **Use a lead containing maximal information.** There is no point in letting available information go down the drain. One never knows when it might be useful; and if one can gather additional data with no additional trouble, why not do so? As an example of lost information that might have been valuable, we are now 20 years into coronary care and do not yet know whether there is any prognostic difference between left and right ventricular extrasystoles. One ongoing study[3] strongly suggests that left ventricular extra- systoles are many times more likely than right ventricular extrasystoles to precipitate ventricular tachycardia or fibrillation. If constant monitoring in its early years had employed a monitoring lead that enabled one to distinguish left

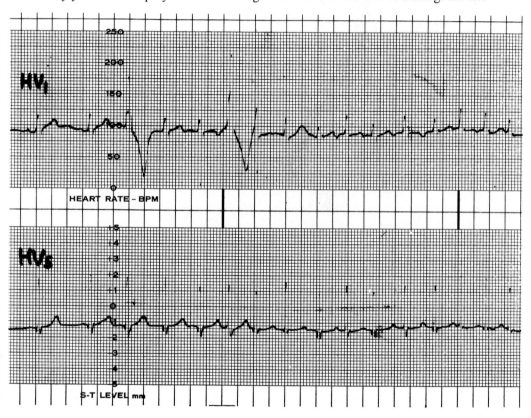

Figure 10.1. Two simultaneous leads from a Holter recording with precordial electrodes at the V_1 and V_5 positions. Two grossly aberrant beats in V_1 produce an almost imperceptible widening of the S wave in V_6.

ONE LEAD IS NOT ENOUGH

from right ventricular ectopic beats, this information might well be in hand today. But a counterfeit lead 2 was used for many years, and if you turn to figure 15.2 you will see how lead 2 can look identical in all four of the Big-4 to be differentiated: left bundle-branch block (LBBB), right bundle-branch block (RBBB), left ventricular ectopics, and right ventricular ectopics. For this reason, if for no other, lead 2 is one of the least satisfactory leads for constant monitoring.

Principle 2. Another principle of good monitoring is that the system should be as **mechanically convenient** as possible; for most systems a maximum of three wires and electrodes is appropriate, and these should be strategically placed so as not to interfere with physical examination of the heart or with the application of emergency countershock.

Principle 3. But no matter how good the monitoring lead is, **one lead is not enough** for all the time; and there are at least four reasons for this: (1) Two dissimilar complexes can look remarkably similar in a single lead; e.g., in figure 10.1, the clearly bizarre and aberrant beats in V_1 would be almost impossible to spot in V_5. (2) A single lead may not show the insignificant item you are looking for—such as the P wave or pacemaker blip. (3) The morphology of, say, RBBB may not be diagnostic in one lead (e.g., V_1) while confidently diagnosable in another (e.g., V_6). (4) The width of a QRS (or other interval) may not be accurately measurable in a single lead—from one angle it may look considerably narrower than it really is (fig. 10.2).

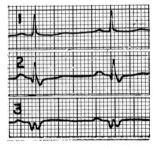

Figure 10.2. From lead 1, no one would think that this patient has intraventricular block with a QRS interval of 0.11 sec as seen in leads 2 and 3. By Einthoven's equation, since the terminal 0.06 sec is a virtually identical negative deflection in leads 2 and 3, that part of the QRS in lead 1 is disarmingly isoelectric.

Table 10.1
Principles of Monitoring

1. Use lead with maximal information
2. Ensure maximal mechanical convenience
3. One lead is not enough
4. Know when to use what other leads

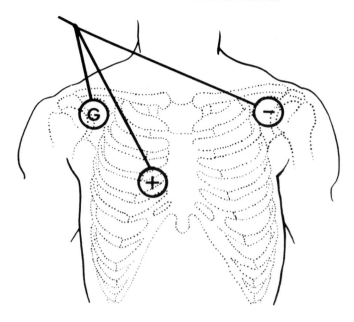

Figure 10.3.   Electrode placement of modified CL$_1$ (MCL$_1$).

Principle 4. A direct consequence of Principle 3 is that one must **know when to use what other leads.**

A monitoring lead that satisfactorily fulfills most of the requirements is the modified CL$_1$ (MCL$_1$) introduced in 1968[2] (fig. 10.3). The positive electrode is placed at the C$_1$ (or V$_1$) position; the negative electrode, at the left shoulder; and the ground (which may be placed anywhere), usually at the right shoulder. This leaves a clear platform for emergency cardioversion and an unencumbered precordium for physical examination. In addition, this lead, since it closely imitates V$_1$, affords several diagnostic advantages: One can immediately distinguish between left and right ventricular ectopy in most instances; RBBB and LBBB can be recognized with ease; and P waves are sometimes best or only seen in a right precordial lead. Most importantly of all, a right chest lead gives one the best chance of distinguishing between left ventricular ectopy and RBBB aberration.

The only disadvantages of lead MCL$_1$, which are minor by comparison with its virtues, are that it fails to recognize shifts of axis and is therefore useless for spotting the development of a hemiblock, and that the polarity of the P wave is not as informative as that in lead 2. However, the P wave morphology in a right chest lead is not all that uninformative: whereas the sinus P wave, when it is diphasic, is usually +−, the ectopic or retrograde P wave when diphasic is usually −+ (fig. 10.4).

The MCL hookup possesses considerable flexibility. When MCL$_1$ fails to provide the answer; it may be helpful to turn to a left chest lead; then it is merely a matter of substituting an electrode at the C$_6$ position to obtain an MCL$_6$, which is a reasonable imitation of V$_6$. Moreover, if the polarity of the retrograde P wave, as familiarly known to us in the limb leads, seems worth recording to document a junctional rhythm, the substituted electrode may be placed low on the left flank below the diaphragm to obtain a reasonable imitation of standard lead 3 (fig. 10.5).

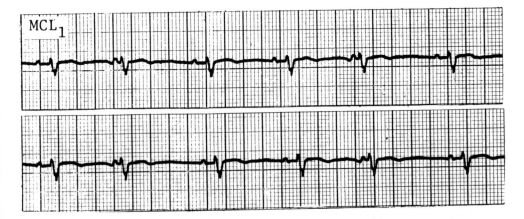

Figure 10.4. Second and fifth beats in each strip are **atrial premature beats.** Note the − + polarity of the ectopic P waves.

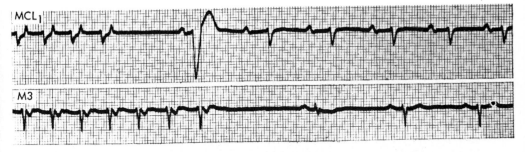

Figure 10.5. Each lead shows the end of a run of **junctional tachycardia** with the retrograde P wave just following the QRS complex. In the second half of each strip, sinus rhythm resumes. Note that the retrograde and sinus P waves are both predominantly positive in MCL$_1$, whereas in M3 the retrograde P waves show the more familiar inversion characteristic of retroconduction in an inferior lead. On each occasion, after the tachycardia ceases, the returning beat is an escape beat.

A left chest lead (V_6 or MCL_6) is not reliable for distinguishing between left and right ventricular ectopy. In figure 10.6, the first extrasystole probably comes from the left ventricle, whereas the second comes from the right ventricle. But in V_6 they both have a very similar LBBB morphology. Unfortunately, in V_6 both left and right ventricular ectopics may be either positive or negative: In left ventricular ectopy the usual QRS in V_6 is mainly negative (rS or QS), but it may be positive as part of the pattern of concordant positivity. Similarly, in right ventricular ectopy the usual QRS in V_6 is positive, but it may be negative as part of the pattern of concordant negativity.

For examples of the sort of information that can be derived from a right chest lead that is not usually available in lead 2, look at figure 10.7. In figure 10.7 *A*, the rSR′ pattern of the sinus beats is typical of RBBB; the qR pattern with early peak in the first extrasystole is typical of ectopy of left ventricular origin; and the rS pattern of the second extrasystole is typical of a right ventricular origin. In figure 10.7 *B*, the atrial fibrillation is interrupted by a burst of bizarre beats that are certain to evoke the "lidocaine reflex"; but the telltale shape (rsR′) of the first of these wide beats tells us that it is a run of aberrantly conducted beats rather than a run of ventricular tachycardia.

Stepwise Approach to Diagnosis

If the diagnosis fails to fall into your lap, then the systematic approach is in order (table 10.2). The first step in any medical diagnosis is to **know the causes** of the presenting symptom. For example, if you want to be a "super" headache specialist, the first step is to learn the 50 causes of headache, which are the common ones, which the uncommon, and how to differentiate them; because "you see only what you look for, you recognize only what you know."[6]

As diagnostic challenges, the arrhythmias are no different—the first step is to know the causes of the disturbance of rhythm that confronts you and there

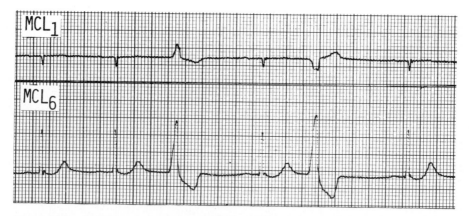

Figure 10.6. Simultaneous recording of MCL_1 and MCL_6. The third beat is a **left ventricular extrasystole** and the fifth beat a **right ventricular extrasystole**. Note that while the distinction is easy in MCL_1, the "LBBB" morphology of the two beats is strikingly similar in V_6.

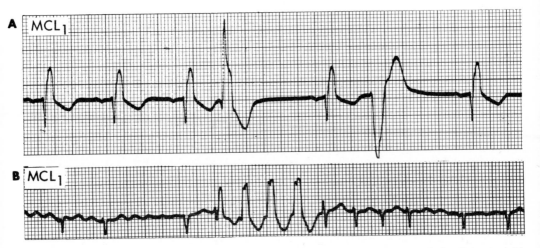

Figure 10.7. The patterns of **RBBB** (sinus beats), **left ventricular ectopy** (fourth beat), and **right ventricular ectopy** (sixth beat) are readily recognized. (*B*) A short run of aberrantly conducted beats during atrial fibrillation; the **aberration** is recognized by the characteristic triphasic (rsR′) contour of the first anomalous beat.

Table 10.2
Approach to Diagnosis

1. Know the causes
2. Milk the QRS
3. Cherchez le P
4. Who's married to whom?
5. Pinpoint the primary

Table 10.3
Eight Basic Rhythm Disturbances

1. Early beats
2. Unexpected pauses
3. Tachycardias
4. Bradycardias
5. Bigeminal rhythms
6. Group beating
7. Total irregularity
8. Regular non-sinus rhythms at normal rates

are only eight basic dysrhythms (table 10.3). "Knowing the causes" of each of these (tables 10.4–10.9) is part of the equipment that you carry around with you—prepared at a moment's notice to use the knowledge when faced with an unidentified arrhythmia.

When a specific arrhythmia confronts you, first **milk the QRS.** There are two reasons for this: first, it is an extension of Willie Sutton's law—Sutton, the bank robber, who robbed banks because that was "where the money was"; and second, because it keeps us in the healthy frame of mind of giving priority to ventricular behavior—in general, it matters comparatively little what the atria are doing so long as the ventricles are behaving themselves.

If the QRS is of normal duration—be sure to check in at least two leads (remember fig. 10.2)—you know that the rhythm is supraventricular and that may tell all you can deduce from such a QRS. But if the QRS is wide and bizarre, you are then faced with the decision whether it is supraventricular with ventricular aberration or is ectopic ventricular; and that is where the fun begins. If you know your morphology, you know what to look for, and you will recognize it if you see it.

During the past decade and a half, the diagnostic morphology of the ventricular complex has come into its own. This began with clinical observation and deductions[1, 5, 7] in which astute coronary care nurses played an important role,[8] and culminated in the confirmatory electrophysiolgical studies of Wellens and his colleagues.[9] Applying the fruits of these labors, Wellens[10] found that inspection of the QRS pattern in the clinical tracing afforded the correct diagnosis in 52 of 56 consecutive wide-QRS tachycardias. Despite the evident

Table 10.4
Causes of Early Beats

1. Extrasystole
2. Parasystole
3. Capture beat, including supernormal conduction during A-V block
4. Reciprocal beat
5. Better (e.g., 3:2) conduction interrupting poorer (e.g., 2:1)
6. Rhythm resumption after inapparent bigeminy

Table 10.5
Causes of Pauses

1. Nonconducted atrial extrasystoles
2. Second degree A-V block
   Type I (Wenckebach, 1899)
   Type II (Wenckebach, 1906; Hay, 1906)
3. Second degree S-A block
   Type I or type II
4. Concealed conduction
5. Concealed A-V extrasystoles

Table 10.6
Causes of Bradycardia[a]

1. Sinus bradycardia
2. Nonconducted atrial bigeminy
3. A-V block; second and third degree
4. S-A block: second and third degree

[a] Note that A-V nodal (idionodal, junctional) and idioventricular rhythms are not *causes* of bradycardia, but *result* from one of the above.

Table 10.7
Causes of Bigeminal Rhythm

1. Extrasystolic
   Ventricular
   Supraventricular
2. Due to 3:2 block
   A-V block, type I and II
   S-A block, type I and II
   Atrial tachycardia or flutter with alternating 2:1 and 4:1 conduction, etc.
3. Nonconducted atrial trigeminy
4. Reciprocal beating
5. Concealed A-V extrasystoles every third beat

Table 10.8
Causes of Chaos

1. Atrial fibrillation
2. Atrial flutter with varying A-V conduction
3. Multifocal atrial tachycardia
4. Shifting (wandering) pacemaker
5. Multifocal ventricular extrasystoles
6. Parasystole
7. Combinations of above

Table 10.9
Regular Rhythms at Normal Rates

1. Normal sinus rhythm
2. Accelerated A-V rhythm
3. Accelerated idioventricular rhythm
4. Atrial flutter with, e.g., 4:1 conduction
5. Sinus or supraventricular tachycardia with (e.g., 2:1) A-V block
6. Ventricular tachycardia with (e.g., 2:1) exit block

availability, simplicity, and accuracy of this method, some authorities persist in ignoring its potential.[4, 11]

If the answer is not afforded by the shape of the QRS complex, the next item to turn to is the P wave—**cherchez le P.** In the past, the P wave, as the key to arrhythmias, has certainly been overemphasized; and a lifelong love affair with P waves has afflicted many an electrocardiographer with the so-called "P-preoccupation syndrome." But there are times when the P wave holds the diagnostic clue and must be accorded the starring role.

In one's search for P waves, there are several clues and caveats to bear in mind. One technique that may be useful is to employ the S_5 lead introduced by French cardiologists 30 years ago. To obtain this lead, the positive electrode is placed at the fifth right interspace close to the sternum (just below the C_1 position), and the negative electrode on the manubrium of the sternum. This will sometimes greatly magnify the P wave, rendering it readily visible when it was virtually indiscernible in other leads. Figure 10.8 illustrates this amplifying

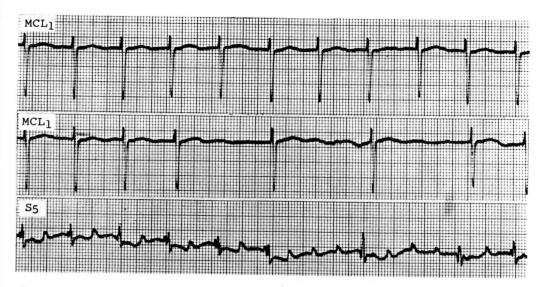

Figure 10.8. The top strip of MCL₁ shows barely perceptible P′ waves of an **atrial tachycardia.** The second strip of MCL₁ shows the effect of carotid sinus stimulation: The ventricular rate halves because of increased A-V block, and additional P′ waves become barely visible through the artifact. In contrast, the strip of lead S₅ (see text) boasts prominent P waves; the beginning of the strip illustrates the "Bix rule" (see text and also fig. 10.9), and the second half of the strip again shows the effect of carotid sinus stimulation.

effect and makes the diagnosis of atrial tachycardia with 2:1 block immediately apparent. If it succeeds, this technique is a great deal kinder to the patient and safer than passing an atrial wire or an esophageal electrode to corral elusive P waves.

Another clue to the incidence of P waves is contained in the **Bix rule,** after the Baltimore cardiologist Harold Bix, who used to say that whenever the P waves of a supraventricular tachycardia were halfway between the ventricular complexes, you should always suspect that additional P waves were hiding within the QRS complex. In the *top strip* of figure 10.9, the P′ wave is midway between the QRS complexes, and one therefore thinks of the "Bix rule." It may be necessary to apply carotid sinus stimulation or other vagal maneuver to bring the alternate P′ waves out of hiding; but in this case, the patient obligingly altered his conduction pattern (*middle strip* of fig. 10.9) and spontaneously exposed the skulking P′ waves. It is clearly important to know if there are twice as many atrial impulses as are apparent because there is the ever-present danger that the *ventricular* rate may double or almost double, especially if the atrial rate were to slow somewhat. It is better to be forewarned and take steps to prevent such potentially disastrous acceleration.

The **haystack principle** can be of great diagnostic importance when you are searching for difficult-to-find P waves or any other inconspicuous deflection. When you have to find a needle in a haystack, if you value your time and energy you would presumably prefer a small rather than large haystack. Therefore, whenever you are faced with the problem of finding elusive items, always give the lead with the least disturbance of the baseline (the smallest

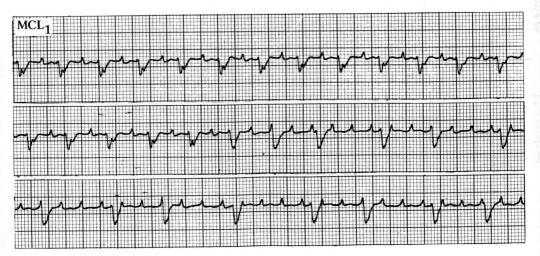

Figure 10.9. The strips are continuous. The *top strip* illustrates the "Bix rule"; toward the end of the *second strip* the conduction ratio changes, and the previously hidden alternate P′ waves are brought to light, revealing an **atrial tachycardia** (rate, 212/min).

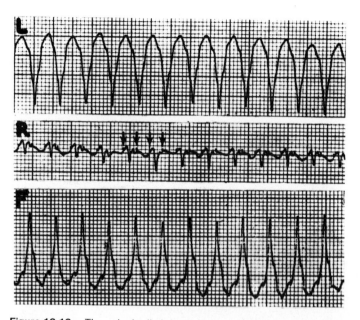

Figure 10.10. The unipolar limb leads from a patient with a **runaway pacemaker**. The pacemaker spikes are not visible in leads aVL and aVF but are plainly seen (*arrows*) in the lead (aVR) with small ventricular complexes.

ventricular complex) a chance to help you. There are some leads that no one would think of looking at to solve an arrhythmia (e.g., aVR), yet the patient illustrated in figure 10.10 died because his attendants did not know or did not apply the haystack principle and make use of aVR. He had a runaway pacemaker at a discharge rate of 440/min with a halved ventricular response at 220/min. Lead aVR was the lead with the smallest ventricular complex, and it was the only lead in which the pacemaker "blips" were plainly visible (*arrows* of fig. 10.10). The patient went into shock and died because none of the attempted therapeutic measures affected the tachycardia, when all that was necessary was to disconnect the wayward pulse generator.

The next caveat is **mind your "Ps."** This means to be wary of things that look like P waves and particularly applies to P-like waves that are adjacent to the QRS complex—they may turn out to be part of the QRS complex. This is a trap for the unwary sufferer from the P-preoccupation syndrome to whom anything that looks like a P wave is a P wave. Many competent interpreters given the strip of lead V_1 or V_2 in figure 10.11 will promptly and confidently diagnose a supraventricular tachycardia for the wrong reasons. In V_1, the QRS seems not to be very wide and appears to be preceded by a small P wave; in V_2, an apparently narrow QRS is followed by an "unmistakable" retrograde P wave. But, in fact, the P-like waves in both these leads are part of the QRS complex. If the QRS duration is measured in V_3, it is found to be 0.14 sec; to attain a QRS of that width in V_1 and V_2, the P-like waves need to be included in the measurement.

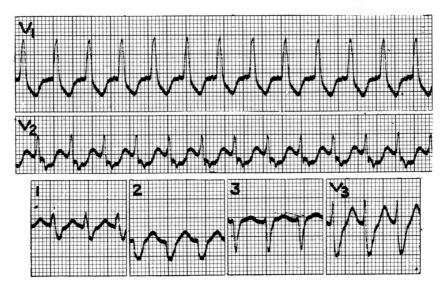

Figure 10.11. The beats in the rhythm strips of leads V_1 and V_2 are readily mistaken for narrow ventricular complexes with constantly related P waves. But the QRS interval, as seen in leads 1 and V_3, clearly measures 0.14 sec. To achieve this width in V_1 and V_2, the P-like waves must be included in the QRS measurement.

Whenever a regular rhythm is difficult to identify, it is always worthwhile to seek and focus on any interruption in the regularity—a process that can be condensed in the three words **dig the break.** It is at a break in the rhythm that you are most likely to find the solution. For example, look at figure 10.12. At the beginning of the strip, where the rhythm is regular at a rate of 200/min, it is impossible to know whether the tachycardia is ectopic atrial or ectopic junctional or a reciprocating tachycardia in the A-V junction; and a fourth possibility is that the little peak is part of the QRS and not a P wave at all (mind your "Ps!"). Further along the strip there is a break in the rhythm in the form of a pause. The commonest cause of a pause is a nonconducted atrial extrasystole, and, sure enough, there at the *arrow* is the culprit—in this situation, a diagnostic ally. As a result of the pause, the mechanism is immediately obvious: When the rhythm resumes, the returning P wave is in front of the first QRS, and the mechanism is evidently an atrial tachycardia.

The next step is to establish relationships or, to put it in more catchy terms, ask yourself **who's married to whom?** This is often the crucial step in arriving at a firm diagnosis. Figure 10.13 illustrates this principle in simplest form. A junctional rhythm is dissociated from sinus bradycardia. On three occasions there are bizarre early beats of a qR configuration that is nondiagnostic. They could be ventricular extrasystoles, but the fact that they are seen *only* when a P wave is emerging beyond the preceding QRS tells us that they are "married to" the preceding P waves and establishes them as conducted (capture) beats with atypical RBBB aberration.

Figure 10.14 illustrates both this principle and the final one, **pinpoint the primary** diagnosis. One must never be content to let the diagnosis rest upon a secondary phenomenon such as A-V dissociation, escape, or aberration—each and all of these are always secondary to some primary disturbance that must be sought out and identified.

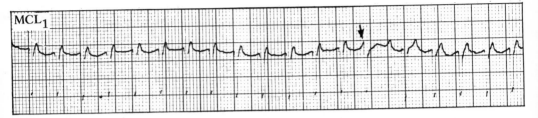

Figure 10.12. The strip begins with an **atrial tachycardia** (rate, 200/min) with 1:1 conduction and a somewhat prolonged P-R interval; this cannot be clearly differentiated from a junctional tachycardia, a reciprocating tachycardia, or even a ventricular tachycardia until the regularity of the rhythm is broken by a nonconducted atrial extrasystole (*arrow*). This break in the rhythm affords the necessary clue since, when the tachycardia resumes, the P' wave precedes the QRS.

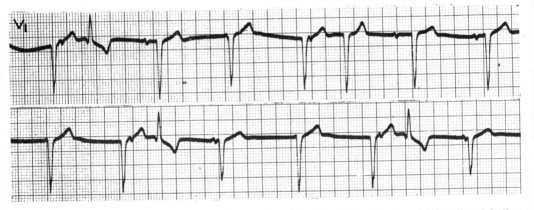

Figure 10.13. **A-V dissociation** between a **sinus bradycardia** (rate, 52/min) and an **A-V junctional rhythm** (rate, 58/min). The early beats are consistently preceded by a sinus P wave just emerging beyond the QRS and are therefore conducted (capture) beats. The strips are continuous.

In figure 10.14, which was obtained from a patient shortly after admission to a coronary care unit on the West Coast, there are a number of wide, bizarre beats that gave the staff concern. One faction, contended that they were ventricular escape beats; the other thought they were conducted, after the longer diastole, with paradoxical critical rate aberration (p. 238). If you ask yourself "Who's married to whom?" it becomes immediately obvious that the beats in question are not related to the P waves. For example, look at the P-R intervals of the last two anomalous beats in the *second strip* and that of the second anomalous beat in the *top strip*. These three intervals are strikingly different measuring 0.31, 0.22, and 0.37 sec, respectively. On the other hand, if you measure the R-R intervals ending with each of these three beats, you find them to be virtually identical; this indicates that the beats in question are

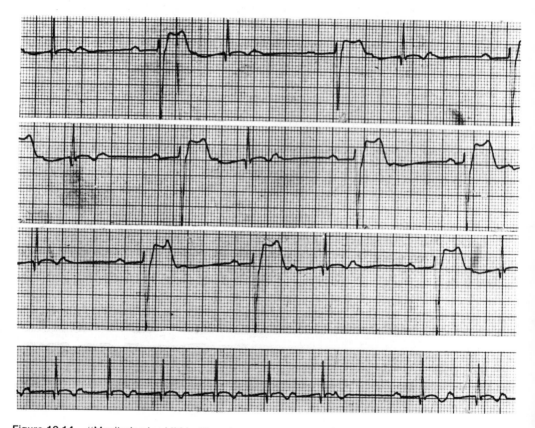

Figure 10.14. "Monitoring lead," identity unknown. The *top three strips* are continuous; the *bottom strip* follows a bolus of lidocaine. The basic disturbance is **type I second degree A-V block.** Following each dropped beat, there is a **ventricular escape beat.** These beats show a variable relationship to the preceding P waves but a constant relationship to the preceding ventricular complexes and are therefore presumably escape beats rather than conducted.

related to the previous QRS rather than to the P wave, which in turn identifies them as escape beats.

In this case, the nurse, regarding them as "PVC's" administered lidocaine and got rid of them (bottom strip). But notice her two mistakes: first, there is nothing "P" about these "VCs"—they are late, not early, beats; and second, one never should treat escape beats—they are rescuing beats, friends in need, and you thank heaven for them. She eliminated them because the lidocaine, as it occasionally will, facilitated A-V conduction, leaving no room or need for escape beats. So by accident she treated the primary disturbance, which was A-V block. What she should have done was apply the fifth principle, "pinpoint the primary," and treat the block with atropine—if indeed the patient required treatment; with an average rate of over 50/min, he may well have been in a satisfactory hemodynamic state and required no immediate therapy.

REFERENCES

1. Marriott, H. J. L.: Differential diagnosis of supraventicular and ventricular tachycardia. Geriatrics 1970: **25**, 91.
2. Marriott, H. J. L., and Fogg, E.: Constant monitoring for cardiac dysrhythmias and blocks. Mod. Concepts Cardiovasc. Dis. 1970: **39**, 103.
3. O'Bryan, C.: Personal communication, 1981.
4. Pietras, R. J., et al.: Chronic recurrent right and left ventricular tachycardia; comparison of clinical, hemodynamic, and angiographic findings. Am. J. Cardiol. 1977: **40**, 32.
5. Sandler, I. A., and Marriott, H. J. L.: The differential morphology of anomalous ventricular complexes of RBBB-type in lead V_1; ventricular ectopy versus aberration. Circulation 1965: **31**, 551.
6. Sosman, M. C.: Quoted by L. Schamroth, in *The Disorders of Cardiac Rhythm*, p. 335. Blackwell, Oxford, 1971.
7. Swanick, E. J., et al.: Morphologic features of right ventricular ectopic beats. Am. J. Cardiol. 1972: **30**, 888.
8. Thorne, D., and Gozensky, C.: Rabbit ears; an aid in distinguishing ventricular ectopy from aberration. Heart Lung 1974: **3**, 634.
9. Wellens, H. J. J., et al.: The value of the electrocardiogram in the differential diagnosis of a tachycardia with a widened QRS complex. Am. J. Med. 1978: **64**, 27.
10. Wellens, H. J. J.: Personal communication, 1981.
11. Zipes, D. P.: Diagnosis of ventricular tachycardia. Drug. Ther. 1979: **9**, 83.

The Extrasystoles

Ectopic beats (Gr. *ek* = out of, *topos* = place) are beats that arise from any focus other than the sinus node. Those originating in the ventricles can be grouped into four categories: extrasystolic, parasystolic, escape(d) and unclassified. The extrasystolic, parasystolic and unclassified beats are all premature, i.e., they end cycles shorter than the cycle of the dominant rhythm, whereas escape(d) beats, by definition, end cycles longer than the dominant cycle. The typical extrasystole bears a constant relationship to the preceding beat of the dominant rhythm, parasystolic beats bear a definite mathematical relationship to each other but not to the dominant rhythm; escape beats, like extrasystoles, occur a constant interval after the preceding dominant beat, but unlike extrasystoles are late rather than early; and the unclassified ectopic beats are inconstantly related to the preceding beat and also bear no relationship to each other. Parasystole and escape will be dealt with in later chapters.

Ventricular Extrasystoles*

"Extrasystole" is probably the most appropriate term to use for those ectopic beats that are both premature and constantly related to the previous beat. Because of this constant relationship they are known as "forced" or "dependent" beats. "Extrasystoles," with all its sibilant sounds, is something of a mouthful and it is phonetically easier to refer to them as "premature beats," although this term has been objected to on the grounds that it does not distinguish them from other early beats. However, the two words, premature beat, as a sort of compound noun has by usage taken on the specific connotation of extrasystole. "Beat" is better than "contraction" because it is a shorter word ("short words are best and the old words when short are best of all"—Churchill) and because it is equally applicable to the electrical and mechanical event, whereas "contraction" is purely mechanical. Hence ventricular premature beat (VPB) is preferred to premature ventricular contraction (PVC).

---

* The uninformed sometimes object to "extra-systole" on the grounds that it is not an extra beat. But the word was never meant to indicate an additional systole any more than extramural means an additional painting on the wall! Extrasystole is a Latin-Greek hybrid that means a systole arising outside (L. *extra* = outside) the normal sinus pacemaker, and by usage has come to mean the sort of premature ectopic beat that is accurately coupled to and depends for its existence on the preceding beat.

The extrasystole together with its preceding parent beat is a "**couplet**," and the interval between them is the "**coupling interval**." When the interval between ectopic beats and the preceding beats is constant, it is known as "**fixed coupling**."

Mechanism

We do not know for certain how all extrasystoles are generated, and it is probable that several mechanisms can account for both the prematurity and the fixed coupling. By far the most popular theory is the reentry theory which undoubtedly accounts for at least some of the VPBs we encounter. The phenomenon of reentry is important to understand not only in approaching the VPB but also because it is the mechanism believed to account for the great majority of our tachycardias, supraventricular and ventricular.

In order to achieve reentry, there are three prerequisities: an available circuit; a difference in the refractory periods of two limbs in the circuit; and slow enough conduction somewhere in the circuit to allow the rest of the circuit to recover responsiveness. In figure 11.1, the three triangular diagrams represent an available circuit in three different stages of recovery. In circuit 1, the descending impulse forks into two limbs of the circuit and finds both still refractory; in circuit 3, both limbs have recovered. In neither of these circumstances can reentry occur. However, in circuit 2, one limb has recovered while the other remains refractory; the refractory limb prevents passage of the impulse when it is first approached and the wave front travels only down the responsive limb. When this wave front reaches the distal end of the refractory region, the region has had time to recover and so the impulse is transmitted backward through the previously refractory patch and regains the original forking-point. At this point the two pathways available to it have by now also recovered and accept the impulse. Thus, it is as though a fresh impulse originated from the forking-point, but in reality it is still the sinus impulse "starting off on a second journey from a foreign port." If this theory is correct, the extrasystole is not a disturbance of impulse formation but rather the result of a disturbance in conduction. The action of some of our antiarrhythmic drugs can be explained on the basis of this theory—they may work by equalizing refractoriness in the limbs of an accommodating circuit and so make reentry impossible.

It has been long and widely believed that the constancy of the coupling interval confirms reentry as the probable mechanism of extrasystoles. But this is not necessarily so,[28] and serious doubt has been expressed that reentry is the usual or even a likely mechanism.[36]

Figure 11.1. Re-entry: for description, see text.

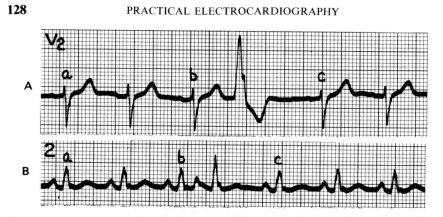

Figure 11.2. Comparison of interval following **ventricular premature beat** (*A*) and that following an **atrial premature beat** (*B*); see text.

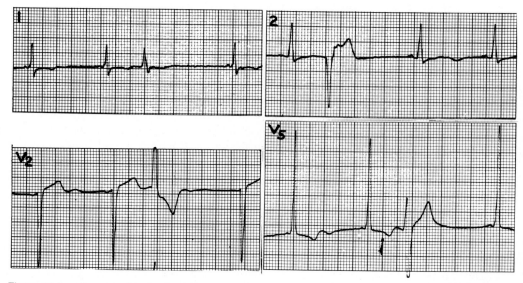

Figure 11.3. The premature beats all have constant coupling intervals and in leads 2, V₂ and V₅ look very different from the conducted sinus beats; however, in lead 1, the VPB bears a striking similarity to the conducted beats.

Diagnosis

The characteristic VPB is wide and bizarre ("sticks out like a sore thumb"), is not preceded by a premature ectopic P wave and is followed by a fully compensatory pause (fig. 11.2, *upper trace*). However, there are exceptions to all of these.

Although the VPB is typically wider than 0.11 sec, it is not always so and probably its most important morphological feature is that it is *different* from the flanking conducted beats. It may only *seem* narrow because part of the complex is isoelectric, and it is striking how often the VPB, in a single lead, can look beguilingly similar to the conducted pattern (fig. 11.3). The moral here, as in so many contexts, is: *when in doubt, take more leads.* On the other hand, it may be a genuinely narrow complex if it arises in one of the ventricular conduction fascicles near its origin (fascicular beat).[34] A rare exception to the typical picture is when an atrial premature beat (APB) or other atrial impulse coincidentally precedes the VPB. The post-extrasystolic cycle may be less than compensatory in several circumstances: when retrograde conduction from the ventricular extrasystole to the atria occurs, discharging the sinus node ahead of its regular schedule (fig. 11.4); when the postectopic cycle ends with an escape beat; and when the VPB interrupts a developing Wenckebach period. To understand these exceptions, it is essential to appreciate the reason for the usual compensatory pause.

If the premature beat does not disturb the sinus rhythm but merely takes the place of a conducted beat (fig. 11.2, *upper trace*), then the interval from the conducted beat before the extrasystole to the conducted beat following the extrasystole will be equal to two sinus cycles—because it *is* two sinus cycles. The compensatory pause is so called because the cycle following the premature beat *compensates* for the prematurity of the extrasystole and the sinus rhythm resumes again on schedule. In figure 11.2 the features of the VPB are contrasted with those of the APB. The sinus rhythm is disturbed by the APB—the sinus node is discharged by the ectopic impulse ahead of schedule—and so its "returning" cycle is also ahead of schedule and the postectopic cycle is less than compensatory. However, at times the atrial impulse discharges and suppresses the sinus node long enough for the returning cycle to be fully compensatory (fig. 11.5). Thus, the compensatory pause is a broken reed as a diagnostic prop and by itself must not be relied upon.

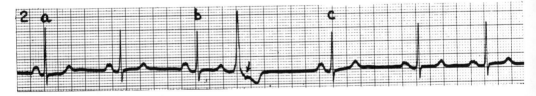

Figure 11.4. Three sinus beats are followed by a VPB with retrograde conduction to the atria (*arrow*). This discharges the sinus pacemaker ahead of schedule and so the returning cycle (*c*) is in turn ahead of schedule, i.e., $b - c$ = less than $a - b$.

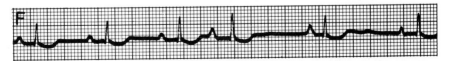

Figure 11.5. Atrial premature beat. The fourth beat is an APB, conducted with a prolonged P-R interval. It suppresses the sinus node with the result that the postextrasystolic cycle is fully compensatory; moreover, the atrial pacemaker is shifted for the last two cycles (atrial escape beats).

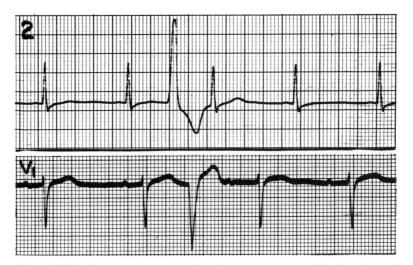

Figure 11.6. *Upper trace* shows a **VPB** sandwiched between two consecutive sinus beats without lengthening their cycle. *Bottom trace* shows another **interpolated VPB** but this one delays the next sinus beat because ("**concealed**") **retrograde conduction** into the A-V junction slows that next descending impulse and prolongs the P-R interval. (See also fig. 11.7.)

Another situation in which the ventricular extrasystole is not followed by a compensatory pause is when it is "interpolated" between two consecutive conducted beats; in such circumstances, the extrasystole is indeed an "extra" beat (fig. 11.6). Interpolated VPBs are often followed by lengthening of the subsequent P-R interval because of retrograde invasion of the A-V junction (concealed retrograde conduction), as in figure 11.6, lower trace. At times an interpolated ventricular bigeminy may progressively lengthen the successive P-R intervals until a beat is dropped and the seeming Wenckebach is completed (fig. 11.7).

Rule of Bigeminy

Simply stated, this "rule" implies that ventricular bigeminy tends to be self-perpetuating because long preceding cycles tend to precipitate a VPB. Once a VPB has materialized, the pause that follows it tends to precipitate another, and so on. In figure 11.8, a right ventricular (RV) extrasystole is followed by the usual lengthened (compensatory) postectopic cycle; this in turn precipitates a left ventricular (LV) extrasystole. The LV extrasystolic mechanism is apparently beholden to the rule of bigeminy and so, once initiated, the bigeminy tends to persist. The importance of the rule is that it acquaints us with the fact that lengthening of the ventricular cycle (slowing the rate) tends to precipitate an extrasystole. Also, by knowing the rule we realize that ventricular bigeminy may not represent such marked myocardial "irritability" as it suggests—preventing only the first extrasystole would prevent them all.

Morphology of Ventricular Ectopic Beats

In figure 11.8, we referred to *right* and *left* VPBs. The ventricle of origin of ectopic beats can best be recognized in lead V_1. If the ectopic ventricular complex in V_1 is predominantly positive, the impulse must be traveling toward the right and therefore coming from the left. Conversely, if the QRS of the ectopic beat is mainly negative in V_1, it must be travelling toward the left and therefore originating on the right. This simple rule of thumb allows one to recognize the ventricular origin of ectopic beats most of the time. This may be of importance in several respects: first, LV premature beats are more often associated with heart disease, whereas RV extrasystoles are commonly seen in normal hearts[18, 34]; then there is some evidence that LV extrasystoles are more likely than RV extrasystoles to precipitate ventricular tachycardia and/or fibrillation in the context of acute myocardial infarction,[31] and it is sometimes useful in confirming which ventricle is being paced by an artificial pacemaker.

Although unfortunately the ventricle of origin cannot always be determined with absolutely certainty from the surface tracing,[11] nevertheless, in a study involving over 1000 consecutive acute myocardial infarctions[31] not one single

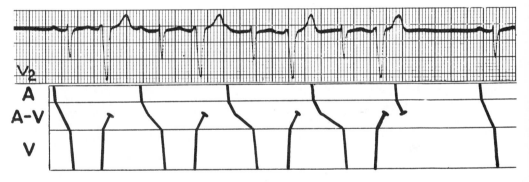

Figure 11.7. The same phenomenon ("**concealed**" **retrograde conduction**) following each of the **bigeminal VPBs**. With each successive VPB, the delaying effect of the retrograde conduction increases until conduction is completely thwarted and a Wenckebach-like sequence is completed.

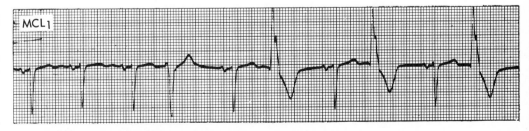

Figure 11.8. The **rule of bigeminy**. The appearance of a right VPB produces a longer (postectopic) cycle and this, by the rule of bigeminy, precipitates a LV bigeminy. In passing, again notice that the left VPBs sport a taller left rabbit ear.

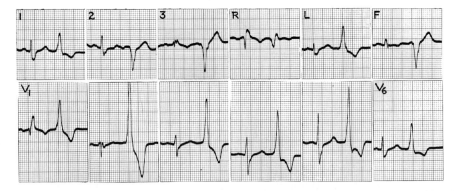

Figure 11.9. A typical pattern of **left ventricular premature beats**. The first beat in each lead is a sinus beat with RBBB; the second beat is a coupled ventricular extrasystole—note that the ectopic complexes are positive in all the chest leads (concordant positivity), and that they manifest a marked left axis deviation in the limb leads.

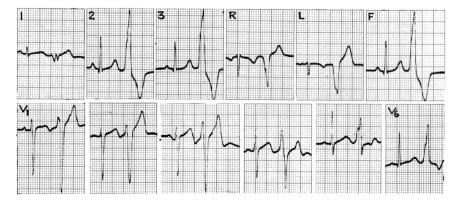

Figure 11.10. A typical pattern of **right ventricular extrasystoles**. In each lead the first beat is a sinus beat and the second a coupled extrasystole having a LBBB pattern in V₆, but wide initial r wave in V₁ and right axis deviation in the frontal plane.

instance of ventricular fibrillation developed among 249 patients who manifested only ectopics with a left bundle-branch block (LBBB) pattern in MCL₁ (presumed *right* ventricular), whereas 82 of 787 (10.4%) that manifested left ventricular ectopics fibrillated. Thus even if the source, as judged by surface morphology, is in doubt, the configuration of the ectopic QRS is helpful in distinguishing potentially malignant from relatively benign ventricular ectopy.

Typical 12-lead patterns of left and right ventricular ectopic beats are illustrated in figures 11.9 and 11.10.

Other morphological features worth noting are: LV ectopics usually produce a monophasic (R) or diphasic (qR) complex in V₁ complemented by a diphasic (rS) or monophasic (QS) complex in V₆ (fig. 11.11). Furthermore, if the upright complex in V₁ has two peaks ("rabbit ears," as coronary care nurses have picturesquely dubbed them),[8] the left ear is often taller than the right (figs. 11.8 and 11.11). RV ectopics, while they may show a typical LBBB pattern in V_6, more often than not have a right axis deviation in the frontal plane and sometimes a wide r ("fat little r wave") greater than 0.04 sec in V_1[34, 40] (fig. 11.12). In artificially paced RV beats, there is almost always a *left* axis deviation with characteristically monophasic complexes in the limb leads (positive in 1

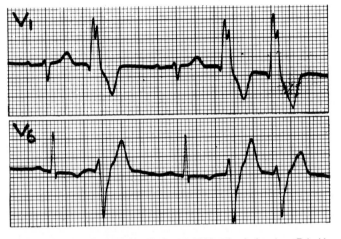

Figure 11.11. Typical morphology of **LV ectopic beats**: qR in V_1 with taller left rabbit-ear, and rS in V_6.

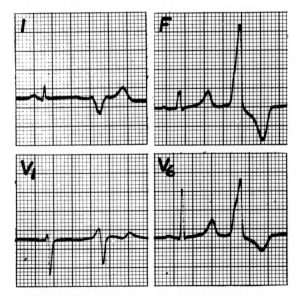

Figure 11.12. A common form of **RV ectopic beats**: a LBBB pattern in V_6, fat initial r wave in V_1 and a right axis deviation in the limb leads.

and aVL, negative in 2, 3 and aVF.)[3, 40] RV ectopics also tend to show a deeper (rS or QS) complex in V_4 than in V_1.[40]

If a ventricular extrasystole follows every sinus beat (fig. 11.13A), the result is bigeminal rhythm (**ventricular bigeminy**). If each sinus beat is followed by two ventricular extrasystoles (fig. 11.13B), the result is **ventricular trigeminy**. This term is also applied (perhaps less correctly) when every third beat (fig. 11.13C) is a VPB. To go beyond threesomes and speak of quadrigeminy, etc., serves no useful purpose. When three consecutive VPBs follow each sinus beat, we already have a better name for it since, by definition, three consecutive VPBs make the shortest definable run of tachycardia; and if every fourth beat is a VPB, no elasticity of terminology can justify implying that the beats are grouped in fours.

In the usual form of bigeminy (fig. 11.13A), in which an extrasystole is substituted for every alternate sinus beat, each extrasystole is followed by a compensatory pause; but it is possible to have interpolated bigeminy producing a form of tachycardia (fig. 11.14) in which, of course, no sinus beats are missing.

When ventricular extrasystoles occur so early that they interrupt the preceding T wave (fig. 11.15A), they carry an ominous significance.[39] A single effective impulse usually elicits a single ventricular response; but at one point in the ventricular cycle—near the apex of the T wave—a single stimulus is likely to evoke repeated responses. This is a dangerous situation, may lead to ventricular

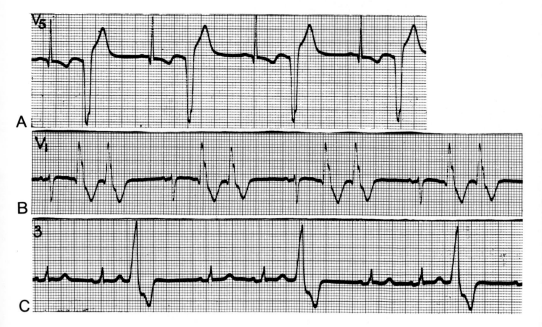

Figure 11.13.   (*A*) **Ventricular bigeminy**—every alternate sinus beat is replaced by a VPB. (*B*) **Ventricular trigeminy**—each sinus beat is followed by two VPBs. (*C*) Every third beat is a VPB—another form of **ventricular trigeminy**.

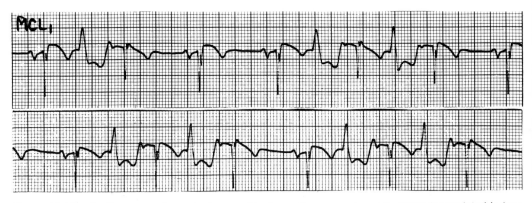

Figure 11.14. On three occasions short runs of tachycardia are produced by VPBs interpolated in two consecutive sinus cycles.

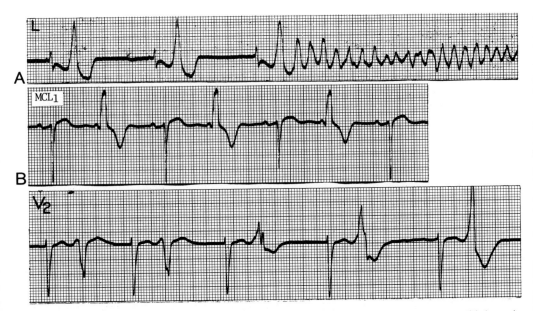

Figure 11.15. (*A*) After two closely coupled (R-on-T) warning ventricular extrasystoles, a third sparks **ventricular fibrillation**. (*B*) At a normal sinus rate (74/min), the ventricular extrasystoles appear after the next sinus P wave and are therefore "**enddiastolic**" **extrasystoles**. (*C*) **Atrial fibrillation** is interrupted by coupled ventricular extrasystoles of varying morphology—**multiform (or multifocal) VPBs** producing bigeminy.

fibrillation (fig. 11.15*A*) and is therefore called the "vulnerable" phase or period in the ventricular cycle. However, a European study[19] that carefully documented the ventricular extrasystoles that initiated fibrillation in 20 consecutive patients demonstrated that over half of the culpable extrasystoles landed beyond the T wave; and so it is not *only* the early ones that matter! Others have also questioned that the threat of "R-on-T" extrasystoles is supreme. Engel[7] reviewed the situation and decided that the R-on-T phenomenon was not the critical determinant of ventricular tachycardia or fibrillation in acute myocardial infarction. Evidence includes the following data: of 44 bouts of ventricular tachycardia in as many patients, only 6 (14%) were initiated by VPBs that landed on T waves[4]; many runs of ventricular tachycardia began with beats that landed beyond the ensuing sinus P wave[41]; and 78% of repetitive VPBs, defined as two or more consecutive ectopic ventricular complexes at a rate of at least 120/min, began with a "late" extrasystole.[33] Nevertheless, the R-on-T beat has by no means lost its sting and, of a series of 48 patients who developed ventricular fibrillation outside the hospital, the initiating beat was an R-on-T extrasystole in more than two thirds.[1a]

When at a normal sinus rate the ectopic beat is late enough to land after the next sinus P wave (fig. 11.15*B*), it is often referred to as an "**end-diastolic**" extrasystole.

When ventricular extrasystoles manifest different patterns in the same lead (as in fig. 11.15*C*), they are assumed to arise from different foci and are often called **multifocal**. It is always possible, however, that variation in shape may result from varying intraventricular conduction rather than from varying sites of origin; in fact, varying patterns of ectopy have been produced from the same artificially stimulated focus.[2a] For this reason, some prefer to use the more cautious term **multiform** rather than multifocal.

Retrograde conduction of ectopic ventricular impulses is common. At times they travel only as far as the A-V junction and then are recognized by lengthening of the ensuing P-R interval—"concealed" retrograde conduction (fig. 11.16*A*); but they often reach the atria and inscribe a retrograde P wave (fig. 11.16*B* and *C*). In fact many years ago Kistin and Landowne[13] detected such P waves, with the help of esophageal electrodes, in nearly half the cases they studied.

Figure 11.16*B* illustrates VPBs with retrograde conduction to the atria, the retrograde P′ wave negatively deforming the ST segment. Note that this P′ wave is negative in contrast with the sinus P waves and that it occurs before the next sinus P wave is due. These two features are characteristic of retrograde P′ waves from VPBs, and when such conduction can be recognized, the R-P′ interval is usually 0.16 to 0.20 sec (measured from the beginning of the QRS to the beginning of the P′ wave). In abnormal hearts this interval may be considerably increased, indicating retrograde V-A block, as in figure 11.16*C* in which the R-P′ interval of the first extrasystole is about 0.28 sec.

Prognostic Implications

Ventricular premature beats are ubiquitous. Most people have them more or less frequently and we sometimes find even continuous ventricular bigeminy in apparently normal hearts. They are usually a benign nuisance. During the acute phase of infarction, they appear in 80 to 90% of patients; but they are

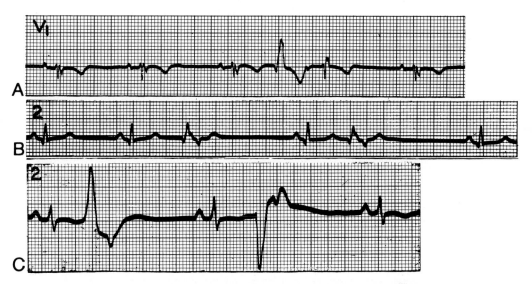

Figure 11.16. (*A*) The fourth beat is an **interpolated VPB**. Notice that it lengthens the P-R interval of the next sinus beat (from 0.16 to 0.22 sec)—evidence of "**concealed**" **(retrograde) conduction** into the A-V junction. (*B*) The two **ventricular extrasystoles** are followed by retrograde (inverted) P waves at normal R-P intervals of 0.17 and 0.19 sec. (*C*) Both **VPBs** are followed by retrograde P waves at abnormally prolonged R-P intervals (0.28 and 0.22 sec).

also found in the majority of actively employed middle-aged men.[9] When brought on by exertion they have been considered a sign of myocardial disease, though this is disputed (see Chapter 27). They are more readily provoked by isometric than by dynamic exercise.[1]

Many studies and much effort have been directed to evaluating the prognostic significance of ventricular extrasystoles following myocardial infarction. In patients who have survived myocardial infarction, complex VPBs (multiform, pairs) have been shown to increase the risk of sudden death[29, 35]; but whether similar ectopy increases the risk of sudden death in normal people has evoked divergent opinion. In a 7-year follow-up of 72 asymptomatic subjects with

Table 11.1
Lown's Grading System of Ventricular Ectopy[20, 21]

Grade	Description of Ventricular Extrasystoles
0	None
1	Less than 30/hour
2	30 or more/hour
3	Multiform
4A	Two consecutive
4B	3 or more consecutive
5	R-on-T

frequent and complex ectopy, none died although a number had angiographically proven significant coronary disease.[10]

Lown's grading system[20, 21] for ventricular ectopy (table 11.1) has become a popular frame of reference for gauging the risk of death after myocardial infarction—the risk supposedly increases as the numerical grade advances from 0 to 5. A subsequent study[2] suggests that the system is flawed in that the R-on-T (grade 5), supposedly the bleakest of indices, is less grave than the finding of paired extrasystoles (grade 4A) or ventricular tachycardia (grade 4B).

Moss[30] suggests a simplified two-level grading: low-risk—late cycle, unifocal, having a 2-year mortality of 10%; and high-risk—early cycle and/or multiform with an associated mortality of 20%. In the final analysis, the prognostic significance of VPBs after myocardial infarction is determined by the recency of the infarct—the longer ago the better—and the severity of the myocardial involvement. The presence of frequent and/or complex VPBs is merely an index of severe myocardial disease and therefore companion to a poor prognosis.

Salient Features of Ventricular Premature Beats

1. Bizarre, premature QRST complex, with prolonged QRS interval and ST segment sloping off in direction opposite to main QRS deflection
2. Morphological details sometimes characteristic
3. Usually followed by *fully* compensatory pause (unless interpolated)
4. P wave usually lost (submerged in ventricular complex), sometimes retrograde

---

Atrial Extrasystoles

The usual atrial extrasystole or premature beat (APB) has three features: a premature, ectopic P wave (the *sine qua non* and often labelled P′); a QRS unchanged from that of the conducted sinus beats; and a post-extrasystolic cycle that is less than compensatory. As a rule all of these characteristics are obvious, as in figure 11.17A; but no one, by itself, is completely reliable: the P′ wave may be unrecognizable as it sits upon the previous T wave; the QRS may show aberrant ventricular conduction; and the pause following the extrasystole may be fully compensatory because, as has been pointed out years ago, ectopic or retrograde atrial impulses have a way of stunning the sinus node and delaying its next discharge, and this delay may be sufficient to make the resulting cycle fully compensatory. It is extremely rare to have all three of these deceptions conspiring at the same time; therefore, if care is exercised, one usually has no trouble in identifying the APB.

In figure 11.17A, B−C is less than A−B; i.e., the postectopic cycle is less than fully compensatory. In figure 11.17B, on the other hand, the atrial ectopic impulse suppresses the sinus node long enough to make B−C actually a little

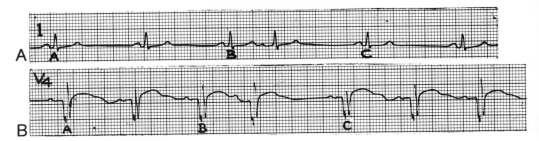

Figure 11.17. The fourth beat in each strip is an APB. In *A*, the extrasystole is followed by a less-than-compensatory pause (*B−C* = less than *A−B*). In *B*, the postectopic cycle is fully compensatory (*B−C* = *A−B*).

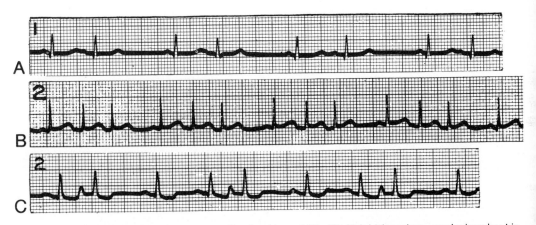

Figure 11.18. (*A*) **Atrial bigeminy**—every other beat is an APB. (*B*) **Atrial trigeminy**—each sinus beat is followed by a pair of APBs. (*C*) Every third beat is an APB, a sequence also, but less correctly, called **atrial trigeminy**.

longer than A−B; i.e., the postectopic cycle is even more than fully compensatory.

When an atrial extrasystole follows every sinus beat, the result is **atrial bigeminy** (fig. 11.18*A*). As with ventricular trigeminy, there are two sequences that are called **atrial trigeminy**: this term is more correctly applied when each sinus beat is followed by a pair of APBs (fig. 11.18*B*), but it is often also used when, as in figure 11.18*C*, an APB occurs every third beat.

Salient Features of Atrial Premature Beats

1. Abnormal, often inverted, premature P′ wave
2. Normal QRST
3. Ensuing interval about equal to, or slightly longer than, the sinus cycle

Atrial extrasystoles are often nonconducted; in fact much the commonest cause of an unexpected pause is the nonconducted APB (fig. 11.19*A*). It is better to refer to such beats as "nonconducted" rather than "blocked" because, by definition, block implies pathology and many such beats fail to be conducted only because they arise so early in the cycle that the A-V tissues are still *normally* refractory. We should always be at pains to differentiate pathological from physiological nonconduction, especially since failure to do this has led to widespread overdiagnosis and overtreatment of heart block (Chapter 24).

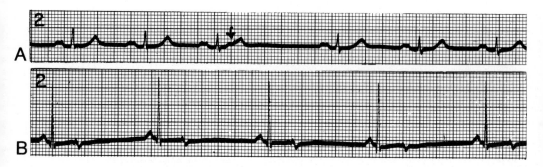

Figure 11.19. (*A*) **Nonconducted APB**: after three sinus beats, an APB (*arrow*) is too early in the cycle to be conducted to the ventricles. (*B*) Each sinus beat is followed by an APB which fails to reach the ventricles—**nonconducted atrial bigeminy**.

** THE COMMONEST CAUSES OF PAUSES ARE NONCONDUCTED ATRIAL PREMATURE BEATS**

Nonconducted atrial bigeminy (fig. 11.19*B*) is quite common and, if the premature P waves are not readily seen, may well be mistaken for sinus bradycardia. Figure 11.20, *A* and *B*, illustrates the development of a much more subtle bigeminy; if the preceding T waves during the regular sinus rhythm were not available for comparison, the slightly deforming P′ waves would not be recognizable. Figure 11.20*C* is from a teenager with nonconducted atrial bigeminy that masquerades as sinus bradycardia and was completely undiagnosable from the rhythm strip but was readily enough recognized from the regularly recurring cannon waves in the neck veins after each ventricular contraction.

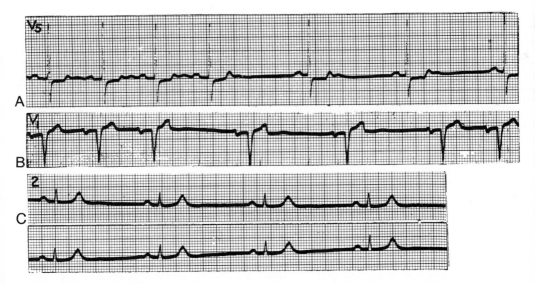

Figure 11.20. (*A*) After four sinus beats in *A* and after three sinus beats in *B*, a run of **nonconducted atrial bigeminy** develops. Note in each strip the subtle deformity of the T wave compared with the preceding T waves, due to superimposed P′ waves. In *C*, the T waves look a little too pointed for natural T waves; but when no previous T waves are available for comparison, it is impossible to diagnose the **atrial bigeminy**.

Often the early APB, instead of being nonconducted, is conducted with delay (prolonged P'-R). In figure 11.21A, the first APB is conducted with a P'-R shorter even than the sinus beats, whereas the second APB, which occurs earlier in the cycle (shorter R-P'), is conducted with a much prolonged P'-R. In figure 11.21B, showing atrial bigeminy, the sinus beats all have normal P-R intervals, and the APBs all have prolonged P'-R intervals. This introduces the important concept of R-P-dependent P-R intervals (the shorter the R-P, the longer the ensuing P-R, and vice versa). This concept is vital to the understanding of type I second degree A-V block and will be taken up in detail in Chapter 23.

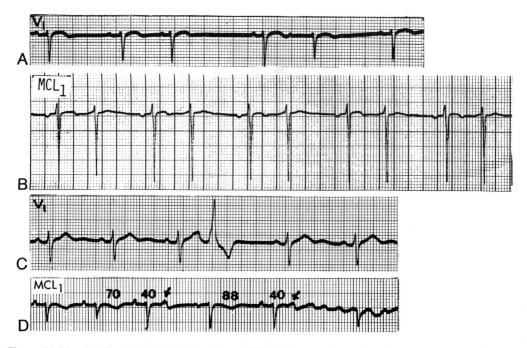

Figure 11.21. (A) The third and fifth beats are **APBs**. Note that the shorter R-P' of the second APB is complemented by a much prolonged P'-R interval. (B) **Atrial bigeminy** in which the P'-R of the APBs is much prolonged compared with the normal P-R of the sinus beats. (C) The fourth beat is an **APB with RBBB aberration**. Note the deformed T wave and the less-than-compensatory postectopic cycle. (D) When the **APB** is premature enough to make the P-P' interval (40) less than half the preceding P-P interval (88), an atrial tachyarrhythmia is triggered.

The APB may traverse the A-V junction at a normal rate only to find that one of the bundle branches or fascicles thereof is still refractory, and then aberrant ventricular conduction occurs (fig. 11.21*C*). In such cases the morphology of the QRS may be indistinguishable from ventricular ectopy, but spotting the preceding P′ wave and finding the postectopic cycle less than compensatory will usually establish its atrial origin.

Just as the more premature ventricular extrasystoles are likely to land in the vulnerable phase of the ventricular cycle and initiate ventricular tachycardia or fibrillation, so the earlier APBs may invade the atria in their vulnerable phase and spark tachycardia, flutter or fibrillation. Killip and Gault[12] offer the rule that, when the P-P′ interval is less than 50% of the previous P-P interval, it is quite likely to initiate an atrial tachyarrhythmia (fig. 11.21*D*).

As a right chest lead (such as MCL₁) is widely used for constant monitoring, it is useful to know that, when sinus beats have diphasic P waves, the positive deflection almost invariably precedes the negative; whereas when ectopic P waves are diphasic, the negative deflection usually precedes the positive (fig. 11.22).

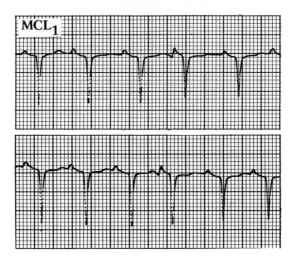

Figure 11.22. The fourth beat in each strip is an **APB**. Note that the diphasic, ectopic P′ wave has a negative/ positive polarity.

A-V Junctional Extrasystoles

Ectopic rhythms arising in the A-V junction may retrogradely activate the atria before, during or after ventricular activation; thus the retrograde P wave may be seen preceding or following the QRS complex, or it may be lost within it. When the P′ wave preceded the QRS complex, the rhythm used to be called "upper nodal"; when the P′ wave followed the QRS, it was called "lower nodal"; and when the P′ wave was lost in the QRS, it was called "midnodal" in accordance with the concept depicted in the *upper diagram* of figure 11.23. We now know, however, that the relationship of P′ to QRS in junctional rhythm is determined more by the rate of propagation in each direction (*lower diagram* in fig. 11.23) than by the level of the initiating pacemaker, and the terms "upper," "lower" and "mid-" have been generally discarded.

The term "nodal," in use for decades, was also partially abandoned several years ago because electrophysiologists reported that there was no evidence of pacemaker activity in the A-V node of animals; as a result, the time-honored "nodal" was largely replaced by "junctional." The question is not yet settled, and there appears to be little harm in retaining "nodal" as the simpler and more traditional term. Scherlag et al.[38] maintain that there are at least two rhythmogenic centers in the A-V junction: the node itself, which has an inherent rate of 45–60/min and responds to atropine by accelerating 20–30 beats/min; and a lower His rhythm with a slower inherent rate (35–45 min) unresponsive to atropine. While adhering to the philosophy that in our present state of

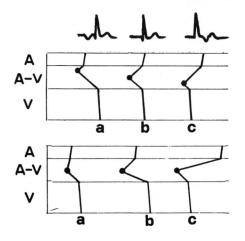

Figure 11.23. The top panel diagrams the concept of "upper," "mid-" and "lower" junctional rhythm. With the impulse travelling at a uniform rate in both directions, the level of origin determines whether atria or ventricles are activated first. In the bottom panel, the relationship of atrial to ventricular activation depends not on the level of the pacemaker, but on the rate of conduction in each direction.

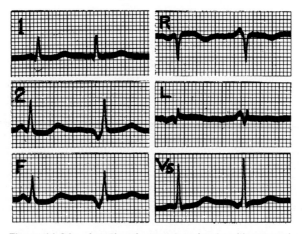

Figure 11.24. Junctional premature beats with antecedent P′ waves. In each lead, the first beat is a sinus beat, and the second, a junctional premature beat with short P′-R interval and typical P-wave polarity.

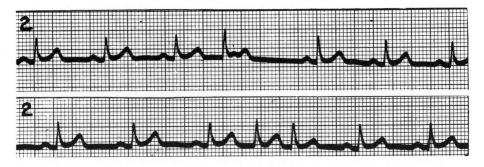

Figure 11.25. Junctional premature beats without retrograde conduction. In the upper strip, the fourth beat is a junctional extrasystole; and in the lower strip, the fourth and fifth beats are a pair of junctional prematures. In neither strip is the regular sinus discharge interrupted by retrograde conduction.

uncertainty it matters little whether we use the traditional or the more recently adopted term, for the sake of consistency we will stick to the current coin, junctional.

Junctional impulses are likely to be conducted retrogradely into the atria, and the usual polarity of the resulting P′ waves is illustrated in the premature beats in figure 11.24: The P′ wave is inverted in leads 2, 3 and aVF and in the left chest leads (V_{5-6}); it is upright in aVR and aVL, almost flat in lead 1 and variable, but often predominantly upright, in V_1.

Figure 11.25 contains junctional premature beats with no sign of retrograde atrial activity. Figure 11.26 shows what are probably junctional premature

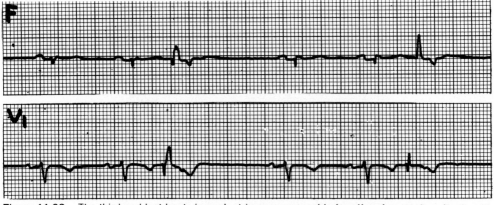

Figure 11.26.   The third and last beats in each strip are presumable **junctional premature beats** with aberrant ventricular conduction of the RBBB type and retroconduction to the atria following the aberrant QRS.

beats with differing degrees of right bundle-branch block (RBBB) aberration and retrograde conduction following the QRS. Although the first premature beat in each strip cannot with any degree of certainty be distinguished from ventricular extrasystoles, the fact that the second premature beat manifests a lesser degree of the RBBB pattern is a strong point in favor of aberration rather than ectopy.

A peculiarity of junctional beats is their tendency to develop aberration (usually minor) regardless of whether they are early (extrasystolic) or late (escape). This has been attributed to either (1) "preferential" conduction, which assumes that the impulse arises near the origin of a paraspecific (Mahaim) fiber and is conducted to the ventricles at least partially via this tract and so writes a distorted ventricular complex; or (2) eccentric placement of the junctional pacemaker so that the impulse is distributed asynchronously to the bundle branches and ventricles (see Chapter 16).

REFERENCES

1. Atkins, J. M., et al.: Incidence of arrhythmias induced by isometric and dynamic exercise. Br. Heart J. 1976: **38,** 465.
1a. Adgey, A. A. J., et al.: Initiation of ventricular fibrillation outside hospital in patients with ischemic heart disease. Br. Heart J. 1982: **47,** 55.
2. Bigger, J. T., and Weld, F. M.: Analysis of prognostic significance of ventricular arrhythmias after myocardial infarction. Shortcomings of the Lown grading system. Br. Heart J. 1981: **45,** 717.
2a. Booth, D. C., et al.: Multiformity of induced unifocal ventricular premature beats in human subjects: electrocardiographic and angiographic correlations. Am. J. Cardiol. 1982: **49,** 1643.
3. Castellanos, A., et al.: Unusual QRS complexes produced by pacemaker stimuli. Am. Heart J. 1969: **77,** 732.
4. Chou, T.-C., and Wenzke, F.: The importance of R-on-T phenomenon. Am. Heart J. 1978: **96,** 191.
5. Coronary Drug Project Research Group: The prognostic importance of premature beats following myocardial infarction; experience in the coronary drug project. J.A.M.A. 1973: **223,** 1116.
6. DeBacker, G., et al.: Ventricular premature contractions; a randomized non-drug intervention trial in normal men. Circulation 1979: **59,** 762.
7. Engel, T. R., et al.: The "R-on-T" phenomenon; an update and critical review. Ann. Intern.

Med. 1978: **88**, 221.

8. Gozensky, C., and Thorne, D.: Rabbit ears; an aid in distinguishing ventricular ectopy from aberration. Heart Lung 1974: **3**, 634.
9. Hinkle, L. E., et al.: The frequency of asymptomatic disturbances of cardiac rhythm and conduction in middle-aged men. Am. J. Cardiol. 1969: **24**, 629.
10. Horan, M. J., and Kennedy, H. L.: Characteristics and prognosis of apparently healthy patients with frequent and complex ventricular ectopy; evidence for a relatively benign syndrome with occult myocardial and/or coronary disease. Am. Heart J. 1981: **102**, 809.
11. Kaplinsky, E., et al.: Origin of so-called right and left ventricular arrhythmias in acute myocardial ischemia. Am. J. Cardiol. 1978: **42**, 774.
12. Killip, T., and Gault, J. H.: Mode of onset of atrial fibrillation in man. Am. Heart J. 1965: **70**, 172.
13. Kistin, A., and Landowne, M.: Retrograde conduction from premature ventricular contractions, a common occurrence in the human heart. Circulation 1951: **3**, 738.
14. Kotler, M. N., et al.: Prognostic significance of ventricular ectopic beats with respect to sudden death in the late postinfarction period. Circulation 1973: **47**, 959.
15. Langendorf, R.: Concealed A-V conduction. Am. Heart J. 1948: **35**, 542.
16. Langendorf, R.: Aberrant ventricular conduction. Am. Heart J. 1951: **41**, 700.
17. Langendorf, R., et al.: Mechanisms of intermittent ventricular bigeminy; I. Appearance of ectopic beats dependent upon the length of the ventricular cycle, the "rule of bigeminy." Circulation 1955: **11**, 442.
18. Lewis, S., et al.: Significance of site of origin of premature ventricular contractions. Am. Heart J. 1979: **97**, 159.
19. Lie, K. I., et al.: Observations on patients with primary ventricular fibrillation complicating acute myocardial infarction. Circulation 1975: **52**, 755.
20. Lown, B., and Wolf, M.: Approaches to sudden death from coronary heart disease. Circulation 1971: **48**, 130.
21. Lown, B., and Graboys, T. B.: Management of patients with malignant ventricular arrhythmias. Am. J. Cardiol. 1977: **39**, 910.
22. Marriott, H. J. L., et al.: Ventricular fusion beats. Circulation 1962: **26**, 880.
23. Marriott, H. J. L.: Differential diagnosis of supraventricular and ventricular tachycardia. Geriatrics 1970: **25**, 91.
24. Marriott, H. J. L., and Fogg, E.: Constant monitoring for arrhythmias and blocks. Mod. Concepts Cardiovasc. Dis. 1970: **39**, 103.
25. Marriott, H. J. L., and Myerburg, R. J.: In *The Heart*, Ed. 5, edited by J. W. Hurst. McGraw-Hill, New York, 1982.
26. Marriott, H. J. L., and Thorne, D. C.: Dysrhythmic dilemmas in coronary care. Am. J. Cardiol. 1971: **27**, 327.
27. Massumi, R. A., et al.: Paradoxic phenomenon of premature beats with narrow QRS in the presence of bundle branch block. Circulation 1973: **47**, 543.
28. Michelson, E. L., et al.: Fixed coupling; different mechanisms revealed by exercise-induced changes in cycle length. Circulation 1978: **58**, 1002.
29. Moss, A. J., et al.: Ventricular ectopic beats and their relation to sudden and nonsudden death after myocardial infarction. Circulation 1979: **60**, 998.
30. Moss, A. J.: Clinical significance of ventricular arrhythmias in patients with and without coronary artery disease. Prog. Cardiovasc. Dis. 1980: **23**, 33.
31. O'Bryan, E. C.: Personal communication, 1981.
32. Pick, A., et al.: Depression of cardiac pacemakers by premature impulses. Am. Heart J. 1951: **41**, 49.
33. Roberts, R., et al.: Initiation of repetitive ventricular depolarizations by relatively late premature complexes in patients with acute myocardial infarction. Am. J. Cardiol. 1978: **41**, 678.
34. Rosenbaum, M. B.: Classification of ventricular extrasystoles according to form. J. Electrocardiol. 1969: **2**, 289.
35. Ruberman, W., et al.: Ventricular premature beats and mortality after myocardial infarction. N. Engl. J. Med. 1977: **297**, 750.
36. Schamroth, L.: *The Disorders of Cardiac Rhythm*, Ed. 2, p. 148. Blackwell, Oxford, 1980.
37. Scherf, D., and Schott, A.: *Extrasystoles and Allied Arrhythmias*, Ed. 2. Grune & Stratton, New York, 1973.
38. Scherlag, B. J., et al.: Differentiation of "A-V junctional rhythms." Circulation 1973: **48**, 304.
39. Smirk, F. H., and Palmer, D. G.: A myocardial syndrome, with particular reference to the

occurrence of sudden death and of premature systoles interrupting antecedent T waves. Am. J. Cardiol. 1960: **6**, 620.

40. Swanick, E. J., et al.: Morphologic features of right ventricular ectopic beats. Am. J. Cardiol. 1972: **30**, 888.
41. Tye, K.-H., et al.: R-on-T or R-on-P phenomenon? Relation to the genesis of ventricular tachycardia. Am. J. Cardiol. 1979: **44**, 632.

Review Tracings

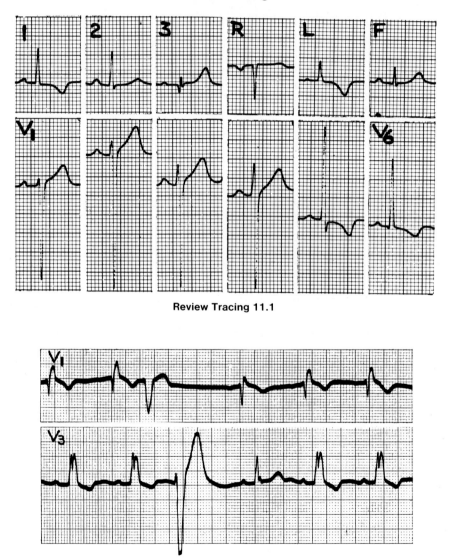

Review Tracing 11.1

Review Tracing 11.2

For interpretation, see page 482

12

Supraventricular Tachycardias

Background

For more than half a century, the mechanisms of the atrial tachyarrhythmias have provided a lively forum for discussion and argument, rising at times to the level of acrimony! After the turn of the century, it all began with the jellyfish when Mayer (1908) demonstrated that a ring of its "umbrella" could sustain a continuously circulating excitation wave. Then Mines (1913) and Garrey (1914) in turn showed that a ring of muscle cut from the atrium of fish or the ventricle of a turtle could similarly sustain a "circus movement."

Encouraged by such demonstrations, Lewis[19] claimed to prove that a similar circus movement, negotiating a sweep round the venae cavae, was responsible for both atrial flutter and fibrillation in man. Atrial and "nodal" tachycardia, on the other hand, he believed were due to the rapid repetitive firing of a single atrial or A-V nodal focus. His views held almost undisputed sway for a quarter century.

Scherf et al., in a series of animal experiments and articles between 1942 and 1950, demonstrated that a circus movement was unlikely to be the mechanism of flutter and fibrillation and concluded that all the atrial tachyarrhythmias were caused by rapid discharge of a single focus. Prinzmetal (1950) enlisted the candid eye of the movie camera and came to the same conclusion.[24] But recently, thanks to the development of sophisticated intracardiac recording techniques, the current crop of cardiac physiologists are convinced that the great majority of our supraventricular tachycardias are due to circus movements (reentry, reciprocation). The mechanisms of atrial flutter and fibrillation for the present remain sub judice.

Classification

It is now clear that the overwhelming majority of "supraventricular tachycardias" (SVT) are in fact reciprocating tachycardias (RT) due to a circulating

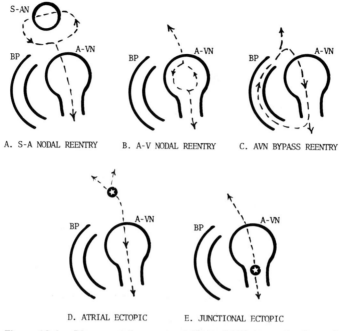

Figure 12.1. Diagrammatic representations of various mechanisms of SVT. S-AN = sinus node; BP = bypass tract; A-VN = A-V node.

wave and not to enhanced automaticity (rapidly firing focus). Such circulating waves have a number of available orbits (fig. 12.1) and, in concert with the rapidly accumulating recent data, SVTs can be reclassified as shown in table 12.1. In fact, such a classification is a bare skeleton, because the number of possible reentry circuits, as Barold says, "staggers the imagination."[2]

To Differentiate or Not to Differentiate

To differentiate the reentry varieties from each other and from their ectopic mimics is often difficult or impossible from the surface tracing and may be achieved only by sophisticated invasive methods. The question naturally arises: Does it matter which mechanism is operative—reentrant or ectopic—from a therapeutic point of view? Indeed, if for no other reason, it is worth making the distinction because, in the intractable case, there is a method tailor-made for the reentry type. For any circulating wave to perpetuate itself, the advancing head must not catch up with the (refractory) tail (fig. 12.2). Thus there must always be a gap of nonrefractory tissue between the head and the tail of the circulating wave. If an extraneous impulse, either natural (premature systole) or artificial (pacemaker stimulus), manages to find the gap between the head and the tail, it will render the gap refractory and the circulating wave will be

Table 12.1
Classification of Supraventricular Tachycardias

A. *Reentry*
   1. S-A nodal (fig. 12.1*A*)
   2. Atrial
   3. A-V junctional (fig. 12.1*B*)
   4. A-V junctional bypass (fig. 12.1*C*)
   5. Kent bundle (WPW)
B. *Ectopic*
   1. Atrial (fig. 12.1*D*)
   2. A-V junctional (fig. 12.1*E*)

Table 12.2
Proportion of SVTs Due to A-V Nodal Reentry (AVNR)

Authors	Total SVTs	AVNR	Percentage
Wellens and Durrer (1975)[31]	54	47	87
Wu et al. (1978)[34]	79	50	63
Farshidi et al. (1978)[9]	60	40	67

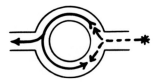

Figure 12.2. A circus movement is interrupted if an extraneous impulse, natural or artificial, "finds the gap" between the head and the tail of the circulating wave.

halted. Thus a temporary pacemaker set to "titrate" the gap is a ready-made method of terminating any circus-movement tachycardia. Furthermore, with more and more victims of intractable tachycardias becoming candidates for surgery, precise definition of the mechanism may be mandatory.

Reentry

For reentry to take place, there are three prerequisites: (1) an available circuit, (2) differing responsiveness in two limbs of the circuit, and (3) conduction slow enough to give the initially unresponsive limb time to recover. In most hearts at normal rates, these conditions are not fulfilled at the time of a normally spreading impulse because all tissues have recovered fully and there are therefore no differences in responsiveness. But an *early* impulse, such as an extrasystole, may find unequal refractoriness since all tissues may not have had

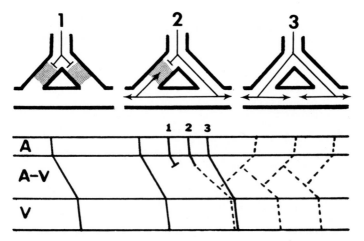

Figure 12.3. The three triangular diagrams represent three stages of recovery in a circuit of conducting tissue. In *1*, both descending limbs of the circuit are refractory; in *2*, one is still refractory, but the other has recovered; and in *3*, both have recovered. Reentry cannot take place at stages 1 or 3; but at the intermediate stage 2, the recovered limb accepts the impulse and, provided conduction is slow enough for the refractory limb to recover, a circus movement is initiated. In the laddergram, the fate of three atrial extrasystoles, 1, 2 and 3, arriving in the A-V junction at the above stages 1, 2 and 3 is diagrammed. Beat 1 is blocked, 3 is conducted normally, and 2 initiates a reciprocating tachycardia in the A-V junction (*dashed lines*).

time to recover fully. Thus most paroxysms of RT are initiated by premature beats. Figure 12.3 illustrates diagrammatically the initiation of RT in the A-V junction by an atrial extrasystole (see the legend to fig. 12.3). The "zone" of prematurity during which an extrasystole can initiate such a tachycardia is known as the "tachycardia-initiating interval." Much the most common mechanism of SVT is A-V junctional reentry (table 12.2).

Although most paroxysms of SVT are initiated by supraventricular extrasystoles, obviously any impulse that reaches an available circuit at a time when it is "ripe" for reentry can initiate RT; and since ectopic ventricular impulses are frequently conducted retrogradely into the junction (and beyond), the SVT may be initiated by ventricular ectopic beats. Figure 12.4 illustrates a reciprocating tachycardia initiated by a single ventricular extrasystole. Figure 12.5 illustrates the initiation of RT by a run of ventricular tachycardia—the first four ectopic impulses are thwarted by the descending sinus impulses; not until the fifth beat of the ventricular tachycardia does the retrograde impulse reach the level of the accommodating circuit (see fig. 12.5, laddergram) and trigger a reentering tachycardia. It then climbs further and activates the atria before the next sinus impulse is due.

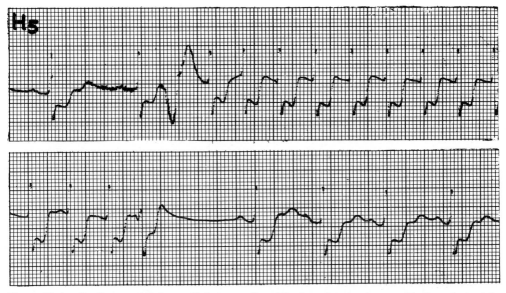

Figure 12.4. Continuous strip from a Holter recording. After two sinus beats, a ventricular extrasystole initiates a **SVT**. Further evidence of its reciprocating nature is that it is also terminated by a premature beat.

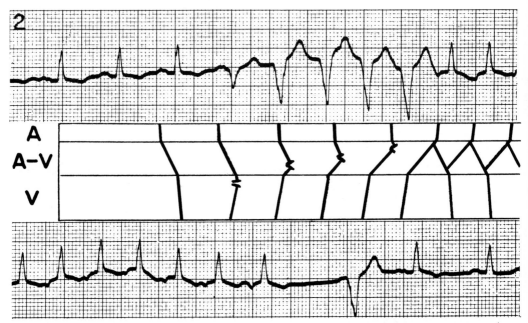

Figure 12.5. After three sinus beats, a run of **ventricular tachycardia** begins with a fusion beat. Three subsequent ectopic ventricular impulses meet the descending sinus impulse progressively higher in the A-V junction (see laddergram). The fifth beat of the tachycardia reaches the atria before the next sinus beat is due and, on the way, finds a "ripe" circuit in the junction and initiates a **reciprocating tachycardia.**

Differentiation between Reentry and Ectopic Tachycardias

There are a number of features in the clinical tracing that may help to distinguish between automatic and reciprocal mechanisms. Some of these aids to identification are dependent upon P-wave detail, and this is frequently obscured because of the inevitable superimposition of the atrial wave upon various parts of the ventricular complex and especially the T wave. Nevertheless, the following points are suggestive of an automatic, ectopic mechanism: (1) the presence of "warm-up" (progressive acceleration for the first few beats); (2) the sameness of all the P′ waves, including the first; and (3) a premature stimulus resetting the tachycardia (in much the same way that an atrial premature beat resets the sinus rhythm). On the other hand, in RT, (1) "warm-up" is absent; (2) the initial (ectopic) P′ wave differs from the subsequent (retrograde) P′ waves; (3) a premature stimulus does not reset, but may terminate the tachycardia (by "finding the gap"): When a tachycardia is terminated by a naturally occurring premature beat (fig. 12.4), it suggests that the extrasystolic stimulus has "found the gap" and therefore favors a reciprocating mechanism; and (4) prolongation of the first P′-R interval is the rule. These differentiating features are illustrated in Figures 12.4, 12.6 and 12.7.

Several other clues point to specific mechanisms: If the P′ wave during the paroxysm is similar to the sinus P waves, there is a likelihood of sinus nodal reentry (fig. 12.8). If the P′ waves are neither of retrograde form and polarity

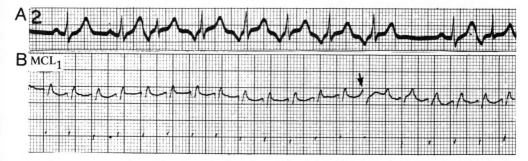

Figure 12.6. (*A*) The P′ waves are identical, and there is slight initial "warm-up"; there is no significant P′-R prolongation, and the diagnosis is, most likely, **ectopic atrial** or **junctional tachycardia**. (*B*) At the beginning of the strip, it is impossible to identify the mechanism—it could be ectopic atrial or junctional or reciprocating. Toward the end of the strip, an atrial extrasystole (*arrow*) provides the probable answer: the premature stimulus does not terminate the tachycardia, but it does "reset" the atrial rhythm; i.e., the two atrial cycles embracing the extrasystole equal less than two cycles of the tachycardia, indicating the diagnosis **atrial tachycardia**.

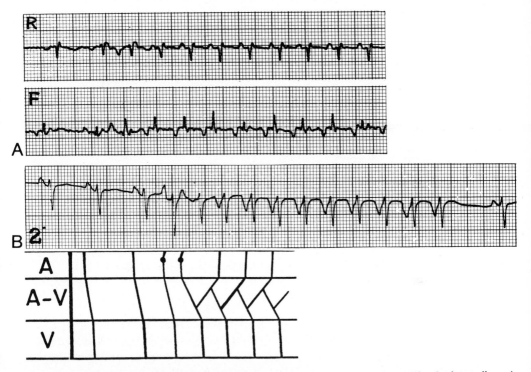

Figure 12.7. (*A*) In each lead, a single atrial extrasystole initiates a run of **reciprocating tachycardia**; note upright retrograde P′ waves in aVR, inverted in aVF. (*B*) It takes "two to tango," and here it took two atrial extrasystoles, the second conducted with delay (long P′-R), to find a "ripe" reentry circuit (see laddergram). The ectopic P′ waves are upright, while the subsequent retrograde P′ waves are sharply inverted.

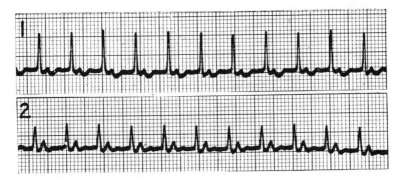

Figure 12.8. Supraventricular tachycardia, possibly due to sinus-nodal reentry. Rate 170; upright P waves are clearly discernible immediately following each QRS with P-R intervals of 0.26 sec.

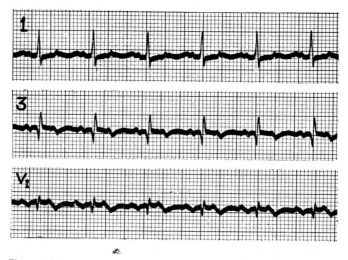

Figure 12.9. An example of probable **ectopic atrial tachycardia** with 2:1 A-V block.

nor like the sinus P waves (fig. 12.9) an ectopic atrial or reentrant atrial tachycardia is likely. The presence of A-V dissociation or A-V block rules out A-V nodal bypass reentry; on the other hand, the presence of ventricular aberration tends to confirm the presence of an A-V nodal bypass; and when the cycle length of the tachycardia increases (rate decreases) with the development of bundle-branch block (BBB), it indicates that the bypass tract is on the same side as the BBB. A negative P′ in lead 1 indicates a probably left-sided bypass.[8a]

Additional clues that may lead one to suspect a reentrant tachycardia using a convenient bypass tract are: (1) the "incessant" form of tachycardia (see below); (2) the tachycardia is initiated when the sinus rate accelerates without the intervention of an APB or prolongation of the P-R interval; and (3) the retrograde P′ waves are associated with an R-P′ shorter than the P′-R.[9]

The relationship of P′ to QRS in various RTs is diagrammatically presented in figure 12.10; and the incidence of functioning concealed bypasses found in some carefully investigated series are listed in table 12.3.

Sinus tachycardia may at times be difficult to differentiate from other forms of SVT if the sinus P wave is unrecognizable because it is perched on the T wave (see fig. 12.11). In such cases, vagal stimulation may provide a ready answer.

Accessory Pathways

Patients with accessory pathways are congenitally equipped with the de luxe milieu for the development of RT since they have two parallel pathways between atria and ventricles, with different conduction velocities and different refractory periods. Either route may act as the anterograde or retrograde pathway; if the wave front travels down the normal conduction system and up the accessory bundle, the QRS complex will be normal; but if it travels down the accessory pathway, the QRS will show the characteristics of preexcitation.

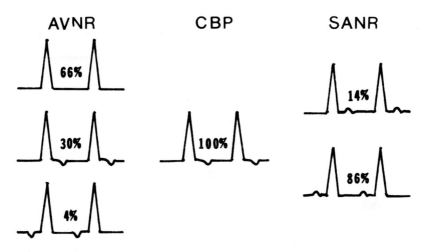

Figure 12.10. Relationship of P to QRS in reentry tachycardias. Series and percentages from Wu et al.[34] Key: AVNR = A-V nodal reentry; CBP = concealed extranodal bypass; SANR = sinus nodal reentry.

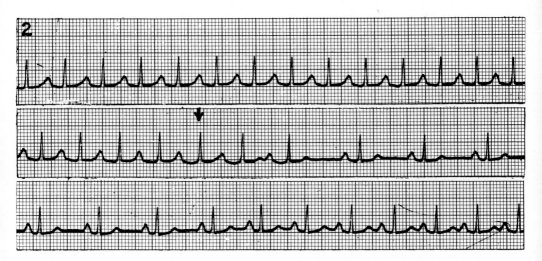

Figure 12.11. In the *top strip*, it is impossible to identify the mechanism of the tachycardia (it could be junctional ectopic, RT, etc.); but carotid sinus stimulation (*arrow*) peels the otherwise unrecognizable P wave off the T wave and makes evident the diagnosis of **sinus tachycardia**.

More and more cases are coming to light in which the accessory pathway is capable of only retrograde conduction (table 12.3). In such patients, the Wolff-Parkinson-White (WPW) pattern fails to show up during sinus rhythm; so a Kent bundle may not be suspected ("concealed WPW"). The importance of recognizing this situation in the intractable tachycardia in whom corrective surgery is being considered is obvious. The RTs complicating preexcitation will be enlarged upon and illustrated in Chapter 18.

In summary, the three most common mechanisms may be suspected from the following observations[34]: A retrograde P wave coincident with the normal QRS (no BBB), with or without evidence of organic heart disease, points to the commonest mechanism of all, **A-V nodal reentry**. A younger subject, a faster rate, BBB during the tachycardia but no organic heart disease indicates a **concealed bypass** in action. P′ waves preceding the normal (no BBB) QRS in the presence of organic disease points to **S-A nodal/atrial reentry**. Based on Wu's series of 66 patients with reentry SVT, the approximate incidence of the above three mechanisms is 76, 14 and 11%.[34]

A Glut of Terms

Apart from the innumerable available circuits, the profusion of descriptive adjectives that have been applied to SVT is nothing short of bewildering; and it is not easy for the clinician to sort out a rational classification. The terms employed fall into two categories: those that apply to clinical behavior—paroxysmal, persistent, permanent, incessant, sustained, nonsustained, chronic, relapsing, repetitive. The second group describe mechanisms—ectopic, automatic, reentrant, reciprocating, circus-movement, slow-fast, fast-slow, orthodromic, antidromic. From this plethora of epithets it is virtually impossible to derive a clear-cut taxonomy.

Paroxysmal retains its traditional meaning—starting and stopping abruptly. Persistent, permanent and incessant appear to be used interchangeably and seem to mean an arrhythmia that is actually neither incessant nor necessarily permanent—as these words were understood before the advent of contemporary electrophysiology—but is definitely persistent in that the tachycardias recur

---

Salient Features of Supraventricular Tachycardia
1. Rapid (100–250), regular, normal QRS complexes
2. Abnormal P waves constantly related to QRS (may not be discernible)
3. ST-T depressions frequently seen

Table 12.3
Proportion of SVTs Using Concealed Bypass (CBP)

Authors	Total SVTs	CBP	Percentage
Wellens and Durrer (1975)[31]	54	5	9
Gillette (1977)[14]	15	10	67
Sung et al. (1977)[27]	46[a]	12	26
Wu et al. (1978)[34]	79	9	11
Farshidi et al. (1978)[9]	60	12	20
Krikler (1978)[17]	20	9	45
	274	57	21

[a] Includes some cases of atrial "flutter-fibrillation."

with annoying perseverance. Here there is overlap with recurrent and repetitive, which mean what they say without a commitment to any particular schedule of recurrence. Clearly there is also overlap with chronic—an arrhythmia that obviously may be recurrent or persistent. Sustained and nonsustained refer to the duration of each bout.

Hence it is evidently possible in the 1980s to have a "chronic, persistent, recurrent, nonsustained, paroxysmal tachycardia"!

On the other side of the ledger, ectopic and automatic are used interchangeably and indicate that the mechanism is a rapidly discharging pacemaking center. Reentrant, reciprocating and circus-movement are all more or less synonymous and mean that the tachycardia concerned is the offspring of a circulating (macro- or micro-) wave. The simple, appealing Anglo-Saxon terms, slow-fast and fast-slow, always apply to reentrant rhythms and inform us which pathway is used for the anterograde (first adjective) and which for the retrograde (second adjective) journey. Orthodromic and antidromic are specifically applied to the reciprocating tachycardias complicating the WPW syndrome and tell us whether the A-V junction was used for the downward anterograde (orthodromic) or upward retrograde (antidromic) journey.

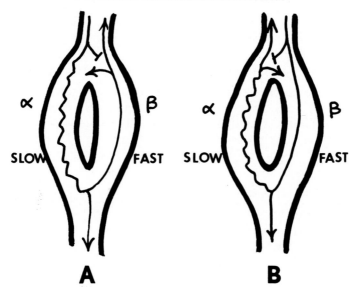

A   **B**

Figure 12.12. Mechanisms of **A-V nodal reentry**. (*A*) Slow-fast: the descending, premature impulse finds the fast (*β*) pathway, with its longer refractory period, still refractory, so travels down the slow (*α*) path producing a prolonged P'-R interval; returning up the now recovered fast pathway it reaches the atria at about the same time that the descending impulse reaches the ventricles, with the result that the P' wave is lost in the QRS. (*B*) Fast-slow: In the less likely event that the fast pathway recovers before the slow, the descending impulse travels down the fast path and rapidly reaches the ventricles; meanwhile the ascending impulse climbs slowly up the now recovered *α* pathway to produce a long R-P' interval.

Dual Pathways in the Junction

Investigators have repeatedly demonstrated that the A-V junction may contain two parallel and conductively independent pathways ("longitudinal dissociation"), one characterized by faster conduction but a longer refractory period (beta, *β*); and the other by slower conduction but a shorter refractory period (alpha, *α*).[28] Thanks to such available pathways, two distinct varieties of A-V nodal reentrant tachycardias may dvelop (fig. 12.12): (1) using the fast pathway downward and the slow pathway upward ("fast-slow"), and (2) using the slow path downward and the fast upward ("slow-fast"). These two forms have different manifestations in the clinical tracing (table 12.4).

Fast-Slow Form. This is the less common form and various authors have called it "persistent," "permanent," "incessant" or "repetitive," in honor of its troublesome quality of being almost always present. It is more common in children than in adults and, since its wave front goes down the fast pathway, does not begin with a prolonged P'-R interval; but since it uses the slow pathway for its return to the atria, the R-P' interval is relatively long. Thus in the clinical tracing it manifests a longer R-P' than P'-R (fig. 12.13*a*).

Slow-Fast Form. This more common form is usually triggered by an atrial premature beat associated with a prolonged P'-R interval—since the early impulse has found the faster path still refractory and has travelled downward by the slower path. In these cases, the P' wave often coincides with the QRS complex—since it travels up the fast pathway—and is therefore often invisible in the surface ECG (fig. 12.13*b*).

By no means do all SVTs fit nicely into one of these pigeon-holes. For example, figure 12.7 illustrated two tachycardias initiated by atrial extrasystoles with prolonged P'-R intervals (slow-fast?) in which the R-P' is longer than the complementary P'-R (fast-slow?).

Table 12.4
Dual Pathways of A-V Junction

	Slow-Fast	Fast-Slow
Synonyms	Paroxysmal	Persistent, etc.
Initial P'-R	Prolonged	Normal
Incidence	Usual form in adults	Especially in children
Triggered by	APB	Spontaneous; APB; VPB
P' relations	Coincides with QRS	R-P' > P'-R

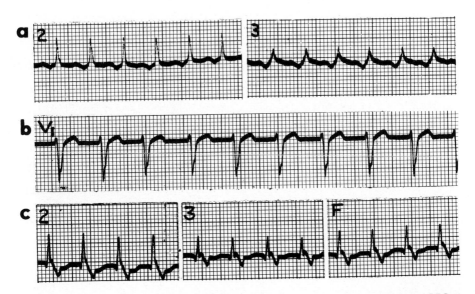

Figure 12.13. Three forms of **junctional tachycardia**. In *a*, the P' waves precede the QRS at a short P'-R interval (R-P' > P'-R = "fast-slow"?). In *b*, the P wave is lost in the QRS—the common "slow-fast" pattern with A-V nodal reentry. In *c*, the P' waves just follow the QRS (R-P' < P'-R = usual pattern of reentry using concealed bypass, or less common "slow-fast" nodal reentry).

Ectopic Tachycardias

With the renewed enthusiasm for circus-movements, the ectopic (automatic) focus tends to be forgotten. But, though the incidence of ectopic atrial and junctional tachycardias is small, they are very real arrhythmias,[16] relatively common in children though rare in adults.[13] It is likely that there are more than one underlying mechanisms: in one series of 52 cases of ectopic atrial tachycardia, most were initiated by late APBs, some began de novo, and a few were ushered in by brief runs of atrial fibrillation.[1]

Two examples of undisputed ectopic atrial tachycardia are the multifocal (or "chaotic") variety (fig. 12.14A), most often associated with chronic lung disease,[20, 26] and the "PAT with block" so often seen as a manifestation of digitalis intoxication (fig. 12.14B). Despite these common associations, it is important to realize that all multifocal tachycardias are not due to lung disease—it may even occur in the newborn[8]; and all "PAT with block" is not caused by digitalis overdosage[23] (fig. 12.15).

Ectopic junctional tachycardia in children may be catastrophic, especially after cardiac surgery.[12]

ST-T Changes

Secondary changes in the ST-T segment may occur. Any tachycardia shortens diastole and therefore curtails coronary blood flow; if the coronaries are already

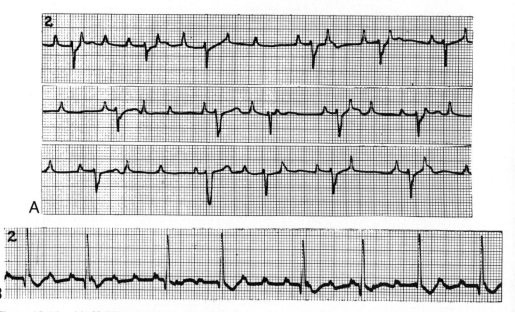

Figure 12.14. (A) **Multifocal atrial tachycardia** in a patient with chronic obstructive lung disease. Note the sharply peaked P-pulmonale even in ectopic P waves, their irregularity in form and rate, and the varying A-V conduction ratio. (B) **Atrial tachycardia** with varying A-V block due to digitalis intoxication.

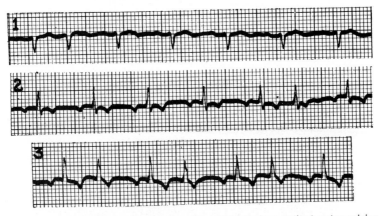

Figure 12.15. **Atrial tachycardia** with A-V block in a patient *not* receiving digitalis. The P′ waves are barely discernible in lead 1 and are inverted in 2 and 3. The A-V block varies between 2:1 and 3:2. In lead 3 the 3:2 ratio is constant, leaving the ventricular beats grouped in pairs—a common cause of bigeminy (see Chapter 23).

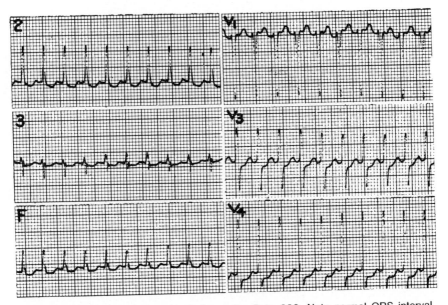

Figure 12.16. **Supraventricular tachycardia.** Rate 230. Note normal QRS interval and ST depression.

diseased, and sometimes even if they are normal, ST-T changes characteristic of myocardial ischemia may develop. These changes consist of depression of the ST segment with inversion of the T wave and are well shown in figure 12.16. ST and T-wave changes of this sort may persist for hours or days after the paroxysm of tachycardia has ceased, the so-called **post-tachycardia syndrome** (fig. 12.17).

Preexisting BBB

Atrial arrhythmias may be complicated by preexisting intraventricular block (fig. 12.18). In such circumstances the QRS complexes will obviously be prolonged, and this combination may be difficult or impossible to differentiate from ventricular tachycardia.

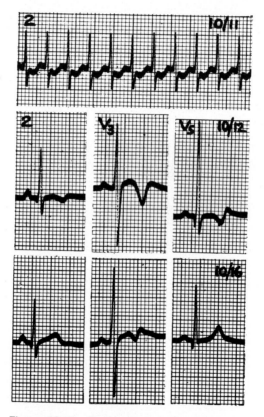

Figure 12.17. Post-tachycardia syndrome. A paroxysm of supraventricular tachycardia is in progress in the upper strip; note associated ST depression. On the following day marked ST-T abnormalities are present; these have disappeared 4 days later. From a 12-year-old boy with a normal heart.

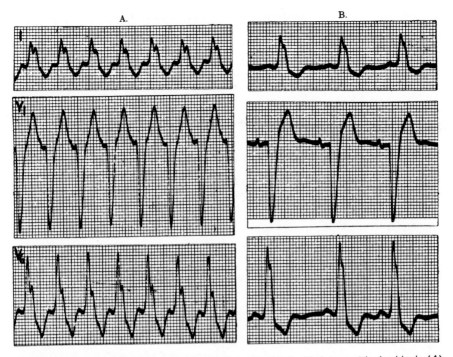

Figure 12.18. Supraventricular tachycardia associated with *intraventricular block.* (*A*) This tracing is indistinguishable from ventricular tachycardia. (*B*) When sinus rhythm is later restored the QRST pattern remains virtually unchanged, proving that a supraventricular rhythm was present in *A*.

References

1. Arciniegas, J. G., et al.: Characterization of the onset of ectopic atrial tachycardia with A-V block (abstr.). Am. J. Cardiol. 1981: **47**, 496.
2. Barold, S. S., and Coumel, P.: Mechanisms of atrioventricular junctional tachycardia; role of reentry and concealed accessory bypass tracts. Am. J. Cardiol. 1977: **39**, 97.
3. Brugada, P., et al.: Observations in patients showing A-V junctional echoes with a shorter P-R than R-P interval. Am. J. Cardiol. 1981: **48**, 611.
4. Coumel, P.: Junctional reciprocating tachycardias. The permanent and paroxysmal forms of A-V nodal reciprocating tachycardias. J. Electrocardiol. 1975: **8**, 79.
5. Denes, P., et al.: Multiple reentrant tachycardias due to retrograde conduction of dual atrioventricular bundles with atrioventricular nodal-like properties. Am. J. Cardiol. 1979: **44**, 162.
6. Epstein, M. L., et al.: Incessant atrial tachycardia in childhood; association with rate-dependent conduction in an accessory atrioventricular pathway. Am. J. Cardiol. 1979: **44**, 498.
7. Epstein, M. L., et al.: Long-term evaluation of persistent supraventricular tachycardia in children; clinical and electrocardiographic features. Am. Heart J. 1981: **102**, 80.
8. Farooki, Z. Q., and Green, E. W.: Multifocal atrial tachycardia in two neonates. Br. Heart J. 1977: **39**, 872.
8a. Farre, J., and Wellens, H. J. J.: The value of the electrocardiogram in diagnosing site of origin and mechanism of supraventricular tachycardia, p. 131. In *What's New in Electrocardiography*, edited by H. J. J. Wellens and H. E. Kulbertus. Martinus Nijhoff, Boston, 1981.
9. Farshidi, A., et al.: Electrophysiologic characteristics of concealed bypass tracts: Clinical and electrocardiographic correlates. Am. J. Cardiol. 1978: **41**, 1052.

10. Gallagher, J. J., et al.: Etiology of long R-P′ tachycardia in 33 cases of supraventricular tachycardia. (abstr.). Circulation 1981: **64** (supp. IV), 145.

11. Gallagher, J. J., et al.: Role of Mahaim fibers in cardiac arrhythmias in man. Circulation 1981: **64,** 176.

12. Garson, A., and Gillette, P. C.: Electrophysiologic studies of supraventricular tachycardia in children; I. Clinical-electrophysiologic correlates. Am. Heart J. 1981: **102,** 233.

13. Gillette, P. C., and Garson, A.: Electrophysiologic and pharmacologic characteristics of automatic ectopic atrial tachycardia. Circulation 1977: **56,** 571.

14. Gillette, P. C.: Concealed anomalous cardiac conduction pathways: A frequent cause of supraventricular tachycardia. Am. J. Cardiol. 1977: **40,** 848.

15. Gillette, P. C.: Advances in the diagnosis and treatment of tachydysrhythmias in children. Am. Heart J. 1981: **102,** 111.

16. Goldreyer, B. N., et al.: The electrophysiologic demonstration of atrial ectopic tachycardia in man. Am. Heart J. 1973: **85,** 205.

17. Krikler, D.: Concealed pre-excitation. J. Electrocardiol. 1978: **11,** 209.

18. Langendorf, R.: Aberrrant ventricular conduction. Am. Heart J. 1951: **41,** 700.

19. Lewis, T.: *The Mechanism and Graphic Registration of the Heart Beat,* Ed 3. Shaw, London, 1925.

20. Lipson, M. J., and Naimi, S.: Multifocal atrial tachycardia (chaotic atrial tachycardia). Clinical associations and significance. Circulation 1970: **42,** 397.

21. Lown, B., et al.: Interrelationship of digitalis and potassium in auricular tachycardia with block. Am. Heart J. 1953: **45,** 589.

22. Lown, B., et al.: Paroxysmal atrial tachycardia with block. Circulation 1960: **21,** 129.

23. Morgan, W. L., and Breneman, G. M.: Atrial tachycardia with block treated with digitalis. Circulation 1962: **25,** 787.

24. Prinzmetal, M., et al.: *The Auricular Arrhythmias.* Charles C Thomas, Springfield, Ill., 1952.

25. Ross, D. L., et al.: Spontaneous termination of circus movement tachycardia using an atrioventricular accessory pathway: incidence, site of block and mechanisms. Circulation 1981: **63,** 1129.

26. Shine, K. I., et al.: Multifocal atrial tachycardia. Clinical and electrocardiographic features in 32 patients. N. Engl. J. Med. 1968: **279,** 344.

27. Sung, R. J., et al.: Clinical and electrophysiologic observations in patients with concealed accessory atrioventricular bypass tracts. Am. J. Cardiol. 1977: **40,** 839.

28. Sung, R. J., and Castellanos, A.: Supraventricular tachycardia; mechanisms and treatment. Cardiovasc. Clin. 1980: **11,** 27.

29. Ward, D. E., et al.: Incessant atrioventricular tachycardia involving an accessory pathway; preoperative and intraoperative electrophysiologic studies and surgical correction. Am. J. Cardiol. 1979: **44,** 428.

30. Wellens, H. J. J.: *Electrical Stimulation of the Heart in the Study and Treatment of Tachycardias.* University Park Press, Baltimore, 1971.

31. Wellens, H. J. J., and Durrer, D.: The role of an accessory atrioventricular pathway in reciprocal tachycardia; observations in patients with and without the Wolff-Parkinson-White syndrome. Circulation 1975: **52,** 58.

32. Wolff, G. S., et al.: The fast-slow form of atrioventricular nodal reentrant tachycardia in children. Am. J. Cardiol. 1979: **43,** 1181.

33. Wu, D., and Denes, P.: Mechanisms of paroxysmal supraventricular tachycardia. Arch. Intern. Med. 1975: **135,** 437.

34. Wu, D., et al.: Clinical, electrocardiographic and elecrophysiologic observations in patients with paroxysmal supraventricular tachycardia. Am. J. Cardiol. 1978: **41,** 1045.

Review Tracings

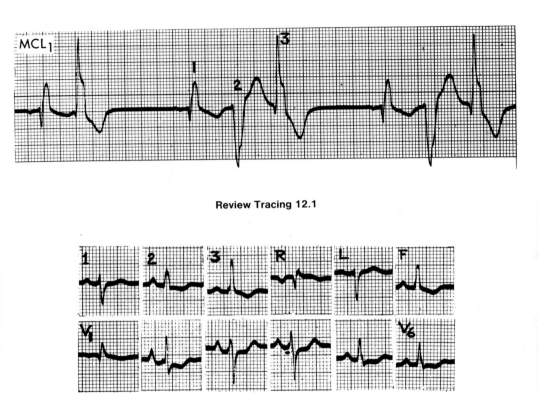

Review Tracing 12.1

Review Tracing 12.2

For interpretation, see page 482

13

Atrial Flutter

The first ECG of atrial flutter in man was published by Einthoven in 1906; it remained for Jolly and Ritchie in 1911 to draw a clear electrocardiographic distinction between fibrillation and flutter.

Electrophysiological Mechanisms

Although the mechanism mediating atrial flutter is not settled—and indeed, different examples of flutter may have different mechanisms—most recent authorities lean toward some form of reentry.[4, 5, 7, 15]

For a quarter of a century, following the claims of Lewis, a circus-movement around the venae cavae was accepted almost universally as the proven mechanism. Scherf[11] and Prinzmetal,[10] independently, then claimed to have demonstrated that the atrial tachyarrhythmias were due to the repetitive firing of a single focus rather than to a reentry mechanism. More recent work suggests that the likely mechanism in most examples of atrial flutter is either a micro-reentry or automatic focus low in the atrium.[6, 7, 12–15]

An apparent prerequisite for the development of atrial flutter is delayed conduction within the atria and/or a disturbance in sinus nodal function.[3, 8, 13]

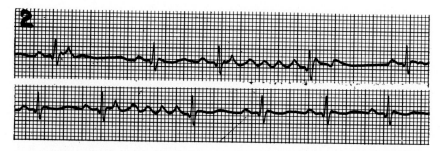

Figure 13.1. The strips are not continuous. Each strip illustrates the initiation of a short, one-second, burst of **atrial flutter**.

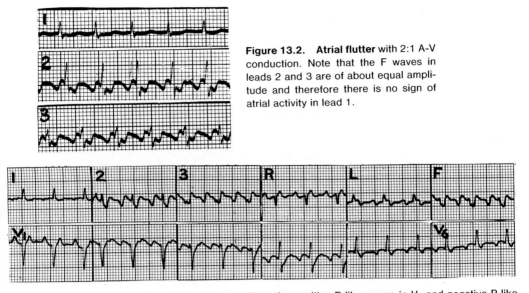

Figure 13.2. Atrial flutter with 2:1 A-V conduction. Note that the F waves in leads 2 and 3 are of about equal amplitude and therefore there is no sign of atrial activity in lead 1.

Figure 13.3. Atrial flutter in a 12-lead tracing. Note the positive P-like waves in V_1 and negative P-like waves in V_5 and V_6. Evidence of atrial activity, as usual, is minimal in lead 1.

The concomitance of a conduction disturbance itself supports the probability of a reentry mechanism. Further support is afforded by the fact that flutter cannot be converted to sinus rhythm by a single atrial extrastimulus.[7, 15]

Flutter may be precipitated by a single atrial extrasystole arising in the atrial vulnerable period; it may persist for only a few seconds (fig. 13.1), though it usually pursues a more chronic course lasting for weeks, months, or years; patients are on record in whom flutter has lasted for more than two decades.

Electrocardiographic Features

In the ECG atrial flutter is recognized by the constantly undulating or zigzagging baseline that has been likened to the teeth of a saw or to a picket fence. This pattern of flutter waves—conventionally labeled "FF"— is usually best seen in leads 2, 3, and aVF; and because the excursion of the flutter waves is approximately equal in leads 2 and 3, by Einthoven's equation (II = I + III) there is little visible evidence of the flutter in lead 1 (fig. 13.2). In the precordial leads, the flutter wave is usually a discrete positive P-like wave in V_1 (figs. 13.3–13.6) with a correspondingly negative P-like wave in V_{5-6} (fig. 13.3). Occasionally, the flutter waves may be so inconspicuous that they can be seen only in lead Vl or in an esophageal lead (see fig. 13.12).

Since the days of Lewis (1913), atrial flutter is sometimes separated into "common" and "uncommon" forms according to the contour of the atrial waves. The atrial waves of the common form have prominent negative components in the inferior leads (2, 3, and aVF) with impressive positive deflections

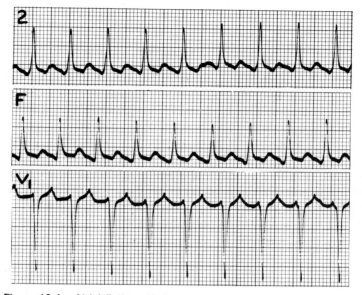

Figure 13.4.   Atrial flutter with 2:1 A-V conduction. Alternate F waves coincide with the ventricular complex, and the diagnosis could easily be missed. Note the positive P-like waves in lead V_1.

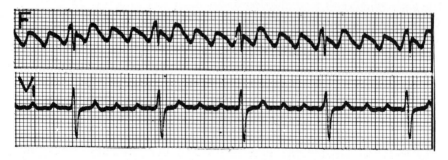

Figure 13.5.   Atrial flutter with 4:1 A-V conduction. The zigzag, "saw-tooth" waves are readily recognized in aVF but assume the usual positive P-like form in V_1.

in aVR and aVL; and the undulation of the baseline is continuous. The uncommon form is any other flutter whose waves fail to conform with *both* these features. The common form supposedly originates in the low (caudad) part of one of the atria, while some at least of the uncommon type arise in the high right atrium (cephalad).

The Birmingham school[12] divides flutter into types I and II. Type I has an inherent rate between 240 and 338/min and is readily converted by atrial pacing; whereas type II fails to respond to atrial pacing and has a faster rate (between 340 and 433/min). Type II may represent an intermediate form between classical atrial flutter and atrial fibrillation.

Untreated, the usual A-V conduction ratio is 2:1 (fig. 13.2–13.4), and when this prevails, it may be difficult to recognize either the flutter or the ratio because every other atrial wave will be partially masked and distorted by the QRS-T conglomerate (fig. 13.4). When the conduction ratio increases because of treatment or disease, the recognition becomes easy since consecutive atrial cycles become plainly visible (fig. 13.5).

Conduction ratios of 2:1 and 4:1 are common and are frequently seen in the same tracing (see figs. 13.11 and 13.16), but odd number ratios (1:1, 3:1, etc.) are rare. Figure 13.6 presents an example of 3:1 conduction; and figure 13.7, with a ventricular rate of about 260/min, is presumably due to atrial flutter with 1:1 conduction.

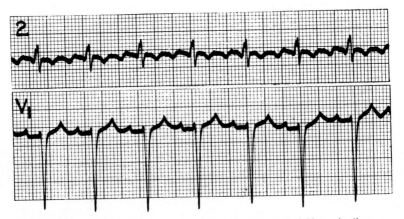

Figure 13.6. **Atrial flutter** at a rate of 306/min with 3:1 A-V conduction—a rare ratio.

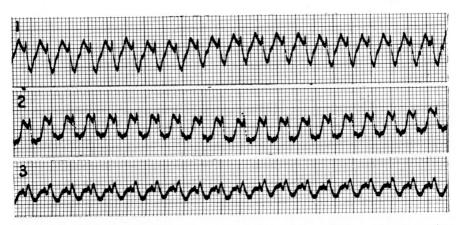

Figure 13.7. **Atrial flutter** at a rate of 256/min with 1:1 A-V conduction and an incomplete right bundle-branch block pattern.

Conduction ratios of 6:1 (fig. 13.8)—and still higher even-number ratios—are sometimes seen. You can tell that there is a stable conduction relationship because the atrial waves retain a constant relationship to the QRS complexes. Compare this with the situation in the two rhythm strips in figure 13.9. In both of these, the relationship of the FF waves to the QRS complexes is constantly changing while the ventricular rhythm is regular; therefore, since the ventricular rate is slow enough, it is reasonable to diagnose atrial flutter with complete A-V block.

There can be considerable variation in the rate of flutter waves (fig. 13.10). Usually between 280 and 320/min, they may be as slow as 200/min and as rapid as over 400/min. The atrial rate may be greatly influenced by drugs. Digitalis tends to accelerate it, whereas quinidine, procainamide, and lidocaine slow the atrial rate. In figure 13.11, the *top strip* was taken while the patient was receiving digitalis alone; quinidine was then started, and 24 hours later, the atrial rate had slowed from 270 to 224/min. In this patient, the drug failed to convert the flutter, and, when it was discontinued, the atrial rate returned to about 275/min.

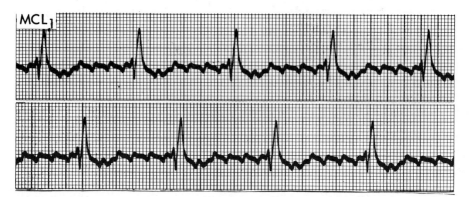

Figure 13.8. The strips are continuous. **Atrial flutter** with 6:1 A-V conduction and right bundle-branch block.

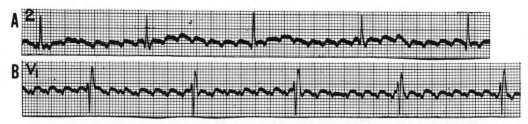

Figure 13.9. Two examples of **atrial flutter** with **complete A-V block**. Note that the relationship of atrial to ventricular complexes is constantly changing, while the ventricular rhythm is independently regular. In *A*, the atrial rate is 310/min, and the junctional escape rate is 42/min. In *B*, the atrial rate is approximatetly 290/min, and the ventricular rate is 44/min. Note the unusual notched morphology of the FF waves.

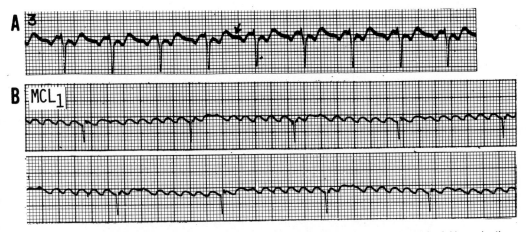

Figure 13.10. (*A*). **Atrial flutter** with the unusually slow atrial rate of 204/min and 2:1 A-V conduction. Note the "isoelectric shelf" between atrial waves (*arrow*). (*B*) Atrial flutter at an unusually rapid rate (about 375/min) with 8:1 A-V conduction.

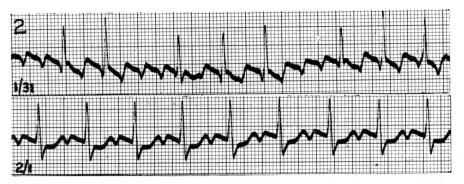

Figure 13.11. **Atrial flutter** before and after quinidine administration. In the *upper strip*, the atrial rate was 270/min with varying 2:1 and 4:1 A-V conduction. After 24-hours' treatment with quinidine (*bottom strip*), the atrial rate is only 224/min with constant 2:1 A-V conduction.

Genesis of Flutter Waves

The genesis of the atrial flutter waves is uncertain. The continuous undulating or zigzag pattern in leads 2 and 3 was one of the points that led Lewis to assume a continuous circulating (circus-movement) wave. But Prinzmetal[10] demonstrated that the continuous zigzag could be "pulled apart" by slowing the atrial rate, leaving an "isoelectric shelf" between consecutive atrial deflections (fig. 13.10*A*). He suggested that the initial negative part of the complex represented depolarization of the atria and the terminal positive part repolarization (Ta or T$_P$ wave).

It is sobering to realize that atrial flutter has yet to be satisfactorily defined. The typical picture is easy to recognize: "saw-tooth" waves in inferior leads at

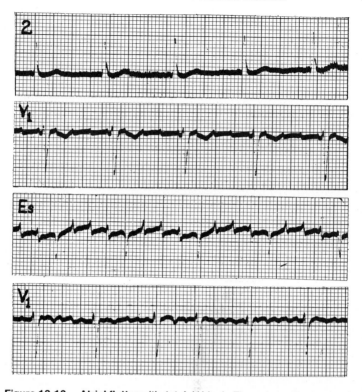

Figure 13.12. **Atrial flutter** with 4:1 A-V block. The only routine lead that showed any sign of atrial activity was V_1. The third strip (Es) is an esophageal lead. The fourth strip is V_1 after digitalization, showing **atrial fibrillation**.

a rate of about 300/min. But there is an extensive borderland between flutter and tachycardia, which no one has as yet satisfactorily staked out; and there may, in fact, be no sharply dividing line between the atrial tachyarrhythmias. Prinzmetal claimed decades ago that the typical pattern of atrial tachycardia, produced in the experimental animal by the application of aconitine to the atrial muscle, could be changed, in turn, to the typical pattern of atrial flutter and on to atrial fibrillation merely by increasing the discharge rate of the ectopic focus by warming it. Figure 13.13 illustrates diagrammatically both the development of Ta waves and the shortening of the isoelectric shelf as the rate increases.

To date, although it is now clear that the majority of supraventricular tachycardias are due to reentry, this "unitary concept" of ectopic atrial arrhythmias remains to be conclusively challenged.

Patterns of A-V Conduction

The most interesting feature of the ECG in atrial flutter is the fascinating variety of conduction patterns that may develop because of the interplay at varying levels in the A-V junction.[1] The untreated 2:1 ratio is due to normal refractoriness in the A-V junction and therefore should not be called 2:1 "block"—the junction is playing its normal physiological role as a shield protecting the ventricles from atrial bombardment. The conduction antics in

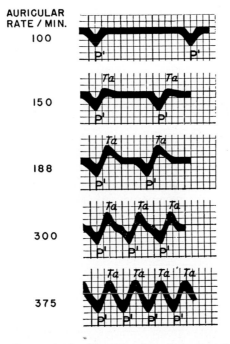

AURICULAR
RATE / MIN.
100

150

188

300

375

Figure 13.13. Illustrating that with increase in rate (1) the Ta wave assumes greater prominence and (2) the isoelectric shelf becomes shorter. (Reproduced with kind permission of the publishers from *The Auricular Arrhythmias*, by Myron Prinzmetal and others, Charles C Thomas, 1951.)

atrial flutter frequently produce a bigeminal rhythm; two of these bigeminal patterns are illustrated in figures 13.14 and 13.15B.

When digitalis or propranolol is administered to reduce the ventricular rate to a normal level, the 2:1 filter continues to operate while the alternate impulses that pass the filter suffer Wenckebach-type conduction delay at a lower level in the junction—perhaps 4:3 conduction at first (fig. 13.16) producing a form of trigeminy, then 3:2 (fig. 13.15B), and finally 2:1 conduction. With 2:1 conduction at the higher level and 2:1 conduction now at the lower level as well, the net A-V ratio becomes the desirable 4:1 goal of therapy, with a now normal ventricular rate of about 75/min (fig. 13.15C).

Pick and Langendorf[11] long ago pointed out that the A-V conduction time in atrial flutter was considerably prolonged owing to the effect of concealed conduction of the very numerous atrial impulses. They calculated that the usual "F-R" interval during 2:1 conduction (measured from the nadir of the atrial wave to the beginning of the ventricular complex) probably measured between 0.26 and 0.46 sec because of the concealed conduction in the A-V junction of the alternate impulses that failed to reach the ventricles. Thus, although the immediately preceding flutter wave does not represent the atrial impulse that is conducted to the ventricles, its changing relationship to the following QRS alerts one's eye to the developing Wenckebach-type conduction; in figure 13.16, the *square brackets* lying on their backs indicate the progressively lengthening A-V interval, though the actual impulse responsible for the ventricular activation is the preceding one, as indicated in the laddergram.

Atrial flutter is relatively uncommon—its incidence in adults is said to be perhaps one-twentieth that of atrial fibrillation. It is most often found in

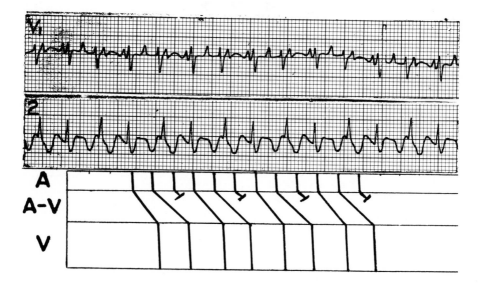

Figure 13.14.   Atrial flutter at a rate of 268/min with 3:2 Wenckebach periods.

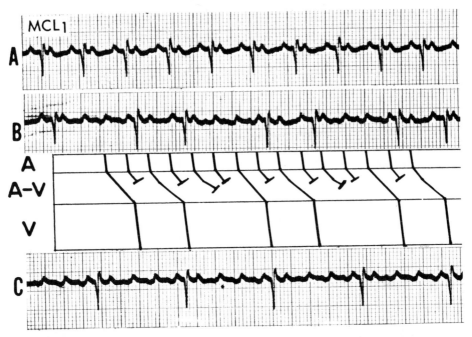

Figure 13.15. Illustrates the effect of propranolol on A-V conduction during **atrial flutter**. (*A*). Before therarpy: Atrial rate is 262/min with 2:1 conduction. (*B*) Less than a minute after 2 mg propranolol had been given intravenously: Atrial rate is unchanged, but the drug has produced 3:2 block of the alternate impulses that have passed the 2:1 filter. This combination of 2:1 filtering at a higher level and 3:2 conduction at a lower level produces alternating 4:1 and 2:1 conduction leaving the ventricular beats in bigeminal rhythm. (*C*) The atrial rate has slowed slightly to 252/min, and the drug has now produced 2:1 block of the alternate impulses so that the net A-V ratio is now 4:1.

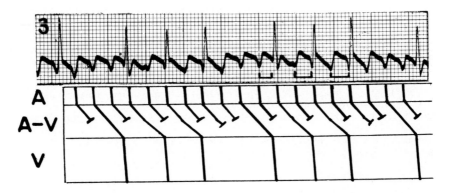

Figure 13.16. **Atrial flutter** at a rate of 306/min with 2:1 filtering at a high level in the junction and 4:3 Wenckebach conduction of the beats that pass the filter. The net result of this is trigeminal grouping of the ventricular beats. The *supine square brackets* highlight the lengthening A-V relationship (see text).

ischemic hearts over the age of 40 years and is strikingly rare in mitral disease compared with atrial fibrillation. It may complicate any form of heart disease, however, and may be precipitated by any acute illness. In the first few years of life, it is much more common than atrial fibrillation, presumably because it requires a greater mass of atrial muscle than the young child possesses to sustain fibrillation.

Salient Features of Atrial Flutter

1. "Saw-tooth" or undulating baseline of "F" waves in inferior leads (2, 3 and aVF)
2. Sharp, P-like waves in V_1
3. Normal QRS complexes in 2:1 to 8:1 A-V ratio
4. T waves may distort the F-wave pattern

References

1. Besoain-Santander, M., Pick, A., and Langendorf, R.: A-V conduction in auricular flutter. Circulation 1950: **2**, 604.
2. Cohen, S. I., et al.: P loops during common and uncommon atrial flutter in man. Br. Heart J. 1977: **39**, 173.
3. Dhingra, R. C., et al.: Clinical significance of prolonged sinoatrial conduction time. Circulation 1977: **55**, 8.
4. Gavrilescu, S. and Cotoi, S.: Monophasic action potential of right human atrium during atrial flutter and after conversion to sinus rhythm: Argument for re-entry theory. Br. Heart J. 1972: **34**, 396.
5. Guiney, T. E., and Lown, B.: Electrical conversion of atrial flutter to atrial fibrillation; flutter mechanism in man. Br. Heart J. 1972: **34**, 1215.
6. Inoue, H., et al.: Clinical and experimental studies of the effects of atrial extrastimulation and rapid pacing on atrial flutter cycle: evidence of macroreentry with an excitable gap. Am. J. Cardiol. 1981: **48**, 623.
7. Josephson, M. E., and Seides, S. F.: *Clinical Cardiac Electrophysiology. Techniques and Interpretations,* pp. 195–202. Lea & Febiger, Philadelphia, 1979.
8. Leier, C. V. et al.: Prolonged atrial conduction. A major predisposing factor for the development of atrial flutter. Circulation 1978: **57**, 213.
9. Neporent, L. M.: Atrial sounds in atrial fibrillation and flutter. Circulation 1964: **30**, 893.
10. Prinzmetal, M., et al.: *The Auricular Arrhythmias.* Charles C Thomas, Springfield, Ill., 1952.
11. Scherf, D., et al.: Mechanism of flutter and fibrillation. Arch. Intern. Med. 1953: **91**, 333.
12. Wells, J. L., et al.: Characterization of atrial flutter; studies in man after open heart surgery using fixed atrial electrodes. Circulation 1979: **60**, 665.
13. Watson, R. M., and Josephson, M. E.: Atrial flutter; I. Electrophysiologic substrates and modes of initiation and termination. Am. J. Cardiol. 1980: **45**, 732.
14. Wellens, H. J. J., et al.: Epicardial excitation of the atria in a patient with atrial flutter. Br. Heart J. 1971: **33**, 233.
15. Wellens, H. J. J.: *Electrical Stimulation of the Heart in the Study and Treatment of Tachycardias,* pp 27–39. University Park Press, Baltimore, 1971.

Review Tracings

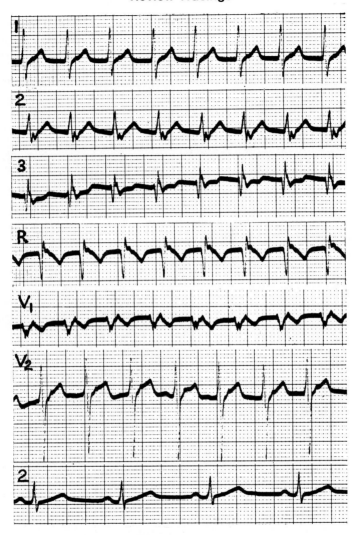

Review Tracing 13.1

For interpretation, see page 482

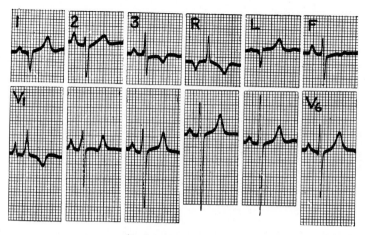

Review Tracing 13.2

For interpretation, see page 482

More Practical Points

Technicians are not expected to learn how to interpret the tracing, but they should be told certain useful points that will make their work more intelligent and more interesting. They should watch the tracing come out of the machine with a trained, alert eye and they should be given the following practical instructions.

Notice carefully the pattern of these four leads:

1. *Lead 1*: If the complexes are all inverted, check your arm electrodes—they are almost certainly reversed (*b* in fig. 3.11, p. 28).
2. *Lead 3*: If the first deflection of the ventricular complex is downward (a Q wave), tell the patient to take a deep breath and hold it for a few heart beats (fig. 26.6, p. 000). This may help to distinguish between important and unimportant Q waves.
3. *Standard limb leads*: If the three main components (P, QRS and T) are virtually invisible in any one of these leads, the probability is that the two electrodes for that lead are attached to the two legs (fig. 3.12)—check your hook-up!
4. *Lead V_6*: If the ventricular complex shows a deep downstroke (S wave) instead of the usual tall upright wave, take a lead further to the left (V_7) to try and get a pattern with the major deflection upward.

14

Atrial Fibrillation

Total irregularity of the arterial pulse, referred to as "delirium cordis," was associated with mitral stenosis in the mid-19th century and was sometimes known as the mitral pulse. Quite independently, a positive systolic wave in the venous pulse was noted in some patients during the latter half of the 19th century and attributed to tricuspid insufficiency. But it was not until Mackenzie (1902) studied such patients with his polygraph that they were both ascribed to a single cause, atrial fibrillation. The first tracings of atrial fibrillation in man were published by Einthoven (1906) and Hering (1908); but it remained for Lewis (1909) to appreciate the significance of the clinical tracing and to introduce the convention of labeling the fibrillatory waves "ff."

Initiation and Mechanism

Just as the ventricles have a vulnerable period, so there is a point in the atrial cycle at which an atrial premature impulse is likely to precipitate an atrial tachyarrhythmia. Killip has formularized the situation as follows: if the P-P' interval (i.e., the interval from the preceding P wave to the premature P' wave) is less than half the preceding P-P interval, it is likely to land in the vulnerable period and spark a tachyarrhythmia; but if the P-P' interval is more than 60% of the preceding P-P interval, it is unlikely to do so[13] (fig. 14.1). Just what the relationship is (if any) between this "vulnerable" period and the "tachycardia-initiating interval" dealt with on page 152 remains to be elucidated.

Sometimes, atrial tachycardia or flutter "degenerates" into atrial fibrillation. Using intra-atrial recordings in patients with acute myocardial infarction, Bennett and Pentacost[3] found that paroxysms of atrial fibrillation always began with a rapid atrial tachycardia showing discrete atrial waves at a rate of about 340/min, and this lasted for up to 30 sec before the fibrillatory pattern took over. Cessation of the arrhythmia was always preceded by reversion to wave form resembling the initiating tachycardia.

The mechanisms of atrial fibrillation are still sub judice.[5] Circus-movement, multiple reentry circuits, and unifocal and multifocal ectopic impulse formation all have their advocates and some supportive evidence.

182

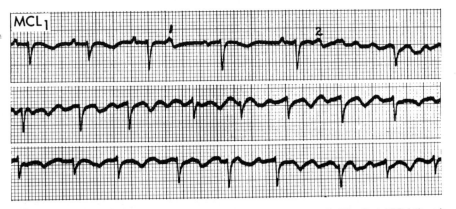

Figure 14.1. **Atrial fibrillation** precipitated by APB (2) in *top strip*. The first APB (1) ends a cycle more than half the preceding cycle; whereas the second APB (2) ends a cycle less than half the preceding P-P interval, therefore lands in the "vulnerable phase" of the atrial cycle and precipitates fibrillation.

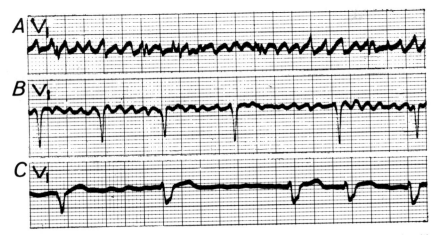

Figure 14.2. Coarse (A), medium (B), and fine (C) **atrial fibrillation**, each with irregular ventricular response.

Electrocardiographic Recognition

In the ECG atrial fibrillation is recognized by irregular undulation of the baseline, usually associated with an irregular ventricular rhythm. The undulations may be gross and distinct (fig. 14.2A), they may be barely perceptible (fig. 14.2C), or they may be intermediate in form (fig. 14.2B); for descriptive purposes these may be called, respectively, coarse, fine, or medium fibrillation. Although the size of the "f" waves seems not to correlate with the size of the atrium or the type of heart disease,[18] large "f" waves are unlikely to be found in the presence of a normal sized left atrium.[1] At times, there may be no recognizable deflection of the baseline, and then the fibrillation may be inferred

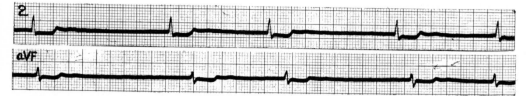

Figure 14.3. "Straight-line" **atrial fibrillation**. There is no discernible undulation of the baseline, but the irregular ventricular response (in the absence of evident atrial activity) makes the presumptive diagnosis of atrial fibrillation.

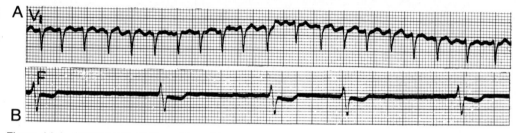

Figure 14.4 (*A*)**Atrial fibrillation** with rapid ventricular response (about 190/min). (*B*) **Atrial fibrillation** with slow ventricular response (about 40/min).

by the irregular ventricular response alone; in this context, the term straight-line fibrillation is sometimes used (fig. 14.3). Fibrillatory (ff) waves are usually best seen in lead V_1 or standard lead 2.

A-V Conduction

The ventricular response to atrial fibrillation is variable. If the A-V junction is normal and unhampered by digitalis or a beta-blocker, rates up to 200/min may develop (fig. 14.4*A*). On the other hand, if the A-V node is diseased or markedly suppressed by drugs, the ventricular response may be markedly reduced (fig. 14.4*B*).

The irregularity of the ventricular response in atrial fibrillation is the result of "concealed conduction" in the A-V junction—the innumerable atrial impulses jostling for penetration get in each other's way, leave the conducting pathways unpredictably refractory and ensure irregular delivery to the ventricles.[14, 15, 17] The same phenomenon also reduces the number of conductible impulses: as in figure 14.5, with a regular supraventricular tachycardia at a rate of 184, all 184 impulses reach the ventricles; but, with the spontaneous onset of atrial fibrillation during the recording of a 12-lead ECG, the number of successful impulses is approximately halved.

When atrial fibrillation complicates the Wolff-Parkinson-White syndrome, the refractory period of the accessory pathway determines the attainable ventricular rate, and rates of well over 200/min, sometimes exceeding 300/min, are found.[4, 23] In this situation, ventricular tachycardia is often erroneously diagnosed (see Chapter 18).

On the other hand, the presence of a regular ventricular rhythm does not exclude the diagnosis of atrial fibrillation. It is not uncommon, as in figure 14.6, *A* and *B*, to have a regular independent ventricular rhythm in the presence of atrial fibrillation because of A-V block. Whenever this is seen, one should consider the possibility of digitalis intoxication.[12] Remember not to call it *complete* A-V block just because there is no conduction—absence of conduction is not necessarily complete block—unless the ventricular rate is slow enough (less than 45/min). Thus in figure 14.6*B*, where the idionodal rate is 36/min, atrial fibrillation with complete A-V block may be diagnosed; but the *upper strip* should be described as atrial fibrillation with some degree of A-V block which, combined with a ventricular (junctional) rate of 51/min, produces complete A-V dissociation.

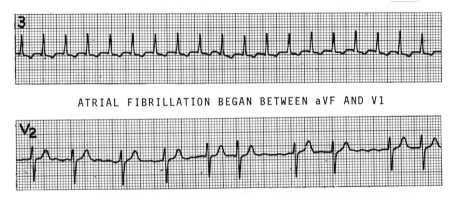

Figure 14.5. **Supraventricular tachycardia** (*top strip*) at rate 184 converting spontaneously to atrial fibrillation (*bottom strip*); during **atrial fibrillation**, the much reduced number of impulses conducted to the ventricles and the ventricular irregularity are accounted for by concealed conduction of innumerable atrial impulses into the A-V junction (average ventricular rate is 100).

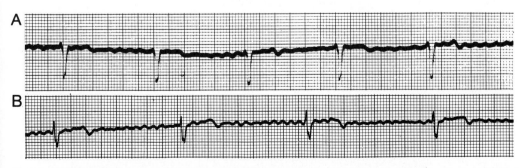

Figure 14.6. Both strips are from lead 3 in different patients. (*A*) **Atrial fibrillation** with independent junctional rhythm (patient had right bundle-branch block with left anterior hemiblock) at a rate of 51/min. (*B*) **Atrial fibrillation** with **complete A-V block** and junctional escape rhythm at a rate of 36/min.

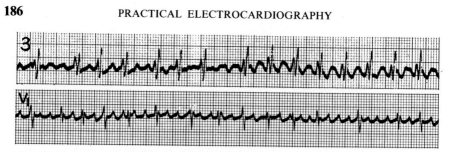

Figure 14.7. Two examples of **atrial flutter-fibrillation**. The atrial waves are too well formed and regular to be called unqualified fibrillation, yet not regular enough to be pure flutter.

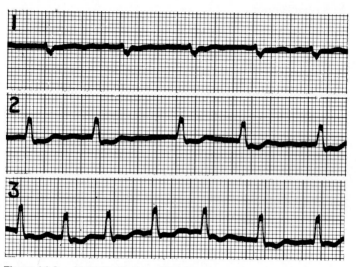

Figure 14.8. **Atrial fibrillation** with right axis deviation; this combination is highly suspicious of mitral stenosis.

Sometimes a mixture of fibrillation with flutter is seen, as in figure 14.7 and may be called **flutter-fibrillation** or **impure flutter**.

A final diagnostic tidbit: The combination of atrial fibrillation with right axis deviation (fig. 14.8) is strongly suggestive of mitral stenosis, especially in the earlier decades.

Salient Features of Atrial Fibrillation

1. Absence of P waves, which are replaced by irregular "f" waves (or no sign at all of atrial activity)
2. Normal QRS complexes, irregular in time and sometimes varying in amplitude

Etiology

Although atrial fibrillation may complicate any cardiac disease and is sometimes seen in the absence of any apparent disease[20] ("lone" fibrillation), the "Big Four" to think of first in causation are mitral disease, ischemic disease, hypertension, and thyrotoxicosis. Advancing age and increased left atrial size are closely related to its development.[11, 21] Chronic atrial fibrillation in the elderly often conceals an underlying sick sinus syndrome, and such patients frequently show the combination of narrowing of the sinus nodal artery, muscle loss in the sinus node, and dilation of the atria, whereas those who develop atrial fibrillation acutely during the last 2 weeks of life as a result of pulmonary embolism or pericarditis usually have atrial dilation without sinus nodal disease.[9]

Chronic atrial fibrillation, once established, usually lasts for life; but occasionally, even when it has persisted 10 or more years after valvotomy for mitral stenosis, it may revert spontaneously to sinus rhythm.[24] Atrial fibrillation developing during the first 72 hours of acute myocardial infarction carries a surprisingly poor prognosis—worse than that of patients resuscitated from major ventricular arrhythmias during the first 24 hours.[8, 10, 16]

Except in myocardial infarction, atrial fibrillation is rare in ischemic heart disease.[19] Whereas in children, atrial flutter is more common than atrial fibrillation, in adult life atrial fibrillation has approximately 20 times the incidence of flutter.[19] Atrial fibrillation is a common complication of chronic constrictive pericarditis though relatively rare in the acute disease.[22] The arrhythmia complicates a significant percentage of all forms of cardiomyopathy[19] and accounts for 20–25% of the tachyarrhythmias associated with the Wolff-Parkinson-White syndrome[6]; it is also fairly common in the Lown-Ganong-Levine syndrome.[2]

References

1. Bartall, H., et al.: Assessment of echocardiographic left atrial enlargement in patients with atrial fibrillation. An electrovectorcardiographic study. J. Electrocardiol. 1978: **11**, 269.
2. Benditt, D. G., et al.: Characteristics of atrioventricular conduction and the spectrum of arrhythmias in Lown-Ganong-Levine syndrome. Circulation 1978: **57**, 454.
3. Bennett, M. A., and Pentacost, B. L.: The pattern of onset and spontaneous cessation of atrial fibrillation in man. Circulation, 1970: **1**, 981.
4. Castellanos, A., et al.: Factors regulating ventricular rates during atrial flutter and fibrillation in preexcitation (Wolff-Parkinson-White) syndrome. Br. Heart J. 1973: **35**, 811.
5. Chung, E. K.: *Principles of Cardiac Arrhythmias*, Ed 2, pp 170–173. Williams & Wilkins, Baltimore, 1977.
6. Chung, E. K.: Tachyarrhythmias in Wolff-Parkinson-White syndrome. J.A.M.A. 1977: **237**, 376.
7. Cohen, S. I., et al.: Concealed conduction during atrial fibrillation. Am. J. Cardiol. 1970: **25**, 416.
8. Cristal, N., et al.: Atrial fibrillation developing in the acute phase of myocardial infarction. Prognostic implications. Chest 1976: **70**, 8.
9. Davies, M. J., and Pomerance, A.: Pathology of atrial fibrillation in man. Br. Heart J. 1972: **34**, 520.

10. Harrison, D. C.: Atrial fibrillation in acute myocardial infarction. Significance and therapeutic implications. Chest 1976: **70**, 3.
11. Henry, W. L., et al.: Relation between echocardiographically determined left atrial size and atrial fibrillation. Circulation 1976: **3**, 273.
12. Kastor, J. A.: Digitalis intoxication in patients with atrial fibrillation. Circulation 1973: **47**, 888.
13. Killip, T., and Gault, J. H.: Mode of onset of atrial fibrillation in man. Am. Heart J. 1965: **70**, 172.
14. Langendorf, R., et al.: Ventricular response in atrial fibrillation; role of concealed conduction in the atrioventricular junction. Circulation 1965: **32**, 69.
15. Lau, S. H., et al.: A study of atrioventricular conduction in atrial fibrillation and flutter in man using His bundle recordings. Circulation 1969: **40**, 71.
16. Lie, K. I., and Durrer, D.: Common arrhythmias in acute myocardial infarction. Cardiovasc. Clin. 1980: **11**, 191.
17. Moore E. N.: Observations on concealed conduction in atrial fibrillation. Circ. Res. 1967: **21**, 201.
18. Morganroth, J., et al.: Relationship of atrial fibrillatory wave amplitude to left atrial size and etiology of heart disease. Am. Heart J. 1979: **97**, 184.
19. Morris, D. C., and Hurst, J. W.: Atrial fibrillation. Curr. Prob. Cardiol. 1980: **5**, 1.
20. Peter, R. H., et al.: A clinical profile of idiopathic atrial fibrillation. Ann. Intern. Med. 1968: **68**, 1296.
21. Probst, P., et al.: Left atrial size and atrial fibrillation in mitral stenosis: Factors influencing their relationship. Circulation 1973: **48**, 1282.
22. Spodick, D. H.: Arrhythmias during acute pericarditis: prospective study of 100 consecutive cases. J.A.M.A. 1976: **235**, 39.
23. Wellens, H. J., and Durrer, D.: Wolff-Parkinson-White syndrome and atrial fibrillation. Am. J. Cardiol. 1974: **34**, 777.
24. Zimmerman, T. L., et al.: Spontaneous return of sinus rhythm in older patients with chronic atrial fibrillation and rheumatic mitral valve disease. Am. Heart J. 1973: **86**, 676.

Review Tracings

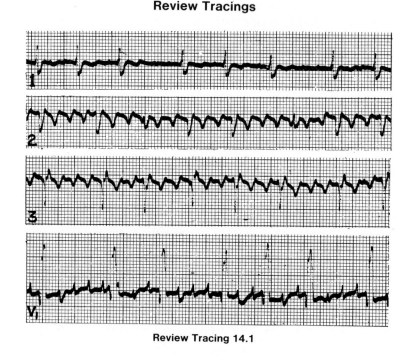

Review Tracing 14.1

For interpretation, see page 482

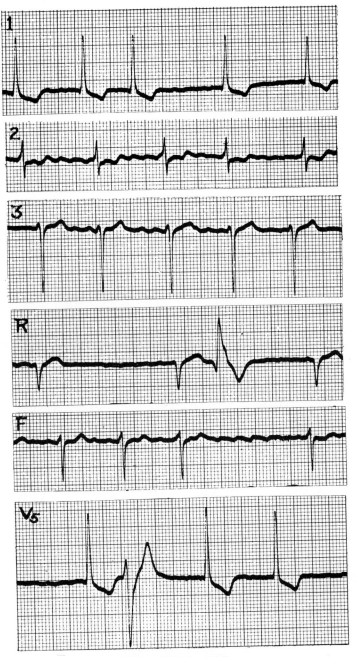

Review Tracing 14.2

For interpretation, see page 482

15

Ventricular Tachyarrhythmias

Ventricular Tachycardia

Ventricular tachycardia (VT) can result from rapid firing by a single focus (enhanced automaticity), or from a circulating wave front using a microscopic Purkinje circuit ("micro-reentry") or a wider sweep using fascicular pathways ("macro-reentry").[1, 2, 11, 74] By definition, VT consists of at least three consecutive, ectopic ventricular QRS complexes recurring at a rapid rate. They are usually regular, despite the widespread doctrine that irregularity helps to identify VT. One of the reasons for this popular belief is that so many examples of atrial fibrillation with Wolff-Parkinson-White (WPW) conduction have been mistakenly published as VT.[31] The P waves are frequently lost in the barrage of ventricular complexes, though they may sometimes be recognized as bumps or notches occurring at a slower rate in no constant relationship to the ventricular complexes (fig. 15.1A). Identification of unrelated P waves is one of the most sought after clues in recognizing VT; yet atrial independence by no means proves a ventricular origin—it just excludes an atrial origin.

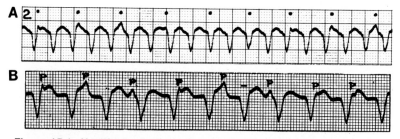

Figure 15.1. Ventricular tachycardia with independent atrial activity. (*A*) Ventricular rate 200/min; atrial activity is indicated by the superposed *dots*. (*B*) Relatively slow ventricular rate (120/min) with independent P waves at slower rate (92/min).

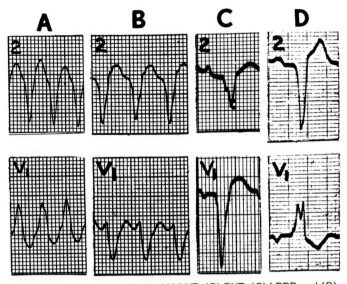

Figure 15.2. Leads 2 and V₁ in (*A*) LVT, (*B*) RVT, (*C*) LBBB and (*D*) RBBB. Note that lead 2 has a QS configuration in all four conditions and that V₁ contains far greater morphological contrast and therefore diagnostic thrust.

Diagnosis

The diagnosis of VT would be an easy task if it were not for close mimicry by supraventricular tachycardia (SVT) with abnormal intraventricular conduction (synonyms: ventricular aberration or aberrancy; aberrant ventricular conduction). For many years the diagnosis of VT hinged upon such features as independent atrial activity (A-V dissociation), irregularity of the tachyarrhythmia, and fusion beats; and often a single lead, even a lead 2, was regarded as adequate for the diagnosis. In recent years the frailty of these diagnostic props became evident, and there has been greater and greater emphasis on the details of QRS morphology in this important differentiation.[30, 44, 50, 63]

First of all, the inadequacy of a lead 2 can be easily appreciated when one finds that it may look so similar in both left ventricular tachycardia (LVT) and right ventricular tachycardia (RVT) and both left and right bundle-branch block. Figure 15.2 displays a lead 2 in each of these four conditions together with the corresponding V₁; in each case the QRS complex in lead 2 is of QS form, and the greater potential of V₁ for differentiating is immediately obvious. This is one of several reasons a right chest lead (e.g., MCL₁) is superior to lead 2 as a constant monitoring lead in intensive care units.

Second, independent atrial activity, although it rules out the diagnosis of atrial tachycardia and favors VT, does not establish a ventricular origin—it still may be a junctional tachycardia with ventricular aberration and independent atria (fig. 15.3). Because of the frequency of retrograde conduction in VT,[22, 60] it is possible to have either constantly related or independent P waves in VT; and it is also possible to have either with SVT and ventricular aberration.

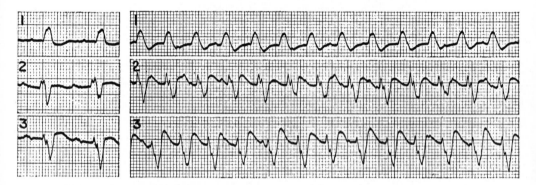

Figure 15.3. Junctional tachycardia with **LBBB** and independent atrial activity. Rhythm strips on right, with their wide QRS complexes and dissociated P waves, suggest ventricular tachycardia; but the identical complexes on the left during conducted sinus rhythm (with prolonged P-R interval) testify to a supraventricular tachycardia.

****YOU CANNOT TELL A PACEMAKER BY THE COMPANY SHE DOESN'T KEEP****

Third, the truth about irregularity is that all paroxysmal tachycardias, regardless of origin, tend to be as regular as clockwork; yet any of them can be irregular. Therefore, in any given case the presence or absence of regularity or irregularity is inconclusive. One of the chief reasons that VT gained the reputation for irregularity is that many examples of atrial fibrillation with WPW conduction have been mistaken for and published as VT.[31]

Fourth, fusion beats (fig. 15.4) are probably the most secure of the clues so far mentioned,[10] but even these show exceptions, as we have been aware since Kistin[23] demonstrated many years ago that aberrantly conducted junctional impulses could fuse with simultaneous sinus impulses. Thus, the presence of fusion is not conclusive evidence of ventricular ectopy.

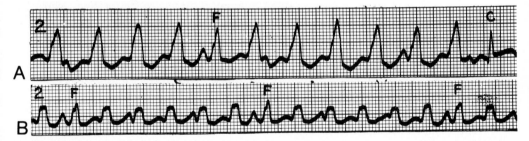

Figure 15.4. (*A*) **Ventricular tachycardia** (rate, 125) showing independent P waves (A-V dissociation) and capture (*C*) and fusion (*F*) beats. (*B*) **Ventricular tachycardia** (rate, 155) showing independent P waves and fusion (*F*) beats.

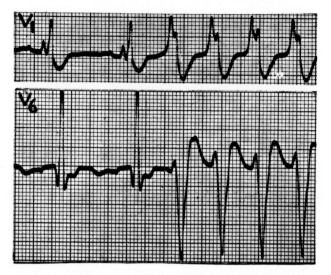

Figure 15.5. Sinus rhythm with **RBBB** interrupted by a run of **left ventricular tachycardia.** Note the ''rabbit ears,'' with left taller than right in V_1, and rS pattern in V_6.

Morphologic Clues. Because of these inherent weaknesses, better clues were sought, and it soon became evident that subtle differences in the shape of the QRS complexes often afforded a reliable indication of their source. In LVT the QRS complex in V_1 is usually either a monophasic R wave or a diphasic qR and only occasionally has a triphasic rsR' pattern. Coronary care nurses[13] were the first to point to the paired peaks—which they soon dubbed "rabbit ears"— in many ectopic beats seen in a right chest lead, such as V_1 or MCL_1, and claim that when the left was taller than the right, it was good evidence for left ventricular (LV) ectopy (figs. 15.5 and 15.6). Note carefully that when the right "ear" is taller than the left, it does not necessarily indicate right bundle-branch block (RBBB) aberration—a misconception that is commonly heard; the truth is that when the right "ear" is taller, the pattern is now in the ball park of aberration, but it remains equally likely to be ectopic ventricular. The sole value of the "rabbit ears" is that when the left is the taller, the odds are heavily in favor of ectopy.

The pattern of LV ectopy most likely to be found in V_6 consists of an rS (present in about 70% of LV ectopy), with conspicuous absence of the normal initial q wave (figs. 15.5 and 15.6*A*). But the rS pattern can be imitated by a combination of RBBB plus left anterior hemiblock; and therefore the rS is not as diagnostic as one would like it to be. A much less common—occurring in about 20% of LV ectopy—but more diagnostic pattern is the QS complex in V_6 (15.6*B*). Notice that this QS pattern may be found complementng the R or

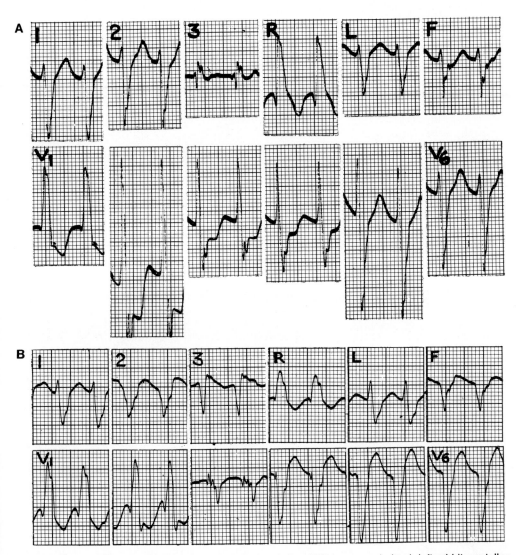

Figure 15.6. (A) **Left ventricular tachycardia** with axis ($-155°$) in no-man's-land, left rabbit ear taller than right in V_1, and rS in V_6. (B) **Left ventricular tachycardia** with axis in no-man's-land ($-135°$), taller left rabbit ear, and QS complex in V_6.

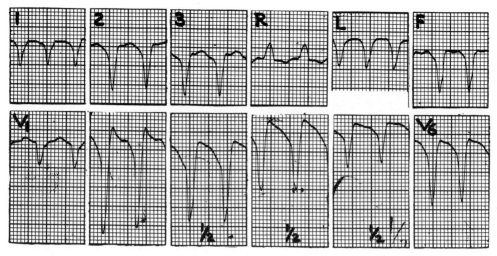

Figure 15.7. Right ventricular tachycardia with axis in no-man's-land and concordant negativity in chest leads.

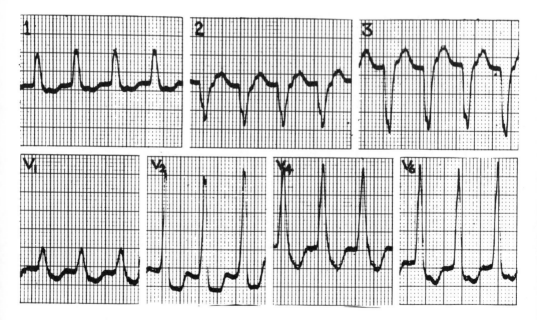

Figure 15.8. Left ventricular tachycardia with marked **left axis deviation**, concordant positivity in chest leads and 1:1 retrograde conduction to the atria—P′ waves are seen just after the QRS in leads 1, 2, 3, and V₆.

qR of LV ectopy in V_1; or it may be part of the concordant negativity pattern of right ventricular (RV) ectopy (fig. 15.7).

"Concordance" of the precordial QRS complexes is another useful clue to ectopy: when all the ventricular complexes from V_1 to V_6 are either positive ("concordant positivity") or negative ("concordant negativity"), ventricular ectopy is strongly favored. Concordant positivity (fig. 15.8) indicates LV ectopy but may be mimicked by type A WPW conduction; if this can be excluded, LV ectopy is confirmed. Concordant negativity (fig. 15.7) indicates RV ectopy, and the only potential mimic is left bundle-branch block (LBBB) when leads have not been taken far enough to the left to obtain the usual left-sided monophasic R waves.

Another clue to RV ectopy forms part of the pattern popularized by Rosenbaum[42] more than a decade ago. He described a pattern of RV ectopy that was quite commonly found in healthy athletic youths who were victims of ectopy but had no other sign of heart disease. It consisted of the pattern of LBBB in V_6 but in company with two other features that are foreign to LBBB—right axis deviation (RAD) in the frontal plane and a "fat little r wave" in lead V_1 (fig. 15.9). When monitoring with a single right-sided lead, such as MCL_1, the

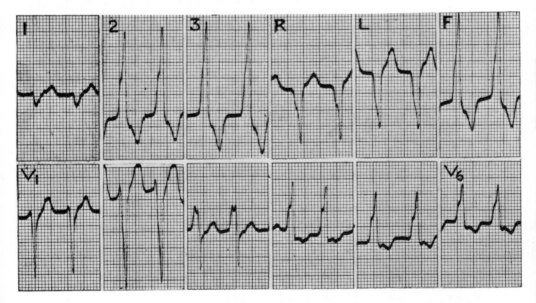

Figure 15.9. Right ventricular tachycardia with **LBBB** configuration in V_6, **right axis deviation** and fat initial r wave in V_1.

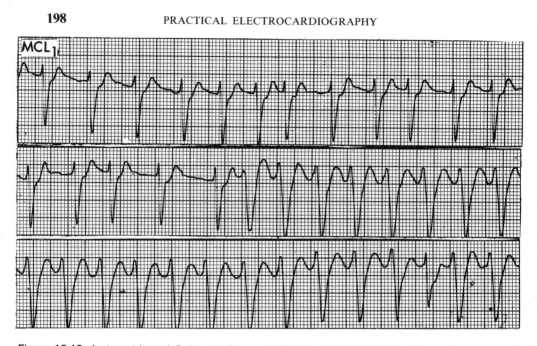

Figure 15.10. In *top strip* and first part of second, there is **atrial fibrillation** with **LBBB**. The abrupt development of a fat initial r wave in the sixth beat in the *second strip* with regularization of the ventricular rhythm signals the development of **right ventricular tachycardia**.

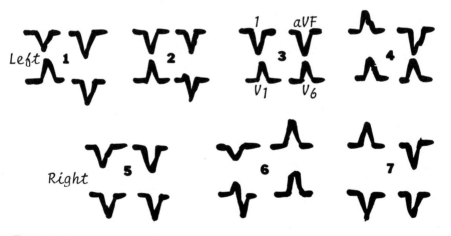

Figure 15.11. Seven **suggestive quartets**: (*1*) axis in no-man's-land, R or qR in V$_1$, QS in V$_6$; (*2*) axis in no-man's-land, R or qR in V$_1$, rS in V$_6$; (*3*) axis in no-man's-land, concordant positivity; (*4*) marked left axis deviation, concordant positivity; (*5*) axis in no-man's-land, concordant negativity; (*6*) right axis deviation, fat r in V$_1$, LBBB pattern in V$_6$; (*7*) marked left axis deviation, concordant negativity.

appearance of fat r waves is, by itself, good evidence in favor of ectopy (fig. 15.10).

A frontal plane axis in the right upper quadrant [between −90° and −180°— "no-man's-land" (NML)] is very seldom found in conducted beats (exceptions: some complex congenital heart lesions, hearts with multiple infarctions, etc.) but is not infrequently found in ectopic ventricular rhythms arising from either right or left ventricle (figs. 15.6 and 15.7). Its presence, then, especially when found in conjunction with other suggestive clues, is good evidence in favor of ectopy.

The clues so far described can be gathered together to compile a table of "suggestive quartets" (fig. 15.11). Leads 1 and aVF indicate the axis, while leads V_1 and V_6 document the precordial pattern in right and left chest leads and concordance if it is present.

It is a rather sad comment on our powers of observation and deduction that for 20 years we have been seeing, without apparently registering the significance of, some of these highly diagnostic patterns in indisputably ectopic rhythms, viz., paced rhythms. Surely when one knows that a certain pattern of conduction is produced by pacing from a known ventricular site, it is a logical conclusion that when the same pattern is seen to occur spontaneously, it is likely also to be ectopic ventricular? Quartet number 3 in figure 15.11 is seen repeatedly in LV pacing, while quartet number 5 sometimes characterizes RV pacing.

All of the above clues owe their recognition to clinical observation and deduction and, until recently, had not been confirmed by acceptable scientific experimentation. But now Wellens[60] has compared the features of 70 instances of VT with 70 SVTs with aberrant conduction, later expanded to 100 of each,[63] the origin of all cases in each series being proven by intracardiac recordings. His findings are confirmatory of the following previously suspected features.

1. Irregularity is of little use in distinguishing VT from SVT. VT was completely regular in the majority (55 of 70); SVT, in a larger majority (65 of 70).

2. Fusion and/or capture beats are seldom seen and then only at the less rapid rates (under 160); they found them in only 4 of 33 sustained VTs.

3. Independent atrial activity (A-V dissociation) favors VT; it was present in 32 of the 70 and was not found in any of the SVTs with aberrant conduction.

4. But *absence* of A-V dissociation is not much in favor of SVT since half of the VTs manifested retrograde conduction (cf. fig. 15.8).

The morphological clues and their diagnostic value, as determined in Wellens' studies,[60, 62, 63] are summarized in table 15.1.

The figures in table 15.1 indicate the number of times the specified pattern was encountered, and of that total how many turned out to be ectopic or aberrant. Take, for example, a QR pattern in V_1: the table tells us that they found it 17 times, 16 of which were indeed ectopic. The reason a superior axis and a wide (>0.14 sec) QRS are unhelpful unless the conduction pattern before the tachycardia developed is known is because, in the presence of *preexisting* BBB, SVT is frequently associated with significant left axis deviation and/or a QRS wider than 0.14 sec.

Other Diagnostic Clues. Another pattern almost diagnostic of VT is shown in figures 15.4 and 15.12 where a suspected VT is punctuated by an occasional fusion (Dressler) beat.[10] These are sometimes to be seen when the ventricular rate is relatively slow and indicate that an impulse from the independently beating atria, happening to arrive at an opportune moment, has been partially conducted. To fulfill the necessary criteria, such beats must be on time or slightly early, never late.

Another useful pointer to VT is the presence of early ventricular capture beats that show a more normal QRS contour than the wide beats of the tachycardia (fig. 15.12). Since the capture beat ends a cycle slightly shorter than the cycles ending with the wider beats, it indicates that the wider beats are probably ectopic ventricular. Because, of all the beats, the *most likely* to be aberrant is the beat that ends the shortest cycle. Since this beat is not aberrant, the wide beats are even less likely to be and are therefore wide and bizarre because of ventricular ectopy rather than aberration.

Left versus Right Ventricular Tachycardia. It is widely accepted that one can distinguish between ectopic beats arising in each ventricle by observing the shape of the ventricular complex in lead V_1; and in general this is certainly

Table 15.1
Diagnosis of Ventricular Tachycardia

	Favoring Ectopy			Favoring Aberration		
V_1	Single peak		15/15	rSR', rsR'		38/41
	Taller left rabbit ear		7/7	M-shaped		19/22
	QR		16/17			
	RS		4/4			
V_6	rS		27/31	qRs		44/47
	QS		17/17			
	QR		8/8			
	Axis −30° to −180°[a]		68/75			
	QRS interval >0.14 sec[a]		59/59			

[a] Of little use if previous tracing not available.

Table 15.2
QRS Morphology/Site of Origin

V_1	LV	RV
⋀	22/22	0/22
⋁	17/17 (sick)	3/3 (well)

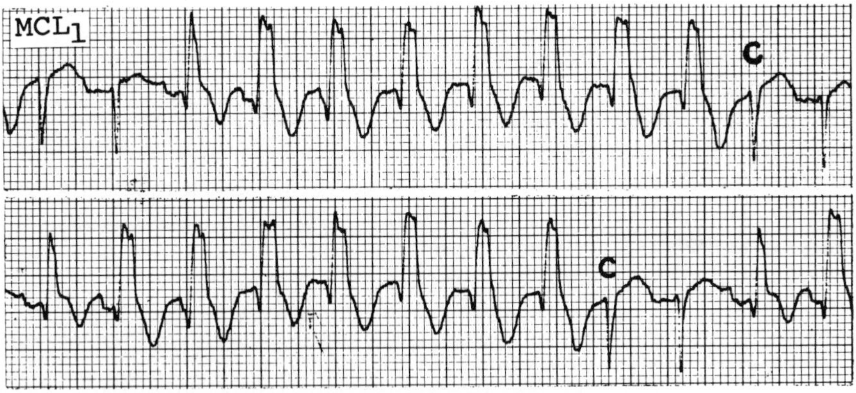

Figure 15.12. Left ventricular tachycardia. The capture beats (c) end cycles that are slightly shorter than the ectopic cycles. Note also: each run of ectopic rhythm begins with a fusion beat and the left "rabbit ear" is taller than the right.

true. However, there are exceptions to every good rule and morphological guidelines are not exempt. Although V_1 is much the best lead for distinguishing between left and right ventricular ectopy, it is not completely reliable in all circumstances. In a series of 39 proven VTs,[17] all of the wide, positive QRS complexes in V_1 were indeed left ventricular; but the wide negative complexes (LBBB pattern) were a different matter (table 15.2). Their origin seemed to vary with the condition of the heart: in normal hearts they represented right ventricular ectopy, but in ischemic hearts the pattern indicated an origin in or near the left septal surface. This LBBB pattern in *left* ventricular rhythms (suggesting a *right* ventricular origin) is attributed to "preferential transseptal activation"[68] resulting in earlier activation of the right ventricle than the left.

Useful as 12-lead QRS morphology is, in the presence of myocardial disease it apparently cannot be relied upon to localize with precision the origin of an ectopic mechanism[68, 73]; this is because the clinical tracing reflects the site of *epi*cardial "breakthrough" which may be many centimeters removed from the *endo*cardial origin of the ectopic impulse.

Nevertheless, the LBBB morphology is of interest and value in another context. In an ongoing study in the Pee Dee area of South Carolina,[37] among over a thousand consecutive patients with acute myocardial infarction, those who have shown *only* the LBBB morphology (usually associated with a right ventricular origin) have never developed ventricular fibrillation and seldom VT; thus, even if they are not in fact right ventricular, they appear to be conspicuously benign.

Varieties of Ventricular Tachycardia

During the past few years, several epithets have been introduced to describe characteristics of VT. It sometimes occurs in short repeated bursts, separated by one or two sinus beats (fig. 15.13), and then is known as **repetitive tachycardia.**[48]

In the term **chronic recurrent ventricular tachycardia**, the meaning of "recurrent" is self-evident, though the distinction from "repetitive" is unclear. At least 3 or 4 discrete, documented episodes are required,[9, 15] and, when "chronic" is added, it is understood that the paroxysms recur over a prolonged period, usually of years, though as little as 1 month is sometimes accepted.[9] Others may require as few as two episodes, but spaced at least a month apart.[39]

It has also become customary to qualify the paroxysms arbitrarily as "sustained" or "nonsustained," depending upon the duration of the individual bursts of tachycardia. The "sustained" variety, usually lasting minutes or hours or days, must last at least longer than 1 min, or require cardioversion before the minute has elapsed.[53] "Nonsustained" is variably defined as lasting less than 10 beats,[15] or less than 60 sec,[53] and ending spontaneously. Frequent isolated VPBs are commonly found between paroxysms.

In patients with chronic recurrent VT, there seem to be striking differences in incidence and prognosis between a RV and LV origin:[39] subjects with LVT tend to be older, male and with diagnosable heart disease; whereas those with RVT tend to be younger, female and without diagnosable heart disease. The

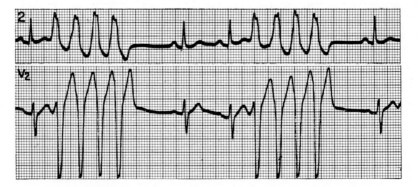

Figure 15.13. Short 4-beat bursts of **ventricular tachycardia.**

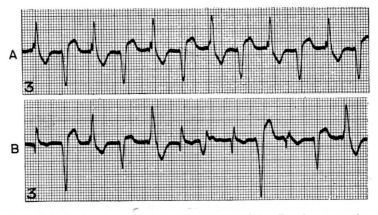

Figure 15.14. Two serious forms of ventricular tachycardia, often presaging ventricular fibrillation. (*A*) **Bidirectional ventricular tachycardia.** (*B*) **Multifocal ventricular tachycardia** (sometimes called **chaotic heart action**).

mechanism of chronic recurrent VT is widely believed to be reentry.[15, 16, 58, 59] However, this is far from certain and Mason[32] gloomily summarizes the status of chronic recurrent VT by reaffirming that the underlying mechanisms are unknown and probably varied. He reiterates the three possibilities, micro-reentry, macro-reentry and automaticity—"with many subdivisions"—and concludes: "Our ignorance is extensive and the result is a disappointing failure to correct or control the arrhythmia in too many patients."

Exercise-induced ventricular tachycardia is almost always provoked by only moderate exertion; it may also be brought on by emotional excitement, upright posture and smoking. It oftens originates in the outflow tract of the right ventricle,[54, 65] and takes the form of rapid, repeated bursts separated by a few sinus beats and perhaps an isolated ventricular extrasystole or two showing the same morphology as the beats of the tachycardia. Its behavior suggests that it arises from a catecholamine-sensitive automatic focus.[65]

The implications of exercise-induced VT are not so grave as they were once thought—the arrhythmia occurs not infrequently in subjects with normal hearts. In one series of 26 people, with exercise-provoked VT, to be sure 16 had ischemic heart disease and 2 had a cardiomyopathy, but the remaining 8 had no evidence of heart disease.[34]

In **bidirectional** tachycardia (fig. 15.14*A*), the wide ventricular complexes alternate in polarity; in **alternating** tachycardia, they merely alternate in amplitude. These two brands are not distinctly separable—often the contour is bidirectional in one lead and alternating in another. The pattern is, however, foreboding and often associated with digitalis toxicity. The mechanisms of these tachycardias are uncertain: some are truly ventricular[6, 7] while others may represent a SVT with RBBB and alternating hemiblock.[7]

Etiology

It is universally known that ventricular extrasystoles can trigger VT. It is much less widely appreciated that single APBs can initiate ventricular ectopic activity, including VT, both in the ischemic and the healthy heart.[35, 61, 66] Figure 15.15 presents two examples of VT precipitated by shortening of the supraventricular cycle.

VT usually affects subjects with organic heart disease, but may on occasion be found in the otherwise normal heart. Lesch was able to collect 34 such cases in 1967[28] and more recently 6 of a series of 17 young patients with VT had no evidence of heart disease.[38] VT may complicate rheumatic disease and was found in 6% of patients with mitral valve prolapse[51]; in some such patients it may assume a "malignant" form.[56]

When VT (or ventricular fibrillation) is found in youth, it is usually associated with one of the following disorders: mitral valve prolapse, cardiomyopathy, myocarditis, hypokalemia (sometimes produced by an energetic slimming program including diuretics), or a long Q-T syndrome.

VT may complicate drug therapy, notably with digitalis, quinidine, procainamide, isopyramide, sympathetic amines and various anesthetics. It may complicate the prolonged QT syndromes and metabolic and electrolyte disorders.

Obviously VT is a major complication of ischemic heart disease, especially with myocardial infarction or cardiac aneurysm. When VT develops within the first 24 hours of acute myocardial infarction, it is probably due to enhanced automaticity[58]; later in the course it is more likely mediated by reentry. In acute myocardial infarction, VT may be precipitated by early ventricular extrasystoles (R-on-T), late extrasystoles and even by *atrial* premature beats.[66] It now seems clear that most VT is precipitated by late beats: of 68 instances, Rothfeld[43]

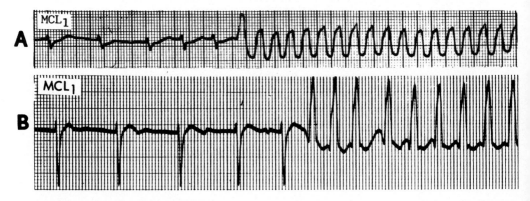

Figure 15.15. Ventricular tachycardia evoked by shortening of the cycle of the supraventricular rhythm. (*A*) In the presence of atrial fibrillation, there is progressive shortening of the conducted cycles until an R-on-T left ventricular extrasystole is provoked. (*B*) An accelerated junctional rhythm is dissociated from the sinus rhythm; the fifth beat, ending a shorter cycle, is a ventricular capture. In this patient, capture beats such as this repeatedly precipitated runs of ventricular tachycardia.

found that 17 (25%) resulted from "R-on-T" beats; 46 (68%) from late extra-systoles; and 5 (7%) from atrial premature beats. And again, in Holtered ambulatory subjects, only 14 of 94 episodes of VT were precipitated by R-on-T extrasystoles.[64]

Other Tachyarrhythmias

Ventricular flutter is the term given by some authorities to a rapid VT giving a modified pattern in the ECG—a regular zigzag—without clearly formed QRS complexes (fig. 15.17B and C). Little is gained in separating it from VT.

Torsades de pointes (twistings of the points): This special form of ventricular tachyarrhythmia with its "tantalizingly euphonious" French name[24] is uncertain of its place in the taxonomy of dysrhythmias. It is often regarded as an intermediary between VT and ventricular fibrillation, and its mechanism is probably a form of reentry,[14] but its exact nature remains to be elucidated.[47] At times it may be due to bifocal ectopic ventricular activity in mutual competition.[67]

Morphologically, it is characterized by wide QRS complexes whose apices, as its elegant name implies, are sometimes positive and sometimes negative—the points swing back and forth above and below the baseline which originally earned it the simple English sobriquet "the swinging pattern" (fig. 15.16). Now it has gathered a number of ponderous titles including atypical,[4] polymorphous[49] and multiform VT—not to be confused with the chaotic or multifocal type illustrated in figure 15.14B. Since morphologically similar tachyarrhythmias may be associated with either prolonged or normal Q-T intervals, and since the distinction has vital therapeutic implications, some authors insist that the term "torsade" be restricted to those polymorphous tachycardias associated with Q-T prolongation.[71]

It is caused by anything that produces or is associated with a prolonged Q-T interval, including drugs (quinidine,[40] procainamide,[49, 71] disopyramide,[36, 55] aprindine,[70] phenothiazines, etc), electrolyte disturbances, insecticide poisoning,[69] subarachnoid hemorrhage[4] and congenital Q-T prolongation. It often develops against a background of bradycardia, especially when due to A-V block[72]; and it has a well established association with Prinzmetal's angina.[27]

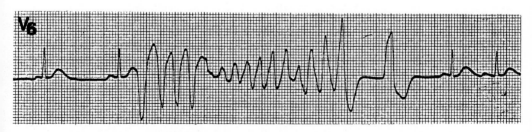

Figure 15.16. Torsades de pointes initiated by an R-on-T ventricular extrasystole.

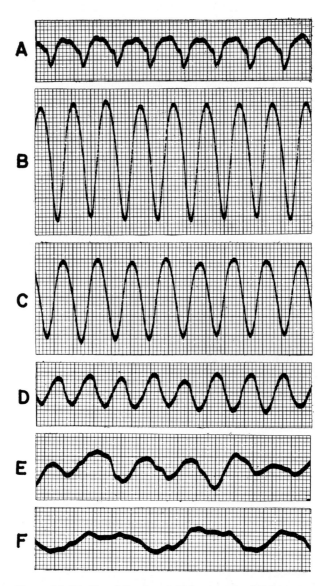

Figure 15.17. The dying heart. Strips from lead 2 taken approximately 1 min apart and illustrating the transitions from ventricular tachycardia through flutter to fibrillation. (*A*) **Ventricular tachycardia.** (*B* and *C*) **Ventricular flutter.** (*D*) Intermediate stage between flutter and fibrillation. (*E* and *F*) **Ventricular fibrillation.**

But its great clinical importance lies in the fact that the usual antiarrhythmic drugs are not only useless but contraindicated since, as causative agents, they make matters worse.

Ventricular fibrillation is usually a terminal, or at a least a catastrophic event; rarely, transient bouts may be responsible for Adams-Stokes attacks. It is easily recognized by the complete absence of properly formed ventricular complexes— the baseline wavers unevenly with no attempt at forming clearcut QRS deflections (fig. 15.17*E* and *F*).

References

1. Akhtar, M., et al: Demonstration of re-entry within the His-Purkinje system in man. Circulation 1974: **50**, 1150.
2. Akhtar, M., et al.: Re-entry within the His-Purkinje system; elucidation of re-entrant circuit using right bundle-branch and His bundle recordings. Circulation 1978: **58**: 295.
3. Atkins, J. M., et al.: Incidence of arrhythmias induced by isometric and dynamic exercise. Br. Heart J. 1976: **38**, 465.
4. Carruth, J. E., and Silverman, M. E.: Torsade de pointes; atypical ventricular tachycardia complicating subarachnoid hemorrhage. Chest 1980: **78**, 886.
5. Cohen, H. C., et al.: Ventricular tachycardia with narrow QRS complexes (left posterior fascicular tachycardia). Circulation 1972: **45**, 1035.
6. Cohen, S. I., et al.: Infra-His bundle origin of bidirectional tachycardia. Circulation 1973: **47**, 1260.
7. Cohen, S. I., and Voukydis, P.: Supraventricular origin of bidirectional tachycardia. Circulation 1974: **50**, 634.
8. Cohn, L. J., et al.: Ventricular tachycardia. Progr. Cardiovasc. Dis. 1966: **9**, 29.
9. Denes, P., et al.: Electrophysiological studies in patients with chronic recurrent ventricular tachycardia. Circulation 1976: **54**, 229.
10. Dressler, W., and Roesler, H.: The occurrence in paroxysmal ventricular tachycardia of ventricular complexes transitional in shape to sinoauricular beats. Am. Heart. J. 1952: **44**, 485.
11. Foster, J. R., and Simpson, R. J.: Initiation of ventricular tachycardia by reentry within the bundle branches. Am. J. Cardiol. 1980: **45**, 895.
12. Goolsby, J. P., and Oliva, P. B.: Electrographic and clinical observations of a recurrent tachyarrhythmia arising from a pacemaker within the distribution of the anterior fascicle. Am. Heart J.: 1974: **88**, 351.
13. Gozensky, C., and Thorne, D.: Rabbit ears; an aid in distinguishing ventricular ectopy from aberration. Heart Lung 1974: **3**, 634
14. Horowitz, L. N.: Torsades de pointes; electrophysiologic studies in patients with transient pharmacologic or metabolic abnormalities. Circulation 1981: **63**, 1120.
15. Josephson, M. E., et al.: Recurrent sustained ventricular tachycardia; 1. Mechanisms. Circulation 1978: **57**, 431.
16. Josephson, M. E., and Seides, S. F.: *Clinical Cardiac Electrophysiology: Techniques and Interpretations*. Lea & Febiger, Philadelphia, 1979.
17. Josephson, M. E., et al.: Sustained ventricular tachycardia: role of the 12-lead electrocardiogram in localizing site of origin. Circulation 1981: **64**, 273.
18. Kastor, J. A., and Goldreyer, B. N.: Ventricular origin of bidirectional tachycardia. Case report of a patient not toxic from digitalis. Circulation 1973: **48**, 897.
19. Keren, A., et al.: Ventricular pacing in atypical ventricular tachycardia. J. Electrocardiol. 1981: **14**, 201.
20. Keren, A., et al.: Etiology, warning signs and therapy of torsade de pointes: A study of 10 patients. Circulation 1981: **64**, 1167.
21. Kistin, A., and Landowne, M.: Retrograde conduction from premature ventricular contractions, a common occurrence in the human heart. Circulation 1951: **3**, 738.

22. Kistin, A. D.: Retrograde conduction to the atria in ventricular tachycardia. Circulation 1961: **24**, 236.

23. Kistin, A. D.: Problems in the differentiation of ventricular arrhythmia from supraventricular arrhythmia with abnormal QRS. Prog. Cardiovasc. Dis. 1966: **9**, 1.

24. Kossmann, C. E.: Torsade de pointes; an addition to the nosography of ventricular tachycardia. Am. J. Cardiol. 1978: **42**, 1054.

25. Koster, R. W., and Wellens, H. J. J.: Quinidine-induced ventricular flutter and fibrillation without digitalis therapy. Am. J. Cardiol. 1976: **38**, 519.

26. Kotler, M. N., et al.: Prognostic significance of ventricular ectopic beats with respect to sudden death in the late postinfarction period. Circulation 1973: **47**, 959.

27. Krikler, D. M., and Curry, P. V. L.: Torsade de pointes, an atypical ventricular tachycardia. Br. Heart J. 1976: **38**, 117.

28. Lesch, M., et al.: Paroxysmal ventricular tachycardia in the absence of organic heart disease; report of a case and review of the literature. Ann. Intern Med. 1967: **66**, 950.

29. Lie, K. I., et al.: Observations on patients with primary ventricular fibrillation complicating acute myocardial infarction. Circulation 1975: **52**, 755.

30. Marriott, H. J. L.: Differential diagnosis of supraventricular and ventricular tachycardia. Geriatrics 1970: **25**, 91.

31. Marriott, H. J. L., and Rogers, H. M.: Mimics of ventricular tachycardia associated with the W-P-W syndrome. J. Electrocardiol. 1969: **2**, 77.

32. Mason, J. W., et al.: Mechanisms of ventricular tachycardia; wide, complex ignorance. Am. Heart J. 1981: **102**, 1083.

33. Meltzer, R. S., et al.: Atypical ventricular tachycardia as a manifestation of disopyramide toxicity. Am. J. Cardiol. 1978: **42**, 1049.

34. Mokotoff, D. M.: Exercise-induced ventricular tachycardia: clinical features, relation to chronic ventricular ectopy, and prognosis. Chest 1980: **77**, 10.

35. Myerburg, R. J., et al.: Ventricular ectopic activity after premature atrial beats in acute myocardial infarction. Br. Heart J. 1977: **39**, 1033.

36. Nicholson, W. J., et al.: Disopyramide-induced ventricular fibrillation. Am. J. Cardiol. 1979: **43**, 1053.

37. O'Bryan, C.: Personal communication, 1981.

38. Pedersen, D. H., et al.: Ventricular tachycardia and ventricular fibrillation in a young population. Circulation 1979: **60**, 988.

39. Pietras, R. J., et al.: Chronic recurrent right and left ventricular tachycardia; comparison of clinical, hemodynamic and angiographic findings. Am. J. Cardiol. 1977: **40**, 32.

40. Reynolds, E. W., and Vander Ark, C. R.: Quinidine syncope and the delayed repolarization syndromes. Mod. Concepts Cardiovasc. Dis. 1976: **45**, 117.

41. Rocchini, A. P.: Ventricular tachycardia in children. Am. J. Cardiol. 1981: **47**, 1091.

42. Rosenbaum, M. B.: Classification of ventricular extrasystoles according to form. J. Electrocardiol. 1969: **2**, 289.

43. Rothfeld, E. L., et al.: Harbingers of paroxysmal ventricular tachycardia in acute myocardial infarction. Chest 1977: **71**, 142.

44. Sandler, I. A., and Marriott, H. J. L.: The differential morphology of anomalous ventricular complexes of RBBB-type in V_1; ventricular ectopy versus aberration. Circulation 1965: **31**, 551.

45. Sclarovsky, S., et al.: Polymorphous ventricular tachycardia; clinical features and treatment. Am. J. Cardiol. 1979: **44**, 339.

46. Smirk, F. H., and Palmer, D. G.: A myocardial syndrome, with particular reference to the occurrence of sudden death and of premature systoles interrupting antecedent T waves. Am. J. Cardiol. 1960: **6**, 620.

47. Smith, W. M., and Gallagher, J. J.: "Les torsades de pointes": An unusual ventricular arrhythmia. Ann. Intern. Med. 1980: **93**, 578.

48. Stock, J. P. P.: Repetitive paroxysmal ventricular tachycardia. Br. Heart J. 1962: **24**, 297.

49. Strasberg, B., et al.: Procainamide-induced polymorphous ventricular tachycardia. Am. J. Cardiol. 1981: **47**, 1309.

50. Swanick, E. J., et al.: Morphologic features of right ventricular ectopic beats. Am. J. Cardiol. 1972: **30**, 888.

51. Swartz, M. H., et al.: Mitral valve prolapse: A review of associated arrhythmias. Am. J. Med. 1977: **62**, 377.

52. Talbot, S., and Greaves, M.: Association of ventricular extrasystoles and ventricular tachycardia with idioventricular rhythm. Br. Heart J. 1976: **38**, 457.

53. Vandepol, C. J., et al.: Incidence and clinical significance of induced ventricular tachycardia. Am. J. Cardiol. 1980: **45,** 725.
54. Vetter, V. L., et al.: Idiopathic recurrent sustained ventricular tachycardia in children and adolescents. Am. J. Cardiol. 1981: **47,** 315.
55. Wald, R. W., et al.: Torsades de pointes tachycardia; a complication of disopyramide shared with quinidine. J. Electrocardiol. 1981: **14,** 301.
56. Wei, J. Y., et al.: Mitral-valve prolapse syndrome and recurrent ventricular tachyarrhythmias: A malignant variant refractory to conventional drug therapy. Ann. Intern Med. 1978: **89,** 6.
57. Wellens, H. J., et al.: Electrical stimulation of the heart in patients with ventricular tachycardia. Circulation 1972: **46,** 216.
58. Wellens, H. J. J.: Pathophysiology of ventricular tachycardia in man. Arch. Intern. Med. 1975: **135,** 473.
59. Wellens, H. J. J., et al.: Observations on mechanisms of ventricular tachycardia in man. Circulation 1976: **54,** 237.
60. Wellens, H. J. J., et al.: The valve of the electrocardiogram in the differential diagnosis of a tachycardia with a widened QRS complex. Am J. Med. 1978: **64,** 27.
61. Wellens, H. J. J., et al.: Initiation and termination of ventricular tachycardia by supraventricular stimuli: Incidence and electrophysiologic determinants as observed during programmed stimulation of the heart. Am. J. Cardiol. 1980: **46,** 576.
62. Wellens, H. J. J.: Personal communication, 1981.
63. Wellens, H. J. J., et al.: Medical treatment of ventricular tachycardia, consideration in the selection of patients for surgical treatment. Am. J. Cardiol. 1982: **49,** 186.
64. Winkle, R. A., et al.: Characteristics of ventricular tachycardia in ambulatory patients. Am. J. Cardiol. 1977: **39,** 487.
65. Wu, D., et al.: Exercise-triggered paroxysmal ventricular tachycardia: A repetitive rhythmic activity possibly related to afterdepolarization. Ann. Intern Med. 1981: **95,** 410.
66. Zipes, D. P., et al.: Atrial induction of ventricular tachycardia; reentry versus triggered automaticity. Am. J. Cardiol. 1979: **44,** 1.
67. D'Alnoncourt, C. N., et al.: "Torsade de pointes" tachycardia: Re-entry or focal activity? Br. Heart J. 1982: **48,** 213.
68. Josephson, M. E., et al.: Relation between site of origin and QRS configuration in ventricular rhythms, p. 200. In *What's New in Electrocardiography*, edited by H. J. J. Wellens and H. E. Kulbertus. Martinus Nijhoff, Boston, 1981.
69. Ludomirsky, A., et al.: Q-T prolongation and polymorphous ("torsade de pointes") ventricular arrhythmias associated with organic insecticide poisoning. Am. J. Cardiol. 1982; **49,** 1655.
70. Scagliotti, D., et al.: Aprinidine-induced polymorphous ventricular tachycardia. Am. J. Cardiol. 1982: **49,** 1297.
71. Soffer, J., et al.: Polymorphous ventricular tachycardia associated with normal and long Q-T intervals. Am. J. Cardiol. 1982: **49,** 2021.
72. Taboul, P.: Torsade de pointes, p. 229. In *What's New in Electrocardiography*, edited by H. J. J. Wellens and H. E. Kulbertus. Martinus Nijhoff, Boston, 1981.
73. Waxman, H. L., and Josephson, M. E.: Ventricular activation during ventricular endocardial pacing. I. Electrocardiographic patterns related to the site of pacing. Am. J. Cardiol. 1982: **50,** 1.
74. Welch, W. J., et al.: Sustained macroreentrant ventricular tachycardia. Am. Heart J. 1982: **104,** 166.

Review Tracings

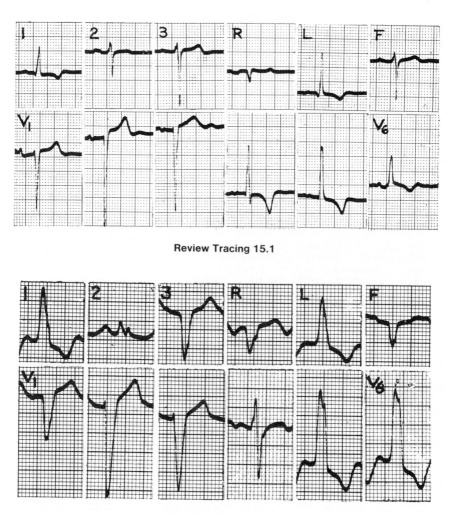

Review Tracing 15.1

Review Tracing 15.2

For interpretation, see page 482

16

Aberrant Ventricular Conduction and the Diagnosis of Tachycardia

Things are seldom what they seem,
Skim milk masquerades as cream—*Gilbert*

Aberrant ventricular conduction (ventricular aberration or aberrancy) is the temporary, abnormal intraventricular conduction of supraventricular impulses, usually due to a change in cycle length. Its importance rests firmly on two facts: (1) it is common—much more common than many realize and (2) it is often overlooked with the result that supraventricular arrhythmias are frequently misdiagnosed as ventricular and treated as such.

Aberration, then, is not a rare curiosity that can be left for the experts in arrhythmias to worry with. Almost all physicians are occasionally called upon to diagnose and treat paroxysmal tachycardia and atrial fibrillation; and they should, therefore, know the fundamental differentiation between supraventricular and ventricular tachycardias. The dilemma arises in those tachycardias with widened, bizarre QRS complexes, which therefore raise the specter of ventricular tachycardia.

Type A Aberration

The Circumstances

When any responsive tissue reacts to a stimulus, the reaction is followed by a dormant interval, the refractory period, during which it cannot respond to a similar stimulus. This period of rest is necessary for the tissue to recoup its spent forces and return to a state in which it can again react normally to the stimulus. Naturally, any such period has a finite, measurable duration; and if the tissue is asked to respond during its refractory period, the response will be absent or at least subnormal. Characteristics of the refractory period differ with

211

different tissues; e.g., in the heart, the bundle branches usually respond with an "all-or-none" response (i.e., if they respond at all, they respond fully and normally), whereas the A-V node over a relatively long period shows a gradual rather than an abrupt improvement in conduction.

The refractory period of the conducting paths is proportional to the length of the preceding cycle (R-R interval); i.e., the longer the cycle and slower the rate, the longer the ensuing refractory period, and vice versa. Ventricular aberration can therefore result either from shortening of the immediate cycle or from lengthening of the preceding one, or from a combination of both (fig. 16.1).

There are three forms of aberration (table 16.1). The common form is due to fascicular refractoriness (type A). To produce aberration of this type, the obvious ploy is to get an impulse to arrive at the ventricular fascicle before it has recovered from its last activation, i.e., while it is still in its refractory period. Clearly, the simplest way to achieve this is either to have a supraventricular premature beat or to accelerate the sinus rhythm. Figure 16.2 illustrates right bundle-branch block (RBBB) aberration of atrial premature beats—the early impulses have taken the right bundle branch (RBB) "by surprise" (while it is still refractory), and it has been unable to respond and conduct.

RBBB aberration is much more common than left bundle-branch block (LBBB) aberration; in fact it is claimed that 80 to 85% of all aberration is of RBBB type.[7, 26] In a relatively sick population, as in a coronary care facility, LBBB aberration assumes greater prominence and accounts for perhaps a third of the aberrant conduction encountered. And in Kulbertus,[10] experimental

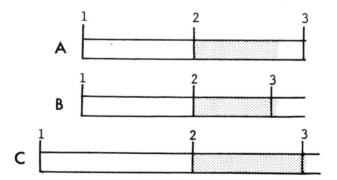

Figure 16.1. In the diagrams, *1, 2,* and *3* are consecutive beats and the *stippled area* represents the refractory period of some part of the conducting system during the second cycle. In *A,* there are two regular cycles with normal conduction. Beat 3 may become aberrant (*lower two diagrams*) if either the first cycle is lengthened or the second cycle is shortened. Shortening of the second cycle (*B*) may bring the beat within the refractory period of part of the conducting system; lengthening of the preceding cycle (*C*) will prolong the refractory period so that the next beat, though no earlier than before, falls within the now longer refractory period.

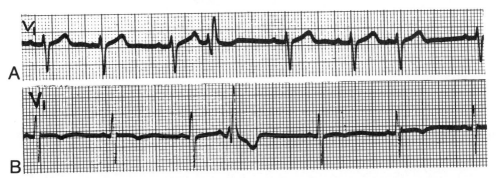

Figure 16.2. In both *A* and *B*, after three normally conducted beats, an **atrial extrasystole** arises, and its impulse arrives at the RBB while it is still refractory; it is therefore conducted with **RBBB aberration.** In *A*, the second and seventh beats are also extrasystoles, but they are less premature and are therefore conducted normally.

Table 16.1
Forms of Ventricular Aberration

Type A	Fascicular refractoriness
Type B	Anomalous supraventricular activation
Type C	Paradoxical critical rate

Table 16.2
Patterns of Induced Aberration[10]

RBBB alone	28	i.e.:
RBBB + LAHB	21	RBBB = 53%
RBBB + LPHB	12	LAHB = 32%
LAHB alone	17	LPHB = 19%
LPHB alone	10	LBBB = 15%
LBBB	10	Uncl = 10%
ILBBB	6	
Unclassified	12	
	116	

study, RBBB accounted for a smaller than expected proportion of the aberrancy produced experimentally. By inducing premature atrial beats in 44 patients, he was able to produce 116 different aberrant configurations (table 16.2), of which RBBB accounted for only 53%.

The Specifics

The first example of ventricular aberration to be published—by Lewis in 1910—showed atrial bigeminy with alternating patterns of aberration. A similar situation is shown in figure 16.3 where the atrial bigeminy is alternately complicated by RBBB and LBBB aberration. Additional points to notice in this tracing are (1) that the increased height of the R wave in lead 1 and the depth of the S wave in V_6 in the RBBB beats presumably indicate an associated left anterior hemiblock and (2) that the earliest indication of RBBB in V_1 may take the form of slurring or notching of the upstroke of the QRS (in fig. 16.3, see first atrial extrasystole in V_1).

The prime importance of aberration is in its mimicry of ventricular ectopy. It is in itself a secondary phenomenon—always the result of some primary disturbance—and never itself requires treatment. At times the morphology of the aberrant complex is indistinguishable from an ectopic pattern; but at other times the aberrant shapes provide broad hints of their supraventricular origin. In the tachyarrhythmias, the most important differentiation is from ventricular tachycardia, though isolated or paired aberrant beats may at times have to be differentiated from ventricular extrasystoles.

The first principle in the diagnosis of aberrancy is: do not diagnose it unless there is *positive* evidence in favor of it. Ectopy is much more common than aberration and, when you hear hoofbeats in this Western World, you do not think first of a zebra: you consider the zebra only if you see its stripes. The positive features in favor of aberration may therefore be called the "stripes" of aberration, and these are listed in table 16.3.

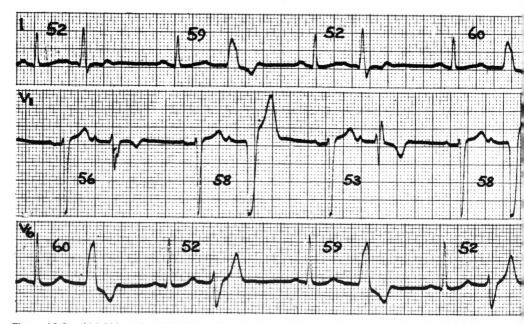

Figure 16.3.   Atrial bigeminy with **alternating aberration.** The shorter extrasystolic cycles end with some form of RBBB aberration, whereas the longer cycles end in LBBB aberration. The beats with RBBB, as evidenced by the slightly increased height of the R wave in lead 1 and the rS pattern in V_6, also show **left anterior hemiblock.** In V_1, the first atrial premature beat shows only the earliest sign of RBBB, i.e., notching of the terminal upstroke.

Table 16.3
The "Stripes" of Aberration

1. Triphasic contours
   a. rsR' variant in V_1
   b. qRs variant in V_6
2. Preceding atrial activity
3. Initial deflection identical with that of conducted beats (if RBBB)
4. Second-in-the-row anomalous beat
5. Alternating BBB patterns separated by single normally conducted beat

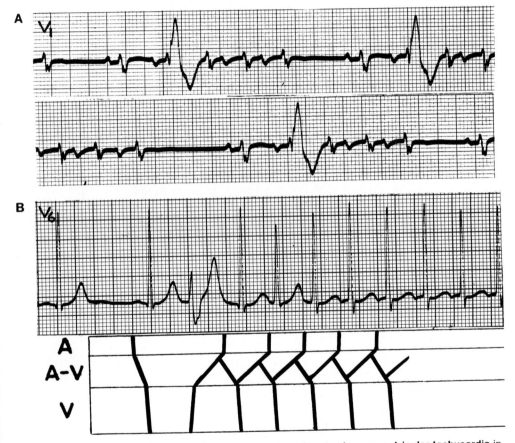

Figure 16.4. (*A*) The strips are continuous. Three short bursts of **supraventricular tachycardia** in which only the first beat (second in the row) develops **ventricular aberration**. (*B*) Here the second in the row of rapid beats is probably a **ventricular extrasystole** initiating a run of reciprocating tachycardia in the A-V junction (see laddergram).

The first four "stripes" are observable in figure 16.4*A* in which the two continuous strips contain three clusters of rapid beats. In each cluster, the second beat alone presents a bizarre appearance, it has a triphasic (rsR') RBBB pattern, its initial deflection is identical with that of the conducted sinus beats, and it is preceded by a premature ectopic P' wave. All of these points clinch the recognition of aberration, and we will take each of them up in turn.

Triphasic V_1/V_6 Morphology. The shape of the QRS complex is virtually diagnostic of aberrancy in many cases; the triphasic contours (rsR′ in V_1 and qRs in V_6) favor the diagnosis of aberration with odds of about 10:1. Figure 16.5*A* illustrates a junctional tachycardia—due to digitalis intoxication—with RBBB aberration; the rSR′ pattern is virtually diagnostic of the supraventricular origin of the tachycardia.

On the other hand, figure 16.5*B* presents a pattern in V_1 which is nondiagnostic: it could be a left ventricular tachycardia, or it could be supraventricular with RBBB aberration. But V_6, with its little q wave, tall thin R wave, and terminal s wave, is excellent evidence of its supraventricular origin. This patient also turned out to have a junctional tachycardia.

Figure 16.6 presents an example in which the characteristic morphology is seen in *both* right and left chest leads. The *top strip* shows the narrow complexes of a supraventricular tachycardia in lead MCL₁, with which the patient was admitted. The second strip shows the development of atrial fibrillation during which a lengthened cycle precipitates aberrancy in the following beat ending a

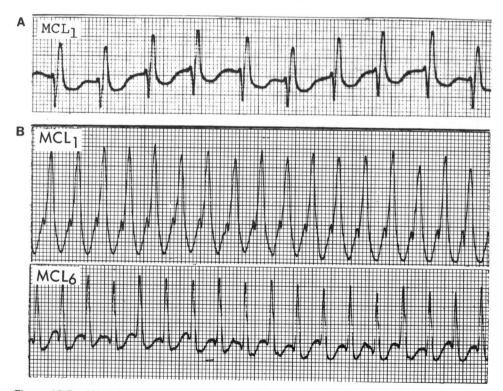

Figure 16.5. (*A*) A tachycardia diagnosable as presumably supraventricular from the triphasic (rSR′) pattern in a right chest lead (MCL₁). (*B*) A tachycardia not identifiable as supraventricular from the right chest lead but readily recognized in a left chest lead (MCL₆) by its triphasic (qRs) contour.

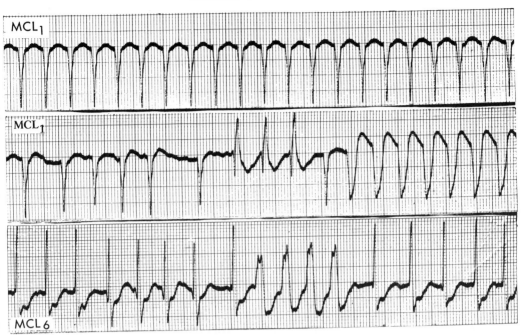

Figure 16.6. *Top strip* shows a regular **supraventricular tachycardia**. In the *middle strip*, **atrial fibrillation** develops and aberration of first **RBBB** and then **LBBB** type appears. In the *bottom strip*, beats 4 to 7 show RBBB aberration, and beats 9 to 12 LBBB aberration. The RBBB aberration is recognizable from its triphasic configuration in both right (rSR′) and left (qRS) chest leads.

shorter cycle (Ashman's phenomenon.)[7] The three aberrant beats have the classical rSR′ pattern of RBBB. A narrow, more normally conducted beat is then followed by regularization of the rhythm and the appearance of LBBB aberration. Meanwhile, in MCL₆, three of the more normally conducted beats are followed by four beats manifesting RBBB aberration of typical qRS form, followed by a single further more normally conducted beat and then LBBB aberration. This tracing therefore illustrates not only the classical QRS morphology of RBBB aberration in both left and right chest leads, but also the phenomenon of alternating, bilateral aberration.

Despite the availability of morphological clues introduced during the past 15 years,[18, 26] and more recently confirmed,[30, 32, 33] many authors persist in ignoring them[1, 24, 34] and continue to give predominant and undue weight to the presence or absence of independent atrial activity.

Identical Initial Deflection. There is no reason why an ectopic ventricular impluse should write an initial deflection indistinguishable from that of a normally conducted beat. On the other hand, since normal ventricular activation begins on the left side, pure RBBB does not interfere with initial activation, and so the initial deflection remains unchanged. If therefore the anomalous beat in question has a pattern compatible with RBBB and begins with a deflection identical with that of flanking conducted beats, it is a point in favor of aberration.

Preceding Atrial Activity. Sometimes the diagnosis of aberration depends upon the recognition of P waves preceding the abnormal ventricular complex. Figure 16.7 illustrates two bursts of anomalous beats whose shape is not the slightest use in distinguishing between aberration and ectopy. It might well be right ventricular tachycardia or supraventricular tachycardia with LBBB aberration. But careful inspection reveals that each bout of tachycardia is preceded by an accelerating atrial rhythm (P′ waves indicated by *arrows*), thus clinching the diagnosis of aberrant conduction. As the atrial cycle shortens, the refractory period of the left bundle branch is encroached upon and the bundle branch fails to conduct.

Figure 16.8 shows another tracing in which the diagnosis of aberration is mainly dependent upon preceding atrial activity. In each of the three strips, the second in a row of rapid beats is anomalous. Is it an aberrant complex because it ends a suddenly shorter cycle? Or is it a ventricular extrasystole initiating a run of reciprocating tachycardia in the A-V junction? The morphology is of no assistance—the right "rabbit ear" is taller than the left so that neither aberration nor ectopy is favored. But if the T wave preceding the anomalous complexes is carefully compared with the T waves of the other sinus beats, it at once becomes plain that something has been added to the pre-anomalous T waves—what else but a superimposed P′ wave confirming aberration!

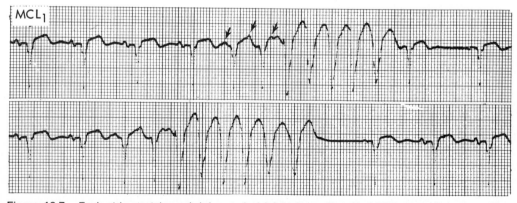

Figure 16.7. Each strip contains a brief run of **atrial tachycardia** with **LBBB aberration**; the telltale antecedent P′ waves (*arrows*) clinch the diagnosis. Note the momentary shift of pacemaker following each burst—the returning P wave differs from the sinus P waves.

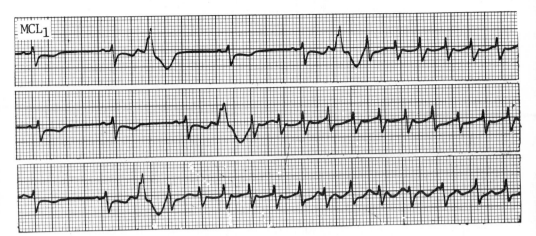

Figure 16.8. Morphologically, the anomalous beats in each strip could be either ectopic ventricular or aberrant. On three occasions, they usher in a run of **supraventricular tachycarda** and so could be aberrant (second in the row) or ventricular extrasystoles initiating runs of reciprocating tachycardia. The differentiation is made by observing the slightly positive deformity (P' waves) preceding each anomalous beat and not seen superimposed on the T waves of the other sinus beats.

Second-in-the-Row Anomaly. The reason only the second in a row of beats tends to be aberrant is because it is the only beat that ends a relatively short cycle preceded by a relatively long one. And since the refractory period of the conduction system is proportional to the preceding ventricular cycle length, the sequence of a long cycle (lengthening the subsequent refractory period) followed by a short cycle provides conditions par excellence for the development of aberration. However, this cycle sequence is not as diagnostic as one would like since the second beat in a row of rapid beats can be a ventricular extrasystole that initiates a run of reciprocating tachycardia in the A-V junction (fig. 16.4B).

Alternating BBB Pattern. When a pattern that could be one BBB is separated from a pattern that could be the other BBB by a single normally conducted beat—as in figures 16.6 and 16.10—the presumption is strong that there is bilateral aberration rather than ectopy from alternate ventricles.

Previous Comparative Tracing. It is obvious that if one is lucky enough to have a previous tracing available which shows the same anomalous pattern at a time when it was known to be aberrant, one can then identify the pattern in

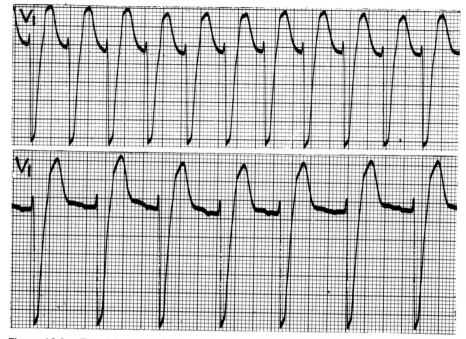

Figure 16.9. *Top strip* during tachycardia shows wide bizarre QRS complexes that could represent right ventricular ectopy or LBBB. *Bottom strip* was taken 1 year earlier and clearly shows a conducted rhythm with the same QRS morphology, thus establishing the supraventricular origin of the later tachycardia.

question. In figure 16.9, the *top strip* shows a tachycardia which could represent a right ventricular tachycardia or a supraventricular tachycardia with LBBB aberration. The *bottom strip* is a tracing from the same patient taken 1 year earlier, and it shows an identical QRS complex during an obviously conducted rhythm. This establishes a supraventricular tachycardia in the top strip.

Ventricular Aberration Complicating Atrial Fibrillation

The common form of ventricular aberration frequently complicates atrial fibrillation. It is probably true to say that when a run of anomalous beats interrupts normal intraventricular conduction during atrial fibrillation, it is more likely due to aberration than to coincidental ventricular tachycardia. Because in the presence of atrial fibrillation one cannot invoke preceding atrial activity as an indication of aberrant conduction, one has to rely more heavily than usual on the morphology of the wide complexes to differentiate aberration from ventricular ectopy. Thus the rsR′ pattern in V_1 or MCL_1 (fig. 16.10*B*) or the qRs pattern in V_6 materially assists in establishing the diagnosis of aberrant conduction.

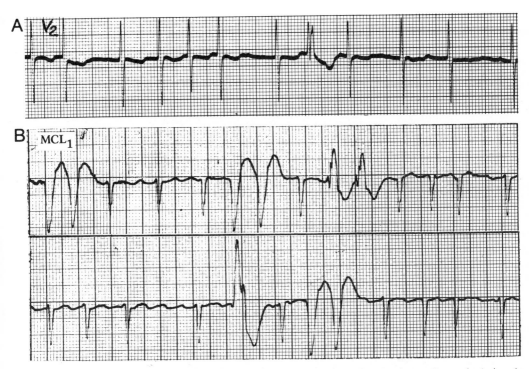

Figure 16.10. (A) The eighth beat has an RsR′ pattern and is undoubtedly aberrantly conducted; note also that the initial R is virtually identical with the R waves of the flanking conducted RS complexes. (B) The strips are continuous. In the top strip, some beats are conducted with **LBBB**, and others with **RBBB aberration.** The RBBB aberration is identified by the rsR′ configuration, whereas the LBBB morphology is of no help and could as well be right ventricular ectopic. In the bottom strip, the fifth beat ends in a longer-shorter cycle sequence but is identified as ectopic left ventricular by the taller left ''rabbit-ear'' configuration.

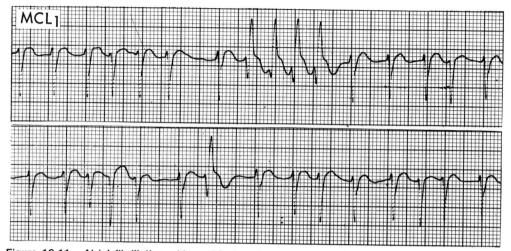

Figure 16.11.   Atrial fibrillation with **ventricular aberration.** The strips are continuous. The run of anomalous beats in the top strip begins with the usual longer-shorter cycle sequence and is identified by the rsR' pattern (RBBB) as aberrantly conducted. In the bottom strip, a single aberrant beat ends a longer-shorter sequence.

Gouaux and Ashman[7] (1947) first drew attention to the fact that aberrant conduction was likely to complicate atrial fibrillation when a longer cycle was succeeded by a shorter cycle (fig. 16.11); and when a long-short sequence produces aberration, it is sometimes referred to as the **Ashman phenomenon.** But it is important to bear in mind that this cycle sequence cannot be used to differentiate aberration from ectopy because, by the "rule of bigeminy," a lengthened cycle also tends to precipitate a ventricular extrasystole (fig. 16.10*B*). And so, a long-short cycle sequence ending with an anomalous complex is as likely to be a ventricular ectopic as an aberrant beat.

There are several other minor clues that help to differentiate aberration from ectopy in the presence of atrial fibrillation.[16]

Presence of Longer Returning Cycle. Ventricular ectopy tends to be followed by a longer returning cycle. This is because many ectopic ventricular impulses are conducted backward into the A-V junction (concealed retrograde conduction) and, if this happens, the A-V junction is left partially refractory by the retrograde invasion so that the next several fibrillatory impulses are unable to penetrate and reach their ventricular destination.

Absence of Longer Preceding Cycle. As indicated above, a long preceding cycle favors both aberration and ectopy and cannot be used as a differentiating point. On the other hand, absence of a longer preceding cycle is evidence against aberration and therefore favors ectopy (fig. 16.12*A*).

Comparative Cycle Sequences. If an anomalous beat ends a longer-shorter cycle sequence, we have seen that differentiation between aberration and ectopy may be difficult. If in such circumstances an even longer cycle followed by an even shorter cycle ends with a normally conducted beat, the evidence against aberration is strong, and the diagnosis of ectopy is favored (fig. 16.12*B*).

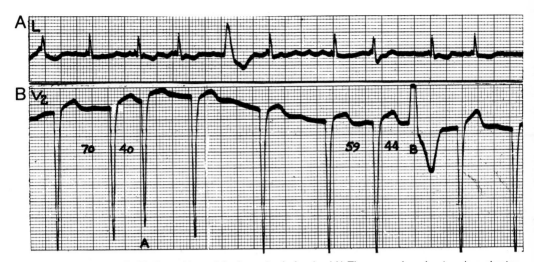

Figure 16.12. Atrial fibrillation with **ventricular ectopic beats.** (*A*) The anomalous beat ends a shorter-longer cycle sequence, identifying it as probably ectopic ventricular. (*B*) The anomalous beat (B) ends a longer-shorter cycle sequence; but beat A, which is not anomalous, ends an even longer-shorter sequence and is not aberrant. Beat B is therefore even less likely to be aberrant and is ectopic ventricular.

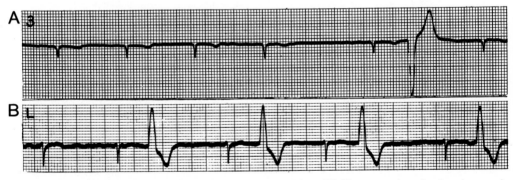

Figure 16.13. Atrial fibrillation with **ventricular extrasystoles.** (*A*) The anomalous beat ends a cycle markedly shorter than any of the conducted beats and is therefore most likely ectopic ventricular. (*B*) The anomalous beats bear an almost constant relationship to the preceding beats (fixed coupling) and are therefore most likely ectopic ventricular.

Undue Prematurity. When sufficient A-V block is present to ensure that all conducted cycles are relatively long, the sudden appearance of an anomalous beat ending a cycle far shorter than any of the normally conducted beats favors the diagnosis of ectopy (fig. 16.13*A*).

Fixed or Constant Coupling. This clue is obviously applicable only if several anomalous beats are available for comparison. If the interval between the normally conducted beat and the ensuing anomalous beat is constant to within a few hundredths of a second, ectopy is favored (fig. 16.13*B*).

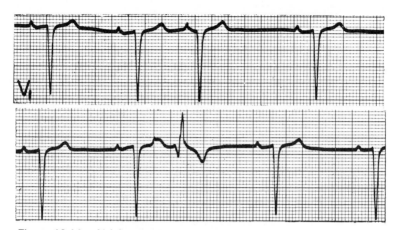

Figure 16.14.   Atrial premature beats. The third beat in each strip is an atrial premature beat; in the upper strip the ectopic P wave is clearly visible and is followed by unchanged conduction to the ventricles. In the lower strip the ectopic beat is much more premature (P wave deforms upstroke of T wave) and finds the right bundle branch still refractory, so that **ventricular aberration** of RBBB type occurs. This beat might easily be mistaken for an ectopic *ventricular* beat.

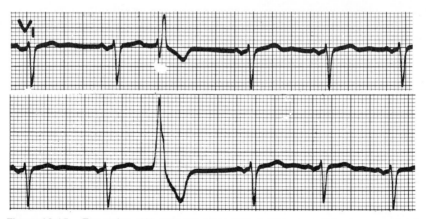

Figure 16.15.   Two strips of V₁ from the same patient. The upper strip shows an **atrial premature beat** with **ventricular aberration**; the lower strip, a left **ventricular premature beat**. Note that the aberrant beat has an initial deflection (r) identical with those of flanking sinus beats and a triphasic (rsR′) contour, whereas the ectopic ventricular beat is monophasic (R), reaches an early peak and has a slurred downstroke. (Reproduced from Sandler and Marriott: The differential morphology of anomalous ventricular complexes of RBBB-type in lead V₁. Circulation 1965;31,551.)

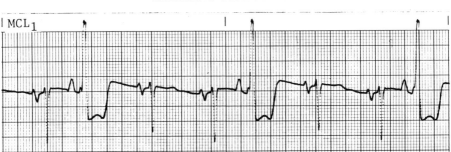

Figure 16.16.   Atrial premature beats. The second, fifth and 8th beats are atrial extrasystoles conducted with a bizarre form of **RBBB aberration.** Note large ectopic premature P waves preceding the aberrant ventricular complexes.

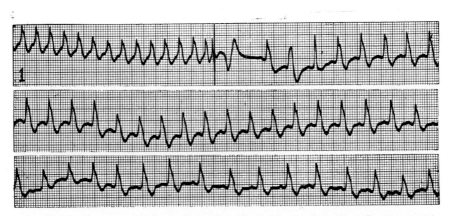

Figure 16.17.   Supraventricular tachycardia with **ventricular aberration.** Continuous strip of lead 1. The record begins with what appears to be a run of ventricular tachycardia. Clinically at rate 245 the first heart sound was constant and there were no irregular cannon waves. After procaine amide the paroxysm gives place to a sinus tachycardia, in which the preceding P waves are well seen at the end of the *bottom strip.* Because the ventricular complexes are identical with those shown during the paroxysmal tachycardia (beginning of *top strip*), there is little doubt that the paroxysm was of supraventricular origin with aberrant ventricular conduction.

For further review, figures 16.14 through 16.23 illustrate aberrant conduction occurring in various supraventricular arrhythmias, and the pertinent points in diagnosis are dealt with in the respective legends. From a study of these examples, it should be evident that confusion can readily occur and that such confusion can have serious consequences.

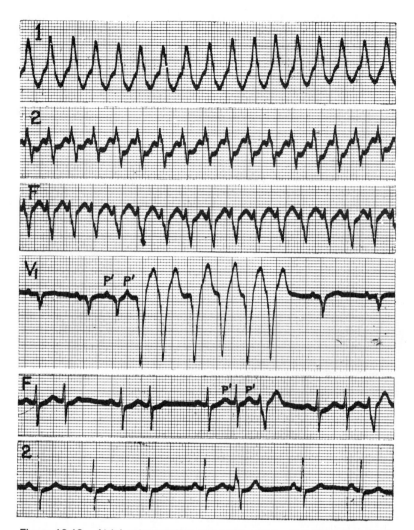

Figure 16.18.   Atrial extrasystoles and **tachycardia** with **LBBB aberration.**
The three upper strips show a pattern suggesting ventricular tachycardia. The
lower three strips demonstrate that the tachycardia is supraventricular with
ventricular aberration; the fourth strip shows the beginning of a paroxysm,
which again looks ventricular but is preceded by the onset of rapid ectopic
atrial activity (P′), indicating that this paroxysm is probably ectopic atrial with
aberrant ventricular conduction. The *bottom two strips* each show telltale
extrasystoles. In lead 2 (*bottom strip*) there is one bizarre premature beat,
which is preceded by an ectopic P wave and followed by a pause that is less
than compensatory. This is then a supraventricular premature beat with aberration, and the aberrant complex is identical with the ventricular complexes
during the paroxysm in the upper lead 2 (*second strip*). In aVF (*fifth strip*) there
are two couplets of atrial bigeminy followed by two triplets of atrial trigeminy. In

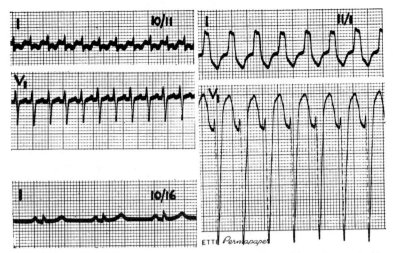

Figure 16.19.   Two paroxysms of **tachycardia** in a boy with no demonstrable heart disease. At left the paroxysm is unmistakably supraventricular. At the right, three weeks later, the QRS pattern has altered markedly and now appears to represent ventricular tachycardia at a considerably slower rate. However, the first heart sound was constant and a lead S_5 demonstrated P waves in relation to each QRS complex. Supraventricular tachycardia with aberrant ventricular conduction is therefore the more likely diagnosis (the possible alternative being ventricular tachycardia with 1:1 retrograde conduction to the atria).

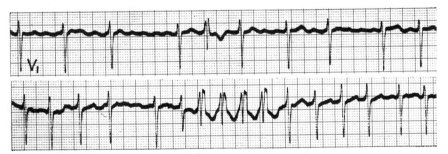

Figure 16.20.   Atrial fibrillation with **aberrant ventricular conduction.** In the upper strip the fifth beat might well be mistaken for an ectopic ventricular beat; however, it is of RBBB (RSR′) form and is more likely an aberrant complex. In the lower strip the fifth beat, which terminates a long diastole, is followed by five aberrant complexes; the first of these shows only minor distortion (slurred upstroke, less deep S wave and frankly inverted T wave) but the following four beats show an RSR′ of RBBB, which could readily be mistaken for a short burst of ventricular tachycardia.

---

these triplets, the second premature beat shows ventricular aberration with bizarre complexes identical with the QRS complexes during the paroxysm in the upper lead aVF (*third strip*). All of this adds up to overwhelming evidence that the "ventricular" tachycardia in the upper three strips is really supraventricular with aberrant ventricular conduction.

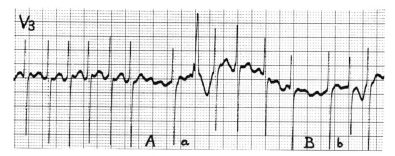

Figure 16.21.   Atrial flutter fibrillation with **aberrant ventricular con-duction**, illustrating the importance of the length of the *preceding* cycle: The rapid ventricular response is interrupted on two occasions by longer than usual diastoles (A and B). These long cycles lengthen the ensuing refractory periods of the conducting tissues. After pause A, therefore, the next short cycle, a, is terminated by a distorted (aberrant) ventricular complex of RBBB form. Pause B is not so long as A and produces less prolongation of the refractory period; the beat terminating the ensuing cycle, b, shows only minor signs of aberration—its T wave is deeply inverted and the QRS has decidedly lower voltage than any of the other beats.

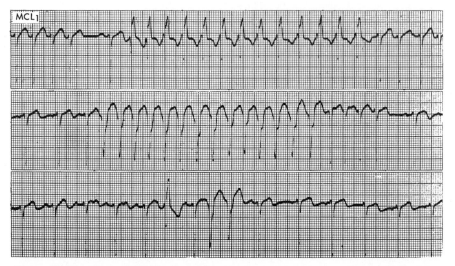

Figure 16.22.   Runs of **atrial tachycardia** with aberrant conduction of RBBB type in the *top strip* and of LBBB type in the *second strip*. Both forms are present in *bottom strip*.

Figure 16.23 illustrates aberrancy that led to regrettable mistreatment. The *top strip* shows the patient's rhythm on admission: atrial tachycardia with 2:1 A-V conduction. He was therefore started on digitalis and by the next morning (*second strip*) frequently manifested 4:1 conduction ratios. Because of this "impairment" of conduction, digitalis was discontinued, and quinidine started. The *bottom strip* was taken the following morning and shows the situation that had developed at about midnight and had led to night-long erroneous therapy for ventricular tachycardia. In fact, the *bottom strip* represents atrial tachycardia with 1:1 A-V conduction and RBBB aberration. The quinidine, perhaps partly by its antivagal effect, but certainly through its slowing effect on the atrial rate—from 210 to 192/min—has enabled the A-V junction to conduct *all* of the ectopic atrial impulses. The resulting much-increased ventricular rate—from approximately 90 to 192/min—had produced a dangerous hypotension from which the patient was finally rescued with the combination of a pressor agent and countershock.

In 1958, Rosenblueth documented the effect of atrial rate on normal A-V conduction by pacing the atria of normal dogs. He found that, at an average rate of 257, the animals developed Wenckebach periods and began to drop beats; and, at an average rate of 285, they developed constant 2:1 conduction. Consider what this means in terms of ventricular rate: at an atrial rate of 286, the ventricular rate will be 143; and, if the atrial rate be slowed only 30 beats/min to 256, the ventricular rate will be 256. In other words, by slowing the atrial rate only 30 beats/min, the ventricular rate has increased 113 beats/min. This is why it can be so dangerous to give an atrial-slowing drug like lidocaine, quinidine or even procainamide in the presence of atrial flutter or fibrillation when the ventricular response is already uncomfortably fast,[20] e.g., if atrial flutter at a rate of 300 is associated with a 2:1 response, producing a ventricular rate of 150, and a drug such as lidocaine is administered, the atrial rate may slow to 250 and A-V conduction may increase to 1:1, producing a dangerous ventricular rate of 250.

From a therapeutic point of view, an extremely important form of aberration may complicate atrial flutter. Uncomplicated and untreated atrial flutter usually manifests an A-V conduction ratio of 2:1. If digitalis or propranolol is then administered, the conduction pattern often changes to alternating 2:1 and 4:1,

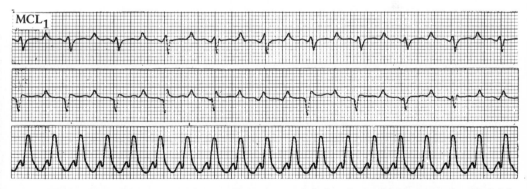

Figure 16.23. The strips are not continuous. Top strip on admission shows **atrial tachycardia with 2:1 A-V conduction.** Middle strip next day shows 2:1 and 4:1 conduction. Bottom strip 24 hours later shows a slower atrial rate with 1:1 conduction and **RBBB aberration**—mistaken for hours and treated as ventricular tachycardia.

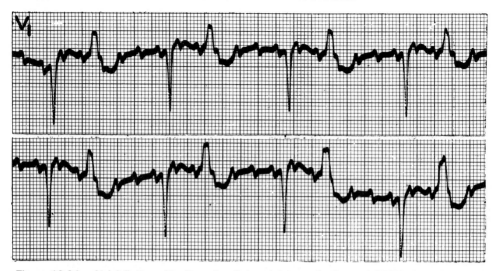

Figure 16.24. **Atrial flutter** with alternating 2:1 and 4:1 conduction and **RBBB aberration** of the beats that end the shorter cycles.

producing alternately longer and shorter cycles; at this stage, the beats that end the shorter cycles may develop aberrant conduction (fig. 16.24). In someone receiving digitalis, this is likely to evoke a diagnosis of ventricular bigeminy and be attributed to digitalis toxocity. Then the still-needed digitalis is wrongfully discontinued, when in fact the situation calls for more digitalis to reduce conduction still further to a constant 4:1 with a then *normal ventricular rate*—always the immediate goal of therapy.

There is a striking tendency, not infrequently seen in aberration complicating tachycardia, for the aberrancy to be bilateral; this is seen in figures 16.10, 16.22 and 16.25. Another intriguing feature shown in these figures is the abrupt switch from one form of aberration to the other—from RBBB to LBBB or vice versa—via a single intervening normally conducted beat. Although unexplained, this phenomenon is sufficiently characteristic to assist in differentiating bilateral aberrancy from bifocal ectopy.

"Critical Rate"

Most of the examples of aberration that we have so far seen have developed because the ventricular cycle, for some reason, suddenly shortened. At times we see the same phenomenon appear as the sinus rhythm *gradually* accelerates. Figure 16.26 presents two examples of slight sinus acceleration in which the cycle gradually shortens until it becomes shorter than the refractory period of one of the bundle branches, whereupon aberrant conduction develops; it will persist until the cycle lengthens enough for normal conduction again to occur. The rate at which the BBB develops is known as the "critical rate," and when such block comes and goes with changes in the heart rate, it is known as "rate-

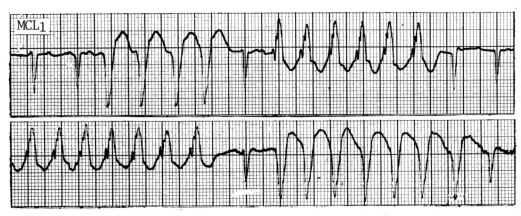

Figure 16.25.   Atrial fibrillation with **bilateral aberration.** Both strips illustrate the abrupt change from one BBB aberration to the other BBB, with a single intervening normally conducted beat.

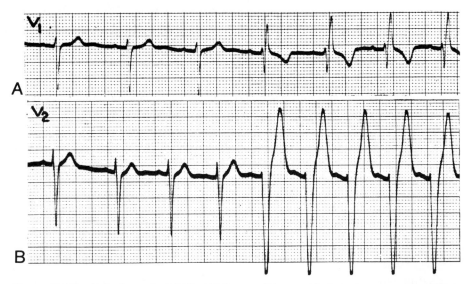

Figure 16.26.   Rate-dependent BBB. (*A*) From a 19-year-old student nurse: as her sinus rate accelerates and the cycle shortens in response to gentle exercise, progressively increasing degrees of RBBB develop ("critical-rate" or "rate-dependent" RBBB). (*B*) From a 64-year-old man with severe coronary disease; as his sinus rate accelerates and the cycle shortens, LBBB develops at a critical rate of just over 100/min.

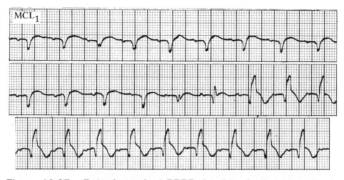

Figure 16.27. **Rate-dependent RBBB** develops in the *second strip* and continues through the *bottom strip*. As the sinus cycle shortens in the middle of the second strip, increasing degrees of RBBB aberration develop. Note that the P-R remains constant.

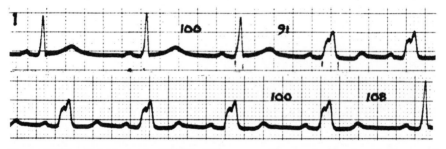

Figure 16.28. **Rate-dependent LBBB.** Strips are continuous. As the sinus rhythm accelerates, LBBB develops when the rate exceeds 60/min (cycle length <100); but for normal conduction to resume, the rate must fall below 60/min (cycle length > 100).

dependent" BBB. Figure 16.27 presents another example of rate-dependent RBBB.

One of the interesting features of rate-dependent BBB is that the critical rate at which the block develops is different (faster) than the rate at which, once established, the BBB disappears. In figure 16.28, as the sinus rhythm accelerates, normal conduction prevails at a cycle of 100 (= rate of 60/min), and the cycle at which the BBB develops is 91 (= rate of 66/min); but as the rate slows, the BBB persists at a cycle of 100 (= rate of 60/min), and for normal conduction to resume, the cycle must lengthen further to 108 (= rate of 56/min).

The two reasons for this difference in rate requirement during acceleration and deceleration are clear but difficult to describe: (1) Since the refractory period of the ventricular conduction system is proportional to the length of the preceding ventricular cycle, it follows that as the rate accelerates the refractory periods get shorter and shorter; i.e., the potential for conduction progressively

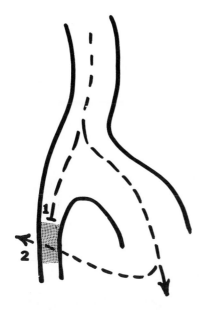

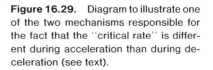

Figure 16.29. Diagram to illustrate one of the two mechanisms responsible for the fact that the "critical rate" is different during acceleration than during deceleration (see text).

improves and therefore there is a tendency to preserve normal conduction. The converse is true as the rate slows. (2) Probably more important is the factor diagrammed in figure 16.29. The *shaded area* in the RBB indicates the refractory segment that precludes conduction when the impulse first arrives (*1*) and so causes RBBB aberration. A moment later, the refractory segment has recovered and, when the transseptal impulse that has meanwhile negotiated the left bundle branch (LBB) approaches it, the RBB is again responsive, and the impulse discharges it (*2*). For the impulse to travel down the LBB and through the septum requires about 0.06 sec; thus the previously refractory RBB is depolarized about 0.06 sec *after the beginning of the QRS complex.* As far as the RBB is concerned, therefore, its cycle begins about 0.06 sec after the beginning of the RBBB QRS complex. When you measure the cycle length conventionally from the beginning of one QRS complex to the beginning of the next, you are not giving the RBB a fair deal since its cycle did not begin until halfway through the first QRS complex. It follows that for normal conduction to resume, the cycle during deceleration (when measured conventionally) must be longer than the "critical" cycle during acceleration by about 0.06 sec. This calculation fits nicely with the observed findings in figure 16.28.

Another way in which the rate dependency of BBB may be revealed is when a sudden lengthening of the ventricular cycle causes the disappearance of a previously present BBB pattern. This is most often seen at the end of the

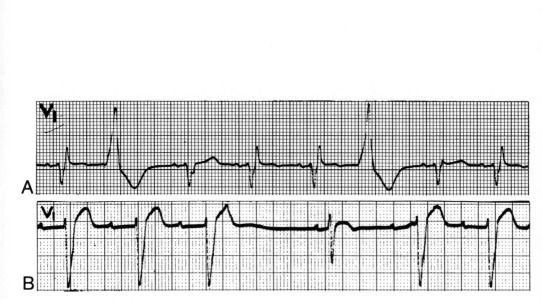

Figure 16.30.   Examples of postextrasystolic revelation of **rate-dependent BBB.** In *A*, after each of the ventricular extrasystoles, the returning sinus beat manifests a lesser degree of RBBB than do the sinus beats ending the normal (shorter) sinus cycles. (*B*) After three sinus beats conducted with first degree A-V block and LBBB, a nonconducted atrial extrasystole results in a prolonged ventricular cycle at the end of which the returning sinus beat is conducted with normal P-R and normal intraventricular conduction, demonstrating that both the A-V delay and the LBBB are rate-dependent.

lengthened cycle following an extrasystole. Figure 16.30 shows two examples of this phenomenon.

The concept of "critical rate" is of greater importance in A-V block than in BBB but has received even less attention. Analogous to the development of BBB at a given "critical rate" is the development of A-V block when the atrial rate reaches a certain critical level and 1:1 conduction gives place to Wenckebach periods and, at a somewhat faster rate, to 2:1 conduction. This is more important than critical-rate BBB because failure to appreciate the role of rate in determining the A-V conduction ratio has often led to unnecessarily aggressive therapy. This whole situation will be dealt with in detail in Chapter 24 on A-V block when the inadequacy of our definitions of the "degrees" of A-V block will be emphasized.

Progressively developing aberration, as in figures 16.26*A* and 16.27, must be differentiated from progressive degrees of fusion as a ventricular ectopic rhythm takes over. If fusion develops by degrees, the P-R interval must progressively shorten (see figs. 17.2 and 21.7*A*); whereas, if aberration gradually widens the QRS, the P-R is likely to remain constant throughout the various stages of increasing aberrant conduction—as in figures 16.26*A* and 16.27.

Type B Aberration

The second form of ventricular aberration, type B (table 16.1), is due to anomalous activation at a supraventricular level, which in turn causes abnormal distribution through the ventricles to produce an aberrant complex. Although not usually included under the heading of ventricular aberration, in the broadest sense of the definition Wolff-Parkinson-White (WPW) conduction is a manifestation of this form of aberration; as a result of anomalous activation and conduction (via a Kent bundle or other bypass tract) above the ventricles, activation of the ventricles themselves is distorted (*1* in fig. 16.31).

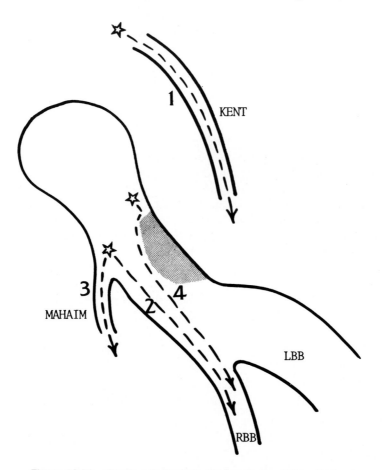

Figure 16.31. Diagram to illustrate the four forms of Type B aberration. (*1*) Kent-bundle (WPW) conduction; (*2*) A-V junctional impulse arising from an eccentrically placed focus spreading preferentially down the ipsilateral bundle branch; (*3*) junctional impulse arising from an eccentrically placed focus spreading preferentially via a Mahaim tract; and (*4*) a junctional impulse arising eccentrically and deflected contralaterally by a patch of diseased tissue.

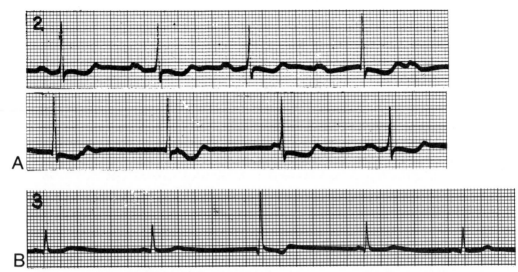

Figure 16.32. Minor **aberration of junctional beats.** (*A*) The two strips are continuous. After three sinus beats showing intraatrial block and first degree A-V block, the fourth sinus impulse is blocked, resulting in four junctional escape beats. Note the slight but definite differences in contour: the junctional beats have small Q waves and taller R waves. (*B*) After two conducted beats, the third beat is exactly on time but without benefit of preceding P wave; its form is obviously changed, but since it is normally narrow, it probably arises in the A-V junction and is conducted with Type B aberration (one obviously cannot absolutely exclude a ventricular septal or fascicular origin.)

A much more common form of aberration of this type is seen with A-V junctional beats. Since there are innumerable potential pacemaker sites in the A-V junction, it follows that most of them cannot be centrally located in the mainstream and are therefore situated off to one side. As most junctional pacemakers are thus eccentrically placed and since longitudinal insulation between parallel fibers in the A-V bundle is effective,[29] it in turn follows that an impulse arising from such a pacemaker tends to be conducted down its side of the junction and the corresponding bundle branch sooner than down the contralateral side and branch (*2* in fig. 16.31); and the QRS complex registers the pattern of more or less conduction delay on the contralateral side. Such a mechanism obviously has nothing to do with cycle length and refractory periods—if the impulse arises eccentrically and spreads asymmetrically, it matters not whether it be an early, punctual or late beat. This is why it is almost the rule for junctional escape beats to show some degree of ventricular aberration. Figure 16.32 presents two examples of minor aberration of junctional escape beats. Although minor aberration is the rule, occasionally it assumes major proportions and can then be mistaken for ventricular ectopy.[9]

A similar form of aberrant conduction can be produced if the eccentrically placed junctional pacemaker, situated near the origin of a Mahaim tract (*3* in fig. 16.31), delivers at least a part of its impulse via the tract and so initiates a distorted QRS complex. Such delivery via "paraspecific" fibers has been called "preferential conduction."[22] A similar form of aberration could result if, owing to disease affecting one side of the junction, the impulse were deflected toward the opposite side (*4* in fig. 16.31) and thus distributed asynchronously via the bundle branches to the ventricles.

Type C Aberration

The third form of aberration, type C (table 16.1), is characterized by the development of abnormal intraventricular conduction only at the end of a *lengthened* cycle; since one would expect conduction to be better after a longer diastolic respite, this form is known as paradoxical critical rate. It is also sometimes referred to as bradycardia-dependent BBB; but this is unsatisfactory as an inclusive term because it is not always necessary to achieve a rate that merits the designation, bradycardia (i.e., under 60/min), for the BBB to develop; e.g., normal conduction may be present at a rate of 82/min, and the BBB may develop only if the cycle length increases to a point equaling a rate of 68/min as in figure 16.33.

So many theories have been advanced to explain this paradoxical phenomenon[6, 21] that it is unlikely that any one of them is universally satisfactory. The currently popular explanation invokes a phase 4 phenomenon. It is well known that as a pacemaking cell spontaneously depolarizes during diastole (phase 4), it becomes less and less responsive to extraneous stimuli. To explain the paradoxical development of BBB after a lengthened cycle, it is assumed that the bundle branch as a whole is functioning as a pacemaker and spontaneously depolarizing. Early in diastole, it will respond to and permit passage of an approaching impulse; but later on, when depolarization has progressed further, it is unresponsive and conduction is therefore impossible. Such an explanation is plausible, but proof is lacking.[6]

At other times, the paradoxical effect appears to be due to vagal influence that both slows the rate and impairs conduction through the bundle branch; this, of course, involves the assumption that the subject is an oddity in whom autonomic innervation extends to the bundle branches. Another possibility in

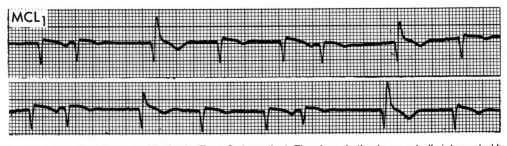

Figure 16.33. Paradoxical critical rate (Type C aberration). The sinus rhythm is repeatedly interrupted by atrial extrasystoles. The conducted beats ending the lengthened postextrasystolic cycles all show RBBB, whereas the shorter sinus cycles and the even shorter extrasystolic cycles show more normal intraventricular conduction.

some cases postulates a critical level of perfusion to a bundle branch, and that perfusion, which is barely adequate at the end of shorter cycles at faster rates, becomes inadequate by the end of the longer diastoles.

The primary importance of all forms of ventricular aberration is that it may be confused with and must be differentiated from ventricular ectopy—a distinction that becomes especially important when we are faced with a wide-QRS tachycardia.

Differentiation between Supraventricular and Ventricular Tachycardias[18, 23]

With close attention to clinical detail, the bedside diagnosis of regular tachycardia can be surprisingly accurate. First some principles, misconceptions and false doctrines:

1. The proper posture for the diagnostician at the bedside is to apply stethoscope to the precordium and eyes to the neck veins *simultaneously.*
2. Clues to search for are:
   a. Presence or absence of cannon "a" waves or flutter waves in the jugular pulse.
   b. Variation in intensity of the first heart sound.
   c. Splitting of the heart sounds.
3. Splitting of the sounds is due to ventricular *asynchrony*, whereas *irregular* cannon waves in the neck and variation in intensity of the first sound are signs of *dissociation* between atria and ventricles.
4. Signs of dissociation are at times more easily identified at the bedside than in the tracing because the independent P waves are often lost in the barrage of ventricular complexes.
5. *Dissociation does not prove ventricular tachycardia*; but it excludes atrial tachycardia and therefore makes ventricular that much more likely. Dissociation can occur between atrial and A-V pacemakers and, if ventricular aberration is also present, the imitation of ventricular tachycardia may be perfect both clinically and electrocardiographically (see fig. 15.3).
6. *Regular* cannon waves—with every beat—may be seen in atrial tachycardia, A-V tachycardia or ventricular tachycardia with 1:1 retroconduction.

The *electrocardiographic* recognition of typical supraventricular tachycardia is easy; the difficulty arises in separating ventricular tachycardia from a supraventricular tachycardia combined with ventricular aberration. In attempting to make this separation, QRS morphology should receive primary attention. If characteristic features are observed, accuracy and speed are both served; but if morphologic clues are absent or equivocal, one must seek elsewhere.

Although the demonstration of dissociation is of limited diagnostic value, evidence of it should always be sought. If P waves are not recognizable even in V_1, more specialized leads may be informative; a precordial lead known as S_5 may be tried[13]: for this the positive electrode is placed in the 5th right interspace close to the sternal border and the negative electrode over the manubrium (with the conventional patient cable, the LA electrode is placed in the 5th interspace with the RA electrode on the manubrium, and the selector switch is set for standard lead 1). If this fails, an esophageal[4, 9] or intracardiac[31] lead will almost always be successful in displaying P waves. Alternatively, if a tracing is taken during the administration of procainamide[2] or acetylcholine[27] intravenously, the ventricular rate will often slow under their influence, and P waves will become apparent in the now lengthened intervals between ventricular complexes. Such maneuvers, however, are seldom necessary or desirable.

With these many principles in mind, we can formulate a systematic approach to the regular tachycardia:

1. *First look at the neck veins and listen to the first heart sound with the patient holding his breath.* If there are irregular cannon waves in the neck and/or the first heart sound varies in intensity from beat to beat, you have evidence of dissociation, and this suggests a ventricular tachycardia. If the first heart sound is of unvarying intensity and there are either no cannon waves or regular cannon waves in the neck, this is against dissociation and the tachycardia is probably supraventricular (exceptions: (a) ventricular tachycardia with retrograde 1:1 conduction; (b) ventricular tachycardia with concurrent atrial fibrillation).

   If an electrocardiograph is available, do not use carotid sinus or other vagal stimulation until after a tracing has been taken, because if the tachycardia is supraventricular, the vagal maneuver may terminate it, leaving no graphic record to document the paroxysm.

2. *Take an electrocardiogram* and look at the QRS pattern. If it is normal in contour and duration, the tachycardia is supraventricular. If it is widened and bizarre, the tachycardia may be either ventricular or supraventricular with aberrant ventricular conduction. If it is widened, study the V_1/V_6 morphology, observe the frontal plane axis and look for the other morphological clues outlined in Chapters 11 and 15. Try to find a lead in which P waves are identifiable and look for Dressler beats. If previous tracings are available, look for isolated extrasytoles and compare their pattern with that of the tachycardia.

3. If the diagnosis is still in doubt, *try carotid sinus massage, eyeball compression or other vagal stimulation.* If the tachycardia is supraventricular, this may terminate it. In atrial flutter vagal stimulation may temporarily halve the rate by increasing the A-V conduction ratio from 2:1 to 4:1. If the tachycardia is ventricular, it will, with very rare exceptions,[7a] be unaffected.

4. If there is still doubt, take a lead S_5; if this is unrevealing, consider passing an *esophageal* or *intracardiac electrode*; a satisfactory esophageal or intracardiac lead will always reveal P waves when they are unidentifiable in conventional leads. However, in practice, these invasive techniques are

almost never needed and should certainly be avoided whenever possible, especially in patients with acute myocardial infarction.

5. If doubt remains, one may administer *procainamide intravenously* with appropriate precautions. If the tachycardia is ventricular, this will be a correct treatment; if it is supraventricular, the drug may momentarily block A-V conduction and reveal the telltale atrial rhythm between the now more widely spaced ventricular complexes.[2] *Acetylcholine* may have a similar effect.[27]

6. If facilities for recording *His-bundle electrograms* are at hand and the clinical circumstances warrant the procedure, this technique may provide the only certain means of differentiating ventricular aberration from ectopy.[5]

In summary:

Clinically

1. Look for
   a. Wide splitting of heart sounds.
   b. Variation in intensity of first sound.
   c. Cannon waves.
2. Observe effect of carotid sinus stimulation.

Electrocardiographically (in records that look like ventricular tachycardia):

1. Study QRS morphology.
2. Identify P waves.
   a. In conventional leads, especially 2 and V_1.
   b. In lead S_5.
   c. In esophageal or intracardiac lead.
   d. During administration of procaine amide or acetylcholine.
3. Look for Dressler beats.
4. Look for isolated extrasystoles in previous tracings.

REFERENCES

1. Bailey, J. C.: The electrocardiographic differential diagnosis of supraventricular tachycardia with aberrancy versus ventricular tachycardia. Pract. Cardiol. 1980: **6**, 118.
2. Bernstein, L. M., et al.: Intravenous procaine amide as an aid to differentiate flutter with bundle branch block from paroxysmal ventricular tachycardia. Am. Heart J. 1954: **48**, 82.
3. Cohen, S. I., et al.: Variations of aberrant ventricular conduction in man. Circulation 1968: **38**, 899.
4. Copeland, G. D., et al.: Clinical evaluation of a new esophageal electrode, with particular reference to the bipolar esophageal electrocardiogram; II. Observations in cardiac arrhythmias. Am. Heart J. 1959: **57**, 874.
5. Damato, A. N., and Lau, S. H.: Clinical value of the electrogram of the conduction system. Prog. Cardiovasc. Dis. 1970: **13**, 119.
6. Gambetta, M., and Childers, R. W.: Reverse rate related bundle branch block. J. Electrocardiol. 1973: **6**, 153.
7. Gouaux, J. L., and Ashman, R.: Auricular fibrillation with aberration simulating ventricular paroxysmal tachycardia. Am. Heart J. 1947: **34**, 366.

7a. Hess, D. S., et al.: Termination of ventricular tachycardia by carotid sinus massage. Circulation 1982: **65**, 627.

8. Kistin, A. D.: Retrograde conduction to the atria in ventricular tachycardia. Circulation 1961: **24**, 236.

9. Kistin, A. D.: Problems in the differentiation of ventricular arrhythmia from supraventricular arrhythmia with abnormal QRS. Prog. Cardiovasc. Dis. 1966: **9**, 1.

10. Kulbertus, H. E., et al.: Vectorcardiographic study of aberrant conduction; anterior displacement of QRS, another form of intraventricular block. Br. Heart J. 1976: **38**, 549.

11. Langendorf, R.: Differential diagnosis of ventricular paroxysmal tachycardia. Exp. Med. Surg. 1950: **8**, 228.

12. Langendorf, R.: Aberrant ventricular conduction. Am. Heart J 1951: **41**, 700.

13. Lian, Cassimatis and Hebert: Intéret de la dérivation précordiale auriculaire S₅ dans le diagnostic des troubles du rythme auriculaire. Arch. Mal. Coeur 1952: **45**, 481.

14. Marriott, H. J. L., and Schamroth, L.: Important dilemmas in cardiac arrhythmias. Md. State Med. J. 1959: **8**, 660.

15. Marriott, H. J. L.: Simulation of ectopic ventricular rhythms by aberrant conduction. J.A.M.A. 1966: **196**, 787.

16. Marriott, H. J. L., and Sandler, I. A.: Criteria, old and new, for differentiating between ectopic ventricular beats and aberrant ventricular conduction in the presence of atrial fibrillation. Prog. Cardiovasc. Dis. 1966: **9**, 18.

17. Marriott, H. J. L., and Menendez, M. M.: A-V dissociation revisited. Prog. Cardiovasc. Dis. 1966: **8**, 522.

18. Marriott, H. J. L.: Differential diagnosis of supraventricular and ventricular tachycardia. Geriatrics 1970: **25**, 91.

19. Marriott, H. J. L., and Thorne, D. C.: Dysrhythmic dilemmas in coronary care. Am. J. Cardiol. 1971: **27**, 327.

20. Marriott, H. J. L., and Bieza, C. F.: Alarming ventricular acceleration after lidocaine administration. Chest 1972: **61**, 682.

21. Massumi, R. A.: Bradycardia-dependent bundle branch block. A critique and proposed criteria. Circulation 1968: **38**, 1066.

22. Pick, A.: Aberrant ventricular conduction of escaped beats: Preferential and accessory pathways in the A-V junction. Circulation 1956: **13**, 702.

23. Pick, A., and Langendorf, R.: Differentiation of supraventricular and ventricular tachycardias. Prog. Cardiovasc. Dis. 1960: **2**, 391.

24. Pietras, R. J., et al.: Chronic recurrent right and left ventricular tachycardia; comparison of clinical, hemodynamic and angiographic findings. Am. J. Cardiol. 1977: **40**, 32.

25. Rubin, I. L., et al.: The esophageal lead in the diagnosis of tachycardias with aberrant ventricular conduction. Am. Heart J. 1959: **57**, 19.

26. Sandler, I. A., and Marriott, H. J. L.: The differential morphology of anomalous ventricular complexes of RBBB-type in lead V₁; ventricular ectopy versus aberration. Circulation 1965: **31**, 551.

27. Schoolman, H. M., et al.: Acetylcholine in differential diagnosis and treatment of paroxysmal tachycardia. Am. Heart J. 1960: **60**, 526.

28. Schrire, V., and Vogelpoel, L.: The clinical and electrocardiographic differentiation of supraventricular and ventricular tachycardias with regular rhythm. Am. Heart J. 1955: **49**, 162.

29. Sherf, L., and James, T. N.: A new electrocardiographic concept: Synchronized sinoventricular conduction. Dis Chest 1969: **55**, 127.

30. Vera, Z., et al.: His bundle electrography for evaluation of criteria in differentiating ventricular ectopy from aberrancy in atrial fibrillation. Circulation 1972: **45** (supp. II), 355.

31. Vogel, J. H. K., et al.: A simple technique for identifying P waves in complex arrhythmias. Am. Heart J. 1964: **67**, 158.

32. Wellens, H. J. J., et al.: The value of the electrocardiogram in the differential diagnosis of a tachycardia with a widened QRS complex. Am. J. Med. 1978: **64**, 27.

33. Wellens, H. J. J., et al.: Medical treatment of ventricular tachycardia; considerations in the selection of patients for surgical treatment. Am. J. Cardiol. 1982: **49**, 187.

34. Zipes, D. P.: Diagnosis of ventricular tachycardia. Drug Ther. 1979: **9**, 83.

Review Tracings

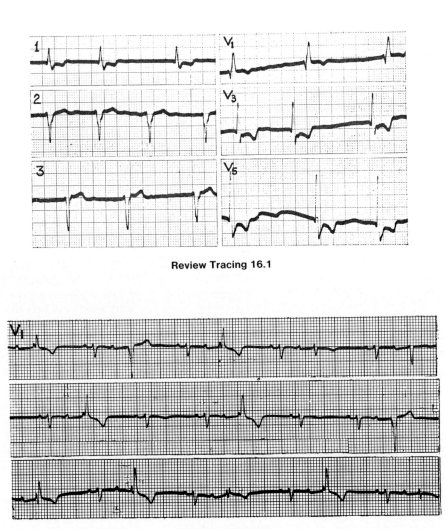

Review Tracing 16.1

Review Tracing 16.2

For interpretation, see page 482

17

Accelerated Idioventricular Rhythm and Parasystole

Accelerated Idioventricular Rhythm (AIVR)

AIVR achieved popularity with the advent of coronary care (CC)—before constant monitoring it was seldom bruited, although examples had been published as early as 1910 by Thomas Lewis. With the spreading CC vogue, the recognition of AIVR became commonplace, and many unsatisfactory terms such as "nonparoxysmal ventricular tachycardia,"[7] "idioventricular tachycardia,"[8] and "slow tachycardia"[1] were applied to it. To emphasize the fact that the ventricular rate was usually closely similar to the sinus rate, Massumi and Ali[5] suggested the term "accelerated isorhythmic ventricular rhythm"; but this is not universally applicable because the rates of the two dissociated pacemakers, though often similar, need not be so; and because sometimes there is consistent 1:1 retrograde conduction and therefore no dissociation.

AIVR is best defined as an automatic ectopic ventricular rhythm at a rate between 50 and 100/min. Unfortunately, definitions have varied; the lower rate limit has ranged from 40 to 60/min, and the upper limit, from 90 to 125/min, which makes comparisons between the various series invalid. Although it is certainly not the monopoly of myocardial infarction, most reported examples have been culled from CC units where it is seen in about 20% of acute infarctions (the range of reported incidence is 8 to 46%). AIVR usually puts in an appearance during the first day or two of acute infarction, though it may appear at any time. At first it was said to be more commonly associated with acute inferior infarctions, but recent studies have found it to be more evenly shared by anterior and inferior infarctions.

AIVR takes over either because the sinus rhythm slows and permits the ectopic rhythm to escape (fig. 17.1) or because the ectopic pacemaker accelerates and temporarily usurps control from the sinus node (fig. 17.2). In either case, since the two rhythms usually have similar rates, the run of AIVR is often ushered in by one or more fusion beats (figs. 17.1 and 17.2). Besides sinus

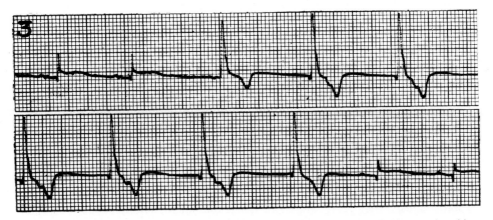

Figure 17.1. Strips are continuous. After two sinus beats, the rhythm abruptly slows and enables an **AIVR** to take over at a rate of 64/min. The third beat in the upper strip is a **fusion beat**. Toward the end of the lower strip, the sinus pacemaker accelerates and recaptures the ventricles.

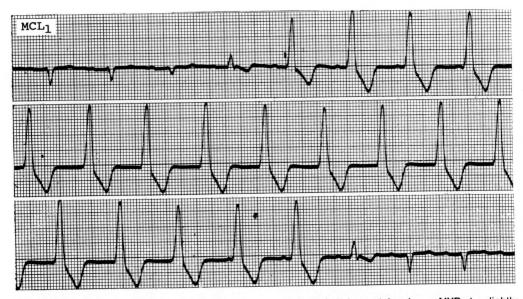

Figure 17.2. Strips are continuous. Sinus rhythm at a rate of 75/min is overtaken by an **AIVR** at a slightly faster rate; the third, fourth and fifth beats are **fusion beats**. In the middle of the bottom strip, the sinus rhythm accelerates and recaptures the ventricles; the sixth beat in this strip is a **fusion beat**.

slowing, other mechanisms that may afford the opportunity for AIVR to escape are A-V block and the postectopic pause following an extrasystole. Occasionally, the run of AIVR begins with a frankly premature beat—a seeming extrasystole—but then settles into a regular automatic rhythm at a modest rate (fig. 17.3). In this situation, one should think of and exclude a parasystolic mechanism (see below). An occasional AIVR may be parasystolic, but the great majority are not.

Once the AIVR gets under way, it usually proceeds as a perfectly regular rhythm, but sometimes it shows progressive acceleration or progressive slowing until it spontaneously ceases (fig. 17.4). Rarely the rhythm may be quite irregular. Usually there is but one accelerated focus, but at times more than one may alternate (fig. 17.5). Sometimes the rate of AIVR is exactly half that of an associated ventricular tachycardia (VT), suggesting that the AIVR may in reality represent VT with a 2 : 1 exit block.[4]

After a varying number of beats, usually ranging between 3 and 10 but sometimes continuing for 20 or 30 beats, the paroxysm ends. It often stops spontaneously (fig. 17.4), but more often the sinus rhythm accelerates and recaptures the ventricles (figs 17.1 and 17.2). As the rates of the two independent pacemakers again approach each other, one or more farewell fusion beats are common (fig. 17.2). In some instances, instead of dissociation between the two pacemakers, there is retrograde conduction to the atria (fig. 17.6).

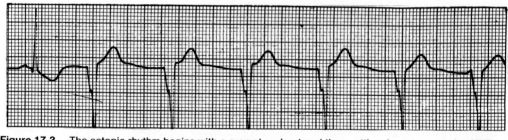

Figure 17.3. The ectopic rhythm begins with a premature beat and then settles down to a regular **AIVR** at a rate of 70/min. A parasystolic mechanism should be considered.

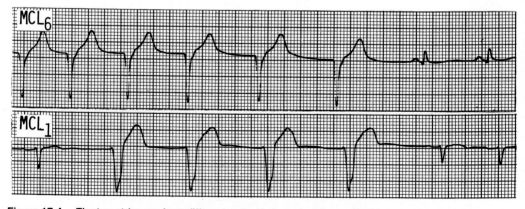

Figure 17.4. The two strips are from different patients. In each strip, an **AIVR** is seen to slow gradually and then spontaneously stop, whereupon the sinus node awakens and resumes control.

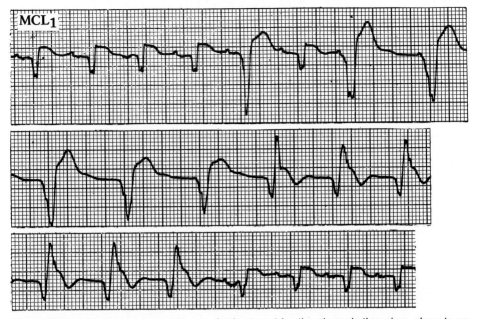

Figure 17.5. The strips are continuous. In the top strip, the sinus rhythm gives place to an irregular **AIVR** from the right ventricle. In the middle of the second strip, control is usurped by a somewhat faster left ventricular **AIVR**.

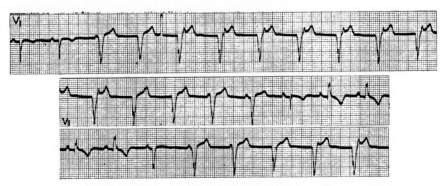

Figure 17.6.   Accelerated ventricular rhythm. In *top strip*, the first two beats *appear to be* normally conducted sinus beats. The sinus rhythm then slows and permits an ectopic right ventricular pacemaker to escape at an almost identical rate. The first two ectopic beats are dissociated from the sinus rhythm, but after that retrograde conduction to the atria develops (narrow positive spike deforming early part of ST segments) and continues to end of strip. *Bottom two strips* are continuous and begin with the accelerated ventricular rhythm with retroconduction in its first beat; then come three dissociated beats, then two fusion beats, the second of which looks like a normally conducted sinus beat. Four sinus beats follow with incomplete RBBB and then the accelerated ventricular rhythm returns via a fusion beat with retroconduction again in the two final beats. Now we can recognize the identity of the first two beats in the *top strip* and the sixth beat in the *second strip*—they look like normal beats because they represent fusion between a right ventricular impulse and a sinus impulse in the presence of RBBB (pp. 284–285).

AIVR is usually benign and neither affects the blood pressure nor presages more serious ventricular arrhythmias. However, like every other cause of A-V dissociation, the loss of the atrial "kick" (contribution to ventricular filling) *may* rarely impair the hemodynamics enough to require corrective therapy. Most observers have found no association between AIVR and ventricular tachycardia[10]; but rather surprisingly at variance with general impressions and experience, some authors[2, 4, 9] have documented a high incidence of true (rapid) VT in patients with AIVR. Nevertheless, the prognosis of patients with myocardial infarction complicated by AIVR appears to be just as good as the prognosis of those without AIVR.[6]

AIVR is also found in childhood and is regarded as benign.[3]

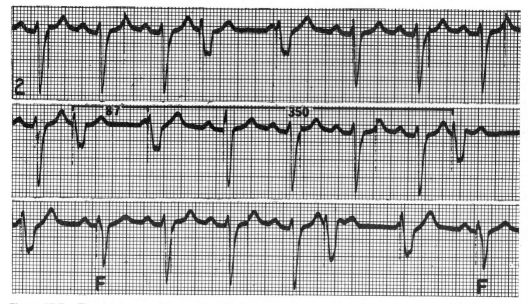

Figure 17.7. The strips are continuous. **Fixed-rate pacemaker** for comparison with ventricular parasystole. Since the pacemaker cannot be turned off by the sinus impulses, it behaves like parasystole, and all longer interectopic intervals are multiples of the pacemaker's cycle.

Parasystole

Dual rhythm is a comprehensive term that covers all situations in which two separate, competing pacemakers are simultaneously operative. Thus complete A-V block, most other forms of A-V dissociation, and the double tachycardias are all classifiable as dual rhythms. Parasystole (Gr. *para* = alongside; *systole* = contraction) is a special form of dual rhythm in which there is a privileged pacemaker whose rhythm, by virtue of local "protection," cannot be disturbed by its competitor: the parasystolic pacemaker cannot be "turned off" or reset by the competing sinus rhythm. The nature of this "protection" is unknown, but in some cases it may be due to the pacemaker's own rapid discharge rate, which assures its constant refractoriness when sinus impulses approach it; a simultaneous exit block (perhaps 4:1, 6:1 or 8:1) produces a slow manifest rate obscuring the underlying real discharge rate.[12, 13]

Ventricular Parasystole

The fixed-rate artificial pacemaker takes the mystique out of parasystole, and figure 17.7 illustrates the "parasystolic" behavior of such a pacemaker: (1) it is "protected" in the sense that nothing can shut it off; therefore (2) whenever its impulse falls at a time when the ventricles are responsive, a QRS accompanies the pacemaker "blip"; but (3) whenever it falls at a time when the ventricles are refractory, the blip is visible (i.e., the pacer discharges and maintains its uninterrupted schedule), but no ventricular complex results; therefore (4) the longer interectopic intervals are multiples of the shortest interectopic interval (e.g., in the second strip, the long interectopic interval, 350, equals four times the shorter interval, 87); and (5) whenever the artificial discharge coincides with sinus conduction into the ventricles, a fusion beat results (F); (6) because parasystole represents an indepedent rhythm and is not beholden to the preceding beat, it will put in an appearance at varying intervals following the sinus beats (variable "coupling"). These six points are all characteristic of parasystolic behavior.

Diagnosis. Parasystole is first suspected in the clinical tracing if ectopic beats show varying coupling intervals; this inconstancy of the coupling interval indicates an indepedent rhythm but does *not* of itself prove parasystole. To do this, one must demonstrate that the independent rhythm is undisturbable, and

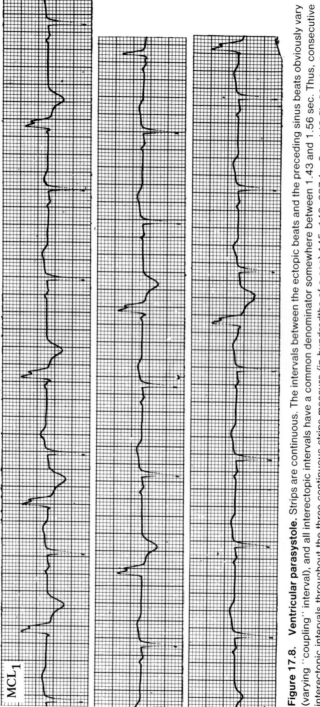

Figure 17.8. Ventricular parasystole. Strips are continuous. The intervals between the ectopic beats and the preceding sinus beats obviously vary (varying "coupling" interval), and all interectopic intervals have a common denominator somewhere between 1.43 and 1.56 sec. Thus, consecutive interectopic intervals throughout the three continuous strips measure (in hundredths of a sec) 145, 146, 287 (= 2 × 143.5), 301 (= 2 × 150.5), 302 (= 2 × 151), 294 (= 2 × 147), 441 (= 3 × 147) and 313 (= 2 × 156.5). Note the fusion beat at the end of the *middle strip.*

this is achieved by showing that the interectopic intervals have a common denominator. Thus, in figure 17.8 the first three ectopic beats all bear obviously differing relationships ("coupling" intervals) to their preceding beats, and the interectopic intervals are, respectively, 145 and 146 hundredths of a sec; all subsequent interectopic intervals are multiples of cycles between 143.5 and 145.6 hundredths.

All examples of ventricular parasystole will presumably produce fusion beats eventually if a long enough trace is taken, but such beats are not essential to the diagnosis. In figure 17.8 the last beat in the second strip is a fusion beat—it is upright like the ectopic beats but narrower, and it is preceded by a sinus P wave with a long enough P-R interval for some conduction into the ventricles (P-R interval of sinus beats = 0.19 sec; P-R of fusion beat = 0.16 sec).

A special pattern of fusion occurs if the ectopic ventricular pacemaker is on the side of a BBB, for then both the QRS of the sinus beat and the QRS of the parasystolic (ectopic) beat are wide; but if each activates its respective ventricle simultaneously, the resulting fusion beat may be quite narrow and may indeed look remarkably normal. Figure 17.9 illustrates such a situation. The sinus beats are conducted with *right* BBB, and the ectopic pacemaker is in the *right* ventricle. The third beat in the bottom strip is a fusion beat with a remarkably normal configuration since the sinus impulse is activating the left ventricle

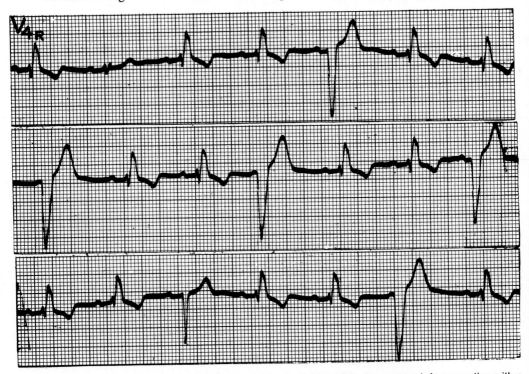

Figure 17.9. The three strips are continuous and show a **right ventricular parasystole** competing with a sinus rhythm with **right bundle-branch block**. The second beat in the *top strip* and the *third* in the *bottom* are fusion beats. There is some variation in the coupling intervals, and the consecutive interectopic intervals measure 249, 242, 240, 238, 237 and 236—the automatic pacemaker is apparently enjoying the phenomenon of "warm-up."

while the ectopic impulse takes care of the right ventricle with precise simultaneity.

In the presence of atrial fibrillation, the diagnosis of fusion is made with less assurance since one never knows exactly when the next fibrillatory impulse is going to be conducted to the ventricles. But in figure 17.10, one can be reasonably certain that the third beat from the end of the second strip (*x*) is a fusion beat since all preceding interectopic intervals measure 162 to 164 and the interval from the first ectopic beat in the bottom strip to the beat in question (*x*) measures 328 (= 2 × 164). It is therefore reasonable to conclude that beat *x* is mainly conducted but contains a small distorting contribution from the ectopic focus.

Since parasystole is an independent, autonomous rhythm that cannot be interrupted, it follows that its impulses must from time to time land on the T waves of the competitive sinus beats. Because of this inevitable R-on-T incidence, parasystole has been declared dangerous, but this is false reasoning. Extrasystoles that alight upon the T wave are admittedly dangerous, but the mechanism of parasystole is quite different from that of the extrasystole, and we have no evidence that (automatic) parasystolic beats on the T wave pose the same threat as (?reentry) extrasystolic beats. Moreover, it is an empirical observation that when a parasystolic discharge coincides with the T wave, it seldom becomes a manifest beat. Parasystole is, in fact, a relatively benign arrhythmia.[11]

Supraventricular Parasystole

All parasystole is not ventricular. Atrial and A-V junctional pacemakers can also assume parasystolic properties. Figure 17.11 shows a continuous tracing from a patient with atrial flutter and varying A-V conduction. Scattered through

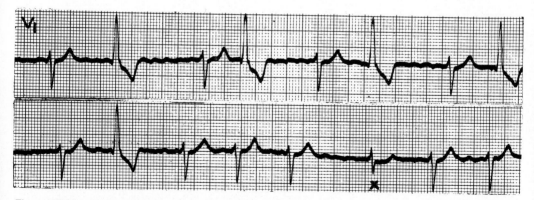

Figure 17.10.   Atrial fibrillation and **ventricular parasystole**. Strips are continuous. This picture of atrial fibrillation with irregular A-V conduction is interrupted by regularly recurring anomalous beats that obviously bear no relationship to the preceding conducted beats yet are themselves regularly spaced (interectopic intervals in the *top strip* are 164, 162 and 163). Clearly they represent a parasystolic rhythm. From the first ectopic beat in the bottom strip to the fusion beat marked *x* is an interval of 328 (= 2 × 164).

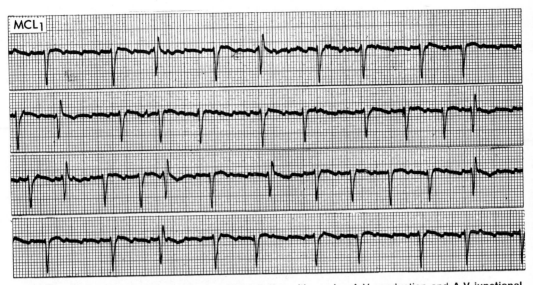

Figure 17.11. The strips are continuous. **Atrial flutter** with varying A-V conduction and **A-V junctional parasystole** with **incomplete RBBB aberration**. Parasystolic measurements: first long interectopic interval (fifth beat in *top strip* to second beat in *second strip*) = 422 = 141 × 3; second long interectopic interval (second beat in second strip to last beat in that strip) = 566 = 141.5 × 4; third long interectopic interval (seventh beat in *third strip* to last beat in that strip) = 278 = 139 × 2; fourth long interectopic interval (last beat in *third strip* to third beat in *bottom strip*) = 272 = 136 × 2.

the tracing are "different" beats that show an rSR′ configuration, and the first thing about these beats that catches the eye is the variation in their intervals from the preceding beats; this immediately makes one suspect an independent pacemaker and suggests parasystole. Then measuring the shortest interectopic intervals, we find that they are almost identical (142, 140, 140, 142). Next we measure the longer intervals and find that they are all approximate multiples (see the legend to fig. 17.11) of the shorter intervals, clinching the diagnosis of parasystole. Since the contour of the parasystolic beats is rSR′, one assumes that they originate in the A-V junction (**junctional parasystole**) and are conducted with incomplete RBBB aberration.

Atrial parasystole is rare. You diagnose it if you can demonstrate (1) that the ectopic P waves vary in their relationship (coupling interval) to the preceding sinus P waves and (2) that the interectopic (P′-P′) intervals all have a common denominator. If sinus and parasystolic impulses simultaneously invade the atrial myocardium, atrial fusion results.

REFERENCES

Accelerated Idioventricular Rhythm

1. Castellanos, A., et al.: Mechanisms of slow ventricular tachycardias in acute myocardial infarction. Chest 1969: **56,** 470.

2. de Soyza, N., et al.: Association of accelerated idioventricular rhythm and paroxysmal ventricular tachycardia in acute myocardial infarction. Am. J. Cardiol. 1974: **34**, 667.
3. Gaum, W. E., et al.: Accelerated ventricular rhythm in childhood. Am. J. Cardiol. 1979: **43**, 162.
4. Lichstein, E., et al.: Incidence and description of accelerated ventricular rhythm complicating acute myocardial infarction. Am. J. Med. 1975: **58**, 192.
5. Massumi, R. A., and Ali, N.: Accelerated isorhythmic ventricular rhythms. Am. J. Cardiol. 1970: **26**, 170.
6. Norris, R. M., et al.: Idioventricular rhythm complicating acute myocardial infarction. Br. Heart J. 1970: **32**, 617.
7. Rothfeld, E. L., et al.: Nonparoxysmal ventricular tachycardia. Circulation 1967: **36** (supp. 2), 227.
8. Schamroth, L.: Idioventricular tachycardia. J. Electrocardiol. 1968: **1**, 205.
9. Talbot, S., and Greaves, M.: Association of ventricular extrasystoles and ventricular tachycardia with idioventricular rhythm. Br. Heart J. 1976: **38**, 457.
10. Yusuf, S., et al.: Heart rate and ectopic prematurity in relation to sustained ventricular arrhythmias. Br. Heart J. 1980: **44**, 233.

Parasystole

11. El-Sherif, N.: The ventricular premature complex: mechanisms and significance. In Mandel, W. J., *Cardiac arrhythmias*, p. 292, edited by W. J. Mandel. J. B. Lippincott, Philadelphia, 1981.
12. Schamroth, L.: Ventricular parasystole with slow manifest ectopic discharge. Br. Heart J. 1962: **24**, 731.
13. Scherf, D., and Bornemann, C.: Parasystole with a rapid ventricular center. Am. Heart J. 1961: **62**, 320.

Review Tracings

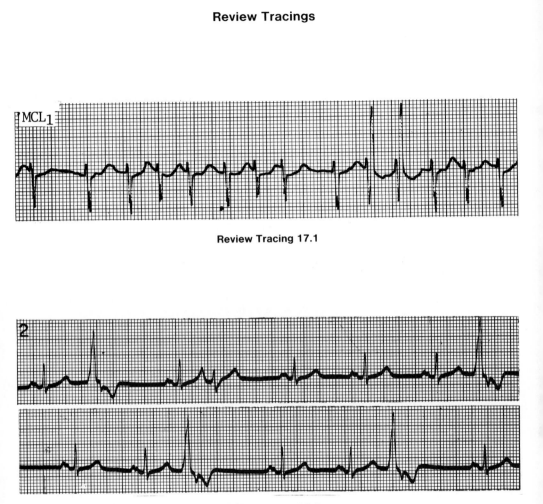

Review Tracing 17.1

Review Tracing 17.2

For interpretation, see page 483

18

Preexcitation

"Preexcitation," the term introduced by Ohnell in 1944, implies that part of the ventricular myocardium is activated before it would have been by an impulse descending via the normal A-V conduction system. The two main variants of preexcitation are the Wolff-Parkinson-White (WPW) and the Lown-Ganong-Levine (LGL) syndromes; these "syndromes" include the predisposition to supraventricular tachyarrhythmias in persons manifesting one of the characteristic electrocardiographic (ECG) patterns.

The first example of preexcitation was published, but not recognized, by the dean of American electrocardiography, Frank Wilson, in 1915. He naturally thought that the widened QRS complex was the result of some form of bundle-branch block; and it was many years before it was appreciated that the QRS might be widened either because part of the ventricular myocardium was activated late (bundle-branch block) or because part was activated early (preexcitation) (fig. 18.1).

WPW Patterns

Prior to 1930, Wolff and White in Boston and Parkinson in London had collected a number of cases with bizarre ventricular complexes and short P-R intervals.[39, 40] In 1930, 20 years before they personally met, they cooperated in a hands-across-the-sea endeavor and published their combined series of 11 cases, again under the heading: "Bundle Branch Block with Short P-R Interval."

As early as 1893, Kent described muscular connections between atria and ventricles but wrongly assumed that they represented pathways of normal conduction from atria to ventricles. Mines, well ahead of his time, in 1914 suggested that these "bundles of Kent" might mediate reentering tachycardias. But it was not until half a century later that the jigsaw fragments were finally coapted and it was fully appreciated that the accessory pathways (AP), the ECG patterns, and the associated reciprocating tachycardias were interdependent.

256

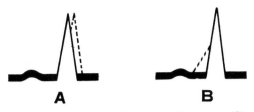

Figure 18.1. (A) Bundle-branch block and (B) Wolff-Parkinson-White syndrome compared diagrammatically.

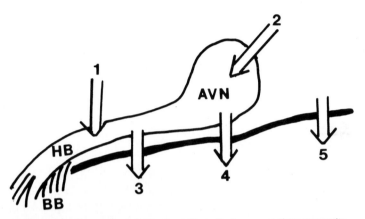

Figure 18.2. The various A-V connections that may mediate preexcitation. Key: AVN = atrioventricular node; HB = bundle of His; BB = bundle branches. 1, atriofascicular connection (James); 2, intranodal bypass; 3, fasciculoventricular connection (Mahaim); 4, nodoventricular connection (Mahaim); and 5, atrioventricular accessory connection (Kent, Paladino).

The classical WPW pattern consists of a short P-R interval (less than 0.12 sec) and a widened QRS complex with a slurred initial component, the "delta" wave, so named by Segers in 1944. The P-R is short because the descending impulse bypasses the normal delay in conduction that is experienced in the A-V node; the delta wave is caused by slow intramyocardial conduction that results when the impulse, instead of being delivered by the normal Purkinje system, finds itself dumped into ventricular myocardium via an anomalous tract; and the widened QRS is the result of the consequent asynchronous activation of the two ventricles. The various tracts that can mediate preexcitation[2] are diagrammed in figure 18.2.

In most cases, the congenital defect that services this conduction anomaly is an imperfect, porous atrioventricular partition with myocardial bridges ("Kent bundles") traversing the pores. In a few cases, the anomalous A-V connection consists of the partnership of a bypass fiber of James with a Mahaim fiber (fig. 18.2).

In preexcitation, the P-R interval is not always abnormally short (fig. 18.3); in fact, of 589 published cases, 23% had P-R intervals of 0.12 sec or longer, and there is a tendency for the P-R to lengthen with age. Nor is the QRS always abnormally broad—in 23% of 598 cases, the QRS measured less than 0.11 sec[35] (fig. 18.4).

Classifications

Classification of WPW patterns began with Rosenbaum and colleagues in 1945. They divided their patients into two groups on the basis of the direction of the *major deflection* in a right-sided chest lead. Since their classification is still popular but their criteria are often misquoted, their exact words are repeated here:

Depending on the form of QRS in the leads from the right side of the precordium, particularly leads V_1, V_2 and V_E, our cases have been divided into two groups: *Group A, in which R is the sole, or by far the largest, deflection in all of these* and *Group B, in which S or QS is the chief QRS deflection in at least one of them* [my italics].

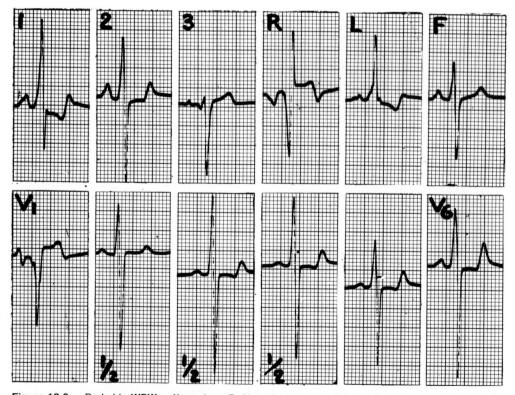

Figure 18.3. Probable **WPW pattern, type B**. Note the normal P-R interval and the entirely negative QS complex in V_1 with elevated ST segment, which could easily be mistaken for anteroseptal infarction. The slurred initial component of the QRS ("delta" wave) is particularly well seen in aVL and V_1. Leads V_{2-4} are recorded at half-standardization.

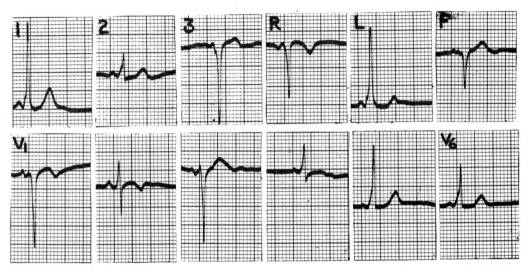

Figure 18.4.   WPW pattern, type B. Note the short P-R interval (0.10 sec) and entirely negative QRS in V_1. Delta waves are well seen in several leads.

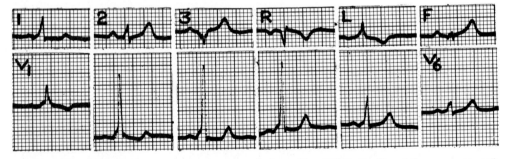

Figure 18.5.   WPW pattern, type A. Note the entirely positive QRS in V_1. The delta waves are well seen in most leads.

It is usually stated that their cases were divided according to the direction of the delta vector, but their own words make plain that this was not so and that the *main deflection* of the QRS provided the differential yardstick. Thus figure 18.5 genuinely belongs to their "Group A"—and everyone else's "type A"—

whereas figure 18.6, despite the positive delta vector in V_1, qualifies for their "Group B."

The simple division into types "A" and "B" is useful in identifying left-sided (type A) versus right-sided (type B) preexcitation. Obviously, right-sided pathways are more accessible to the surgeon than septal or left-sided tracts.

Grant[15] in 1958 pointed out that this differentiation was based on a relatively insignificant shift of the ventricular vector and introduced a new classification based on the axis of the delta wave in the frontal plane: type I—the commonest—had a delta-wave axis in the neighborhood of −30° and so produced Q waves in leads, 2, 3 and aVF simulating inferior infarction (fig. 18.7). Type III—the least common—had a delta-wave axis of about +105° and so produced small wide Q waves in leads 1 and aVL simulating anterior or lateral infarction. Type II had an axis between the other two, at about +50°.

Sherf and Neufeld,[35] in their excellent text, prefer a combination of precordial and limb lead patterns so that types A and B are subdivided into those with superior and inferior displacement of the frontal plane axis; thus the main categories in their classification are:

$$AS = \text{type A with superior axis}$$
$$AI = \text{type A with inferior axis}$$
$$BS = \text{type B with superior axis}$$
$$BI = \text{type B with inferior axis}$$

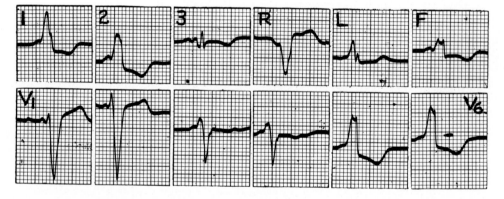

Figure 18.6.   WPW pattern, type B. Note the initially positive but mainly negative QRS complex in V_1. This pattern could well be mistaken for left bundle-branch block, but the P-R interval is only 0.09 sec.

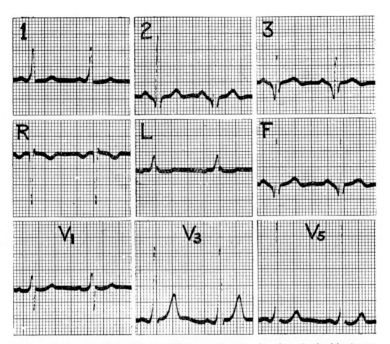

Figure 18.7.   Wolff-Parkinson-White syndrome, showing atypical features: the P-R interval is normal at 0.16 sec, the QRS slightly prolonged at 0.10 to 0.11 sec. Delta waves are clearly seen in leads 1, V₃ and V̇₅. The slurred initial component in leads 2, 3 and aVF takes the form of wide Q waves, which may be mistaken for those of inferior myocardial infarction if the overall pattern is not recognized.

These four categories accounted for approximately 90% of their large series of 215 patients, but the remaining 10% required no less than 6 additional subsets. Figure 18.8 presents an example of their type AI.

Thanks to modern investigative and surgical techniques, it has been possible to identify the location of the AP in a large number of patients and correlate it with the clinical 12-lead tracings. In this way, the Duke group have been able to tabulate the tentative ECG findings for 10 locations around the periphery of the A-V rings and in the septum.[11] For example, when the right posterior crux is the site of the preexcitation pathway, an abrupt transition from an isoelectric delta wave with rS pattern in V_1 to a positive delta wave and Rs in V_2 is often found. Or again, if the pathway of preexcitation is at the lateral extremity of the mitral ring, the delta wave is negative in 1 and aVL but positive across the precordium from V_1 to V_6 (fig. 18.8). When the preexcitation conduction was mediated via James and Mahaim fibers, the delta vector was found by Lev and associates to be negative in leads 2, 3, aVF, and V_1 while positive in 1, aVL, and V_{2-3}.[23]

The main function of a classification of WPW patterns is to aid in the localization of the APs. As more and more information is gathered electro-

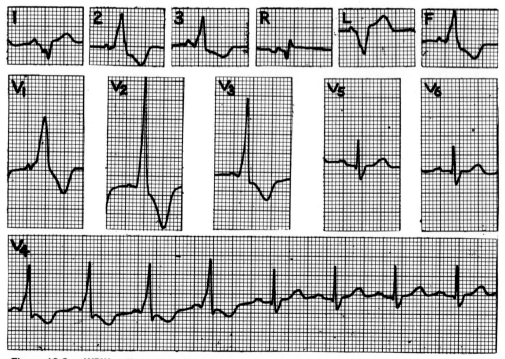

Figure 18.8. WPW pattern, type AI of Sherf and Neufeld. The negative delta vector in leads 1 and aVL indicates probable left-lateral preexcitation. During the recording of lead V_4, the pattern spontaneously changes from preexcitation with short P-R interval (0.09 sec) to incomplete right bundle-branch block with normal P-R (0.17) sec.

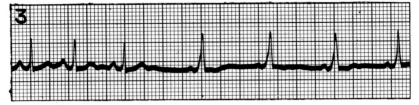

Figure 18.9. After three sinus beats with P-R of 0.13 sec, there is a sinus pause which ends with atrial escape (note change in P-wave contour). The ectopic atrial pacemaker apparently has access to a preexcitation pathway, and the P-R shortens to 0.08 sec as the QRS assumes a delta wave and widens.

physiologically and surgically and localization becomes more and more precisely correlated with the clinical ECG, types "A" and "B" will surely become outmoded. Meanwhile, however, these two types comprise the most used—and most misquoted!—classification.

One of the interesting, and not fully explained, facets of the WPW syndrome is that the pattern of preexcitation may develop only with a change in the atrial pacemaker from sinus to ectopic (fig. 18.9). One possible explanation is that the ectopic atrial focus is situated[44a] in or near the posterior internodal tract which contains fibers that bypass the A-V node.[34]

Determinants of QRS Width

The width of the QRS depends upon the size of the delta wave, which in turn depends on the number of lengths (milliseconds) by which the accessory impulse wins the steeplechase to the ventricles. And this in turn depends on the interplay of several factors[38]: the location of the AP; conduction time from sinus node to A-V node and to AP; conduction time down the AP (whose length may range from 1 to 10 mm); and conduction time over the normal A-V pathways. The result is that the QRS may be anything from normal in duration and barely distorted if the impulse via the A-V junction arrives first, to grossly widened and bizarre if the accessory impulse wins by a wide margin and activation results exclusively from its spread.

Since depolarization is abnormal, repolarization must also be and there are always consequent ST-T abnormalities.

Incidence, Associations and Imitations

If there is any topic in electrocardiography that has received attention in print more in proportion to its fascination than to its prevalence, it is the WPW syndrome. This is understandable since the syndrome not only produces disturbances of rhythm and conduction that attract and hold the fascinated eye, it is also the meeting place of numerous paracardiological disciplines, including anatomy, embryology, physiology, electrophysiology, and pediatrics. During the past decade, apart from more than a thousand papers, several comprehensive reviews,[4, 9-11, 19, 26] each with its own peculiar virtues, and at least one small but comprehensive book[35] on preexcitation have been published. Yet the syndrome is encountered only about 15 times among 10,000 electrocardiograms.

It affects males about twice as often as females and is found in all age groups. In young subjects, it occurs predominantly in those with no other sign of heart disease; however, it is found in a significant number of young patients with hypertrophic cardiomyopathy, and type B WPW occurs in 25% of those with Ebstein's disease.[33] An association has also been claimed with corrected transposition of the great arteries, tricuspid atresia, endocardial fibroelastosis and mitral valve prolapse.[11]

Although the substrate for WPW conduction (accessory pathways) is congenital, evidence of preexcitation may not appear until late in life. It may, for instance, come to light only after a myocardial infarction has impaired conduction through the A-V node, and so give the appearance of being an "acquired" WPW.[12, 14] In others, completion of the "syndrome," i.e., the development of tachycardia, may not occur till late in life. Of the infants who start life with the full-blown syndrome, the great majority happily "outgrow" their predisposition to tachyarrhythmias within a few years.[13]

Patterns of preexcitation may at least partially mimic a number of other entities. Type "A," with the wide positive QRS in V_1, may simulate right bundle-branch block, right ventricular hypertrophy, or a true posterior infarction. Type "B" may be mistaken for left bundle-branch block (figs 18.6 and 18.10), or even left ventricular hypertrophy (fig. 18.4). A negative delta wave, producing Q waves in appropriate leads, may imitate anteroseptal or inferior

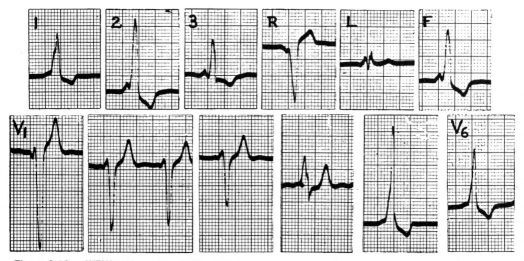

Figure 8.10. **WPW pattern, type B**. The P-R interval is about 0.09 sec, and the widened QRS has a slow initial component well seen in several leads. The overall QRS pattern could be mistaken for left bundle-branch block.

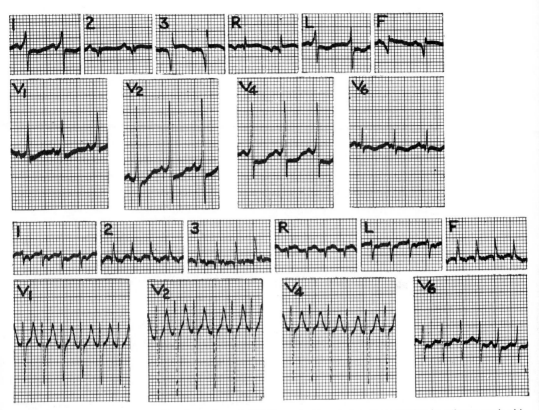

Figure 18.11. The upper tracing shows **type A WPW** conduction during sinus rhythm in a three-week-old baby. The lower tracing shows SVT with narrow QRS, indicating that the A-V junction serves as the anterograde pathway, and the accessory bundle as the retrograde pathway.

infarction. The QS complex in V_1 in figures 18.3 and 18.4 could easily be mistaken for anteroseptal necrosis. The deep, wide Q wave in lead 3 in figures 18.7 and 18.11 combined with the ST elevation, is certainly highly suggestive of acute inferior infarction, but figure 18.11 is derived from a three-week-old infant with the WPW syndrome.

Ruskin[32] found 31 (70%) of 44 consecutive patients with WPW patterns had delta vectors that produced Q waves mimicking myocardial infarction. One third of the 44 patients were referred to the laboratory with the diagnosis of myocardial infarction. On the other hand, the Q wave of genuine infarction may be masked by a positive delta wave of preexcitation.[14]

In turn, the short P-R and wide QRS of the WPW can be simulated by the dissembling pacemaker catheter.[28, 36] If the catheter becomes looped in the right atrium in the presence of a sinus rhythm faster than the paced rhythm, each atrial contraction may thrust the catheter tip against the ventricular endocardium and produce an ecotpic QRS at a short and constant P-R interval.

Diagnostic Measures

In the patient with a history of tachycardia but whose tracing during sinus rhythm manifests a normal P-R without widening of the QRS, to prove the presence of an accessory pathway it may be necessary to pace the atria at increasing rates or to stimulate the atria at increasingly premature intervals (single atrial-test stimuli). But several noninvasive maneuvers may be successful in making the diagnosis: vagal stimulation,[30] by impairing conduction in the A-V node and so favoring conduction via the AP may reveal a delta wave; intravenous digoxin, by simultaneously inhibiting conduction in the A-V node and facilitating it in the AP, may bring a delta wave to light. On the other hand, drugs that block the accessory pathway (such as procainamide, ajmaline, lidocaine or disopyramide) or that abbreviate conduction in the A-V node (atropine, isoproterenol) may visibly normalize the initial portion of the suspect QRS complex.

Arrhythmias Associated with WPW Syndrome

The clinical importance of preexcitation resides almost entirely in its predisposition to tachyarrhythmias. The WPW heart is custom-made for the accommodation of reentering rhythms because it is equipped with two parallel pathways with differing conductive characteristics. The accessory pathway (AP) usually conducts much faster than the A-V node but usually has a longer

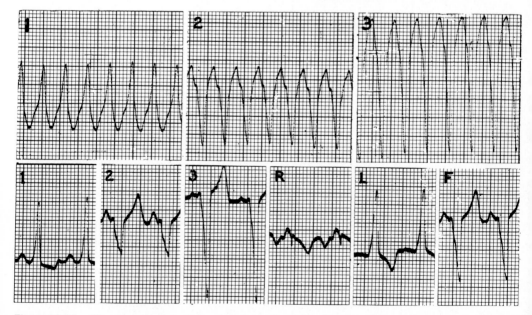

Figure 18.12. The *upper tracing* shows a regular tachycardia with wide QRS complexes, easily mistaken for ventricular tachycardia. The *lower tracing* shows the patient's limb leads during sinus rhythm and reveals the **W-P-W pattern**. This identifies the tachycardia as RT using the accessory bundle as the anterograde path.

refractory period. With the normal sinus cycle, the descending impulse usually finds both A-V junction and AP responsive and so traverses both avenues to the ventricles, and the dichotomized impulse produces fusion beats within the ventricles. The pattern of fusion obviously depends upon the amount of preexcitation (duration of delta wave), which in turn depends upon the time required for each wave front to reach and spread down its respective path.

Reciprocating Tachycardia

An early beat, on the other hand, such as an atrial extrasystole, may find the AP still refractory after the A-V node has recovered and so its impulse travels only down the orthodox conduction routes; however, by the time it reaches the ventricular end of the AP, that may have recovered and, if the impulse then travels retrogradely through the AP to the atria, the stage is set for reciprocation (reentry, circus-movement). A ventricular ectopic beat may achieve the same success by finding one retrograde pathway receptive while the other remains unresponsive.

Most reciprocating tachycardias have a normal QRS since they travel anterogradely through the junction (fig. 18.11); but in a minority, the AP may have recovered while the A-V node is still refractory and then the impulse travels exclusively down the AP and may complete the circuit in the reverse direction (sometimes called "antidromic," as opposed to "orthodromic," tachycardia). In such cases, the QRS during the tachycardia has the wide, bizarre QRS of the WPW syndrome (fig. 18.12). An occasional patient with a wide-QRS tachycardia enjoys the luxury of two (or more) APs and the circulating wave uses both—one for the downward and one for the upward journey.[11]

Two important diagnostic pitfalls should be appreciated: (1) Just because the patient is known to have preexcitation—as revealed during sinus rhythm—this does not prove that the tachycardia circuit includes the AP. In an important

Table 18.1
Tachyarrhythmias in 161 WPWs

RT[a]	89
RT + AF[a]	32
AF	15
RT + AF + VF[a]	13
AF + VF	5
VF	4
RT + VF	3
Total WPWs	161

[a] RT, reciprocating tachycardia; AF, atrial fibrillation; VT, ventricular fibrillation.

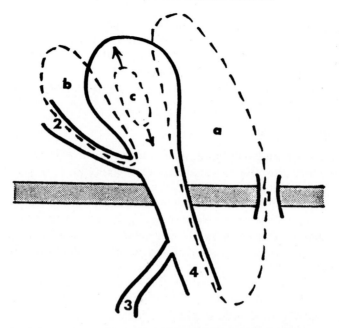

Figure 18.13.   Reentry circuits in WPW syndrome. (*1*) Accessory pathway (Kent bundle), (*2*) bypass tract (James fiber), (*3*) Mahaim fiber, (*4*) bundle of His. Circuit *a* consists of a Kent bundle and the normal A-V pathways; circuit *b* consists of a bypass tract and the A-V junction; circuit *c* is confined to the A-V node.

minority—5% in Wellens' series[38]—despite the presence of an AP, the circulating wave gyrates exclusively within the A-V junction (fig. 18.13, circuit "c"), obviously a fact of paramount importance if surgical intervention is contemplated. (2) In some patients, the AP conducts retrogradely but not anterogradely. Thus the patient may sustain a reciprocating tachycardia without ever showing the telltale WPW pattern during sinus rhythm; and since the 12-lead tracing is innocent of delta waves, the mechanism may not be suspected. This situation is referred to as "concealed WPW" and accounts for a significant minority of supraventricular tachycardias.[41, 44, 47] Although subject to misdiagnosed tachycardia, they are protected from frantic ventricular rates if they develop atrial fibrillation by the long refractory period of their AP.

An unusual mode of onset of the tachycardia may afford a clue to the existence of a concealed AP. Gradual, progressive shortening of the sinus cycle with the sudden development of retrograde conduction, without prior lengthening of the P-R interval, may suggest this form of tachycardia.[11]

Atrial Flutter and Fibrillation

Atrial flutter in the WPW syndrome occurs but rarely (fig. 18.14). Atrial fibrillation, on the other hand, is quite common and assumes great importance because of the extremely rapid ventricular rates that may develop. The major determinant of the rate of the ventricular response is the length of the refractory

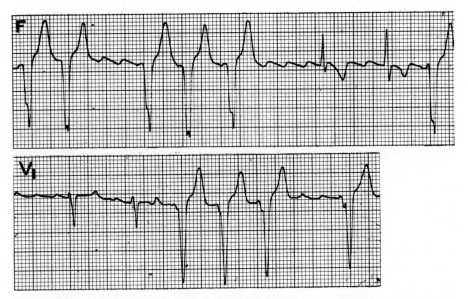

Figure 18.14. **Atrial flutter** in a patient with the **WPW syndrome**. Both normal conduction and preexcitation are evident in each lead. The flutter waves are readily apparent in the longer diastoles.

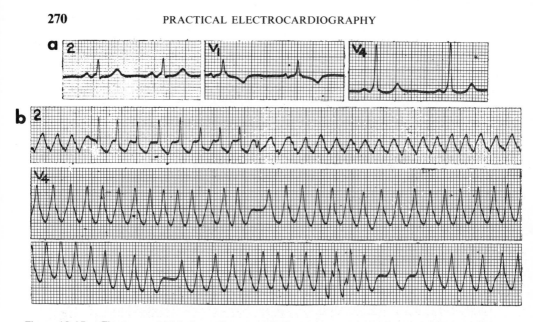

Figure 18.15. The top panel (*a*) shows the **preexcitation pattern**, while the rhythm strips (*b*) illustrate the typical picture of **atrial fibrillation** during anomalous pathway conduction with a ventricular response at 280/min. Several beats in the first half of lead 2 are evidently conducted via normal pathways at a somewhat slower rate. Note that occasional cycles are more than twice the length of the shortest cycles.

period of the AP.[4, 9] If that refractory period is very short, rates in the neighborhood of 300/min may be achieved (figs 18.15 and 18.16) and then there is serious danger of ventricular fibrillation developing, either because the descending impulse arrives in the vulnerable phase of the ventricular cycle; or because the wild tachycardia evokes serious hypoxia.

It can be extremely difficult, and sometimes impossible, to differentiate ventricular tachycardia from atrial fibrillation with WPW conduction.[25] The QRS morphology can be helpful but one must realize that some of the features so characteristic of ventricular ectopy may be imitated by WPW conduction: the taller left "rabbit-ear" and "concordant positivity" in the chest leads can be simulated by type A WPW, and the "fat" initial r wave in V_1 by type B.

Numerous examples of atrial fibrillation with WPW conduction have been published as irregular ventricular tachycardia[25]; this has earned the undesirable title of "pseudoventricular tachycardia." The true nature of most of these can be suspected at a glance from two characteristic features: (1) the cycle length at times is as short as 0.20 sec, the equivalent of a rate of 300/min; and (2) in other places there are cycles more than twice as long as the shortest cycles. This greater than 100% variation in cycle length would represent a remarkable degree of irregularity in genuine ventricular tachycardia which, in the large majority of cases, is perfectly regular.[49]

Atrial fibrillation may be initiated by an atrial extrasystole arising during the vulnerable phase of the atrial cycle or by a ventricular extrasystole conducted retrogradely to the atria and arriving in their vulnerable phase. The extremely rapid ventricular rate that may develop may precipitate ventricular fibrillation.

Procainamide, quinidine, and lidocaine (fig. 18.16) prolong the refractory period and slow conduction in the AP,[45] whereas digitalis at least in some patients has the unhappy effect of shortening the refractory period, may therefore further increase the already-rapid ventricular rate, and has been repeatedly implicated in the development of ventricular fibrillation.[46]

Ventricular Fibrillation

Although ventricular fibrillation is sometimes the presenting arrhythmia, it usually appears in the wake of atrial fibrillation[4a]; and the patient whose R-R interval during atrial fibrillation drops to or below 0.20 sec is at particular risk of developing ventricular fibrillation.

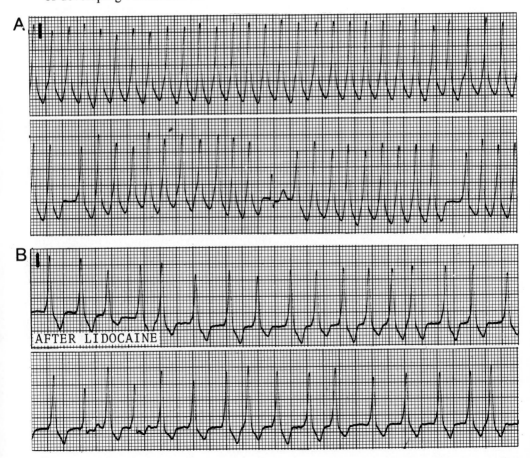

Figure 18.16. (A) The strips are continuous. From a young woman with **atrial fibrillation** and the **WPW syndrome**. Note the rate of 290/min, the occasional normal conduction, and the occasional cycle more than twice the length of the shortest cycles. (B) The strips are continuous and illustrate the slowing effect of lidocaine (rate, about 165/min).

Incidence

The precise incidence of the various tachycardias complicating the WPW syndrome is not known. Clearly the largest published series are preselected since they consist largely of intractable tachycardias referred to sophisticated centers for investigation. In Wellens' series of 149 patients with WPW arrhythmias,[38] about 70% had supraventricular tachycardia alone, 20% had only atrial fibrillation, and the remainder had both SVT and atrial fibrillation. Campbell found atrial fibrillation in 16 per cent of his WPW patients.[3] In the first 161 patients referred to Duke, the incidence of tachyarrhythmias is shown in table 18.1.

LGL Syndrome

In 1952, Lown, Ganong, and Levine[24] published a series of cases with P-R intervals of 0.12 or 0.13 sec, snapping first heart sounds, and no organic heart disease. Two thirds of the patients were women, and a minority of them suffered from paroxysms of tachycardia. Since that time anything with a short P-R and normal QRS has been called LGL syndrome. Because of the inconsistency of usage and because there is doubt that the described features really represent a clinical entity, Sherf and Neufeld[35] suggest that the term LGL syndrome be dropped entirely and replaced by the noncommittal but accurately descriptive term "short-PR-normal-QRS syndromes," of which figure 18.17 is an example.

The majority of workers have found that the shortened P-R interval is due to less-than-normal delay in the A-V node as manifested by an abbreviated A-H interval in the His-bundle electrogram—?intranodal bypass, see figure 18.2.[20] It is of interest to note that the incidence of short P-R interval and long

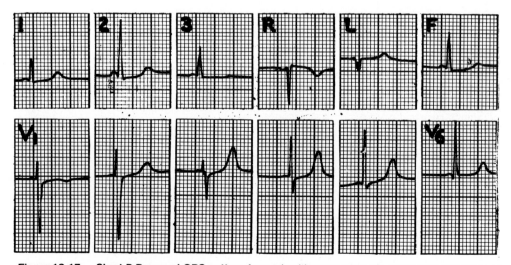

Figure 18.17.   Short-P-R-normal-QRS pattern from a healthy asymptomatic nurse with no history of palpitations or tachycardia. Note the short P-R interval (0.08 sec) with normal QRS complex.

P-R interval is exactly the same—1.3%—in a healthy young population, suggesting that neither is necessarily abnormal and each may represent the extremities of a normal bell-shaped curve of P-R incidence. On the other hand, the short-PR-normal-QRS combination may at times be due to conduction via an extranodal bypass tract but with conduction thereafter via normal His-Purkinje pathways—1 and HB in figure 18.2.

Arrhythmias in Short-PR-Normal-QRS Syndrome

Arrhythmias in the so-called LGL syndrome have not been studied in the same detail as those complicating the WPW syndrome. Although the anatomical substrate for this syndrome at least at times presumably involves an A-V nodal bypass, this bypass apparently played no part in the RTs in a small series studied at Duke.[42] Of 12 patients, 6 had supraventricular tachycardia; 2, atrial fibrillation; and 4, ventricular tachycardia. Four of the RTs were due to reentry in the A-V node, while two used a concealed bypass tract. That the arrhythmias complicating this syndrome may also be life-threatening is indicated by the fact that 3 of the 4 patients with ventricular tachycardia required resuscitation.

REFERENCES

1. Bashore, Th. M., et al.: Ventricular fibrillation in the Wolff-Parkinson-White syndrome. Circulation 1976: **11**, 187.
2. Becker, A. E., et al.: The anatomical substrates of Wolff-Parkinson-White syndrome. Circulation 1978: **57**, 870.
3. Campbell, R. W. F., et al.: Atrial fibrillation in the preexcitation syndrome. Am. J. Cardiol. 1977: **40**, 514.
4a. Cosio, F.G., et al.: Onset of atrial fibrillation during antidromic tachycardia: Association with sudden cardiac arrest and ventricular fibrillation in a patient with Wolff-Parkinson-White syndrome. Am. J. Cardiol. 1982: **50**, 353.
4. Chung, E. K.: Wolff-Parkinson-White syndrome—current views. Am. J. Med. 1977: **62**, 252.
5. Dreifus, L. S., et al.: Ventricular fibrillation: a possible mechanism of sudden death in patients with Wolff-Parkinson-White syndrome. Circulation 1971: **43**, 520.
6. Durrer, D., et al.: Pre-excitation revisited. Am. J. Cardiol. 1970: **25**, 690.
7. Durrer, D., et al.: The role of premature beats in the initiation and the termination of supraventricular tachycardia in the Wolff-Parkinson-White syndrome. Circulation 1967: **36**, 644.
8. Ferrer, M. I.: New concepts relating to the preexcitation syndrome. J.A.M.A. 1967: **201**, 1038.
9. Ferrer, M. I.: Preexcitation. Am. J. Med. 1977: **62**, 715.
10. Gallagher, J. J., et al.: Wolff-Parkinson-White syndrome; the problem, evaluation and surgical correction. Circulation 1975: **51**, 767.
11. Gallagher, J. J., et al.: The preexcitation syndromes. Prog. Cardiovasc. Dis. 1978: **20**, 285.
12. Gavrilescu, S., et al.: Accelerated atrioventricular conduction during acute myocardial infarction. Am. Heart J. 1977: **94**, 21.
13. Giardina, A. C. V., Ehlers, K. H., and Engle, M. A.: Wolff-Parkinson-White syndrome in infants and children: a long term follow up study. Br. Heart J. 1972: **34**, 839.
14. Goel, B. G., and Han, J.: Manifestations of the WPW syndrome after myocardial infarction. Am. Heart J. 1974: **87**, 633.
15. Grant, R. P., et al.: Ventricular activation in the pre-excitation syndrome (Wolff-Parkinson-White). Circulation 1958: **18**, 355.
16. Hejtmancik, M. R., and Herrmann, G. R.: The electrocardiographic syndrome of short P-R interval and broad QRS complexes. A clinical study of 80 cases. Am. Heart J. 1957: **54**, 708.
17. Herrmann, G. R., et al.: Paroxysmal pseudoventricular tachycardia and pseudoventricular fibrillation in patients with accelerated A-V conduction. Am. Heart J. 1957: **53**, 254.

18. James, T. N.: The Wolff-Parkinson-White syndrome. Ann. Intern. Med. 1969: **71,** 399.
19. James, T. N.: The Wolff-Parkinson-White syndrome: evolving concepts of its pathogenesis. Prog. Cardiovasc. Dis. 1970: **13,** 159.
20. Josephson, M. E., and Kastor, J. A.: Supraventricular tachycardia in Lown-Ganong-Levine syndrome; atrionodal versus intranodal reentry. Am. J. Cardiol. 1977: **40,** 521.
21. Kariv, I.: Wolff-Parkinson-White syndrome simulating myocardial infarction. Am. Heart J. 1958: **55,** 406.
22. Lev, M., et al.: Anatomic findings in a case of ventricular pre-excitation (WPW) terminating in complete atrioventricular block. Circulation 1966: **34,** 718.
23. Lev, M., et al.: Mahaim and James fibers as a basis for a unique variety of ventricular preexcitation. Am. J. Cardiol. 1975: **36,** 880.
24. Lown, B., et al.: The syndrome of the short P-R interval, normal QRS complex and paroxysmal rapid heart action. Circulation 1952: **5,** 693.
25. Marriott, H. J. L., and Rogers, H. M.: Mimics of ventricular tachycardia associated with the W-P-W syndrome. J. Electrocardiol., 1969: **2,** 77.
26. Narula, O. S.: Wolff-Parkinson-White syndrome: A review. Circulation 1973: **47,** 872.
27. Newman, B. J., et al.: Arrhythmias in the Wolff-Parkinson-White syndrome. Prog. Cardiovasc. Dis. 1966: **9,** 147.
28. Ohe, T., et al.: Catheter-induced isorhythmic idioventricular rhythm. Chest 1980: **78,** 638.
29. Prinzmetal, M., et al.: Accelerated conduction. In *The Wolff-Parkinson-White Syndrome and Related Conditions.* Grune & Stratton, New York, 1952.
30. Przyblyski, J., et al.: Unmasking of ventricular preexcitation by vagal stimulation or isoproterenol administration. Circulation 1980: **61,** 1030.
31. Rosen, K. M.: A-V nodal reentrance: an unexpected mechanism of paroxysmal tachycardia in a patient with preexcitation. Circulation 1973: **47,** 1267.
32. Ruskin, J. N., et al.: Abnormal Q waves in Wolff-Parkinson-White syndrome: Incidence and clinical significance. J.A.M.A. 1976: **235,** 2727.
33. Schiebler, G. L., et al.: The Wolff-Parkinson-White syndrome in infants and children. Pediatrics 1959: **24,** 585.
34. Sherf, L., and James, T. N.: A new look at some old questions in clinical electrocardiography. Henry Ford Hosp. Med. Bull. 1966: **14,** 265.
35. Sherf, L., and Neufeld, N. H.: *The Pre-excitation Syndrome: Facts and Theories.* Yorke Medical Books, New York, 1978.
36. Voukydis, P. C., and Cohen, S. I.: Catheter-induced arrhythmias. Am. Heart J. 1974: **88,** 588.
37. Wellens, H. J. J., and Durrer, D.: The role of an accessory atrioventricular pathway in reciprocal tachycardia. Circulation 1975: **52,** 58.
38. Wellens, H. J. J., et al.: The Wolff-Parkinson-White syndrome. In *Cardiac Arrhythmias, Their Mechanisms, Diagnosis and Management*, p. 342, edited by W. J. Mandel. J. B. Lippincott, Philadelphia, 1980.
39. Wolff, L.: Syndrome of short P-R interval with abnormal QRS complexes and paroxysmal tachycardia (Wolff-Parkinson-White syndrome). Circulation 1954: **10,** 282.
40. Wolff, L.: Wolff-Parkinson-White syndrome: historical and clinical features. Prog. Cardiovasc. Dis. 1960: **2,** 677.
41. Barold, S. S., and Coumel, P.: Mechanisms of atrioventricular tachycardia: Role of reentry and concealed accessory bypass tracts. Am. J. Cardiol. 1977: **39,** 97.
42. Benditt, D. G., et al.: Characteristics of atrioventricular conduction and the spectrum of arrhythmias in Lown-Ganong-Levine syndrome. Circulation 1978: **57,** 454.
43. Castellanos, A., et al.: Factors regulating ventricular rates during atrial flutter and fibrillation in pre-excitation (Wolff-Parkinson-White) syndrome, Br. Heart J. 1973: **35,** 811.
44. Gillette, P. C.: Concealed anomalous cardiac conduction pathways; a frequent cause of supraventricular tachycardia. Am. J. Cardiol. 1977: **40,** 848.
44a. Kennelly, B.M.: The short PR interval. In *What's New in Electrocardiography* p. 172, edited by H.J.J. Wellens and H.E. Kulbertus. Martinus Nijhoff, Boston, 1981.
45. Sellers, T. D., et al.: Effects of procainamide and quinidine sulfate in the Wolff-Parkinson-White syndrome. Circulation 1977: **55,** 15.
46. Sellers, T. D., et al.: Digitalis in the pre-excitation syndrome. Analysis during atrial fibrillation. Circulation 1977: **56,** 260.
47. Sung, R. J., et al.: Mechanisms of reciprocating tachycardia during sinus rhythm in concealed

Wolff-Parkinson-White syndrome. Circulation 1976: **54,** 338.

48. Wellens, H. J., and Durrer, D.: Wolff-Parkinson-White syndrome and atrial fibrillation: Relation between refractory period of accessory pathway and ventricular rate during atrial fibrillation. Am. J. Cardiol. 1974: **34,** 777.

49. Wellens, H. J. J., et al.: The value of the electrocardiogram in the differential diagnosis of a tachycardia with a widened QRS complex. Am. J. Med. 1978: **64,** 27.

Review Tracings

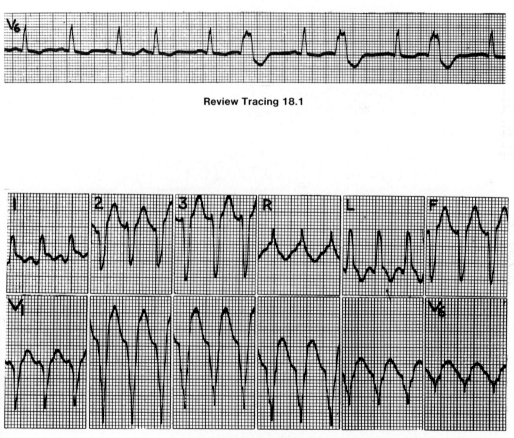

Review Tracing 18.1

Review Tracing 18.2

For interpretation, see page 483

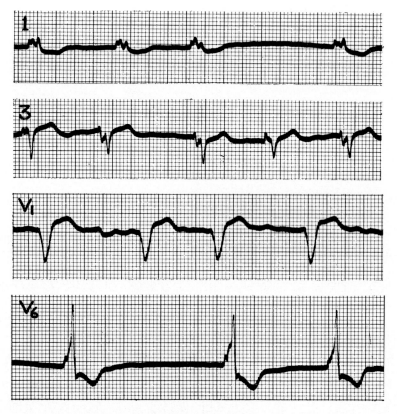

Review Tracing 18.3

For interpretation, see page 483

19

Fusion Beats—
Ventricular and Atrial

The fusion (summation or combination) beat is unrecognizable clinically and is a purely electrocardiographic diagnosis. It is the complex (ventricular or atrial) that results when two (or more) impulses simultaneously activate parts of the same myocardial territory (ventricular or atrial myocardium). The simultaneously spreading impulses, therefore, produce a hybrid complex usually possessing recognizable features of the patterns produced by each alone.

Theoretically, fusion could result from any number of simultaneously spreading impulses, but in practice it is obviously almost always between just two. However, triple fusion has occasionally been recognized in the presence of a WPW syndrome and an ectopic ventricular rhythm.[2, 3]

Ventricular Fusion

The ventricular fusion beat is thought to be of considerable value in recognizing ectopic ventricular rhythms; most authorities believe that the presence of fusion favors ectopy with 85 to 90% odds. The argument runs as follows: if a supraventricular impulse manages to enter the ventricles and merge with a second simultaneously spreading impulse, that second impulse must have arisen within the ventricle itself since—the argument goes—if two supraventricular impulses are heading for the ventricles, the first one to get to the A-V junction will leave the junction refractory and prevent passage of the second; if fusion occurs, therefore, one of the impulses must not be supraventricular and must be ventricular.

By and large, this is probably true; but Kistin[5] demonstrated long ago that it was possible for a descending sinus impulse to fuse with an aberrantly conducted junctional beat. The explanation for this was that the junctional impulse spreads via paraspecific (Mahaim) fibers to the ventricle, leaving the A-V junction clear for the passage of the simultaneous sinus impulse. It is also true that the majority of Wolff-Parkinson-White (WPW) beats represent fusion

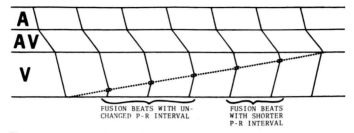

FUSION BEATS WITH UN-
CHANGED P-R INTERVAL

FUSION BEATS
WITH SHORTER
P-R INTERVAL

Figure 19.1. Ladder diagram illustrating progressively "higher" levels of fusion within the ventricles. The first beat represents a pure sinus beat; the last beat, a pure ventricular ectopic. Note that at first the P-R intervals remain the same as that of the sinus beat (as long as the sinus impulse invades the ventricles before or no later than the ectopic center fires); but when the ectopic center fires before the sinus impulse has arrived, the P-R becomes shorter than that of the sinus beat.

between the two wave fronts of the dichotomized sinus impulse, some of which spreads normally through the A-V junction and some through the accessory pathway (bundle of Kent). There is no question that it is possible to have fusion between two supraventricular impulses; nevertheless, the usefulness of fusion beats in favoring ventricular ectopy cannot be denied.

Ventricular fusion may result from various pairs of impulses (table 19.1) but is generally seen between a descending sinus and an ectopic ventricular impulse. The ectopic contributor may be an extrasystole, ventricular tachycardia (VT), accelerated idioventricular rhythm (AIVR), parasystole, or an escape or paced beat. Less often, the supraventricular contributor may be an ectopic atrial or junctional impulse. Ventricular fusion can also result from the simultaneous spread of two ectopic ventricular impulses, as when two idioventricular pacemakers, one in each ventricle, are competing for control.

There are three main principles in the diagnosis of ventricular fusion:[6]

1. You must have demonstrable reason to believe that two impulses were due at the moment that fusion is postulated. (This is so obvious that one feels that it should not have to be stated, but it emphatically requires to be stated because fusion beats are plucked out of thin air, without reason, more than any other electrocardiographic item.)
2. The contour of the fusion beat should be intermediate in shape and duration between the QRS contours of the two supposedly fusing impulses. (There are two exceptions to this to be discussed later.)
3. The P-R interval of a fusion beat may be the same as that of the conducted sinus beats, or it may be shorter (fig. 19.1); but if it is shorter, it will not as a rule be more than 0.06 sec shorter than the basic P-R. (In one exceptional circumstance, the P-R may actually be longer; this is when the subject has R-P dependent P-R intervals, i.e., has the potential for varying P-R intervals à la Wenckebach. In such a patient, if the sinus

Table 19.1
Potential Partners in Fusion (Any of the Impulses in A Can Fuse with Any in B)

A	B
Sinus	Ectopic ventricular
Ectopic atrial	Extrasystole
Junctional	Tachycardia
Ectopic ventricular	Accelerated idioventricular
	Parasystole
	Escape
	Pacemaker
	Junctional conducted
	preferentially
	Sinus or ectopic atrial
	conducted by Kent bundle

impulse arises early in diastole, it may be conducted with delay and fuse after a prolonged P-R interval.)

Fusion with Ventricular Extrasystoles

In order for a sinus impulse to fuse with a premature beat, the beat must usually qualify as an "end-diastolic" extrasystole; i.e., at normal sinus rates, the ectopic beat must occur late enough to follow the next sinus P wave. Figure 19.2 shows a ventricular bigeminy in which the coupling intervals are long enough to deposit the extrasystoles after the next sinus P waves. Ventricular fusion beats (labelled 1, 2, 3 and 4) result from the gradually lengthening coupling interval. The first two extrasystoles capture the whole myocardium; but, beginning with the third extrasystole, there is time for the sinus impulse to enter the ventricles before they have been completely activated from the ectopic center. As the coupling interval and with it the P-R interval lengthens, the sinus contribution to the ventricular fusion complex increases (see fig. 19.2, ladder diagram).

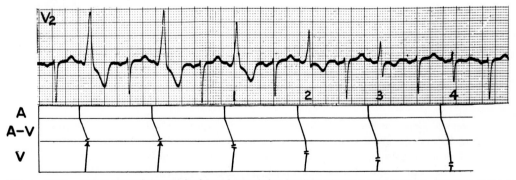

Figure 19.2. "End-diastolic" **ventricular extrasystoles** landing after the next P wave. After the first two extrasystoles, their coupling intervals progressively lengthen so that fusion occurs (beats 1, 2, 3 and 4) at progressively "lower" levels in the ventricles with more and more contribution from the sinus impulse. The P-R interval of beat 4 is as long as that of the sinus beats.

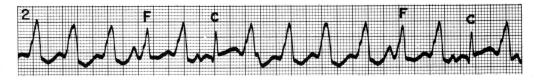

Figure 19.3.   Ventricular tachycardia (rate, 126/min) interrupted by two **fusion beats** (F) and two capture beats (C) in a patient with acute inferior infarction.

Occasionally, the coincidence of a more or less simultaneous atrial and ventricular extrasystole produces ventricular fusion.

Fusion during VT

The value of fusion beats in the diagnosis of VT was emphasized by Dressler,[1] and such beats are often referred to as Dressler beats. Their presence is considered excellent evidence in favor of VT, but their value is limited by the fact that they are seldom seen in the faster tachycardias—if the rate is much over 150/min, one is unlikely to find fusion beats. All of the examples published by Dressler had a rate less than 150/min. Figure 19.3 shows an example of fusion beats punctuating VT. Note that the rate of the tachycardia is only about 126/min and that there are capture beats (C) as well as fusion beats (F).

Fusion during AIVR

AIVR is a common source of fusion and for the good reason that its rate is often closely similar to the competing sinus rate. For this same reason, it is not surprising that the championship for consecutive fusion beats has been won by this rhythm! Figure 19.4 is a champion tracing boasting no less than 37 consecutive fusion beats. The beat marked "*x*" in the top strip is the last of the pure ectopic beats, and that marked "*x*" in the bottom strip is the first of the pure sinus beats. Between these 2 beats lie the 37 fusion beats showing contribution by the ectopic and sinus impulses in varying proportions.

Since many examples of AIVR have rates little different from the sinus, it is quite common for short runs of AIVR to begin and end with fusion beats. Figure 19.5 illustrates just such a run of AIVR.

Fusion with Ventricular Parasystole

If two independent rhythms with different rates continue to beat regularly and if one of them is ectopic ventricular and "protected" from (cannot be discharged by) the other, i.e., is parasystolic, it is a mathematical certainty that at some point their discharges will coincide and produce fusion. Ventricular parasystole, therefore, if long enough strips are taken, will always manifest

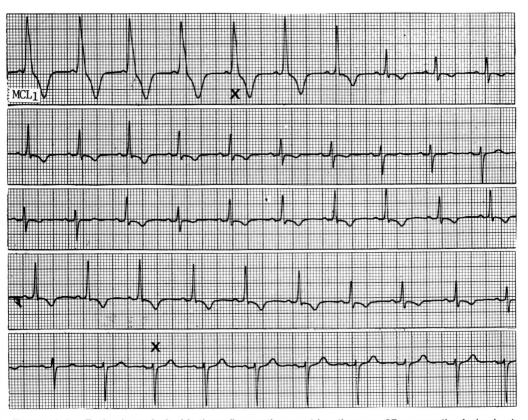

Figure 19.4.   Fusion in profusion! In these five continuous strips, there are 37 consecutive fusion beats between the complexes marked ''x.'' The **AIVR** from the left ventricle (seen pure in the first five beats of the top strip) and the sinus rhythm (seen pure in the last eight beats in the bottom strip) have identical rates; slight beat-to-beat fluctuations in the cycle length of one or other pacemaker alters the contribution to the fusion complex by each pacemaker but is not enough to disengage them.

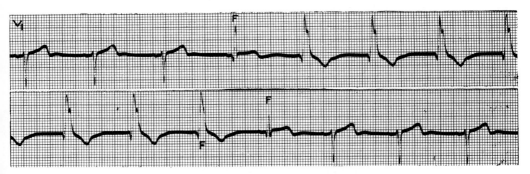

Figure 19.5.   The strips are continuous. **AIVR** from the left ventricle (rate, 58/min) taking over from a sinus rhythm with an almost identical rate that slows slightly. The run of AIVR is ushered in and out by **fusion beats** (F).

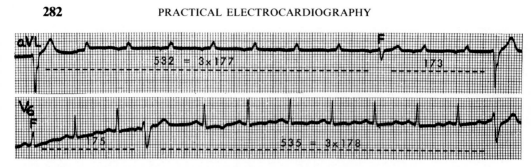

Figure 19.6.   Ventricular parasystole with **fusion beats.** The diagnosis of parasystole is established by the varying "coupling" intervals and the fact that the longer interectopic interval is a multiple of the shorter interectopic interval—from fusion beat (F) to next ectopic beat—in each lead.

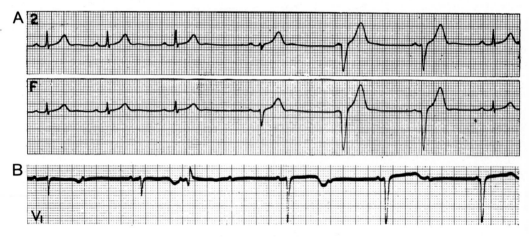

Figure 19.7.   Ventricular escape. A. In each strip, the sinus rhythm slows and allows an idioventricular center to escape for three beats. The first and third of these escapes in each strip form **fusion beats.** B. The strip begins with 2:1 A-V block (note the different P-R intervals of the conducted beats—presumably type I block with R-P dependent P-R intervals); then a ventricular extrasystole is followed by a longer cycle which enables an idioventricular pacemaker to escape. The first of the three escape beats is narrower than the last two, is preceded by a P wave at a conductible interval and is clearly a **fusion beat.**

fusion beats. This is not to say that fusion is necessary for the diagnosis, only that it is an inevitable eventual finding. Figure 19.6 is an example of ventricular parasystole with fusion.

Fusion with Ventricular Escape Beats

This fusion-producing combination is seen, for example, when an AIVR escapes from an even slower sinus rhythm; or when, in the presence of incomplete A-V block, conduction occurs at the same time that an idioventricular pacemaker escapes.

Figure 19.5 illustrated the beginning of a run of AIVR which took over from the sinus rhythm because the sinus rhythm slowed; the AIVR is, therefore, by definition an escape rhythm.

Figure 19.7*A* shows progressive slowing of the sinus rate with consequent escape by an idioventricular pacemaker at a rate of 48/min. The fifth beat in each strip is a full-blown ectopic beat (idioventricular); the fourth and sixth beats are fusion beats.

Figure 19.7*B* begins with 2:1 A-V block and ends with 2 idioventricular beats. The fourth beat in the strip is somewhat narrower than the idioventricular beats, is preceded by a P wave at a conductible interval and is therefore a fusion beat.

Fusion with Paced Beats

The pacemaker is a splendid fusion factory: the demand model is a perfect artificial analog of ventricular escape, and the fixed-rate pacemaker is an equally perfect analog of ventricular parasystole. Both types of pacemaker, therefore, produce fusion beats in exactly the same way as their natural prototypes. Figure 19.8*A* shows a demand pacemaker producing fusion beats as the sinus rhythm accelerates and takes control: as the sinus P wave emerges in front of the pacemaker "blip," partial conduction occurs and fusion (F) results. Figure 19.8*B* illustrates a fixed-rate pacemaker ignoring in its autocratic way the sinus beats in the top strip and finally fusing with one (F) toward the end of the bottom strip.

"Two Wrongs Sometimes Make a Right"

"Two wrongs sometimes make a right" is the picturesque way in which Schamroth indicates that there are circumstances in which two impulses, each

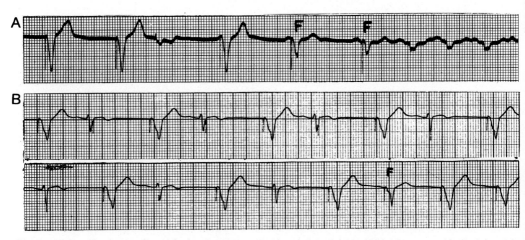

Figure 19.8. Two examples of **fusion** between paced and sinus beats. (*A*) In the second half of the strip, a demand right ventricular pacemaker produces fusion with an accelerating sinus rhythm. (*B*) The two strips are continuous. A fixed-rate right ventricular pacemaker beats relentlessly in competition with the sinus rhythm to produce a form of "escape-capture" bigeminy in the top strip. Toward the end of the bottom strip, it at last achieves fusion (F).

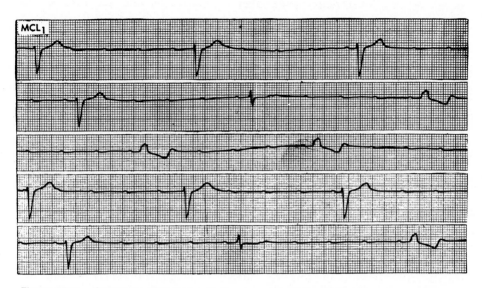

Figure 19.9.   **Complete A-V block** with two competing idioventricular pacemakers, one in each ventricle (right ventricular in *first* and *fourth strips*, left ventricular in *third strip*). In the *second* and *fifth strips*, the middle beats are narrow **fusion beats** thanks to simultaneous activation of the two ventricles.

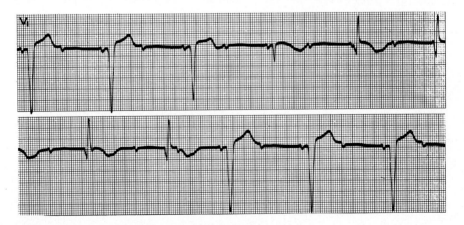

Figure 19.10.   The strips are continuous. The basic rhythm is **2:1 A-V block**, probably type II, with **LBBB** seen at the beginning of the top strip and in the second half of the bottom strip. The last two beats in the *top strip* and the first two in the *bottom strip* represent an idioventricular rhythm from the left ventricle. The third and fourth beats in the *top strip* are **fusion beats**—note the normal appearance of beat 4.

of which on its own produces an abnormal complex, may create a normal-looking complex when they fuse. This may happen when two idioventricular centers, one in each ventricle, are competing for control. Each center by itself would produce a wide ectopic complex; but if they both activate their respective ventricles simultaneously, the resulting fusion complex will be normally narrow and bear no resemblance to either of its "component" complexes (fig. 19.9).

It may also happen if there is an ectopic center on the same side as a BBB. In this case, if the ectopic focus discharges at the same moment that the sinus impulse enters the contralateral ventricle, the resulting fusion complex will be normally narrow (fig. 19.10), though each impulse on its own produces a wide complex.

In both these circumstances, the principle enunciated earlier, that fusion complexes are intermediate in form and width, is violated.

Fusion between Supraventricular Impulses

I pointed out above that fusion, though useful in the diagnosis of ectopy, *could* occur between two supraventricular impulses. In the WPW syndrome, the famous "concertina" effect is due to a progressively changing contribution from each of the two wave fronts of the dichotomized sinus impulse. The first four beats in the bottom strip of figure 19.11 show progressive widening of the QRS, with concomitant shortening of the P-R, as more and more of the QRS is accounted for by accessory-pathway conduction and less and less by orthodox conduction.

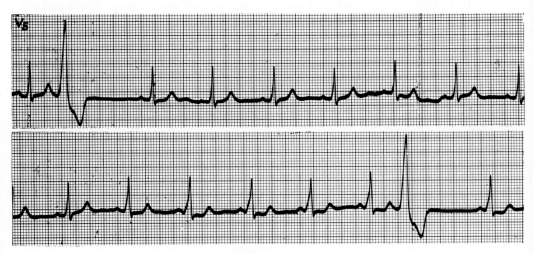

Figure 19.11. The strips are continuous. **WPW syndrome** interrupted by two ventricular extrasystoles. The "concertina" effect is seen at the beginning of the *bottom strip* where the first three or four beats manifest progressive widening of the QRS with corresponding shortening of the P-R.

Fusion between two supraventricular impulses can also occur when an aberrantly conducted junctional impulse fuses with a simultaneously descending sinus impulse.[5] Figure 19.12 illustrates a probable example of this: the independent beats have an incomplete RBBB pattern, whereas the conducted sinus beats have no r', suggesting that the independent focus is situated leftward in the junction and experiences delay in reaching and traversing the RBB (see Chapter 16). The fourth beat in the top strip and third in the bottom strip are presumable fusion beats between sinus and A-V impulses.

Atrial Fusion

When two impulses simultaneously invade the atria, atrial fusion results. This is most often seen in the presence of a wandering pacemaker when pacemaking is shifting back and forth between sinus node and A-V junction. In such a case, if the junctional pacemaker sends its retrograde impulse into the atrium at the same time that the sinus impulse is also activating atrial muscle, an atrial fusion beat results (fig. 19.13). Atrial fusion may also be seen when an ectopic ventricular pacemaker succeeds in pushing its impulse retrogradely into the atria at a time when the sinus impulse is also on the go (fig. 19.14).

When Kistin[4] demonstrated, with the help of esophageal leads, that retrograde conduction to the atria was a common event with ventricular extrasystoles yet was seldom seen in the clinical tracing, he suggested that their absence could be explained by assuming that they produced relatively isoelectric, and therefore invisible, atrial fusion beats.

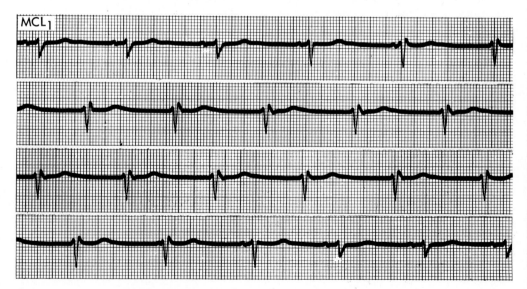

Figure 19.12. The strips are continuous. After three sinus beats, a presumable junctional rhythm escapes because the sinus rhythm slows. The escaping rhythm is characterized by rSr' configuration suggesting incomplete RBBB, probably because the junctional pacemaker is situated toward the left side. The fourth beat in the *top strip* and the third in the *bottom strip* are **fusion beats**.

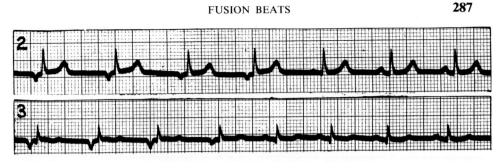

Figure 19.13.   Shifting pacemaker. In each lead, **junctional rhythm** with retrograde conduction shifts to sinus rhythm. In lead 2, the third, fourth and fifth P waves are intermediate in form between retrograde and sinus P's and presumably represent **atrial fusion.** In lead 3, only the fourth P wave is due to fusion.

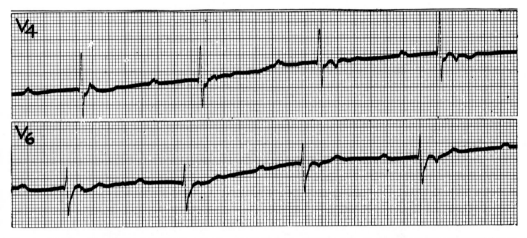

Figure 19.14.   Complete A-V block, yet retrograde V-A conduction occurs after the third and fourth beats in V$_4$ and after the fourth beat in lead V$_6$. Following the second QRS in V$_4$ and following the second and third QRS in V$_6$, sinus and retrograde P waves coincide to produce **atrial fusion.**

REFERENCES

1. Dressler, W., and Roesler, H.: The occurrence in paroxysmal ventricular tachycardia of ventricular complexes transitional in shape to sinoauricular beats. Am. Heart J. 1952: **44,** 485.
2. Dubb, A., and Schamroth, L.: Ventricular parasystole with the Wolff-Parkinson-White syndrome. Chest 1979: **75,** 607.
3. Kinoshita, S., et al.: Triple ventricular fusion due to intermittent ventricular parasystole in the Wolff-Parkinson-White syndrome. Am. Heart J. 1981: **102,** 290.
4. Kistin, A. D., and Landowne, M.: Retrograde conduction from premature ventricular contractions, a common occurrence in the human heart. Circulation 1951: **3,** 738.
5. Kistin, A. D.: Problems in the differentiation of ventricular arrhythmia from supraventricular arrhythmia with abnormal QRS. Prog. Cardiovasc. Dis. 1966: **9,** 1.
6. Marriott, H. J. L., et al.: Ventricular fusion beats. Circulation 1962: **26,** 880.

Review Tracings

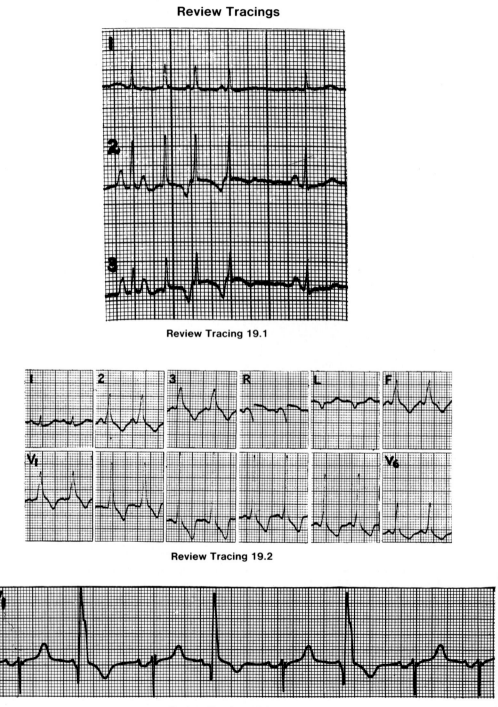

Review Tracing 19.1

Review Tracing 19.2

Review Tracing 19.3

For interpretation, see page 483

20

Subsidiary Supraventricular Rhythms

This chapter deals with a number of ectopic rhythms arising in either the atria or the A-V junction. Some are well defined and understood; the identity of others is less secure.

A-V Junctional Rhythms

A-V junctional rhythm was first experimentally produced in the animal by Engelmann in 1903. When Tawara described the A-V node three years later, the rhythm that Engelmann described became "nodal." Zahn then, in 1913, introduced the concept of "upper," "middle," and "lower" nodal rhythm based on the temporal relationship of atrial to ventricular activation; and in the following year, Meek and Eyster described the electrocardiographic features that were generally accepted for decades. Modern methods of investigation, however, have cast doubt on the A-V node as a source of spontaneous impulse formation, on the concept of "upper," "middle," and "lower" junctional rhythms, and on our ability to recognize the source of the atrial impulse from the pattern of the P wave in the surface electrocardiogram.

The A-V junction is divided into four parts[6]: the "approaches" to the A-V node; the A-V node proper; the penetrating portion of the A-V bundle (bundle of His), which enters the central fibrous body and is in danger of strangulation if that body becomes calcified; and the nonpenetrating, nonbranching portion. The branching portion which spawns the bundle branches is regarded as subjunctional.[6] Just where in this junctional conglomerate automatic impulses arise is still a matter of debate. It is widely accepted that the bundle of His possesses pacemaking potential; it is considered probable that the N-H region (junction of node with bundle) also possesses automaticity; and it is widely doubted that the node itself can form impulses. However, Scherlag[17] asserts that there are two forms of junctional rhythm, one that arises in the A-V node proper and one that arises in the His bundle; the characteristics of these two forms are summarized in table 20.1.

Table 20.1
Characteristics of Junctional Rhythms[17]

	Nodal Rhythm	His Rhythm
Intrinsic rate	45–60/min	35–45/min
Atropine effect	Rate increased by 35–45/min	No significant rate change

To avoid terminological controversies, I shall use the noncommittal terms "A-V junctional," "junctional," or just plain "A-V," which has enjoyed uninterrupted usage since 1915.

Junctional Rhythm

In A-V junctional rhythm, the impulse travels anterogradely and retrogradely at the same time, to write a normal QRS-T (unless aberrant) and a retrograde P wave. Depending upon the rate of conduction in each direction, the P wave may be inscribed shortly in front of the ventricular complex, may follow the QRS, or it may be lost within it. An example of junctional rhythm with short P-R interval is illustrated in figure 20.1, and one with the retrograde P waves following the QRS in figure 20.2.

Figure 20.1 also shows the usual retrograde P-wave polarity in the 12-lead tracing: The axis of the P wave is in the neighborhood of −90°—it is nearly isoelectric in lead 1, frankly inverted in leads 2, 3, and aVF, and upright in aVR and aVL; it is usually inverted in left chest leads (V₅₋₆) and at least partly upright in V₁.

Though there is little doubt that the majority of retrograde P waves manifest this polarity, one should know and keep in mind that retrograde conduction can produce positive P waves in leads 2, 3, and aVF[10, 20] and in fact the

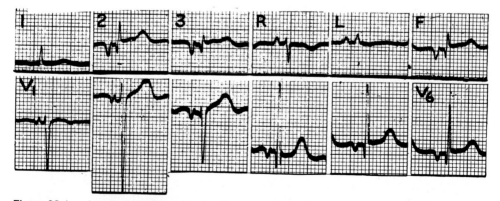

Figure 20.1.   Junctional rhythm showing the typical polarity of retrograde P waves: flat in lead 1; inverted in 2, 3, aVF, and left chest leads; upright in aVR and aVL; and at least partly upright (often − +) in lead V₁. The P-R interval is about 0.12 sec.

localizing status of human P waves is so uncertain that we can echo the gloomy pronouncement of Waldo and James[21] that neither P-wave polarity nor the P-R interval are dependable guides to the origin of the atrial impulse.

The various rhythms that originate in or occupy the A-V junction are listed in table 20.2. The rhythms "by default" put in an appearance only if the higher pacemaker, the sinus node, fails to maintain control; this may happen if the sinus node itself slows or fails or if block prevents its impulses from reaching the ventricles.

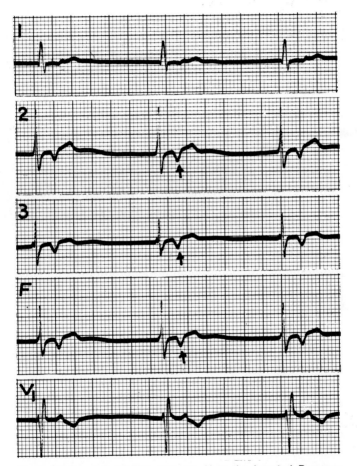

Figure 20.2. A-V rhythm, rate 47. Note the inverted P waves (arrows) following the QRS in 2, 3 and aVF with upright P waves in V₁.

A-V junctional rhythm, therefore, since it is always secondary to failure of the higher mechanism, is never in itself a primary diagnosis; and the same is true of all rhythms by default. When a single junctional beat comes to the rescue after a longer cycle than the dominant cycle, it is an escape beat (fig. 20.3). Junctional escape beats seldom show manifest retrograde conduction to the atria—the escaping junctional QRS stands either isolated or attended by the adjacent, dissociated sinus P wave. In both of the examples in figure 20.3, the absence of retrograde conduction is attributable to the adjacent sinus activity, which obviously precludes retrograde conduction to the atria. But in other instances, where there is no nearby sinus P wave, retrograde P waves are often noticeably absent. In such cases, either there is no retrograde conduction or, alternatively, the retrograde P wave coincides with and is lost within the QRS complex.

When the junction escapes for several consecutive beats without retrograde conduction, a run of "idiojunctional" rhythm results. The prefix "idio-" (as also in idioventricular) implies that the ventricles have their own pacemaker to themselves—not shared with the atria (from the Greek, *idios*, which means "one's own," "private," "personal"). In figure 20.4, after two sinus beats there is a pause, and before the next tardy atrial impulse can be conducted, the junction takes over and retains control of the ventricles for five beats before the sinus node recaptures the ventricles in the next-to-last beat. This then is a run of idiojunctional rhythm dissociated from the concomitant sinus bradycardia.

Salient Features of A-V Rhythms

1. Abnormal P waves closely preceding or following QRS; or absent P waves
2. Normal QRST sequence

Table 20.2
A-V Junctional Rhythms

By Default	By Usurpation
A-V junctional escape	A-V extrasystoles
	Manifest
	Concealed
A-V junctional rhythm	A-V parasystole
Idiojunctional rhythm	Accelerated A-V rhythm
	Accelerated idiojunctional rhythm
	A-V tachycardia
	Reciprocating
	Ectopic

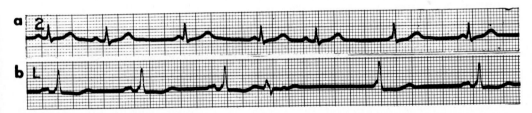

Figure 20.3.   Junctional escape beats. In *a*, the third, fourth, sixth, and seventh beats are junctional escapes owing to the lengthened sinus cycles. In *b*, the fourth beat is a ventricular extrasystole with retrograde conduction; the postextrasystolic pause ends with a junctional escape beat.

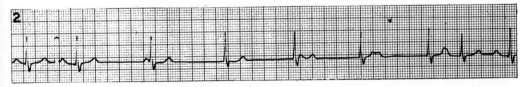

Figure 20.4.   After two sinus beats with first degree A-V block, a sinus pause permits an A-V pacemaker to escape at a rate of about 54/min. The resulting **idiojunctional rhythm** produces a run of A-V dissociation until the sinus pacemaker recaptures the ventricles for the last two beats.

Shifting or Wandering Pacemaker

The terms "shifting" and "wandering" pacemaker often are—but should not be—applied when the P wave changes with usurping ectopic atrial beats. The terms are appropriate when two (usually sinus and junctional) or more competing supraventricular rhythms, having approximately the same rate, vie with one another for control of the heart. Two typical examples are shown in figure 20.5. In lead 1 of figure 20.5*A*, after three sinus beats, an A-V rhythm takes over without measurable change in the atrial rate. In lead 2, the sinus node regains control in the middle of the strip when the A-V pacemaker pauses perceptibly. Often, as is seen in figure 20.5*B*, atrial fusion beats intervene between the pure sinus and pure retrograde P waves.

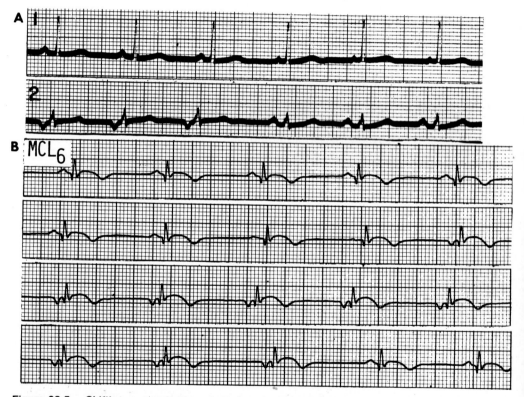

Figure 20.5.   Shifting or **wandering pacemaker.** In *A*, the first three beats in lead 1 are sinus; then, without any measurable change in cycle length, pacemaking shifts to the A-V junction. In lead 2, after three junctional beats, the sinus node regains control at the end of a slightly longer cycle. In *B*, the four strips are continuous. The top strip shows only sinus rhythm, and the third strip shows only junctional rhythm. The last three beats in the second strip show atrial fusion. In the bottom strip, after three junctional beats, the sinus node takes over again for the last two beats.

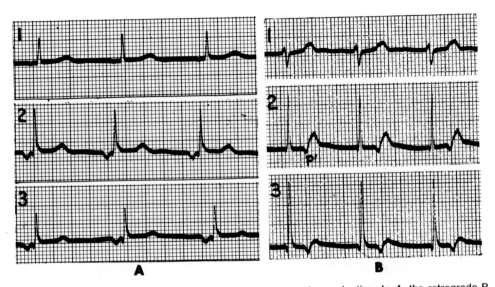

Figure 20.6.   Accelerated junctional rhythm with retrograde conduction. In *A*, the retrograde P waves closely precede the QRS (P-R = 0.12 sec). In *B*, the retrograde P waves follow the QRS at an R-P interval of 0.19 sec.

Accelerated Junctional Rhythm

When the junction seizes control by firing before the next expected beat of the dominant rhythm, it is said to take over "by usurpation." Junctional extrasystoles, junctional parasystole and the junctional tachycardias have been dealt with in previous chapters.

If the junctional rate exceeds 60/min but is less than 100/min, it is usually referred to as an accelerated rhythm. Figure 20.6 presents two examples of accelerated A-V junctional rhythm in which the junctional pacemaker controls both ventricles and atria: in *A*, the retrograde P waves closely precede the QRS complexes with typical retrograde polarity; in *B*, the retrograde P waves follow the QRS at a normal R-P interval.

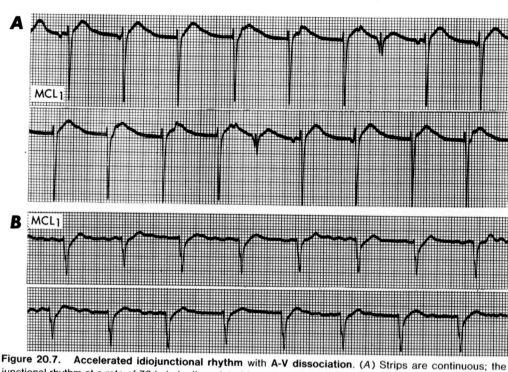

Figure 20.7.   Accelerated idiojunctional rhythm with **A-V dissociation.** (*A*) Strips are continuous; the junctional rhythm at a rate of 76/min is dissociated from the sinus rhythm (rate 72/min). The seventh beat in the *top strip* and the fifth in the *bottom strip* are ventricular capture beats with prolonged P-R intervals and ventricular aberration. (*B*) Strips are continuous. **Atrial fibrillation** with some degree of A-V block and an accelerated idiojunctional rhythm at a rate of 72/min.

On the other hand, figure 20.7*A* illustrates an idiojunctional rhythm which usurps control from a slower sinus pacemaker; the two rhythms remain dissociated except for the two ventricular captures by the sinus node. Figure 20.7*B* illustrates an accelerated idiojunctional rhythm dissociated from fibrillating atria—a combination that should always make one think of the possibility of digitalis intoxication.

Accelerated junctional rhythms are one of the relatively common causes of A-V dissociation, especially seen in acute inferior myocardial infarction, rheumatic fever, and digitalis intoxication.

Ectopic Atrial Rhythms

Left Atrial Rhythms

Our time-honored concepts of A-V rhythm were upset by Mirowski who drew attention to the fact that we have based our diagnosis of junctional activity on the P-wave pattern in the limb leads alone and ignored their morphology in the chest leads.[12] He maintained that many of the rhythms that we call junctional are really of left atrial origin and he suggested that an important criterion for left atrial rhythm was an inverted P wave in V_6, often associated with an upright P wave in V_1. His argument does not explain why "left atrial" rhythms should so often have short P-R intervals, and for the moment the matter must remain unsettled. Meanwhile he has done us a service in focussing attention on the precordial P waves in tracings that show typical "retrograde" P waves in the limb leads.

Probably more helpful in the diagnosis of left atrial rhythm are the rather specific "dome-and-dart" P wave in V_1 (fig. 20.8) and/or the frankly inverted P wave in standard lead 1.[1, 22]

Slow Atrial Rhythm

This is defined[3] as an atrial rhythm at a rate between 50 and 80/min, with P waves different from the sinus P waves and with a normal or slightly longer than normal P-R interval. Thus most examples of "coronary sinus rhythm," as described below, qualify for this category; but slow atrial rhythm does not require P waves of retrograde form, they must merely be *different* from the sinus P wave. This rhythm may be an index of an underlying sick sinus (p. 318).

An alternative and preferable term is **ectopic atrial rhythm**[5]—to be preferred because the changed form of the P wave, presumably due to a shift in the pacemaker, is its characteristic feature rather than an identifying rate which, after all, is in the sinus range; and rates of up to 80/min hardly qualify as "slow."

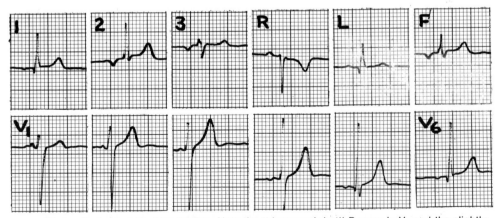

Figure 20.8. Probable **left atrial rhythm.** Note the "dome-and-dart" P wave in V_1 and the slightly inverted P wave in lead 1.

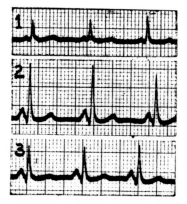

Figure 20.9. An example of a short-PR-normal-QRS "syndrome," often called Lown-Ganong-Levine (LGL) syndrome and formerly sometimes known as coronary nodal rhythm. The P-R interval is only 0.08 sec.

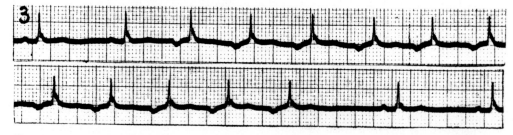

Figure 20.10. Strips are continuous. An example of what has been known as coronary sinus rhythm, but is better called ectopic atrial rhythm. After two sinus beats, the ectopic focus takes over for an 11-beat run, followed by a return to sinus rhythm.

Outmoded Atrial Rhythms

A question is still occasionally asked concerning the nature of the following two terms:

Coronary nodal rhythm was formerly applied by some authorities when the P-R interval was abnormally short (less than 0.12 sec) and followed by a normal QRS complex[2, 8] (fig. 20.9). Others called it the Lown-Ganong-Levine (LGL) syndrome,[9] and this is dealt with in Chapter 18.

Coronary sinus rhythm was the term Scherf[14, 15] applied when the P waves had a typical retrograde morphology but were associated with a normal (rather than short) P-R interval (fig. 20.10).

REFERENCES

1. Bix, H. H.: The electrocardiographic pattern of initial stimulation in the left auricle. Sinai Hosp. J. 1953: **2**, 37.
2. Eyring, E. J., and Spodick, C. H.: Coronary nodal rhythm. Am. J. Cardiol. 1960: **5**, 781.
3. Ferrer, M. I.: Significance of slow atrial rhythm. Am. J. Cardiol. 1980: **46**, 176.
4. Fisch, C., and Knoebel, S. B.: Junctional rhythms. Prog. Cardiovasc. Dis. 1970: **13**, 141.
5. Gaughan, G. L., and Gorfinkel, H. J.: Physiologic and biologic variants of the electrocardiogram. Cardiovasc. Clin. 1977: **8**, 7.

6. Hecht, H. H., et al.: Atrioventricular and intraventricular conduction: revised nomenclature and concepts. Am. J. Cardiol. 1973: **31**, 232.

7. Hoffman, B. F., and Cranefield, P. F.: The physiological basis of cardiac arrhythmias. Am. J. Med. 1964: **37**, 670.

8. Katz, L. N., and Pick, A.: *Clinical Electrocardiography. The Arrhythmias.* Lea & Febiger, Philadelphia, 1956.

9. Lown, B., et al.: The syndrome of the short P-R interval normal QRS complex and paroxysmal rapid heart action. Circulation 1952: **5**, 693.

10. MacLean, W. A. H., et al.: P waves during ectopic atrial rhythms in man. A study utilizing atrial pacing with fixed electrodes. Circulation 1975: **52**, 426.

11. Marriott, H. J. L.: Nodal mechanisms with dependent activation of atria and ventricles. In *Mechanisms and Therapy of Cardiac Arrhythmias*, 14th Hahnemann Symposium, Grune & Stratton, New York, 1966.

12. Mirowski, M.: Left atrial rhythm. Diagnostic criteria and differentiation from nodal arrhythmias. Am. J. Cardiol. 1966: **17**, 203.

13. Pick, A.: Mechanisms of cardiac arrhythmias: from hypothesis to physiologic fact. Am. Heart J. 1973: **86**, 249.

14. Scherf, D., and Gurbuzer, B.: Further studies on coronary sinus rhythm. Am. J. Cardiol. 1958: **16**, 579.

15. Scherf, D., and Harris, R.: Coronary sinus rhythm. Am. Heart J. 1946: **32**, 443.

16. Scherf, D., and Cohen, J.: *The Atrioventricular Node and Selected Cardiac Arrhythmias.* Grune & Stratton, New York, 1964.

17. Scherlag, B. J., et al.: Differentiation of "A-V junctional rhythms." Circulation 1973: **48**, 304.

18. Somlyo, A. P., and Grayzel, J.: Left atrial arrhythmias. Am. Heart J. 1963: **65**, 68.

19. Spodick, D. H., and Colman, R.: Observations on coronary sinus rhythm and its mechanism. Am. J. Cardiol. 1961: **7**, 198.

20. Waldo, A. L., et al.: Sequence of retrograde activation of the human heart. Correlation with P wave polarity. Br. Heart J. 1977: **39**, 634.

21. Waldo, A. L., and James, T. N.: A retrospective look at A-V nodal rhythms. Circulation 1973: **47**, 222.

22. Beder, S.D., et al.: Clinical confirmation of ECG criteria for left atrial rhythm. Am. Heart J. 1982: **103**, 848.

Review Tracings

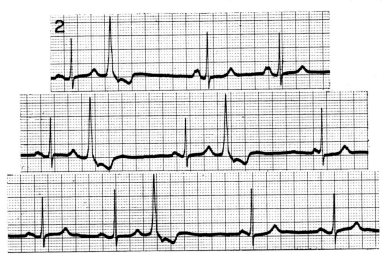

Review Tracing 20.1
For interpretation, see page 483

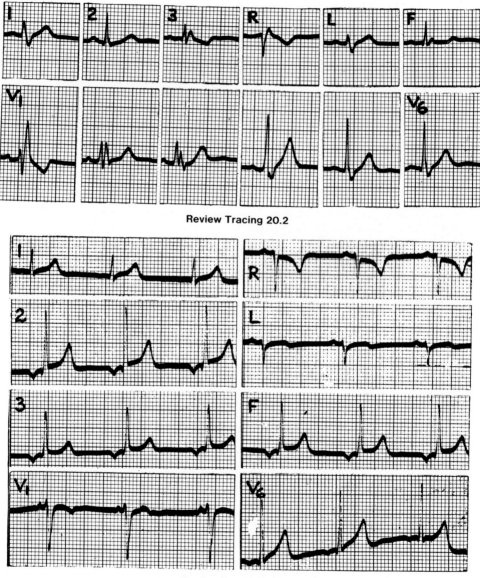

Review Tracing 20.2

Review Tracing 20.3

For interpretation, see page 483

21

Escape and Dissociation

The dysrhythmic disturbances so far considered have been primary disorders of either impulse formation or conduction. The two phenomena, escape and dissociation, discussed in this chapter, are NOT primary diagnoses—they are, like jaundice or headache, symptomatic of some underlying primary disturbance to which they are secondary.

Escape

The escape(d) beat is an ectopic, automatic beat that ends a cycle longer than the cycle of the dominant rhythm. It is a rescuing beat—a friend in need—and as such, of course, should *never* be treated. The escape beat arises because, for some reason, the higher pacemaker has failed to maintain control and so a pause has been provided that has given the escaping pacemaker time for its slope of diastolic depolarization to reach threshold. Just as the fixed-rate pacemaker is a precise artificial analogue of parasystole, so the demand pacemaker is the analogue of spontaneous escape rhythms. Normally, all potential escape foci are subdued by the faster beating sinus node, and it is only when this hegemony falters that an escaping rhythm (or a demand pacemaker) has the opportunity to assert itself.

Escape can result from three of the four mechanisms that can produce A-V dissociation:

1. Slowing of primary pacemaker
    Sinus bradycardia
2. Block of primary impulses
    Incomplete S-A block
    Incomplete A-V block
    Complete A-V block
3. Pause producers
    Extrasystoles
    Termination of tachycardia

These three mechanisms are illustrated in figure 21.1.

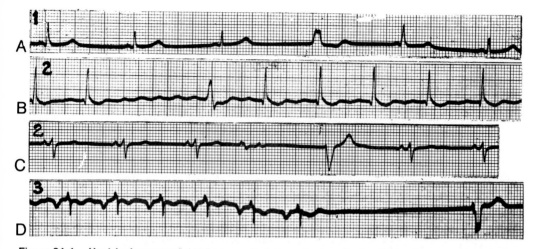

Figure 21.1.   **Ventricular escape.** (*A*) As a result of sinus slowing, the fourth beat is a ventricular escape, and the fifth a fusion beat. (*B*) An atrial tachyarrhythmia (?flutter) with predominantly 3:1 conduction. After the second beat, several consecutive atrial impulses are blocked, producing a pause that enables a ventricular pacemaker to escape. (*C*) The fourth beat is a VPB; the longer postextrasystolic cycle provides the opportunity for another ectopic ventricular pacemaker to escape. (*D*) The pause following the abrupt cessation of an ectopic atrial rhythm enables a ventricular pacemaker to escape.

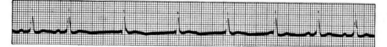

Figure 21.2.   Transient sinus slowing induced by a deep breath. After the second beat, the sinus rhythm slows and junctional escape results for four beats. The sinus node then accelerates and resumes control for the last two beats.

Usually the escaping pacemaker is in the A-V junction (**junctional escape**), but, if this also defaults, a Purkinje focus in the ventricles may take over (**ventricular escape**). **Atrial escape** is not much talked about, yet it is a common finding after ectopic atrial activity.

Junctional Escape

When something goes wrong with the normal formation or conduction of the sinus impulse, the next officer in the pacemaking hierarchy is the A-V junction; so the most common form of escape is junctional. Junctional escapes are recognized by their unchanged or only slightly changed QRS complex ending a cycle longer than the dominant cycle and, for some reason, they are usually *not* associated with retrograde conduction. At times this absence of retroconduction is obviously because the atria have already been activated by the sinus impulse (see fig. 21.2); but even when there is no neighboring sinus activity, there is a conspicuous scarcity of visible retrograde atrial activation in association with single junctional escape beats.

At times junctional escape beats are characterized by marked aberration, and then distinction from ventricular escapes may be difficult and is sometimes impossible. Neither does fusion in such a case clinch the diagnosis of ectopy since Kistin[3] years ago demonstrated that aberrantly conducted junctional beats could fuse with sinus impulses (see Chapter 19).

Ventricular Escape

Ventricular escape is diagnosed when the QRS of the rescuing beat is wide and bizarre. It may be diagnosed with some confidence if the complex manifests a shape characteristic of ventricular ectopy (Chapters 11 and 15); otherwise there is always the possibility that the escaping beat is junctional with type B aberration (p. 237). Figure 21.1 illustrates presumed ventricular escape resulting from each of the three mechanisms listed above.

Atrial Escape

Atrial escape beats are seldom heard of, although they are commonly seen, especially after ectopic atrial activity or retrograde conduction has suppressed the sinus node. They are recognized by the altered P wave that ends a cycle longer than the sinus cycle. Figure 21.3 illustrates atrial escape beats following an APB, following a ventricular extrasystole with retrograde conduction and interrupting a sinus pause.

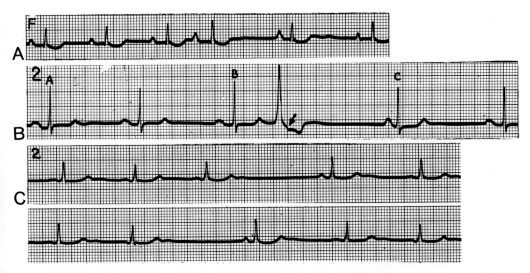

Figure 21.3. Atrial escape. (*A*) The fourth beat is an obvious APB followed by a more-than-fully-compensatory cycle. Note that the two returning beats are atrial escapes. (*B*) After three sinus beats, the VPB with retrograde conduction (*arrow*) discharges the sinus node ahead of schedule so that the returning beat, despite being an atrial escape, is also ahead of schedule; i.e., B − C = less than A − B. (*C*) In each strip, a sinus pause is interrupted by an atrial escape beat.

A-V Dissociation

A-V dissociation is a much-sinned-against term. The only way to avoid confusion is to define it simply as "the independent beating of atria and ventricles, *period*." It is important to think of it always as a symptom rather than a diagnosis—it is a secondary phenomenon due to one of four primary mechanisms, and one should no more use A-V dissociation as a diagnosis than jaundice or headache. A-V dissociation is not the same as A-V block (though they have sometimes been used interchangeably), but block is one of the *causes* of dissociation.

There are also three other things to remember about dissociation: (1) it is not the same thing as shifting pacemaker, though there is overlap between the two in the form of atrial fusion beats. (2) Regardless of the mechanism causing it, A-V dissociation deprives its host of his atrial "kick." (3) Fusion beats and A-V dissociation, though usually not thought of as close relatives, are virtually the same thing, both being due to two independently beating pacemakers—the only difference between the two being the site at which their impulses rendezvous. Each of these three items will be taken up in a later paragraph.

A-V dissociation is always secondary to one or more of four mechanisms (table 21.1): sinus bradycardia; blockade of primary impulses (incomplete or complete A-V block, incomplete S-A block); acceleration of subsidiary pacemakers (accelerated idionodal or idioventricular rhythm; junctional or ventricular tachycardia); or a pause producer (extrasystoles, ending of tachycardia).

The atria and ventricles may be dissociated momentarily, as in the ventricular extrasystole or ventricular escape without retrograde conduction; the dissociation may be temporary, as when it is due to sinus bradycardia or to accelerated idioventricular rhythm; or it may be permanent, as in complete heart block.

Table 21.1
Causes of A-V Dissociation

Mechanism	Diagnosis	Other Terms
1. Slowing of sinus node	Sinus bradycardia	
2. Block of sinus impulses	S-A block A-V block	Dissociation by "default"
3. Acceleration of subsidiary pacemaker	Accelerated idiojunctional or idioventricular rhythm Junctional or ventricular tachycardia	Dissociation by "usurpation"
4. Postextrasystolic pause permitting escape	Atrial, junctional or ventricular extrasystole	
5. Combinations of above		

A-V Dissociation due to Sinus Bradycardia

A perfectly healthy athlete may develop dissociation as a result of his physiological bradycardia. Figure 21.4 is from a Japanese wrestler in the pink of condition. He has a normal sinus bradycardia at a rate of about 45/min. But if his sinus rate slows to 44 or 43, his A-V junctional pacemaker is waiting in the wings ready to step on to the stage at 44/min. This is exactly what happens in the top strip: the P waves approach and flirt with the QRS complexes, never quite disappearing within them, until the sinus node slightly accelerates and recaptures the ventricles at the end of the bottom strip. Obviously, a pathological bradycardia, as in a patient with acute inferior infarction (fig. 21.5), can similarly produce dissociation.

When dissociation develops because the sinus rhythm slows, it is sometimes called dissociation *by default*. And when the rates of the two independent pacemakers are virtually identical, as in figure 21.4, French cardiologists coined the term "isorhythmic dissociation."[10]

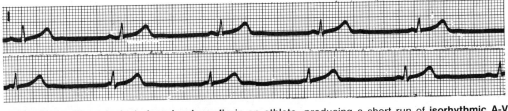

Figure 21.4. Physiological **sinus bradycardia** in an athlete, producing a short run of **isorhythmic A-V dissociation.**

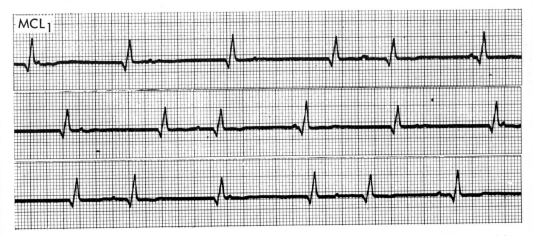

Figure 21.5. The strips are continuous. **Sinus bradycardia** with arrhythmia (rate, about 45/min) in a patient with myocardial infarction and RBBB. Because of the bradycardia, a **junctional escape** rhythm takes over at a slightly faster rate. The early beats seen in each strip—with prolonged P-R intervals when the complementary R-P is relatively short—are capture beats (ventricular captures).

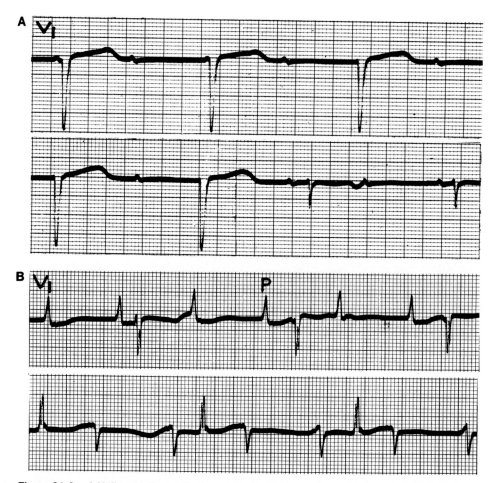

Figure 21.6.   **A-V dissociation** owing to A-V block. (*A*) Strips are continuous. **2:1 A-V block**, as evidenced at the end of the second strip, producing dissociation. The idioventricular pacemaker is escaping at a rate of 39/min, slightly faster than the conductible rate of 37/min. (*B*) Strips are continuous. **Complete A-V block** with resulting dissociation in a man of 32 with severe cardiomyopathy. The atrial rate is 78, and the ventricular (junctional) rate is 36/min.

A-V Dissociation due to Block

Incomplete S-A block, by reducing the number of sinus impulses, operates exactly like sinus bradycardia to produce dissociation. Complete S-A block obviously cannot produce dissociation from a sinus rhythm since there are no sinus impulses from which to dissociate. Only if an ectopic atrial or junctional pacemaker escapes, can dissociation develop.

Both incomplete and complete A-V block can result in A-V dissociation. If, because of incomplete A-V block, insufficient impulses reach the ventricle, then a lower pacemaker may take over if its escape rate is faster than the rate of *conductible* impulses. Figure 21.6A illustrates a short period of A-V dissociation resulting from incomplete (2:1 at this atrial rate) A-V block. This sort of dissociation is often mistakenly called complete block by those who do not fully understand the roles of the various determinants of conduction (atrial rate, ventricular escape rate, R-P interval, etc.). A-V dissociation due to genuine complete A-V block is shown in figure 21.6B.

A-V Dissociation due to Acceleration of Lower Pacemakers

Accelerated A-V junctional (idionodal) rhythm, by snatching control from the slower sinus pacemaker, can lead to dissociation as illustrated in figure 21.7. Clearly, a faster junctional rhythm, junctional tachycardia, can do the same thing with even greater ease. If retrograde conduction is facile, the junctional pacemaker may take charge of both atria and ventricles, and then there is no dissociation.

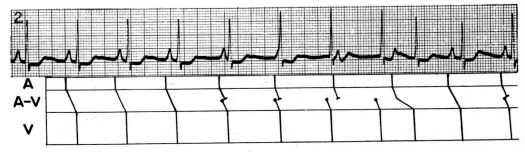

Figure 21.7.   A-V dissociation due to usurpation by an **accelerated idionodal rhythm** (rate, about 78/min) from a sinus rhythm with a perfectly normal rate of 74/min. From a girl of 12 years with digitalis intoxication shortly after mitral valvotomy.

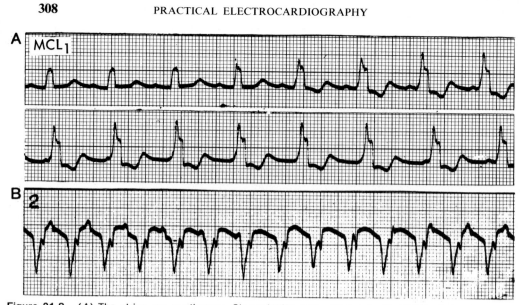

Figure 21.8. (*A*) The strips are continuous. Sinus rhythm (rate, 84/min) with RBBB gives place to a usurping **accelerated idioventricular rhythm** from the left ventricle at a slightly faster rate. Beats 4, 5 and 6 in the top strip are fusion beats. (*B*) A "double tachycardia"—**ventricular tachycardia** (rate, 150/min) dissociated from an **atrial tachycardia** (rate, 136/min).

Exactly the same things can be said of accelerated idioventricular rhythm and ventricular tachycardia. Figure 21.8 illustrates dissociation resulting from each of these rhythms. When a lower pacemaker produces dissociation by beating faster than the normal sinus thythm, it is sometimes known as dissociation by *usurpation.*

A-V Dissociation due to Pause Producers

Anything that produces a cycle longer than the cycle of a potential subsidiary pacemaker offers the opportunity for that pacemaker to escape and maintain its own rate and rhythm independent of the sinus rhythm. Thus the ventricular extrasystole, which often provides a fully compensatory cycle, and even the atrial extrasystole, which lengthens the ensuing cycle by the amount that the ectopic impulse suppresses the sinus node, may give a lurking junctional or ventricular pacemaker, with an intrinsic cycle length shorter than the pause provided, the opportunity it has been waiting for. In figure 21.9, a ventricular extrasystole is followed by a pause long enough to enable a junctional pacemaker to escape, and a short run of A-V dissociation follows.

A-V Dissociation due to Combinations of Above Mechanisms

Sometimes there is a conspiracy of two or more of the above mechanisms, each of which contributes something to the cause of dissociation. For example, in figure 21.10*A* the sinus rhythm slows to bradycrotic range, which enables an enhanced junctional pacemaker (accelerated junctional rhythm) to take over. Figure 21.10*B* shows a combination of A-V block with an accelerated junctional rhythm producing dissociation. Figure 21.10*C* shows the triple combine—all due to digitalis—of sinus bradycardia, some degree of A-V block and a junctional tachycardia all contributing to the A-V dissociation. Figure 21.10*D* shows the combined effect of a nonconducted atrial extrasystole and an accelerated idioventricular rhythm.

A-V DISSOCIATION, LIKE JAUNDICE, IS A SYMPTOM, NOT A DIAGNOSIS

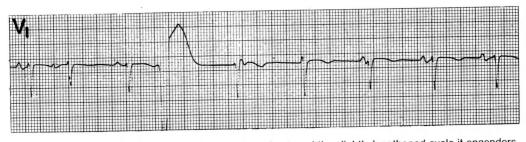

Figure 21.9. The second beat is an atrial premature beat, and the slightly lengthened cycle it engenders precipitates a ventricular extrasystole (rule of bigeminy). As a result of the lengthened postectopic cycle, an **accelerated junctional rhythm** escapes at a rate of 75/min, producing a four-beat run of A-V dissociation.

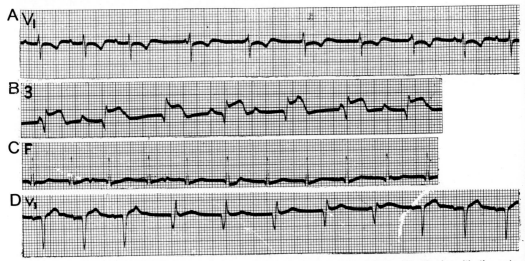

Figure 21.10. **A-V dissociation** due to combinations of factors. (*A*) **Sinus arrhythmia** with the rate dropping low enough (to about 58/min) so that an **accelerated junctional rhythm** takes over at 72 to 75/min. (*B*) **A-V block** of some unknown degree + **accelerated junctional rhythm**, in a patient with acute inferior infarction. (*C*) **Sinus bradycardia** + some degree of **A-V block** + **junctional tachycardia**, in a patient with digitalis intoxication. (*D*) A **nonconducted atrial premature beat** producing a long enough cycle for an **accelerated idioventricular rhythm** to take over at a rate of 80/min for 5 beats.

Capture(d) Beats

Since many examples of A-V dissociation occur without benefit of A-V block, in such cases, whenever the atrial impulse arrives at the A-V junction at a time when it is not refractory, the impulse is conducted to the ventricles. When a conducted beat interrupts or follows a period of dissociation, it is called a "capture(d) beat." If, as is usually the case, the atrial impulse captures the ventricles, it is called ventricular capture; if, as occasionally happens, an independent ectopic ventricular rhythm sends an impulse back to activate the atria, it is called atrial capture. I emphasize this point because the incorrect epithet is sometimes seen in print; e.g., ventricular capture (when the sinus impulse is capturing the ventricles) is miscalled sinus capture.

Capture beats are recognized by the preceding P wave and the fact that they end a cycle shorter than the dominant cycle, i.e., they are premature; usually they occur singly (fig. 21.11*B*) but sometimes they are seen in pairs (fig. 21.11*A*). If the ventricles are under junctional control, the capture beat has the same configuration as the independent junctional beats (fig. 21.7). The capture

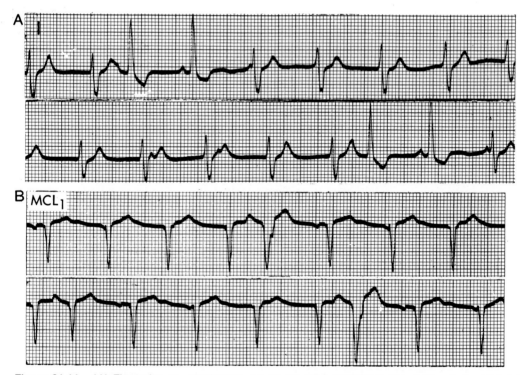

Figure 21.11. (*A*) The strips are continuous. An **accelerated idioventricular rhythm** (rate, 80/min) dissociated from sinus rhythm (rate, 76/min). Paired capture beats are seen in each strip. (*B*) The strips are continuous. An **accelerated junctional rhythm** (rate, 84/min) dissociated from a slightly slower sinus rhythm. One ventricular capture in each strip develops LBBB aberration because of its prematurity.

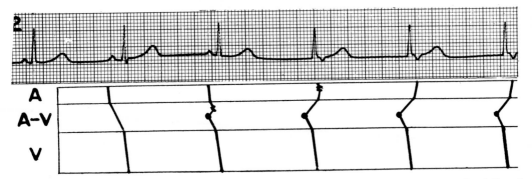

Figure 21.12. An orderly march from sinus rhythm to A-V junctional rhythm via dissociation (beat 3) and atrial fusion (beat 4).

beat will be different from the beats of the independent rhythm if the independent rhythm is ectopic ventricular (fig. 21.11*A*) or if, with a junctional rhythm, the capture beat develops aberration because of its prematurity (fig. 21.11*B*).

A-V Dissociation versus Fusion

Though seldom thought of in the same context, dissociation and fusion have identical causes and are really different expressions of the same thing. Required are two independent pacemakers, e.g., the sinus node and an ectopic ventricular pacemaker as in figure 21.8*A*, each more or less simultaneously delivering its impulse. If the timing is such that the two impulses meet in the A-V junction, the result is A-V dissociation; if the sinus impulse fires ahead of the ectopic ventricular center, they will meet in the ventricular muscle and produce ventricular fusion; if the ventricular center discharges its impulse before the sinus discharge, the ventricular impulse may reach the atrium before the sinus impulse has entirely activated the atrial myocardium, and then an atrial fusion beat results. So the only difference between the three phenomena is the rendezvous they choose for their collision. In fact, a fusion beat can be considered in terms of partial dissociation: an atrial fusion is dissociation between part-of-the-atria and the-rest-of-the-atria-and-the-ventricles; and a ventricular fusion beat is dissociation between part-of-the-ventricles and the-rest-of-the-ventricles-and-the-atria.

Next, the question is often asked of a tracing such as that seen in figure 21.7: "The pacemaker changes from sinus to A-V junction—why isn't that a shifting pacemaker?" The answer is: shifting or wandering pacemaker is used only when the pacemaker for the entire heart changes (see fig. 20.5). In figure 21.7 the ventricles' pacemaker indeed changes from sinus node to A-V junction, but the atria remain independently under sinus control, and so the term does not apply. On the other hand, figure 21.12 presents a genuine shifting pacemaker—control of both atria and ventricles shifts from sinus node to A-V junction.

But there is an overlap between the two in the shape of atrial fusion. Above, I was at pains to point out that fusion was tantamount to partial dissociation.

And in shifting pacemaker there is often intervening atrial fusion between the full-blown sinus control and junctional control; thus partial dissociation (fusion) forms a bridge between the two shifting rhythms, and therefore the terms "dissociation" and "shifting pacemaker" are certainly not mutually exclusive.

"Interference"

The terminology of this subject has been unnecessarily confused. The use of the term A-V dissociation as though it were a *diagnosis* is the first point of confusion. The second is in the application of the term interference. Sometimes it refers to the fact that one pacemaker interferes with the rhythm of a second pacemaker. This was the sense implied by Mobitz when he originally introduced the term **interference-dissociation**, and by Scherf when he later modified the term to **dissociation with interference.** Other authorities[2] ignore this use of the term and employ it in an entirely different sense, though a sense no less correct in the terminology of electrophysics. Their "interference" refers to the meeting of two opposing impulses with resulting extinction of both; such interference is seen in fusion beats (p. 277 ff.) and obviously must occur in A-V dissociation as the independent atrial and ventricular impulses meet, presumably within the A-V junction, and extinguish each other. Thus the "interference" (capture) beat of the first school is the only beat that shows no "interference" of the second type! This paradox is naturally perplexing to the uninitiated, and as neither school ever refers to the perfectly acceptable usage of the other, the confusion is further confounded. Until the terminology of both schools has been grasped, much confusion can be avoided by eschewing the term interference and referring to the conducted beats as capture beats or ventricular captures. The term interference-dissociation has been appropriately shelved as a "functional misnomer and superfluous term."[1]

Conclusion

A-V dissociation is an education in the arrhythmias. We have seen that it can be caused by sinus bradycardia; by accelerated junctional rhythm and junctional tachycardia; by accelerated idioventricular rhythm and ventricular tachycardia; by incomplete S-A block and incomplete and complete A-V block; and by the pause producers—the extrasystoles and the sign-off of any ectopic tachycardia. Moreover, one cannot delve deeply into the mechanisms of dissociation or witness many examples of it without encountering and studying related phenomena like escape beats and rhythms, including A-V junctional rhythm and idioventricular rhythm; atrial and ventricular fusion; and reciprocal beats and rhythm. And what else is there?

The whole subject of A-V dissociation has been fully and repeatedly reviewed[4, 5, 8, 9] and readers who wish to pursue its ramifications and entanglements further are referred to these articles.

REFERENCES

1. Hecht, H. H., et al.: Atrioventricular and intraventricular conduction: revised nomenclature and concepts. Am. J. Cardiol. 1973: **31,** 232.
2. Katz, L. N., and Pick, A.: *Clinical Electrocardiography. The Arrhythmias.* Lea & Febiger, Philadelphia, 1956.
3. Kistin, A. D.: Problems in the differentiation of ventricular arrhythmia from supraventricular arrhythmia with abnormal QRS Prog. Cardiovasc. Dis. 1966: **9,** 1.
4. Mariott, H. J. L., et al.: A-V dissociation: a re-appraisal. Am. J. Cardiol. 1958: **2,** 586.
5. Menendez, M. M., and Marriott, H. J. L.: A-V dissociation revisited. Prog. Cardiovasc. Dis. 1966: **8,** 522.
6. Pick, A.: Aberrant ventricular conduction of escaped beats. Preferential and accessory pathways in the A-V junction. Circulation 1956: **13,** 702.
7. Pick, A., and Dominguez, P.: Nonparoxysmal A-V nodal tachycardia. Circulation 1957: **16,** 1022.
8. Pick, A.: A-V dissociation. A proposal for a comprehensive classification and consistent terminology. Am. Heart J. 1963: **66,** 147.
9. Schott, A.: Atrioventricular dissociation with and without interference. Prog. Cardiovasc. Dis. 1959: **2,** 444.
10. Schubart, A. F., et al.: Isorhythmic dissociation: atrioventricular dissociation with synchronization. Am. J. Med. 1958: **24,** 209.

Review Tracings

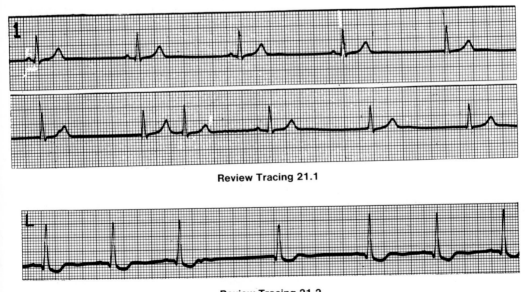

Review Tracing 21.1

Review Tracing 21.2

For interpretation, see page 483

Review Tracing

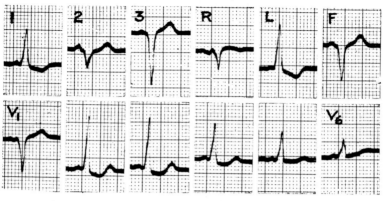

Review Tracing 21.3

For interpretation, see page 483

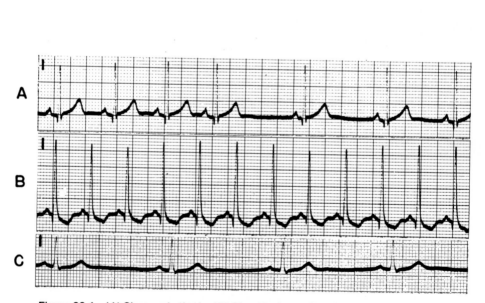

Figure 22.1   (A) Sinus arrhythmia. (B) Sinus tachycardia. (C) Sinus bradycardia.

22

Sinus Rhythms, the Sick Sinus and Intra-Atrial Block

Sinus Rhythms

The normal rate of impulse formation by the sinus node is generally accepted as 60 to 100/min. Above 100 the rhythm is called **sinus tachycardia** (fig. 22.1*B*); below 60, **sinus bradycardia** (fig. 22.1*C*). Sinus tachycardia results from exercise, eating, emotion, pain, hemorrhage, shock, fever, thyrotoxicosis and infections; it is a common reaction to heart disease, including myocardial infarction and heart failure per se, and may be caused by many drugs, such as caffeine, nicotine, adrenaline, atropine, amyl nitrite and quinidine. Sinus bradycardia is seen as a normal variation, especially in well-trained athletes, whose heart rates may be in the thirties at rest—and often not much more with moderate exertion; it is a physiological reaction to sleep, fright, carotid sinus massage or ocular pressure, and it may also result from disease processes, such as obstructive jaundice (effect of bile salts on sinus node), sliding hiatal hernia,[12] glaucoma (oculocardiac reflex), carotid sinus sensitivity and increased intracranial pressure; it is often seen in convalescence and as a result of digitalis therapy. It may be the first, or only, manifestation of the so-called "sick sinus syndrome" (see below). Sinus bradycardia is associated with a significant percentage of acute inferior wall infarctions; provided it is not severe enough to cause hemodynamic deterioration, it seems to be a favorable prognostic sign.[5, 14]

When the sinus node forms impulses irregularly, we have **sinus arrhythmia** (fig. 22.1*A*). This is of two varieties: one that waxes and wanes with the phases of respiration, the heart accelerating with inspiration and slowing with expiration; and a less common type in which the changes of rate bear no relationship to the phases of respiration. Sinus arrhythmia is a perfectly normal finding, but it may on occasion produce such marked irregularity that it can be confused clinically with other more important arrhythmias.

315

When the heart actually drops a beat, it means either that the S-A node has failed to release the impulse (S-A block) or, much more likely, that the impulse after traversing the atria has been unable to get through the A-V conducting tissues (A-V block). Both these types of block may be recognized in any lead in which P waves are clearly formed.

S-A Block

The hallmark of S-A block is a missing P wave, but there are no less than four reasons why P waves may be absent: (1) failure of the sinus node to form impulses (generator failure); (2) failure of the impulse to emerge from the sinus node (exit block); (3) failure of the emerging impulse to activate the atria (inadequate stimulus); and (4) failure of the atria to respond to the impulse (atrial paralysis). Strictly speaking, only the second of these is true S-A block, but it is often impossible to determine which mechanism is responsible for the missing P wave(s) and S-A "block" is too often loosely and erroneously diagnosed. It should be diagnosed only when a mathematical relationship between the longer and shorter sinus cycles can be demonstrated; or when the sinus cycles show the characteristic sequence of a Wenckebach period (see p. 325).

S-A block may be incomplete or complete:

1. **Incomplete S-A block** consists in the more or less infrequent failure of the impulse to emerge from the S-A node, with the result that occasional beats are completely dropped. This is recognized in the tracing by the occasional absence of the entire P-QRS-T sequence (figs. 22.2 and 22.3) and its type and "degree" are recognized by establishing a mathematical relationship between the longer and shorter atrial (P-P) cycles. When no such relationship can be established, **sinus pause** is a useful and appropriate term for the abnormally long cycle, qualified by a statement of its duration, e.g., "a 4.5 second sinus pause."

2. **Complete S-A block** exists when no impulses emerge from the S-A node and therefore no P waves are inscribed. Other terms that are sometimes applied when P waves are absent are: sinus arrest, sinus or atrial standstill and atrial paralysis. In general, these are better avoided because they are often loosely used and only vaguely defined. Atrial paralysis is of course the appropriate

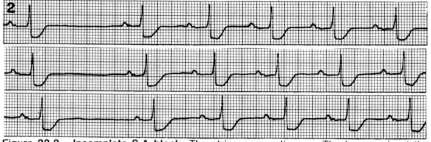

Figure 22.2.   Incomplete S-A block. The strips are continuous. The long cycle at the beginning of each strip is due to a dropped sinus beat—an entire P-QRS-T sequence is missing.

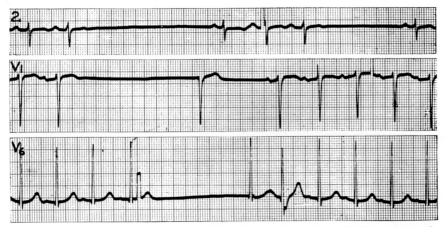

Figure 22.3. Runs of sinus rhythm at a rate of about 100 are punctuated by periods of **S-A block.** Two such periods occur in lead 2. In V₁ the period of atrial standstill is interrupted by an **A-V junctional escape** beat. In V₆ a similar pause is terminated by an escape beat which is followed by a run of sinus rhythm, the first beat of which shows **ventricular aberration** of RBBB form.

term when potassium intoxication is known to be responsible for disappearance of the P waves.

In the absence of S-A leadership, one of two things can happen: either (a) a lower pacemaker, usually in the A-V junction but sometimes in the ventricles, comes to the rescue and takes over the job of pacemaking, or (b) asystole persists and the patient dies. If (a) occurs and the ventricles proceed to beat independently, **junctional** or **ventricular escape** is said to have occurred and the heart's rhythm is called **idiojunctional** or **idioventricular**. Complete S-A block is thus one of the mechanisms leading to the development of idioventricular rhythm.

Complete S-A block is recognized in the electrocardiogram by the complete absence of the entire P-QRS-T sequence, i.e., by a straight and unadorned baseline; this continues until, if the patient is fortunate, independent QRST complexes appear at a slow rate while P waves remain absent.

Salient Features of S-A Block

1. *Incomplete: occasional absence of P-QRS-T sequence*
2. *Complete:*
   a. *P waves absent*
   b. *QRST sequence at slow rate*
   c. *QRS interval normal or prolonged, depending on site of ventricular pacemaker*

S-A block is rather rare, but it can be produced by a wide variety of causes: *drugs,* such as digitalis, quinidine and salicylates; *diseases,* such as coronary disease and acute infections; *physiological* disturbances, such as carotid sinus sensitivity and increased vagal tone.

Sick Sinus Syndrome

This catchy alliterative title was first used to characterize the situation when the sinus node failed to wake up following cardioversion of atrial fibrillation.[11] Most authorities now include any form of sinus nodal depression including marked sinus bradycardia, prolonged sinus pauses (sinus arrest), and sinoatrial block.[7] It is particularly applied to the **tachycardia-bradycardia syndrome**[13]— although its use is this context is inappropriate[9]—in which bursts of an atrial tachyarrhythmia, often atrial fibrillation, alternate with prolonged periods of sinus nodal and junctional inertia (fig. 22.4). Apart from these florid manifestations, the "syndrome" may initially present as paroxysmal atrial fibrillation; as failure of the sinus rhythm to accelerate appropriately in response to fever or exercise; or as "lone" atrial fibrillation.

Although the sick sinus predominantly affects the elderly, no age is immune and the disease has been recognized as early as the first day of life.[4]

Temporary and reversible manifestations of the syndrome can be caused by digitalis, quinidine, beta-blockers, or aerosol propellants. The chronic progressive syndrome is particularly associated with ischemic disease but may result from inflammatory diseases, cardiomyopathy, especially amyloidosis,[6] collagen disease, metastatic disease, surgical injury, etc. In many cases no cause is evident and they are classified as idiopathic; in these it may be part of a sclerodegenerative process also affecting the lower reaches of the cardiac conduction system, especially the A-V node (binodal disease).

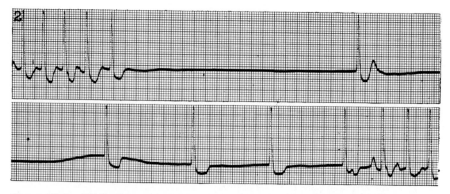

Figure 22.4. "**Sick sinus syndrome,**" better called **tachycardia-bradycardia** ("tachy-brady") syndrome. Irregular atrial tachycardia followed by a prolonged sinus pause punctuated by all too few, badly needed A-V escape beats.

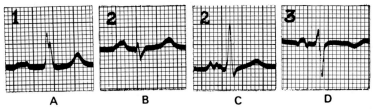

Figure 22.5. Intra-atrial block. Four samples from four different patients. *A* and *B* show widening of P wave without significant notching; *C* and *D* show marked notching with wide peak interval (more than 0.04 sec).

The diagnosis can usually be made from the standard ECG or a 24-hour Holter recording, always of course carefully correlated with the clinical history. In some cases additional more sophisticated tests may be required, of which the best is the sinus node recovery time after rapid atrial pacing.[3, 8]

Sinus node disorders probably account for half the permanent pacemakers implanted in the United States today.[10]

Intra-atrial Block

If the impulse takes longer than normal to activate the atria, i.e., if the P wave is widened, intra-atrial block is said to be present. The upper normal limit of P-wave duration is not universally agreed upon, but the most satisfactory limit is probably 0.11 sec. The criterion, therefore, for diagnosing intra-atrial block is a P wave with a duration of 0.12 sec or more (fig. 22.5). Further evidence of block is to be found in deep notching of the P wave with a distance between peaks ("peak interval") of more than 0.04 sec (fig. 22.5C).

Intra-atrial block is not uncommon and is most often seen in coronary disease, mitral disease and in association with left ventricular hypertrophy.[2] It probably often represents left atrial enlargement rather than true block.

REFERENCES

1. Bower, P. J.: Sick sinus syndrome. Arch. Intern. Med. 1978: **138**, 133.
2. Bradley, S. M., and Marriott, H. J. L.: Intra-atrial block. Circulation 1956: **14**, 1073.
3. Chung, E. K. : Sick sinus syndrome; current views. Mod. Concepts Cardiovasc. Dis. 1980: **49**, 61 and 67.
4. Ector, H., et al.: Sick sinus syndrome in childhood. Br. Heart J. 1980: **44**, 684.
5. Epstein, S. E., et al: The early phase of acute myocardial infarction; pharmacologic aspects of therapy. Ann. Intern. Med. 1973: **78**, 918.
6. Evans, R., and Shaw, D. B.: Pathological studies in sinoatrial disorder (sick sinus syndrome). Br. Heart J. 1977: **39**, 778.
7. Ferrer, M. I.: *The Sick Sinus Syndrome.* Futura Publishing, Mt. Kisco, N.Y., 1974.
8. Gann, D., et al.: Electrophysiologic evaluation of elderly patients with sinus bradycardia. Ann. Intern. Med. 1979: **90**, 24.
9. Kaplan, B. M., et al.: Tachycardia-bradycardia syndrome (so-called "sick sinus syndrome"). Am. J. Cardiol. 1973: **31**, 497.
10. Kaplan, B. M.: Editorial: Sick sinus syndrome. Arch. Intern. Med. 1978: **138**, 28.
11. Lown, B.: Electrical reversion of atrial fibrillation. Br. Heart J. 1967: **29**, 469.

12. Marks, P., and Thurston, J. G. B.: Sinus bradycardia with hiatus hernia. Am. Heart J. 1977: **93,** 30.
13. Moss, A. J., and Davis, R. J.: Brady-tachy syndrome. Prog. Cardiovasc. Dis. 1974: **16,** 439.
14. Norris, R. M., et al.: Sinus rate in acute myocardial infarction. Br. Heart J. 1972: **34,** 901.
15. Shaw, D. B., et al.: Survival in sinoatrial disorder (sick sinus syndrome). Br. Med. J. 1980: **1,** 139.

Review Tracing

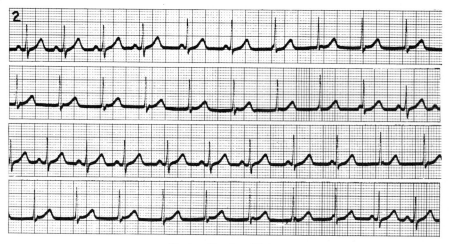

Review Tracing 22.1

For interpretation, see page 483

Review Tracings

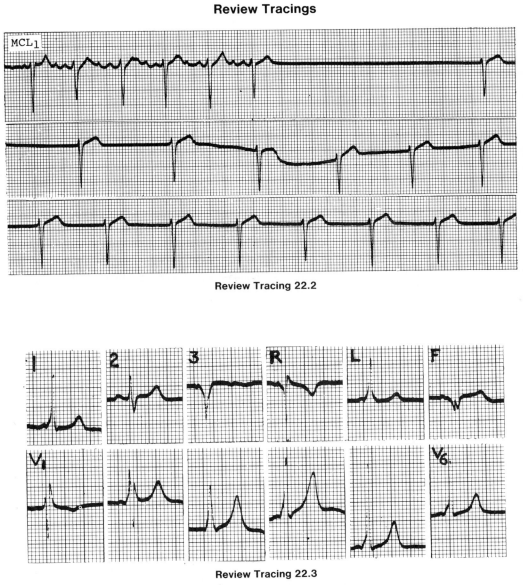

Review Tracing 22.2

Review Tracing 22.3

For interpretation, see page 483

Atrioventricular Block: Conventional Approach

To do justice to this important and much mishandled subject, it will be expedient to divide this account into two parts: This chapter treats the subject in time-honored, conventional terms and, without introducing inaccuracies, avoids the inconsistencies and misconceptions that have plagued the diagnostic criteria for A-V block and which are tackled in the following chapter.

It is conventional to divide atrioventricular (A-V) block into three grades or "degrees." First and second degree block are incomplete whereas third degree is synonymous with complete block.

"First Degree" A-V Block

The "normal" P-R interval measures between 0.12 and 0.20 sec. First "degree" A-V block is generally defined as a prolongation of A-V conduction time (P-R interval) to 0.21 sec or more. In the analysis of records from supposedly normal young people, the incidence of a prolonged P-R interval is between 0.5%[7] and 1.6%.[26] Whether such otherwise normal subjects should be considered to have a "degree" of block is a moot point. Figure 23.1 illustrates two examples of first degree block: the first minor, with a P-R of 0.24 sec; the second shows a P-R lengthening of a higher order.

"Second Degree" A-V Block

By definition, second degree block is present when one or more, but not all, atrial impulses fail to reach the ventricles *because of impaired conduction*. Such failure may occur at any level of the ventricular conduction system.

Wenckebach, in Vienna in 1899, described the dropped beat after progressive lengthening of the previous conduction times; and then in 1906, he in Austria and Hay in Scotland described a second form of block in which the conduction time remained constant before the beat was unexpectedly dropped. Both of these astute observers made their discoveries without benefit of electrocardiograph by studying the waves in the jugular pulse and noting the interval between the "a" and "c" waves as a measure of A-V conduction time. It

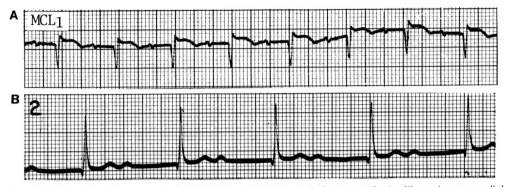

Figure 23.1. Two examples of **first degree A-V block**. *A* is from a patient with acute myocardial infarction and minor P-R prolongation to 0.24 sec. *B* shows marked prolongation to 0.57 to 0.60 sec.

remained for Mobitz in 1924, equipped with electrocardiograph, to suggest that the two forms of block be called, respectively, type I and type II. Classical examples of type I are presented in figures 23.2 and 23.7 and of type II in figure 23.10.

And so it is perfectly correct to refer to these two forms of A-V block as Mobitz type I and Mobitz type II; or, as is less commonly done,[11] Wenckebach type I and Wenckebach type II. What is historically incorrect—a mistake made in many places including the 4th edition of this text—is to call type I "Wenckebach-type" block and type II "Mobitz-type" block. It seems far best to call them simply type I and type II and drop the eponyms except in reference to the "Wenckebach phenomenon" or "Wenckebach period" to describe the distinctive features of progressive delay in conduction culminating in a "dropped beat."

Type I A-V Block

Type I A-V block is relatively benign. The block usually occurs in the A-V node[4, 17] and is usually associated with acute reversible conditions, such as acute inferior myocardial infarction, rheumatic fever, digitalis or propranolol effect. Generally a transient disturbance, it seldom progresses to complete A-V block, although of one series of 16 children manifesting Wenckebach periods, 7 went on to complete block.[28] Chronic type I second degree A-V block may be found in many conditions including chronic ischemic heart disease, aortic valve disease, mitral valve prolapse, atrial septal defect, amyloidosis, Reiter's syndrome, and mesothelioma of the A-V node. In healthy trained athletes, the incidence of both "first" and "second degree" block is surprisingly high.[24, 27] In one series, of 35 endurance athletes, prolongation of the P-R interval was found in 13 (37%) compared with a 15% incidence in as many controls; and "second degree" block was found in 8 (23%) of the athletes compared with 6% in the control subjects.

The most classical form of type I block is the **Wenckebach phenomenon** in which the P-R interval may begin within normal limits but is usually somewhat prolonged; then with each successive beat the P-R interval gradually lengthens until finally an impulse fails to reach the ventricles and a beat is dropped. Following the dropped beat the P-R interval reverts to normal, or near normal, and the sequence is repeated. At times the P-R interval may stretch to surprising lengths, rarely even to 0.80 or 0.90 sec; intervals of 0.50 or 0.60 are not uncommon.

Progressive lengthening of the P-R interval occurs because each successive beat arrives earlier and earlier in the relative refractory period of the A-V node and therefore takes longer and longer to penetrate it and reach the ventricles. In tachycardias it may be a physiological mechanism, but at normal rates it implies definite impairment of A-V conduction although it is occasionally reported in apparently normal hearts.[2] The progressive lengthening usually follows a predictable pattern: the maximal increment of one P-R over its predecessor develops between the first and second cycles and in subsequent cycles the increment is less and less. This in turn leaves its mark on the rhythm of the ventricles: following the pause of the dropped beat, the R-R intervals tend to shorten (fig. 23.2); and the long cycle (containing the dropped beat) is less than two of the shorter cycles—because it contains the shortest P-R interval. Recognition of this pattern enables one to spot the phenomenon in action even when there are no P-R intervals available to measure, as when there is a Wenckebach out of the sinus node (see p. 335).

"Footprints" of the Wenckebach

1. Small groups of beats, especially pairs, trios, etc.
2. Progressive shortening of the cycle of the receiving chambers (ventricles or atria).
3. The longest cycle (of the dropped beat) less than twice the shortest cycle.

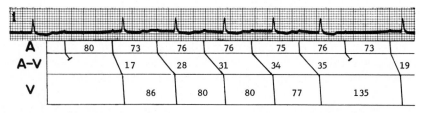

Figure 23.2.   Wenckebach phenomenon. Figures indicate intervals in hundredths of a second. The P-R intervals progressively lengthen until a beat is dropped. Note that the biggest increment (11) is in the second P-R (28) over the first (17) and that there is a tendency for the increments to become less and less (11-3-3-1). The effect of this is to cause progressive shortening of the ventricular cycles (86-80-80-77).

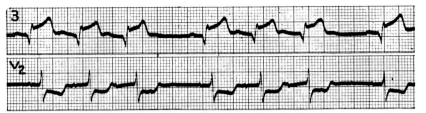

Figure 23.3. Sinus tachycardia with 4:3 **Wenckebach periods** which result in the beats being grouped in threes (trigeminy).

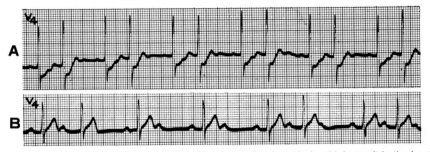

Figure 23.4. (*a*) Sinus tachycardia with 3:2 **Wenckebach periods** which result in the beats being grouped in pairs (bigeminy). B. Sinus tachycardia with 3:2 **Wenckebach periods** separated by an intervening run of 2:1 A-V block.

"Footprints" of the Wenckebach. The characteristic cycle-sequences that result from this form of conduction can be figuratively referred to as the "footprints" of the Wenckebach. These are three in number: (1) the beats tend to cluster in small groups and particularly in pairs (this is because 3:2 Wenckebachs are more common than 4:3, which in turn are more common than 5:4, and so on). (2) In each group of beats, the first cycle is longer than the second cycle, and indeed, there is a tendency for progressive shortening to occur in succeeding cycles. At first, this seems like a paradox—that as the P-R lengthens, the ventricular cycle shortens—but it will become clear later with a look at the diagram in figure 23.6. (3) The longest cycle—that of the dropped beat—is less than twice the shortest cycle.

The clue that often alerts one to an underlying Wenckebach mechanism, especially during tachycardia, is the presence of pairs or small groups of beats (figs. 23.3 and 23.4*A*); this is thanks to the common occurrence of short (3:2, 4:3, etc.) Wenckebach periods, which also often alternate with 2:1 conduction (fig. 23.4*B*).

****ALL THAT'S BIGEMINAL ISN'T EXTRASYSTOLIC****

When you look at figure 23.5, you immediately see the "footprints," and although P waves and therefore P-R intervals are obscure, you know that there is a Wenckebach at work: the beats are grouped in pairs and trios; in three out of the four trios, the first cycle is longer than the second cycle; and the longest cycles separating the groups are less than twice the shortest cycles. Since the first beat of each group is preceded by a P wave at a constant, prolonged P-R interval, you know that it is an A-V Wenckebach, even though you cannot see the succeeding P-R intervals.

The reason for the second and third "footprints" becomes apparent with a little study of figure 23.6. This is an idealized diagram of an A-V Wenckebach, highlighting the classical features of its structure; namely, (1) the largest increase in the P-R is in the second over the first—it jumps from 22 to 22 + 12 = 34 (all intervals are expressed in hundredths of a second); after that, the increase in each P-R over its predecessor is progressively smaller. Thus, although the P-R gets longer and longer, it is lengthening by less and less. Since the R-R (ventricular) cycle is composed of the sinus cycle plus the increment of the P-R and the increment is shrinking, the R-R interval will correspondingly shrink (92 to 85 to 83).

When it comes to the double cycle of the dropped beat, 140 is less than twice the shortest cycle (83); and this is because this double cycle, instead of containing an increment, contains a P-R decrement—the P-R drops from 42 to 22, a decrease of 20. The long cycle, therefore, equals 80 + 80 − 20 = 140.

Now let us look at an actual Wenckebach and compare its structure with the idealized one in figure 23.6. In figure 23.7, the sinus cycle is a constant 75 to 76; the second P-R jumps by 10 over the first, from 21 to 31, and the third then increases by only 4 to 35. RESULT: the ventricular cycle shortens from 85 (75 + 10) to 79 (75 + 4). And when it comes to dropping a beat, the P-R shrinks back toward normal and becomes only 23; so the cycle of the dropped beat is 76 + 75 = 151 minus the *decrement* (35 − 23 = 12), and 151 − 12 = 139.

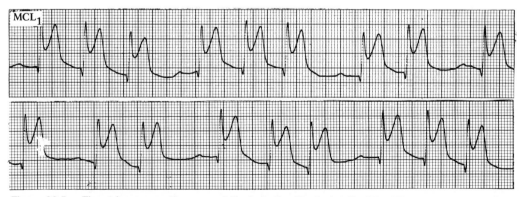

Figure 23.5.   The strips are continuous and illustrate the **"footprints" of the Wenckebach** in a patient with an **acute anteroseptal infarction**. The grouping of beats in pairs and trios and the cycle sequences (see text) identify the presence of Wenckebach-type conduction.

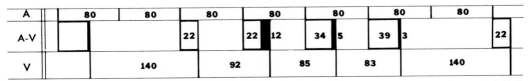

A	80	80	80	80	80	80	80	
A-V		22	22	12	34	5	39	3	22
V	140		92		85		83	140

Figure 23.6. Idealized schema of an A-V Wenckebach—measurements are in hundredths of a second. Note the following: even the first P-R is prolonged (22); the largest P-R increment is in the second P-R (34) over the first (22); the cycles of the receiving chambers (ventricles) progressively shorten; and the cycle of the dropped beat (140) is less than twice the shortest cycle (83).

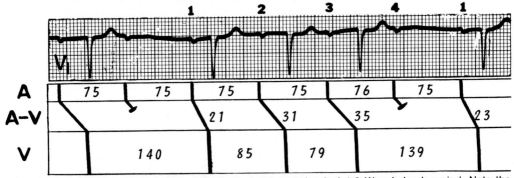

A	75	75	75	75	76	75
A-V			21	31	35	23
V	140		85	79	139	

Figure 23.7. **Type I second degree A-V block** showing a classical 4:3 Wenckebach period. Note the following typical features: (*1*) even the shortest P-R is longer than normal; (*2*) the QRS is of normal duration; (*3*) the larger P-R increment is in the second (31) over the first (21); (*4*) the first cycle (85) in the group of three beats is longer than the second (79); and (*5*) the longest cycle (139) is less than twice the shortest (79).

Those then are the features of a classical Wenckebach period; but do not expect all of them to be classical or you will be disappointed. In fact the majority of all Wenckebach periods contain some deviation from the classical structure[5, 18]; but, if you are conversant with the typical features and with the likely deviations from them, virtually all Wenckebachs are readily recognized. Likely divergences from the "norm" include the following: the first increment may not be the largest; every P-R may not lengthen over the previous one; the last increment may be larger than the preceding one; and the last increment may be the largest.[5]

R-P/P-R Reciprocity. I have indicated that the earlier the impulse arrives in the A-V node's refractory period, the longer it takes to get through to the ventricles; and the later it arrives, the less time it takes. Although we cannot tell from the surface ECG when the impulse reaches the junction, we have a rough but excellent guide in the relationship of the P wave to the preceding QRS complex—the R-P interval, measured from the beginning of the QRS to the beginning of the ensuing P wave. And if you look at the tracings of typical Wenckebachs (figs. 23.2 and 23.7) you can easily see that the P-R progressively lengthens *as the P wave retreats toward the preceding QRS.* This is diagrammatically expressed in figure 23.8, and we can articulate this relationship as

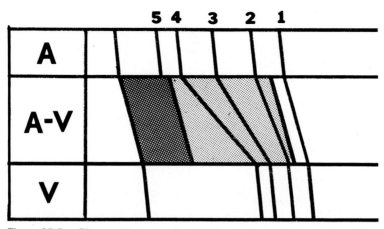

Figure 23.8.   Diagram illustrating the effect on A-V conduction as successive atrial impulses (1–5) arrive in the A-V junction earlier and earlier in its refractory period. *Dark stippling* = absolute refractory period; *light stippling* = relative refractory period.

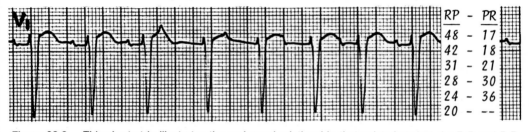

RP	–	PR
48	–	17
42	–	18
31	–	21
28	–	30
24	–	36
20	–	––

Figure 23.9.   This short strip illustrates the reciprocal relationship that exists between the R-P and P-R intervals in subjects with type I conduction delay (see text).

"R-P/P-R reciprocity"; and we can state that the hallmark of type I block in the surface tracing is "R-P dependent P-R intervals." This dependence is elegantly demonstrated in figure 23.9, where there are P-R intervals ranging from a normal 0.17 sec to more than twice that length, and the variation is secondary to the varying R-P interval. After three sinus beats that are normally conducted with a P-R of 0.17 sec, there is a single atrial premature beat that either is conducted with a much prolonged P-R interval of about 0.49 sec or is not conducted and permits an accelerated junctional pacemaker to escape at a cycle length of 0.67 sec. The next, slightly delayed sinus P wave lands on the T wave of this beat and is conducted with a P-R of 0.36 (R-P/P-R = 24/36). The next three sinus P waves land at slightly but progressively longer R-P intervals and are consequently conducted with slightly but progressively shorter P-R intervals (see inset table). In the last four beats, you see exactly what happens in a Wenckebach period but in reverse—the P-R intervals get shorter and shorter because the R-P gets longer and longer; whereas in the Wenckebach period, the P-R intervals get longer and longer because the R-P intervals get shorter and shorter. In each case, the dependence of the P-R on its antecedent R-P is evident.

Type II A-V Block

This much less common form of second degree block is also much more serious. It is usually associated with a BBB pattern and the site of the block is usually below the bundle of His; i.e., in the presence of BBB, the dropped beats are due to intermittent block in the other bundle branch.[4, 17] Type II block is therefore usually a form of bilateral BBB and progresses to complete A-V block with Adams-Stokes seizures. It is recognized when at least two regular and *consecutive* atrial impulses are conducted with the same P-R interval before the dropped beat (fig. 23.10). In this form of block, in contrast with type I block, the P-R interval is independent of its associated R-P. In figure 23.10 the P-R labelled "*1*", after a long R-P, is exactly the same (0.18 sec) as is the P-R (labelled "*2*") that complements a much shorter R-P. Figure 23.11*A* is another

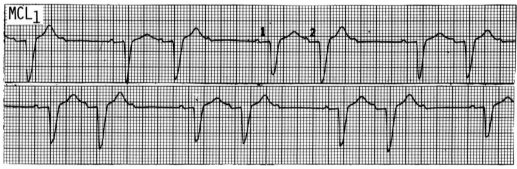

Figure 23.10.   The strips are continuous and show **type II second degree A-V block** with 3:2 conduction. Note the following typical features: (*1*) the P-R interval is constant and of normal duration (0.18 sec); and (*2*) **LBBB** is present.

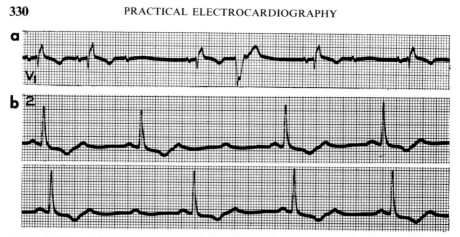

Figure 23.11. (a) **Second degree A-V block, type II.** Two consecutive P-R intervals are unchanged before the dropped beat. The conducted beats have a normal P-R interval and show RBBB; the 4th beat is a right ventricular premature beat. (B) **High grade A-V block.** Sinus rhythm with 2:1 and 3:1 A-V block.

example of type II block; note that the P-R remains unchanged (and normal) despite longer and shorter R-P intervals, i.e., there is no R-P/P-R reciprocity.

High Grade (or Advanced) Second Degree A-V Block

High grade block may be diagnosed when, at *reasonable atrial rates* (not, for example, at a frantic 300/min, as in atrial flutter), two or more consecutive atrial impulses fail to be conducted *because of the block itself*—and not because of interference by an escaping subsidiary pacemaker. In figure 23.11*B*, on two occasions there are two consecutive atrial impulses that fail to reach the ventricles; and that failure is in the presence of a normal atrial rate (about 85) and is entirely due to the block itself since there is no intruding escape rhythm. Another example of high grade block is illustrated in figure 23.12.

Ideal Criteria for Diagnosing High Grade Block

1. Two, or more than two, consecutive atrial impulses blocked.
2. A reasonable atrial rate (?under 135/min).
3. No escaping pacemaker preventing conduction.

Complete ("Third Degree") A-V Block

When *no* impulses can pass the A-V barrier, complete A-V block has developed. Bilateral bundle-branch block, or trifascicular block, rather than blockade at the A-V node or in the main bundle, is usually the cause of complete A-V block.[13, 14, 21, 23] Lev's and Lenegre's diseases, by producing bilateral bundle-branch block, are probably the commonest causes of complete "A-V" block.

As with the less common complete S-A block, two possibilities now exist: Either the ventricles remain inactive (**ventricular asystole**) and the patient dies, or more likely the A-V node (or a lower pacemaker) takes over and controls the ventricles (**junctional** or **ventricular escape**). In this event the atria continue to beat in their own time, and the ventricles beat in a slower tempo, **idiojunctional** or **idioventricular rhythm**. For example, the atria may continue to beat at a sinus rate of 96, while the ventricles perform at 28 (fig. 23.13). This independence is readily recognized in the tracing by the lack of relationship between the slow ventricular complexes and the more frequent P waves. Each maintains its own rhythm without regard for the other, except that in about 20% of

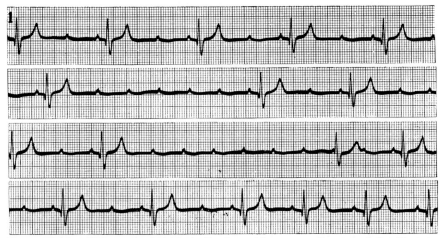

Figure 23.12. **High grade A-V block** (the four strips are continuous). A 3:1 block is present in the *top strip*. The *second strip* contains a 7:1 period. A slightly longer period of ventricular standstill in the *third strip* is terminated by a junctional escape beat. In the *bottom strip* there is 3:1 and 2:1 block. Shallow T$_P$ waves are clearly visible following each of the non-conducted P waves.

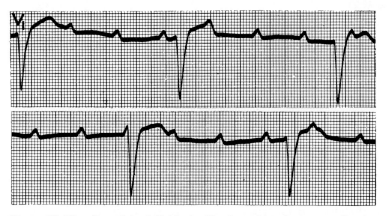

Figure 23.13. **Complete A-V block.** The two strips form a continuous record. P waves and QRS complexes are independent, at ventricular rate of 28, and atrial of 96.

331

complete A-V blocks, although anterograde conduction is impossible, retrograde conduction to the atria can occur[9, 25] (fig. 23.14).

If the escaping rhythm is initiated in the A-V junction, the QRS interval and complex will be normal (unless there is concomitant BBB) and the term **idiojunctional** may be applied to the rhythm. If the rescuing pacemaker is in the ventricular muscle itself, then the QRST complex is bizarre with prolonged QRS interval and has the form of an ectopic ventricular beat (figs. 23.13 and 23.14).

It is perhaps worth clarifying the difference between *idio*junctional and just plain junctional rhythm. The prefix idio- is from the Greek *idios,* meaning private, and idiojunctional (or idioventricular) implies that the ventricles have their own private pacemaker all to themselves and are beating independently of the atria: the atria are beating in their own rhythm, or fibrillating, or they are inactive. Junctional rhythm, on the other hand, means that both the ventricles and the atria are under A-V control—the junction is the pacemaker of the whole heart.

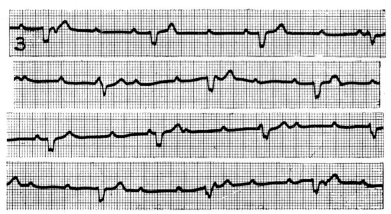

Figure 23.14.   Complete A-V block with idioventricular rate of 36, and atrial of 104. The four strips are continuous. Atrial and ventricular activities are independent except for the first and last ventricular beats—each of these is conducted retrogradely to the atria (note inverted P waves deforming the ST segments of these beats).

Ideal Criteria for Diagnosing Complete Block

1. Complete absence of A-V conduction (P waves and QRS complexes entirely independent and the ventricles beating regularly).
2. A slow ventricular rate (?under 45/min).
3. Plenty of P waves (deployed across all phases of the ventricular cycle).

Pseudo-A-V Block

This term is sometimes applied to the masquerade perpetrated by concealed junctional impulses (fig. 23.15): first degree A-V block, second degree type I and type II and "high grade" A-V block can all be imitated by concealed junctional extrasystoles or parasystole.[3, 6, 16] The importance of this is that, although the presence of such A-V ectopy probably indicates significant junctional disease,[17] accurate differentiation from true A-V block is clearly desirable.

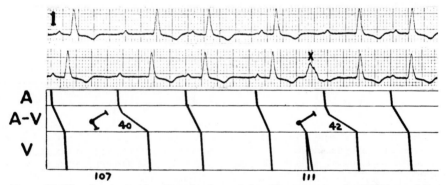

Figure 23.15.   Concealed junctional extrasystoles. The premature beat (x) toward the end of the *second strip* has the appearance of an interpolated ventricular extrasystole with concealed retrograde conduction into the A-V junction lengthening the ensuing P-R. But the pauses in the *top strip* and at the beginning of the second strip contain the same lengthened P-R without evidence of the extrasystole. The supposed "ventricular" extrasystole must therefore be a (concealed) junctional beat with LBBB aberration (see laddergram).

Wenckebach Phenomenon at Large

A context in which the Wenckebach phenomenon is commonly seen, though perhaps not always recognized, is when the conduction ratio in atrial flutter is satisfactorily reduced—by digitalis, propranolol or verapamil—from 2:1 to 4:1. Often there is an intermediate stage when 2:1 and 4:1 conduction alternate (producing bigeminal grouping) caused by the development of 3:2 Wenckebach conduction of the impulses that have succeeded in passing the 2:1 filter higher up (fig. 23.16).

All Wenckebachs are not atrioventricular, and all A-V Wenckebachs are not anterograde; and therefore you cannot recognize all of them by lengthening P-R intervals—you recognize them by spotting the "footprints" described earlier in this chapter. The phenomenon can develop anywhere that conduction occurs: out of the sinus node,[22] out of an ectopic focus, between pacing stimulus and ventricular myocardium,[10, 19] in a bundle branch,[20] in the junction below a

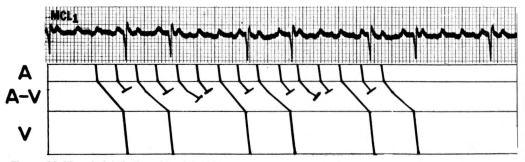

Figure 23.16. Atrial flutter with alternating 4:1 and 2:1 conduction caused by the administration of propranolol. Half the atrial impulses are "filtered"—we should not say "blocked" at this atrial rate—at an upper level in the A-V juncation, while the alternate impulses that pass through the "filter" develop a 3:2 Wenckebach.

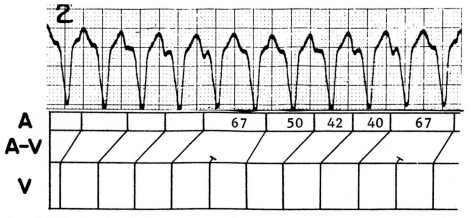

Figure 23.17. Ventricular tachycardia (rate, 150/min) with **retrograde 5:4 Wenckebach** period.

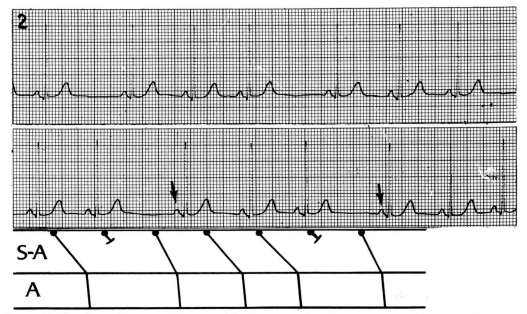

Figure 23.18.   The strips are continuous and illustrate group beating due to 4:3 and 3:2 **sinus Wencke-bachs**. One 4:3 period in the bottom strip is diagrammed.

junctional pacemaker, etc. In the two examples here illustrated, the characteristic footprints are detected in the spacing of the P waves. Figure 23.17 shows a ventricular tachycardia with retrograde Wenckebach conduction to the atria in a ratio of 5:4 (see laddergram).

The next example parades its P waves but shows no sign of lengthening P-R intervals. Figure 23.18 is from an eight-year-old boy with streptococcal tonsillitis, and his beats are grouped in threes, always with the first cycle longer than the second; and the shortest cycle is more than half the longest cycles. In this case, the first complexes to manifest the typical grouping are the P waves (the QRS's just follow the P waves obediently), and so the "receiving" chambers are the atria, which means that the Wenckebach must be occurring proximal to the atria, i.e., in the sinus node. This is, therefore, type I 4:3 exit block out of the sinus node.

To diagram this sort of block, first draw in a bar in the atrial tier to represent each P wave; then measure the total Wenckebach period, i.e., from the first P wave of one group to the first P wave of the next group (*arrows*) = 252; then divide this total period by the number of cycles, not forgetting to count the dropped beat: 252/4 = 63. Then with your dividers set for a cycle of 63, mark out pacemaker "blobs" at the top of the S-A tier, beginning at some reasonable interval in front of the first P-wave bar; finally, connect blobs to bars—as in the figure 23.18 laddergram.

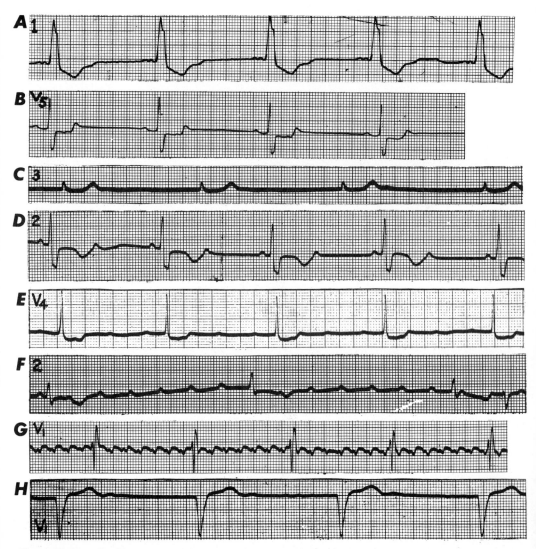

Figure 23.19. (*A*) **Sinus bradycardia**, rate 40/min. (*B*) **Nonconducted atrial bigeminy**, with incomplete RBBB; ventricular rate 38/min. (*C*) Probable **complete S-A block** with junctional escape at 30/min. (*D*) **2:1 A-V block**, probably type II (normal P-R + RBBB); ventricular rate 38/min. (*E*) Sinus tachycardia with **3:1 A-V block**; ventricular rate 39/min. (*F*) Sinus tachycardia with **complete A-V block** and idiojunctional rhythm at rate 21/min. (*G*) Atrial flutter with **complete A-V block** and idiojunctional rhythm with incomplete RBBB at rate 42/min. (*H*) Atrial fibrillation with **complete A-V block** and idioventricular rhythm (or idiojunctional with LBBB) at rate 30/min.

Marked Bradycardia

As complete A-V block is the last cause of bradycardia we shall encounter in this adventure through electrocardiography, it is appropriate to recapitulate its several causes. When the ventricular rate is under 45/min, the mechanism may be:

1. Sinus bradycardia (fig. 23.19*A*)
2. Nonconducted atrial bigeminy (fig. 23.19*B*)
3. S-A block, incomplete or complete (fig. 23.19*C*)
4. A-V block, incomplete or complete, e.g.:
   a. Sinus rhythm with 2:1 block (fig. 23.19*D*)
   b. Sinus tachycardia with 3:1 block (fig. 23.19*E*)
   c. Sinus rhythm or tachycardia with complete block (fig. 23.19*F*)
   d. Atrial flutter with complete block (fig. 23.19*G*)
   e. Atrial fibrillation with complete block (fig. 23.19*H*)

Prolonged QRS Interval

We are now also in a position to summarize the conditions associated with prolonged intraventricular conduction:

1. Ectopic ventricular mechanisms:
   a. Ventricular premature beats (extrasystoles)
   b. Ventricular escape beats
   c. Ventricular tachycardia
   d. Idioventricular rhythm
   e. Accelerated idioventricular rhythm
   f. Ventricular parasystole
   g. Paced ventricular rhythm
2. Slowed intraventricular conduction
   a. Intraventricular block (BBB)
   b. Aberrant ventricular conduction
3. Conduction to one ventricle accelerated:
   a. Wolff-Parkinson-White syndrome

REFERENCES

1. Barold, S. S., and Friedberg, H. D.: Second degree atrioventricular block: A matter of definition. Am. J. Cardiol. 1974: **33**, 311.
2. Brodsky, M., et al.: Twenty-four hour continuous electrocardiographic monitoring in fifty male medical students without apparent heart disease. Am. J. Cardiol. 1977: **39**, 390.
3. Castellanos, A., et al.: Pseudo AV block produced by concealed extrasystoles arising below the bifurcation of the His bundle. Br. Heart J. 1974: **36**, 457.
4. Damato, A. N., and Lau, S. H.: Clinical value of the electrogram of the conduction system. Prog. Cardiovasc. Dis. 1970: **13**, 119.
5. Denes, P., et al.: The incidence of typical and atypical atrioventricular Wenckebach periodicity. Am. Heart J. 1975: **89**, 26.
6. Fisch, C., et al.: Electrocardiographic manifestations of concealed junctional ectopic impulses. Circulation 1976: **53**, 217.

7. Johnson, R. L., et al.: Electrocardiographic findings in 67,375 asymptomatic individuals. VII. A-V block. Am. J. Cardiol. 1960: **6,** 153.
8. Katz, L. N., and Pick, A.: *Clinical Electrocardiography. The Arrhythmias.* Lea & Febiger, Philadelphia, 1956.
9. Khalilullah, M., et al.: Unidirectional complete heart block. Am. Heart J. 1979: **97,** 608.
10. Klein, H. O., et al.: The Wenckebach phenomenon between electric pacemaker and ventricle. Br. Heart. 1976: **38,** 961.
11. Knoebel, S. B., et al.: The role of transvenous pacing in acute myocardial infarction. Heart Lung 1972: **1,** 56.
12. Langendorf, R., and Pick, A.: Atrioventricular block, type II (Mobitz)—its nature and clinical significance. Circulation 1968: **38,** 819.
13. Lenegre, J.: Etiology and pathology of bilateral bundle branch block in relation to complete heart block. Prog. Cardiovasc. Dis. 1964: **6,** 409.
14. Lepeschkin, E.: The electrocardiographic diagnosis of bilateral bundle branch block in relation to heart block. Prog. Cardiovasc. Dis. 1964: **6,** 445.
15. Levy, M. N., et al.: The AV nodal Wenckebach phenomenon as a possible feedback mechanism. Prog. Cardiovasc. Dis. 1974: **16,** 601.
16. Lindsay, A. E., and Schamroth, L.: Atrioventricular junctional parasystole with concealed conduction simulating second degree AV block. Am. J. Cardiol. 1973: **31,** 397.
17. Narula, O. S.: Wenckebach type I and type II atrioventricular block (revisited). Cardiovasc. Clin. 1974: **6,** 138.
18. Narula, O. S.: *His Bundle Electrocardiography and Clinical Electrophysiology,* pp. 146–160. F. A. Davis, Philadelphia, 1975.
19. Peter, T., et al.: Wenckebach phenomenon in the exit area from a transvenous pacing electrode. Br. Heart J. 1976: **38,** 201.
20. Rosenbaum, M. B., et al.: Wenckebach periods in the bundle branches. Circulation 1969: **40,** 79.
21. Rosenbaum, M. B., et al.: Anatomical basis of AV conduction disturbances. Geriatrics 1970: **25,** 132.
22. Schamroth, L., and Dove, E.: The Wenckebach phenomenon in sinoatrial block. Br. Heart J. 1966: **28,** 350.
23. Steiner, C., et al.: Electrophysiological documentation of trifascicular block as the common cause of complete heart block. Am. J. Cardiol. 1971: **28,** 436.
24. Strasberg, B., et al.: Natural history of chronic second-degree atrioventricular nodal block. Circulation 1981: **63,** 1043.
25. Taboul, P., et al.: Retrograde conduction in complete A-V block. Br. Heart J. 1976: **38,** 706.
26. Van Hemel, N. M., and Robles de Medina, E. O.: Electrocardiographic findings in 791 males between the ages of 15 and 23 years; I. Arrhythmias and conduction disorders (Dutch). Cardiovasc. Dis. Cardiovasc. Surg. 1975: **23,** abs. 91.
27. Viitasalo, M. T., et al.: Ambulatory electrocardiographic recording in endurance athletes. Br. Heart J. 1982: **47,** 213.
28. Young, D., et al.: Wenckebach atrioventricular block (Mobitz type I) in children and adolescents. Am. J. Cardiol. 1977: **40,** 393.
29. Zipes, D. P., et al.: Artificial atrial and ventricular pacing in the treatment of arrhythmias. Ann. Intern. Med. 1969: **70,** 885.

Review Tracings

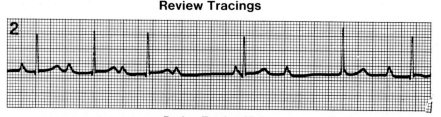

Review Tracing 23.1
For interpretation, see page 483

Review Tracings

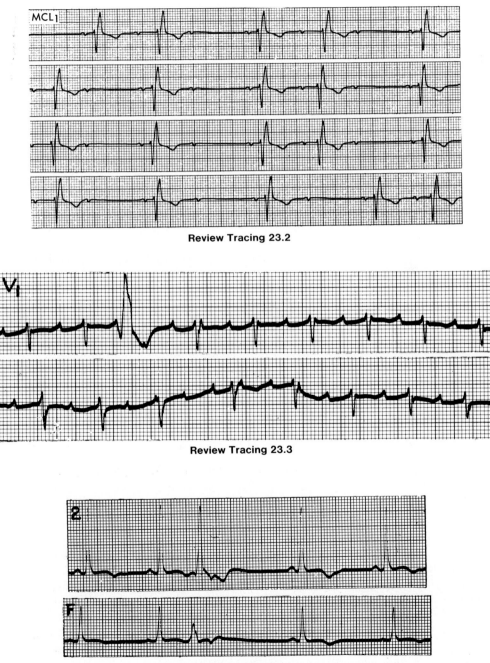

Review Tracing 23.2

Review Tracing 23.3

Review Tracing 23.4

For interpretation, see page 484

24

A-V Block: Growing Pains

Chapter 23 presented a conventional but oversimplified approach to A-V block. In it I was careful not to include any of its several aspects that have led to misconception and controversy. But now the time has come.

Up to a quarter of a century ago, there was no consistently effective therapy for heart block and therefore the finer points of classification in relation to prognosis were academic and relatively unimportant. But then the artificial pacemaker made the scene and revolutionized therapy. At last there was a really efficient and reliable way to stimulate the reluctant heart. And so we have since stumbled through an era of extremely effective and sophisticated therapy unaccompanied by needed refinements in diagnosis and prognosis.

One of the first steps in understanding the vagaries of A-V conduction is to appreciate that there are several determinants of A-V conduction besides the state of the conducting system (table 24.1); and of these the atrial and ventricular *rates* are paramount, as I shall repeatedly emphasize in the next few pages.

Causes of Confusion

There are three main reasons (table 24.2) the approach to A-V block remains confused.

1. Defective Definitions

Almost without exception, authors who write about complete and other serious grades of A-V block fail to define their terms and to state precisely what they are discussing. Take complete A-V block for example. Since it is not defined, presumably it is tacitly assumed that everyone knows how everyone else uses the term; but this is far from true. Consider the three situations depicted in figure 24.1. When the strip in figure 24.1*A* was circularized to cardiology departments, over half of the 550 respondents called it complete block, and many similar tracings have been published as such.[2, 11, 12, 17, 23] Others have alluded to tracings like that in figure 24.1*C* as complete block.[10, 14] Whereas figure 24.1*B* is the only one of the three that fulfills the criteria for complete A-V block outlined in the previous chapter.

340

Table 24.1
Main Determinants of A-V Conduction

1. State of A-V junction and bundle branches
   a. Physiologic refractoriness
   b. Pathologic refractoriness
2. Autonomic influences
3. Atrial rate
4. R/P relationships
5. Ventricular rate
6. Level of ventricular pacemaker

Table 24.2
Reasons for Confusion and Controversy

1. Authors seldom if ever define their terms
2. "Degrees" do not necessarily tally with severity of block
3. Several misconceptions lead to overdiagnosis and overtreatment

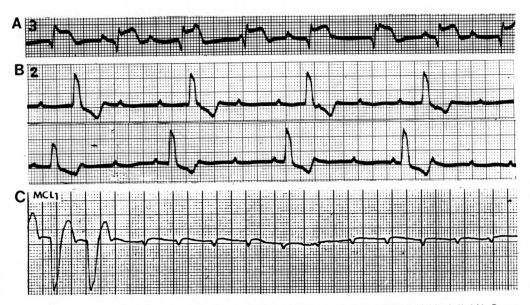

Figure 24.1. Three dissimilar situations that are frequently called "complete A-V block." (*A*) *Some* (undetermined) degree of A-V block combining with an accelerated junctional rhythm to produce complete A-V dissociation; conveniently called "**block-acceleration dissociation.**" Acute inferior infarction; prognosis excellent. (*B*) Genuine **complete A-V block** with idioventricular rhythm, rate 37/min. (*C*) Abrupt cessation of A-V conduction with no rescuing (escaping) pacemaker; conveniently distinguished from A and B by calling it "**spontaneous ventricular asystole**" initiated by A-V block. Prognosis: dismal.

Thus, when authors report on a series of patients with (undefined) "complete A-V block," the reader has no idea what "mix" of conduction disturbances is being included. Yet when prognostic implications are being considered and therapeutic recommendations made, it is vital to separate the three manifestations of block seen in figure 24.1, both from each other and from other forms of A-V conduction disturbance. When the worst manifestation of A-V block during acute infarction is that represented by *A* in figure 24.1, the mortality is less than 10%; whereas the mortality associated with the situation depicted in *C* is over 90%, and the mortality of *B* is somewhere in between. It is clearly unrealistic to gather three such disparate entities under one heading.

Similar strictures apply to use of the terms "high grade," "advanced," and "type II" block.

2. The Non-degrees of Block

"Degrees," as we use the term, do not necessarily represent grades of severity—as they presumably should. For example, a patient with first degree block at a rate of 60 may have worse block than a patient with 2:1 block at a rate of 100. This is because the first patient may develop 2:1 block if his rate increases from 60 to 75, whereas the second patient may achieve 1:1 conduction with only first degree block if his rate slows from 100 to 80. Obviously a person with 2:1 block at 75 has worse block than one with 1:1 conduction at 80.

Consider the *bottom strips* in figures 24.2 and 24.3: 24.2 has 2:1 block and 24.3 has none. But if you look at their respective *top strips*, you see that in fact 24.3 has worse block than 24.2: because 24.2 is able to maintain 1:1 conduction at an atrial rate of 100, whereas 24.3 develops 2:1 block at a rate of only 84. As long as our "degrees" are mainly predicated upon conduction *ratio* to the neglect of the more important *rate*, chaos will continue to reign.

Table 24.3
Misconceptions about A-V Conduction

1. That 2:1 A-V block is type II
2. That 2:1 A-V block is high grade
3. That when most of the atrial impulses are not conducted, the block is high grade
4. That when none of the atrial impulses is conducted, the block is complete

3. Common Misconceptions

Several misconceptions (table 24.3) have further fostered confusion. **Misconception 1:** *That 2:1 block is high-grade block.* Many respected authorities[4, 9, 26] describe 2:1 block as "high grade" or "advanced." Yet it is quite illogical to base the grade of block on the conduction ratio without taking rate into consideration. Because it is obvious that 2:1 conduction can be anything from a disaster to a blessing: at an atrial rate of 65, 2:1 block is indeed a disaster and deserves the title "high grade"; but, at an atrial rate of 125, 2:1 conduction may well be a blessing. Clearly blocks should not be branded by ratio alone.

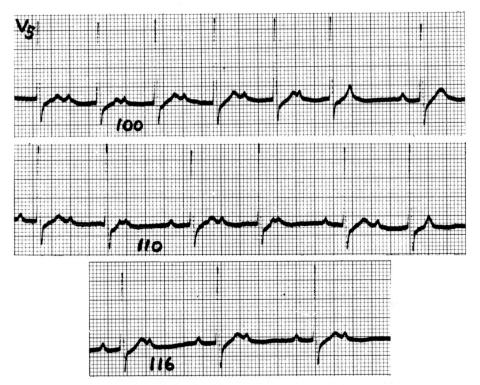

Figure 24.2.   Illustrating the effect of atrial rate on the A-V conduction ratio: at a rate of 100/ min, 1:1 conduction with prolonged P-R interval; at 110, 3:2 Wenckebach periods; at 116, 2:1 conduction.

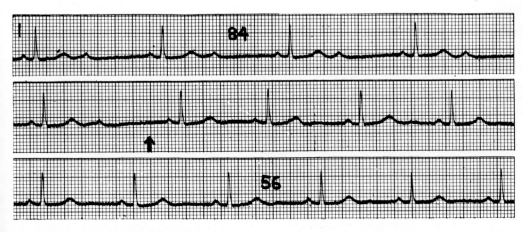

Figure 24.3.   Also illustrating the influence of atrial rate on the A-V conduction ratio. At a sinus rate of 84/ min (*top strip*), there is 2:1 conduction. At the *arrow*, carotid sinus stimulation slows the sinus rate to 56/ min. and 1:1 conduction results. Strips are continuous.

Misconception 2: *That 2:1 A-V block is necessarily type II.* Although 2:1 block, especially in the acute setting of myocardial infarction, is much more often type I than type II, many authorities automatically assign it to type II, apparently because the P-R intervals of the conducted beats are constant. This indicates both a misunderstanding of the constant P-R criterion and failure to understand the nature and nuances of type I block. The misapprehension is further promoted by such inadequate descriptions of type II block as "constant P-R intervals for conducted sinus beats irrespective of the ratio of atrial to ventricular depolarizations,"[25] and "A-V block with constant P-R intervals."[7] Even the definition ". . . failure of a ventricular response, without antecedent progressive lengthening of A-V conduction time"[10] omits the crucial point that the lack of progressive P-R lengthening must characterize the conduction of *consecutive* atrial impulses and leaves a loophole through which 2:1 block can squeeze.

In order to apply the constant P-R criterion for type II block, it is essential that *consecutive* atrial impulses be conducted with identical P-R intervals before the dropped beat; and that the P-R, when conduction resumes after the dropped beat, remains the same. This implies that the P-R remains unchanged regardless of its associated R-P—in contrast with type I in which the P-R and the R-P are reciprocally related. In type I block with 2:1 conduction, provided the sinus

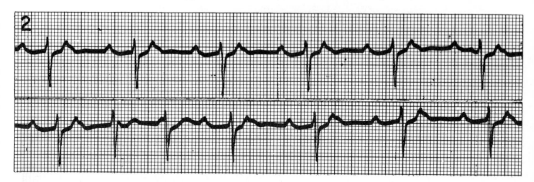

Figure 24.4. Strips are continuous. **Sinus tachycardia,** rate 116/min. with **2:1 A-V block** in the *top strip;* bottom strip begins with a **4:3 Wenckebach period.** The long P-R and absence of BBB, in the top strip alone, strongly suggest that the block is type I.

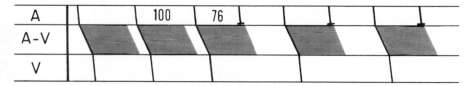

Figure 24.5. Ladder diagram, illustrating how an increase in atrial rate, without change in the refractory period (degree of block), can alter the conduction ratio from 1:1 to 2:1. First two cycles represent a rate of 60/min, last five cycles, a rate of 78/min—numbers are hundredths of a second. *Shaded area* represents an unchanging refractory period.

rhythm is regular, the R-P interval will be constant and so the P-R will be constant because, you will remember, the P-R in type I block is "R-P dependent."

Figure 24.4 presents an example of type I 2:1 A-V block in which the P-R intervals are constant at 0.32 sec until the ratio changes to a classical 4:3 Wenckebach at the beginning of the *second strip*; thus the 2:1 block is associated with all the typical findings of pure type I block: prolonged P-R, no BBB and a nearby Wenckebach period. It should be obvious that when the classical form of Wenckebach conduction alternates with 2:1 conduction, as in figure 24.4, the *type* of block has not changed. When the conduction ratio in Wenckebach periods changes from, say, 5:4 to 4:3, or from 4:3 to 3:2, there is no doubt in anyone's mind that the *type* of block is unchanged; why, when it goes one stage further and becomes 2:1, should there be an immediate diagnostic urge to switch the type and with it the prognostic significance?

When the conduction ratio changes because of an increase in atrial rate from, say, 1:1 with first degree block to 2:1, it is often described as a change for the worse in the *degree of block*,[6] when in reality the grade of block itself has not changed. Let us drive this point home with a fictitious laddergram.

In figure 24.5, the shaded area represents the refractory period (or degree of block) which remains unchanged throughout. But if the atrial rate accelerates so that the cycle shortens from 100 to 76, 2:1 conduction develops: the conduction ratio has changed to 2:1 from 1:1, but the grade of block has advanced not at all. The primary change is the atrial rate and the secondary change is the conduction ratio. It should be clear that we cannot assess the severity, or the change in severity, of any block from a conduction ratio *alone*.

Misconception 3: *That when most of the atrial impulses are not conducted, the block is high grade or advanced.* Loose definitions often imply that high grade (advanced) block is present when the conduction ratio is 3 or more to 1; or when "most" or "more than half" of the atrial impulses are not conducted. But, as with 2:1 block, the seriousness of a 3 or more to 1 ratio is also dependent on the atrial rate at which it develops; and when less than half the atrial impulses are conducted, the seriousness of the situation depends on the reasons for nonconduction. It is possible for even mild block to so conspire with atrial and ventricular rates that almost no conduction occurs (fig. 24.6). Therefore, to make the diagnosis of high grade block, it is necessary to demonstrate that the absence of conduction is due to the block itself and is not the result of an escape rhythm interfering with conduction. In figure 24.6, the block is evident but the opportunism of the ventricular pacemaker makes an important contribution to the prevailing nonconduction; and the fact that conduction can occur with prolonged P-R when the R-P interval reaches 0.60 sec (fifth beat in top strip) indicates that the patient is capable of 1:1 conduction with only first degree block at a rate of 64—hardly high grade block! *Moral:* If *any* beats are conducted, they are the ones that should receive attention, for they contain more information about the patient's conduction capabilities than any or all of the nonconducted beats. And if you calculate the rate represented by the cycle of the captured beat, this gives you the rate at which the patient is capable of 1:1 conduction and which can conveniently be called the "1:1 conduction equivalent."

Figure 24.7 consists of another example of partial A-V block which many would call "high grade" because only one out of every five atrial impulses is conducted—altogether there are 39 atrial impulses and only 8 are conducted. But both the atrial and ventricular rates are largely contributing to the nonconduction, and not just once but on eight occasions the patient is informing us that when the R-P reaches 0.54 sec he is perfectly capable of conducting with a slightly prolonged P-R interval—another way of telling us that if we could give him an atrial rate of 78 instead of 109/min, he would conduct every beat with a little first degree block! Again, hardly high grade block, but similar tracings are often published as such.[2, 8, 21, 22]

Misconception 4: *That when none of the atrial impulses is conducted, the block is complete.* Complete temporary absence of conduction (as in fig. 24.1*A*) is often accepted as evidence of complete A-V block; and this is again because the importance of rate is not appreciated. To repeat: when associated with appropriate atrial and ventricular rates, just mild block may prevent most or all conduction. Evidence that such a situation may represent the mildest of blocks

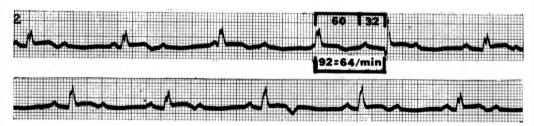

Figure 24.6. Strips are continuous. Out of 21 atrial impulses, only one is conducted to the ventricles (capture beat). That beat informs us that with an R-P of 60, conduction can take place with a prolonged P-R of 32; the cycle length of 92 represents a rate of 64/min which tells us that it would be reasonable to expect 1:1 conduction (with only first degree block) at that atrial rate.

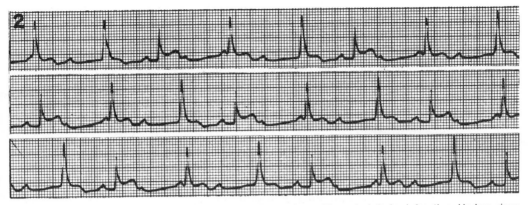

Figure 24.7. The strips are continuous, from another patient with acute inferior infarction. He has sinus tachycardia (rate, 109/min) with some (undetermined) degree of A-V block and a junctional escape rhythm at 60/min. There are 39 atrial impulses, of which only 8 are conducted with prolonged P-R intervals (0.24 sec).

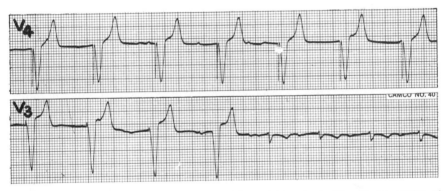

Figure 24.8. **Artificial pacemaker** pacing right ventricle at rate 62 with resumption of sinus rhythm at end of *second strip*. Note that none of the sinus impulses in the *top strip* is conducted, but this is not because of complete A-V block as conduction in the *second strip* testifies. Conduction in the *top strip* fails because of a conspiracy between *some* degree of A-V block, a ventricular (escape) rate of 62, and probably retrograde conduction into the A-V junction from the paced beats. Yet 1:1 conduction with mere **first degree A-V block** is possible at a sinus rate of 78—as evidenced in the second strip.

is afforded by the sequences depicted in figure 24.8. Here the pattern in lead V₄ is similar to that in figure 24.1*A* except that the ventricular rhythm is paced and its rate is only 62/min. In the course of this lead, the P wave emerges in front of the QRS, moves successively back towards the T wave, without conduction occurring, i.e., there is A-V dissociation. But in lead V₃, when the atrial impulse arrives at the critically "right" moment (i.e., when the R-P is exactly right), it is conducted with a prolonged P-R and narrow QRS complex and conduction continues through the rest of the strip. Far from warranting a diagnosis of complete block, impairment of conduction in the A-V junction is obviously minor. And it is this minor degree of block with which the attendant atrial and ventricular rates team up to produce A-V dissociation. The block in figure 24.1*A* may be just as minor as the block in figure 24.8 fortuitously proved itself to be.

There is no neat existing term to describe this situation accurately; to do it justice, some such recital as the following must be used to describe the situation in figure 24.1*A*: "some (undetermined) degree of block which, combined with an atrial rate of 90 and an accelerated junctional rhythm at rate 68, produces complete A-V dissociation." To characterize this dysrhythmia—where absence of conduction is due to two main causes, A-V block and accelerated subsidiary pacemaker—I have suggested the term "block/acceleration dissociation."[13]

Behavior versus Anatomy

And now we come to a knotty problem indeed. I have talked of type I and type II block in the way the terms are generally used, connoting behavior.[1, 10, 19, 27] We have seen that type I behavior (progressive lengthening of conduction times when impulses arrive earlier and earlier in a pathologically prolonged refractory period) is characteristic of the A-V node; and type II behavior ("all-or-none" conduction) is characteristic of infranodal sites (His-Purkinje system). Although type II behavior never occurs in the A-V node, type I behavior can, and occasionally does, occur anywhere in the conduction system. Thus with block in the His bundle, if it manifests type I behavior, the surface ECG will be indistinguishable from a Wenckebach occurring in the A-V node (except that the increments will tend to be smaller); and if it manifests type II behavior, type II block may be seen without BBB. The His bundle therefore may be responsible both for imitating A-V nodal block and for concealing infranodal block.

From the point of view of significance and prognosis, the anatomical level of the block is more important than its behavior; and so it would be ideal if, from the clinical tracing, we could infallibly distinguish between nodal (and call it type I) and infranodal (and call it type II) block. Unfortunately this cannot be done and the only sure way of localizing the level of the block is with intracardiac recordings—which are often neither available nor desirable. However, with a knowledge of the attributes and associations of both types of block (table 24.4), one can usually make an intelligent and correct inference from the clinical setting and the surface ECG.[27]

Moreover, it is also claimed that, in the presence of a narrow QRS (i.e., no BBB), A-V nodal block can be differentiated from infranodal block in most cases by observing the effects of atropine and carotid sinus massage. Atropine "improves" nodal block (shortens the P-R interval and/or increases the proportion of conducted beats) and "worsens" (decreases the proportion of beats conducted) infranodal block; whereas carotid sinus massage "worsens" nodal block (decreases proportion of beats conducted) and "improves" infranodal block (increases proportion of beats conducted).[12a]

Steps in the Right Direction

The difficulties that beset block are not easily resolved, but there are some remedial steps that can be taken:

1. The simple division into three degrees is too simple; clearly *additional categories are needed.* Take for example the category of ventricular asystole, exemplified by figure 24.1*C*, which has never been cleanly separated from complete block. But there are at least two other forms of ventricular asystole that in turn deserve separation from the spontaneous form (fig. 24.1*C*), namely that which results from a lengthening of the atrial cycle (attributed to a phase 4 phenomenon)[5] (fig. 24.9*A*) and that due to vagotonia, as from vomiting (fig. 24.9*B*). Undoubtedly these three forms of block-cum-asystole have differing

Table 24.4
Established Associations of Type I and Type II Block

Characteristic	Type I	Type II
Clinical	Usually acute	Usually chronic
	Inferior infarction	Anteroseptal infarction
	Rheumatic fever	Lenegre's disease
	Digitalis	Lev's disease
	Propranolol	Cardiomyopathy
Anatomical	Usually A-V nodal—sometimes His bundle	Always subnodal—usually bundle branches
Electrophysiologic	Relative refractory period	No relative refractory period
	Decremental conduction	All-or-none conduction
Electrocardiographic	R-P/P-R reciprocity	Stable P-R
	Prolonged P-R	Normal P-R
	Normal QRS duration	Bundle-branch block

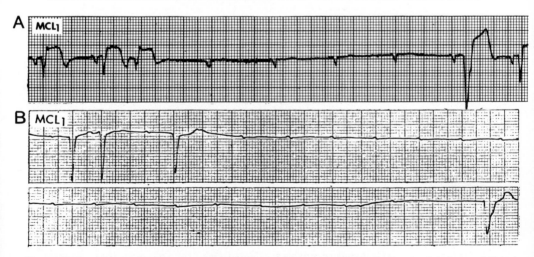

Figure 24.9. Two more examples of **transient ventricular asystole.** In *A*, the asystole is precipitated by an atrial premature beat that suppresses the sinus node and thus lengthens the sinus cycle. In *B*, the asystole is vagally induced—the patient vomited.

mechanisms and prognoses and require different therapeutic approaches; and each, therefore, deserves a category to itself. As a tentative improvement on the outworn three-degree classification, I have suggested the outline presented in table 24.5.[15]

2. Since the "degrees" of block, as presently defined—or not defined!—have created more confusion than they have contributed precision, *degrees should be de-emphasized*, perhaps even abandoned. Note that the term "degree" is not included in table 24.5.

3. In veiw of the major role that both atrial and ventricular rates play in determining the frequency and ratio of A-V conduction, *rates should be included* in all definitions and diagnostic categorizations of A-V block. Rates should be emphasized at the expense of ratios, instead of ratios at the expense of rates.

If these three suggestions were implemented, perfection would not be achieved but it would represent three sizeable steps in the right direction.

Table 24.5
Categories of A-V Conduction Disturbance

1. Prolonged P-R interval
2. Block/acceleration dissociation
3. Occasional "dropped" beats
    a. Type I (Wenckebach periodicity)
    b. Type II
4. 2:1 A-V Block
    a. Type I
    b. Type II
5. High grade block
    a. Type I
    b. Type II
6. Complete block
    a. Junctional escape
    b. Ventricular escape
7. Transient ventricular asystole
    a. Spontaneous
    b. Phase 4 (?)
    c. Vagal

REFERENCES

1. Barold, S. S., and Friedberg, H. D.: Second degree atrioventricular block; a matter of definition. Am. J. Cardiol. 1974: **33**, 311.
2. Beregovich, J., et al.: Management of acute myocardial infarction complicated by advanced atrioventricular block. Am. J. Cardiol. 1969: **23**, 54.
3. Chung, E. K.: *Principles of Cardiac Arrhythmias*, p. 271. Williams & Wilkins, Baltimore, 1971.
4. Chung, E. K.: How to approach cardiac arrhythmias. Heart Lung 1972: **1**, 523.
5. Corrado, G., et al.: Paroxysmal atrioventricular block related to phase 4 bilateral bundle branch block. Am. J. Cardiol. 1974: **33**, 553.
6. Danzig, R., et al.: The significance of atrial rate in patients with atrioventricular conduction abnormalities complicating acute myocardial infarction. Am. J. Cardiol. 1969: **24**, 707.
7. DePasquale, N. P.: The electrocardiogram in complicated acute myocardial infarction. Prog. Cardiovasc. Dis. 1970: **13**, 72.

8. Hart, H. H., and Schamroth, L.: A study in A-V block. Heart Lung 1976: **5**: 633.
9. Josephson, M. E., and Seides, S. F.: *Clinical Cardiac Electrophysiology. Techniques and Interpretations,* p. 80. Lea & Febiger, Philadelphia, 1979.
10. Langendorf, R., and Pick, A.: Editorial: Atrioventricular block, type II (Mobitz)—its nature and clinical significance. Circulation 1968: **38**, 819.
11. Lie, K. I., et al.: Mechanism and significance of widened QRS complexes during complete atrioventricular block in acute inferior myocardial infarction. Am. J. Cardiol. 1974: **33**, 833.
12. Lie, K. I., et al.: Incidence, prognostic significance and therapeutic implications of arrhythmias in acute myocardial infarction. Hart Bull. 1974: **5**, 17.
12a. Mangiardi, L. M., et al.: Bedside evaluation of AV block with narrow QRS complexes: usefulness of carotid sinus massage and atropine administration. Am. J. Cardiol. 1982: **49**, 1136.
13. Marriott, H. J. L.: AV block; an overdue overhaul. Emerg. Med. 1981: **30**, 85.
14. Marriott, H. J. L.: Second-degree AV block. Prim. Cardiol. 1981: Oct., p. 33.
15. Marriott, H. J. L., and Myerburg, R. J.: Recognition of arrhythmias and conduction abnormalities. In *The Heart,* p. 544, edited by J. W. Hurst. McGraw-Hill, New York, 1982.
16. McNally, E. M., and Benchimol, A.: Medical and physiological considerations in the use of artificial cardiac pacing. Part I. Am. Heart J. 1968: **75**, 380.
17. Narula, O. S., et al.: Analysis of the A-V conduction defect in complete heart block utilizing His bundle electrograms. Circulation 1970: **41**, 437.
18. Narula, O. S.: *His Bundle Electrocardiography and Clinical Electrophysiology,* pp. 146–161. F. A. Davis, Philadelphia, 1975.
19. Pick, A., and Langendorf, R.: *Interpretation of Complex Arrhythmias,* pp. 217–223. Lea & Febiger, Philadelphia, 1979.
20. Rosen, K. M., et al.: Mobitz type II block with narrow QRS complex and Stokes-Adams attacks. Arch. Intern. Med. 1973: **132**, 595.
21. Schamroth, L.: *The disorders of Cardiac Rhythm,* p. 536. Blackwell Scientific Publications, Oxford, 1971.
22. Scheinman, M., and Brenman, B.: Clinical and anatomic implications of intraventricular conduction blocks in acute myocardial infarction. Circulation 1972: **46**, 753.
23. Scherf, D., and Dix, J. H.: The effects of posture on A-V conduction. Am. Heart J. 1952: **43**, 494.
24. Singh, S., and Fletcher, R. D.: The site of myocardial infarction: Effect on presentation and management. Pract. Cardiol. 1980: **6**, 35.
25. Stock, R. J., and Macken, D. L.: Observations on heart block during continuous electrocardiographic monitoring in myocardial infarction. Circulation 1968: **38**, 993.
26. WHO/ISC Task Force: Definition of terms related to cardiac rhythm. Am. Heart J. 1978: **95**, 796.
27. Zipes, D. P.: Second-degree atrioventricular block. Circulation 1979: **60**, 465.

Review Tracing

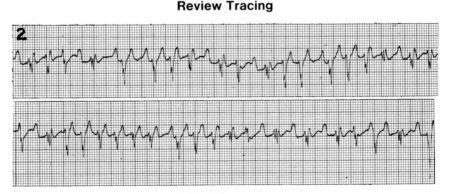

Review Tracing 24.1

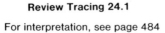

For interpretation, see page 484

Review Tracings

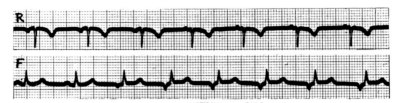

Review Tracing 24.2

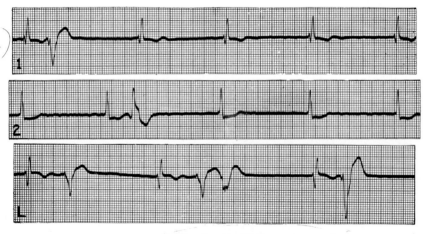

Review Tracing 24.3

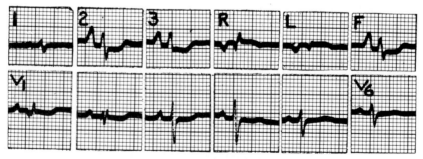

Review Tracing 24.4

For interpretation, see page 484

25

Artificial Pacemakers

The introduction of artificial pacemakers opened a new chapter in arrhythmias, both by producing their own new crop[6] and by shedding new light on long recognized mechanisms.[7] But the wonder machines of medicine are not without their own peculiar problems, and the artificial pacemaker is no exception. It may sometimes snatch the moribund from the jaws of death or restore a near-normal life-style to the cardiac cripple; but it can also spark fatal arrhythmias, induce hiccups, infection or thrombophlebitis, interfere with the golfer's swing, perforate the myocardium, and perpetrate numerous deceptions in the electrocardiogram.

The pacemaker's relationship to the cardiac arrhythmias has many and varied points of contact: It has aided in unraveling the mechanisms of several arrhythmias,[8] including those associated with the Wolff-Parkinson-White syndrome[10]; it has imitated time-honored patterns of arrhythmia; and it has produced its own vintage. As the state of the pacemaker art has progressed, the pacemaker has evolved its own set of pranks and created its own booby traps for the diagnostician.

The 1970s saw a revolution in pacemaker technology so that the field sprouted with more complex models: A-V sequential, automatic antitachycardia, multiprogrammable, etc. By 1978, more than a third of all implanted pacemakers in the United States were programmable; and the advantages of programmability indicate that, in the foreseeable future, all or most pacemakers implanted will be of this genre.[1] Since models have proliferated and many pacemakers can alter their signatures at the will of their programmers, the electrocardiography of pacemakers has become so diverse and complex that it is often impossible to attempt interpretation without a foreknowledge of the model concerned and how it is programmed. Now rate, sensitivity, output and refractory period are all noninvasively programmable, and pacemaking sophistication has reached such a pitch that nothing less than a multichaptered book can possibly do it justice; fortunately such a book is now available.[1a]

For convenience in terminology, one must be familiar with the three-letter code introduced in 1974 and presented in Table 25.1. Thus, for example, a "VVI" model is the common demand pacemaker that paces the ventricle, senses ventricular activity and is inhibited by such sensing.

Types of Pacemakers

There are four *basic* types of artificial pacemakers[2]:

1. Fixed-rate—recognized in the electrocardiogram by the fact that pacemaker "blips" occur with relentless regularity, their rhythm unaffected by the intervention of naturally occurring beats (fig. 25.1).

2. Demand (ventricular-inhibited)—recognized by the fact that, when a natural beat occurs, the regular rhythm of the pacemaker blips is interrupted (fig. 25.2); then, after a predetermined "escape" interval, the pacemaker fires again unless another natural beat anticipates it.

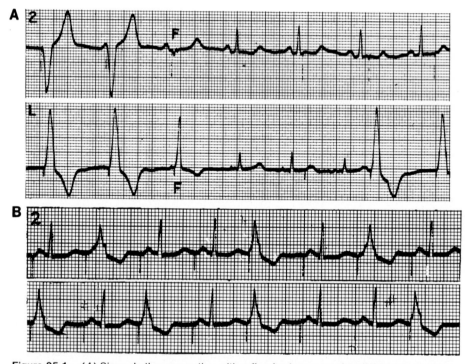

Figure 25.1. (*A*) Sinus rhythm competing with a **fixed-rate pacemaker (VOO)** with resulting fusion beats (*F*). Note that regular rhythm of pacemaker blips is not disturbed by the natural beats. (*B*) **Fixed-rate atrial pacemaker (AOO)**: each P wave is immediately preceded by a pacemaker "blip." The paced rhythm is interrupted by frequent ventricular premature beats which happen to coincide with the next expected P waves so that they look like paced ventricular beats.

Table 25.1
Types of Pacemakers[a]

	Paced	Sensed	Response
Fixed-rate ventricular	V	O	O
P-triggered ventricular	V	A	T
QRS-triggered ventricular	V	V	T
QRS-inhibited ventricular (demand)	V	V	I
Fixed-rate atrial	A	O	O
Demand A-V sequential	D	V	I
Fixed-rate A-V sequential	D	O	O
Fixed-rate A-V simultaneous	D	O	O
Atrial synchronous, ventricular demand	V	D	D
Universal, fully automatic	D	D	D

[a] Key: V = ventricle, A = atrium, D = both ventricle and atrium, O = neither chamber; T = triggered, I = inhibited.

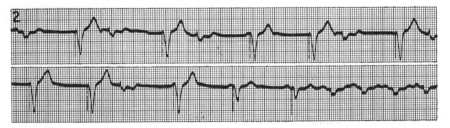

Figure 25.2. Demand pacemaker (VVI). Note that when a natural beat occurs, the pacemaker shuts off. The sinus beats are conducted with intraventricular block and the fifth and sixth beats in the *bottom strip* are fusion beats. In the *top strip*, the first and fourth paced beats are followed by retrograde P waves which in turn are followed by probable reciprocal beats.

3. Atrial-triggered—recognized by the fact that the ventricular blips always follow a P wave at a fixed interval (fig. 25.3).

4. Ventricular-triggered—this seldom seen pacemaker is recognized by the fact that the blip is in, not immediately before, the QRS complex of natural beats.

Notes: (a) If there are no natural beats (fig. 25.4), you cannot distinguish between a fixed rate and demand pacemaker; because the demand pacemaker, if it is not interrupted by natural beats, will continue to fire regularly. (b) The demand pacemaker operates exactly like a ventricular escape rhythm, whereas the fixed rate pacemaker functions like ventricular parasystole. Both are therefore potent manufacturers of fusion beats. (c) Both atrial-triggered and ventricular-triggered pacemakers become demand pacemakers when there are no natural complexes to trigger them.

Dysrhythms Produced by Pacemakers

Early Beats

In several situations, the pacemaker may create early beats. Figure 25.5*A* illustrates a fixed-rate pacemaker which, since it is not turned off by the sinus beats, produces three early beats. A demand pacemaker which fails to sense obviously amounts to a fixed-rate pacemaker and similarly produces early beats when its effective stimulus interrupts the basic rhythm. In figure 25.5*B*, the non-sensing demand pacemaker begins its short three-beat tenure with an early beat.

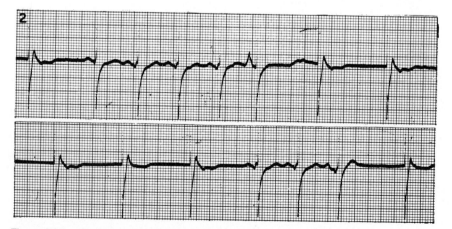

Figure 25.3.   Atrial-triggered pacemaker (VAT). Note that all the P waves are followed, at a fixed interval, by a pacemaker "blip." When no P waves appear in time to trigger the pacemaker, it escapes like a demand pacemaker.

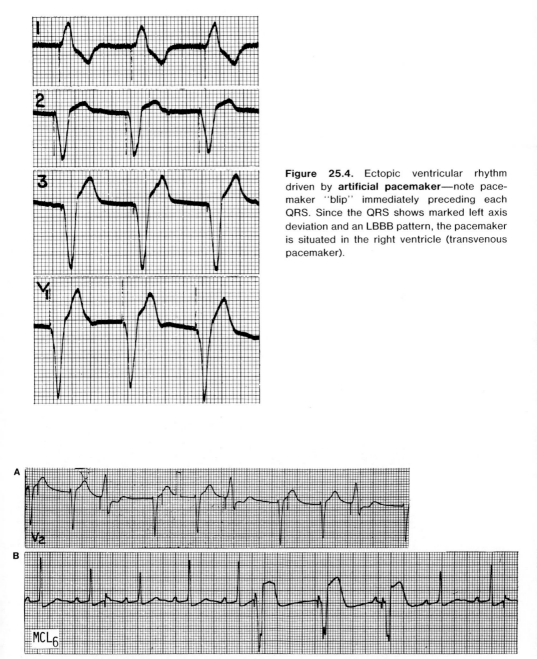

Figure 25.4. Ectopic ventricular rhythm driven by **artificial pacemaker**—note pacemaker "blip" immediately preceding each QRS. Since the QRS shows marked left axis deviation and an LBBB pattern, the pacemaker is situated in the right ventricle (transvenous pacemaker).

Figure 25.5. (A) **Fixed-rate pacemaker** which, since it is not shut off by the sinus beats, produces early (parasystolic) paced beats. B. **Demand pacemaker** which intermittently fails to sense—see spikes after second, fifth and last beats. The stimulus following the fifth sinus beat is slightly later than the other two and therefore produces a ventricular response and retains control for three consecutive beats.

At times, a failing, ineffective pacemaker retains the capability to pace only at a point early in the ventricular cycle. In figure 25.6, there is complete A-V block with an escaping idioventricular rhythm at a rate of about 36/min. The pacemaker (implanted epicardially in the left ventricle) consistently fails to pace except when its stimulus happens to land at the end of the idioventricular T wave. On the two occasions when it lands there (third beat in top strip and fourth beat in bottom strip), it effectively stimulates the left ventricle. When excitability is better earlier than later in the ventricular cycle, it is credited to "supernormal" excitability. This is, however, a misnomer because the excitability is not better than *normal*, as the term implies, but it is better than expected, judging from the evident lack of excitability later in the cycle.

Another form of "supernormality" produces a special form of ventricular capture. In the presence of anterograde A-V block, the ventricular pacemaker initiates retrograde conduction into the A-V junction and there sets up a refractory period containing a "supernormal" phase during which anterograde conduction becomes possible. In figure 25.7, only when the P wave lands on the T wave is the impulse conducted, and it is conducted with a perfectly normal P-R interval (as is often seen with type II A-V block), whereas P waves landing elsewhere in the ventricular cycle are invariably blocked. Thus, when P waves land at the summit of the T wave, conduction is better than expected and therefore qualifies as "supernormal."

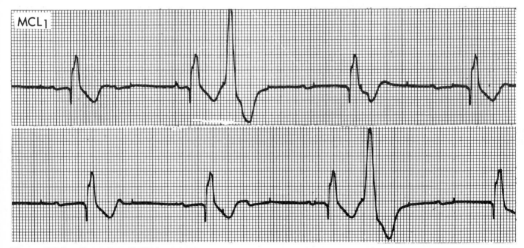

Figure 25.6.   Complete A-V block with idioventricular escape at a rate of 36/min. Pacemaker stimuli are entirely ineffective except when they fall at a critical time following an idioventricular beat—presumably in the "supernormal" phase of excitability.

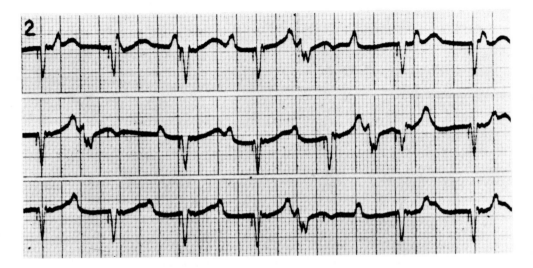

Figure 25.7. Fixed-rate pacemaker in the presence of A-V block. Conduction of the sinus impulse occurs only when the P wave lands on the summit of the T wave. Since sinus impulses later in the ventricular cycle are not conducted, conduction earlier in the cycle is unexpected and is therefore probably due to a **"supernormal" phase** set up by retrograde conduction into the A-V junction from the previous paced beat.

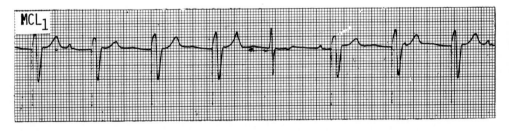

Figure 25.8. The right ventricular paced rhythm (rate, 70/min) is dissociated from the sinus rhythm (rate, 50/min) except for the fifth beat, which is slightly early and is a **capture beat** conducted with a long P-R interval. Note that the ventricular capture is the only beat that is *not* paced.

It is a pity that "capture" has crept into the pacemaker vernacular to connote successful pacing. Semantically, this is acceptable enough; but on grounds of legitimate priority, the "capture(d)" beat has for decades been a conducted beat interrupting any form of A-V dissociation; and the pity in the pacemaker context is that the only beat that by priority of nomenclature has the right to be called "captured" is the one beat that is not paced (fig. 25.8)!

Bigeminal Rhythm

There are several ways in which pacemakers can produce bigeminal grouping, and some of these are illustrated in figures 25.9 to 25.11. A relatively common mechanism is the escape-capture sequence. In this, the longer cycles end with a paced (escape) beat, and the subsequent shorter cycles end with a conducted beat (fig. 25.9). For this to happen, it is necessary for the spontaneous sinus discharge rate to be considerably slower than that of the noncompetitive pacemaker's escape rate or that of the competitive pacemaker's fixed rate.

Retrograde conduction into the A-V junction and often into the atria is common in any form of ectopic ventricular rhythm, and paced ventricular rhythms are no exception. If retrograde conduction is sufficiently delayed and the ascending impulse finds a circuit in the A-V junction ripe for reentry, the impulse may be reflected back to the ventricles to produce a reciprocal beat or ventricular "echo." If this happens after every paced beat, as in figure 25.10, the result is reciprocal bigeminy.

Yet another form of bigeminy will result if the failing pacemaker succeeds in pacing only twice out of every three attempts. Figure 25.11 illustrates such a pacemaker implanted on the left ventricle; firing at a rate of 80/min, it paces successfully twice and then records a dismal failure with every third discharge.

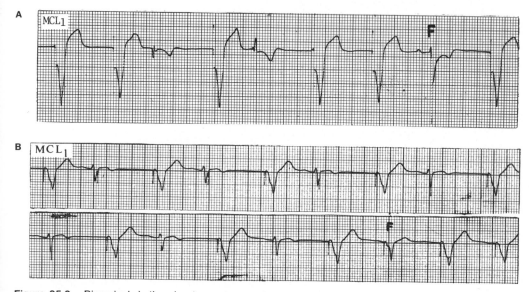

Figure 25.9. Bigeminal rhythm due to escape-capture sequences. In *A*, the **demand pacemaker** has a rate of 70/min, and the competing sinus rhythm is irregular at a rate of 44 to 50/min; as a result, two pairs of beats appear, each pair consisting of a paced beat followed by a conducted (capture) beat. The eighth beat (*F*) is a fusion beat. In *B*, the **fixed-rate pacemaker** has a rate of 72/min, while the sinus discharge rate is only 34/min. The *top strip* consists entirely of escape-capture sequences; the seventh beat (*F*) in the *bottom strip* is a fusion beat.

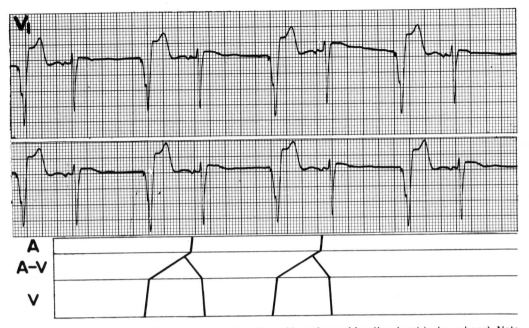

Figure 25.10. Bigeminal rhythm due to paced rhythm with **reciprocal beating** (ventricular echoes). Note that the retrograde P waves, as usual in V_1, have a negative-positive contour.

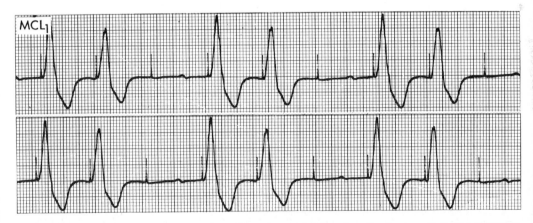

Figure 25.11. Bigeminal rhythm due to the failure of every third pacing stimulus to activate the ventricles.

Tachyarrhythmias

It is painfully well known that artificial pacemaker stimuli, when they land in the vulnerable period of the ventricles, can precipitate ventricular tachycardia or fibrillation. Pacing stimuli can be and frequently are used to deliberately produce supraventricular or ventricular tachycardia for the purpose of diagnosis and to evaulate the efficacy of drugs in their control.

Three other ways in which the pacemaker can produce a dangerous tachycardia are illustrated in figures 25.12 to 25.15. If a fixed-rate (or failing demand) pacemaker at a rate of, say, 70 intersperses its stimuli midway between the competing sinus beats which also enjoy a rate of about 70, the result will be a series of interpolated paced beats producing in effect a tachycardia at a rate of 140. Interpolated tachycardia, at a somewhat slower rate, is illustrated in figure 25.12.

A malfunctioning pacemaker may go berserk and fire at several hundred times a minute ("runaway pacemaker"), sometimes driving the ventricles in a wild tachycardia. The pacemaker in figure 25.13 is firing at a rate of 440/min with a 2:1 exit block between the pacemaker electrode and the responsive myocardium, so that the resulting ventricular tachycardia has a rate of 220/min. Unfortunately, the cause of this patient's predicament was not recognized, and instead of isolating the offending pulse generator, he was treated with drugs and cardioversion with the unhappy result that he died within the hour.

His tracing illustrates another important point, the so-called "haystack principle": If you have to find a needle, would you rather have a large or little haystack? As with the haystack, so with the electrocardiogram: If you have difficulty finding something that is inconspicuous—like small P waves, pacer spikes, etc.—always give the lead with the smallest disturbance of the base line a chance to help you. If only the attendants of this unfortunate patient had looked at aVR, the runaway blips would have sprung immediately to sight. But who would think of using aVR in search of an arrhythmic diagnosis?

Like other electrocardiographic manifestations of electrical activity, the pacemaker spike has magnitude and direction and, though easily seen in most

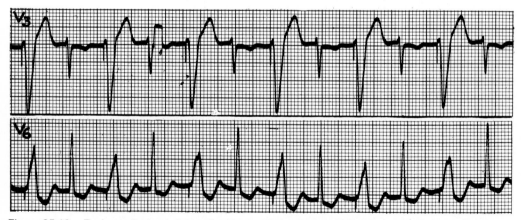

Figure 25.12. Tachycardia due to interpolated paced beats from a **fixed-rate pacemaker**: Both sinus and paced rhythms have a rate of 62/min, producing an interpolated tachycardia at a rate of 124/min.

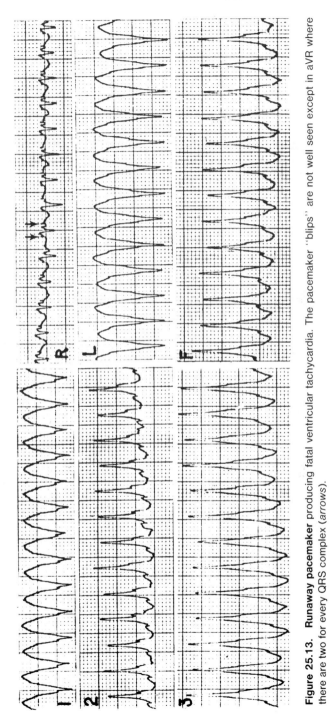

Figure 25.13. Runaway pacemaker producing fatal ventricular tachycardia. The pacemaker "blips" are not well seen except in aVR where there are two for every QRS complex (*arrows*).

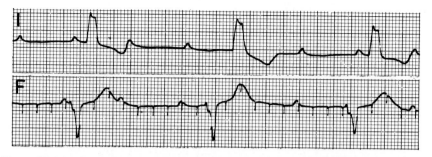

Figure 25.14. Complete A-V block with ineffective **runaway pacemaker.** ''Blips'' are visible at rate 350 in aVF; note that there is no sign of pacemaker activity in lead 1.

leads, may be inconspicuous or quite invisible in others (fig. 25.14)—a potential source of frustration and misdiagnosis (see below).

The introduction of a dual chamber pacemaker is equivalent to implanting an accessory pathway and is therefore an invitation to reentry. As retrograde conduction is common in any ectopic ventricular rhythm—a fact at first overlooked or underestimated by pacemaker innovators—atrial sensing sets the stage for a reentering tachycardia. The sequence of events following a ventricular premature beat is diagrammed in figure 25.15A and illustrated in figure 25.15B—the vicious circle of an "endless loop" tachycardia.[4a]

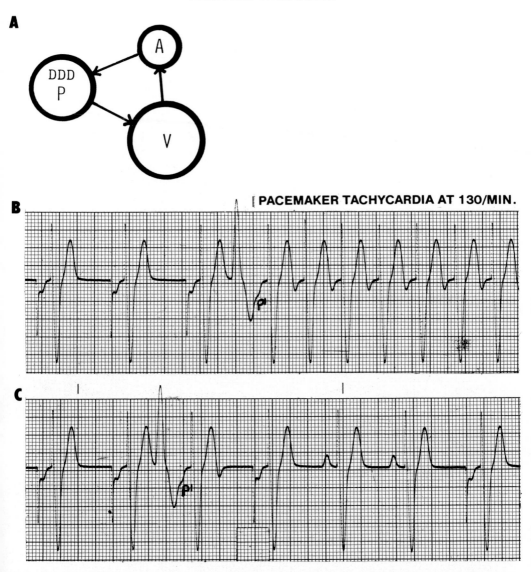

Figure 25.15. (A) Diagram of the sequence of events in "endless loop" tachycardia. (A = atrium; V = ventricle; P = pacemaker.) (B) **Fully automatic (DDD) pacemaker** producing **endless loop tachycardia** in response to a ventricular premature beat. At beginning of strip, pacer is operating in the A-V sequential mode. The fourth beat is a ventricular extrasystole with retrograde conduction (P'); the retrograde P' wave is sensed and, after the preset A-V delay of about 0.16 sec, the ventricle is paced. This beat in turn conducts retrogradely and the vicious circle continues. (C) The programmable atrial refractory period has been lengthened so that a similar premature beat fails to initiate a tachycardia because the retrograde P' now arrives during the atrial refractory period and is therefore not sensed. The sixth and seventh beats in this strip show this versatile pacemaker in the ventriclar mode, i.e., natural P waves are sensed and the ventricles paced after the preset A-V delay.

Miscellaneous Deceptions

Apart from imitating the natural arrhythmias, the pacemaker can produce its own peculiar crop of rhythm disturbances. In figure 25.16, there are two families of cycles, a longer and a shorter, suggesting a faulty pacemaker; the longer cycles are all equal, and the shorter cycles are also equal. Whenever one is faced with this situation, one should measure the short cycle carefully and subtract it from the longer cycle measuring backward *from the end of the longer cycle.* In this tracing (fig. 25.16), if you do this, you find that you exactly reach the summit of the T wave, and this immediately gives us the answer: The pacemaker is intermittently sensing the T waves—and enthusiastic sensing is no crime!

The escaping interval of a demand pacemaker may be longer or shorter than expected.[3] Some models have had "hysteresis" (Gr. *hysteros* = later) built into them; i.e., after being shut off by a natural beat, the first returning beat is *later*

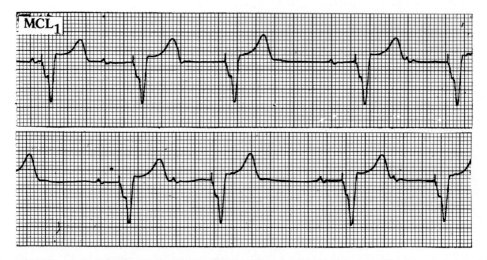

Figure 25.16. A normally functioning **demand pacemaker** deceived by T waves. The pacemaker cycle is 0.96 sec, and the longer cycles of 1.38 sec result when the pacemaker senses the preceding T wave.

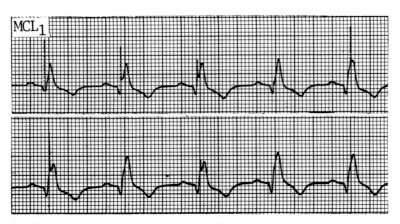

Figure 25.17.   Sinus rhythm with RBBB and a normally functioning, right ventricular **demand pacemaker.** Pacemaker artifacts are superimposed on the ventricular complexes as much as 0.08 sec after beginning of the QRS because of the circuitous path taken by the sinus impulse to reach the sensing electrode.

than the set rate of the pulse generator would lead one to expect. On the other side of the coin, "partial sensing" may produce an ensuing cycle that is shorter than the full escape cycle of the pacer. It is important to be aware of these phenomena so as not to be too hasty in condemning the pacemaker as faulty.

Tracings such as that in figure 25.17 are often misinterpreted as indicating faulty sensing because in many beats the QRS complex contains the pacemaker spike indicating that the demand mode failed to sense the natural depolarization. But it is a question of geography[9]: The pacemaker's electrodes are situated within the *right* ventricle, and the conducted beats show a *right* bundle-branch block (RBBB) pattern. This means that, for the conducted impulse to reach the sensing electrode, it must travel down the left branch and work its way through the septum; depending on the exact location of the electrode, this journey may take up to about 0.08 sec.[4] Thus, in the presence of RBBB and a right ventricular demand pacemaker, the pacemaker spike may be found within the QRS as late as 0.08 sec after the beginning of the complex without implying faulty sensing.

Figure 25.18 illustrates another form of deception. Throughout lead 1 and the first three beats in lead 2, one would diagnose a ventricular-triggered pacemaker since the ventricular complex contains the pacing spike within it. But the last beat in lead 2 belies this diagnosis since the premature complex does not trigger the pacemaker but is *followed by* its spike. The spike is therefore constantly related not to the QRS but to the P wave, which it follows at the fixed preset interval of 0.20 sec. The sequence of events was as follows: The patient had an atrial-triggered pacemaker implanted because of high grade type II A-V block. With the regular paced rhythm and consequent better perfusion, conduction was restored, and as is usual with type II block, the P-R interval was normal (0.16 sec) and shorter than the preset P-to-spike interval; therefore, when conduction resumed, the conducted QRS began before the spike was evoked by the P wave.

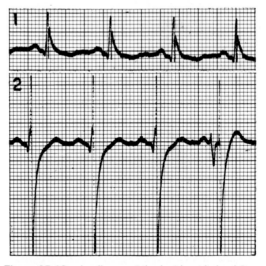

Figure 25.18.   In all except the last beat in lead 2, a pacemaker artifact interrupts the ventricular complex suggesting a ventricular-triggered pacemaker. However, the last beat in lead 2 is premature, does not elicit a pacemaker response, and so argues that it is not a ventricular-triggered model. The stimulus artifact is, however, constantly related to the P wave (P-to-blip interval = 0.20 sec) indicating an **atrial-triggered pacemaker.**

In figure 25.19, a supposedly atrial-triggered pacemaker is, in fact, ignoring the atrial stimulus and responding to the ventricular. The pacer spike is accurately coupled to the QRS (at 0.17 sec) instead of to the P wave. Because the atrial impulse is inherently too feeble or because the atrial electrode has been displaced, the pulse generator is responding to the more remote though stronger ventricular stimulus. It does not respond to *every* ventricular beat, however, because of the built-in 2:1 block that automatically develops when the atrial rate exceeds 110/min.

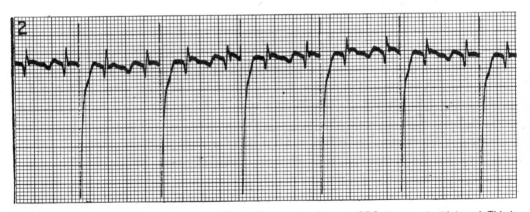

Figure 25.19.   This **unipolar pacemaker** artifact follows every alternate QRS at a constant interval. This is an atrial-triggered model that is being triggered not by the atrial impulse but by every alternate ventricular impulse.

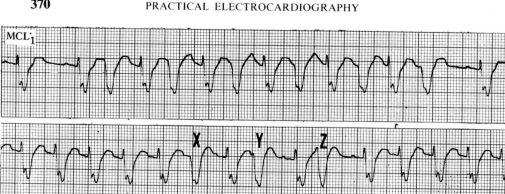

Figure 25.20. A **demand pacer** on standby, whose stimuli are invisible in this monitoring lead, intermittently failing to sense. *Top strip*: tachycardia produced by interpolated pacer beats in which the "blips" are invisible. *Bottom strip*: The coupling interval of consecutive paced beats (*X, Y, Z*) varies, but the interectopic interval is constant—like a bona fide parasystole.

Figure 25.20 recapitulates several of the points already made and illustrates how an innocent pacemaker can perpetrate a double deception. The patient was admitted with an acute anterior infarction. Shortly after admission, he developed sinus tachycardia with 2:1 conduction and left bundle-branch block. Because of these blocks, his cardiologist put in a temporary demand pacemaker on standby. A few hours later, he developed runs of interpolated ventricular bigeminy producing, in effect, a significant tachycardia with a ventricular rate of 138/min (fig. 25.20, *top strip*). These runs of interpolated tachycardia recurred despite the use of lidocaine in increasing dosage and supplemented with procainamide. It was then noticed that the coupling intervals showed variation (as in fig. 25.20, *X, Y*, and *Z* in *bottom strip*), and what was worse, they were consecutively shortening for three beats until the third beat (*Z*) bisected the T wave. After a while, one of the attendants spotted the fact that though the coupling intervals varied, the interectopic intervals were constant— and this suggested *parasystole*. At this point, it did not take long to recall that a fixed-rate pacemaker is parasystolic and that perhaps the troublesome and unresponsive ectopy was due to the pacemaker. With the pacemaker turned off completely, the ectopy immediately stopped, and it was then realized that the pacemaker was guilty of an almost unbelievable double deception: Its demand mode was intermittently failing, and the pacemaker spikes were invisible in the monitoring lead!

REFERENCES

1. Barold, S. S., et al.: The third decade of cardiac pacing; multiprogrammable pulse generators. Br. Heart J. 1981: **45**, 357.

1a. Bognolo, D.: *Practical Approach to Physiologic Cardiac Pacing.* Tampa Tracings, Tarpon Springs, 1983.

2. Castellanos, A., and Lemberg, L.: *Electrophysiology of Pacing and Cardioversion.* Appleton-Century-Crofts, New York, 1969.

3. Castellanos, A., and Lemberg, L.: Pacemaker arrhythmias and electrocardiographic recognition of pacemakers. Circulation 1973: **47,** 1382.

4. Castellanos, A., et al.: A study of arrival of excitation at selected ventricular sites during human bundle branch block using close bipolar catheter electrodes. Chest 1973: **63,** 208.

4a. Furman, S., and Fisher, J. D.: Endless loop tachycardia in an AV universal (DDD) pacemaker. PACE 1982: **5,** 486.

5. Kastor, J. A., and DeSanctis, R. W.: Reciprocal beating from artificial ventricular pacemaker; report of a case. Circulation 1967: **35,** 1170.

6. Kastor, J. A., and Leinbach, R. C.: Pacemakers and their arrhythmias. Prog. Cardiovasc. Dis. 1970: **13,** 240.

7. Katz, A. M., and Pick, A.: The transseptal conduction time in the human heart. Circulation 1963: **27,** 1061.

8. Langendorf, R., and Pick, A.: Artificial pacing of the human heart; its contribution to the understanding of arrhythmias. Am. J. Cardiol. 1971: **28,** 516.

9. Vera, Z., et al.: Lack of sensing by demand pacemakers due to intraventricular conduction defects. Circulation 1975: **51,** 815.

10. Wellens, H. J. J.: Contribution of cardiac pacing to our understanding of the Wolff-Parkinson-White syndrome. Br. Heart. J. 1975: **37,** 231.

Review Tracings

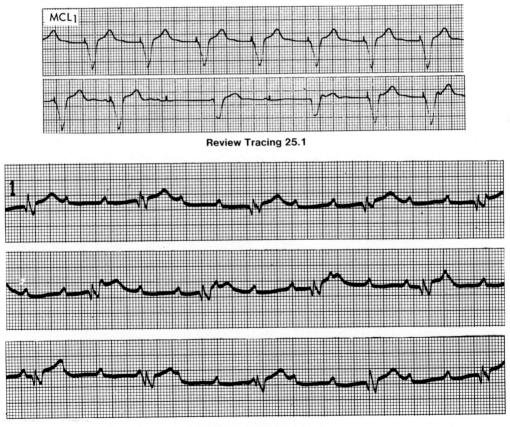

Review Tracing 25.1

Review Tracing 25.2

For interpretation, see page 484

Review Tracings

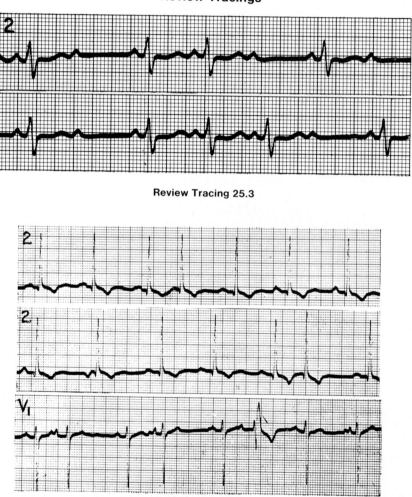

Review Tracing 25.3

Review Tracing 25.4

For interpretation, see page 484

26

Myocardial Infarction

Experimental Considerations

If a branch of a dog's coronary is tied and an electrode is placed on an area of myocardium supplied by the occluded vessel, the T waves in the derived tracing soon become inverted. If the ligature is then removed and the flow of blood to the muscle re-established, the inverted T waves soon return to normal. The T-wave inversion is therefore clearly the result of simple ischemia. Inverted T waves form the basis of the **pattern of ischemia** in the clinical tracing.

If when T inversion occurs the ligature is allowed to remain in place, a dramatic change in the pattern shortly develops: within a minute or two the ST segment becomes strikingly elevated, dragging up with it and obliterating the inverted T wave. If at this stage the tie is removed, the tracing, gradually passing back through the inverted T stage, again reverts to normal. ST elevation, representing a stage beyond ischemia but still reversible, is known as the **pattern of injury.**

If when the pattern of injury is fully developed the tie is left in place, a further striking change eventually occurs. The entire QRS complex becomes inverted to produce a QS complex, while the ST segment comes back to the isoelectric line and the T wave once more assumes an upright contour. If this pattern is allowed to persist for long before the ligature is removed, it is found to be irreversible—no matter how long you wait, a QS pattern will continue to be recorded from the damaged area. Irreversible structural changes have occurred, and the new pattern is called the **pattern of necrosis.**

The reason necrosis produces Q waves is as follows: If a segment of myocardium is knocked out, electromotive forces cease to traverse it. There is thus a loss of forces directed toward the electrode placed over the inert muscle, and this results in a negative deflection (Q wave). By the same token there will be a relative gain in forces directed away from the inert area, and this may be indicated by increase in the size of the positive deflection (R wave) in leads taken from other surfaces of the heart. This concept is helpful in explaining some of the less classical patterns of infarction encountered.

The explanation for ST-segment elevation is less secure but it is believed that the major cause is a loss of resting membrane potential which depresses the baseline (T-Q segment), leaving the ST segment relatively elevated.[65]

Clinical Infarction

The two main types of infarction used to be called anterior and posterior. But because the term "posterior" is anatomically inaccurate, as it was applied to the surface of the heart resting on the diaphragm, it has become more common to use the terms "inferior" or "diaphragmatic" when referring to lesions of this wall.

If you hold a heart in your hand, it is at once obvious that there are no clearcut surfaces or boundaries; any "walls" defined are at best rough approximations. The four walls usually referred to in discussions of infarction are anterior, lateral, inferior and true posterior (to distinguish it from the false posterior of the older terminology).

The three changes observed in the experimental heart—T-wave inversion, ST elevation and the appearance of Q waves—form the basis of infarction patterns as we see them clinically. Around any patch of infarcted muscle there is a less damaged zone which produces the pattern of injury; and outside this an even less affected area which produces the pattern of ischemia. In the experimental heart these zones can be "tapped" individually with small electrodes placed directly on the epicardium (**direct leads**). Clinically the nearest one can get is several centimeters from the myocardium on the outside of the chest (**semidirect leads**). A natural result of this is that the precordial pattern is usually a composite picture combining the patterns of ischemia, injury and necrosis all in one QRST sequence—the relatively distant electrode is influenced by all three zones instead of only one.

The first step, then, in diagnosing infarction from the electrocardiogram is to know what changes to look for. Those changes are (1) the **fresh appearance of Q waves or the increased prominence of pre-existing ones,** (2) **ST-segment elevations** and (3) **T-wave inversions.** Only Q-wave changes are diagnostic of infarction (necrosis), but changes in the ST segments and T waves may provide strong presumptive evidence. The Q, ST and T changes all have special characteristics: The Q wave is often wide as well as deep; any Q measuring 0.03 sec or more in width is highly suspicious of infarction. The deviated ST segments typically show an upward convexity. The fully developed T waves are pointed and consist of two symmetrical limbs, well likened to an arrowhead. These three changes are summarized in figure 26.1. Note that these changes are registered in **leads that face the area of damage,** and it is convenient to refer to them collectively as "indicative" changes. Opposite, or "reciprocal," changes (i.e., no Q wave with perhaps some increase in height of R wave, depressed ST segments and tall upright T waves) meanwhile appear in leads facing the diametrically opposed surface of the heart. Fortified with a little imagination

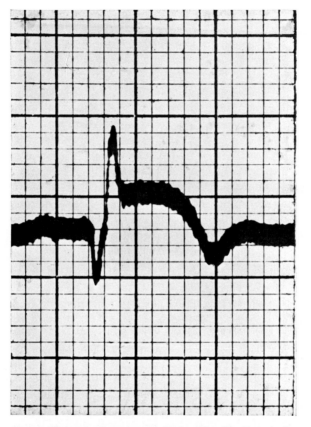

Figure 26.1   Acute myocardial infarction. The three indicative changes–Q wave, ST elevation and T inversion.

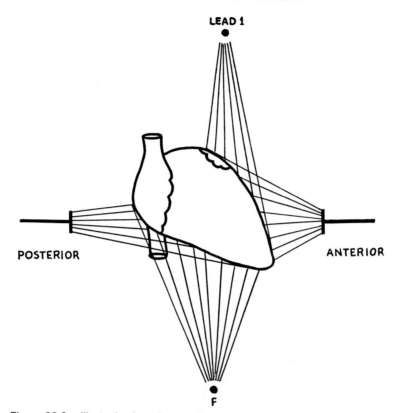

Figure 26.2. Illustrating how the anterior chest leads and lead 1 both face the same "anterior" (really anterosuperior) surface of the heart, while the posterior chest leads and the positive pole (*F*) of leads 2, 3 and aVF face the inferior (diaphragmatic) surface.

and with a glance at figure 26.2, it is relatively simple to decide what changes will occur in which leads when various surfaces of the heart are involved. Leads whose positive poles face the inferior surface (2, 3 and aVF) are most important in the diagnosis of **inferior** infarction. Reciprocal changes are usually seen in leads 1, aVL and some of the precordial leads. In **anterior** infarction indicative changes occur in precordial leads and in leads 1 and aVL, while reciprocal changes develop in leads 2, 3 and aVF. In **lateral** wall infarction leads 1, aVL and V_5 and V_6 are most likely to show indicative changes, and reciprocal changes may sometimes develop in leads taken farthest to the right (V_1, V_{3R}, etc.). None of the routine 12 leads faces the **posterior** surface of the heart, and so infarction of this wall must be inferred from reciprocal changes occurring in anterior leads, especially V_1 and V_2.

The limb lead patterns associated with the two main types of infarction, anterior and inferior, are perhaps worth summarizing first and separately. Anterior infarction produces indicative changes in lead 1 and for this reason is sometimes called Q_1T_1 type infarction. Inferior infarction produces indicative changes in lead 3 and is therefore called Q_3T_3 type infarction. In anterior infarction indicative changes are also seen in aVL and reciprocal changes appear in 2, 3 and aVF. In inferior infarction indicative changes are also found in 2 and aVF, while reciprocal changes develop in 1 and aVL. These changes are summarized in figure 26.3. Remember, however, that the characteristic changes of infarction may appear *only* in the precordial leads, the limb leads remaining normal or near normal.

Salient Features of Acute Myocardial Infarction

	Anterior	Inferior
1. Indicative changes (Q, ST elevation, T inversion) in leads:	1, aVL, anterior chest	2, 3, aVF, posterior chest
2. Reciprocal changes in leads:	2, 3, aVF, posterior chest	1, aVL, anterior chest
3. Progressive changes in pattern from day to day		

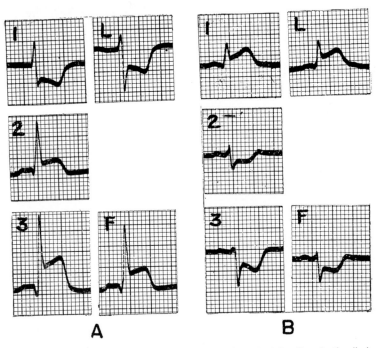

A   B

Figure 26.3. Characteristic early changes of acute infarction in the limb leads. (*A*) Inferior infarction. (*B*) Anterior infarction.

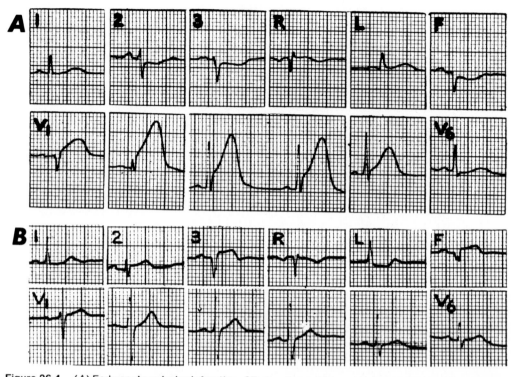

Figure 26.4. (*A*) Early **acute anterior infarction.** ST elevation, with loss of its normal concavity, is evident in four of the five chest leads, with minor reciprocal depression in leads 2, 3 and aVF. (*B*) Early **acute inferior infarction.** There are Q waves in leads 3 and aVF, indicative ST elevation in leads, 2, 3 and aVF and reciprocal depression in leads 1 and aVL, but no such depression in the V leads.

Figure 26.4 illustrates the typical changes of early acute myocardial infarction, anterior (*A*) and inferior (*B*). Note that the ST elevation of anterior infarction (fig. 26.4*A*) is much more pronounced in the chest leads than in the standard limb leads, while reciprocal depression of the ST segment is definite but relatively minor in leads 2, 3 and aVF. In figure 26.4*B* there is ST elevation in leads 2, 3 and aVF with reciprocal depression in leads 1 and aVL; notice that there is no reciprocal ST depression in the precordial leads. The idealized patterns of evolution of both anterior and inferior infarctions are presented in figure 26.5. The reciprocal ST-T changes diagrammed in V_3 with inferior infarction may represent more than mere reciprocity; for it is said that ST-segment depression in anterior leads (V_{1-4}) in the presence of acute transmural inferior infarction usually indicates additional significant ischemia elsewhere[22, 58, 60]: some authors claim further myocardial damage in the posterolateral region,[22] while others find that such "reciprocal" ST depression indicates serious involvement of the anterior descending artery and foretells a stormy course.[58, 60] Depression only in leads 1 and/or aVL, on the other hand, is not indicative of additional involvement and represents a pure "reciprocal" change.[58] However, the issue of reciprocal changes in chest leads is not settled and others express the opinion that precordial ST depression frequently occurs *early* in acute inferior infarction, is not generally caused by significant anterior ischemia, nor associated with more left ventricular dysfunction than is found in patients without such ST depression.[72]

Additional "improved" criteria for the diagnosis of acute inferior infarction, requiring the simultaneous recording of the three standard limb leads, have been proposed.[76]

Evaluation of Q_3

As a prominent Q wave in lead 3 is one of the hallmarks of inferior infarction but is also sometimes a normal finding, its evaluation is often difficult.[68] It is more likely to be abnormal if it is wide (more than 0.03 sec), if it is associated with Q waves also in 2 and aVF, and if it is followed by a slurred upstroke into the R wave.

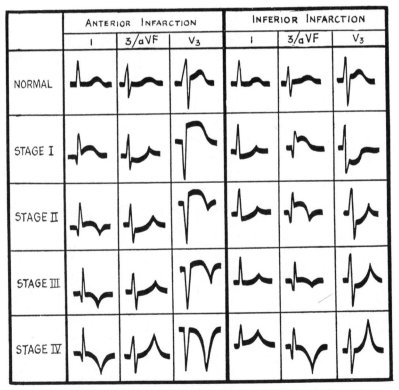

Figure 26.5. Acute myocardial infarction. Stages of evolution in the patterns of anterior and inferior infarctions.

A simple test is sometimes helpful: deep inspiration will usually cause an innocuous (positional) Q_3 to disappear or materially decrease; whereas the Q_3 of infarction is relatively unaffected by this simple maneuver[18] (fig. 26.6, *A–D*). However, the test is not always reliable,[36] to which strip *E* in figure 26.6 bears testimony.

At times, but by no means invariably, it is helpful to refer the decision to the aV leads,[46] for lead 3, connecting left arm and left leg, represents the difference between aVF and aVL ($3 = aVF - aVL$). If the initial deflection of the QRS in aVF is less positive (or more negative) than the corresponding deflection in aVL, there will be an initial negative (Q) wave in 3. And so if there is no Q wave in either aVL or aVF but the R wave in aVF is not so tall as the R in aVL (fig. 26.7*A*), there will be a Q wave in 3. This will clearly not be a pathological Q wave, as it results simply from difference in the height of normal R waves. In such a situation the aV leads give an immediate favorable answer. If on the other hand there is a Q wave in aVF (fig. 26.7*B*), one has merely transferred the burden of proof to aVF and it then has to be decided whether the Q there is of abnormal significance or not.

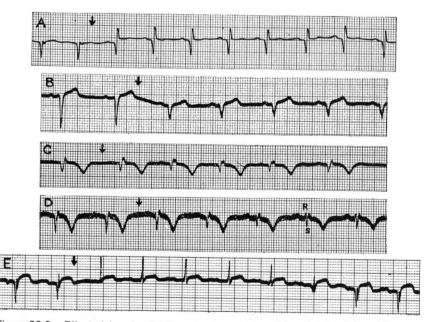

Figure 26.6.   Effect of deep inspiration on Q_3 in patients with inferior infarction. Inspiration began at the arrow in each strip. Note that there is relatively little effect on the negative wave in *A*, *B*, *C* and *D*. In *D* the Q wave is replaced by a small initial R wave, but an appreciable negative (S) wave persists. In *E*, however, the pathological Q wave is entirely drawn up.

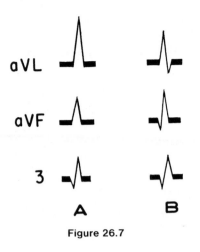

Figure 26.7

Localization of Infarction

Localization of the infarct from the ECG is far from precise.[55, 62] It is however usually possible to identify the main area of involvement and to some extent gauge the infarct's size. Localization is mainly based on the previously stated principle that indicative changes (those epitomized in fig. 26.1, p. 375) occur in leads facing the damaged surface of the heart. Thus if indicative changes are seen in all the precordial leads from V_1 to V_6, we diagnose an **extensive anterior** or **anterolateral infarction**[38] (Figs. 26.8 to 26.11). If such changes occur in only one or more of leads V_1 to V_4, the infarct is labelled **anteroseptal**[37] (fig. 26.12, p. 384). If the limb leads indicate an inferior infarction, but indicative changes are present also in leads V_5 and V_6, we would call it an inferior infarction with lateral extension or an **inferolateral infarction**[41] (figs. 26.13 to 26.15). If the only changes seen are in 1 and aVL, it would suggest **lateral infarction**,[42] and so on.

Subendocardial infarction[9, 30, 35, 49, 50, 70] is diagnosed if (1) the clinical picture justifies the diagnosis of infarction and (2) several of the limb and precordial leads show ST depression and T wave inversions (fig. 26.16) that persist. The subendocardial layer of myocardium is particularly vulnerable because, being close to the ventricular cavity, it is subjected to particularly high pressure during systole and is therefore the earliest zone to "feel the pinch" when coronary adequacy falters.

Right ventricular infarction: significant ST elevation in lead V_4R in patients with inferior wall infarction is said to be diagnostic of a right ventricular infarct[6, 17]; indeed, ST elevation of 1 mm or more in any of the leads V_4R to V_6R is claimed to have 90 per cent sensitivity and specificity.[73]

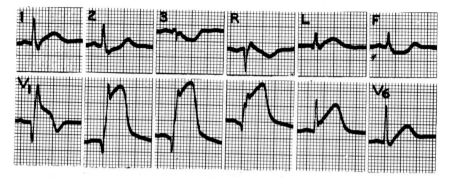

Figure 26.8   Acute anterior myocardial infarction. Note ST elevation in V_{1-5}, and loss of the normal upward concavity of the ST segment in 1, aVL and V_{2-6}, with reciprocal changes in 2, 3 and aVF. Q waves have developed in the right chest leads, and the pattern of RBBB has appeared, indicating septal involvement.

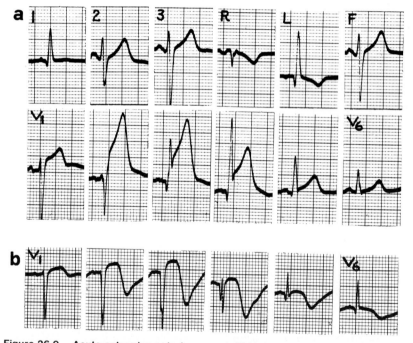

Figure 26.9.   Acute extensive anterior myocardial infarction. In a, note probable left anterior hemiblock in the limb leads with high ST take-off and tall T waves in precordial leads; in b, 2 days later, "coving" of ST segments with deep inversion of T and U waves, while simultaneously R waves have dwindled in V_{1-2}, a QS complex has appeared in V_3, and Q waves have developed or deepened in V_{4-6}.

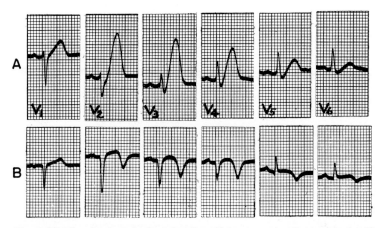

Figure 26.10.   Acute anterior infarction. Note unusual early stage in *A*, with tall T waves and *depressed ST* take-off. *B*, taken a few days later, shows typical evolution of anterior infarction.

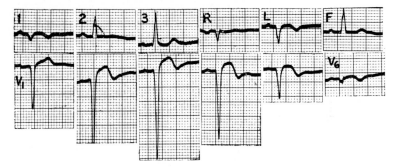

Figure 26.11.   Old anterior myocardial infarction with persistent ST elevation in precordial leads 3 years after the infarction. A ventricular aneurysm was demonstrated.

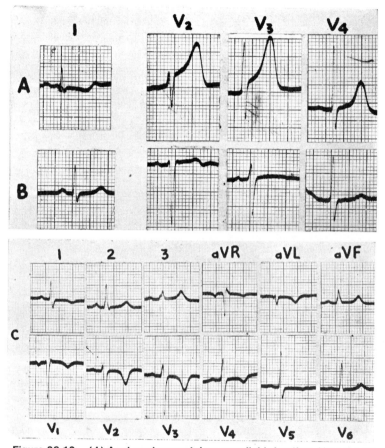

Figure 26.12. (*A*) **Acute anteroseptal myocardial infarction.** Note the tall T waves in V$_{2-4}$, where they will later be deeply inverted. (*B*) Taken just a few hours later; note striking changes in T waves; tracing is now remarkably normal. (*C*) Taken 6 days later; shows fully developed pattern of anteroseptal infarction. Note that no pathological Q waves have developed, but the infarction can be diagnosed with certainty from the striking evolution in the ST-T pattern.

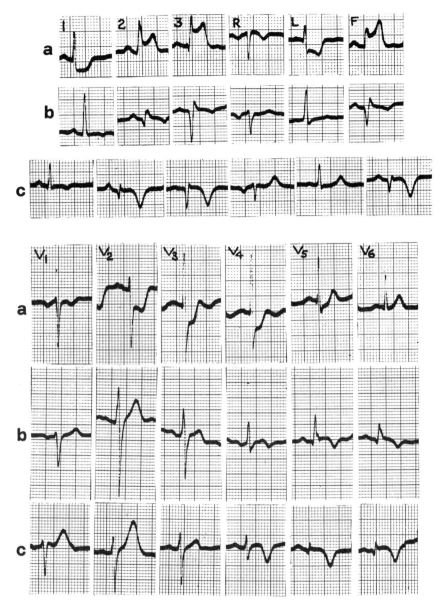

Figure 26.13. Acute inferolateral myocardial infarction. Tracing *a* was taken 3 days before *b*, and *b* 6 days before *c*. Note in *a* indicative changes in 2, 3 and aVF with reciprocal changes in 1, aVL and the chest leads V_{2-5}. Subsequent evolution demonstrates indicative changes in the left chest leads as well, so that the infarction is inferolateral. Note also that the QRS axis shifts from about $+60°$ to $-30°$ (thanks to the development of infarction Q waves, not to left anterior hemiblock) and that the R waves in left chest leads have shrunk away.

Atrial infarction also usually complicates the inferior wall infarct. It must be suspected when, in the presence of ventricular infarction, an atrial arrhythmia develops. Other clues include abnormal P-wave contour and any significant P-R segment displacement (see fig. 26.25), especially widespread P-R segment depression in the presence of an atrial arrhythmia, elevation of the P-R segment in left chest leads with reciprocal depression in right chest leads, or elevation in lead 1 with reciprocal depression in lead 3.[33]

Complex Patterns

Frequently the pattern observed is not so "pure" as the ones so far described. If the anterior and inferior walls of the left ventricle are both involved in the process, **antero-inferior infarction** (fig. 26.17 and 26.18), varying combinations

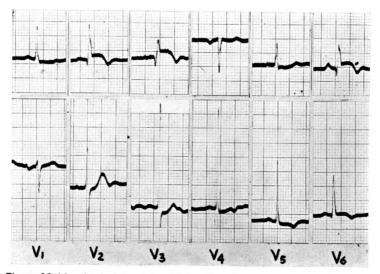

Figure 26.14.   Acute inferolateral infarction. Note indicative changes in 2, 3 and aVF. The ST-T changes in V_6 suggest lateral wall involvement as well.

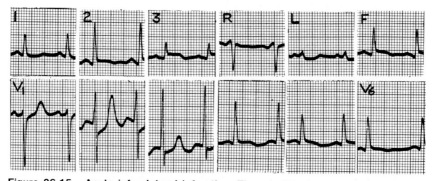

Figure 26.15.   Acute inferolateral infarction. There is ST elevation in 2, 3, aVF and V_{4-6}, with classical reciprocal changes in V_{1-3}.

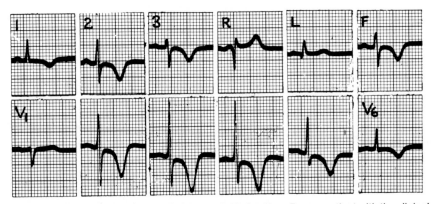

Figure 26.16. Probable **acute subendocardial infarction.** From a patient with the clinical picture of infarction; note widespread ST-T depression in limb and chest leads, but no associated Q waves.

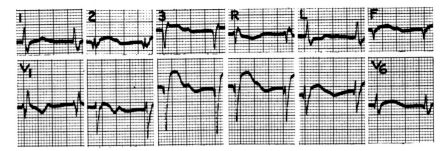

Figure 26.17. Antero-inferior myocardial infarction. Note that indicative changes are evident in both anterior (V_{2-6}) and inferior (2, 3, and aVF) leads; RBBB has also developed, indicating septal involvement. There is also marked prolongation of the P-R interval to about 0.40 sec.

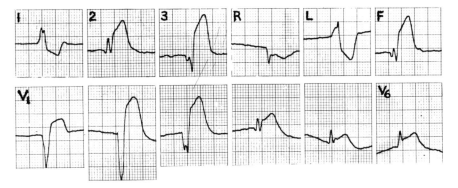

Figure 26.18. Acute antero-inferior infarction. Note the diagnostic "indicative" ST elevation across the precordium (V_{1-6}) and in the "inferior" leads (2, 3 and aVF) as well with reciprocal changes in the lateral leads (1 and aVL). There is also a **LBBB** pattern.

of the changes typical of each may occur.[39] Sometimes an inferior infarction develops in a heart that has suffered a previous anterior infarction, or vice versa; in such circumstances the current infarction, producing changes opposite (or reciprocal) to the changes of the previous infarction, may tend to "normalize" the tracing so that it looks "better" than it did before the second occlusion. Some patients may have two transmural infarctions, one recent and one old, and consequently have a poor prognosis yet have no sign of a Q wave.

Bundle-branch block, producing as it does bizarre QRS, ST and T changes of its own, may mask the changes of a superimposed infarction. A sometimes difficult diagnosis is that of infarction in the presence of left bundle-branch block.[4, 12] If a previous tracing is available showing the uncomplicated block pattern, then the appearance of fresh Q waves (especially over the left ventricle, where they are not found in uncomplicated left bundle-branch block) is good evidence of acute infarction. Q waves in 1, aVL or V_6 in the presence of left bundle-branch block (fig. 26.19) are strongly suspicious of anteroseptal infarction,[26, 53] as are notched S waves in V_3 or V_4.[74] A decrease in amplitude of R waves over the left ventricle,[29] is a clue suspicious of acute infarction. At times, the diagnosis may be disarmingly easy if the primary ST-T changes of acute injury replace the secondary changes of the LBBB (figs. 26.18 and 26.19). Similarly, the diagnostic ST-T changes of acute infarction may show through the bizarre pattern of ventricular pacing[44] and other forms of ventricular ectopy.

Right bundle-branch block is less likely to cause confusion.[13] Both anterior and inferior infarction patterns can be seen superimposed on the block pattern

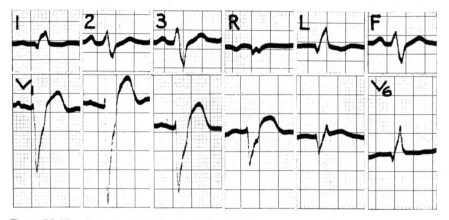

Figure 26.19.   Anteroseptal infarction. The QRS pattern is characteristic of LBBB except that there are unexpected Q waves in 1, aVL and V6. The rSr′ in V_5 suggests the possibility of ventricular aneurysm.[16] Note characteristic *upward convexity* of elevated ST segments V_{2-4}.

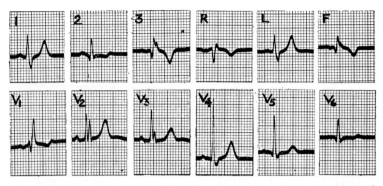

Figure 26.20. Acute inferior infarction with right bundle-branch block. Q and T changes are evident in 2, 3 and aVF, with reciprocal T-wave changes in V_{2-4}.

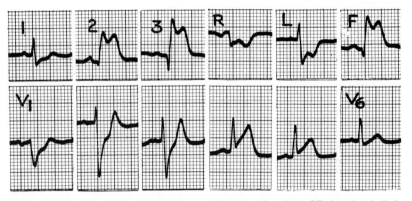

Figure 26.21. Acute **infero-apical** myocardial infarction. Note ST elevation in 2, 3, aVF, V_4 and V_5 with reciprocal depression in other leads. Q waves are developing in 2, 3 and aVF.

(figs. 26.8, 26.17 and 26.20). The block may have preceded the infarction or may have resulted from it; indeed, the presence of bundle-branch block may be considered an integral part of the pattern of **septal infarction**.[46]

A less thoroughgoing involvement of both anterior and inferior walls is presented in figure 26.21 where indicative changes are confined to only V_4 and V_5 in the chest series: an **infero-apical infarction.**

Along with the inferior wall, there may be involvement of the posterobasal region of the left ventricle; this directly posterior involvement is recognized by reciprocal changes in anterior leads (V_1, V_2) including an increase in height and width of their normally small R waves. Figure 26.22 illustrates such an **inferoposterior infarction** with classical indicative changes in the inferior leads and increased prominence of the R waves in V_1 and V_2.

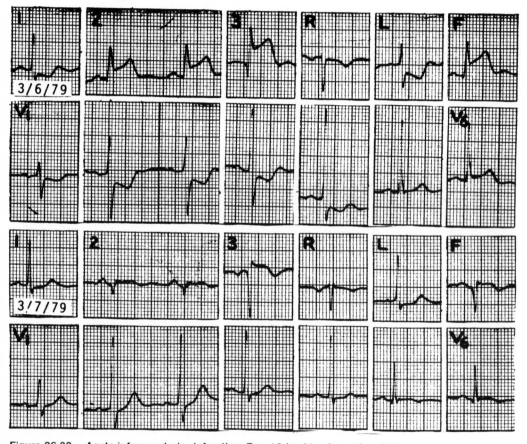

Figure 26.22.   Acute inferoposterior infarction. Two 12-lead tracings taken 24 hours apart and showing evolution both in the indicative changes in leads 2, 3 and aVF and in the reciprocal changes in anterior leads V_1 and V_2. Note the virtually complete loss of R waves in the inferior leads as the Q waves develop, and the abnormally prominent R waves in V_1 and V_2 which double in size by the second day. Judging by the ST-T changes in V_5 and V_6, there is probably also involvement of the lateral wall as well.

Further Observations

Some important general points:

1. *Time relationships* are important. Rarely, no changes develop in the tracing for several days or even for 2 or 3 weeks. Usually, however, they begin to make their appearance within the first few hours. ST-segment changes appear early and progress. At this stage the T waves, later to become inverted, actually become taller and appear as an upward extension of the rising ST segments[2] (figs. 26.9, 26.10 and 26.12). This early tall T wave may be mistaken for the later tall T wave of reciprocal leads, and an early anterior infarction may thus be wrongly labelled as inferior. Sometimes this tall T wave is associated with striking depression of the ST segment,[10] and then of course the reciprocal pattern of an inferior infarction is even more closely simulated (fig. 26.10*A*). To add to the confusion similar tall T waves are occasionally seen as an early stage of inferior infarction[66]; in such cases this may well represent a premonitory stage of diaphragmatic wall ischemia before actual infarction has occurred. Similar but persistent tall T waves are a not uncommon finding in patients with angina[20] (see Chapter 27, fig. 27.4).

Q waves may appear early or may not develop for several days. Whenever the various changes appear they tend to evolve in a fairly typical sequence (fig. 26.5). In the indicative leads the ST segments rise higher and higher and then begin to return to the baseline, while the T waves develop progressively deeper inversion; finally, after weeks or months, the T waves may become shallower and finally return to normal. Thus ST changes are usually the most transitory; the T changes are more lasting; but the Q waves are the most likely to remain as a permanent record of the myocardial scar. Even well established Q waves, however, may at times completely disappear; in fact, diagnostic Q waves are lost within three years in approximately 14 per cent of patients with myocardial infarction.[77] Persistent ST segment elevation[15] (fig. 26.11) the explanation for which is quite uncertain,[54] or the presence of an rsR′ pattern in V$_5$ or V$_6$[16] suggests the possibility of ventricular aneurysm.

The model sequence of changes depicted diagrammatically in figure 26.5 is not invariable, but there is always some "evolution" of the pattern along similar lines, and to diagnose an *acute* infarction such evolution must be in evidence. For there is no means of being certain, in a single tracing, whether the typical changes of infarction are due to an acute process or are the remnants of an old one. ST segment deviations are least likely to represent an old process, but even they may sometimes endure for a long time and rarely are permanent. Progressive changes from day to day are the conclusive evidence of an active, acute process.

2. The electrocardiogram should be considered *confirmatory* of the clinical impression, and should not supersede it. If the patient is suspected clinically of having sustained a myocardial infarct, he should be treated accordingly even if his tracing is completely normal. The looked-for changes may be late to appear

or, rarely, they may never appear in the routine leads although the infarction is a clinical certainty. For factors favoring missed diagnoses, see page 395.

3. The Q waves of infarction may be better revealed in ectopic ventricular beats than in the conducted sinus beats[3,5] (fig. 26.23).

4. A T-wave pattern of some importance is the T_1-lower-than-T_3 pattern. T_1 is often found normally lower than T_3 in vertical hearts, i.e., when the QRS axis is in the neighborhood of +90°. It is also abnormally present in early left ventricular overload, before frank inversion of T_1 has occurred. If both vertical heart and left ventricular overload can be excluded such a pattern is extremely suspicious of an anterior infarction, either old or recent.[11]

5. Apart from the changes specific for acute infarction, other abnormalities frequently appear. The tracing sometimes shows low voltage and this is associated with a doubled mortality rate.[56] The QT duration is frequently prolonged, reaching its maximum in the second week. Any arrhythmia or block may develop, and continuously monitored series indicate that some form of rhythm disturbance occurs in 75 to 95% of all patients. In order of frequency, the commonest to develop are ventricular premature beats, supraventricular premature beats, atrial fibrillation, ventricular tachycardia, accelerated idioventricular rhythms and supraventricular tachycardia. Sinus bradycardia, first degree A-V block, type I A-V block, and complete A-V block with narrow escaping ventricular QRS complexes (idiojunctional rhythm) characteristically complicate acute inferior infarction; whereas BBB, type II A-V block, and complete A-V block with wide QRS complexes (idioventricular rhythm) more often result from anterior infarction.

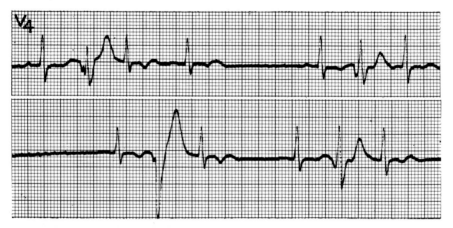

Figure 26.23. Anterior infarction, the indicative Q waves of which are obvious in the ventricular extrasystoles and absent in the conducted beats. (From a 52-year-old physician who had an anterior infarction 2 years previously.)

Infarction without Q Waves

Q waves have come to be regarded as the hallowed hallmark of infarction. But there is nothing sacred about Q waves as such. Their importance is that they represent the replacement of electrical forces directed toward the electrode by oppositely directed forces, i.e., replacement of impulses (dipoles) travelling toward the electrode by impulses travelling away from it. This being so, loss of R wave with or without gain in depth of S wave might well carry the same significance as a Q wave. Indeed, in some circumstances this is true. Loss of QRS amplitude over the left ventricle has already been mentioned as a clue to infarction in the presence of left bundle-branch block.

Furthermore, Q waves have been regarded for decades as an index of transmural (through-and-through; full-thickness) infarction and therefore as a discriminator between transmural and subendocardial infarction. Yet long ago Prinzmetal's team demonstrated that the subendocardium was *not* electrocardiographically silent; and so the mistaken significance of Q waves could have been corrected a quarter century ago. But established traditions die hard and slowly, and still the belief lingers that Q waves are the monopoly of transmural infarcts. The truth is that, although statistically Q waves are more commonly seen in transmural than in nontransmural (subendocardial) infarction, both brands of infarcts are seen both with and without Q waves. These waves are, therefore, in themselves useless in discriminating between them.[28,48,52,55,59,62]

Again, reversal of the normal trend toward heightening of R waves in the first three or four precordial leads may be a helpful sign. In these leads we have seen that the height of the R wave normally increases from right to left. If, however, these R waves dwindle progressively from right to left, it is suspicious of anteroseptal infarction; but it is important to remember that both "poor" and "reversed" progression of the precordial R wave may also be seen in ventricular hypertrophy, left or right, and even in some normal subjects. And even complete loss of R waves (i.e., QS complexes) in V_1 through V_3 is not necessarily evidence of anterior infarction and is seen in left ventricular hypertrophy and other situations (see below).

In true posterior or inferoposterior infarction the only changes may be reciprocal ones observed in the anterior chest leads. At times in true posterior or in lateral infarction[31,70] the sole or chief change may be an increase in the

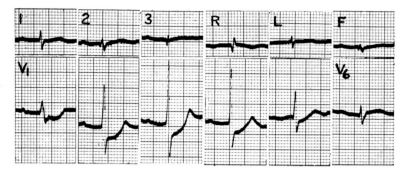

Figure 26.24. Probable **acute posterior infarction.** Note prominent and wide R waves in V₁ and V₂ accompanied by reciprocal ST-T changes in the same leads; these features in anterior leads suggest an acute infarction of the opposite, i.e., posterior, wall.

height of R waves over the right precordium (V₃ᵣ, V₁, V₂). Similarly, an increased width of the R wave to 0.04 sec or more in V₁ and V₂ may be diagnostic of true posterior infarction[23] (fig. 26.24).

Another infarction pattern, of which the most striking feature is *left axis deviation*, was described by Grant.[24] Its characteristics are (1) an initial wide R wave (0.04 sec or more) followed by a deep S wave in aVF, and (2) marked left axis deviation of more than −30°. A careful study with autopsy correlation showed that many patients with this pattern had infarction of the anterolateral wall. He attributed the axis shift to "peri-infarction block," but subsequent work[7] indicates that this pattern is more often found with LVH or diffuse scarring of the left ventricle than with a discrete infarction. Its probable anatomic basis is left anterior hemiblock (see p. 86). Left anterior hemiblock can also eliminate the Q waves of inferior infarction by substituting r waves for them in 2, 3 and aVF (fig. 26.25). Thus the diagnosis of inferior infarction in the presence of anterior hemiblock presents a special problem, since they both produce significant left axis deviation—the infarction with Q waves, the hemiblock with S waves.

Grant also pointed out that *right axis deviation* may sometimes result from infarction of the diaphragmatic wall[23]; the probable explanation for this is left posterior hemiblock.

In a few patients with anteroseptal infarction and intermittent RBBB, the initial q wave of infarction may appear in V₁ only in association with the RBBB and be replaced by an initial r wave during normal conduction.[75]

Q Waves without Infarction

Just as the absence of Q waves does not exclude, so their presence does not prove, infarction. One of the commonest errors of over interpretation is in the reading of anteroseptal infarction from QS complexes in V₁ and V₂—a pattern much more often produced by left ventricular hypertrophy alone. The following conditions can produce pathological Q waves that simulate those of myocardial infarction:

1. Ventricular hypertrophy, left or right[43, 63]
2. Diffuse myocardial disease[45, 47, 64]
3. Hypertrophic cardiomyopathy
4. Anterior and posterior hemiblock
5. Focal septal block[21]
6. Localized myocardial replacement
7. Acute extracardiac catastrophes, e.g., pancreatitis,[19] pulmonary embolism, pneumonia,[34] etc.
8. Ventricular preexcitation[67]

In addition, significant Q waves may occur as a transient manifestation of myocardial ischemia[57]; and they are rarely seen in apparently normal youths.[32]

Concluding Notes on Diagnosis

The electrocardiogram is not infallible in the diagnosis of infarction. It has been estimated that with 12 routine leads only 80 to 90% of cases are diagnosable. Factors to bear in mind as probable causes of missed diagnoses are:

1. Failure to take serial tracings.
2. Failure to take additional exploratory chest leads in doubtful cases
3. Presence of bundle-branch block
4. Digitalis action tending to neutralize ST elevations
5. Simultaneous infarcts neutralizing each other's patterns
6. Masking by hemiblock

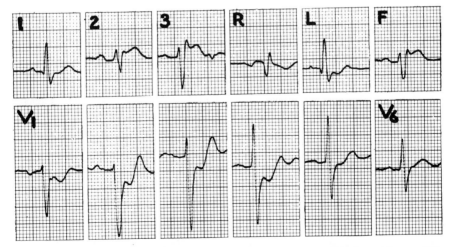

Figure 26.25. Acute inferior infarction with left anterior hemiblock and incomplete **RBBB.** The Q waves of inferior infarction are kept at bay by the r waves of the hemiblock in 2, 3 and aVF, but the ST elevation in those leads with reciprocal depression in 1, aVL and V_{1-5} are diagnostic. Depression of the P-R segment, best seen in leads 2 and aVF, bespeak an **atrial infarction** as well.

REFERENCES

1. Abbott, J. A., and Scheinman, M. M.: Nondiagnostic electrocardiogram in patients with acute myocardial infarction: clinical and anatomic correlations. Am. J. Med. 1973: **55**, 608.
2. Bayley, R. H., et al.: Electrocardiographic changes (local ventricular ischemia and injury) produced in the dog by temporary occlusion of a coronary artery, showing a new stage in the evolution of a myocardial infarction. Am. Heart J. 1944: **27**, 164.
3. Benchimol, A., et al.: The ventricular premature contraction. Its place in the diagnosis of ischemic heart disease. Am. Heart J. 1963: **65**, 334.
4. Besoain-Santander, M., and Gomez-Ebensperguer, G.: Electrocardiographic diagnosis of myocardial infarction in cases of complete left bundle branch block. Am. Heart J. 1960: **60**, 886.
5. Bisteni, A., et al.: Ventricular premature beats in the diagnosis of myocardial infarction. Br. Heart J. 1961: **23**, 521.
6. Braat, S., et al.: The value of right precordial leads in detection of right ventricular infarction; a comparison with ^{99m} Tc-pyrophosphate scintigraphy (abstr.). Circulation 1981: **64** (supp. IV), 86.
7. Castle, C. H., and Keane, W. M.: Electrocardiographic "peri-infarction block." A clinical and pathologic correlation. Circulation 1965: **31**, 403.
8. Class, R. N., et al.: Diphtheritic myocarditis simulating myocardial infarction. Am. J. Cardiol. 1965: **16**, 580.
9. Cook, R. W., et al.: Electrocardiographic changes in acute subendocardial infarction. I. Large subendocardial and nontransmural infarcts. Circulation 1958: **18**, 603. II. Small subendocardial infarcts. Ibid.: 613.
10. Dressler, W., and Roesler, H.: High T waves in the earliest stage of myocardial infarction. Am. Heart J. 1947: **34**, 627.
11. Dressler, W., and Roesler, H.: The diagnostic value of the pattern T_1 lower than T_3 ($T_1 < T_3$) compared with the information yielded by multiple chest leads in myocardial infarction. Am. Heart J. 1948: **36**, 115.
12. Dressler, W., et al.: The electrocardiographic signs of myocardial infarction in the presence of bundle branch block. I. Myocardial infarction with left bundle branch block. Am. Heart J. 1950: **39**, 217.
13. Dressler, W., et al.: The electrocardiographic signs of myocardial infarction in the presence of bundle branch block. II. Myocardial infarction with right bundle branch block. Am. Heart J. 1950: **39**, 544.
14. Dunn, W. J., et al.: The electrocardiogram in infarction of the lateral wall of the left ventricle: a clinicopathologic study. Circulation 1956: **14**, 540.
15. East, T., and Oram, S.: The cardiogram in ventricular aneurysm following cardiac infarction. Br. Heart J. 1952: **14**, 125.
16. El-Sherif, N.: The rsR′ pattern in left surface leads in ventricular aneurysm. Br. Heart J. 1970: **32**, 440.
17. Erhardt, L. R., et al.: Single right-sided precordial lead in the diagnosis of right ventricular involvement in myocardial infarction. Am. Heart J. 1976: **91**, 571.
18. Evans, W.: The effect of deep inbreathing on lead III of the electrocardiogram. Br. Heart J. 1951: **13**, 457.
19. Fulton, M. C., and Marriott, H. J. L.: Acute pancreatitis simulating myocardial infarction in the electrocardiogram. Ann. Intern. Med. 1963: **59**, 730.
20. Freundlich, J.: The diagnostic significance of tall upright T wave in the chest leads. Am. Heart J. 1956: **52**, 749.
21. Gambetta, M., and Childers, R. W.: Rate-dependent right precordial Q waves: "septal focal block." Am. J. Cardiol. 1973: **32**, 196.
22. Goldberg, H. L., et al.: Anterior S-T segment depression in acute inferior myocardial infarction: Indicator of posterolateral infarction. Am. J. Cardiol. 1981: **48**, 1009.
23. Grant, R. P., and Murray R. H.: QRS complex deformity of myocardial infarction in the human subject. Am. J. Med. 1954: **17**, 587.
24. Grant, R. P.: Left axis deviation. An electrocardiographic-pathologic correlation study. Circulation 1956: **14**, 233.
25. Grant, R. P.: Peri-infarction block. Prog. Cardiovasc. Dis. 1959: **2**, 237.
26. Horan, L., et al.: The significance of diagnostic Q waves in the presence of bundle branch block. Chest 1970: **58**, 214.

27. Hurd, H. P., et al.: Comparative accuracy of electrocardiographic and vectorcardiographic criteria for inferior myocardial infarction. Circulation 1981: **63**, 1025.
28. Ideker, R. E., et al.: Q waves and transmural infarcts; the terms are not the same (abstr.). Am. J. Cardiol. 1981: **47**, 463.
29. Kennamer, R., and Prinzmetal, M.: Myocardial infarction complicated by left bundle branch block. Am. Heart J. 1956: **51**, 78.
30. Levine, H. D., and Ford, R. V.: Subendocardial infarction: report of six cases and critical survey of the literature. Circulation 1950: **1**, 246.
31. Levy, L., et al.:Prominent R wave and shallow S wave in lead V_1 as a result of lateral myocardial infarction. Am. Heart J. 1950; **40**, 447.
32. Likoff, W., et al.: Myocardial infarction patterns in young subjects with normal coronary arteriograms. Circulation 1962: **26**, 373.
33. Liu, C. K.: Atrial infarction of the heart. Circulation 1961: **23**, 331.
34. Mamlin, J. J., et al.: Electrocardiographic pattern of massive myocardial infarction without pathologic confirmation. Circulation 1964: **30**, 539.
35. Massumi, R. A., et al.: Studies on the mechanism of ventricular activity. XVI. Activation of the human ventricle. Am. J. Med. 1955: **19**, 832.
36. Mimbs, J. W., et al.: The effect of respiration on normal and abnormal Q waves: an electrocardiographic and vectorcardiographic analysis. Am. Heart J. 1977: **94**, 579.
37. Myers, G. B., et al.: Correlation of electrocardiographic and pathologic findings in anteroseptal infarction. Am. Heart J. 1948: **36**, 535.
38. Myers, G. B., et al.: Carrelation of electrocardiographic and pathologic findings in large anterolateral infarcts. Am. Heart J. 1948: **36**, 838.
39. Myers, G. B., et al.: Correlation of electrocardiographic and pathologic findings in anteroposterior infarction. Am. Heart J. 1949: **37**, 205.
40. Myers, G. B., et al.: Correlation of electrocardiographic and pathologic findings in posterior infarction. Am. Heart J. 1949: **38**, 547.
41. Myers, G. B., et al.: Correlation of electrocardiographic and pathologic findings in posterolateral infarction. Am. Heart J. 1949: **38**, 837.
42. Myers, G. B., et al.: Correlation of electrocardiographic and pathologic findings in lateral infarction. Am. Heart J. 1949: **37**, 3.
43. Myers, G. B.: QRS-T patterns in multiple precordial leads that may be mistaken for myocardial infarction. Circulation 1950: **1**, 844 and 860.
44. Niremberg, V., et al.: Primary ST changes; diagnostic aid in paced patients with acute myocardial infarction. Br. Heart J. 1977: **39**, 502.
45. Oram, S., and Stokes, W.: The heart in scleroderma. Br. Heart J. 1961: **23**, 243.
46. Osher, H. L., and Wolff, L.: The diagnosis of infarction of the interventricular septum. Am. Heart J. 1953: **45**, 429.
47. Perez-Trevino, C., et al.: Glycogen storage disease of the heart. Am. J. Cardiol. 1965: **16**, 137.
48. Pipberger, H. V., and Lopez, E. A.: "Silent" subendocardial infarcts; fact or fiction? Am. Heart J. 1980: **100**, 597.
49. Prinzmetal, M., et al. Studies on the mechanism of ventricular activity; VI. The depolarization complex in pure subendocardial infarction; role of the subendocardial region in the normal electrocardiogram. Am. J. Med. 1954: **16**, 469.
50. Pruitt, R. D., et al.: Certain clinical states and pathologic changes associated with deeply inverted T waves in the precordial electrocardiogram. Circulation 1955: **11**, 517.
51. Pruitt, R. D., et al.: Simulation of electrocardiogram of apicolateral myocardial destructive lesions of obscure etiology (myocardiopathy). Circulation 1962: **25**, 506.
52. Raunio, H., et al.: Changes in the QRS complex and ST segment in transmural and subendocardial myocardial infarctions. Am. Heart J. 1979: **98**, 176.
53. Rhoads, D. V., et al.: The electrocardiogram in the presence of myocardial infarction and intraventricular block of the left bundle-branch block type. Am. Heart J. 1961: **62**, 78.
54. Richter, S., et al.: Functional significance of electrocardiographic changes after left ventricular aneurysmectomy. J. Electrocardiol. 1978: **11**, 247.
55. Roberts, W. C., and Gardin, J. M.: Locations of myocardial infarcts: A confusion of terms and definitions. Am. J. Cardiol. 1978: **42**, 868.
56. Rotmensch, H. H., et al.: Incidence and significance of the low-voltage electrocardiogram in acute myocardial infarction. Chest 1977: **71**, 708.
57. Rubin, I. L., et al.: Transient abnormal Q waves during coronary insufficiency. Am. Heart J. 1966: **71**, 254.

58. Salcedo, J. R., et al.: Significance of reciprocal S-T segment depression in anterior precordial leads in acute inferior myocardial infarction; concomitant left anterior descending coronary artery disease? Am. J. Cardiol. 1981: **48**, 1003.
59. Savage, R. M., et al.: Correlation of postmortem anatomic findings with electrocardiographic changes in patients with typical anterior and posterior infarcts. Circulation 1977: **55**, 279.
60. Shah, P. K., and Berman, D. S.: Implications of precordial S-T segment depression in acute inferior myocardial infarction. Am. J. Cardiol. 1981: **48**, 1167.
61. Sokolow, M.: The clinical value of the unipolar extremity (aV) leads. Ann. Intern. Med. 1951: **34**, 921.
62. Sullivan, W., et al.: Correlation of electrocardiographic and pathologic findings in healed myocardial infarction. Am. J. Cardiol. 1978: **42**, 724.
63. Surawicz, B., et al.: QS- and QR-pattern in leads V_3 and V_4 in absence of myocardial infarction: electrocardiographic and vectorcardiographic study. Circulation 1956: **12**, 391.
64. Tavel, M. E., and Fisch, C.: Abnormal Q waves simulating myocardial infarction in diffuse myocardial diseases. Am. Heart J. 1964: **68**, 534.
65. Vincent, G. M., et al.: Mechanisms of ischemic ST-segment displacement: evaluation by direct current recordings. Circulation 1977: **56**, 552.
66. Wachtel, F. W., and Teich, E. M.: Tall precordial T waves as the earliest sign of diaphragmatic wall infarction. Am. Heart J. 1956: **51**, 91.
67. Wasserburger, R. H., et al.: Noninfarctional $QS_{2,3,aVF}$ complexes as seen in the Wolff-Parkinson-White syndrome and left bundle branch block. Am. Heart J. 1962: **64**, 617.
68. Weisbart, M. H., and Simonson, E.: The diagnostic accuracy of Q_3 and related electrocardiographic items for the detection of patients with posterior wall myocardial infarction. Am. Heart J. 1955: **50**, 62.
69. Yu, P. N. G., and Blake, T. M.: The significance of QaVF in the diagnosis of posterior infarction. Am. Heart J. 1950: **40**, 545.
70. Yu, P. N. G., and Stewart, J. M.: Subendocardial myocardial infarction with special reference to the electrocardiographic change. Am. Heart J. 1950: **39**, 862.
71. Zema, M. J., et al.: Electrocardiographic poor R-wave progression; correlation with postmortem findings. Chest 1981: **79**, 195.
72. Croft, C. H., et al.: Clinical implications of anterior ST segment depression in patients with acute inferior myocardial infarction. Am. J. Cardiol. 1982: **50**, 428.
73. Croft, C. H., et al.: Detection of acute right ventricular infarction by right precordial electrocardiography. Am. J. Cardiol. 1982: **50**, 421.
74. Havelda, C. J., et al.: The pathologic correlates of the electrocardiogram: complete left bundle branch block. Circulation 1982: **65**, 445.
75. Rosenbaum, M. B., et al.: Abnormal Q waves in right sided chest leads provoked by onset of right bundle-branch block in patients with anteroseptal infarction. Br. Heart J. 1982: **47**, 227.
76. Warner, R., et al.: Improved electrocardiographic criteria for the diagnosis of inferior myocardial infarction. Circulation 1982: **66**, 422.
77. Wasserman, A. G., et al.: Prognostic implications of diagnostic Q waves after myocardial infarction. Circulation 1982: **65**, 1451.

Review Tracings

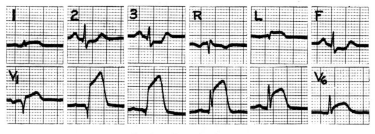

Review Tracing 26.1

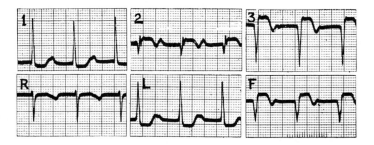

Review Tracing 26.2

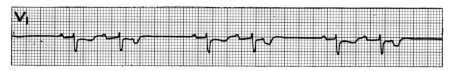

Review Tracing 26.3

For interpretation, see page 484

Review Tracing

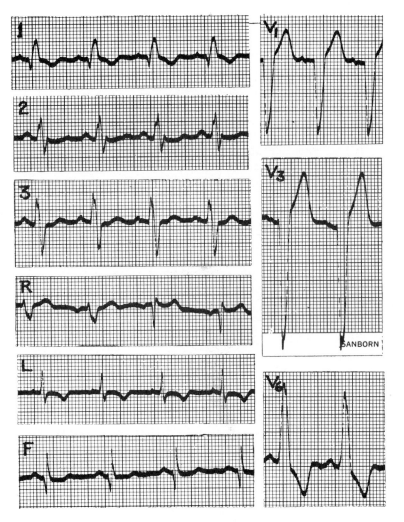

Review Tracing 26.4

For interpretation, see page 484

Some Electrocardiographic Milestones

1858 Kolliker and Muller in Germany demonstrated that contraction of heart muscle was accompanied by electrical activity.

1887 Waller in England recorded the first electrocardiogram in man using a capillary electrometer.

1903 Einthoven in Holland introduced the string galvanometer electrocardiograph and employed the classical standard limb leads in human electrocardiography.

1914 Lewis in England introduced a two-string electrocardiograph. Our knowledge of the sequence of myocardial activation is based on his studies with this machine. Lewis also introduced the concept of the "intrinsic deflection."

1927 Craib introduced the doublet (dipole) concept.

1932 Wolferth and Wood in America demonstrated the value of precordial leads.

1934 Wilson in America introduced the central terminal and with it the unipolar or V leads.

1935 Wilson in America demonstrated the superiority of multiple precordial leads over one such lead.

1938 Schellong in Germany and Wilson and Johnston in America described techniques for recording the frontal plane electrocardiogram as a vector figure using the cathode-ray oscillograph.

1969 Scherlag in America developed the technique for His-bundle electrography.

27

Coronary Insufficiency and Related Matters

Coronary insufficiency may be suspected when ST segments are significantly depressed below the baseline formed by the T-P segment (figs. 27.1 and 27.2). But a number of other conditions cause ST-T changes which may readily be confused with those of coronary disease. These will be dealt with later in this chapter.

An ST-T pattern particularly suggestive of coronary insufficiency is a horizontal ST segment (also known as "plane" depression[33]) making a sharp angle with the proximal shoulder of the still upright T wave (figs. 27.1 and 27.2). Normally the ST segment and T wave should merge smoothly and imperceptibly.

At times the most striking or only evidence of coronary insufficiency is inverted U waves (fig. 27.3). At other times pathologically tall precordial T waves are the sole manifestation of myocardial ischemia (fig. 27.4).

Another sometimes helpful sign of coronary insufficiency is a post-extrasystolic T-wave change.[64, 73] The T wave of the sinus beat following the premature beat changes form and often polarity; sometimes this is accompanied by abnormal lengthening of the Q-T interval (fig. 27.5). Levine called this the

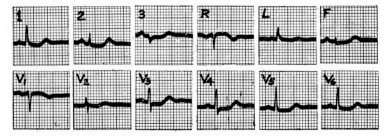

Figure 27.1. Coronary insufficiency. Note horizontally depressed ST segments in many leads.

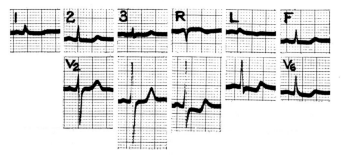

Figure 27.2. Coronary insufficiency. ST depression in many leads with sharp-angled ST-T junctions.

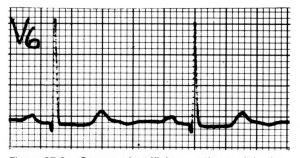

Figure 27.3. Coronary insufficiency—three subtle signs: horizontality of ST segments, sharp-angled ST-T junctions, U-wave inversion.

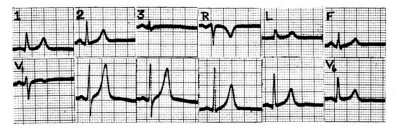

Figure 27.4. Coronary insufficiency. Abnormally tall precordial T waves are the only electrocardiographic sign of myocardial ischemia in this patient with typical angina.

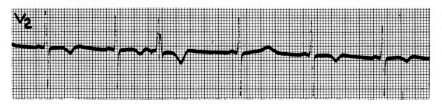

Figure 27.5. Post-extrasystolic T-wave change. After two sinus beats comes a supraventricular premature beat with ventricular aberration. The sinus beat *following* the extrasystole shows a complete change in polarity of the T wave with prolongation of the Q-T interval.

"poor man's exercise test" since the change is included in the initial tracing and so obviates the need and expense of a subsequent exercise test. Useful as this change may be in drawing attention to the possibility of myocardial disease, there is little doubt that it is also often seen in normal hearts.[32, 35, 61] Engel found postextrasystolic T-wave changes in 13 of 19 (68%) subjects with normal hearts compared with 29 of 36 (81%) of patients with proven coronary disease.[32]

Another minor sign which may direct attention to the presence of coronary disease is the TV_1-taller-than-TV_6 pattern. In most normal hearts the T wave in V_6 is taller than the T wave in V_1, which indeed is often inverted. If TV_1 is not only upright but taller than TV_6, it suggests an abnormality of the left ventricular myocardium and is seen in left ventricular overloading as well as coronary disease.[89]

In some patients with coronary insufficiency, diagnostic ST-T changes develop only during an attack of anginal pain (fig. 27.6). Conversely, since ECG abnormalities develop in 97% of patients with unstable angina,[98] absence of ST segment shifts during pain virtually rules out the diagnosis of unstable angina. In the "variant" form of angina,[101] ST *elevation* develops.

Finally, the presence of coronary disease is *not excluded* by a normal tracing.[84] Of 37 patients having multivessel disease and markedly positive exercise tests (3 mm or more ST depression), 30 (81%) had normal resting ECGs.[140] Figure 27.7 is the tracing from a 42-year-old man who had a proved myocardial infarction two years previously and who has suffered from angina of effort since then. The ECG is within normal limits.

Exercise (Stress) Testing

Sometimes the presence of coronary disease can be demonstrated only when the ventricular myocardium is stressed and its oxygen requirement thus increased. The most commonly applied stress is exercise, and the most commonly used form of exercise is the treadmill[4, 83, 107]; the original Master's two-step test, bicycle ergometry and other tests are less frequently employed. Since the previous edition of this book, a veritable spate of articles on stress testing has flooded the cardiological journals as more and more criteria and more and more lead systems have been introduced in an effort to enhance its diagnostic accuracy. In consequence, this chapter has been greatly expanded; but, despite the multiplicity of methods, expansion of criteria and deluge of words, results continue to be plagued by an unsatisfactory proportion of false-positives and false-negatives. For details, beyond the scope of this text, you are referred to excellent reviews.[2, 31, 54, 87, 145]

Recording techniques during exercise have varied considerably. While most bipolar leads place the exploring (positive) electrode at C5, the indifferent (negative) electrode has been variously placed on the manubrium (CM5), the right arm (CR5), the right shoulder (CS5), the right axilla (CX5), the back (CB5), or even the head (CH5). Other systems employ multiple leads and, although approximately 90% of abnormal responses are detected by a C5 lead,

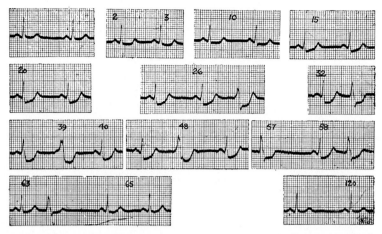

Figure 27.6. Coronary insufficiency. Lead 2 taken during an attack of chest pain which lasted less than a minute. Top left corner strip taken shortly before pain began spontaneously; figures on subsequent strips represent number of seconds after onset of pain. Notice marked progressive ST-T depression and appearance of frequent ectopic ventricular beats. At the end of 2 min, pattern has returned to normal.

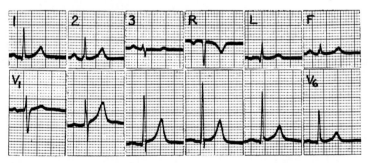

Figure 27.7. Normal tracing in a patient with previous myocardial infarction and subsequent angina of effort.

the more leads used the greater the potential for a positive yield. Therefore more and more investigators are employing multiple leads.

Normal Responses to Exercise

Before attempting to recognize the abnormal, one must be thoroughly familiar with the normal responses to exercise. In the ECG, these include increased P-wave amplitude, shortened P-R interval, decreased R wave amplitude, a rightward axis shift, depression of the early part of the ST segment so that it becomes upsloping to a T wave diminished in amplitude; in some leads the T wave may become taller while it inverts in others. Extrasystoles frequently develop at the height of an exercise test; they may be considered an integral part of an abnormal response, but in themselves are not necessarily an indication of heart disease[59]—see below.

Normal hemodynamic responses include tachycardia and an increase in systolic blood pressure; the normal ranges of these responses to submaximal exercise (achievement of 85% of predicted maximal heart rate for age), as encountered in hundreds of healthy men,[141] are tabulated in table 27.1.

Table 27.1
Normal Responses to Exercise in Healthy Men[141]

	Baseline	Submaximal Response	Recovery at	
			2 Min	5 Min
Heart rate	52–82	158–190	102–138	88–116
Systolic blood pressure	110–140	160–208	140–194	120–158
Diastolic blood pressure	70–90	60–90	60–90	60–86

ST Segment Criteria

The "graded" exercise test aims at standardizing the load on the coronary circulation (which, after all, is what is being tested) rather than that on the skeletal muscles; and uses as its end point 85% of the age-predicted maximal heart rate.[114] Regardless of the form of exercise/stress test, the electrocardiographic endpoint for a positive result is the same. The time-honored criterion for a positive test is a 1- to 2-mm **depression of the ST segment** 0.08 sec beyond the J point (figs. 27.8 and 27.9). Horizontal or downsloping depression of ST segments have been considered most significant and upsloping segments relatively benign; but more recent investigation suggests that significant depression associated with upsloping ST segments is hardly less abnormal.[126] An upsloping ST that still remains 1 mm or more below the baseline 0.08 sec after the J point[103]; or a depression of the J point of more than 2 mm with upsloping ST still 2 mm below the isoelectric line 0.08 sec later[55] are cited as positive criteria.

Not only are the depth and shape of the ST depression important, the rate at which the abnormal changes develop is a reliable index of the presence and severity of the coronary disease.[85] Nearly 90% of patients with left main coronary artery disease have a markedly positive test with 2 mm or more depression of the ST segment, a positive ST response as early as stage I, need to terminate the test during the first few minutes, or exertional hypotension.[152]

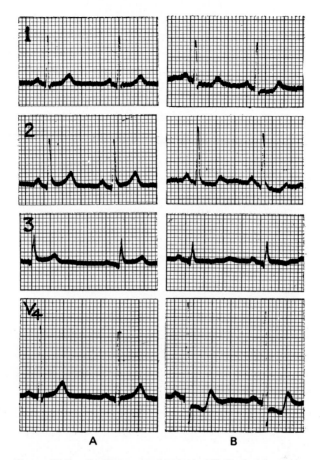

Figure 27.8. Positive exercise test. (*A*) Control tracing
before exercise: within normal limits. (*B*) Two minutes after
exercise: striking downsloping ST depression and increased
height of R wave in V_4 with lesser ST-T changes in 1 and 2.

A sequential pattern of ST depression is said to exclude false-positive results
and to be predictive of the severer grades of coronary disease[17]; this
"evolutionary" pattern ideally consists of the following sequence: J-point
depression with upsloping ST→horizontal ST→downsloping ST→inversion of
first part of T wave→complete T-wave inversion→gradual return to baseline.

Instead of the classical depression of the ST segment, exercise may produce **ST elevation**[19] (fig. 27.10*A*). This was found in 47 of 720 patients (6.5%)[137] and in another series, in 29 of 840 subjects (3.5%)[10]; of the 21 who had coronary arteriography, 19 had 75% or greater narrowing of the left anterior descending artery and 18 manifested left ventricular dyskinesia. ST elevation is undoubtedly correlated with the more severe grades of myocardial ischemia[142] and is most often seen in patients with previous myocardial infarction. In such patients, the immediate cause of this response to exercise appears to be "depressed left ventricular function"[124] or "abnormal wall motion."[123] In those who have neither previous infarction nor ventricular aneurysm, including those with variant angina, ST elevation is probably the result of coronary spasm.[120, 121, 137]

Exercise-induced ST elevation is an accurate localizer of the underlying myocardial mischief and implies critical stenosis of the artery supplying subjacent myocardium. ST elevation in anterior chest leads or aVL often indicates proximal left anterior descending obstruction.[28, 70] When the sole abnormal finding in patients with previous infarction is ST elevation, it suggests the

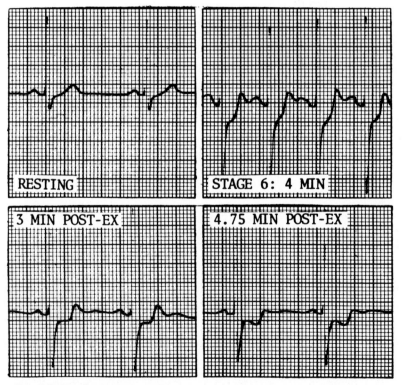

Figure 27.9.   Positive treadmill test showing in succession upsloping, horizontal and downsloping ST segments.

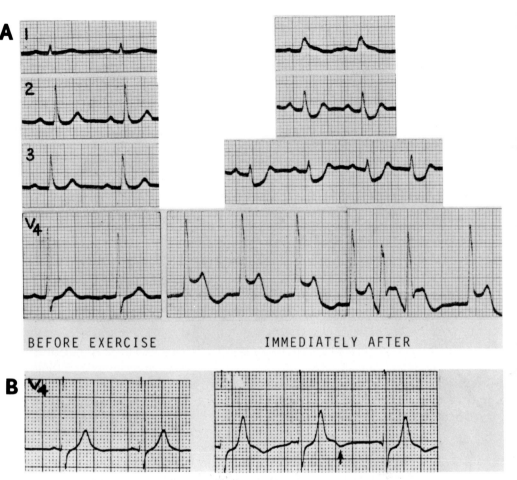

Figure 27.10. (*A*) Positive exercise test showing ST elevation immediately after exercise in leads 1 and V₄ with reciprocal depression in leads 2 and 3. Note the pair of ectopic beats in lead V₄. (*B*) There is slight upsloping ST depression and minor inversion of U waves in the control tracing before exercise; after exercise there is further depression of the J-point, but the most striking change is the deep inversion of the U wave (*arrow*).

involvement of only one vessel; but if concomitant ST depression is found in other leads it is said to suggest that other vessels are also involved.[22]

In patients with ventricular aneurysm, the ST elevation accurately indicates its site.[123] The location of coronary artery spasm is often accurately reflected: ST elevation in V_2 and V_3 indicates spasm of the left anterior descending artery, whereas elevation in lead 3 or aVF suggests spasm in either the right coronary or the circumflex artery. Elevation in V_1 signals spasm of the left anterior descending or the right coronary artery.[71] When ST depression during exercise is followed by anginal pain and ST elevation in the recovery period, it may predict imminent myocardial infarction in the indicated territory.[58]

Additional Criteria

Since dependence on ST-T changes alone produces a crop of false-positive and false-negative tests, considerable attention has been focussed on other variables. Many investigators have advocated that multiple criteria be simultaneously employed—the so-called "multivariate" approach—to enhance the diagnostic reliability of treadmill testing. The many parameters that have been variously invoked are listed in table 27.2.

Changes in **QRS amplitude** may be diagnostically helpful. Since in the normal person the RS amplitude responds to exercise by shrinking,[15, 133, 141] some observers have said that if it decreases you can rule out coronary disease.[143] In the presence of ischemic disease, the amplitude of the R wave often increases with exercise and, if this signal is read in conjunction with ST-T responses, the sensitivity of the exercise stress test is claimed by some to be significantly enhanced[12, 15, 132]; and, especially in women, analysis of R-wave changes is said to be a useful adjunct to ST criteria.[150] Changes in QRS amplitude may be especially helpful in situations where the repolarization moiety has been rendered less useful by preexisting abnormality as, for instance, the presence of digitalis effect[12] or bundle-branch block.[132]

According to Berman,[12] one of the most sensitive indices of coronary disease is an increase in R-wave amplitude in multiple leads taken in conjunction with ST shifts of 1 mm or more. He recommends continuous monitoring with a single lead supplemented by 12-lead tracings every three minutes during exercise and at 1, 3, 5 and 8 min during recovery. Using this method, a positive test requires 1 mm or more ST shift—down or up—at 0.08 sec after the J point *plus* an increase in the sum of QRS amplitudes (R in aVL, aVF, V_3, V_4, V_5, and V_6 + S in V_1 and V_2).

The small **septal q wave** normally increases with exercise and thus may help to identify false-positive ST changes[92]; failure to increase indicates abnormal septal activation because of ischemia. The development of anterior hemiblock along with QS complexes in V_1 to V_3 has been reported as a sign of exercise-induced septal ischemia.[147]

The helpfulness of QRS changes is disputed by others[8, 38, 133]; indeed some assert that most patients with severe coronary disease safely exercise to high levels and enjoy a reduction in their R-wave amplitude and others regard the R wave changes as so unpredictable as to be useless in the diagnosis of coronary heart disease.[148]

T-wave changes alone are not enough to make the diagnosis of coronary heart disease. For a long time it was thought that exercise differentiated between normal and abnormal T-wave inversion—that it left the abnormal T inverted or exaggerated the abnormality, but "normalized" the normally inverted T

Table 27.2
Multivariate Approach in Diagnosis

Observed Items	Foreboding Responses
ST depression	>2 mm
	Downsloping > horizontal > upsloping
	Early onset (stage I)
	Persistence of change
	Presence in 5 or more leads
ST elevation	Development of
RS amplitude	Increase[12, 15, 46, 132]
Septal q	Failure to increase[92]
U wave	Inversion[42]
VPBs	Repetitive
Peak heart rate	<120/min[87]
Peak blood pressure	<130 mm Hg
Time tolerated	<6 min
Angina	Development of
Standing or hyperventilation	Inappropriate increase in heart rate response[47]

wave. But recent studies demonstrated that, although normally inverted T waves are twice as likely to be "normalized" by exercise, no less than 27% of inverted ischemic T waves are also normalized.[3] This effect is not altogether surprising since spontaneous bouts of clinical ischemia are also at times associated with an "improved" T-wave pattern.[95]

In some patients, abnormal **U-wave inversion** (fig. 27.10B) may be the most diagnostic feature; it suggests significant ischemic disease and especially signals a lesion in the proximal left anterior descending.[42]

It used to be thought that when exercise precipitated **ventricular extrasystoles** it was a sign of coronary artery disease; but it is now known that exercise often produces VPBs in the fit and healthy. In a group of 345 regularly exercising normal men and women, VPBs were provoked by exercise in 35% of the men and in 14% of the women.[29] The tendency to ectopy increased with increasing heart rate and its incidence was similar to that in a cohort of patients who had had myocardial infarctions. Another study suggests that if the axis of the extrasystolic QRS is superiorly directed (left axis deviation or "no man's land"), it may be a specific index of coronary artery disease.[75]

Further efforts to improve the accuracy of treadmill testing for ischemic disease have included the following suggestions: precordial surface mapping with 16 leads[37]; maximal (as opposed to submaximal) testing combined with consideration of clinical symptoms and hemodynamic changes, plus a knowledge of reasons for falsely positive or negative tests[145]; a treadmill exercise score (TES) combining the following numerous parameters: Depth of J-point depression, horizontal or downsloping ST segment, promptness of onset of ST depression, development of ST depression at low heart rates, persistence of ST depression after exercise stops, and inadequate heart-rate response.[52]

Misleading Responses

Many factors besides coronary artery disease influence the interpretation of the electrocardiographic response to exercise. These include heart disease (other than ischemic), preexisting abnormality in the resting ECG, the number and location of the leads available for scrutiny, electrolyte disturbances and drug therapy.[18, 31, 36, 118]

The effect of digitalis is disputed: Some investigators claim that the influence of digitalis promotes falsely positive tests[67, 131] whereas earlier studies[6, 113] led to the conclusion that the administration of digitalis would not. A more recent study[119] determined that indeed digoxin caused a positive test in 25% of healthy men, especially over the age of 60 years; and that the ST-T changes so produced were indistinguishable from the genuine earmarks of ischemic disease. On the other hand, the positive test provoked by digitalis may serve to unmask latent coronary disease.[119] The effect of digoxin on the response to exercise is attenuated by propranolol.[67]

Among the numerous causes of falsely positive tests are the Wolff-Parkinson-White syndrome,[125] hyperventilation,[53, 60] and the prolapsing mitral valve.[39] Women are notorious for producing false-positive tests in as many as half to two-thirds of those tested.[30] ST-T changes in the presence of LBBB are not reliable indices of coronary disease[96] and, in patients with RBBB, ST depression confined to leads V_{1-3} may represent falsely positive tests whereas changes in leftward leads (V_{4-6}) may be more diagnostic.[128]

One must be cautious in interpreting the post-exercise tracing of hypertensive patients receiving thiazides. These drugs may reduce the patient's potassium stores without altering the ECG; in such a situation, exercise may bring to light the latent pattern of hypokalemia[41] whose ST depression may be mistaken for myocardial ischemia. ST-T changes may result solely from the upright posture and these must not be mistaken for displacement indicating ischemia.[56]

Although post-exercise changes are helpfully diagnostic of ischemic disease in the clinical suspect, they are not specific, since patterns indistinguishable from those typical of ischemia develop after exercise in other forms of heart disease.[51] It is therefore better to say that the typical changes indicate myocardial *disease*, often but not necessarily ischemic. Thus the term "false-positive" may at times be a misnomer: It is the myocardium that produces the tracing and therefore the test result; and the fact of angiographically clean coronary vessels does not exonerate the heart muscle[30]—which may be the seat of noncoronary disease, such as cardiomyopathy or rheumatic disease, giving it abundant right to protest appropriately, not falsely, to unwanted stress.

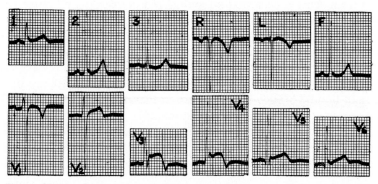

Figure 27.11. From a normal Negro man of 24 years. Note marked ST elevation and T-wave inversion in V_3 and V_4.

On the other side of the coin, falsely negative tests may be found in the presence of severe coronary artery disease: In one study, 15 of 26 critical stenoses of the left coronary artery were associated with negative stress tests.[130] Although a negative test can therefore not be relied upon to exclude significant coronary disease, according to some investigators it virtually excludes the existence of significant left main disease.[94]

The exercise test has its uses but must be regarded as a test of limited value because (a) a negative test fails to rule out significant disease and (b) a positive test, in the presence of atypical chest pain, is difficult to interpret since falsely positive tests are rife.[25]

Electrocardiographogenic Disease

Abnormalities in the ECG do not necessarily indicate cardiac disease, much less coronary disease.[65, 76, 82] When deviations from the normal, especially those affecting the ST segments and T waves, are encountered in the middle-aged and elderly, they are much too glibly interpreted as "coronary insufficiency." Statistically such inferences are no doubt often right, but the habit is bad practice and is scientifically unsound; too many people are limping their ways through life maimed by the unkind cuts of electrocardiographic interpretation.[99] Remember the following facts before attaching the "cardiac" or "coronary" label:

1. The range of normal is wide and its limits cannot be satisfactorily defined.[116] Changes well outside the accepted range are undoubtedly at times normal variants. Examples of this are the persistent "juvenile" precordial pattern particularly seen in healthy young Negroes[48, 68, 102] (fig. 27.11), unusual S-T elevation (fig. 27.12), also especially common in Negroes (fig. 27.11)[129] and often referred to as "early repolarization"—a misnomer![151] It must be differentiated from acute myocardial infarction and pericarditis,[122, 149] see page 463. The ST elevation of "early repolarization" may be restored to the baseline with exercise or isoproterenol.[1, 91, 144] Apparent ST depression due to carryover of T_P wave[136] may suggest myocardial ischemia. Other potential mimics include: ST-T depression in "suspended" hearts[34] (fig. 27.13), precordial T-wave inversion during pregnancy, prolonged P-R intervals in occasional healthy hearts[74, 110] and a right bundle-branch block pattern in marathon runners,[9] whose cardiovascular competence can hardly be questioned.

Striking T-wave inversion, ominously reminiscent of myocardial ischemia, and sometimes leading to unnecessary hospitalization, is found in well-trained, top-ranking athletes, such as professional bicyclists and marathon

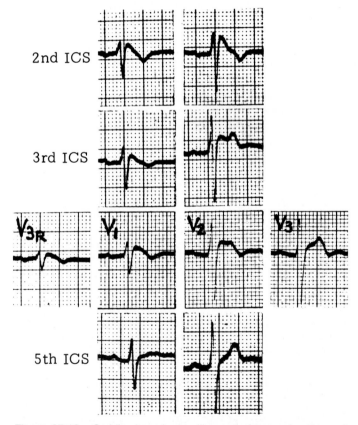

Figure 27.12. Saddle-shaped, step-like and plateau elevations of precordial ST segments from a healthy dentist of 32 years. Notice the variation from interspace to interspace; thus misplacement of the electrode from day to day may trap the unwary into thinking that "evolution" is occurring.

runners.[49, 50, 93, 144] ST and T-wave changes, simulating those of ischemic heart disease, have been reported in normal men with normal coronary arteriograms[127]; and about one third of normal men show 1 mm ST depression and/or labile T-wave inversion of up to 3 mm during ambulatory monitoring.[146] In normal youths, suspicious T-wave changes may be the result of increased sympatho-adrenal activity.[5]

2. Numerous extracardiac factors can produce patterns similar to those seen in myocardial disease. Without necessarily impairing cardiac competence, many factors can cause changes in the repolarization processes of the ventricles which are reflected in the ECG in T-wave or ST-segment alterations. The T wave and to a lesser extent the ST segment are unstable members that are easily upset by a great variety of major and minor provocations. Among the many stimuli that can affect them are eating,[105, 112, 136] drinking ice water,[26] posture,[110] hyperventilation[135]; emotional disturbances such as the startle reaction, fear or anxiety[72, 90] and neurocirculatory asthenia[115]; numerous drugs, including digitalis, quinidine, procainamide, adrenaline, isuprel, insulin; extracardiac diseases such as electrolyte imbalances, the acute abdomen, shock, hiatal hernia, gallbladder disease, cerebrovascular accidents,[16] psychosis and endocrine and metabolic disturbances.

3. Cardiovascular disease other than coronary may counterfeit the changes of ischemic heart disease. Such mimics include myocarditis,[97] cardiomyopathy, hypertension and other diseases producing ventricular hypertrophy.

4. Finally the heart may be the victim of a disease that is not primarily cardiac, let alone coronary. Pulmonary embolism, anemia, hypothyroidism, myocarditis[23] from infections (e.g., pneumonia, infectious mononucleosis), sarcoidosis, hemochromatosis, primary amyloidosis, beriberi, scleroderma, disseminated lupus, Friedreich's ataxia, progressive muscular dystrophy and myasthenia gravis all may produce changes in the tracing indicative of myocardial

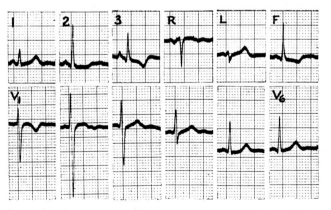

Figure 27.13. Abnormal ST-T pattern in leads 2, 3 and aVF in a young woman with a "suspended" heart but no cardiac disease.

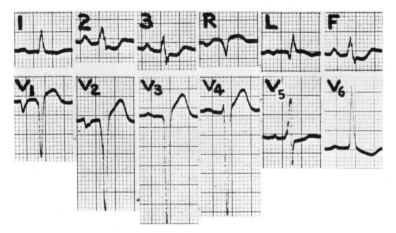

Figure 27.14. Left ventricular hypertrophy and **incomplete LBBB.** From a patient with severe aortic stenosis and no sign of anterior infarction at autopsy.

Table 27.3
Mimics of Anteroseptal Infarction

1. Left ventricular hypertrophy
2. Incomplete left bundle-branch block
3. Hemiblock, anterior or posterior
4. Myocardial replacement (neoplasm, sarcoid, etc.)
5. Cardiomyopathy
6. Wolff-Parkinson-White syndrome

involvement and quite indistinguishable from some of the alterations resulting from coronary disease.

Numerous conditions can produce Q waves that may be mistaken for those of myocardial infarction; most of these are listed in table 27.3. Among the more common Q-wave producers is ventricular hypertrophy: Left ventricular hypertrophy, with or without the coexistence of incomplete LBBB, can produce QS complexes in V_{1-2} and even in V_3 (fig. 27.14), often erroneously mistaken for evidence of anteroseptal infarction—probably the single most common mistake made in everyday ECG interpretation.

In a carefully autopsied Japanese series of 63 patients with QS complexes in one or more anterior precordial leads, correlation with anteroseptal infarction was as indicated in table 27.4.

Hypertrophic cardiomyopathy can often be suspected from the presence of gross Q waves that simply do not look like the Q waves of infarction; and a further helpful detail in this connection is the fact that the T waves are discordant,[45] i.e., whereas in myocardial infarction the T wave is inverted in the leads that show significant Q waves, the T waves in hypertrophic cardiomyopathy are upright in the leads that sport Q waves (see figs. 29.9 and 30.23). Transient Q waves may develop with the coronary spasm of variant angina and even in occasional cases of acute pericarditis,[88] hypoglycemia, hyperkalemia, shock, acute pancreatitis and phosphorus poisoning.

Therefore in assessing the tracing that does not conform with our accepted standards we should remember the whole array of common and uncommon possibilities and we should ask ourselves three questions: (1) Could this be a normal variant? (2) Could these abnormalities be due to extracardiac factors, physiological or pathological? and (3) Could these changes be due to heart disease other than coronary?

The danger of attributing changes of the first and second category to heart disease is that the patient is branded as a cardiac. The danger of labelling the third group as "coronary" is that the physician in charge of the case may be thereby blinded to the true nature of the cardiac involvement and of the underlying primary disease. We should often be content to state that the pattern is abnormal but nonspecific. We should also certainly be at pains to spread the gospel that AN "ABNORMAL" TRACING DOES NOT NECESSARILY MEAN AN ABNORMAL HEART.

In many ways this is the most important section of this book. For if the lesson that it attempts to teach is well learned, it may save many from cardiac invalidism. The whole subject of "coronary mimicry" in the ECG was reviewed elsewhere[76] with detailed discussion and a full bibliography and has also formed the subject of an excellent monograph.[45]

Table 27.4
Correlation of QS Complexes with Anteroseptal Infarction

Leads Showing QS Complexes	No.	Anteroseptal Infarction	
		No.	Percent
V_1, V_2, V_3, V_4	3	3	100
V_1, V_2, V_3	9	6	66
V_1, V_2	15	3	20
V_2	8	1	12
V_1	25	1	4
V_2, V_3	2	0	0
V_3	1	0	0

REFERENCES

1. Alimurung, B.: The influence of early repolarization variant on the exercise electrocardiogram; a correlation with coronary arteriograms. Am. Heart J. 1980: **99**, 739.
2. Amsterdam, E. A., et al.: Toward improved interpretation of the exercise test. Cardiology 1980: **66**, 236.
3. Aravindakshan, V., et al.: Electrocardiographic exercise test in patients with abnormal T waves at rest. Am. Heart J. 1977: **93**, 706.
4. Aronow, W. S.: Thirty-month follow-up of maximal treadmill stress test and double Master's test in normal subjects. Circulation 1973: **47**, 287.
5. Atterhog, J.-H., et al.: Sympathoadrenal and cardiovascular responses to mental stress, isometric handgrip and cold pressor test in asymptomatic young men with primary T wave abnormalities in the electrocardiogram. Br. Heart J. 1981: **46**, 311.

6. Bartel, A. G., et al.: Graded exercise stress tests in angiographically documented coronary artery disease. Circulation 1974: **49**, 348.

7. Baron, D. W., et al.: R wave amplitude during exercise. Relation to left ventricular function and coronary artery disease. Br. Heart J. 1980: **44**, 512.

8. Battler, A., et al.: Relationship of QRS amplitude changes during exercise to left ventricular function, volumes, and the diagnosis of coronary artery disease. Circulation 1979: **60**, 1004.

9. Beckner, G. L., and Winsor, T.: Cardiovascular adaptations to prolonged physical effort. Circulation 1954: **9**, 835.

10. Belic, N., and Gardin, J. M.: ECG manifestations of myocardial ischemia. Arch. Intern. Med. 1980: **140**, 1162.

11. Bellet, S., et al.: Radioelectrocardiography during exercise in patients with angina pectoris. Comparison with the postexercise electrocardiogram. Circulation 1962: **25**, 5.

12. Berman, J. L., et al.: Multiple-lead QRS changes with exercise testing: diagnostic value and hemodynamic implications. Circulation 1980: **61**, 53.

13. Blackburn, H., and Katigbak, R.: What electrocardiographic leads to take after exercise? Am. Heart J. 1964: **67**, 184.

14. Blackburn, H., et al.: The exercise ECG test. At what intervals to record after exercise. Am. Heart J. 1964: **67**, 186.

15. Bonoris, P. E., et al. Evaluation of R wave amplitude changes versus ST-segment depression in stress testing. Circulation 1978: **57**, 904.

16. Burch, G. E., et al.: A new electrocardiographic pattern observed in cerebrovascular accidents. Circulation 1954: **9**, 719.

17. Chahine, R. A., et al.: The evolutionary pattern of exercise-induced ST segment depression. J. Electrocardiol. 1979: **12**, 235.

18. Chaitman, B. R., et al.: Improved efficiency of treadmill exercise testing using a multiple lead electrocardiographic system and basic hemodynamic exercise response. Circulation 1978: **57**, 71.

19. Chaitman, B. R., et al.: S-T segment elevation and coronary spasm in response to exercise. Am. J. Cardiol. 1981: **47**, 1350.

20. Chun, P. K. C., et al.: ST-segment elevation with elective DC cardioversion. Circulation 1981: **63**, 220.

21. Coulshed, N.: The anoxia test for myocardial ischaemia. Br. Heart J. 1960: **22**, 79.

22. deFeyter, P. J., et al.: Clinical significance of exercise induced ST segment elevation. Correlative angiographic study in patients with ischaemic heart disease. Br. Heart J. 1981: **46**, 84.

23. de la Chapelle, C. E., and Kossmann, C. E.: Myocarditis. Circulation 1954: **10**, 747.

24. Demoulin, J. C., et al.: Prognostic significance of electrocardiographic findings in angina at rest. Therapeutic implications. Br. Heart J. 1981: **46**, 320.

25. Detry, J.-M. R., et al.: Diagnostic value of history and maximum exercise electrocardiography in men and women suspected of coronary heart disease. Circulation 1977: **56**, 756.

26. Dowling, C. V., and Hellerstein, H. K.: Factors influencing the T wave of the electrocardiogram. II. Effects of drinking ice water. Am. Heart J. 1951: **41**, 58.

27. Dunn, R. F., et al.: Exercise-induced ST-segment elevation; correlation of thalium-201 myocardial perfusion scanning and coronary arteriography. Circulation 1980: **61**, 989.

28. Dunn, R. F., et al.: Exercise-induced ST-segment elevation in leads V_1 or aVL; a predictor of anterior myocardial ischemia and left anterior descending coronary artery disease. Circulation 1981: **63**, 1357.

29. Ekblom, B., et al.: Occurrence and reproducibility of exercise-induced ventricular ectopy in normal subjects. Am. J. Cardiol. 1979: **43**, 35.

30. Ellestad, M. H., et al.: The false positive stress test. Am. J. Cardiol. 1977: **40**, 681.

31. Ellestad, M. H., et al.: Stress testing; clinical application and predictive capacity. Prog. Cardiovasc. Dis. 1979: **21**, 431.

32. Engel, T. R.: Postextrasystolic T wave changes and angiographic coronary disease. Br. Heart J. 1977: **39**, 371.

33. Evans, W., and McRae, C.: The lesser electrocardiographic signs of cardiac pain. Br. Heart J. 1952: **14**, 429.

34. Evans, W., and Lloyd-Thomas, H. G.: The syndrome of the suspended heart. Br. Heart J. 1957: **19**, 153.

35. Fagin, I. D., and Guidot, J. M.: Post-extrasystolic T wave changes. Am. J. Cardiol. 1958: **1**, 597.

36. Fortuin, N. J., and Weiss, J. L.: Exercise stress testing. Circulation 1977: **56,** 699.
37. Fox, K., et al.: Precordial electrocardiographic mapping after exercise in the diagnosis of coronary artery disease. Am. J. Cardiol. 1979: **43,** 541.
38. Froelicher, V. F., et al.: Variations in normal electrocardiographic response to treadmill testing. Am. J. Cardiol. 1981: **47,** 1161.
39. Gardin, J. M., et al.: Pseudoischemic "false positive" S-T segment changes induced by hyperventilation in patients with mitral valve prolapse. Am. J. Cardiol. 1980: **45,** 952.
40. Gazes, P. C., et al.: The diagnosis of angina pectoris. Am. Heart J. 1964: **67,** 830.
41. Georgopoulos, A. J., et al.: Effect of exercise on electrocardiogram of patients with low serum potassium. Circulation 1961: **23,** 567.
42. Gerson, M. C., et al.: Exercise-induced U-wave inversion as a marker of stenosis of the left anterior descending coronary artery. Circulation 1979: **60,** 1014.
43. Gerson, M. C., et al.: Relation of exercise-induced physiologic S-T segment depression to R wave amplitude in normal subjects. Am. J. Cardiol. 1980: **46,** 778.
44. Goldberger, A. L.: Q wave T wave vector discordance in hypertrophic cardiomyopathy: Septal hypertrophy and strain pattern. Br. Heart J. 1979: **42,** 201.
45. Goldberger, A. L.: *Myocardial Infarction: Electrocardiographic Differential Diagnosis,* Ed. 2. C. V. Mosby, St. Louis, 1979.
46. Greenberg, P. S., et al.: Predictive accuracy of Q-X/Q-T ratio, Q-Tc interval, S-T depression, and R wave amplitude during stress testing. Am. J. Cardiol. 1979: **44,** 18.
47. Greenberg, P. S., et al.: Use of heart rate responses to standing and hyperventilation at rest to detect coronary artery disease: correlation with the S-T response to exercise. J. Electrocardiol. 1980: **13,** 373.
48. Grusin, H.: Peculiarities of the African's electrocardiogram and the changes observed in serial studies. Circulation 1954: **9,** 860.
49. Hall, R. J., and Gibson, R. V.: Anterior T wave changes in the ECG of an athlete. Br. Med. J. 1978: **2,** 738.
50. Hanne-Paparo, N., et al.: T-wave abnormalities in the electrocardiograms of top-ranking athletes without demonstrable organic heart disease. Am. Heart J. 1971: **81,** 743.
51. Hellerstein, H. K., et al.: Two step exercise test as a test of cardiac function in chronic rheumatic heart disease and in arteriosclerotic heart disease with old myocardial infarction. Am. J. Cardiol. 1961: **7,** 234.
52. Hollenberg, M., et al.: Treadmill score quantifies electrocardiographic response to exercise and improves test accuracy and reproducibility. Circulation 1980: **61,** 276.
53. Kemp, G. L., and Ellestad, M. H.: The significance of hyperventilation and orthostatic T wave changes on the electrocardiogram. Arch. Intern. Med. 1968: **121,** 518.
54. Koppes, G., et al.: Treadmill exercise testing. Curr. Probl. Cardiol. 1977: **7,** Nos. 8 and 9.
55. Kurita, A., et al.: Significance of exercise-induced junctional S-T depression in evaluation of coronary artery disease. Am. J. Cardiol. 1977: **40,** 492.
56. Lachman, A. B., et al.: Postural ST-T wave changes in the radioelectrocardiogram simulating myocardial ischemia. Circulation 1965: **31,** 557.
57. Lahiri, A., et al.: Exercise-induced S-T segment elevation in variant angina. Am. J. Cardiol. 1980: **45,** 887.
58. Lahiri, A., et al.: Exercise-induced ST segment elevation. Electrocardiographic, angiographic and scintigraphic evaluation. Br. Heart J. 1980: **43,** 582.
59. Lamb, L. E., and Hiss, R. G.: Influence of exercise on premature contractions. Am. J. Cardiol. 1962: **10,** 209.
60. Lary, D., and Goldschlager, N.: Electrocardiographic changes during hyperventilation resembling myocardial ischemia in patients with normal coronary arteriograms. Am. Heart J. 1974: **87,** 383.
61. Leachman, D. R., et al.: Evaluation of postextrasystolic T wave alterations in identification of patients with coronary artery disease or left ventricular dysfunction. Am. Heart J. 1981: **102,** 658.
62. Lepeschkin, E., and Surawicz, B.: Characteristics of true-positive and false-positive results of ECG Master two step exercise tests. N. Engl. J. Med. 1958: **258,** 511.
63. Lepeschkin, E.: Exercise tests in the diagnosis of coronary heart disease. Circulation 1960: **22,** 986.
64. Levine, H. D., et al.: The clinical significance of postextrasystolic T wave changes. Circulation 1952: **6,** 538.

65. Levine, H. D.: Non-specificity of the electrocardiogram associated with coronary artery disease. Am. J. Med. 1953: **15**, 344.
66. Levine, H. J.: Mimics of coronary heart disease. Postgrad. Med. 1978: **64**, 58.
67. LeWinter, M. M., et al.: The effect of oral propranolol, digoxin and combination therapy on the resting and exercise electrocardiogram. Am. Heart J. 1977: **93**, 202.
68. Littmann, D.: Persistence of the juvenile pattern in the precordial leads of healthy adult Negroes, with report of electrocardiographic survey on three hundred Negro and two hundred white subjects. Am. Heart J. 1946: **32**, 370.
69. Lloyd-Thomas, H. G.: The effect of exercise on the electrocardiogram in healthy subjects. Br. Heart J. 1961: **23**, 260.
70. Longhurst, J. C., and Kraus, W. L.: Exercise-induced ST elevation in patients with myocardial infarction. Circulation 1979: **60**, 616.
71. MacAlpin, R. N.: Correlation of the location of coronary arterial spasm with the lead distribution of ST segment elevation during variant angina. Am. Heart J. 1980: **99**, 555.
72. Magendantz, H., and Shortsleeve, J.: Electrocardiographic abnormalities in patients exhibiting anxiety. Am. Heart J. 1951: **42**, 849.
73. Mann, R. H., and Burchell, H. B.: The sign of T-wave inversion in sinus beats following ventricular extrasystoles. Am. Heart J. 1954: **47**, 504.
74. Manning, G. W.: Electrocardiography in the selection of Royal Canadian Air Force Aircrew. Circulation 1954: **10**, 401.
75. Mardelli, T. J., et al.: Superior QRS axis of ventricular premature complexes: An additional criterion to enhance the sensitivity of exercise stress testing. Am. J. Cardiol. 1980: **45**, 236.
76. Marriott, H. J. L.: Coronary mimicry: normal variants, and physiologic, pharmacologic and pathologic influences that simulate coronary patterns in the electrocardiogram. Ann. Int. Med. 1960: **52**, 411.
77. Marriott, H. J. L.: Electrocardiographogenic suicide and lesser crimes. J. Florida Med. Assoc. 1963: **50**, 440.
78. Marriott, H. J. L.: Normal electrocardiographic variants simulating ischemic heart disease. J.A.M.A. 1967: **199**, 103.
79. Marriott, H. J. L., and Nizet, P. M.: Physiologic stimuli simulating ischemic heart disease. J.A.M.A. 1967: **200**, 715.
80. Marriott, H. J. L., and Menendez, M. M.: Noncoronary disease simulating myocardial ischemia or infarction. J.A.M.A. 1967: **201**, 53.
81. Marriott, H. J. L.: Dangers in overinterpretation of the electrocardiogram. Heart Bull. 1967: **18**, 61.
82. Marriott, H. J. L., and Slonim, R.: False patterns of myocardial infarction. Heart Bull. 1967: **16**, 71.
83. Martin, C. M., and McConahay, D. R.: Maximal treadmill exercise electrocardiography. Circulation 1972: **46**, 956
84. Martinez-Rios, M. A., et al.: Normal electrocardiogram in the presence of severe coronary artery disease. Am. J. Cardiol. 1970: **25**, 320.
85. Mary, D. A. S. G., et al.: Use of submaximal ST segment/heart rate relation during maximal exercise testing to predict severity of coronary artery disease (abstr.). Br. Heart J. 1981: **45**, 342.
86. Master, A. M. and Rosenfeld, I.: Two-step exercise test: current status after twenty-five years. Mod. Concepts Cardiovasc. Dis. 1967: **36**, 19.
87. McNeer, J. F., et al.: The role of the exercise test in the evaluation of patients for ischemic heart disease. Circulation 1978: **57**, 64.
88. Meller, J., et al.: Transient Q waves in Prinzmetal's angina. Am. J. Cardiol. 1975: **35**, 691.
89. Meyer, P., and Herr, R.: L'intéret du syndrome éléctrocardiographique TV1 > TV6 pour le dépistage précoce de troubles de la repolarisation ventriculaire gauche. Arch. Mal. Coeur 1959: **52**, 753.
90. Mitchell, J. H., and Shapiro, A. P.: The relationship of adrenalin and T wave changes in the anxiety state. Am. Heart J. 1954: **48**, 323.
91. Morace, G.: Effect of isoproterenol on the "early repolarization" syndrome. Am. Heart J. 1979: **97**, 343.
92. Morales-Ballejo, H., et al.: Septal Q wave in exercise testing: Angiographic correlation. Am. J. Cardiol. 1981: **48**, 247.
93. Nishimura, T., et al.: Noninvasive assessment of T-wave abnormalities on precordial electrocardiograms in middle-aged professional bicyclists. J. Electrocardiol. 1981: **14**, 357.

94. Nixon, J. V., et al.: Exercise testing in men with significant left main coronary disease. Br. Heart J. 1979: **42**, 410.
95. Noble, J., et al.: Normalization of abnormal T waves in ischemia. Arch. Intern. Med. 1976: **136**, 391.
96. Orzan, F., et al.: Is the treadmill exercise test useful for evaluating coronary artery disease in patients with complete left bundle branch block? Am. J. Cardiol. 1978: **42**, 36.
97. Palank, E. A., et al.: Fatal acute bacterial myocarditis after dentoalveolar abscess. Am. J. Cardiol. 1979: **43**, 1238.
98. Papapietro, S. E., et al.: Transient electrocardiographic changes in patients with unstable angina: Relation to coronary arterial anatomy. Am. J. Cardiol. 1980: **46**, 28.
99. Prinzmetal, M., et al.: Clinical implications of errors in electrocardiographic interpretations: heart disease of electrocardiographic origin. J.A.M.A. 1956: **161**, 138.
100. Prinzmetal, M., et al.: A variant form of angina pectoris. Am. J. Med. 1959: **27**, 375.
101. Prinzmetal, M., et al.: Variant form of angina pectoris: previously undelineated syndrome. J.A.M.A. 1960: **174**, 1794.
102. Reiley, M. A., et al.: Racial and sexual differences in the standard electrocardiogram of black versus white adolescents. Chest 1979: **75**, 474.
103. Rijneki, R. D., et al.: Clinical significance of upsloping ST segments in exercise electrocardiography. Circulation 1980: **61**, 671.
104. Robb, G. P., and Marks, H. H.: Latent coronary artery disease. Determination of its presence and severity by the exercise electrocardiogram. Am. J. Cardiol. 1964: **13**, 603.
105. Rochlin, I., and Edwards, W. L. J.: The misinterpretation of electrocardiograms with postprandial T-wave inversion. Circulation 1954: **10**, 843.
106. Roesler, H.: An electrocardiographic study of high takeoff of R (R′)-T segment in right precordial leads. Altered repolarization. Am. J. Cardiol. 1960: **6**, 920.
107. Roitman, D., et al.: Comparison of submaximal exercise test with coronary cineangiocardiogram. Ann. Intern. Med. 1970: **72**, 641.
108. Roman, L., and Bellet, S.: Significance of the QX/QT ratio and the QT ratio (QTr) in the exercise electrocardiogram. Circulation 1965: **32**, 435.
109. Scherf, D.: Development of the electrocardiographic exercise test. Standardized versus nonstandardized test. Am. J. Cardiol. 1960: **5**, 433.
110. Scherf, D., and Dix, J. H.: The effects of posture on A-V conduction. Am. Heart J. 1952: **43**, 494.
111. Scherf, D., and Schaffer, A. I.: The electrocardiographic exercise test. Am. Heart J. 1952: **43**, 927.
112. Sears, G. A., and Manning, G. W.: Routine electrocardiography: postprandial T-wave changes. Am. Heart J. 1958: **56**, 591.
113. Senat, I., et al.: Effects of digoxin on the S-T segment during treadmill exercise testing (abstr.). Circulation 1974: **50**, (suppl. III), 245.
114. Sheffield, L. T., et al.: Exercise graded by heart rate in electrocardiographic testing for angina pectoris. Circulation 1965: **32**, 622.
115. Silverman, J. J., and Goodman, R. D.: Extraordinary alteration of P-R interval in neurocirculatory asthenia. Am. Heart J. 1951: **41**, 155.
116. Simonson, E.: Editorial: Principles for determination of electrocardiographic normal standards. Am. Heart J. 1956: **52**, 163.
117. Simonson, E., and Keys, A.: The effect of an ordinary meal on the electrocardiogram. Normal standards in middle aged men and women. Circulation 1950: **1**, 1000.
118. Sketch, M. H., et al.: Reliability of single lead and multiple lead electrocardiography during and after exercise. Chest 1978: **74**, 394.
119. Sketch, M. H., et al.: Digoxin-induced positive exercise tests: Their clinical and prognostic significance. Am. J. Cardiol. 1981: **48**, 655.
120. Specchia, G., et al.: Coronary arterial spasm as a cause of exercise-induced ST-segment elevation in patients with variant angina. Circulation 1979: **59**, 948.
121. Specchia, G., et al.: Significance of exercise-induced ST-segment elevation in patients without myocardial infarction. Circulation 1981: **63**, 46.
122. Spodick, D. H.: Differential characteristics of the electrocardiogram in early repolarization and acute pericarditis. N. Engl. J. Med. 1976: **295**, 523.
123. Sriwattanakomen, S., et al.: S-T segment elevation during exercise: Electrocardiographic and arteriographic correlation in 38 patients. Am. J. Cardiol. 1980: **45**, 762.
124. Stiles, G. L., et al.: Clinical relevance of exercise-induced S-T segment elevation. Am. J. Cardiol. 1980: **46**, 931.

125. Strasberg, B., et al.: Treadmill exercise testing in the Wolff-Parkinson-White syndrome. Am. J. Cardiol. 1980: **45**, 742.

126. Stuart, R. J., and Ellestad, M. H.: Upsloping S-T segments in exercise stress testing. Am. J. Cardiol. 1976: **37**, 19.

127. Taggart, P., et al.: Electrocardiographic changes resembling myocardial ischaemia in asymptomatic men with normal coronary arteriograms. Br. Heart J. 1979: **41**, 214.

128. Tanaka, T., et al.: Diagnostic value of exercise-induced S-T depression in patients with right bundle branch block. Am. J. Cardiol. 1978: **41**, 670.

129. Thomas, J., et al.: Observations on the T wave and S-T segment changes in the precordial electrocardiogram of 320 young Negro adults. Am. J. Cardiol. 1960: **5**, 468.

130. Timmis, G. G., et al.: The diagnostic inadequacy of exercise testing in critical left coronary artery disease. J. Electrocardiol. 1977: **10**, 321.

131. Tonkon, M. J., et al.: Effect of digitalis on the exercise electrocardiogram in normal adult subjects. Chest 1977: **72**, 714.

132. Uhl, G. S., and Hopkirk, A. C.: Analysis of exercise-induced R wave amplitude changes in detection of coronary artery disease in asymptomatic men with left bundle branch block. Am. J. Cardiol. 1979: **44**, 1247.

133. Wagner, S., et al.: Unreliability of exercise-induced R wave changes as indexes of coronary artery disease. Am. J. Cardiol. 1979: **44**, 1241.

134. Wasserburger, R. H., and Alt, W. J.: The normal RS-T segment elevation variant. Am. J. Cardiol. 1961: **8**, 184.

135. Wasserburger, R. H., et al.: The effect of hyperventilation on the normal adult electrocardiogram. Circulation 1956: **13**, 850.

136. Wasserburger, R. H., et al.: The T-a wave of the adult electrocardiogram: an expression of pulmonary emphysema. Am. Heart J. 1957: **54**, 875.

137. Waters, D. D., et al.: Clinical and angiographic correlates of exercise-induced ST-segment elevation; increased detection with multiple electrocardiographic leads. Circulation 1980: **61**, 286.

138. Weiner, D. A.: Exercise testing for the diagnosis and severity of coronary disease. J. Cardiac Rehabil. 1981: **1**, 438.

139. Weiner, D. A., et al.: Identification of patients with left main and three vessel coronary disease with clinical and exercise test variables. Am. J. Cardiol. 1980: **46**, 21.

140. Williams, D. O., and Most, A. S.: Clinical, angiographic and hemodynamic characteristics of patients with a strongly positive exercise test. Am. Heart J. 1980: **66**, 241.

141. Wolthuis, R. A., et al.: The response of healthy men to treadmill exercise. Circulation 1977: **55**, 153.

142. Yasui, H.: Comparison of coronary arteriographic findings during angina pectoris associated with ST elevation or depression. Am. J. Cardiol. 1981: **47**, 539.

143. Yiannikas, J., et al. Analysis of exercise-induced changes in R wave amplitude in asymptomatic men with electrocardiographic ST-T changes at rest. Am. J. Cardiol. 1981: **47**, 238.

144. Zeppilli, P., et al.: T wave abnormalities in top-ranking athletes: Effects of isoproterenol, atropine, and physical exercise. Am. Heart J. 1980: **100**, 213.

145. Zohman, L. R., and Kattus, A. A.: Exercise testing in the diagnosis of coronary heart disease; a perspective. Am. J. Cardiol. 1977: **40**, 243.

146. Armstrong, W. F., et al.: Prevalence and magnitude of S-T segment and T wave abnormalities in normal men during continuous ambulatory monitoring. Am. J. Cardiol. 1982: **49**, 1638

147. Bateman, T., et al.: Transient appearance of Q waves in coronary disease during exercise electrocardiography. Am. Heart J. 1982: **104**, 182.

148. Fox, K., et al: Inability of exercise-induced R wave changes to predict coronary artery disease. Am. J. Cardiol. 1982: **49**, 674.

149. Ginzton, L. E., and Laks, M. M.: The differential diagnosis of acute pericarditis from the normal variant: new electrocardiographic criteria. Circulation 1982: **65**, 1004.

150. Ilsley, C., et al.: Influence of R wave analysis upon diagnostic accuracy of exercise testing in women. Br. Heart J. 1982: **48**, 161.

151. Mirvis, D.: Evaluation of normal variations in S-T segment patterns by body surface isopotential mapping: S-T segment elevation in absence of heart disease. Am. J. Cardiol. 1982: **50**, 122.

152. Stone, P. H., et al.: Patterns of exercise treadmill test performance in patients with left main coronary artery disease. Am. Heart J. 1982: **104**, 13.

Review Tracings

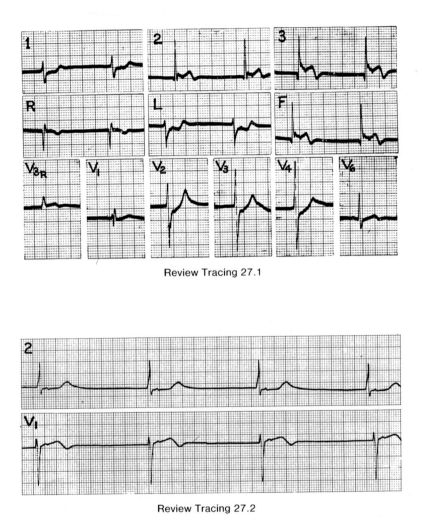

Review Tracing 27.1

Review Tracing 27.2

For interpretation, see page 485

Review Tracings

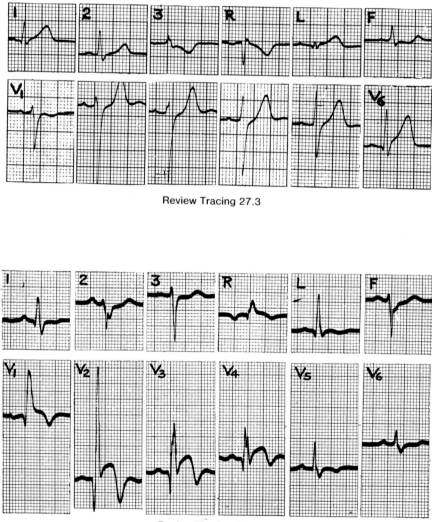

Review Tracing 27.3

Review Tracing 27.4

For interpretation, see page 485

28

Drug Effects:
Digitalis and Quinidine

Digitalis is to the electrocardiogram what syphilis was to medicine—the great imitator. It can mimic heart disease and it can cause almost all manner of blocks and arrhythmias.

Digitalis Effect

1. *ST-T changes:* digitalis causes depression of the ST segments with flattening and inversion of T waves. At the same time the relative Q-T duration is shortened in contrast to quinidine effect (see below). The shape of the depressed segment is often characteristic—sagging, with its concavity upward—and has been said to look as though a finger had been hooked over it to drag it down (figs. 28.1 and 28.2); sometimes it is more like a reversed

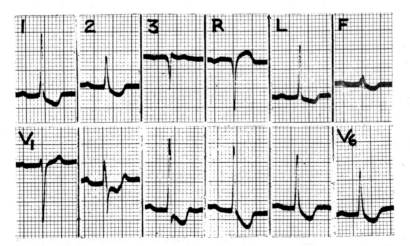

Figure 28.1. **Digitalis effect.** Note sagging ST segments in most leads, with short Q-T interval.

check mark, as in figure 28.8. These are not indications of digitalis *intoxication* but rather of simple digitalis *effect*, unless they occur in leads with predominantly negative QRS deflections (see below). They may be anticipated in most patients who are approaching adequate digitalization and are not an indication for reducing dosage. These changes occur in animals with approximately 25% of the lethal dose.

ST depression and inversion of T waves usually occur only in those leads with tall R waves. It is claimed that such displacement of ST segments and T waves in the direction opposite to the main QRS deflection means a uniform therapeutic action on the myocardium; but that depression of ST and inversion of T in leads with mainly negative QRS complexes (fig. 28.2) indicates that the drug is causing relative ischemia in the subendocardial muscle layers, and is therefore an indication to reduce the dose.

2. The *P-R interval* lengthens; modest prolongation is regarded as effect rather than toxicity and is likely due to the vagal effect exerted by the glycosides.

Digitalis Intoxication

Digitalis intoxication is always a clinical diagnosis, never a purely electrocardiographic one. There are no rhythmic or conductive disturbances that are peculiar to digitalis toxicity. Of course, there are circumstances in which the electrocardiographer may *suspect* the diagnosis, as when one of the disturbances especially typical of digitalis overdosage (e.g., ventricular bigeminy, accelerated junctional rhythm or type I A-V block) is seen in the presence of typical sagging ST-T changes. But it remains only a suspicion, and it is left to the clinician, weighing all the evidence, to establish the diagnosis.

A Bostonian wag has been credited with the observation that "lanatoside has replaced homicide as the nation's number one killer." Certainly, the intent of this remark has been true; many in the past have been intoxicated with a too large maintenance dose of digitoxin or by the too enthusiastic use of potassium-depleting diuretics in patients receiving a digitalis preparation. But more recently, the trend seems to have reversed itself to some extent, probably because of the present vogue of treating congestive heart failure with diuretics and vasodilators to the exclusion of digitalis.

It is impossible to determine accurately the comparative frequency of the various disturbances that result from digitalis intoxication. This is because it depends how far the toxicity is allowed to run riot. If a series of intoxications is based on fatal cases, the incidence of the more serious effects, such as complete A-V block or ventricular tachycardia will be exaggerated; whereas, if the series involves patients in whom the drug was discontinued at the earliest sign of intoxication,[4] the incidence of complete block and ventricular tachycardia will be minimized.

When digitalis is given in excess or when its toxic effects are felt because of a lowered potassium, the dysrhythmic manifestations can be divided into two

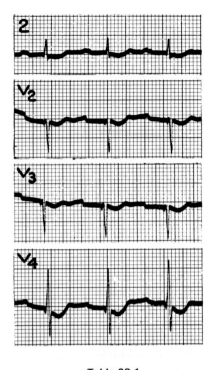

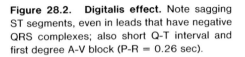

Figure 28.2. Digitalis effect. Note sagging ST segments, even in leads that have negative QRS complexes; also short Q-T interval and first degree A-V block (P-R = 0.26 sec).

Table 28.1
Main Excitant Disturbances

Ventricular extrasystoles—especially bigeminal and multiform
Atrial tachycardia
A-V junctional tachycardia
Accelerated junctional rhythm
Ventricular tachycardia
Bidirectional tachycardia
Ventricular fibrillation

categories: the excitant (table 28.1) and the suppressant effects (table 28.2). Often, there is a combination of excitant and suppressant effects (table 28.3).

Excitant Effects

Except in children, in whom supraventricular disturbances are more common, ventricular extrasystoles are the most frequently seen cardiac manifestations of digitalis overdosage. However, they are of course common in both health and disease of any kind and are in no sense diagnostic of digitalis intoxication. Furthermore, although it is not widely realized, digitalis is often an effective drug for reducing or eliminating ventricular extrasystoles that are not caused by the drug.[9, 14] When they are caused by digitalis, they tend to be bigeminal and, according to Scherf,[13] will always show variation in morphology if long enough strips are taken. Sometimes the bigeminy due to digitalis may be "concealed;" i.e., bigeminal runs may not be seen, but all interectopic intervals will contain only odd numbers of sinus beats.[12] Ventricular extrasystoles will be illustrated in the later section on "Combined Effects."

Atrial tachycardia caused by digitalis tends to possess P′ waves of normal sinus polarity but of smaller than average amplitude; they may be somewhat irregular in time and variable in shape ("multifocal atrial tachycardia"). The arrhythmia is often associated with varying ratios of A-V conduction ("PAT with block") and will also be illustrated in the later section on "Combined Effects."

A-V junctional tachycardia is another fairly common manifestation of digitalis intoxication. Whereas the drug usually slows sinus nodal pacemakers, it tends to enhance the automaticity of junctional pacemakers. Sometimes it produces a genuine tachycardia, as in figure 28.3; but at other times it induces a more modest enhancement to a rate between 60 and 100/min, and the disturbance is then most appropriately termed accelerated junctional or idionodal rhythm (AINR), illustrated in figure 28.4.

Figure 28.3*A* illustrates an A-V junctional tachycardia caused by digitalis in the presence of atrial fibrillation. The junctional discharge is almost precisely regular at a rate of 140/min.

The patient who authored figure 28.3*B* was a man who was being relentlessly nudged toward his death by repeated intravenous doses of digoxin. His RBBB was present on admission, and the first evidence of intoxication he manifested was the junctional tachycardia. In the second strip, the junctional tachycardia gives place to a second excitant manifestation of toxicity, ventricular tachycardia

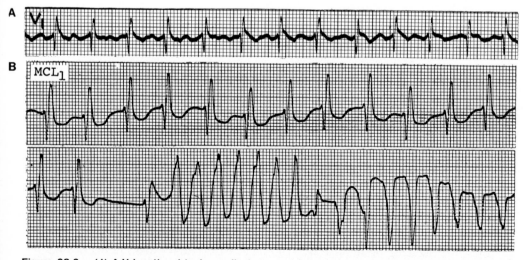

Figure 28.3. (*A*) **A-V junctional tachycardia** (rate, 140/min) with incomplete RBBB in the presence of atrial fibrillation. (*B*) The strips are continuous. Two excitant manifestations of digitalis intoxication: **A-V junctional tachycardia** (rate, 125/min) with RBBB in the *top strip*; in the *lower strip*, the A-V tachycardia suddenly pauses (?exit block), and the lengthened cycle precipitates **ventricular tachycardia** of the "swinging" variety.

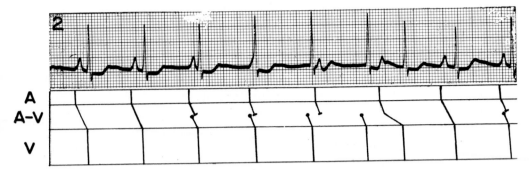

Figure 28.4.   **Digitalis intoxication: Accelerated junctional rhythm** (rate, 78/min) usurps control from a sinus rhythm (rate, 70 to 75/min). The seventh beat is a capture beat conducted with prolonged P-R interval.

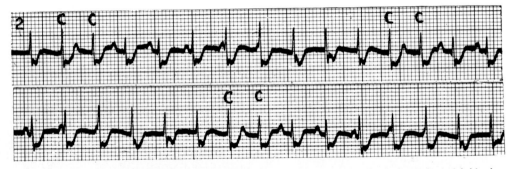

Figure 28.5.   **Digitalis intoxication.** Strips are continuous. Simultaneous but independent **atrial tachycardia** (rate, 172/min) and **junctional tachycardia** (rate, 154/min). Pairs of captured beats (*CC*) are recognized by the slight shortening of the ventricular cycles.

of the "swinging" variety (torsades de pointes); i.e., the polarity of the QRS swings between positive and negative.

The patient in figure 28.4 is a girl of 12 who required a mitral commissurotomy. After successful surgery her digitalis dosage was not reduced, and she soon developed signs of intoxication. Her earliest sign of cardiotoxicity was the AINR illustrated, a rhythm that frequently leads to A-V dissociation—as in figure 28.4—by usurping control from the somewhat slower sinus rhythm.

Digitalis toxicity is much the most common cause of "double tachycardia,"[3] i.e., the simultaneous existence of two rapidly firing but independent foci, such as the simultaneous atrial and junctional tachycardia in figure 28.5. Figure 28.6

presents an example of the so-called bidirectional tachycardia. This is not a specific term—it is purely descriptive, indicating just what you see in the rhythm strip and implying no particular mechanism. Whatever the underlying dysrhythmic mechanism, the pattern is frequently seen in digitalis intoxication. The mechanism is sometimes bifocal (or at least biform!) ectopic ventricular[5, 10] and sometimes A-V junctional with RBBB and alternating hemiblocks.[11] Another possibility in some cases is an interpolated ventricular bigeminy with fortuitously equal coupling and postectopic intervals.[6]

Atrial flutter and atrial fibrillation have only occasionally been described as manifestations of digitoxicity.[1, 4]

Suppressant Effects

Digitalis has a suppressant effect both on impulse formation in the sinus node and on conduction out of the node. Figure 28.7*A* shows both sinus bradycardia and a simultaneous 5:4 Wenckebach out of the sinus node (see ladder diagram).

When digitalis impairs conduction in the A-V junction, its effect is on the A-V node itself and therefore the pattern of conduction disturbance is of the "type I" variety. Figure 28.7*B* presents a 6:5 Wenckebach period in a patient with mild digitalis toxicity.

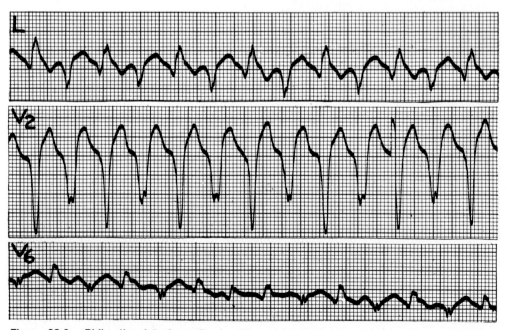

Figure 28.6.   Bidirectional tachycardia. In aVL and V₆, there is a tendency for the ventricular complexes to be alternately positive and negative. In V₂, the QRS amplitude alternates ("alternating tachycardia").

Table 28.2
Main Suppressant Disturbances

Sinus bradycardia
S-A block
Type I A-V block
Complete A-V block

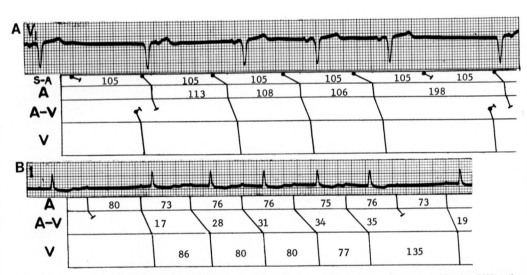

Figure 28.7.   Digitalis intoxication. (A) Sinus bradycardia complicated by a **sinus exit block of Wenck-ebach type**. The second and last beats are junctional escape beats (see laddergram). Wenckebach-type conduction is inferred from the progressive shortening of the atrial (P-P) interval (113, 108, 106)—"footprints" of the Wenckebach. (B) **Second degree A-V block, type I:** The typical Wenckebach period shows progressive lengthening of the P-R interval until the sixth beat is dropped (6:5 A-V block)—see laddergram.

Figure 28.8 is from a young man who swallowed an unknown number of digoxin tablets in a suicide attempt; as usual in the normal heart, there is disturbance of conduction without provocation of ectopy.[16]

It is doubtful if digitalis ever produces type II A-V block or bundle-branch block (BBB). However, in advanced stages of intoxication in severely diseased hearts, it is possible that digitalis may impair conduction in the ventricular expressways. This may indeed be the underlying mechanism in some patterns of bidirectional tachycardia.

Combined Effects

One of the commonest combinations of excitant and suppressant effects is the partnership of atrial tachycardia with A-V block—glibly known as "PAT with block." This is a sinister combination carrying a high mortality if the offending drug is not immediately discontinued. It is said to be more likely to

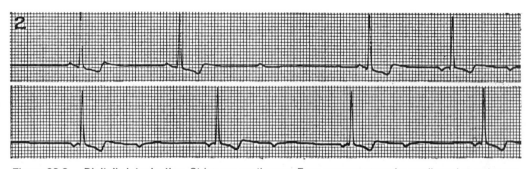

Figure 28.8. Digitalis intoxication. Strips are continuous. From a young man who swallowed an unknown number of digoxin tablets in a suicide attempt. The sinus rhythm has been slowed to slightly under 50/min. Toward the end of the *top strip*, an ectopic atrial or junctional pacemaker takes over. Note that there is impressive **A-V block**—2:1 in *bottom strip*—yet no prolongation of the P-R interval.

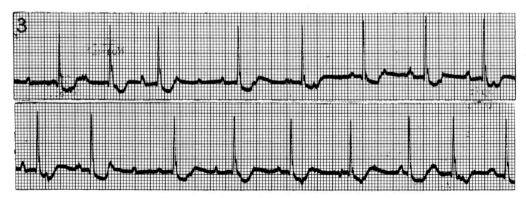

Figure 28.9. Digitalis intoxication. The strips are continuous. **Multifocal atrial tachycardia** with **varying A-V block**. Note the variable P-wave morphology, irregular atrial rhythm, changing A-V conduction ratio and the sagging ST segments characteristic of **digitalis effect**.

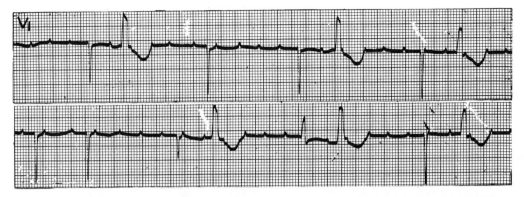

Figure 28.10. **Digitalis intoxication.** Strips are continuous. **Atrial tachycardia** with **varying A-V block** and numerous **ventricular extrasystoles** tending to bigeminy. Note irregularity of the atrial rhythm. From a 30-year-old black woman with postpartum cardiomyopathy who was mistakenly given an overdose of intravenous digoxin.

develop in patients with cor pulmonale and hypoxia.[2] Figure 28.9 is a classical example of this combine: The P′ waves are variable in shape, irregular in rhythm and of normal polarity for the most part; and the A-V conduction ratio, though mostly 2:1, is variable. The sagging ST segments are characteristic of digitalis effect. Figure 28.10 also shows this combination but, in addition, contains ventricular extrasystoles. The tracing is from a 30-year-old black woman with postpartum cardiomyopathy who was mistakenly given 2 mg digoxin intravenously. Not surprisingly, she manifests atrial tachycardia with varying block interspersed with ventricular extrasystoles tending to occur in bigeminal rhythm.

Table 28.3
Combined Disturbances

Atrial tachycardia with A-V block (''PAT with block'')
Sinus bradycardia with A-V junctional tachycardia
Regular accelerated junctional rhythm in presence of atrial fibrillation
Double tachycardias, atrial and A-V junctional
Etc

Figure 28.11 presents a third example of "PAT with block" in which you can compare the P′ waves of the toxic tachycardia with the patient's sinus P waves.

Figure 28.12*A* illustrates another threefold effect of digitalis overdosage: sinus bradycardia, a minor degree of A-V block and junctional tachycardia.

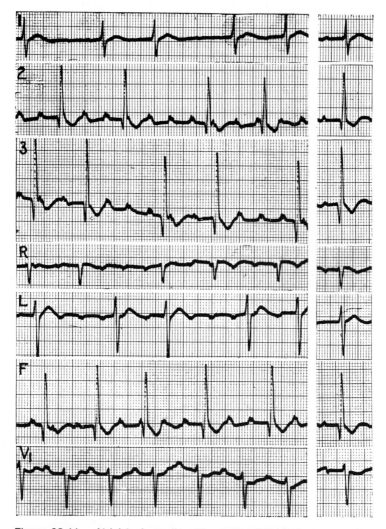

Figure 28.11. **Atrial tachycardia with varying A-V block** as a result of **digitalis intoxication.** Note that the P waves are almost normally directed (axis +90°), that the A-V conduction ratio varies and that the atrial rhythm is not precisely regular. The single column of complexes on the right is to show for comparison the form and direction of P waves (axis +60°) when sinus rhythm was restored.

Figure 28.12*B* illustrates a patient with atrial fibrillation in whom the digitalis has produced some degree of A-V block and an accelerated junctional rhythm, the combination of which has caused complete A-V dissociation.

Figure 28.13 is from a patient with atrial fibrillation, true posterior infarction and digitalis intoxication. Lead V_3 shows the accelerated A-V junctional rhythm resulting from the toxicity. Leads V_2 and V_4 show the same accelerated rhythm but with Wenckebach periods out of (exit block) or below the A-V pacemaker; V_2 shows 5:4 and 4:3 Wenckebachs, while V_4 shows the even more common 3:2 ratio producing bigeminal grouping (see laddergram).

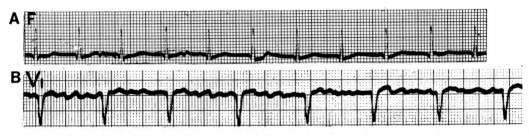

Figure 28.12. Digitalis intoxication. (*A*) **Sinus bradycardia** (rate, 55/min) with some degree of **A-V block** and **junctional tachycardia**—all due to digitalis. The third and fifth beats end slightly shorter cycles and are presumably conducted with prolonged P-R intervals; elsewhere the two rhythms are dissociated. (*B*) **Atrial fibrillation** with some degree of **A-V block** and independent **accelerated idionodal rhythm** (rate, 70/min). The degree of block and enhancement of A-V automaticity necessary to produce the dissociation are both due to digitalis.

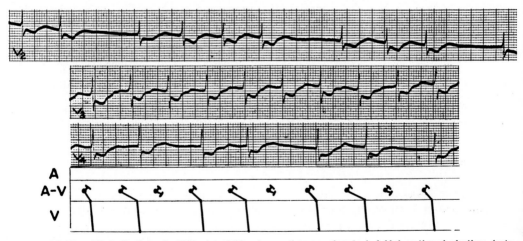

Figure 28.13. Digitalis intoxication. Lead V_3 shows the **accelerated A-V junctional rhythm** (rate, 98/min) resulting from digitalis toxicity. Leads V_2 and V_4 show the same accelerated junctional rhythm complicated by **Wenckebach periods** out of (exit block) or below the A-V pacemaker—V_2 shows 5:4 and 4:3 Wenckebachs, while V_4 shows the even more common 3:2 ratio producing bigeminal grouping (laddergram).

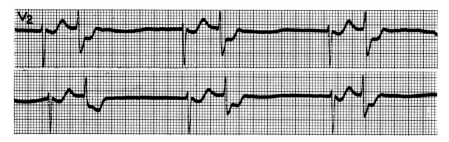

Figure 28.14.   Digitalis intoxication. Note (1) **atrial fibrillation** with regular independent idionodal rhythm, (2) **ventricular bigeminy** with multiform ectopic QRS complexes and (3) ST sagging in a lead with negative QRS complexes.

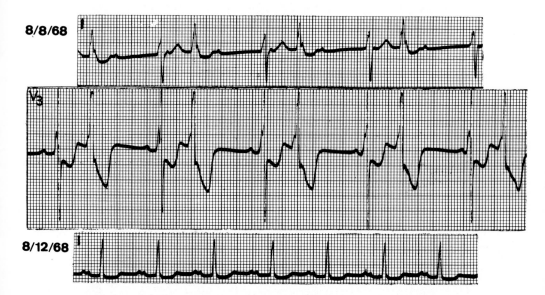

Figure 28.15.   Digitalis intoxication. From a 10-year-old black boy who was mistakenly maintained on a double dose of digitalis preparations after mitral valve surgery. On 8/8/68, he had developed an **accelerated idioventricular rhythm** (rate, 64/min) with **ventricular bigeminy** dissociated from his sinus rhythm (rate, 90/min). There is also some degree of **A-V block**—note the P waves in lead 1 landing beyond the T waves which should be conducted but are not. Both digitalis preparations were discontinued, and by 8/12/68 he reverted to sinus rhythm (rate, 80/min) with first degree A-V block. Note the P-mitrale in lead 1 on both days.

Figure 28.14 is from a patient with atrial fibrillation and severe digitalis intoxication. First of all, there is at least high-grade and probably complete A-V block with resultant escaping idionodal rhythm at the slow rate of about 40/min. There is ventricular bigeminy and, as is always the case,[13] the extrasystolic complexes vary in shape ("variform" or "multiform" rather than "multifocal"). Another (nondysrhythmic) sign referred to on page 426 and said to be diagnostic of digitalis intoxication is the sagging of the ST segment in leads *in which the QRS is predominantly negative*[8]: In the supraventricular beats the QRS is dominated by its S wave, while the ST segment has the typical, scooped-out, sagging aspect so characteristic of digitalis.

Figure 28.15 is from a 10-year-old black boy who, after mitral valve surgery, was mistakenly maintained on a double dose of digitalis. On 8/8/68, he had developed an accelerated idioventricular rhythm, dissociated from his sinus rhythm, with ventricular bigeminy. There is also some degree of block since the atrial impulses in lead 1 land beyond the T wave and yet are not conducted. Four days later, after discontinuing the digitalis, he had reverted to sinus rhythm uncomplicated except for residual first degree A-V block.

Finally, figure 28.16 is from the same patient as figure 28.3*B*—in a later stage of intoxication. He shows a combination of the same A-V junctional tachycardia with RBBB, now with intermittent A-V block below the level of the A-V pacemaker and, in the *middle strip*, the development of a right ventricular tachycardia at a modest rate. The fusion beats (*F*) in the middle of the *bottom strip* are a nice example of the "normalization" that results when BBB is present and a ventricular impulse, arising on the same side as the BBB, fuses with a simultaneous supraventricular impulse (see p. 285).

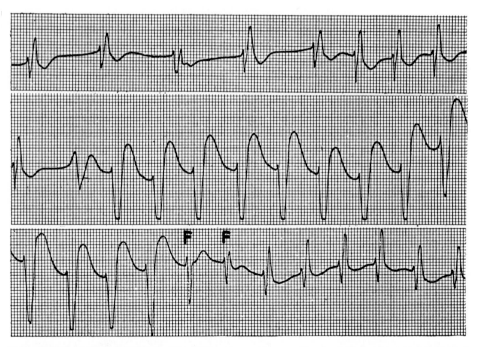

Figure 28.16.   Digitalis intoxication. Strips are continuous. The *top strip* begins with **junctional tachycardia** at first with probable 2:1 exit block or block below the A-V pacemaker; the strip ends with 1:1 conduction. After another blocked beat at the beginning of the *second strip*, a right **ventricular tachycardia** takes over (rate, 112/min). In the *bottom strip*, there are two "normalized" **fusion beats** (*F*) between the impulses of the two tachycardias.

Quinidine Effect and Toxicity

Compared with digitalis, quinidine causes qualitatively and quantitatively different changes in the tracing. It regularly lengthens the QT interval in contrast to digitalis effect. It is less likely to cause lengthening of the P-R interval but much more likely to prolong the QRS. Its influences may be summarized as follows:

1. *ST-T changes.* T waves become depressed, widened, notched and finally inverted. Meanwhile the Q-T interval lengthens (fig. 28.17). The ST segment is less likely to become depressed than with digitalis administration.

2. *Blocks* of all types can occur. S-A block may produce fatal atrial asystole. Prolongation of the QRS is frequently seen and is important to the

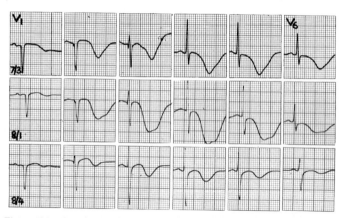

Figure 28.17.   Quinidine effect. From a patient with extensive anterior infarction who was receiving quinidine. Between 7/31 and 8/1 the quinidine effect increases—the broad T-U complex widens still further. On 8/1 quinidine was discontinued and by 8/4 the quinidine effect has largely disappeared.

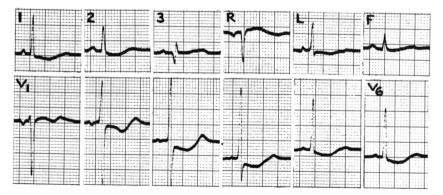

Figure 28.18.   Digitalis plus quinidine effects producing a pattern indistinguishable from that of hypokalemia (see p. 467).

therapist: if this interval increases during treatment by 25 to 50%, it is an indication to discontinue the drug.

3. *Ventricular ectopic rhythms* are occasionally produced.

The combined effects of digitalis and quinidine (fig. 28.18) can closely mimic the pattern of hypokalemia[15] (see also figs. 30.13 and 30.14).

REFERENCES

1. Agarwal, B. L., et al.: Atrial flutter; a rare manifestation of digitalis intoxication. Br. Heart J. 1972: **34**, 330.
2. Agarwal, B. L., and Agarwal, B. V.: Digitalis-induced paroxysmal atrial tachycardia with AV block. Br. Heart J. 1972: **34**, 330.
3. Castellanos, A., et al.: Digitalis-induced arrhythmias; recognition and therapy. Cardiovasc. Clin. 1969: **1** (No. 3), 108.
4. Church, G., et al.: Deliberate digitalis intoxication; a comparison of the toxic effects of four glycoside preparations. Ann. Intern. Med. 1962: **57**, 946.
5. Cohen, S. I., et al.: Infra-His origin of bidirectional tachycardia. Circulation 1973: **47**, 1260.
6. Gavrilescu, S., and Luca, C.: His bundle electrogram during bidirectional tachycardia. Br. Heart J. 1975: **37**, 1198.
7. Kastor, J. A.: Digitalis intoxication in patients with atrial fibrillation. Circulation 1973: **47**, 888.
8. Lepeschkin, E.: *Modern Electrocardiography*, pp. 297–299. Williams & Wilkins, Baltimore, 1951.
9. Lown, B., et al.: Effect of a digitalis drug on ventricular premature beats. N. Engl. J. Med. 1977: **296**, 301.
10. Morris, S. N., and Zipes, D. P.: His bundle electrocardiography during bidirectional tachycardia. Circulation 1973: **48**, 32.
11. Rosenbaum, M. B., et al.: The mechanism of bidirectional tachycardia. Am. Heart J. 1969: **78**, 4.
12. Schamroth, L., and Marriott, H. J. L.: Concealed ventricular extrasystoles. Circulation 1963: **27**, 1043.
13. Scherf, D., and Schott, A.: *Extrasystoles and Allied Arrhythmias*, Ed. 2, p. 586. Heinemann, London, 1973.
14. Scherf, D., and Schott, A.: *Extrasystoles and Allied Arrhythmias*, Ed. 2, pp. 592, 990, 993. Heinemann, London, 1973.
15. Surawicz, B.: Electrolytes and the electrocardiogram. Am. J. Cardiol. 1963: **12**, 656.
16. Vanagt, E. J., and Wellens, H. J. J.: The electrocardiogram in digitalis intoxication, p. 315. In *What's New in Electrocardiography*, edited by H. J. J. Wellens and H. E. Kulbertus. Martinus Nijhoff, Boston, 1981.

Review Tracings

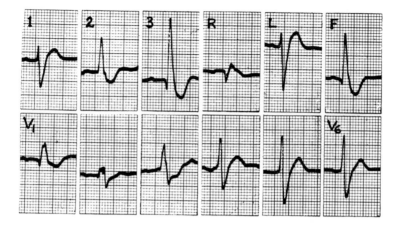

Review Tracing 28.1

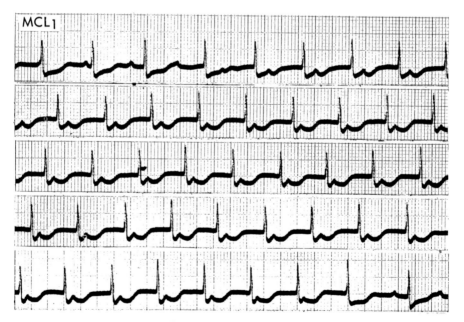

Review Tracing 28.2

For interpretation, see page 485

Review Tracings

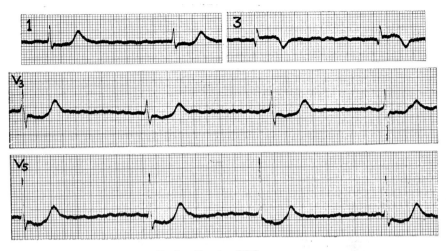

Review Tracing 28.3

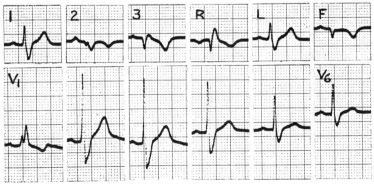

Review Tracing 28.4

For interpretation, see page 485

29

The Heart in Childhood and Congenital Lesions

Several points are of importance in interpreting the electrocardiogram in chidren. First and foremost, variations in the normal are more diverse than they are in adult tracings, so that one should be even more careful in declaring a youthful tracing abnormal than that of an adult. The rate is relatively faster, and the P-R and QRS intervals relatively shorter in childhood.

At birth the right ventricular wall is almost as thick as the left, and this leads to a different balance of power. Apart from the common occurrence of right axis deviation, tall R waves are frequently seen in precordial leads to the right of the precordium with deep S waves in left chest leads. Thus a pattern resembling right ventricular hypertrophy in the adult may be a perfectly normal finding in the child.

A further important point to remember is that T waves may be normally inverted further to the left of the precordium in the child. The percentage incidence of T-wave inversion in the first four chest leads is as follows[22, 28]:

	V_1	V_2	V_3	V_4
6–12 mo	100	91	57	4.3
1–3 yr	96	77	38	4
8–12 yr	82	13.2	4.45	0

Congenital Heart Disease

Many congenital lesions may be associated with a normal electrocardiogram. Normal tracings are more often seen in lesions that place primary stress on the left ventricle, such as aortic stenosis, coarctation of the aorta, ventricular septal defect and patent ductus; they are less often seen in association with lesions that stress the right ventricle, such as pulmonic stenosis and atrial septal defect. Complex defects are only rarely associated with a normal tracing. A normal tracing, therefore, by no means excludes a congenital lesion.

442

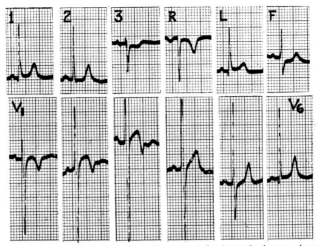

Figure 29.1.   From a patient with **patent ductus arteriosus**, showing left ventricular diastolic overloading. Note high voltage of QRS
complexes, with tall upright T waves in V_{5-6}. U waves are inverted
in 1, 2 and V_6.

Again, there may be great differences between the tracings from different
patients with the same deformity; for example, in mild patent ductus or
ventricular septal defect the tracing will probably be normal. Later the pattern
of left ventricular diastolic overloading may develop (fig. 29.1). When pulmonary hypertension becomes significant, right ventricular hypertrophy will be
added to the left ventricular overloading pattern. Finally, when pulmonic
hypertension is marked, the pattern may become that of right ventricular
hypertrophy alone.

In congenital heart disease few patterns are diagnostic and those that are are
associated with the rarer malformations: for example, when the left coronary
arises from the pulmonary artery (anomalous left coronary artery), the electrocardiographic pattern is usually diagnostic—Q waves, ST elevation and T-wave
inversion are present in leads 1, aVL and the left chest leads, giving a pattern
identical with that of lateral infarction.[13] The electrocardiogram of dextrocardia
with situs inversus is also almost specific, and those of the ostium primum/
common A-V canal group and Ebstein's disease are relatively so (see below).
Although the tracing is seldom truly diagnostic, it often serves as a helpful
guidepost and it is convenient to gather the most useful pointers under the
headings of the four main components of the tracing:

P waves

1. In isolated dextrocardia the P wave in lead 1 is normally upright, whereas in dextrocardia with situs inversus it is inverted (left-sided venous atrium and vena cava); indeed all complexes in lead 1 are inverted (fig. 29.2).
2. **P-congenitale** consists of tall and peaked P waves in leads 1 and 2, with tall, mainly positive P waves in right chest leads (fig. 29.3). The frontal plane axis is generally between +30° and +45°, in contrast with one to the right of +60° in P-pulmonale. P-congenitale is found mainly in cyanotic forms of congenital disease but also in pure pulmonic stenosis. The tallest P waves occur in tricuspid disease (stenosis or atresia) and in Ebstein's disease (fig. 29.4).

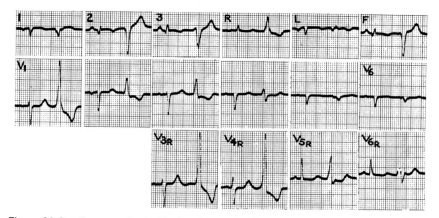

Figure 29.2.　From a patient with **situs inversus**, acute inferior infarction and ventricular bigeminy. Note inverted P and QRS in lead 1 and dwindling S wave across left precordium. When precordial leads are taken to the right (V$_{3R}$-V$_{6R}$), the normal transition from rS to R occurs.

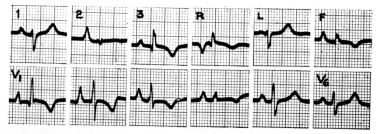

Figure 29.3.　From a 44-year-old patient with **pulmonic stenosis**. Tracing shows right ventricular hypertrophy and strain (systolic overloading). Note P-congenitale, indicating right atrial enlargement, with prominent R waves in right precordial leads, marked right axis deviation (+150°) and relatively low equiphasic complexes in V$_{5-6}$.

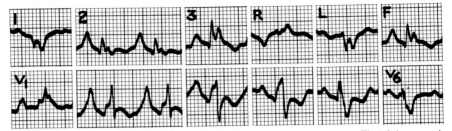

Figure 29.4. **Ebstein's anomaly.** From a 36-year-old woman with severe Ebstein's anomaly. Note low voltage, atypical RBBB and enormous P waves.

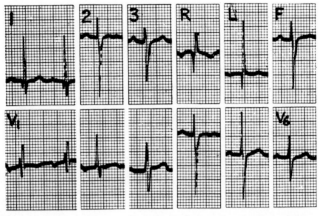

Figure 29.5. From a 13-year-old boy with an **ostium primum** atrial septal defect, cleft mitral valve and small ventricular septal defect (incomplete **A-V communis**); note the almost diagnostic combination of marked left axis deviation of the early portion of the QRS with incomplete RBBB.

QRS Complex

1. Determination of the **mean QRS axis** may provide a helpful initial clue to diagnosis. Diagrams illustrating the distribution of congenital malformations in the various segments of the hexaxial reference system have been published, and these may profitably be consulted.[10, 15, 23] When **left axis deviation** is seen in a patient with cyanotic disease, the most likely diagnosis is tricuspid atresia; but other possibilities include transposition of the great vessels, single ventricle and a number of other anomalies.[20] When the initial portion of the QRS complex shows marked left axis deviation while the terminal part shows a right bundle-branch block, the overwhelming probability is a lesion of the ostium primum/ A-V communis group (endocardial cushion defect) (fig. 29.5). Such a pattern is unfortunately also sometimes seen in secundum defects.[14]

2. The patterns of **ventricular hypertrophy** are obviously of considerable diagnostic importance; right ventricular hypertrophy is seen in pure pulmonic stenosis (fig. 29.3), atrial septal defect and most of the cyanotic lesions. In the tetralogy of Fallot, the dominant R wave in V_1 of right ventricular hypertrophy usually changes to RS or rS by V_2 (fig. 29.6) whereas in pure pulmonic stenosis the R wave usually remains dominant in the first 3 or 4 chest leads (fig. 29.3).

Left hypertrophy is seen in aortic stenosis, coarctation of the aorta, ventricular septal defect and patent ductus. In aortic stenosis, an R/T ratio of more than 10 in V_5 or V_6 indicates severe obstruction.[11] Note that ventricular hypertrophy and axis deviation do not necessarily go hand in hand. Indeed, left axis deviation is seen in less than 25% of cases showing left ventricular hypertrophy, and right axis deviation is present in less than 66% of those showing right ventricular hypertrophy.

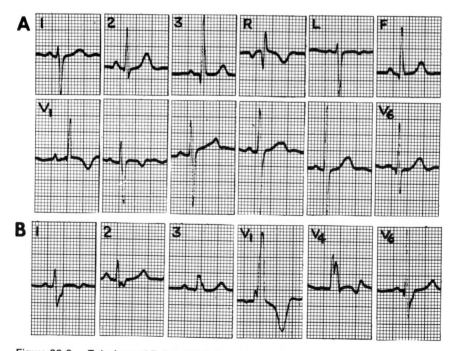

Figure 29.6.   Tetralogy of Fallot. (A) Note marked right axis deviation ($+120°$), tall R in V_1 and deep S waves through V_6; also that S waves become dominant at V_2 while T waves are upright at V_3 (compare pattern of pure pulmonic stenosis, fig. 29.3). (B) Development of RBBB following surgical correction.

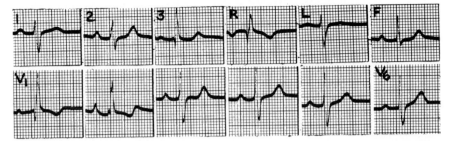

Figure 29.7.   Atrial septal defect. Typical RBBB pattern of right ventricular diastolic overloading. Note also 1st degree A-V block and pointed right precordial P waves suggesting right atrial hypertrophy.

3. **Bundle-branch block.** The pattern of right bundle-branch block is commonly seen as a hemodynamic expression of right ventricular diastolic overloading (fig. 29.7). The classic example is atrial septal defect, and up to 90% of patients with this lesion manifest right bundle-branch block. RBBB is also frequently seen in the hemodynamically similar total anomalous pulmonary venous return and turns up occasionally in a variety of other lesions. It is a well-recognized complication of surgery for ventricular septal defect (fig. 29.6). In Ebstein's disease right bundle-branch block is the rule, but in this condition the QRS complexes of the right precordial leads are typically of quite low voltage (fig. 29.4). Left bundle-branch block is rare but is occasionally seen in aortic stenosis and in other lesions placing predominant strain on the left ventricle. It regularly occurs following surgery for septal hypertrophy.

4. **Pre-excitation.** The WPW syndrome has been described in a variety of congenital lesions, but much its commonest associations are Ebstein's anomaly and primary cardiomyopathy.[17, 24]

5. The **Katz-Wachtel phenomenon** consists of equiphasic complexes in two or more limb leads, often with similar equiphasicity in the midprecordial leads. This is seen in many congenital lesions, but is perhaps most common in ventricular septal defect (fig. 29.8).

6. Prominent **Q waves** in the right precordial leads are evidence of right *atrial* hypertrophy; prominent Q waves in left chest leads, or in 2, 3, and aVF, sometimes reaching a depth of 10 mm, are most suspicious of ventricular septal defect (fig. 29.8). Prominent Q waves in limb and left chest leads are also typical of hypertrophic cardiomyopathy (fig. 29.9).

T Waves

In differentiating Fallot's tetralogy from the trilogy (pulmonic stenosis, atrial septal defect and right ventricular hypertrophy) or from pure pulmonic stenosis, T-wave behavior may be helpful. In the tetralogy precordial T waves are usually inverted only in leads taken to the right of the sternum (fig. 29.10), whereas in the trilogy or pure pulmonic stenosis they are frequently inverted as far to the left as V_4 or V_5 (fig. 29.3).

U Waves

These have been largely neglected in descriptions of the electrocardiogram in congenital heart disease; but inverted U waves are a common finding in left chest leads as an early sign of left ventricular overloading, systolic or diastolic.

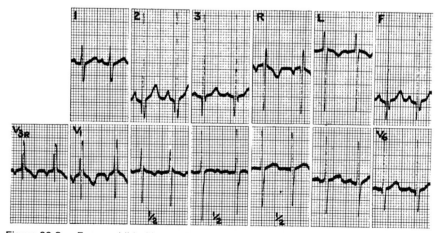

Figure 29.8.   From a child with **ventricular septal defect**. Note deep Q waves in 2, 3 and aVF, incomplete RBBB pattern and equiphasic RS pattern in midprecordial leads.

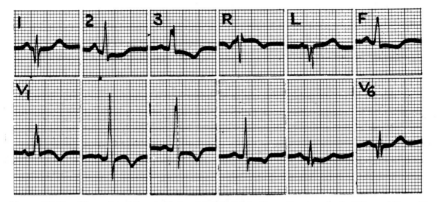

Figure 29.9. Hypertrophic cardiomyopathy. Note deep Q waves in 1, aVL and V₆, with reciprocal tall R in right chest leads, indicating septal hypertrophy.

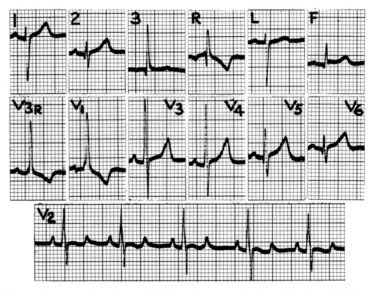

Figure 29.10. Tetralogy of Fallot. Note marked right axis deviation (+150°) with right ventricular hypertrophy. T waves become upright in V₂ (compare with persistent inversion through V₄ in pure pulmonic stenosis—fig. 29.3).

Individual Defects

The cardinal features of the electrocardiogram in the commoner congenital lesions and in those with distinctive features are as follows:

Ventricular Septal Defect (VSD) (fig. 29.8)

Prominent Q waves in left chest leads or in 2, 3 and aVF. High voltage equiphasic QRS complex in midprecordial leads in 50 to 75%.

Pattern of RBBB, complete or more often incomplete, in 20 to 30%.
Depending on severity and stage, may be normal, or show LVH, combined
ventricular hypertrophy or RVH; LVH is often of diastolic overloading type.

Patent Ductus Arteriosus (figs. 29.1 and 29.11)

Similar to VSD; but left atrial enlargement and 1st degree A-V block are more
common and RBBB patterns less common than in VSD.

Atrial Septal Defect (fig. 29.7)

Patterns of RBBB in majority—up to 90% in some series.
P-congenitale in some.
First degree A-V block and atrial arrhythmias in a few.

Aortic Stenosis

Normal in at least 25% of those with significant obstruction.
Varying stages of LVH in most of remainder.
LBBB in a few.

Hypertrophic Cardiomyopathy (HCM) (fig. 29.9)

Axis usually normal.
Delta waves are common; occasional WPW.
Prominent Q waves, especially in leads 2, 3, aVF, V_{5-6}, with tall R waves in
right chest leads (evidence of septal hypertrophy). Progression from this to
LVH.

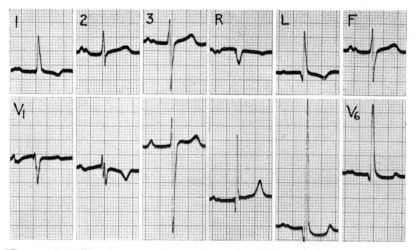

Figure 29.11. From a 24-year-old patient with **patent ductus arteriosus**. Note
wide notched P waves (intra-atrial block, evidence of left atrial enlargement), first
degree A-V block (P-R = 0.30 sec) and high voltage QRS complexes with ST-T
changes indicating left ventricular hypertrophy and strain.

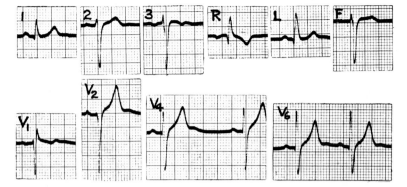

Figure 29.12. From a 15-year-old boy with **coarctation of the aorta**. Note unusually marked left axis deviation (−75°), presumably due to left anterior hemiblock.

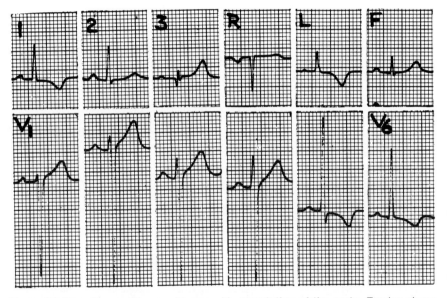

Figure 29.13. From a 32-year-old man with **coarctation of the aorta**. Tracing shows typical pattern of left ventricular hypertrophy and strain (systolic overload).

Coarctation (figs. 29.12 and 29.13)

Normal or LVH.

Pulmonic Stenosis (PS) (fig. 29.3)

RVH with rR or qR in V_1 when RV pressure is equal to or higher than LV pressure; Rs or rS in V_1 when RV pressure is less than LV pressure.
P-congenitale.
In severe PS, R waves dominant and T waves inverted V_1 to V_3 or V_4.

Tetralogy of Fallot (figs. 29.6 and 29.10)

RVH with dominant R and inverted T in V_1; abrupt change to rS with upright T in V_2 or V_3 (cf. pulmonic stenosis).
P-congenitale.

Transposition of Great Vessels

RVH with a) qR in V_1 suggests intact ventricular septum; b) rsR' in V_1 suggests VSD.
P-congenitale.
T waves taller in right than left chest leads.

Corrected Transposition (Inversion of Ventricles) (fig. 29.14)

qR in V_1 with no q and RS in V_6.
P-congenitale.
Some degree of A-V block.

Endocardial Cushion Defect (fig. 29.5)

Left axis deviation of initial portion of QRS with incomplete RBBB pattern.
Occasional first degree A-V block.

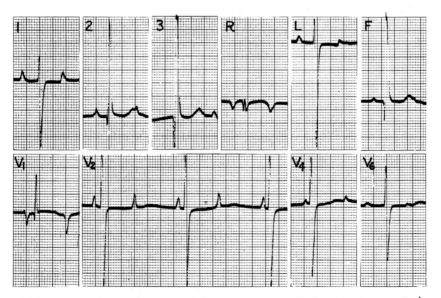

Figure 29.14.   Corrected transposition of the great vessels. Note the left ventricular (qR) pattern in V_1 with absent Q and deep S in V_6—typical of **ventricular inversion**; also the P-congenitale type of right atrial enlargement and the high grade (probably complete) A-V block. (Reproduced from H. J. L. Marriott: *Bedside Diagnosis of Heart Disease.* Tampa Tracings, 1967.)

Ebstein's Anomaly (fig. 29.4)

Right atrial enlargement without RVH.
Low amplitude, atypical RBBB pattern.
WPW syndrome (type B) in 10%.
First degree A-V block in 15 to 20%.
Arrhythmias, especially atrial tachycardia.

Tricuspid Atresia

LVH, or at least left axis deviation, in 80 to 90%.
Right atrial overload.

REFERENCES

1. Beregovich, J., et al.: The vectorcardiogram and electrocardiogram in persistent common atrioventricular canal. Circulation 1960: **21**, 63.
2. Beregovich, J., et al.: The vectorcardiogram and electrocardiogram in ventricular septal defect. Br. Heart J. 1960: **22**, 205.
3. Braudo, M., et al.: A distinctive electrocardiogram in muscular subaortic stenosis due to septal hypertrophy. Am. J. Cardiol. 1964: **14**, 599.
4. Braunwald, E., et al.: Idiopathic hypertrophic subaortic stenosis. I. A description of the disease based upon an analysis of 64 patients. Circulation 1964: **30**, Supp. IV-3.
5. Brink, A. J., and Neill, C. A.: The electrocardiogram in congenital heart disease: with special reference to left axis deviation. Circulation 1955: **12**, 604.
6. Brumlik, J. V.: Principles of electrocardiographic interpretation in congenital heart disease. In *Advances in Electrocardiography*, p. 203. Grune & Stratton, New York, 1958.
7. Burchell, H. B., et al.: The electrocardiogram of patients with atrioventricular cushion defects (defects of the atrioventricular canal). Am. J. Cardiol. 1960: **6**, 575.
8. Dack, S.: The electrocardiogram and vectorcardiogram in ventricular septal defect. Am. J. Cardiol. 1960: **5**, 199.
9. de Oliviera, J. M., and Zimmerman, H. A.: The electrocardiogram in interatrial septal defects and its correlation with hemodynamics. Am. Heart J. 1958: **55**, 369.
10. de Oliviera, J. M., et al.: The mean ventricular axis in congenital heart disease: a study considering the natural incidence of the malformations. Am. Heart J. 1959: **57**, 820.
11. Fowler, R. S.: Ventricular repolarization in congenital aortic stenosis. Am. Heart J. 1965: **70**, 603.
12. Grant, R. P., et al.: Symposium on diagnostic methods in the study of left-to-right shunts. Circulation 1957: **16**, 791.
13. Kuzman, W. J., et al.: Anomalous left coronary artery arising from the pulmonary artery. Am. Heart J. 1959: **57**, 36.
14. Harrison, D. C., and Morrow, A. G.: Electrocardiographic evidence of left-axis deviation in patients with defects of the atrial septum of the secundum type. N. Engl. J. Med. 1963: **269**, 743.
15. Landero, C. A., et al.: The mean manifest electrical axes of ventricular activation and repolarization processes (ÂQRS and ÂT) in congenital heart disease; frontal and horizontal planes. Am. Heart J. 1959: **58**, 889.
16. Pryor, R., et al.: Electrocardiographic changes in atrial septal defects: ostium secundum defect versus ostium primum (endocardial cushion) defect. Am. Heart J. 1959: **58**, 689.
17. Schiebler, G. L., et al.: The Wolff-Parkinson-White syndrome in infants and children. Pediatrics 1959: **24**, 585.
18. Scott, R. C.: The electrocardiogram in atrial septal defects and atrioventricular cushion defects. Am. Heart J. 1961: **62**, 712.
19. Scott, R. C.: The electrocardiogram in ventricular septal defects. Am. Heart J. 1961: **62**, 842.

20. Shaher, R. M.: Left ventricular preponderance and left axis deviation in cyanotic congenital heart disease. Br. Heart J. 1963: **25**, 726.
21. Sodi-Pallares, D., and Marsico, F.: The importance of electrocardiographic patterns in congenital heart disease. Am. Heart J. 1955: **49**, 202.
22. Sodi-Pallares, D., et al.: Electrocardiography in infants and children. Pediatr. Clin. North Am. 1958: **5**, 871.
23. Sodi-Pallares, D., et al.: The mean manifest electrical axis of the ventricular activation process (ÂQRS) in congenital heart disease: a new approach in electrocardiographic diagnosis. Am. Heart J. 1958: **55**, 681.
24. Swiderski, J., et al.: The Wolff-Parkinson-White syndrome in infancy and childhood. Br. Heart J. 1962: **24**, 561.
25. Toscano-Barboza, E. M., et al.: Atrial septal defect. The electrocardiogram and its hemodynamic correlation in 100 proved cases. Am. J. Cardiol. 1958: **2**, 698.
26. Toscano-Barboza, E. M., and DuShane, J. W.: Ventricular septal defect. Correlation of electrocardiographic and hemodynamic findings in 60 proved cases. Am. J. Cardiol. 1959: **3**, 721.
27. Wigle, E. D., and Baron, R. H.: The electrocardiogram in muscular subaortic stenosis. Circulation 1966: **34**, 585.
28. Ziegler, R. R.: *Electrocardiographic Studies in Normal Infants and Children.* Charles C Thomas, Springfield, Ill., 1951.

Review Tracing

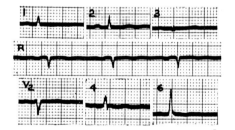

Review Tracing 29.1

For interpretation, see page 485

Review Tracings

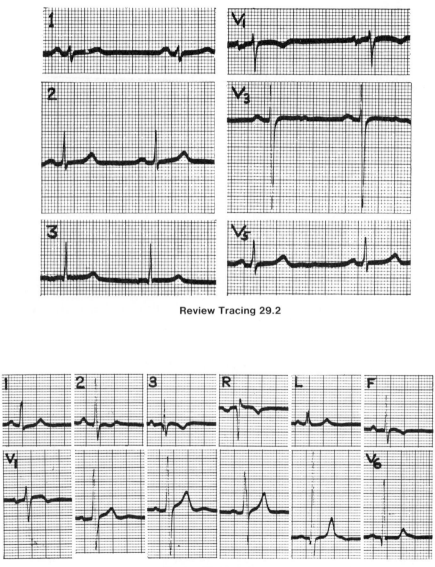

Review Tracing 29.2

Review Tracing 29.3

For interpretation, see page 485

30

Miscellaneous Conditions

Valvular Lesions

The electrocardiogram plays only a small part in the diagnosis of valvular lesions. Mitral stenosis is the only one which may claim anything like a specific pattern.[21] The **P-mitrale** pattern, consisting of wide, notched P waves in leads 1 and 2, with flat, diphasic or inverted P waves in 3, is frequently found (fig. 30.1). P-wave notching is sometimes best seen in midprecordial leads (e.g., V_3). The combination of right axis deviation (with or without right ventricular hypertrophy) and the P-mitrale pattern or atrial fibrillation is strongly sugges-

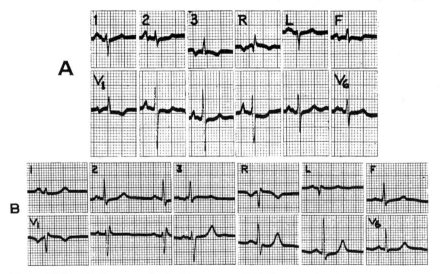

Figure 30.1. (*A*) From a patient with severe **mitral disease**, showing evidence of left atrial and right ventricular enlargement. Note P-mitrale with wide notched P waves, marked right axis deviation (+150°) with prominent R in V_1 and equiphasic complexes in left chest leads. (*B*) From a 31-year-old woman with pure mitral stenosis. Note P-mitrale, low voltage QRS in lead 1 (P and R about same height) and rSr' pattern of RVH in V_{1-2}. (Reproduced from H.J.L. Marriott: *Bedside Diagnosis of Heart Disease.* Tampa Tracings, 1967.)

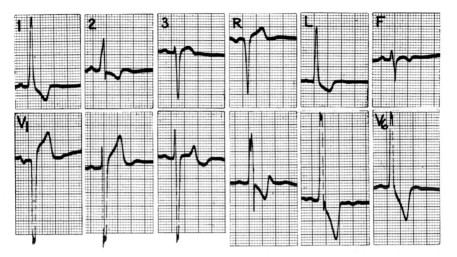

Figure 30.2.   From a patient with severe **syphilitic aortic insufficiency**, showing classical pattern of marked left ventricular hypertrophy and strain.

tive of mitral stenosis. The combination of right axis deviation with atrial fibrillation (see fig. 14.8, p. 186) in a patient under 40 is practically diagnostic of mitral stenosis; but it is occasionally found in thyrotoxicosis and in atrial septal defect. When upright, the QRS in lead 1 is often strikingly low and may be rivalled by the height of the P wave (fig. 30.1*B*).

The effect of other valvular lesions can be predicted from the known mechanical effects on the heart. Aortic or mitral regurgitation predominantly affects the left ventricle and initially produces a pattern of left ventricular diastolic overloading; later they, like aortic stenosis, produce the typical pattern of left ventricular hypertrophy and strain (fig. 30.2). Signs of left atrial overload are common in mitral regurgitation.[39, 40]

In 50 subjects with pure severe aortic stenosis at autopsy, the electrocardiograms taken within two months of death showed left axis deviation in only 12; LBBB in 4 and left ventricular hypertrophy in 44 of the remaining 46, with left atrial overload in 15; ventricular extrasystoles and prolonged P-R intervals in 7 each, and atrial fibrillation in 5.[69]

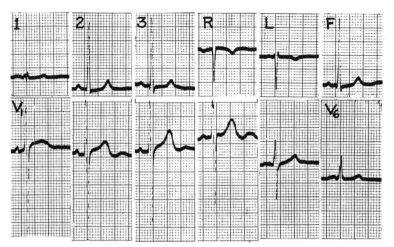

Figure 30.3. From a patient with combined **mitral** and **aortic disease**. Tracing suggests biventricular hypertrophy: the high QRS voltage in 2, 3, aVF and V_{1-4} indicates left ventricular enlargement, to which the inverted U waves in 2, 3 and aVF lend supporting evidence; whereas the prominent R waves in V_{1-2}, together with the axis, which approaches $+90°$, are evidence of right ventricular hypertrophy. The flat, wide and notched P waves in 1 and V_{5-6} indicate left atrial enlargement as well.

Combined mitral and aortic lesions often produce patterns suggesting enlargement of both ventricles (fig. 30.3). Tricuspid stenosis is suggested when right atrial enlargement is associated with a prolonged P-R interval without preponderance of either ventricle; lead V_1 not infrequently shows a low voltage rsr' complex. Pulmonic stenosis was dealt with in Chapter 29.

Acute Cor Pulmonale

The pattern of acute cor pulmonale develops within a few minutes of a massive pulmonary embolism[15, 37] or may develop in the course of other conditions producing acute cor pulmonale.[29] Its greatest importance diagnostically is that its pattern somewhat resembles that of inferior myocardial infarction, and as the clinical picture also may well be confused with myocardial infarction, the distinction may be a difficult one. In the typical case, a Q wave develops in lead 3 and the ST segment becomes elevated with shallow inversion of the T wave. Meanwhile lead 1 has developed somewhat "reciprocal" changes: an S wave appears (indicating a not surprising tendency to develop right axis deviation); the ST segment is depressed while the T remains upright. All these changes are compatible with inferior infarction. Lead 2, however, tends to follow lead 1 and shows no Q wave, but an S wave, a slightly depressed ST segment and an upright T wave; whereas in inferior infarction lead 2 tends to follow lead 3 with a Q, an elevated ST and inverted T.

In the precordial leads, elevated ST segments and inverted T waves are sometimes seen over the right ventricle, while S waves may become more

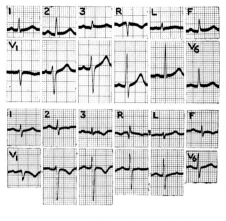

Figure 30.4. Acute cor pulmonale from pulmonary embolism. *Upper tracing*, taken 1 year before lower, within normal limits: note upright T waves in 2, 3 and aVF with normal shallowly inverted T in V_1; virtual absence of S waves in limb leads and in V_{5-6}. *Lower tracing* taken shortly after onset of symptoms: note simultaneous inversion of T waves in 2, 3 and aVF and V_{1-3}; development of significant S waves in all limb leads and in V_{5-6}.

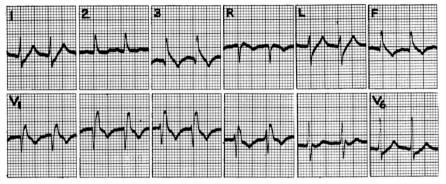

Figure 30.5 Acute cor pulmonale (from a patient with massive pulmonary embolism). Note simultaneous inversion of T waves in inferior (3, aVF) and anteroseptal (V_{1-4}) leads, and development of RBBB.

prominent over the left ventricle (indications of right ventricular dilation). The S wave in V_1 may become slurred and the R/S ratio decrease in two successive precordial leads.[47] Transient right bundle-branch block may appear. Many of these changes are to be seen in figures 30.4 and 30.5.

The differences between this pattern and that of inferior infarction may thus be summarized as follows:

1. Lead 2 tends to follow lead 1 rather than 3.
2. The changes may be fleeting and evolve and recede in a matter of hours or days rather than weeks or months.
3. ST-T deviations in limb leads are slight, whereas they may be major in inferior infarction; and in right precordial leads they resemble the anteroseptal rather than the inferior infarction pattern.

A helpful aphorism: If you find yourself diagnosing inferior infarction from the limb leads, and anteroseptal damage or infarction from the chest leads, think of pulmonary embolism.

Chronic Cor Pulmonale

In the presence of chronic lung disease, the four indications that the right ventricle is beginning to feel the strain are[19] rightward shift of the QRS axis by more than 30°; inverted, diphasic or flattened T waves in leads V_1-V_3; ST depression in leads 2, 3 and aVF; and right bundle-branch block.

Florid chronic cor pulmonale, most often seen in emphysema, is characterized by right axis deviation and sometimes the pattern of right ventricular hypertrophy and strain. Enlargement of the right atrium is manifested by the **P-pulmonale** pattern (fig. 30.6; also fig. 3.1, p. 15), consisting of a low P in lead 1 with tall, pointed P waves in 2, 3 and aVF. The single most characteristic electrocardiographic feature of diffuse lung disease is said to be a P-wave axis between +70° and +90°.[20] The P waves in right precordial leads are usually also pointed, or are diphasic with a distinct intrinsicoid deflection; and the P-terminal force is said to be often abnormally large.[66] Low voltage is not infrequently present, and T_1 is often of lower voltage than T_3.

Frequently, instead of the fullblown pattern of right ventricular hypertrophy and strain with tall R waves in V_1, an intermediate pattern is seen with deep S waves across the precordium from V_1 to V_6 (fig. 30.6). The Q-T interval in cor pulmonale, unlike that in other forms of heart failure, is not prolonged.[1] This may at times be a helpful differential point.

Salient Features of Chronic Cor Pulmonale

1. Right axis deviation
2. Right ventricular hypertrophy, or simply rS complexes across precordium
3. P-pulmonale pattern
4. Often low voltage QRS, and T_1 lower than T_3

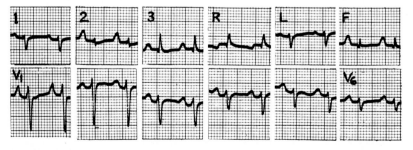

Figure 30.6. **Chronic cor pulmonale.** Note P-pulmonale pattern, marked right axis shift (+150°) and deep S waves across precordium with low R waves in left chest leads.

The five most typical findings in emphysema[28] have been grouped together into a "pentalogy": (1) prominent P waves in 2, 3 and aVF; (2) exaggerated T_P waves producing more than 1-mm depression of the ST segment in 2, 3 and aVF; (3) rightward shift of the QRS axis; (4) marked "clockwise rotation" in the precordial leads; and (5) low voltage of the QRS complexes, especially over the left precordium (V_{4-7}). The QRS axis in the frontal plane is surprisingly sometimes in the neighborhood of $-90°$, i.e. marked *left* axis deviation[24] (fig. 30.7). Thus the axis tends to be vertically down or up ($+90°$ or $-90°$) and is seldom inclined much to either side. This is because in emphysema the QRS is predominantly posterior (dominant S in V_{1-6}) and relatively little deviation up or down will swing the frontal axis through $180°$. Schaeffer[42] found that 15% of patients with chronic obstructive pulmonary disease had left axis deviation, while 9% had dominant S waves in the three standard limb leads ($S_1S_2S_3$ pattern). It is also not uncommon for Q waves simulating inferior infarction to develop in leads 2, 3 and aVF with simultaneous appearance of S waves in lead 1.

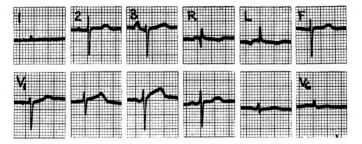

Figure 30.7. From a patient with chronic lung disease. Note marked *left* axis deviation ($-60°$).

Acute Pericarditis

In acute pericarditis, from whatever cause, the characteristic finding is an elevation of ST segments with upward *concavity* in many leads, including all three standard leads. The T wave remains upright at first, except in lead 3, where it may be inverted. Lead 3 is also often an exception in the shape of its ST segment, which may present an upward convexity. In most cases, the P-R segment is depressed in the limb leads and V_{2-6}[50]; in fact, P-R segment displacements were present in 28 (63%) of 44 consecutive cases.[8] These changes characterize the first or **ST stage** of acute pericarditis (fig. 30.8).

In a sizeable minority, the classical electrocardiographic constellation will not appear; out of the same 44 consecutive cases, 19 (43%) were atypical in some way. Eight had no ST elevation in the limb leads including three who showed no abnormalities of any kind; and in four, the *only* sign was P-R segment displacement.[8]

The second stage, or **T stage**, presents widespread T-wave inversion (fig. 30.9). At this stage the ST segments have returned to the isoelectric level. During both stages low voltage is a common finding. In the average case of acute pericarditis resolving in the course of 3 or 4 weeks, these stages each last for about 10 days to 2 weeks.

In mild cases, the ST stage may resolve with or without some T-wave flattening but without proceeding to the inverted T-wave stage.[52]

The changes in pericarditis are probably due to two causes:

1. Short circuiting of impulses by pericardial fluid or thickened pericardium causes the low voltage.
2. Spread of the inflammation to the immediately subjacent layer of myocardium (i.e., subepicardial myocarditis) accounts for the ST- and T-wave changes.

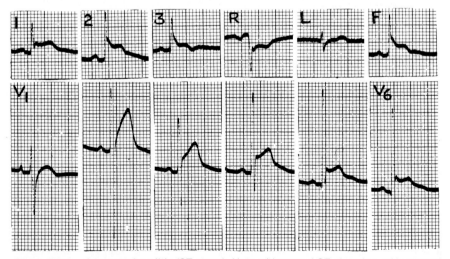

Figure 30.8. **Acute pericarditis** (ST stage). Note widespread ST elevation, with upward concavity in 1, 2, aVF, and V_{4-6}.

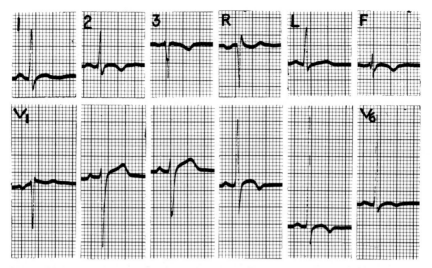

Figure 30.9. **Acute pericarditis** (T stage). Note T-wave inversions in 2, 3, aVF and V₄₋₆.

Table 30.1
Differentiation of Acute Pericarditis and Acute Infarction

	Acute Pericarditis	Acute Infarction
ST reciprocity (between 1 and 3)	Absent. Elevation in both 1 and 3	Present. Elevated in one, depressed in the other
ST shape	Concave upward	Convex upward
Q waves	Absent	Present
Period of evolution	Few weeks	Months

If the subepicardial involvement is localized rather than diffuse, ST-segment elevation may be restricted to a few leads with reciprocal depression elsewhere, closely imitating myocardial infarction; but, although R waves may be diminished, pathological Q waves usually do not develop.[9] Although Q waves are not expected in the absence of necrosis, in an occasional patient the subepicardial myocarditis may be severe enough to cause the temporary appearance of Q waves[60] thus enhancing the simulation of myocardial infarction.

The four most striking differences between acute pericarditis and acute infarction are tabulated in table 30.1.

Acute pericarditis must also be differentiated from the "early repolarization" syndrome. According to Spodick, pericarditis is more likely to present with ST elevation in both limb and precordial leads; an ST axis to the left of the T-wave axis, and ST *depression* in V₁ also favor the diagnosis of pericarditis. On the other hand, a vertical ST axis to the right of the T-wave axis and an isoelectric ST segment in V₆ favor early repolarization.[51] Exercise[2] and isoproterenol[34] may restore the elevated ST segments of early repolarization to the baseline—a palpably unlikely effect in acute pericarditis!

Another differentiating point, recently claimed to be of value, is the ST/T ratio in V_6.[65] Using the end of the P-R segment as baseline, if the apex of the T wave is more than 4 times higher than the onset of the S-T segment, it is said to be normal (i.e., "early repolarization"); if less than 4 times, pericarditis is suggested.

Chronic Constrictive Pericarditis

In the chronic constrictive or adhesive type of pericarditis, changes in the tracing are relatively fixed and nonprogressive. They are not unlike the findings in the T stage of the acute disease, two of the most characteristic features being low voltage and inverted T waves. Flat or inverted T waves are present in all cases, abnormal P waves in about three quarters of the cases and low voltage in over half.[12]

Such changes are found in all or at least many leads. It is of practical importance to note the degree of inversion of the T waves, for the depth of inversion is usually proportional to the degree of pericardial adherence to the myocardium[17]; deep T waves are associated with intimate adherence, which makes surgical stripping difficult or impossible, whereas flat or barely inverted T waves usually indicate a relatively easy surgical undertaking.

Atrial fibrillation is persistently present in over a third of the cases.[12]

One other characteristic which deserves passing mention is that the axis of the heart does not alter, as it does normally when the patient turns from one side to the other; for being bound by adhesions it is not free to swing from side to side with change in position. This electrocardiographic feature corresponds with the clinical finding of a fixed apex beat.

Pericardial Effusion

A triad that is virtually diagnostic of pericardial effusion is: low voltage, S-T segment elevation and electrical alternans (fig. 30.10). Total alternans, i.e., alternation of P waves as well as QRS, is almost pathognomonic of effusion due to malignancy.[4, 36]

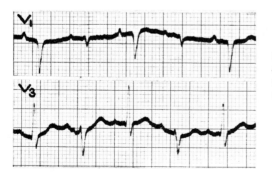

Figure 30.10. Malignant *pericardial effusion*. Note "total alternans" (i.e., alternation of P as well as QRS) in presence of regular sinus tachycardia, rate 118.

Salient Features of Chronic Pericarditis

1. Low voltage
2. Flat or inverted T waves
3. Fixed axis
4. Possible P-mitrale pattern or atrial fibrillation

Myxedema

The diagnosis of myxedema should certainly never depend upon electrocardiographic changes though it may be suspected when flattening or shallow inversion of many T waves is seen without comparable ST displacement (fig. 30.11). Its cardinal characteristics are three:

1. Low to inverted T waves in all or many leads
2. Low voltage
3. Sinus bradycardia (uncommon)

The QT interval is also always prolonged but, because of the low/flat T waves, its measurement is often difficult (58).

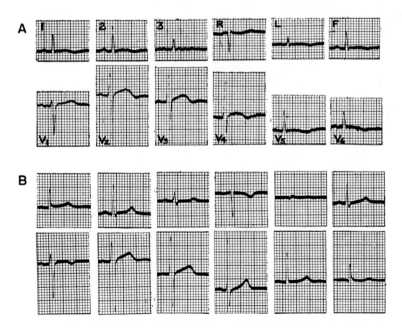

Figure 30.11. Myxedema. Tracing *A* was taken before treatment; note shallow inversion of T waves in many leads. *B* was taken after 10 weeks of treatment with thyroid extract; the previously inverted T waves are now upright.

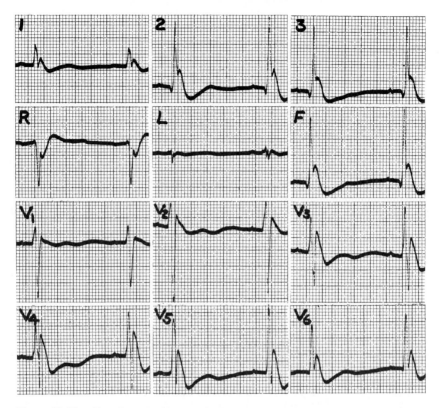

Figure 30.12.   Hypothermia. Note marked elevation of the "J deflection" maximal in midprecordial leads.

Hypothermia

When the body temperature falls below 30°C, characteristic changes develop in the electrocardiogram (fig. 30.12). All intervals—R-R, P-R, QRS and Q-T—may lengthen, and elevated "J deflections" appear especially in left chest leads. Atrial fibrillation may develop at about 29°C.[16]

Hypokalemia

The electrocardiogram may be of great value in the diagnosis of this not uncommon and dangerous situation. A significant potassium deficit may be encountered in many metabolic disorders, including cirrhosis of the liver, diabetic coma after vigorous treatment, hypochloremic alkalosis from whatever cause (vomiting, diuresis, etc.) and in situations where excessive amounts of corticosteroids are being secreted (Cushing's syndrome, primary aldosteronism) or administered. The typical signs of potassium lack in the tracing may appear when the serum potassium is within normal limits, and conversely the tracing may be normal and show no evidence of potassium deficiency when hypokalemia is chemically proven. As the heart is most dangerously affected by too much or too little potassium, it may well be that the electrocardiogram is the most sensitive indicator of the immediate threat to life. Furthermore, an electrocardiogram can sometimes be taken when facilities for serum determinations are not available. It is therefore well worth while to know the electrocardiographic changes that a potassium deficit can initiate (figs. 30.13 and 30.14).

As the effect of potassium depletion progresses, there is gradual depression of the ST segment, lowering of the T wave and increase in the height of the U wave. As the potassium concentrations fluctuate, the T and U waves seesaw— as the T wave decreases in height, the U wave increases, and vice versa. When T and U are approximately equal, a "camelhump" effect (fig. 30.14A) is produced; when the U wave becomes taller than the T wave (figs. 30.13 and 30.14B), the plasma potassium is usually under 2.7 mEq per liter.[59]

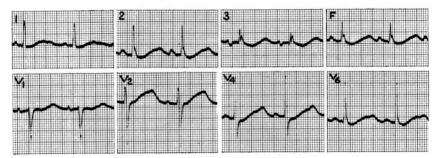

Figure 30.13. Hypokalemia. Note characteristic pattern with ST depression and extremely prominent U waves.

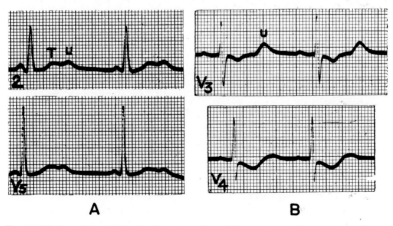

A   B

Figure 30.14. Hypokalemia. Tracings A and B are from different patients. A shows early changes of hypokalemia with prominent U wave merging to form continuous undulating wave with T wave. B shows changes of advanced hypokalemia (1.8 mEq per liter) in a patient with cirrhosis; note ST-T depression with very prominent U waves in V_3.

In hypokalemia the P wave becomes larger and wider and the P-R interval prolongs somewhat. In advanced stages, the QRS complex widens uniformly and the ST segment is markedly depressed with T-wave inversion. The fully developed pattern is seen in figure 30.14*B*. These changes rapidly revert to normal with administration of potassium salts.

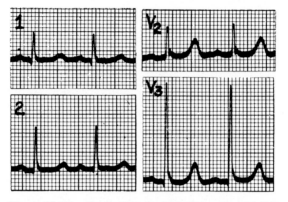

Figure 30.15.   Hypocalcemia. Note the prolonged Q-T interval in an otherwise normal tracing. Q-T = 0.40 sec (upper limit of normal for this rate and sex is 0.35 sec). Patient's serum calcium was 7.0 mg per 100 ml, other electrolytes being normal.

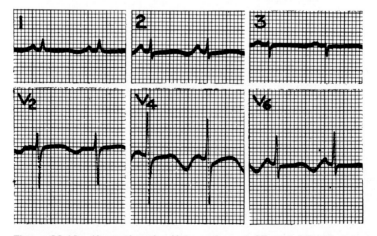

Figure 30.16.   Hypocalcemia. Note prolonged ST and QT with late inversion of T waves. From a patient with serum calcium of 4.2 mg per 100 ml.

Hypocalcemia

Calcium deficiency produces a prolonged Q-T interval. This lengthening is effected through elongation of the ST segment, the T wave remaining relatively normal (fig. 30.15); terminal T-wave inversion, however, occurs in some leads in about a third of the cases (fig. 30.16).

Hyperkalemia

The earliest sign of potassium intoxication is the appearance of tall, thin T waves (fig. 30.17). Later the P-R interval becomes prolonged, the ST segment becomes depressed and the QRS interval lengthens. Finally the P waves

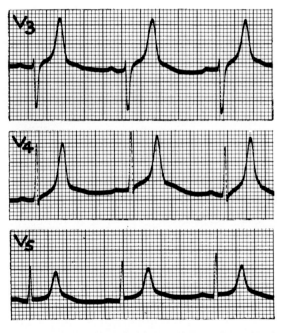

Figure 30.17. Hyperkalemia. Note tall, pointed, "pinchbottomed" T waves. (K = 6.1 mEq per liter.)

disappear and the QRS widens further (fig. 30.18) until ventricular fibrillation closes the picture. Disappearance of the P waves does not necessarily indicate a cessation of S-A node activity; despite atrial paralysis, sinus impulses may proceed to the A-V junction via specialized "internodal" conducting tracts without writing P waves, and thence onward to control the ventricles (**sino-ventricular rhythm**).[46]

Hypercalcemia

The most striking change in the electrocardiogram is a shortening of the Q-T interval, but particularly of the distance from the beginning of the QRS to the *apex* of the T wave (Q-aT interval). This change gives the proximal limb of the T wave an abrupt slope to its peak that is most characteristic (fig. 30.19*A*). In some cases the P-R interval is prolonged.

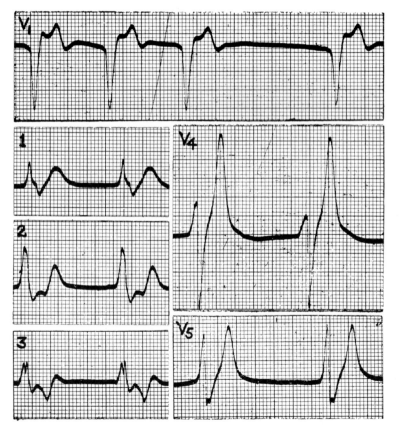

Figure 30.18.   Hyperkalemia. This tracing shows evidence of advanced potassium intoxication: tall peaked T waves, absent P waves, widened QRS complexes and irregular rhythm. From a patient with serum potassium level of 8.1 mEq per liter.

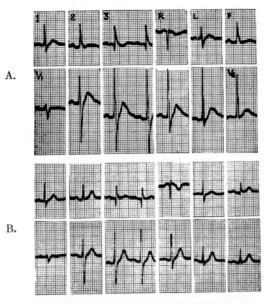

A.

B.

Figure 30.19. From a patient with **hyperparathy-roidism.** (*A*) Before parathyroidectomy (serum calcium 15 mg.). Note virtual absence of ST segment, early peak of T wave and relatively gradual downslope of descending limb of T wave. (*B*) After parathyroidectomy (serum calcium 10.7 mg). Note normal contour of ST-T pattern. (Reproduced with permission from G. H. Beck and H. J. L. Marriott: The electrocardiogram in hyperparathyroidism. *American Journal of Cardiology,* 1959: **3**, 411.)

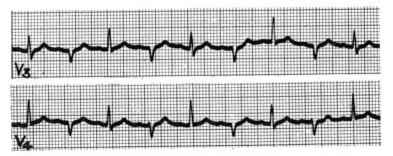

Figure 30.20. **Electrical alternans.** Note alternating direction of QRS complexes.

Electrical Alternans

This abnormality is readily recognized by the alternating amplitude of QRS complexes in any or all leads (fig. 30.20). It is much less common than, but has the same prognostic significance as, its mechanical counterpart, *pulsus alternans.* Electrical alternans is an important part of the pattern of pericardial effusion[31] (see p. 464).

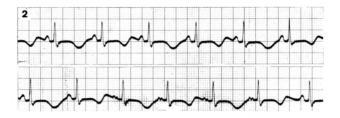

Figure 30.21.   Alternation of T-U complex. Strips are continuous. Note shifting atrial pacemaker in *bottom strip.*

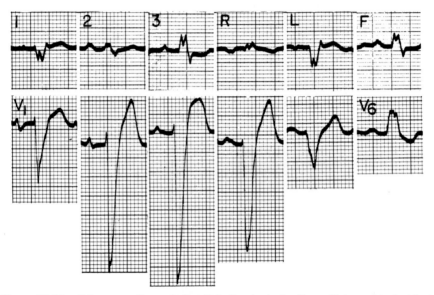

Figure 30.22.   Primary cardiomyopathy. Note the atypical pattern of intraventricular block with notching and slurring of the QRS in limb leads. P waves are also wide and notched with evidence of left atrial enlargement.

Alternation may affect only the T wave,[27] only the U wave,[35] or both simultaneously (fig. 30.21); such alternation has been described in electrolyte disturbances and in terminal states.

Cardiomyopathy

Any electrocardiographic abnormality may accompany a cardiomyopathy,[30] and none is diagnostic, with the possible exception of the progressive pattern—from septal hypertrophy (see fig. 29.9) to generalized LVH—seen in the prolonged follow-up of hypertrophic cardiomyopathy.[6] There are, however, a few tendencies worth noting: a BBB pattern tends to be atypical and splintered (fig. 30.22); the association of the preexcitation syndrome with familial cardio-

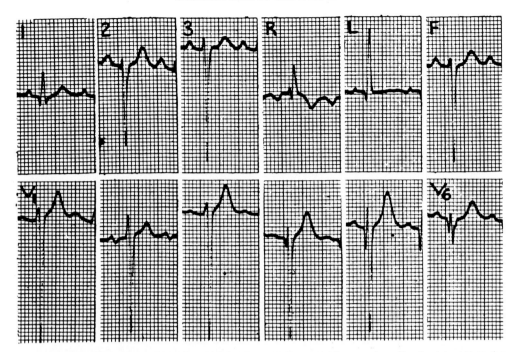

Figure 30.23.   Hypertrophic cardiomyopathy. From a 29-year-old, asymptomatic physician. Note the marked left axis deviation (−75°) and prominent but narrow Q waves V$_{4-6}$.

myopathy, obstructive or nonobstructive; and the tendency to *right* ventricular hypertrophy and *right* BBB in endomyocardial fibrosis. The unusual combination of *left* bundle-branch block with *right* axis deviation, as in figure 30.22, may be uniquely characteristic of a primary cardiomyopathy.[68]

Hypertrophic cardiomyopathy (HCM) [*aliases*: muscular subaortic stenosis; idiopathic hypertrophic subaortic stenosis (IHSS); asymmetric septal hypertrophy (ASH); hypertrophic obstructive cardiomyopathy (HOCM)] has been given so many names that by 1981 a list containing no less than 46 terms could be compiled.[32] HCM can produce a variety of 12-lead patterns[3, 49]: more than 20% may be entirely normal[45]; many show the classical picture of left ventricular hypertrophy; others present with marked left axis deviation (fig. 30.23), presumably due to left anterior hemiblock; infants with HCM commonly present with a pattern of *right* ventricular hypertrophy.[67] The combination of *left* ventricular with right *atrial* hypertrophy is suspicious.[22] But perhaps the most suggestive clue of all is the finding of obviously pathological Q waves that just do not look like the Q waves of infarction—this broad hint is contained in both figure 30.23 and 29.9. Such "pseudoinfarction" Q waves are to be found in 20 to 25%.[33, 45] Subjects with HCM have an increased incidence of both supraventricular and ventricular arrhythmias.[64]

In cardiac amyloidosis[18] the diagnosis may be suspected from the combination of low voltage, marked left axis deviation and QS or tiny rS complexes from V_1 to V_3 or V_4 (fig. 30.24).

Glycogen storage disease tends to produce oversized QRS complexes in all leads in company with a short P-R interval.[41]

Intracranial Hemorrhage

Intracerebral or subarachnoid hemorrhage can produce dramatic changes in the electrocardiogram.[10, 25, 56] Precordial T waves become wide and prominent, usually inverted but sometimes upright, and are continuous with large U waves, giving the effect of a long drawn out T-U complex (fig. 30.25). Bradycardia frequently accompanies these changes.

Mysteriously, the development of a cerebrovascular accident has been reported to abruptly replace the deeply negative T waves of subendocardial infarction with normally upright T waves.[23]

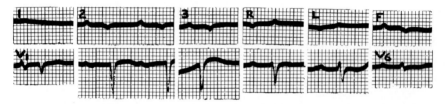

Figure 30.24. Primary amyloidosis. Note low voltage, marked left axis deviation (of what's left of the QRS), QS complexes V_{1-3}, abnormal P waves, and prolonged P-R. (Reproduced with permission from H. J. L. Marriott: Correlations of electrocardiographic and pathologic changes. In *Pathology of the Heart and Blood Vessels*, Charles C Thomas, Springfield, Ill., 1968.) Ed. 3, Chap. XX, edited by S. E. Gould.

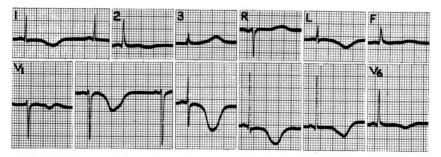

Figure 30.25. Intracerebral hemorrhage. Note bradycardia, large inverted precordial T and U waves.

Low Voltage with Inverted T Waves

It is opportune to review the several conditions which can cause low voltage QRS with inverted T waves in all or most leads:

1. Any diffuse myocardial involvement
   a. Diffuse ischemic disease
   b. Heart failure treated with digitalis
   c. Myxedema
   d. Cardiomyopathy
2. Pericarditis
   a. Acute ("T stage")
   b. Chronic constrictive

ST-T Depression

When ST segments are depressed and T waves flat to inverted in many leads, one should think of:

1. Digitalis effect
2. Diffuse ischemic disease
3. Left ventricular strain
4. Combined anterior and inferior infarction (antero-inferior infarction)
5. Subendocardial infarction
6. Hypokalemia

As well as the above causes of ST-segment and T-wave changes, the many factors that can influence these labile members of the electrocardiogram (pp. 413–417) should be constantly borne in mind.

REFERENCES

1. Alexander, J. K., et al.: The Q-T interval in chronic cor pulmonale. Circulation 1951: **3**, 733.
2. Alimurung, B.: The influence of early repolarization variant on the exercise electrocardiogram; a correlation with coronary arteriograms. Am. Heart J. 1980: **99**, 739.
3. Bahl, O. P., and Massie, E.: Electrocardiographic and vectorcardiographic patterns in cardiomyopathy. Cardiovasc. Clin. 1972: **4**,(1), 95.
4. Bashour, F. A., and Cochran, P. W.: The association of electrical alternans with pericardial effusion. Dis. Chest 1963: **44**, 146.
5. Bellet, S.: The electrocardiogram in electrolyte imbalance. Arch. Intern. Med. 1955: **96**, 618.
6. Braudo, M., et al.: A distinctive electrocardiogram in muscular subaortic stenosis due to septal hypertrophy. Am. J. Cardiol. 1964: **14**, 599.
7. Bronsky, D., et al.: Calcium and the electrocardiogram. I. The electrocardiographic manifestations of hypoparathyroidism. Am. J. Cardiol. 1961: **7**, 823. II. The electrocardiographic manifestations of hyperparathyroidism and of marked hypercalcemia from various other etiologies. Ibid.: **7**, 833.
8. Bruce, M. A., and Spodick, D. H.: Atypical electrocardiogram in acute pericarditis; characteristics and prevalence. J. Electrocardiol. 1980: **13**, 61.
9. Bullington, R. H., and Bullington, J. D.: "Pseudo-infarction" phenomenon of acute pericarditis. J.A.M.A. 1959: **171**, 2205.
10. Burch, G. E., et al.: A new electrocardiographic pattern observed in cerebrovascular accidents. Circulation 1954: **9**, 719.
11. Charles, M. A., et al.: Atrial injury current in pericarditis. Arch. Intern. Med. 1973: **131**, 657.

12. Dalton, J. C., Pearson, R. J., and White, P. D.: Constrictive pericarditis: a review and long term follow-up of 78 cases. Ann. Intern. Med. 1956: **45**, 445.

13. Demerdash, H., and Goodwin, J. F.: The cardiogram of mitral restenosis. Br. Heart J. 1963: **25**, 474.

14. Dreyfus, L. S., and Pick, A.: A clinical correlation study of the electrocardiogram in electrolyte imbalance. Circulation 1956: **14**, 815.

15. Eliaser, M., and Giansiracusa, F.: The electrocardiographic diagnosis of acute cor pulmonale. Am. Heart J. 1952: **43**, 533.

16. Emslie-Smith, D., et al.: The significance of changes in the electrocardiogram in hypothermia. Br. Heart J. 1959: **21**, 343.

17. Evans, W., and Jackson, F.: Constrictive pericarditis. Br. Heart J. 1952: **14**, 53.

18. Farrokh, A. et al.: Amyloid heart disease. Am. J. Cardiol. 1964: **13**, 750.

19. Ferrer, M. I.: Clinical and electrocardiographic correlations in pulmonary heart disease (cor pulmonale). Cardiovasc. Clin. 1977: **8**(3), 215.

20. Fowler, N. O., et al.: The electrocardiogram in cor pulmonale with and without emphysema. Am. J. Cardiol. 1965: **16**, 500.

21. Fraser, H. R. L., and Turner, R.: Electrocardiography in mitral valvular disease. Br. Heart J. 1955: **17**, 459.

22. Goodwin, J. F., et al.: Obstructive cardiomyopathy simulating aortic stenosis. Br. Heart J. 1960: **22**, 403.

23. Gould, L., et al.: Electrocardiographic normalization after cerebral vascular accident. J. Electrocardiol. 1981: **14**, 191.

24. Grant, R. P.: Left axis deviation. An electrocardiographic-pathologic correlation study. Circulation 1956: **14**, 233.

25. Hersch, C.: Electrocardiographic changes in subarachnoid haemorrhage, meningitis, and intracranial space-occupying lesions. Br. Heart J. 1964: **26**, 785.

26. Hull, E.: The electrocardiogram in pericarditis. Am. J. Cardiol. 1961: **7**, 21.

27. Kimura, E., and Yoshida, K.: A case showing electrical alternans of the T wave without change in the QRS complex. Am. Heart J. 1963: **65**, 391.

28. Littman, D.: The electrocardiographic findings in pulmonary emphysema. Am. J. Cardiol. 1960: **5**, 339.

29. Mack, I., Harris, R., and Katz, L. N.: Acute cor pulmonale in the absence of pulmonary embolism. Am. Heart J. 1950: **39**, 664.

30. Marriott, H. J. L.: Electrocardiographic abnormalities, conduction disorders and arrhythmias in primary myocardial disease. Prog. Cardiovasc. Dis. 1964: **7**, 99.

31. McGregor, M., and Baskind, E.: Electrical alternans in pericardial effusion. Circulation 1955: **11**, 837.

32. McKenna, W. J., and Goodwin, J. F.: The natural history of hypertrophic cardiomyopathy. Curr. Probl. Cardiol. 1981: **6**(4), 1.

33. McMartin, D. E., and Flowers, N. C.: Clinical-electrocardiographic correlations in diseases of the myocardium. Cardiovasc. Clin. 1977: **8**(3), 191.

34. Morace, G.: Effect of isoproterenol on the "early repolarization" syndrome. Am. Heart J. 1979: **97**, 343.

35. Mullican, W. S., and Fisch, C.: Postextrasystolic alternation of the U wave due to hypokalemia. Am. Heart J. 1964: **68**, 383.

36. Nizet, P. M., and Marriott, H. J. L.: The electrocardiogram and pericardial effusion. J.A.M.A. 1966: **198**, 169.

37. Phillips, E., and Levine, H. D.: A critical evaluation of extremity and precordial electrocardiography in acute cor pulmonale. Am. Heart J. 1950: **39**, 205.

38. Phillips, R. W.: The electrocardiogram in cor pulmonale secondary to pulmonary emphysema: a study of 18 cases proved by autopsy. Am. Heart J. 1958: **56**, 352.

39. Rios, J. C., and Goo, W.: Electrocardiographic correlates of rheumatic valvular disease. Cardiovasc. Clin. 1973: **5**(2), 247.

40. Rios, J. C., and Leet, C.: Electrocardiographic assessment of valvular heart disease. Cardiovasc. Clin. 1977: **8**(3), 161.

41. Ruttenberg, H. D., et al.: Glycogen-storage disease of the heart. Am. Heart J. 1964: **67**, 469.

42. Schaeffer, J., and Pryor, R.: Pseudo left axis deviation and the $S_1S_2S_3$ syndrome in chronic airway obstruction. Chest 1977: **71**, 453.

43. Scott, R. C.: The electrocardiogram in pulmonary emphysema and chronic cor pulmonale. Am. Heart J. 1961: **61,** 843.
44. Selvester, R. H., and Rubin, H. B.: New criteria for the electrocardiographic diagnosis of emphysema and cor pulmonale. Am. Heart J. 1965: **69,** 437.
45. Shah, P. M.: Clinical-electrocardiographic correlations: Aortic valve disease and hypertrophic subaortic stenosis. Cardiovasc. Clin. 1977: **8**(3), 151.
46. Sherf, L., and James, T. N.: A new electrocardiographic concept: synchronized sinoventricular conduction. Dis. Chest 1969: **55,** 127.
47. Smith, McK., and Ray, C. T.: Electrocardiographic signs of early right ventricular enlargement in acute pulmonary embolism. Chest 1970: **58,** 205.
48. Spodick, D. H.: Electrocardiographic studies in pulmonary disease. I. Electrocardiographic abnormalities in diffuse lung disease. Circulation 1959: **20,** 1067.
49. Spodick, D. H.: Hypertrophic obstructive cardiomyopathy of the left ventricle (idiopathic hypertrophic subaortic stenosis. Cardiovasc. Clin. 1972: **4**(1), 133.
50. Spodick, D. H.: Electrocardiogram in acute pericarditis. Distributions of morphologic and axial changes by stages. Am. J. Cardiol. 1974: **33,** 470.
51. Spodick, D. H.: Differential characteristics of the electrocardiogram in early repolarization and acute pericarditis. N. Engl. J. Med. 1976: **295,** 523.
52. Spodick, D. H.: Pathogenesis and clinical correlations of the electrocardiographic abnormalities of pericardial disease. Cardiovasc. Clin. 1977: **8**(3), 201.
53. Surawicz, B., and Lepeschkin, E.: The electrocardiographic pattern of hypopotassemia with and without hypocalcemia. Circulation 1963: **8,** 801.
54. Surawicz, B., et al.: Quantitative analysis of the electrocardiographic pattern of hypopotassemia. Circulation 1957: **16,** 750.
55. Surawicz, B.: Electrolytes and the electrocardiogram. Am. J. Cardiol. 1963: **12,** 656.
56. Surawicz, B.: Electrocardiographic pattern of cerebrovascular accident. J.A.M.A. 1966: **197,** 913.
57. Surawicz, B., and Lasseter, K. C.: Electrocardiogram in pericarditis. Am. J. Cardiol. 1970: **26,** 471.
58. Surawicz, B., and Mangiardi, M. L.: Electrocardiogram in endocrine and metabolic disorders. Cardiovasc. Clin. 1977: **8**(3), 243.
59. Surawicz, B.: The interrelationship of electrolyte abnormalities and arrhythmias, p. 83. In *Cardiac Arrhythmias: Their Mechanisms, Diagnosis and Management,* edited by W. J. Mandel. J. B. Lippincott, Philadelphia, 1980.
60. Tiefenbrunn, A. J., and Roberts, R.: Elevation of plasma MB creatine kinase and the development of new Q waves in association with pericarditis. Chest 1980: **77,** 438.
61. Wasserburger, R. H., et al.: The T-a wave of the adult electrocardiogram: an expression of pulmonary emphysema. Am. Heart J. 1957: **54,** 875.
62. Wasserburger, R. H., et al.: The electrocardiographic pentalogy of pulmonary emphysema. Circulation 1959: **20,** 831.
63. Weaver, W. F., and Burchell, H. B.: Serum potassium and the electrocardiogram in hypokalemia. Circulation 1960: **21,** 505.
64. Bjarnson, I.: Cardiac arrhythmias in hypertrophic cardiomyopathy. Br. Heart J. 1982: **48,** 198.
65. Ginzton, L. E., and Laks, M.M.: The differential diagnosis of acute pericarditis from the normal variant; new electrocardiographic criteria. Circulation 1982: 65, 1004.
66. Lynch, P., and Webb-Peploe, M.M.: The P terminal vector in lead V_1 of the electrocardiogram in cor pulmonale. J. Electrocardiol. 1982: **15,** 205.
67. Maron, B. J., et al.: Hypertrophic cardiomyopathy in infants: clinical features and natural history. Circulation 1982: **65,** 7.
68. Nikolic, G.: Personal communication, 1982.
69. Siegel, R. J., and Roberts, W. C.: Electrocardiographic observations in severe aortic valve stenosis. Am. Heart J. 1982: **103,** 210.

Review Tracings

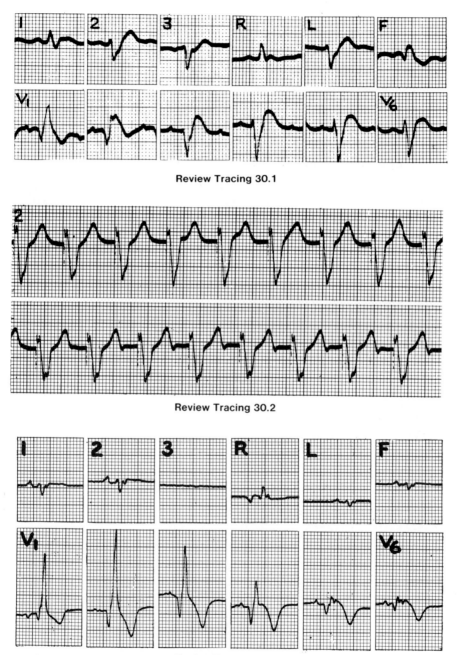

Review Tracing 30.1

Review Tracing 30.2

Review Tracing 30.3

For interpretation, see pages 485–486

Review Tracing

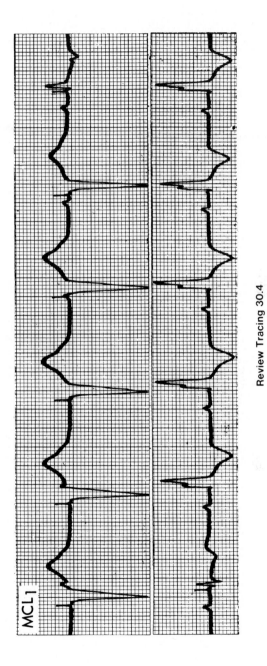

MCL₁

Review Tracing 30.4

For interpretation, see page 486

Review Tracing

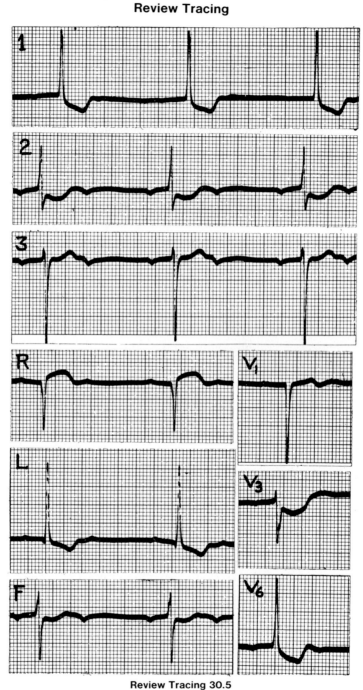

Review Tracing 30.5
For interpretation, see page 486

Review Tracing

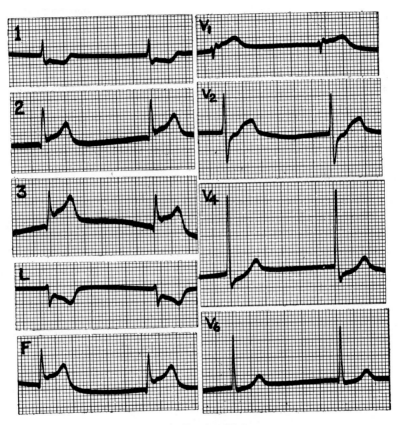

Review Tracing 30.6

For interpretation, see page 486

Review Tracings:
Interpetations

11.1, page 148: Left ventricular hypertrophy and strain. (From a 34-year-old man with coarctation of the aorta.)

11.2, page 148: (1) Right bundle-branch block. (2) The third beat in each lead is a ventricular premature beat. (3) Thanks to the respite of the long compensatory pause, the beat following the extrasystole is conducted with less block—incomplete RBBB—a manifestation of "critical rate."

12.1, page 167: The numbered beats are: sinus with RBBB (1), right ventricular extrasystole (2), and left ventricular extrasystole (3).

12.2, page 167: Right ventricular hypertrophy and strain with right atrial hypertrophy as well. From a patient with pulmonic stenosis and tricuspid insufficiency resulting from the malignant carcinoid syndrome.

13.1, page 179: Supraventricular tachycardia, probably "slow-fast" reciprocating tachycardia in the A-V junction. Sinus rhythm restored in the bottom strip.

13.2, page 180: (1) P-congenitale (right atrial hypertrophy). (2) Right ventricular hypertrophy and strain. Axis $-160°$. From a patient with pulmonic stenosis.

14.1, page 188: (1) Atrial flutter with varying A-V block (atrial rate about 330, ventricular about 102). (2) Right bundle-branch block, incomplete.

14.2, page 189: (1) Atrial fibrillation; at times (beginning of lead 2, end of lead aVF) atrial activity is regular enough to be called flutter; so rhythm might be called flutter-fibrillation. (2) Two ectopic ventricular beats. (3) Left ventricular hypertrophy and strain. From a patient with rheumatic heart disease with mitral and aortic involvement.

15.1, page 210: (1) Left ventricular hypertrophy and strain. (2) Intra-atrial block (presumable evidence of left atrial enlargement). (3) The left axis deviation ($-40°$) indicates the likelihood of left ventricular disease besides hypertrophy and incomplete left anterior hemiblock is probable.

15.2, page 210: LBBB with slight left axis deviation ($-25°$).

16.1, page 243: (1) Atrial fibrillation. (2) Right bundle-branch block with (3) primary T-wave changes (to which digitalis might be contributing). (4) Marked left axis deviation (close to $-90°$) presumably due to left anterior hemiblock.

16.2, page 243: (1) Numerous atrial premature beats with (2) prolonged P-R intervals and (3) varying patterns of RBBB and LBBB aberration.

17.1, page 255: (1) Atrial fibrillation with rapid ventricular response. (2) Incomplete RBBB aberration of two beats.

17.2, page 255: (1) Abnormally notched P waves (intra-atrial block). (2) Fourth beat in top strip is an atrial extrasystole with minor aberration. (3) Ventricular extrasystoles with retrograde conduction to atria.

18.1, page 275: (1) Fourth beat is an atrial extrasystole; this slightly lengthens the next cycle, enough to precipitate (2) ventricular bigeminy ("rule of bigeminy"). (3) Nonspecific ST-T changes.

18.2, page 275: Ventricular tachycardia: Note marked left axis deviation (−80°) and concordant negativity in chest leads.

18.3, page 276: (1) Atrial fibrillation, with slow to moderate ventricular response. (2) Left bundle-branch block.

19.1, page 288: After one sinus beat, these three simultaneous leads illustrate an atrial premature beat, conducted with a prolonged P-R interval, initiating reentry in the A-V junction which lasts for only two cycles. Note the deeply inverted, retrograde P waves in leads 2 and 3.

19.2, page 288: (1) Sinus tachycardia. (2) Wolff-Parkinson-White syndrome ("type A").

19.3, page 288: (1) Increased "P-terminal force" indicating left atrial enlargement. (2) Three left ventricular extrasystoles, in bigeminal rhythm, the second produces a fusion beat.

20.1, page 299: (1) Intra-atrial block (P-mitrale). (2) Shifting atrial pacemaker. (3) Ventricular extrasystoles with retrograde conduction to atria. (4) Junctional escape beats terminate the pauses following the extrasystoles. From a patient with severe mitral stenosis.

20.2, page 300: Right bundle-branch block

20.3, page 300: Accelerated junctional (or ectopic atrial) rhythm (rate 72/ min).

21.1, page 313: (1) Sinus bradycardia, resulting in (2) A-V junctional escape and A-V dissociation. The third beat in bottom strip is a capture beat.

21.2, page 313: (1) Following the third sinus beat, there is a nonconducted atrial premature beat which, in turn, is followed by a junctional escape beat. (2) Digitalis effect.

21.3, page 314: Wolff-Parkinson-White syndrome ("type B").

22.1, page 320: (1) Sinus arrhythmia. (2) Accelerated idiojunctional rhythm at rate 90/min resulting in intermittent isorhythmic A-V dissociation. Note the slightly changed QRS morphology in the junctional beats (taller R and shallower S wave)—type B aberration.

22.2, page 321: Tachycardia-bradycardia syndrome consisting of (1) atrial fibrillation and (2) sinus arrest with junctional escape. The escape rhythm gradually accelerates until, in the bottom strip, the rhythm is "accelerated idiojunctional."

22.3, page 321: Wolff-Parkinson-White syndrome; note the unusual rSR′ imitation of RBBB in lead V₁.

23.1, page 338: (1) Type I A-V block with a 4:3 Wenckebach period. (2) Two junctional escape beats. (From an asymptomatic 6-year-old girl.)

23.2, page 339: (1) 3:2 A-V Wenckebach periods and 2:1 A-V block, presumably type I. (2) Right bundle-branch block. (*Note:* The "A-V" block *could* be due to simultaneous LBBB, i.e., type II.)

23.3, page 339: (1) Atrial tachycardia with varying A-V block, mostly 2:1. (2) One left ventricular extrasystole. (The block is presumably type I—prolonged P-R intervals and absence of BBB.)

23.4, page 339: (1) Abnormal non-specific ST-T pattern. (2) The third beat in each lead is a ventricular premature beat. (3) Following the premature beats retrograde conduction to the atria occurs (retrograde P waves deforming the ST segments). (4) Post-extrasystolic T-wave changes (increase in depth of T-wave inversion) are noted in the cycles following the premature beats. From a patient with severe hypertension.

24.1, page 351: (1) Atrial tachycardia, rate 224/min. (2) Wenckebach periods (5:4, 4:3, 3:2, etc.). (3) Abnormal axis deviation, probably left. The marked apparent variation in QRS morphology is entirely due to the varying relationship to large, positive P waves.

24.2, page 352: Shifting (wandering) pacemaker. Third P wave in each strip is an atrial fusion beat.

24.3, page 352: (1) Atrial fibrillation. (2) Complete A-V block with idioventricular rhythm at rate 38/min. (3) Multiform ventricular premature beats. This combination suggests digitalis intoxication.

24.4, page 352: (1) P-pulmonale (right atrial hypertrophy). (2) Low voltage of QRS with dominant S waves V_{3-6}. From a patient with severe emphysema.

25.1, page 371: (1) Partially ineffective right ventricular pacemaker. (2) Two right ventricular escape beats.

25.2, page 371: (1) Sinus tachycardia controlling atria. (2) Complete A-V block with idioventricular rhythm at rate 40/min. Note the shallowly inverted T_P waves following most of the P waves.

25.3, page 372: Type II A-V block. The P-R interval of the conducted beats is constant and normal (0.15 sec) and there is intraventricular block (QRS interval = 0.11 sec).

25.4, page 372: (1) Intra-atrial block. (2) First degree A-V block (P-R interval 0.22 to 0.24 sec). (3) Shifting atrial pacemaker. (4) Numerous atrial premature beats, in V_1 producing bigeminy. The third atrial premature beat in V_1 shows (5) aberrant ventricular conduction of RBBB type. (6) Left ventricular hypertrophy and strain (judging by the high voltage of the QRS and ST-T pattern).

26.1, page 399: Acute extensive anterior myocardial infarction.

26.2, page 399: (1) First degree A-V block (P-R = about 0.34 sec). (2) Acute inferior infarction.

26.3, page 399: (1) Sinus tachycardia, rate 102. (2) Nonconducted atrial premature beat every third beat. (3) Slight prolongation of the second P-R interval in each pair of sinus beats (indicates potential Wenckebach periodicity).

26.4, page 400: Atypical intermittent left intraventricular block, probably rate-related. Precordial leads show classical LBBB, but the block is not typical since there is a prominent Q wave in lead 1, which strongly suggests anteroseptal infarction. In aVR the block changes to an unblocked pattern that persists through aVL and aVF.

27.1, page 423: (1) A-V junctional rhythm with retrograde conduction. (2) Imcomplete RBBB. (3) Acute inferior myocardial infarction.

27.2, page 423: (1) Sick sinus, permitting (2) junctional escape with slow junctional rhythm at rate 31/min with retrograde conduction. (Note that the escaping junctional rhythm is not the *primary* diagnosis—the primary disturbance is in the sinus node and this allows the rescuing A-V pacemaker to take over.)

27.3, page 424: Early acute lateral infarction (early ST elevation in leads 1, aVL and V6 with reciprocal changes in 3, aVF and V_{1-3}).

27.4, page 424: (1) Right bundle-branch block. (2) Anteroseptal infarction. (3) Marked left axis deviation, presumably due to anterior hemiblock.

28.1, page 440: (1) Right bundle-branch block (with marked right axis deviation of about $+120°$, presumably due to left posterior hemiblock). (2) First degree A-V block. (3) Digitalis effect.

28.2, page 440: Type I A-V block with a 42:41 Wenckebach period. The dropped beats occur after the third beat at the beginning of the *top strip* and before the last beat in the *bottom strip*.

28.3, page 441: (1) Atrial fibrillation. (2) High grade A-V block; ventricular rhythm is completely regular (except for two beats referred to under (3) below) at rate 32—idionodal rhythm. (3) The fourth beat in V_3 and the third in V_5 have a somewhat different form from the dominant beats in their respective leads, have a shorter QRS interval and are slightly earlier than the next expected idioventricular beat; these then are presumably conducted supraventricular beats arising in the fibrillating atria. (4) Acute inferior infarction.

28.4, page 441: (1) Right bundle-branch block. (2) Inferior myocardial infarction.

29.1, page 454: Low voltage of QRS with flattened T waves, without much ST displacement. A nonspecific pattern but most suspicious of hypothyroidism. (From a patient with severe myxedema.)

29.2, page 455: (1) Sinus bradycardia with arrhythmia, rate 43 to 55. (2) Intra-atrial block (P-wave duration = 0.14 sec) with P-mitrale; note horizontal axis of P waves ($+20°$) with vertical axis of QRS ($+90°$)—this combination is highly suggestive of mitral stenosis. (From a patient with rheumatic heart disease.)

29.3, page 455: Abnormal nonspecific tracing because of ST-T abnormalities and inverted U waves (V_{5-6}). (From a 22-year-old man with rheumatic aortic and mitral regurgitation.)

30.1, page 478: (1) Acute anterior infarction. (2) RBBB. (3) Left anterior hemiblock.

30.2, page 478. Artificial pacemaker with dissociated atrial activity in the top strip; in bottom strip, 1:1 retrograde conduction (retrograde P waves produce sharp negative deformity at end of T-wave downstroke).

30.3, page 478: (1) RBBB. (2) Extensive anterior infarction of uncertain date, probably recent. (3) LA and RL electrodes reversed. (Whenever the tracing in a bipolar lead is a virtual straight line—as in lead 3—that lead is probably recording the potential difference between the two legs which is virtually nil; in this case the retaken limb leads—see below—reveal marked left axis deviation (−60°) indicating presumable left anterior hemiblock.)

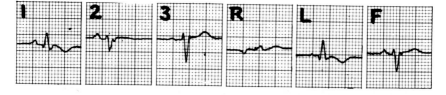

30.4, page 479: (1) Sinus bradycardia. (2) First degree A-V block. (3) Right bundle-branch block. (4) Right ventricular demand pacemaker, producing three fusion beats (last two beats in top strip and first in bottom strip.)

30.5, page 480: (1) P waves are inverted in 2, 3 and aVF, upright in aVR; this is therefore an ectopic atrial rhythm. (2) 2:1 A-V block (atrial rate 84, ventricular 42) with prolonged P-R in conducted beats, presumably type I block. (3) Left ventricular hypertrophy and strain. (4) Digitalis effect.

30.6, page 481: (1) Junctional rhythm. No P waves are visible preceding the QRS complexes; tiny notches are apparent at the very beginning of the ST segments in several of the leads—these are presumably retrograde P waves. (2) Acute inferior infarction.

Index

NOTE: All initial entries are nouns. Boldface page numbers refer to primary discussions.